# Crucible
## of
# Struggle

# Crucible
## of
# Struggle

*A History of Mexican Americans
from Colonial Times to the Present Era*

ZARAGOSA VARGAS
*University of North Carolina, Chapel Hill*

New York    Oxford
OXFORD UNIVERSITY PRESS
2011

Oxford University Press, Inc., publishes works that further Oxford University's objective of excellence in research, scholarship, and education.

Oxford  New York
Auckland  Cape Town  Dar es Salaam  Hong Kong  Karachi
Kuala Lumpur  Madrid  Melbourne  Mexico City  Nairobi
New Delhi  Shanghai  Taipei  Toronto

With offices in
Argentina  Austria  Brazil  Chile  Czech Republic  France  Greece
Guatemala  Hungary  Italy  Japan  Poland  Portugal  Singapore
South Korea  Switzerland  Thailand  Turkey  Ukraine  Vietnam

For titles covered by Section 112 of the US Higher Education Opportunity Act, please visit www.oup.com/us/he for the latest information about pricing and alternate formats.

Published by Oxford University Press, Inc.
198 Madison Avenue, New York, New York 10016
http://www.oup.com

Oxford is a registered trademark of Oxford University Press

**Library of Congress Cataloging-in-Publication Data**
Vargas, Zaragosa.
  Crucible of struggle: a history of Mexican Americans/Zaragosa
Vargas—1st ed.
    p.   cm.
  Includes bibliographical references and index.
  ISBN 978-0-19-515851-9 (alk. paper)—ISBN 978-0-19-515850-2
1. Mexican Americans—History. 2. Mexican Americans—Social Conditions.
3. Immigrants—United States—History. 4. United States—Relations—Mexico.
5. Mexico—Relations—United States. I. Title.
  E184.M5V343,2010
  973'.046872—dc22
                                                                2010009162


Printing number: 9 8 7 6 5 4 3 2

Printed in the United States of America
on acid-free paper

*For Zaneta, Lina, and Marcel*

# CONTENTS

꼬ᄀ

PREFACE   xii

ACKNOWLEDGMENTS   xviii

A NOTE ON TERMINOLOGY   xx

Chapter 1   **The Era of the Spanish Northern Frontier
to 1821   1**
Spanish Institutions and Mixed-Race Society of the Northern
Frontier   3
The Founding of New Mexico   8
Resisting Spanish Colonization: The Pueblo Revolt of 1680   11
Duty to the Crown and Church Fulfilled: The Spanish
Reconquest of New Mexico   13
A Buffer Zone Against Expansion: Spanish Colonial Texas   20
The Apache and Comanche Threat in Texas   22
The Condition of the Spanish Texas Colony in the Early
Nineteenth Century   24
Guarding the Western Periphery: Spanish Colonial Alta
California   25
Mexican Independence Comes to the Northern Frontier   30
Conclusion   31

Chapter 2   **Life and Society in Mexico's Northern
Borderlands, 1821–1846   39**
Indian Relations on the Northern Frontier After Mexican
Independence   42
Men of the Plains: New Mexican Ciboleros and
Comancheros   45
The Opening of Commercial Markets: The Taos Trade Fair
and the Santa Fe Trail   46

Conflict in New Mexico: The 1837 Revolt    48
Tejano Life on the Texas Frontier Under Mexico    50
The Never-Ending Indian Menace: Comanche Raids
    in Texas    51
The Growing Conflict in Texas with Mexico    52
The Drive for Texas Independence    54
Making California Mexican    63
The California Missions: Making Indians Faithful and
    Industrious Christians    65
The Golden Age of California Ranching    67
The Californio Era Revolts Against Mexican Rule    70
Conclusion    71

Chapter 3    **Mexican Americans in the Era of War
    and American Westward Expansion**    79

The Southwest on the Eve of the Mexican War    81
The Outbreak of War    84
The American Occupation of New Mexico    85
The 1847 Taos Revolt Against American Occupation
    of New Mexico    88
The American Occupation of California    91
The Battles at Monterrey and Buena Vista    94
The Enduring Paradox: The Treaty of Guadalupe Hidalgo    101
Conclusion    105

Chapter 4    **Mexican Americans from the 1850s
    to the End of the Civil War**    112

Mexican Americans in the Postconquest Southwest    113
The Californio Banditti Joaquín Murieta and Tiburcio
    Vasquez    119
Juan Cortina: Champion and Hated Villain of the Texas Border
    Region    123
Mexican Americans in the American Civil War    127
Mexican Americans Fight in the Indian Wars    134
Conclusion    137

Chapter 5    **Mexican Americans in the Southwest,
    1870 to the Early Twentieth Century**    144

The Mexican Americans of California    145
The Tejanos and Mexicans of Texas    146
Disenfranchising Tejano Voters as Political Strategy    151
The Mexicans of Arizona and New Mexico    152
The United States and the New Mexico Land Grants
    Question    156
Las Gorras Blancas and the Struggle to Protect Land Grants    158

Statehood for New Mexico and Arizona?   162
The New Southwest Economy and the First Modern Phase
    of Mexican Immigration to the United States   165
Conclusion   170

Chapter 6   **Mexican Immigration, Work, Urbanization,
and Americanization, 1910–1929**   177
Mexican Labor Strife and Struggle   179
Tejano Freedom Fighters: The Plan de San Diego   183
The Killing Fields of South Texas   185
Immigration from Mexico During the Years 1910–1920   188
Mexicans, World War I, and the 1920–1921 Depression   189
Mexican Immigration from 1920 to 1929   191
Mexican Los Angeles   193
Mexicans in the Rocky Mountain and Plains States   194
Mexicans in the Urban Industrial Heartland of the Midwest   196
Mexicans and Social and Cultural Change and
    Americanization   199
Mexican Mutualism and Fraternalism   201
Conclusion   205

Chapter 7   **The Mexican American Struggle for Labor
Rights in the Era of the Great Depression**   213
The Plight of Mexicans in the Early Years of the Great
    Depression   215
The Repatriation Campaign Unfolds   217
Mexicans in the Era of the National Recovery Act   221
Mexican Women Workers Battle for Equality   223
Mexican Coal Miners' Wage War in Gallup   225
Tejano Struggles for Unionism in South Texas   228
Emma Tenayuca Brings Social Justice to San Antonio's
    Mexicans   229
The 1938 Strike by San Antonio's Pecan Shellers   230
The UCAPAWA Organizes Colorado's Mexican
    Farmworkers   232
Mexican American CIO Unionists Organize Los Angeles
    and Southern California   233
Conclusion   236

Chapter 8   **The Mexican American People in the World
War II Era**   243
Mexican Americans on the Eve of the Second World War   245
Justice Delayed: The Sleepy Lagoon Incident   250
Mexican Americans and the Sinarquista Menace   252

America's War at Home: The Los Angeles Zoot Suit Riots   253
Mexican American GIs on the Pacific and European War
    Fronts   255
Mexican Americans Fight Against Discrimination: The Case
    of Los Angeles   259
Mexican American Women War Workers   260
Braceros: The Mexican Contract Labor Program Begins   263
American Race Relations and Mexican Americans   263
Conclusion   265

Chapter 9    **Mexican Americans in the Postwar Years,**
              **1946–1963**   272
Forgotten: The Status of Mexican Americans in Postwar
    America   274
Mexican Americans in the Early Postwar American Labor
    Movement   276
The Radicalism of ANMA   280
Mexican Americans and the Community Service
    Organization   282
Mexican Americans Caught in the Web of the Red Scare   284
Mexican Americans in the Dragnets of Operation Wetback and
    Operation Terror   286
Civil Rights Litigation by Mexican Americans   288
Don't Bow to the Powers That Be: Shifts in the Mexican
    American Rights Movement   291
Mexican Americans and the Democratic Party   292
Conclusion   297

Chapter 10   **Mexican Americans in the Protest Era,**
              **1964–1974**   306
Viva La Huelga!: Gaining Ground for Farmworkers   309
The People's Choice: Reies López Tijerina and the New Mexico
    Land Grants Movement   313
Cultural Nationalism and Community Control: The Crusade
    for Justice   318
A Search for Identity: The Chicano Student Movement   321
Righteous Discontent: The Chicana Women's Movement   324
Raza Sí!  Guerra No!: The National Chicano War
    Moratorium   325
"Pardon My English": La Raza Unida Party   331
Conclusion   335

Chapter 11   **Mexican Americans at the End of the**
              **Twentieth Century**   344
Mexican Americans and Reagan's "New Morning in
    America"   347

"Tú Voto Es Tú Voz" (Your Vote Is Your Voice): Mexican
     Americans and the Political Process   349
Mexican Americans and the Civil Wars in Central America   352
Unemployment, Drugs, Gang Warfare, and the 1992 Rodney
     King Riots   353
The 1986 Simpson-Mazzoli Act or IRCA, the English-Only
     Movement, and Proposition 187   356
"Fight the Power": From the Bakke Decision
     to Proposition 209   359
Mexican American Workers Organize   363
"NAFTA's Gonna Shaft Ya": Mexican Americans and the North
     American Free Trade Agreement   366
Latino: A New National Identity and Continued Latino
     Immigration   369
Conclusion   370

Chapter 12   **Epilogue: Mexican Americans in the New
           Millennium**   378


INDEX   392

# PREFACE

꩜

The broad demographic shift in the racial and ethnic composition of the United States' population through unparalleled immigration from Mexico, Central and South America, and the Spanish-speaking Caribbean has resulted in the Latinization of America. Latinos are a major political, economic, and cultural force who are changing the national identity of the United States. With its inclusive diversity, Latino culture is considered to be a prototype of a future American culture that has recast the pervading notion of a black-and-white America. Presently exceeding forty-five million people, Latinos have replaced African Americans as the nation's largest minority group. As the fastest growing and youngest minority, Latinos are projected to make up 25 percent of the United States population by the middle of this century, and they will have a greater presence by century's end, when half of the United States may be Latino. Despite this huge demographic reality, mainstream America knows relatively little about the history of Latinos.[1]

Mexicans make up the vast majority of Latinos. About twenty-six million Mexicans make up two-thirds of the nation's Latinos, and their numbers are increasing faster than those of all other Latino groups. Mexicans are both the oldest settlers of the United States and the nation's largest and most recent immigrant arrivals. Mexican Americans have been contributing to the shaping of the nation since the late sixteenth century. At this time men and women of mixed racial background helped colonize and settle the Southwest before the English colonization of North America. These ancestors of Mexican Americans shaped the regional landscape of the Southwest and in turn were shaped by it, in the process helping define America's perception of the region. Mexicans in the present period continue to fashion much of the social, cultural, political, and economic reality of the Southwest and other regions that now include the South. The growing importance of this minority group in American society calls for a fresh assessment of Mexican American history. It is necessary to recognize and understand this history, for it is a means of counteracting the relative historical invisibility of the Mexican population, shunted off to the margins of American history, and the profound resistance to reconceptualizing this history.

Mexican American history emerged from and was indelibly marked and inspired by the political and social activism of the 1960s that influenced other new approaches to historical writing. Seeking to provide innovative views of a long misunderstood history that had been generally neglected in accounts of America's past, Mexican American historians altered the focus of the new narrative to present the role of Mexican Americans as primary historical actors and determinants of Mexican American history. The outcome of this paradigm shift in Mexican American historiography was clearly a revised account that applied methods of the new social history and that had an impact on these scholars. New studies written by Mexican American historians made substantive contributions to this contemporary American historical scholarship.[2] Historians of Mexican American history in the late 1970s and 1980s began a process of reinterpretation, all pointing the way toward the type of historiographical developments and research that emerged in the 1980s and the 1990s that reconceptualized the Mexican American experience in a broader context.

The new generation of historians has broadened and developed our knowledge of Mexican Americans in the United States. Books on urban life, labor, immigration, politics, and a host of other themes examine the Mexican American population in more detailed and innovative ways in addressing ethnicity, race relations, Catholicism, and other topics.[3] The twentieth century is the period to which Mexican American historians have turned; however, the late eighteenth and nineteenth centuries have been well served by the appearance of works in the field, some that pay more attention to American Indian and Mexican perspectives, for example. They evince the authors' awareness of the importance of this and other issues in the new borderlands scholarship. These histories, for example, trace the historical interaction among California Indians, Mexicans, and Anglos through the framework of relations of production and labor demands; examine the issues of sex, power, and gender in colonial New Mexico; or situate the United States-Mexico borderlands within a transnational perspective to explore national identity formation among the Spanish speaking in the years leading up to the Mexican-American War.[4] Mexican American historiography has increasingly incorporated gender as an analytical category in studies of the late colonial period and the nineteenth and twentieth centuries. Women historians provide a new interpretation of Mexican American history because they have investigated the roles of class, race relations, and sexuality in relations of power in this history.[5]

Mexican American history continues to be influenced by the shifts and debates in the broader field of American history. The discipline is headed in varied and complicated directions as innovative methods and perspectives have surfaced and established domains that will be supplanted by other methodologies as more scholarship emerges. Most Mexican American historians are not engaged in writing about a separate historical experience but in integrating Mexican Americans into the broader study of the American experience.

With the exception of Carey McWilliams's lucid history *North from Mexico,* first published in 1949, there is a dearth of readable and comprehensive surveys of the history of persons of Mexican descent in the United States.[6] McWilliams—attorney, writer, activist, and editor of *The Nation* magazine—informed his readers what was being forgotten: the significant social and cultural contributions of Mexicans to the larger history of the American Southwest region; their role in shaping the economy; the legal codes regarding mining, water, range lands, and community property that affected them; and their general survival on the frontier. Mexican culture was ignored, supplanted by a mythic Spanish heritage based on the memoirs of the Spanish-speaking elites and used to romanticize a simple and virtuous pastoral past.[7]

In 1972, one of the first revisionist surveys published was *Occupied America: A History of Chicanos* by Rodolfo Acuña.[8] The most important aspect of *Occupied America* is the interpretative framework. The book begins in the period when the United States takes possession of the Southwest and reinterprets the life of the Mexican American community from this historical juncture to the 1960s (then the present day) as one of occupation. It traces the conquest of northern Mexico by the United States and the violation of the civil rights of Mexican Americans from the 1800s to the present, while providing an analysis of the class politics within the Mexican American community. Acuña basically carries forward the critical point made by McWilliams—that Mexican Americans are the only ethnic minority other than Native Americans who were added to the United States by conquest and who were accorded treaty protection. Whereas the provisions of the 1848 Treaty of Guadalupe Hidalgo were quickly forgotten, Acuña argues that the structure of colonialism was not. Instead, Acuña contends that Mexican Americans, regardless of when their families entered the Southwest, are a colonized people. The agencies of the southwestern states and the federal government serve the purpose of disenfranchising Mexican Americans and restricting them to relatively low social and political spheres.[9]

Acuña's work is a detailed and moving history that laid the groundwork for a provocative recentering of Mexican American history. As noted, the field has been transformed dramatically in the more than three decades since the publication of *Occupied America*. The works provide a textured social critique and examine particular regions, eras, persons, or organizations in much more detail than can be done in a work as broadly defined as Acuña's *Occupied America*.

There is certainly ample room for an interpretative account of Mexican American history, especially one that rethinks its chronological conceptualization and integrates the latest and best available scholarship. A sound knowledge of the distinct historical experiences of Mexican Americans, along with a clear understanding of the social, economic, and political variations among the regions of the Southwest, is necessary to accurately convey their contributions to the American experience. *Crucible of Struggle: A History of Mexican Americans from Colonial Times to the Present Era* attempts to present an informed assessment of Mexican American life from the Spanish colonial period to the twenty-first century that is national in scope.

The concept of this book emerged from my work on *Major Problems in Mexican American History*, when I first outlined the historical patterns I saw in Mexican American history. My work shares some of the same themes with the continuing variety and depth of scholarship in Mexican American history, and it demonstrates as well the vitality and strength of this scholarship. As the title suggests, the Mexican American freedom struggle and how this theme has changed over time stands at the core of this synthesis. It examines how the 1836

Texas Revolt, the Mexican War, the Civil War, World War II, the Great Depression, the Chicano movement, and other important and epoch-making events all altered and shaped the context of the Mexican American struggle for equality and freedom. *Crucible of Struggle* places the history of Mexican Americans directly in the mainstream of American history. The Mexican American experience cannot be understood without analyzing the long history of United States involvement in Mexico, from territorial expansion in the early nineteenth century to formulating the North American Free Trade Agreement (NAFTA) and immigration policy in the late twentieth and early twenty-first centuries. Thus *Crucible of Struggle* not only analyzes the nature of the Mexican American quest for equality and freedom but also does so in the context of the larger economic and political changes in the United States.

*Crucible of Struggle* investigates the realities that Mexican Americans confronted and in turn affected on myriad levels. It also celebrates the resolute spirit of a people in the face of overwhelming odds and the persistence of a community over the generations. The history that follows is meant to be suggestive rather than exhaustive or conclusive. Hopefully it will stimulate more research, further debate, and additional studies. Its relevance is far reaching in light of the recent demographic shifts that make Latinos the nation's fastest growing population. History has placed Latinos at center stage as the United States is forced to adjust to an ever-changing international order.

*Crucible of Struggle* emphasizes social, economic, and political history over cultural interpretation. In terms of organization, the book follows a chronological framework that covers a period of more than four hundred years and sweeps through the colonial period and nineteenth and twentieth centuries in order to reinterpret the Mexican American experience. It addresses significant differences in the Mexican American experience between and within subregions of the Southwest. Little-known segments usually ignored or only briefly touched on in the chronicling of Mexican American history receive special emphasis. The content and outlook shifts from period to period. The book attempts to balance detail with discussion of the themes that give an overall perspective and an integrated view of the whole Mexican American experience.

There are twelve chapters, five of them concerned with the nineteenth century and six with the twentieth century. The chapters reflect the turning points in social, political, and economic relations and the dynamic forces that produced them. Chapter 12 is an epilogue that considers the implications of the dramatic growth of the Latino population in the early twenty-first century. Each chapter is divided into subsections. Chapters 1 through 5 deal with the formative stages of Mexican life and society in the Southwest: the nature and consequence of Spanish colonialism and the themes of settlement and Indian resistance; the development of the northern frontier region during the transition from Spanish to Mexican and finally American rule, focusing on the shift of the economic production of mission lands to the native Californians through secularization; the social interactions between Mexicans, Indians, and entrepreneurs in the New Mexico territory who connected it to the United States through the Sante Fe Trail; the encroachment on Texas by the westward movement of Anglo slaveholders that culminates in the Texas Revolt of 1836;

the Manifest Destiny ideology that gained expansion into California and culminated in the Mexican War and the disruptions and transformations of Mexican life caused by this war; Mexican Americans in the Civil War and relations with Indians; the rise of capitalist agriculture in the 1870s and 1880s; and agrarian protest and populism. Also, along with race relations, there is a thematic emphasis on the effect of late-nineteenth-century railroad building on the economics of northern Mexico and the United States and Mexican migration. It is at this time that Mexican migrants arrived as birds of passage, intending to return to Mexico with newly acquired wealth but instead remaining and sending for their family members.

Chapters 6 through 11 take up the themes of the first wave of Mexican immigration to the United States from the 1910 Mexican Revolution to the early Great Depression; the challenges Mexicans faced in the initial years during which they arrived in large numbers and initiated community formation and adaptation in their new homeland; repatriations; the surge of union activism among mine, cannery, and agricultural workers that was emblematic of larger struggles already evident in the 1930s; the appeal of communism and the struggle against fascism; the domestic and overseas warfront experiences of Mexican Americans during World War II; the progress and achievements of Mexican Americans in their challenge of racial norms in the 1950s; the key issues of the cold war and McCarthyism; the failure of President Johnson's Great Society to bring social and economic equality to Mexican Americans; the rise of Mexican American social protest movements in the 1960s and 1970s to secure full citizenship; Chicano movement ideology; mobilizing against the long and unpopular war in Vietnam; Mexican Americans and the culture wars and social polarization of the 1980s and 1990s and the struggle over affirmative action; and the ongoing process of globalization as embodied in the North American Free Trade Agreement, when the new rapid and intensive immigration from Mexico became noticeable. The epilogue, Chapter 12, contains a discussion of the recent years since 2000 with a focus on immigrant social movements and policy debates regarding immigration reform, and it confronts and discusses other contemporary issues facing Latinos of Mexican background. Throughout the book I have attempted to include and acknowledge the presence and contributions of women whose lives have been underdocumented and need to be written into the history. Their many contributions have earned them the honor of remembrance.

*Crucible of Struggle: A History of Mexican Americans from Colonial Times to the Present Era* is thus a story of the denial of equality and freedom and the development of strategies by Mexican Americans for achieving these elusive goals. It is mindful of the earliest Spanish frontier but also rethinks the chronological conceptualization of Mexican American history by discussing and giving an up-to-date view of Mexican American history that reflects the state of current research.

## NOTES

1. Joseph A. Rodríguez and Vicki L. Ruiz, "At Loose Ends: Twentieth-Century Latinos in Current United States History Textbooks," *Journal of American History* 86, no. 4 (March 2000): 1689–99; Vicki L. Ruiz, "Nuestra America: Latino History as United States History," *Journal of American History* 93, no. 3 (December 2006): 655–72.

2. Albert Camarillo, *Chicanos in a Changing Society: From Mexican Pueblos to American Barrios in Santa Barbara and Southern California, 1848–1930* (Cambridge, MA: Harvard University Press, 1979); Richard Griswold del Castillo, *The Los Angeles Barrio, 1850–1890: A Social History* (Berkeley: University of California Press, 1979); Juan Gómez-Quiñones, *Sembradores, Ricardo Flores Magón y El Partido Liberal Mexicano: A Eulogy and Critique,* rev. ed. (Los Angeles: Chicano Studies Center Publication, University of California, Los Angeles, 1977.)

3. George Sánchez, *Becoming Mexican American: Ethnicity, Culture, and Identity in Chicano Los Angeles, 1900–1945* (Oxford, UK: Oxford University Press, 1993); Stephen J. Pitti, *The Devil in Silicon Valley: Northern California, Race, and Mexican Americans* (Princeton, NJ: Princeton University Press, 2003); David G. Gutiérrez, *Walls and Mirrors: Mexican Americans, Mexican Immigrants, and the Politics of Ethnicity* (Berkeley: University of California Press, 1995); Neil Foley, *The White Scourge: Mexicans, Blacks, and Poor Whites in Texas Cotton Culture* (Berkeley: University of California Press, 1997); Roberto Treviño, *The Church in the Barrio: Mexican American Ethno-Catholicism in Houston* (Chapel Hill: University of North Carolina Press, 2006).

4. David Weber, *The Mexican Frontier, 1821–1846* (Albuquerque: University of New Mexico Press, 1982); Douglas Monroy, *Thrown Among Strangers: The Making of Mexican Culture in Frontier California* (Berkeley: University of California Press, 1993); Ramon Gutiérrez, *When Jesus Came the Corn Mothers Went Away: Marriage, Sexuality, and Power in New Mexico, 1500–1846* (Stanford, CA: Stanford University Press, 1991); James Brooks, *Captives and Cousins: Slavery, Kinship, and Community in the Southwest Borderlands* (Chapel Hill: University of North Carolina Press, 2002); Andrés Reséndez, *Changing Identities at the Frontier: Texas and New Mexico, 1800–1850* (Cambridge: Cambridge University Press, 2004).

5. Vicki L. Ruiz, *From Out of the Shadows: Mexican Women in Twentieth-Century America* (New York: Oxford University Press, 2008); Deena González, *Refusing the Favor: The Spanish-Mexican Women of Santa Fe: 1820–1880* (New York: Oxford University Press, 2001); Gabriela Arredondo, *Mexican Chicago: Race, Identity, and Nation, 1916–39* (Urbana: University of Illinois Press, 2008); among other studies.

6. *North from Mexico* was reissued in paperback in the late 1960s and was updated by Matt S. Meier in an expanded 1990 edition for Greenwood Press to cover the period from 1945 to 1988. The other three surveys are: *The Chicanos: A History of Mexican Americans* written by Matt S. Meier and Feliciano Ribera, published in 1972 by Hill and Wang for its American Century Series and reissued in 1993 as a second edition under the new title *Mexican Americans/American Mexicans: From Conquistadores to Chicanos; North to Aztlán: A History of Mexican Americans in the United States* by Richard Griswold del Castillo and Arnoldo de Leon, published in 1996 by Twayne Publishers as part of its Immigrant Heritage of America Series; and *Mexicanos: A History of Mexicans in the United States,* written by Manuel G. Gonzales and published by Indiana University Press in 1999.

7. For example, McWilliams notes that in 1900, the Sons of the Golden West were asked for a list of prominent men in the history of Los Angeles. When the list was submitted, there was not one Spanish name. An excellent account of Carey McWilliams's life and career is Peter Richardson's *American Prophet: The Life and Work of Carey McWilliams* (Ann Arbor: University of Michigan Press, 2005).

8. Harper and Row produced a second edition of Acuña's survey in 1980 as *Occupied America II.* Harper and Row published a third edition of *Occupied America* in 1988 and a fourth in 2000, and Acuña readopted the chronological framework of the first edition.

9. In the preface to the third edition of *Occupied America,* Acuña tells us that this style of analysis was informed by contemporary critiques of more traditionally understood colonialism in Africa and Asia, especially Franz Fanon and Chinua Achebe.

# ACKNOWLEDGMENTS

*✦*

In the community of scholars, I would like to mention all of those who have had a profound intellectual influence on me. I especially want to thank Alan M. Wald, David Montgomery, Nelson Lichtenstein, Eileen Boris, Gerald Horne, David G. Gutiérrez, Ramón A. Gutiérrez, David J. Weber, Robin D. G. Kelly, Pekka Hämäläinen, Michael K. Honey, Linda Gordon, and Nancy MacLean. Others who deserve my thanks include Louis A. Perez, Jr., Lloyd Kramer, Katherine DuVal, W. Miles Fletcher, Joe Glatthaar, Jacquelyn Dowd Hall, Jerma A. Jackson, Heather Williams, and Lars Schoultz, in addition to my colleagues and my friends in my new home at the University of North Carolina, Chapel Hill.

The archivists and staff who were particularly helpful with my research, and colleagues and friends who assisted me in procuring archival material and images that appear in this book are: Dr. Thomas Kreneck and Grace Charles, Special Collections, at Texas A&M University–Corpus Christi for their archival help with their expert and ready assistance in finding materials as well as obtaining the photograph of the Viva Kennedy Club; Professor Ann Massmann of the Center for Southwest Research at the University of New Mexico for her assistance in navigating the Reies López Tijerina Collection as well as arranging a meeting with the staff members who processed Tijerina's papers for the Center and offered valuable insights. Christine Marin and Neil E. Millican, Chicano Research Collection, Arizona State University, for their guidance in finding information and for prompt processing of my request for photographs from their rich collection; Dr. William Estrada for permitting me use of the photograph of Ernesto Galarza from his own personal collection as well as providing me fascinating historical background on Galarza the "barrio boy"; Katherine Reeve of the Arizona Historical Society in Tucson for obtaining a photograph of the Camp Grant massacre trial participants the day before her staff photographer lost his job to state budget cuts and consequent staff reductions; Michael Hironymous of the Nettie Lee Benson Latin American Collection of the University of Texas, Austin, for his assistance in acquiring the Sons of America image and willingness to comb the Raza Unida Party archives for a photograph of this group's activities; Patrick Lemelle of the Institute of Texan Cultures at the University of Texas, San Antonio, for his helpfulness and sleuthing to find his archive's copy of a photograph of Gregorio Cortez when another major university, which was the primary repository for the photograph, could not; Daniel Kosharek of Palace of the Governors, Sante Fe, New Mexico; Michelle Frauenberger of the Franklin Delano Roosevelt Presidential Library in Hyde Park, New York; Victor Hotho of the Texas State Preservation Board; Clare Flemming of the Academy of Natural Sciences, Philadelphia; Susan Synder of the Bancroft Library, the University of California, Berkeley; Carol Nishijima, Department of Special Collections, the University of California, Los Angeles Library; and David Nacke at the University of New Mexico.

A special thanks to artist and longtime friend Barbara Carrasco for assisting me in obtaining the use of the photograph of Dolores Huerta registering members at the NFWA founding convention; and to photographer and longtime friend Harry Gamboa, Jr., for his expert aesthetic and ability to recognize when he is at the perfect place at the optimal time to take a shot that will be historically significant and included in this book.

I thank Oxford University Press freelance acquisitions editor Bruce Borland for originally inviting me in 2000 to work on this book. Thanks also to Oxford University Press's reviewers Luis Leobardo Arroyo, California State University, Long Beach; Francisco E. Balderrama, California State University Los Angeles; Lawrence Culver, Utah State University; and Carmen R. Lugo-Lugo, Washington State University for their critical and constructive reviews of my manuscript. At Oxford University Press I would like to thank executive editor Brian Wheel who gave me vital support, and so many encouraging words, from the beginning to the end of the formal publication process; editorial assistant Danniel Schoonebeek; senior production editor Barbara Mathieu for her expert laying out of this book; copyeditor Elaine Kehoe's efficient preparation of this manuscript for publication; and the creative book cover by Liz Demeter and interior design by Binbin Li. Many thanks to the many people at Oxford University Press whose names I do not know who labored to convert my manuscript into a book.

Finally, and most of all, a very special thanks is due to my beautiful and loving wife S. Zaneta Kosiba-Vargas who came into my life and changed me forever. Thank you for your unceasing love, companionship, and encouragement and for standing by my side all of these years. This book is dedicated to you Zaneta and our gifted daughter Lina and our precious grandson Marcel. Lina, you are so close to my heart. Marcel, your birth marked my emotional rebirth and your special love was a source of inspiration in writing this book.

# A NOTE ON TERMINOLOGY

The terminology varies from chapter to chapter and in some cases within a chapter. The terms *Tejano* and *Californio* are used to designate persons of Mexican American and Mexican background in Texas and California, respectively. *Anglo* is the term of usage in the Southwest, both in the past and in present times. It functions much in the same way as the term *white*. I use the term *Mexican* when I want to emphasize a moniker that whites use to define both U.S.-born Mexicans and Mexican nationals. The term *Chicano* connotes political awareness or consciousness and refers to U.S.-born persons of Mexican descent. As a final remark on terminology, the term *Latino* is all-inclusive. It is used to refer to immigrants to the United States from Mexico, Central America, and the Spanish-speaking Caribbean. *Latino* is used to reflect the shift in self-identification of the Spanish-speaking population from Mexican to Latino, especially in the final chapter and epilogue. Otherwise I use the term *Mexican American*.

# CHAPTER 1

✦

# The Era of the Spanish Northern Frontier to 1821

The history of the inhabitants of Spain's vast northern frontier—the modern Southwest area of New Mexico, Arizona, Texas, and California—unfolded within the context of the various rivalries among European colonial powers for control of North American trade, influence over the Indians, and possession of empires. Unlike England, France, or Russia, Spain's rivals in the Americas, the purpose of the Spanish *entrada* (entrance) into the northern frontier was to look for riches, with the religious conversion of Indians playing a secondary role. The Spanish era consisted of three periods. The first period of initial colonization lasted from the arrival of Juan de Oñate in New Mexico in 1598 to the Pueblo Revolt of 1680. The second began with the reconquest of New Mexico in 1693 by Juan de Vargas and lasted until the inspection of the northern frontier by Visitador General José de Gálvez in 1765 during the Bourbon Reforms. The third period was from the Bourbon reorganization of the northern frontier until Mexican Independence in 1821. By the early eighteenth century, Spanish explorers had mapped most of the territory and established more than three hundred settlements, thereby extending Spain's presence in this vast region.[1]

The desire of the Spanish Crown was to establish permanent settlements on its northern frontier as buffers against European enemies and hostile Indians. Missions, presidios, and pueblos (towns) were the most important institutions. Spain's missionary impulse, developed through centuries of warfare, was longer lasting than it was with other European powers. Missionary efforts were designed to spread the Catholic faith in the heathen wilderness. As teachers, civilizers, and lawgivers, Spanish missionary priests imposed European culture on the Indians to make them loyal and obedient Christians. Known for their missionary work, the Franciscans preached to the Indians but also exploited their labor to the benefit of agricultural development, as in Alta California, where the missions held most of the better land. In Texas, missions failed to convert Indians to the Catholic faith or produce many goods, the same shortcomings of the few missions established in the New Mexico province. Power struggles arose between religious and secular authorities on the northern frontier over their access to Indian labor and commerce. Bound by notions of self-interest and religious conviction to protect the

1

Indians, the Church deplored the excessive actions against them, especially Spanish soldiers' raping Indian women. The fear of Indian rebellion fostered the Church's dependence on civil-military authority. The "harvesting of Indian souls" by the missionary priests and the Spanish states' costly and erratic pattern of Indian diplomacy eventually created for its colonists a condition of endemic warfare with several powerful Indian nations, among them the Comanche. By 1800, Spain had yet to overcome the Indian threat to its northern frontier settlements.[2]

Imperial Spain regarded the northern frontier of New Spain (Mexico) as a territorial buffer zone between empires. Marginal to Spain's economic needs, the vast region was, furthermore, expensive to maintain. With its overall objective being the colonization of lands for defensive purposes against its European rivals, Spain established an institutional presence in the northern frontier through the presidios. These frontier outposts became melting pot communities, owing to Spain's inability to adequately man them with soldiers and through the practice of Spanish males taking Indian and mixed-race spouses or *negro* (African) concubines. From these presidios militias made up of Spanish and Indian allies launched expeditions into the Indian strongholds resisting subjugation.

The settlers faced constant attacks by Apaches, Comanches, and other nomadic Indians who raided the frontier settlements or defended their territory from Spanish encroachment. The Spaniards took advantage of a royal decree that permitted the enslavement of unconverted Indians who made unprovoked attacks on Spanish colonists. Indian reaction to this imperial policy of colonization and slavery was resistance, and in the New Mexico province it produced the Pueblo Revolt of 1680. The bloody episode scaled the end to thirteen years of Spanish rule in the New Mexico province.

A succession of raids and counterraids by Spanish colonists and their Indian allies rapidly developed into widespread warfare. This gave rise to retaliatory attacks in which captives were taken and traded. The demand for captives intensified fighting between the nomadic Indian tribes, which the Spanish learned to exploit by purchasing captives from all groups. The Spanish also used diplomacy in their dealings with the Indian tribes. Through the policy of peace by purchase, put into effect in the late eighteenth century, the Spanish supplied Indians with food, clothing, and other items that they could procure only by raiding or trading captives.[3] Guided by their self-interests, the Indians of the northern frontier would ally with one or the other European rivals to leverage favors from them.

Those who occupied the land for Spain on the northern frontier lived in small, isolated self-sufficient *poblaciones*, or communities. The use of the soldier as colonist formed part of the Spanish colonization strategies to the early nineteenth century. Individual and communal land grants were rewards for service to the Spanish Crown, and the occupation of expansive lands was achieved by rancher-farmers. Colonists and Indians influenced one another in their techniques of hunting and warfare. Trade conducted between the New Mexican colonists and nomadic Indian tribes of the southern plains was a key activity during the last decades of the eighteenth century. The commercial interests of New Mexico's residents likewise structured and restructured relations and alliances with the area Indians with whom they traded. Because no mineral wealth was found to encourage population growth in such an inhospitable land, the northern frontier settlements grew slowly.

By 1800, the newly created United States was already the chief threat to New Spain's northern periphery. Bourbon Spain's confrontation with the United States meant a new series of crises—disputes over the boundary with Florida and over navigation on the Mississippi River and competition for the loyalty of the Indians in the contested lands. Nevertheless, the northern frontier society that emerged was economically, socially, and politically diverse; it was a product of interactions among settlers, Indians, and foreign immigrants in which exploitation, power struggles, and cooperation over material and spiritual values unfolded. The regionally disconnected northern societies, islands of Spanish royal power beset by dangers, also showed a decided tendency toward defining themselves separately from and resisting control by New Spain, emphasizing individualism, self-reliance, dependence on one another, and the intermingling of races.[4] This is the frontier society that the ambitious and expansionist-minded Americans came upon as they made their way into the Southwest. Mexico City's lack of communication and control over the northern frontier made it difficult to provide the settlers with protection from the Americans.

## SPANISH INSTITUTIONS AND MIXED-RACE SOCIETY OF THE NORTHERN FRONTIER

Spain used three basic institutions to settle the northern frontier: the mission, the presidio, and the town, all focal points of Spanish civilized society. This was in contrast to central Mexico, where the Spanish developed an economy based on agriculture and mining using Indian tribute labor (a system by which labor was exacted from the Indians). The missions as a conquest institution allowed the Spanish to control and settle the northern frontier. In New Mexico, missions were built at the edge of Indian villages; in Texas, missions merged with settlements established around military presidios; and in Alta California, a mission was a self-sustaining community and the basic institution of settlement. The missions would operate for as long as it took to convert and civilize the Indians, duly estimated at ten years.[5] To achieve conversion to Christianity, priests used trickery, bribery, and force.

Spanish settlers had little contact with the missions or priests because the missions' purpose was full cultural and social reorientation of the Indian, achieved through promoting community life, or *congregación*. This purpose implied a reorganization of the various Indian economies based on mission needs. The neophytes were taught to make wine, shoes, and candles; to tan hides and make tallow; to cultivate gardens, vineyards, orchards, and grain fields; and to build aqueducts, dams and reservoirs. Consequently, the mission Indians learned carpentry and masonry to construct buildings. The Spanish brought Indian auxiliaries with them as aides in the civilizing of the Indians. As models, teachers, and colonists, the auxiliaries instructed the northern Indians in social life, work, and minor political office holding. The Indians felt the oppressive, authoritarian character of the Catholic regime through punishment. Indeed, the mission priests unmercifully made regular use of every form of corporal punishment against recalcitrant Indians, including whipping posts, stocks, branding, mutilation, prison cells, and execution.[6] As an additional safeguard against rebellion, the Indians were forbidden to bear arms or ride horses. This legacy of brutality and harsh treatment of the Indians sears the Catholic missionary's humane image. Subjected to a state of hopeless servitude, the Indians believed the missionaries were the devil incarnate. Slavery to the Indians was annihilation, and they resisted Spanish incursion with rebellion.

Spain's vast, far-flung empire had many frontiers facing hostile Indians and European rivals; thus it was never able to garrison all the dangerous flash points effectively. Based on the model for the protection of the mining areas of New Spain, the presidio or fort was the defensive arm of Spanish colonization. From the presidios full-scale military campaigns were launched against marauding Indians in the immediate area and far afield. In the eighteenth century the presidios eclipsed the missions as a dominant Spanish northern frontier institution. Manned by soldier-settlers, for the most part, the presidios gave rise to the towns of Santa Fe in New Mexico, El Paso and San Antonio in Texas, Tucson in Arizona, and Monterey, San Francisco, and San Diego in Alta California.[7]

The new Bourbon administration that assumed power in 1707 was determined to centralize power in the Spanish monarchy. The status of the northern frontier changed dramatically after 1750 when Spain, pressed by growing foreign pressure, sought to strengthen and coordinate the defensive margins of its possessions to consolidate New Spain's northern presidial line. A response to the Seven Years' War (1756–1763), the Bourbon Reforms in Spain's northern frontier provinces resulted in territorial expansion, political consolidation, increased defenses against foreign invasion, and economic growth through trade. In 1776, an office of commandant-general was set up to provide all the northern provinces with more effective government and better defense.[8] As its chief administrator, Teodoro de Croix strengthened the existing frontier fortifications, the new forts stretching from Texas to the California coast. New Mexico, an interior Spanish province, was left outside of this line of defense, though a garrison was established in this province.[9]

Duty on the dangerous and remote northern frontier was avoided, and most troops were kept in Mexico City. Only when there was political turmoil or imminent foreign invasion were the presidios properly manned or reinforced. As a result, forced conscription was used to fill the ranks of the presidio soldiers; vagabonds, criminals, and Indians (kept in chains to prevent their escape) composed many of the militia companies formed by the Spanish.[10]

Manning the military garrisons was difficult because manpower was in short supply. Just under a thousand soldiers and officers commissioned by the Spanish Crown served on the northern frontier. The presidio soldiers were veteran Indian fighters with prior experience at other presidios on Spain's northern frontier. Fifty-nine soldiers were assigned to the two presidios in Texas, half the force required by each fort. New Mexico had one garrison with one hundred soldiers, but a third of the men lacked military equipment. In Arizona less than a dozen soldiers manned the presidios at Tubac and Tucson. In Alta California, presidios were established at San Diego (1769), Monterey (1770), San Francisco (1776), and Santa Barbara (1782). Half the soldiers guarded the missions, and the rest served at presidios or presidial towns. There were four hundred soldiers in Alta California during the Spanish period, distributed among the four presidios and twenty-one missions.[11]

Presidio soldiers faced long duty assignments, were poorly paid, and had little chance of promotion. The soldiers were unhappy with their duty, and insubordination, desertion, and other disciplinary problems limited their efficiency; poor communication and few or no provisions further hindered defense.[12] The poorly clad men had to purchase overpriced uniforms, horses, and weapons, for much of the money Spain provided for its frontier defense wound up in the pockets of corrupt officials. Going months without pay, the hard-pressed soldiers sold their guns and ammunition and asked for permission to hunt, farm, and ranch to feed themselves and their families. Owing to trying circumstances, soldiers usually exacted food and rations from the frontier citizenry, and some even resorted to stealing.[13]

The presidios were an economic burden for the impoverished northern settlements, because the civilian communities were required to provide the garrison soldiers and their families with food and shelter. For example, the pueblo of San José in northern Alta California, this province's first Spanish civilian settlement, grew grain and vegetables to support the military outpost at San Francisco, as well as the Santa Clara mission. The pueblo of Los Angeles served a similar purpose. Twelve families had been recruited to raise crops and livestock for the four area presidios.[14]

The small presidial communities such as San Diego, Santa Barbara, Monterey, San Francisco, Tucson, and Nogales did not develop into municipalities until after the end of the Spanish era. As a condition of owning land within a five-mile radius of a presidio, the settlers all along the frontier fought in campaigns against the highly mobile Indian raiders who swept through the country and were difficult to subdue.[15]

**Santa Clara Mission in 1849.**
CREDIT: msc.12.11. Andrew P. Hill painting. SCU General Photograph Collection-Mission Santa Clara, Sketches & Paintings. Courtesy of Santa Clara University Library, Department of Archives and Special Collection.

The protection of the far-flung northern colonies against ascending Indian raids grew to depend on an informal civilian militia recruited from the nearby ranches and towns, who supplied their own weapons and horses. Owing to the severe shortages of guns and ammunition, and having adjusted to pioneer conditions, the volunteer forces frequently pursued and fought the Indians in their own way, with bows and arrows and lances. The weary combatants showed themselves to be able soldiers, but there were not enough of them. The weak system of defense against raiding Indians, who struck quickly and without warning, contributed to the growing alienation of the northern frontier settlements from the government in Mexico City.[16] Nevertheless, the protection of homes, families, and property and the emergent sense of community encouraged settlers to volunteer as militia, including Indian allies. The promise of spoils, namely Indian captives who could be forced into service as ranch hands and servants, also served as an inducement.

The subjects of a strong and absolute monarchy, the pioneers had either journeyed north with permission, been sent there by royal order, or been recruited by Spanish officials given authorization to open new lands for the Crown. Settlers went north with offers of land, seeds, tools, titles of nobility, exemption from taxes, and the promise of military protection.[17] Once on the frontier, the settlers could not leave or travel without official consent, as settlement was part of a royal plan. Laws also governed land tenure, methods of irrigation, and the laying out of towns, and there were restrictions on trade with foreigners. Integrated into a social system that was an extension of the larger Spanish colonial society, the settlers essentially were captives of the Spanish Crown's bureaucracy. Moreover, New Spain was a rigidly race- and class-stratified society.

At the top of New Spain's caste system were the *peninsulares* (European-born Spaniards) and the *creoles* (Spaniards born in the Americas). Most administrative officials were peninsulares, whereas creoles dominated the political realm, the Catholic Church, and bureaucracies and owned land and mines. These upper-class Spaniards perpetuated income inequality and an authoritarian-paternalistic rule over a broad peasant substratum comprised of mestizos, that is, people of mixed Indian, European, and Negro blood. Miscegenation was known as *mestizaje*. The elaborate Spanish caste system distinguished sixteen kinds of mestizos. Mestizos were considered racially inferior, a low-status caste. Although legally free, mestizos had to pay taxes and render military service. Throughout Spanish colonial America the term *indio* (Indian) had heavily negative connotations. It was term of denigration and also one that suggested aggression.[18]

In the Spanish Americas an individual's social status, wealth, occupation, and legitimate or illegitimate birth strongly correlated with his or her racial and ethnic origins. Mestizos, together with Negroes, mulattos, *afromestizos* (African Indians or *zambos*), and *genízaros* (detribalized or Hispanicized captive Indians), composed the vast majority of settlers. Along with soldiers of black ancestry, Negroes came to the northern frontier involuntarily as slaves or servants, and mulatto women and children were brought illegally by soldiers. Other offspring derived from further intermixing between mestizo, mulatto, and zambo. The nearly impermeable caste system, based on racial distinction and social standing, that would take hold for centuries was quite fluid and ambiguous on the northern frontier. Despite its many hardships, the northern frontier offered mixed-blood settlers opportunities of social mobility that were closed to them in Mexico. Military service was one sure method of attaining social status. Many mestizos and other mixed-blood people obtained government positions owing to the absence of Spaniards to fill the offices. For example, the lieutenant governor of New Mexico in 1680, Alonzo García, was a mestizo, and many of the leaders of the Pueblo Revolt, such as Alonzo Catití, were mestizos disaffected with the Spanish. The large number of mestizos and mulattoes were evidence that miscegenation between Spanish and Indians was widespread and indiscriminate, despite religious regulations. During the Bourbon reforms, wealthy colonists of mixed-race background purchased certificates of whiteness, whereas other mixed-race individuals reclassified themselves Spaniards. In time, the frontier population became "whiter," as mestizos declared themselves Spanish and Indians and mulattoes declared themselves mestizos.[19]

Along with the blurring of racial "boundaries," settlers on the northern frontier simultaneously transformed Spanish culture through adjustments in their dress, diet, medicine, homes, and communities. Whereas Spaniards maintained dress appearances to distinguish themselves from Indians, the common Hispano man and woman who had contact with Indians often mingled European and Indian clothing. They donned moccasins, dressed in buckskins and coarse woolens and flannels. In addition to adopting the Indians' agricultural plants and cultivation and harvesting methods, settlers adopted Indian food preparation methods,

*Cuadro de Castas.*
Different castes of Mexico, late 18th century.
CREDIT: Museo Nacional del Virreinato, Instituto Nacional de Antropología e Historia.

**How the California Indians Fight, 1791.**
CREDIT: MS 1726-47. Courtesy of Museo Naval, Madrid.

implements, and other indigenous influences. Colonial settlers and Indians in essence forged pacts of interdependence. Moreover, the northern Indians mixed into the lower segments of Spanish settler society.[20]

Spread over a larger territory, Indians remained warlike and a formidable presence and an obstacle to Spanish expansion. Maintained to prevent further encroachment by Spain's foreign rivals and to defend against hostile Indian tribes, the northern frontier settlements served basically as defensive positions until the end of Spanish rule in 1821. Initiative was discouraged, and individual interests were subordinated to those of the military. Spanish institutions and culture as a result took on derived or hybrid forms. The settlers reproduced the Spanish hierarchical and patriarchal social structures through the acquisition of titles, land, and Indian servants. However, few settlers became wealthy.[21]

## THE FOUNDING OF NEW MEXICO

Missions were the harbingers of European civilization in New Spain. The seventeenth century was the missionary era on the northern frontier. Through the passage of the Laws of Discovery, religious forays received royal sanction if missions were established to convert Indians to Catholicism. This military protection with financial backing facilitated Franciscan proselytizing efforts by terrifying Indians into submission. As Spanish settlement advanced steadily northward, Franciscans learned that the area Indians traded with other Indians who lived even further north.

In 1581, Captain Francisco Sánchez Chumascado and Fray Agustín Rodríguez led a party of three Franciscan friars, nine soldiers, nineteen Indian auxiliaries, and six hundred head of livestock three hundred miles into present-day New Mexico. Antonio de Espejo led another entrada the following year. Espejo's exaggerated reports reminded Spanish officials of the many prospective Indian converts to Christianity and, more important, of the potential to discover mineral wealth. This news encouraged the subsequent conquest and colonization of New Mexico.[22] The Spanish believed the subjugation of the Indians was justified because it brought cultural and religious superiority to a people deemed *barbároso* (barbarous). Ignoring royal legislation on the treatment of the Indians, a pattern of Spanish brutality toward the Indians was established in New Mexico by the first explorers and colonists, as an increasingly bitter conflict emerged between Franciscan missionaries, governors, and settlers over control of Pueblo land, labor, and tribute.

In 1595, King Philip II of Spain opened New Mexico to colonial expansion. Universally obsessed with the lust for gold and silver, Spain's original attraction to the northern region was its potential wealth, though later the dominating motive in the settlement of New Mexico was religious—to spread the Catholic faith among the Indians and destroy their religions. Spain's approach to New Mexico once more was a long overland march from the mining area of Zacatecas, Mexico.[23]

In 1598, with a contract for a colonization expedition, though with little financial support from Spain, Juan de Oñate, a successful and wealthy silver miner, eagerly set off from Zacatecas with an elaborate and well-organized expedition of settler colonists into the northern region (previously explored by his father's friend Francisco Vasquez de Coronado fifty years earlier).[24] Oñate's party consisted of about 129 colonists, some accompanied by their families; nine Franciscan friars; several hundred Indians; 61 wagonloads of goods; and 7,000 domestic animals. The troops and settlers included Spaniards, Greeks, Flemish, Creole Spaniards, mestizos, Indians, and, although barred, mulatto slaves. Mestizos predominated. Oñate was awarded titles and authorized to grant titles, and he was invested with civil and military authority over the settlement. The Spaniard was also designated the primary beneficiary of any riches discovered, as well as Indian labor.[25] Oñate would depend on intimidation and violence to control the Pueblo Indians.

On April 30, 1598, the Oñate expedition crossed the Río Grande and stopped near present San Elizario, Texas. Invoking the King's name, it took formal possession of the territory. Continuing north along the Río Grande, the expedition paused at each Indian settlement and obtained their formal allegiance to the authority of their new king and new God. Spanish law demanded that if the Indians resisted, their lands would be confiscated, and they would be put to the sword or enslaved. By the early seventeenth century, the northern Spanish colonies institutionalized slavery and other forms of servitude.[26]

The Franciscans converted the Indians to Christianity, scoring considerable success with the youths the priests took away from their parents. The Acoma and Hopi Indians were hostile toward the Franciscans and steadfastly resisted Christian conversion. In response to their maltreatment and impoverishment, the subjugated Indian pueblos began to intrigue to free themselves from Spanish tyranny.

Violence and terror based on patriarchal codes of honor was a principal Spanish tactic that underlined Juan de Oñate's colonizing plan. In early December 1598, one of Oñate's lieutenants, his nephew Juan de Saldívar, and thirty of his men demanded alliance of the Acoma Pueblo and attempted to exact tribute from the Indians. They refused Saldívar. Angered, the Spanish officer seized corn, beans, squash, and clothing from the Indians and, as a lesson for their insubordination, unleashed a campaign of torture, slaughter, and rape. The Acomas retaliated; they lured Saldívar and ten of his men to the top of the mesa and butchered the soldiers. Oñate in reprisal declared war on the Acoma and ordered his soldiers to punish them for going to war against the Spanish. On January 23, 1599, soldiers under Vicente de Saldívar completely destroyed the Acoma pueblo and killed all the inhabitants they could find in a full-scale assault. When the carnage was over, the Indian dead totaled eight hundred men, women, and children. Oñate's men took eighty men and five hundred women and children captive. Demanding swift and exemplary punishment, on February 12, 1599, the Indian prisoners were marched to San Juan, where the adults, including women over twelve years of age, were given a criminal sentence of twenty years that legalized their enslavement. Many of the enslaved Indians were sent south under escort to work in the mines. The Indian girls and boys under age twelve were placed under the care of the Fray Alonzo Martínez and Vicente de Saldívar to perform domestic labor. In a final act of retribution, Oñate forced all the adult male Indian captives to have a foot cut off, an act carried out in public on different days and at different pueblos. He then sentenced them to twenty years of enslavement to his soldiers. These brutal actions served as a warning to other Indians who chose to challenge Spanish authority. Similar incidents of pillaging, burning, and murdering marked the colonial diplomacy of the Oñate expedition. In 1607, the King of Spain banished Oñate for life from the New Mexico province for mismanagement, despotism, and maltreating the Indians and settlers.[27]

Juan de Oñate's failure to discover wealth, his misrule of the New Mexico province, and constant Indian raiding and rebellion convinced Spanish royal officials to abandon the lands. However, the Franciscan missionaries did not want the Indians to lapse into heathenism and appealed to the King of Spain to reconsider. In 1609, the King appointed Pedro Peralta the governor of New Mexico, established Santa Fe as the new provincial capital in 1610, and sent additional soldiers to the northern province.[28]

During the next several decades, a string of permanent Spanish settlements was established in New Mexico along the Río Grande extending from present-day Socorro in the south to the Taos Valley in the north, an upper region more remote physically and socially. By 1680 there were three thousand Spanish colonists settled on communal land grants to give them better defense against the Indians. The early farms were self-sufficient because the colonist and his family did the work. The men hunted, cleared the land, built homes, farmed, and performed domestic chores such as butchering and blacksmithing. Women were employed at housework and, with their children, took care of stock and poultry and engaged in domestic industries with the men. Other settlers lived in clusters of farms and ranches close to Pueblo Indians, their source of labor. Marriage and population growth were necessary to stabilize the colony and spread Spanish power, and owing to the shortage of Spanish women, male settlers took wives from among local Indian women. Hard-pressed Indian parents often encouraged such unions of their daughters for economic reasons. The Spanish had acquired the best farm-lands, thus forcing the Indians into poorer lands.[29]

Approximately fifty thousand Pueblo Indians lived in the New Mexico prov-ince, and through baptismal and doctrinal education twenty thousand had been converted to Christianity. Indian tribute and trade in Indian slaves with the south-ern mining districts was the sole source of wealth. Commercial workshops (*obrajes*) at the Indian pueblos and at Santa Fe were set up on tribute and captive Indian labor, producing blankets, hides, ropes, leather, and other products that were traded at mining districts. Because of years of tribulation through enslavement and disease-induced population collapse, the absolute prohibition of traditional reli-gious practices and the destruction of religious images by missionary zealots sparked several Indian revolts. The embittered and angry Indians cared little for Christianity. The Pueblo Revolt of 1680 was the worst of this cycle of warfare.[30] It was triggered by the whipping of its leaders, but its causes were related to a variety of grievances—specifically, the desire to cast off the yoke of the Catholic Church.

## RESISTING SPANISH COLONIZATION: THE PUEBLO REVOLT OF 1680

The Pueblo Indians were growing more desperate and resentful owing to decades of escalating death rates from disease, drought, and famine and increasing raids of their villages and settlements by Navajo and Apache Indians. Moreover, in 1664 New Mexico's governor had imposed restrictions on Pueblo trade with nomadic Indians and instituted labor drafts. Brutality inflicted by the Spanish included the rape of Indian women, who lived in fear of physical abuse by the soldiers. The destruction of kivas, the public humiliation of holy men, and the suppression of ceremonial practices reached a critical juncture in the 1670s. The Pueblo Indians turned to spiritual sources to fuel their resistance. They followed the mulatto prophet Popé of the Naranjo family of the San Juan Pueblo, who harbored con-tempt for Spanish rule. Led by Popé, who held an important religious office, the Indians began to formulate a strategy to overthrow their Spanish overlords, whom they called disparagingly "the demons of hell." [31]

The greatest of all Indian revolts on the northern frontier broke out in 1680 under the leadership of Popé. The crisis came to a head in 1675 when the Spanish interro-gated forty-seven Pueblo Indian holy men on charges of practicing sorcery and plot-ting rebellion. As a way to intimidate the Pueblos, four of the religious leaders were hanged, and the others were flogged. A large number of Indian warriors threatened Governor Juan Francisco Treviño with attack and succeeded in obtaining the release of the holy men. One of these was Popé. Following his release, Popé led the intertribal movement to expel the hated Spanish oppressors and their culture from New Mexico.[32]

The headquarters of the plotters was Taos Pueblo. There Popé and his con-spirators, among them sympathetic Apaches, mixed bloods, and mestizos, devised a plan; each Pueblo at a prearranged signal was to destroy its mission churches and the holy images and then kill the resident priests and settlers. Once the outlying

Spanish settlements were wiped out, the rebel forces would converge on the capital of Santa Fe and destroy it.[33]

Popé set August 11, 1680, as the date of reckoning. The rebel leader dispatched runners to take his message to all the pueblos. The runners carried calendars, cords of knotted maguey fiber marking the number of days until the uprising. Each morning the Pueblo leaders untied one knot from the cords. The last knot untied signaled the insurgency. However, the plot was betrayed because two Pueblo Indian runners were captured at Tesuque pueblo, alerting Governor Otermín of the plot. Their strategy compromised, Pueblo leaders sent runners out with new instructions to begin the rebellion a day earlier, on August 10.[34]

That morning the surprise attacks began and extended from the northern Tewa pueblo of Taos to the Tewa villages north of Santa Fe. A wave of high anxiety soon gripped the non-Indian inhabitants as the insurgents burned and pillaged farms and settlements and massacred every Spanish man, woman, and child they found. However, the capture of the runners upset the well-made plot for insurrection; some outlying pueblos received word of the changed plans too late and other pueblos not at all. Though caught off-guard, most of the terror-stricken Spanish settlers were able to escape the onslaught.[35]

Hysterical with fear of being annihilated by the siege, the settlers gathered for protection at Santa Fe, at Isleta pueblo, or at the pueblos that did not take part in Popé's rebellion. Governor Otermín sent out heavily armed relief parties to escort several hundred settlers to Santa Fe, where on their arrival they prepared frantically for its defense. Over a thousand men, women, and children, led by Lieutenant Governor Alonso García, the head of Spanish authority in the *río arriba* (upper Río Grande) region, fortified themselves at Isleta pueblo seventy miles south of Santa Fe. In the meantime, the revolt gained force. The rebel assaults spread south to the *río abajo* area (lower Río Grande). The situation looked hopeless for the colonists.

On August 15, five days into the revolt, nearly two thousand Pueblo Indians and their mixed-blood and mestizo allies, armed with bows and arrows and the guns, lances, swords, and leather armor taken from their victims, laid siege to Santa Fe. The rebels had superiority in numbers and weapons; just one hundred of the thousand Spaniards who took refuge in Sante Fe were armed. The Pueblos cut off the colonists' water supply. On September 21, after two days without water, with food supplies dwindling and no hope for reinforcements, an overwhelmed and frightened Otermín ordered the abandonment of New Mexico. Four hundred colonists and twenty-one Franciscans died violently in the siege of Santa Fe. Rotting corpses were everywhere. The insurgents reserved special vengeance for the priests; the Indians first tortured the clerics, while laughing at their victims and mocking their faith, and then slaughtered them, leaving their mutilated corpses on the church altars to rot or be eaten by wild animals.[36]

Lieutenant Governor García abandoned Isleta but halted his retreat to wait for Otermín and the refugees from Santa Fe. The terrified colonists, including Indians from Isleta pueblo fearing retribution for aiding the Spaniards, retreated to El Paso del Norte, the New Mexico province's southernmost settlement. Two thousand refugees spent the winter near El Paso del Norte. Popé's uprising succeeded in driving the Spanish out of the region for thirteen years. Rebels throughout northern New Spain spread news of the success of the Pueblo Revolt. Spanish administrators wanted to abandon the New Mexico colony. However, reports of the French presence west of the Mississippi and of the mishap of French explorer Rene-Robert Cavelier, Sieur de La Salle, on the Texas coast prompted Spain to make a permanent royal commitment in New Mexico. Governor Otermín began planning to take back the province from the united northern Indians who had rejected the yoke of Spanish and religious oppression.[37]

## DUTY TO THE CROWN AND CHURCH FULFILLED: THE SPANISH RECONQUEST OF NEW MEXICO

Pueblo Indian unity splintered as traditional intervillage feuds, jealousies, and disagreements resurfaced. Popé's decrees became more and more reactionary; the holy man took up a role similar to a Spanish governor and was finally deposed in 1690. Diego de Vargas, New Mexico's newly appointed governor, was assigned the reconquest of New Mexico. The drive to reconquer New Mexico was fueled by the threat posed by foreign encroachment in Spanish Florida, to the newly opened silver mines of northern Mexico, and by Spanish revenge and reward in service to the Crown.[38]

On August 17, 1692, Governor Vargas, leading fifty soldiers, three friars, and Pueblo Indian allies, left San Lorenzo near El Paso del Norte for the journey north to retake Santa Fe. In early September, Vargas arrived at Santa Fe. Through a combination of diplomacy and intimidation, twenty-three Indian pueblos were returned to Spanish rule. In October 1693, amid growing Indian and French threats to the northern frontier, Vargas returned to New Mexico with seventy families, eighteen Franciscan friars, and a number of Tlaxcalan Indian auxiliaries to recolonize the northern province. The colonists who arrived at Santa Fe in December found the town once again defended by Tewa and Taos Pueblo Indians.[39]

Having failed to persuade the Indians to surrender, Vargas ordered the taking of Santa Fe by force, which the governor did after two days of heavy fighting. Indians were hunted down without mercy and slaughtered. Seventy Indians were formally charged with treason against the Crown and the Church and immediately executed. Several hundred Indian men, women, and children were sentenced to ten years' domestic servitude. Incensed by the executions the Spanish carried out, Pueblo Indians continued to resist the military campaign. By the summer of 1696, the situation worsened; it turned into a general rebellion. In the Second Pueblo Revolt, five Franciscans died martyrs' deaths at the hands of the insurgents who laid waste to the hated churches and convents. Warfare between the Indians and the settler colonists continued for several years. Weakened and decimated by the prolonged fighting, the Indians eventually succumbed to Spanish coercion. Additional Spanish families arrived in Santa Fe, the missions were reestablished, and the pueblos were repopulated.[40]

For the next eighty years, the Pueblo Indians and the Spaniards maintained an uneasy alliance in the New Mexico province. The Indians reluctantly accepted the Christian faith and rendered services to the Crown in return for military protection. The specter of Apache and Navajo mounted raiders made mutual protection necessary. Along with the raiding and warfare, Spanish diseases triggered a series of lethal plagues that decimated much of the Pueblo Indian population.[41]

Settlement of New Mexico continued and concentrated around Santa Fe and El Paso del Norte. Most of the settlers of the río arriba area resided near Santa Fe, while those in the río abajo area lived on the ranches along the Río Grande and on the larger estates concentrated around El Paso del Norte. In 1706, Francisco Cuervo y Valdéz founded an administrative unit he named San Felipe de Albuquerque. It consisted of thirty-five families numbering 252 people. Albuquerque's population grew to 600 by 1745 and by 1790 had nearly doubled to 1,115. Communities were founded farther out on the New Mexico frontier, such as Santa Rosa de Lima, San Miguel del Vado, Cebolleta, and Belén. New communities were granted legal rights over local water, woodlands, and land through *composiciones de tierra* (certificates of occupancy rights).[42]

Individual grants, private grants, and communal grants were conferred to New Mexican colonists as stipulated in the recently published *Recopilación*. Individual land grants were made to persons who pledged to attract settlers and supervise a settlement in areas exposed to Indian raids to create a defensive perimeter between populated areas and nomadic Indians. Private grants were bestowed for individual service to the Spanish Crown. The community land grants were the most important grants, as these were awarded to settle and defend the New Mexican frontier. Each individual was given a parcel of land on which to build a home and develop the land. The remainder of the community grant was used in common by all the *vecinos* (settlers). The vecinos were given tax exemptions and the right to possess firearms, but they were not allowed to leave the community grants without permission. Common lands could not be sold. Because of constant Indian raiding, grants were made, then abandoned, then made again, and abandoned once more. Nevertheless, the early pioneers made a commitment to live on New Mexico's frontier and endured the attendant dangers and hardships to keep hold of their land.[43]

Spanish policy dictated that colonies could not compete with Spain in commercial enterprises. However, colonists were encouraged to develop agricultural (as well as mining) activities and to engage in raising livestock. New Mexico's settlers cultivated corn, beans, and squash. They also introduced tomatoes, chilies, wheat, apples, pears, peaches, cantaloupes, watermelons, and grapes. In addition, the colonists raised chickens, goats, pigs, oxen, burros, horses, and sheep, owing to the demand for wool and mutton. New Mexicans preferred sheep to cattle and horses because sheep were difficult to stampede and thus less attractive to Indian raiders who were growing increasingly proficient in their predatory activities. The number of sheep was great. A census taken in 1757 reported that Spanish settlers and Pueblo Indians possessed 112,182 sheep, 16,157 cattle, and 7,356 horses. By the end of the Spanish colonial era there were more than 200,000 sheep in the New Mexico province, despite periodic disease, and sheepherders in search of new pasturelands, water, and salt had moved into the present Texas Panhandle. Minus pregnant ewes and those with lambs, more than 200,000 sheep made the long and arduous trek south into Mexico for market.[44]

Trade was the next most important economy in New Mexico after farming and livestock raising. New Mexicans went without manufactured goods and worked instead with crudely fashioned axes and hoes and wove their own cloth. The settlers obtained their manufactured products from Chihuahua, though this was sporadic at first. Because of the imposed trade restrictions with the other countries, the northern frontier settlements developed a black market with France and England, as well as the Netherlands. Settlers traded with the French for contraband goods they brought to Taos. The French had reached New Mexico from Illinois and Louisiana. The settlers obtained most of their goods from nomadic Indian tribes and by attending trade fairs such as the one held at Taos. The trade fair was also used for the barter of slaves, and the New Mexicans were prepared to purchase them.[45]

Along with bringing hides, animals, jerky, tallow, and pelts to the fairs, the western Comanches brought Pawnee and Wichita Indian captives to exchange for baked bread, knives, gunpowder, and other merchandise. To get a higher price, the Indian slavers abused their captives with heated arrow points, whippings, and other cruelty. Because adult males were usually killed in the raids and wars, women and children made up many of the Indian captives at the northern trade fairs. About five thousand Indians were ransomed and entered New Mexican society as genízaros between 1700 and 1880. This figure may be low, however; slavery was an extensive practice. Genízaros were baptized, raised in Spanish households, and assumed Spanish surnames; they could acquire land and within three generations gain their freedom.[46] The Indians procured more captives for trade owing to their growing dependence on European manufactured goods, particularly firearms. Highly valued, guns were acquired from the French, who were spreading them among the Plains Indians, or else from the Pawnees through trading or raiding for captives, as well as horses; the latter were valued as a weapon of war and as a marker of wealth. Contraband trade and slave routes extended to the Great Basin and became the mainstay of the economies of many northern New Mexican villages into the early nineteenth century.[47] A system of trade also developed in New Mexico with the settlements and the towns in the interior of New Spain via the Chihuahua trade route.

Located 265 miles south of present El Paso, the town of Chihuahua dominated New Mexico's trade. The annual caravan sponsored by the Spanish government supplied New Mexico with provisions, but these were costly, as Chihuahua's merchants monopolized the market. New Mexico's governors, its *ricos* (wealthy New Mexicans), and the caravan contractors likewise profited from the sale of goods.[48]

The trade caravans left New Mexico in November at the end of the annual Taos trade fair. Plunder obtained through barter at Taos, which included Indian captives along with sheep and raw wool, hides, pine nuts, grain, salt, and blankets, was sent to Chihuahua. Military convoys, prisoners, mail, and civilians also made the long forty-day journey. Iron tools and weapons, boots, shoes, tobacco, foodstuffs, domestic and imported fabrics, and furniture were sent north to New

Mexico. The prices for the goods from Mexico were exorbitant, four times greater than their actual costs. Consequently, New Mexicans remained in perpetual debt to Chihuahua merchants, who also monopolized the sale of supplies to the northern garrisons.[49]

Nevertheless, New Mexico was integrated into the expanding mercantile economy of New Spain through the growth of the overland trade with Chihuahua and with the silver mining areas of northern Mexico. Chihuahua's monopoly of the New Mexico market lasted until the early nineteenth century. At this time American merchants from Missouri arrived in New Mexico with competitively priced goods of higher quality. They opened up the celebrated Santa Fe trade. Mexican independence would eventually lead to the abolishment of two centuries of Spanish trade controls, allowing the United States to compete.

The small New Mexico settlements could not protect themselves against the constant Indian attacks because they lacked presidios. Governor Juan Bautista de Anza therefore ordered the merger of the province's settlements so that each would have a minimum of twenty families and all homes would be equipped with gun ports. The consolidation of the settlements did not work because the vecinos ignored the governor's order to give up their farms for the confines of a village and villagers strongly objected to being relocated to larger communities. New Mexico's growing mixed-race peasantry carried the burden of frontier settlement and defense, holding the line against the mounted Indian raiders. The frontier environment continued to emphasize their fighting style and operations; the citizen soldiers used bows and lances and, because there were more horses, launched mounted offensive campaigns and surprise attacks against the horse nomads. Sharing in this frontier defense were Pueblo Indians and genízaros, the latter drawn from the Apache, Comanche, Kiowa, or Pawnee captives purchased at the trade fairs.[50]

Genízaros were adopted into New Mexican families beginning in the mid-eighteenth century, many as women and children. Subordinate and powerless and without the racial status of the settlers, they worked as indentured ranchers, herders, and domestics; women Indian slaves provided "sexual comfort," as they had been obtained with a primary goal of sexual exploitation. Their *coyote* progeny (intermixed persons with one Indian parent and one mestizo parent) became the basis of a larger frontier settler population. Genízaros also helped protect the settlements from Indian attacks and served as interpreters on military campaigns and slaving parties. As a reward for their militia service, genízaros were granted land or homes in *barrios* (neighborhoods) within Spanish settlements and also formed separate communities. Belén, Abiquiú, and other genízaro settler communities were strategically located to provide protection. Genízaros thus not only bore a significant portion of New Mexico's northern frontier defense, but they also made expansion of New Mexico possible. Genízaros and their descendants in essence were the vanguard of Spanish territorial expansion, spreading north into southern Colorado, east into the Texas Panhandle and Oklahoma, and west into central Arizona.[51]

To emphasize, raiding by nomadic Indians was endemic on the northern frontier during the Spanish era. The Indians staged surprise attacks and ambushes

**Hos-Ta (the Lightning): Governor of the Jemez Pueblo, 1849.**
Pueblo Indian auxiliaries such as Hos-Ta were sometimes termed *genízaros*. They intermixed and were of genízaro ancestry.
CREDIT: Coll. 146, Kern's No. 4.  Courtesy of the Academy of Natural Sciences, Ewell Sale Stewart Library.

and used overwhelming speed in eluding pursuit and unbounded courage in attacks that included hand-to-hand combat. The Indian raids that plagued the settlements were the result of Spain's unreliable policies, an underfunded military, the slaving, thefts, and aggression by the colonists against the Indians, displacement by European encroachment, and Indians' obtaining guns, lead, powder, and horses from French interlopers. The arming of the Indian tribes of the northern frontier eventually eliminated the Spanish military advantage over the Indians. By the 1760s, the cycle of Indian raids and retaliatory campaigns against these attacks was a life-and-death struggle for those living in the northern borderland.[52]

Indian tribes surrounded New Mexico. The Spanish province's northern and eastern frontier abutted the Comanche and Jicarilla Apache lands; to the northwest lived the Utes; northwestern and western New Mexico was Navajo territory; and various Apache tribes inhabited New Mexico's southwest, south, and southeast regions. The Apaches attacked Spanish settlements along the greatest part of the northern frontier and for a long time could not be controlled. Apache war parties, running to as many as two hundred warriors, formed to avenge the killing of tribesmen. Apache raiding parties numbered between twelve to fifteen men and took prisoners to use as captives or to kill. The Apaches proved especially troublesome to the New Mexican settlers, isolating them and making life extremely dangerous, as they raided with virtual impunity wherever they desired, taking a heavy toll on settlers through burning, robbing, and murdering.[53] It was the unending raids by western Comanches that posed the greatest threat to New Mexico's survival.

Hunting and raiding were the Comanches' chief occupations. Migrating southeast from the Rocky Mountains in the late seventeenth and early eighteenth centuries, the Comanches acquired horses through trading and raiding and began to compete for access to the buffalo hunting grounds. The western Comanches soon extended their power throughout northeastern New Mexico, eastern Colorado, and western Texas as far as present San Antonio. The western Comanches

**Comanche Family, by Lina Sanchez y Tapia, 1828.**
CREDIT: Watercolor. 4016.336.3. Courtesy of Gilcrease Museum, Tulsa, Oklahoma.

opposed Spanish intrusion into their far-flung domain and carried their raids into Spanish settlements on their borders. Many New Mexicans died in the unceasing Comanche attacks and the punitive expeditions that followed each other with regularity and kindled violence on both sides.[54]

The struggle for domination of the northern frontier that pitted Indian and Spaniard against each other raged on. New Mexico surpassed the northern departments in actions against Indians, especially the Comanches, who posed the greatest threat to New Mexico's survival. In two campaigns in 1774, New Mexicans killed nearly 500 Comanche men, women and children. The Indians, however, were unrelenting in their attacks. Between 1767 and 1777, the governor of New Mexico reported 106 assaults by Comanches, in addition to 77 by Apaches and 12 by Navajos, resulting in the deaths of 382 colonists and Pueblo Indians and the captivity of 94 others. Because Indian raids jeopardized the very existence of New Mexico, as well as the other northern Spanish provinces, Spain implemented an aggressive policy to defeat the hostile Indian tribes. New Mexican Governor Juan Bautista de Anza realized that to establish peace with the hostile Indians the power of the western Comanches had to be broken. To accomplish this, de Anza in August 1779 launched a surprise military campaign in the western Comanches' homeland in present southeastern Colorado. Six hundred Spanish soldiers, vecinos, and Pueblo Indians, augmented with two hundred Ute and Jicarilla Apache Indian auxiliaries, killed the powerful western Comanche chief Cuerno Verde and defeated his tribe in a battle near present Pueblo, Colorado. Raiding by the western Comanches into New Mexico nonetheless continued. Further efforts by Spain to negotiate peace with the western Comanches were hindered by the diversion of Spanish resources to support the American Revolution against England.[55]

The incessant raiding by the Apaches and Comanches affected agriculture, ranching, and trade. Finally, in February 1786, Governor de Anza made a formal treaty of peace and alliance with the powerful western Comanches through their representative Ecueracapa. Acknowledging that defense and retaliation against the western Comanches was almost impossible and costly, New Mexico colonial officials worked out a "peace by purchase" policy. Spain gave the western Comanches arms, ammunition, horses, clothing, and other gifts, including money, and access to the annual trade fairs; they also agreed to cooperate with the Comanches against mutual enemies. The Comanches pledged peace and honored the treaty for several decades. Spain also used its policy of gift giving to maintain alliances with the eastern Comanches in Texas and the Utes and Jicarilla Apaches, and it later strengthened relations with the Navajos.[56]

In addition to Indian raiding, New Mexico colonists suffered from smallpox and other diseases that were frequent visitors to the northern frontier. The lethal smallpox virus had reached epidemic proportions five years earlier in 1780–1781. It spread slowly along the settled parts of the Río Grande, infecting, disfiguring, and killing about a quarter of New Mexico's population, and it took a serious toll among the Indian population as well.[57]

New Mexico existed as little more than an insecure, remote settlement on Spain's northern frontier; that is, until 1806, with the arrival of the U.S. government-sponsored expedition of American Zebulon Pike. More Americans followed in his wake, bringing guns and ammunition and other goods, which they traded with the New Mexicans and Indians. The hardships of colonial life on the frontier and the hostile Indian tribes discouraged settlers from moving to Texas, one of the least populated provinces of New Spain.

## A BUFFER ZONE AGAINST EXPANSION:
## SPANISH COLONIAL TEXAS

During the first half of the eighteenth century, Spanish colonization was extended through present Arizona and Texas. A part of Colonia del Nuevo Santandar that extended north from Tampico, Mexico, Texas was conquered, pacified, and settled as a defensive measure to protect Spanish possessions in the Gulf of Mexico, where further advances by England and France through aggression or contraband trade had to be guarded against. Texas would also serve as a buffer zone against American expansion into Spanish territory, as well as an outpost against the menace of Apache and Comanche Indian marauders who ravaged this region of the northern frontier. Soldiers, Franciscan missionaries, and settlers would not have been sent to Texas had Spain not feared that this northern province would be occupied by foreign powers seeking to gain north Mexico's mines and the trade of New Spain's frontier. As with its other northern possessions, Spain's support of Texas was inadequate because of its crumbling international power.[58]

Spain set up a series of presidios, missions, and towns to develop the province of Texas. Forty different mission sites were established in Texas lasting from one year to one hundred years, though no more than a dozen missions operated at any one time. Eight presidios and ten civilian settlements were occupied concurrently. Spanish officials ordered a mission/presidio built at Nacogdoches in eastern Texas in 1716, and additional missions and settlements made up of Spaniards, mestizos, and mulattos were established in this region. On May 5, 1718, Martín de Alarcón, the newly appointed governor of Texas, founded the presidio San Antonio de Béxar, the mission San Antonio de Valero (the Alamo), and the town of Villa de Béxar on the upper San Antonio River. Thirty Spanish soldiers and their families were Béxar's first settlers. Mission San José y Miguel de Aguayo was five miles south of the Alamo. The other three missions along the San Antonio River were Nuestra Señora Purisima Concepción de Acuña, San Juan Capistrano, and San Francisco de la Espada established in 1731.[59] Spanish efforts to colonize and develop Texas would be centered at Béxar.

In 1722, the presidio La Bahía and towns and missions were established on Matagorda Bay. Nearby were the future sites of missions Espíritu Santo and Rosario.[60] La Bahía supplied food for east Texas missions and Béxar. Inspector General Pedro Rivera visited the mission and presidio during his inspection. He reported that ninety soldiers and over four hundred Aranama Indians were with the mission. Around 1749, Governor José de Escandón ordered the mission and presidio of La Bahía moved near present Goliad on the San Antonio River.[61]

The Texas province was developed from 1746 to 1757, though preparations were made as early as 1738. The Spanish established the province because of the

French movement down the Mississippi River from Canada to the Gulf of Mexico. Following the start of the war between France and Spain in June 1719, hostilities between these two countries extended to their North American possessions. They were focused on the Texas coastal region extending from Tampico in the south to Matagorda Bay in the north. By 1750, José de Escandón established twenty-three towns and fifteen missions in the region. Only two towns, Laredo and Dolores, were in the Texas province.[62]

Ranching and subsistence agriculture underscored the development of Texas, owing to abundant and unoccupied pasturage land. The ranches were connected through trade, marriage, *compadrazgo* (godparenthood), and extended family ties that obligated the ranchers to help each other in times of need or crisis, such as raids by Indians. Ranching developed quickly, as the major Spanish expeditions to the Texas province left cattle, horses, sheep, and goats in their wake to roam and reproduce. Another factor was the demand for beef from miners expanding into northern Mexico and later from American soldiers fighting in the American Revolution. Texas had three ranching centers by the late eighteenth century. The ranches around Nacogdoches raised horses, and the abundant grazing lands in the San Antonio and La Bahía regions and in the lower Río Grande Valley raised both horses and cattle. Together these ranching centers formed part of the ranching region that extended from San Antonio to Laredo along the Río Grande to the Gulf of Mexico to La Bahía de Espíritu Santo and northwest to San Antonio.[63]

Awarded abundant land grants, the San Antonio and La Bahía missions contributed to the growth of ranching in Spanish Texas. The four hundred sheep and three hundred cattle that crossed the Río Grande into the Texas province with the Marqués de San Miguel de Aguayo in 1721 stocked the first mission herds. Eventually, thousands of horses, cattle, goats, and sheep managed by Indian vaqueros and shepherds grazed along the San Antonio and Guadalupe Rivers from San Antonio to La Bahía. Livestock constituted the principal wealth of the Texas missions. The mission-controlled ranches totaled more than one million acres for raising cattle, sheep, buffalo, and mustangs.[64] By the late eighteenth century the control that the missions held over cattle raising declined as Spanish colonial administrators took over the cattle ranching. The secularization of the missions that began in 1793 and officially ended in 1824 allowed local settlers to acquire the former Church lands. The Texas frontier developed high levels of inequality based on the provincial elites' protection of ranch properties and the commodification of labor.

Colonists moved their livestock onto unclaimed pasturelands north of the Río Grande and developed huge ranches. For example, José Vásquez Borrego obtained the rights to over 300,000 acres in present Webb and Zapata counties in South Texas and established the ranch Nuestra Señora de Dolores. The Dolores ranch had 3,000 cattle, 3,400 horses, and 2,650 mules and donkeys and was worked by thirty families. Ranching became essential to the South Texas economy; area ranchers drove horses and cattle to markets in Coahuila and Nuevo Leon, Mexico, and took herds to Louisiana.[65]

Béxar, whose economy was based on ranching, the military, and trade, was the most important settlement in Texas, and it eventually became the capital of this Spanish province. Presidio soldiers were a key component of Béxar's population, serving to defend the region against Indians and as the Crown's presence on the frontier. Many soldiers after their discharges remained in the pueblo as permanent settlers and married into local families. In 1731, the three missions and their mission populations in eastern Texas were relocated on the San Antonio River. In the same year, fifty-five Canary Islanders from outside Mexico City were settled in Béxar. The largest settlement in Texas, Béxar was a racially diverse group of Indian, negro, and European origin born either in Texas or northern Mexico. Peninsular Spaniards made up less than 2 percent of the population. Distinguishable divides based on class and race in terms of political power, economic resources, and social status bound Béxar's mixed-race population.[66]

In 1760, Béxar had nearly six hundred settlers. The settlements of east Texas around Nacogdoches, San Augustine, and Los Adaes combined had about five hundred inhabitants. There were two hundred colonists living at La Bahía.[67] The first census of the Texas province taken in 1777 recorded 3,103 residents, including the priests and the mission Indians. Half the population had originated in Coahuila, Mexico. One in two settlers was male. Half of the Texas colony was enumerated as Spaniard or mestizo, mulattoes composed a fourth of the population, and mission Indians made up the remainder. There were only twenty slaves reported in Texas. The three population centers of Béxar, La Bahía, and Nacogdoches and the ranches and farms between them suffered severe economic hardship because of their great distance from Mexico City. As a result the settlers developed a contraband trade in furs, stolen livestock, guns, and tobacco with French, Americans, and Indians in Nacogdoches and Louisiana. The colonies protected themselves from Indian raids by mobilizing civilian militias. Twenty thousand Indians inhabited the Texas province, outnumbering the non-Indian population almost seven to one.[68]

## THE APACHE AND COMANCHE THREAT IN TEXAS

Whereas New Mexico's development was stimulated by Indian trading, the growth of frontier Texas was hampered by Indian raiding. The settlers of Spanish Texas shared dangers on the remote frontier from mounted nomads, especially the Lipan Apache and Comanche Indians, who moved with stealth and speed and raided the settlements with a vengeance. The settlers received little assistance with the Indian depredations and relied mainly on themselves to hold the land. As in the New Mexico province, this need for self-defense demanded and produced a spirit of mutual helpfulness among the settlers. The Lipan Apaches were in retreat from the Comanches, who, lured by French trade along the Red River, were migrating into northern Texas. The Lipan Apaches moved into southern Texas, where they wiped out or absorbed the area Coahuiltec, Chiso, Jano, and Manso Indians. Pressed into the hill country of central Texas, the Lipan Apaches staged raids on San Antonio for horses, other livestock, and guns and ammunition and also began raiding into northern Mexico.[69]

Béxar's war-weary settlers were unable to make peace with the pernicious Apaches, whose raids turned increasingly more violent with the killing of ranchers and the taking of hostages. The governor of Texas, Fernando Pérez de Almazán, eventually secured a truce with the Apaches so that by 1725 campaigns against them stopped, leading to a decline in their raiding over the next six years. During this lull, Inspector Pedro de Rivera, through the Regulation of 1729, recommended the reduction of the garrison at Béxar. The law also barred governors and commanders from waging war on friendly Indians, discouraged campaigns by non-hostile Indian tribes against hostile Indians, and encouraged brokering peace with enemy Indian tribes.[70]

Owing to the dismal condition of Spain's northern frontier as a result of mismanagement, Spain found it necessary to order an examination of the entire frontier. In 1765, Spain appointed Marqués de Rubí to visit the entire frontier from Sonora to Texas. Traveling overland seventy-five hundred miles, Rubí described the scattered nature of the colonial settlements, the workings of the missions, and the increasing destructive Apache and Comanche raids. The Marqués reported that Spain's presidio in Texas was a waste of money and recommended a realignment of the presidio for offensive and defensive actions against the Apaches. As a result of Rubí's recommendations, military command was centralized on the northern frontier; the presidio system was reduced to fifteen at 120-mile intervals extending from the Gulf coast of Mexico in the east to the Gulf of California in the west. Only two presidios were in Texas: one at San Antonio de Béxar and the other at La Bahía. Marqués de Rubí furthermore recommended that all posts in east Texas be abandoned, including the former capital Los Adaes. In assessing the Indian problems, the royal official advised that Spain stress trade over war in order to cultivate friendship with the northern Indian tribes to eliminate the Apache menace.[71]

The Apaches and Spaniards continued to wage war on each other. The latter believed the solution to this hostility was to convert the Apaches to Christianity, but these efforts failed dismally. With the exception of the missions at Béxar, La Bahía, and Nacogdoches, the Spanish mission system in Texas ended in 1793, when Viceroy Revilla Gigedo ordered the secularization of the Texas missions.[72] Adding to the misery and demoralization from Apache raids were the swift confrontations with Comanches.

In Texas, the Comanchería extended eastward from the present panhandle to north Texas and south to San Antonio. For a quarter century, Comanche raids struck continuously throughout eastern Texas. In 1772, the *Regulations and Instruction for the Presidios . . . of New Spain* gained peace with the eastern Comanches through trade and gifts even as it called for the extermination of the southern Apaches.[73]

In 1778, the governor of Texas signed a treaty with the eastern Comanches by using his alliances with other northern Indian tribes to bring pressure on them. The Comanches continued their raids into Texas until the major smallpox epidemic of 1780–1781 swept through the Indian tribes and brought with it a huge mortality rate. In 1785, Governor Domingo Cabello y Robles made a truce with the Comanches that ushered in thirty years of peaceful relations. The peace ended when American traders along the Red and Arkansas rivers began the illegal trading of guns to the Comanches for horses, which in turn renewed Comanche raiding in Texas.[74]

The eastern Comanches became the allies of the Spanish in destroying the Apaches. In 1790, a Spanish army entered Texas from Coahuila to address Apache depredations. Joined by soldiers and civilians from Béxar and by eastern Comanches, the army routed a large band of Lipan and Mescalero Apaches at Soledad Creek in present Duval County. Pressure from both Comanches and Spaniards forced Apache leaders to arrange a peace settlement. The Spanish made treaties with the Apaches, but nonetheless they remained enemies, because the Lipan Apaches now attacked settlements along the Río Grande.[75] Relations between the Texas Spanish colonists and the eastern Comanches remained uneasy. With the start of Mexico's War for Independence in 1810, Spain paid less and less attention to the Indian attacks in Texas.

## THE CONDITION OF THE SPANISH TEXAS COLONY IN THE EARLY NINETEENTH CENTURY

Texas remained poorly defended and sparsely settled. In 1803, less than four thousand Spanish colonists lived in Texas, over half at San Antonio de Béxar and the remainder at La Bahía and Nacogdoches. As elsewhere in the Spanish borderlands, the start of the Wars for Independence soon interfered with Spain's support of the Texas province.[76] Moreover, tensions between Spain and the new United States grew.

Through the Pinckney Treaty of 1795, Spain guaranteed American navigation rights on the Mississippi River and the right to deposit goods for export at New Orleans. American frontiersmen and colonists, many of whom had territorial ambitions, now threatened Spain with invasion into and settlement of Texas. Because Spain was unable to colonize the Louisiana Territory and the northern *Provincias Internas* (Internal Provinces) of New Mexico, Texas, Coahuila, and Chihuahua, it embraced a policy of controlled immigration. In 1796, the Commandant of the Provincias Internas, Pedro de Nava, issued an order banning foreigners without documentation from entering Texas. Nava directed his order at the American adventurers intruding into Texas who could upset trade relations with Texas Indians by furnishing them with guns, powder, whiskey, and other goods in exchange for livestock and captives.[77] This proved to be too late in light of unfolding international events.

Spain in 1803 delivered Louisiana to France under the Treaty of San Ildefonso. One month later, France turned Louisiana over to the United States. President Thomas Jefferson's administration soon launched a campaign to include Texas in the purchase, which in turn brought more restless North Americans—adventurers, opportunists, filibusters, and refugees—across the ill-defined border of Texas.[78] The Americans were strengthening their garrisons at Natchitoches in Louisiana. Spanish colonial officials called for more troops to defend Texas against the aggressive United States. Commandant of the Provincias Internas Nemesio Salcedo feared the United States because it was negotiating with the Indians and encouraging trespassing by traders into Texas. In late 1805, open conflict between American and Spanish forces over the disputed Texas border erupted. Salcedo and Texas

Governor Antonio Cordero ordered six hundred troops to Nacogdoches. The American troops at Natchitoches were under the command of James Wilkerson. Wilkerson, the highest ranking American general in the west, double agent for Spain, trader, and land speculator, offered to withdraw his troops east of Hondo River if Spain pulled back its forces west of the Sabine River. In 1806, Wilkinson negotiated the "neutral ground agreement," which provided for neutral territory between the Sabine near Nacogdoches and the Arroyo Hondo River to the east. Because civilians of both nations could settle in this area, it became a netherworld for thieves, contraband smugglers, fugitive slaves, and deserters from American military forces. In addition, there remained a considerable number of American interlopers in the area greatly interested in making all of Texas their home.[79]

In the same year of the neutral ground agreement, Nemesio Salcedo issued orders banning the entrance of all foreigners into Texas. Salcedo authorized his nephew Manuel María de Salcedo, the new governor of Texas, to deal with the immigrants already in Texas. To counteract the influx of American squatters and to hold Texas, the governor promoted more active Spanish settlement, and he also took measures to deal with the Indian menace. In the spring of 1810, Governor Salcedo made an inspection tour of east Texas. Sympathizing with the problems of the American squatters, the governor counseled those he believed to be potential Spanish citizens. This abrupt change in policy would have long-range repercussions, because the United States gained title to the land from Spain.[80] Circumstances impelled the geographic extension of Spain in California. It was a matter of expanding or losing California to other European rivals casting hungry glances at the region.

## GUARDING THE WESTERN PERIPHERY: SPANISH COLONIAL ALTA CALIFORNIA

Spanish exploration of California began in the eighteenth century; colonization did not begin until 1769, following news that Russians had crossed the Bering Strait and claimed Alaska and all the northwest Pacific coast extending down to California. Russian fur traders were steadily moving southward along the Pacific coastline, trapping and trading with the Indians and founding outposts and settlements. Russia's southernmost colony was several miles north of San Francisco Bay at present Fort Ross, California.[81]

At the end of the Seven Years' War, Spain was the sole rival of England in North America. Following the French and Indian War, English fur traders moved into the Pacific Northwest and the South Pacific. This English presence likewise posed a potential challenge to Spanish claims. As visitor-general of New Spain, the skilled and knowledgeable José de Gálvez began the defensive modernization of the northern provinces through their reorganization and consolidation under separate command. It included pushing forward Spain's presence on the western coast with the occupation of Alta California. To guard against the attack on northern Mexico's silver mining districts, Gálvez obtained permission from King Charles III of Spain to occupy and establish garrison sites and settlements at the ports of San Diego and Monterey in Alta California.[82]

In 1769, when Spanish officials commenced the so-called Sacred Expedition to establish the first missions and presidios in Alta California, Gálvez, together with a small military force of Spanish soldiers and several Franciscan missionaries under his command, traveled overland and by sea from Baja California. Gaspar de Portolá led a separate sixty-three-man land expedition to San Diego. Further north, encamping his expedition near some asphalt pits, Gálvez named the site *El Pueblo de Nuestra Señora la Reina de Los Angeles de Porciuncula*—Our Lady of the Angels. Gálvez placed Alta California under military governorship and turned missionary duties over to the Franciscans. He ordered Captain Portolá to treat the "Indians well" as "any molestations or violence toward the Indian women . . . could . . . endanger the success of the expedition."[83] In the same year, Captain Fernando de Rivera y Moncada, governor of Baja California, led a division of cuero dragoons overland from Loreto, Baja California, to San Diego. The mission and presidio at San Diego were the first Spanish colonies established in California. In 1773, Rivera was appointed military governor of Alta California, succeeding Pedro Fages. Four years later, Philipe de Neve replaced Rivera as governor and in 1779 de Neve recruited soldiers and settlers for Los Angeles and Santa Barbara.[84] More Spanish followed.

In 1774, Captain Juan Bautista de Anza, military commander of the Tubac presidio in present Arizona, led Spain's second and largest colonization effort, an expedition overland to Alta California to establish a mission at San Francisco. The captain was directed by the viceroy to enlist married and marriageable soldiers. The former were to bring their wives and children. The 240-member expedition was made up of recruits from Sonora and Sinaloa, including 34 women and 115 children, and made the 165-day arduous journey through Arizona across the Colorado River and deserts and mountains to the San Gabriel Mission and beyond. Drawn from presidios, villas, pueblos, mining communities, and ranches, the soldiers, settlers, and their families, all of mestizo and mulatto backgrounds, were offered mules, horses, cattle (totaling six hundred head of livestock), and transportation costs as incentives. The expedition members were also given two years' pay, five years' rations, and a full set of clothing.[85]

In the spring of that year de Anza colonists reached Monterey and in the following year were at the San Francisco Bay. Spain divided the Alta California province into four presidio districts. Concurrent with the founding of the missions, the establishment of the four presidios in California was done for the protection of the colonists and the missions. The 1781 regulation for governing Alta California provided two hundred soldiers to defend the northern province. The new mission St. Francis of Assisi and the presidio at San Francisco were founded on September 17, 1776. In the same year the capital of the Californias under royal orders was transferred to Monterey from Loreto in Baja California. Alta and Baja California, Nueva Vizcaya, Coahuila, Texas, Sinaloa, and Sonora were placed into a single unit, the Internas Provincias, to better govern Spain's northern frontier. Although the Franciscan missions became self-supporting, problems remained in feeding the presidios' soldiers. Supply lines from San Blas on Mexico's west coast were difficult to maintain, and the mission fathers protested against royal requisitions on their crops and herds to feed the garrisons. Therefore, in 1779, Governor Philip de Neve issued the *Reglamento para el governo de las provincias de Californias.* Towns were established in the northern and southern Alta California province to develop the agricultural resources of these regions in order to supply presidios with grain for sale. In exchange for their allotted agricultural and communal land, livestock, seeds, and tools, the colonists had to erect public buildings, a central plaza, churches, and dams and irrigation projects.[86]

Governor de Neve collected fourteen families from the presidios at Monterey and San Francisco and established the town of San José de Guadalupe southeast of mission Santa Clara de Asís in 1777 across from Mission Santa Cruz.[87] Four years later, in 1781, the governor founded the town of Los Angeles with eleven families consisting of twelve men, eleven women, and twenty-three children. The town's first settlers were of mixed race and recruited from Sonora and Sinaloa. In 1797, Branciforte (Santa Cruz) across from Mission Santa Cruz was the last pueblo established in Alta California.[88]

Alta California's settlements were the smallest outposts in Spanish America, numbering less than a thousand settlers who were for the most part members of Mexico's lower strata. They consisted of artisan families and convict-settlers and were descendents of Indians, Africans, and Spaniards. Over 70 percent came from the ranching and mining districts of the present Mexican states of Sinaloa, Sonora, and Baja California. Many of these individuals remained in California after their colonization contracts expired. Women were absent in the colonizing parties before 1774, as most of the military personnel left their wives, daughters, or mothers in Mexico or Spain. These women stayed at home and managed their homes and raised their children, as in the case of upper-class Spanish women. The lower-class, mixed-race women worked outside the home to support their families. Because of long enlistments, two-thirds of the presidio soldiers in Alta California took Hispanicized Indian women from Baja or Alta California as common-law wives. Until 1791, the soldiers received livestock and mission lands as inducements to marry Indian women. In 1781, six hundred persons, exclusive of Indian groups, lived at Alta California's four presidios, two pueblos, and eleven missions. Nine years later, in 1790, the total population of Alta California numbered 970 whites, mestizos, and mulattoes. Most of these settlers had arrived in Alta California between 1769 and 1781. This population grew to 1,800 in 1800. It suffered deprivation and physical hardship. The irregular arrival of supply ships and food that arrived spoiled caused near starvation among the colonists, who lacked water for drinking and cooking. Mexico's wars of independence disrupted Spain's colonization efforts in Alta California and the rest of the northern frontier, as well. Alta California's population numbered 3,200 in 1821 on the eve of Mexico's independence. The population growth was the result of natural birth increases plus the immigration of new colonists to Alta California.[89]

Monterey became the hub of social and political life in Alta California. By 1830 Monterey had a population of 950 persons, making it the largest settlement in northern Alta California. San Francisco was small; it had 130 residents in 1787. San Diego was the next largest colony. In 1790, Santa Barbara had a population of 237 persons, but the town grew rapidly with the development of ranching in central California. In 1810, about 850 persons lived in Santa Barbara.

Grants of land were awarded to encourage agriculture in Alta California, to reward soldiers for their service, and to provide for settlers who held no property. These land grants could be small or as large as eleven leagues (one league equaled 4,400 acres). The Spanish government granted thirty of the more than eight hundred ranch grants made. The majority of the land grants would be awarded during the Mexican period. Land grants encouraged soldiers originally recruited from presidios in Sonora, Sinaloa, and Baja California to remain in Alta California at the end of their military service. Ex-presidio soldiers, all of them of mixed-race background from Mexico's low economic strata that included criminals and vagabonds, made up the ranks of the California ranchers. Some controlled private grants as large as three hundred thousand acres. Through royal land grants, the soldiers became part of a provincial Spanish aristocracy within a single generation that distinguished itself culturally and ethnically from the Indians. Most important was the fact that colonists who fought for Spain were rewarded with the honorific title of *hidalgo* (Spanish noblemen). The forebears of Californio governors Manuel Alvarado and Pío Pico and of the generals Manuel Vallejo and José María Castro were all presidio soldiers. Some of the prominent Californio families, such as De la Guerra, Ortega, Peralta, Valencia, Sánchez, Bernal, Alviso, Galindo, Carrillo, and Moraga, among others, were also descendants of presidio soldiers. Wealth permitted these Californios mobility into categories of higher status, and with time hidalgo took on the outward signs of mobility without regard for merit or mixed racial heritage.[90]

The development of Alta California was an outgrowth of the Jesuit missionary effort in Baja California to defend the northern frontier, to pacify and convert the Indians to Christianity, and to settle the region. The missions of Alta California encompassed most of the coastal region. The Franciscans founded the missions between 1769 and 1823 from San Diego in the south to Sonoma in the north. Each mission was a day's journey from the next. Indian auxiliaries brought up from Baja California aided greatly in this endeavor. A total of twenty-one missions were established. Conversion of the Indians in the newly discovered lands fulfilled the goal of Christianizing and civilizing Indians and incorporating them into the Spanish Empire. The prospective neophytes were instructed in Spanish language, customs, economies, and skills to assimilate them. California's economic development required a labor force inculcated with a European work ethic, and to do this physical coercion had to be used. There were between 335,000 and 350,000 Indians in Alta California, the Indian tribes each numbering between 50 and 500 persons. As the Spanish Crown pursued its goal of Christianization and Hispanicization, it destroyed the California Indians through a sustained policy of military campaigns, incarceration, corporal punishment, forced labor, exposure to deadly European diseases and epidemics, and poor sanitation and malnutrition in crowded mission environments that essentially became death camps.[91]

As loyal subjects of the King of Spain, the California Indians through baptism were regarded as prospective converts to Christianity. The Jesuits baptized about 12,000 California Indians between 1769 and 1830, and after them the Franciscans baptized 80,000 between 1700 and 1752. California's mission Indian population in 1784 was 4,650; it was 21,000 at the time of secularization in 1833. The missionaries were responsible for the transformation of the California Indian into that type of common European laborer, the serf. The Spanish-speaking women colonists such as Eulalia Pérez and Apolinaria Lorenzana, who arrived in California after 1774, helped the missionary priests by teaching Indian women neophytes Spanish and domestic chores. The Indian women were taught how to grind corn, cook, do needlework, sew, weave, and wash clothing. The women colonists worked as matrons watching over the Indian women. They also supervised the cooking and distribution of food and inspected and distributed supplies. The widespread rape of Indian women was a main catalyst for Indians' resistance. As a result of the soldier's assaults and rapes, Indian women and children contracted syphilis and other sexually transmitted diseases, all of which by 1800 were rampant.[92]

The missions, presidios, towns, and ranchos along California's coastal strip had been built by and were all mutually dependent on compulsory Indian labor. Between 1782 and 1832, for example, mission Indian labor produced 2.5 million pounds of wheat and other agricultural crops and took care of 308,000 cattle, sheep, goats, pigs, horses, and mules. The Franciscans failed to turn the California Indians into Christians, for conversion did not necessarily signify the renunciation of traditional Indian beliefs. California mission Indians resisted colonization; they refused to adopt Spanish languages and customs, and many escaped the rigors of bondage. Occasionally the California Indians organized conspiracies and rebellions, as did the Chumash Indians in 1824, to challenge the inhumane mission system.[93] The missions unquestionably initiated the inevitable and alarming downward spiral of the California Indian.

California was caught up in the whirlwind of British and American mercantile expansion into the Pacific area. In 1789, a Spanish expedition sent from Mexico north to Nootka Sound on the western shore of Vancouver Island found British, American, and Portuguese ships in the harbor. When England threatened war, Spain renounced its claims to the Pacific area. In 1790, Spain signed the Nootka Treaty, the first withdrawal from Spanish territory in America that reversed Spain's longtime expansionist foreign policy. This exposed Alta California to more threats of foreign invasion.[94]

As the Pacific Northwest opened to foreigners, European and North American visitors became more common in Alta California. They found Alta California to be a society administered by a military governor and a mission system, without schools, manufactures, and defenses, and inhabited by just over fifteen hundred non-Indian people. Travelers complained of difficulties in obtaining supplies, the lack of transportation, the absence of skilled workmen, and the poor condition of houses.

Alta California was indeed poor and backward. The inhabitants were confined to a small coastal strip extending from San Diego in the south to San Francisco in the north. However, the population was widely dispersed owing to the development of the ranch economy in the province based on land grants. Most of the land grants were located in the central part of Alta California, where sufficient water and good grazing lands were abundant.[95]

# MEXICAN INDEPENDENCE COMES
# TO THE NORTHERN FRONTIER

Support for Mexico's war for independence (1810–1821) in the northern provinces was mixed. Dissension and quarrels arose between local Spanish royalists
and insurgents, both of whom solicited aid from Indians and the North Americans.[96] Located far from Mexico, Alta California avoided the revolutionary
movement because the Californios created a landed society nearly free of
Spanish control. Alta California consequently escaped the vicissitudes of imperial politics. New Mexico likewise remained untouched. This was not the case
in Texas. Spanish rule in Texas was contested violently and with civil war
when news of Father Miguel Hidalgo's insurrection reached this northern
province. Drawing men and matériel from neighboring Louisiana, the defense
of the Spanish Crown against Creole nationalists in Texas fell to Royalist governor Manuel María Salcedo. Salcedo quickly organized resistance to the insurrection with the aid of Royalist *Tejanos* (Texas Mexicans) such as José Erasmo
Seguín. One decade later, Seguín would welcome the American emigrant Moses
F. Austin to Texas.[97]

On April 6, 1813, the insurgents in Texas declared the province independent
of Spain and one week later introduced a constitution. Meanwhile, the United
States was set on a course to gain the coveted borderland territory of Spanish
Florida and Texas—to monopolize the entire western hemisphere by commercial
penetration of Spanish America. In 1819, the Adams-Onís Treaty (Transcontinental Treaty) between the United States and Spain made the Sabine and Red
rivers the border of New Spain. Texas remained a buffer zone against the rapidly
advancing Americans, who were infiltrating both Louisiana and Texas and supplying weapons and ammunition to the Indians hostile toward the Spanish.
A much-weakened Spain could not provide for the adequate defense of its northern frontiers. Texas was already an asylum for deserters, criminals, and other
fugitives from justice engaged in shady dealings. Some American adventurers
who hungered for land continued to claim that the Louisiana Purchase extended
to the Río Grande. They launched filibustering expeditions into Texas, caring
little for the rights of ownership. Looking to advance their interests, American
slaveholders likewise entered Texas south of the Red River. In 1820, Spain
changed its long-standing policy of prohibiting foreigners from settling in New
Spain. Texas governor Antonio María Martínez and the Béxar *ayuntamiento*
(municipal government) had petitioned the Spanish Cortes for a colonization
project, which was approved. The new change in Spanish policy would have
long-term consequences.[98]

Mexico, which lost 10 percent of its population and about half its labor force
during its war for independence, was unable to populate Texas with its own colonists. What is more significant is that independent Mexico had to confront the
United States. Much of Mexico's northern frontier could not thwart the nation-
building on which the increasingly confident and assertive United States
embarked.[99] Peace lasted for fifteen years, shattered by a revolt that gave birth to
the Texas republic.

# CONCLUSION

Spain's involvement in 150 years of wars on the European continent determined its colonial policies and its ability to maintain and hold its colonial possessions. The Spanish empire was territorial, but Spain was unable to establish a well-defended northern frontier, a patchwork of regions encompassing contested ground. Although Spanish power was oppressive, it was also weak, isolating, and dissolving. The Spanish central government in Mexico City did not consider the problems and interests that developed in the northern frontier colonies. As a result it failed to secure the loyalty of its citizens in this region. The small number of frontier settlers, overwhelmingly made up of mixed-race peasants, suffered the consequences of low imperial priorities, isolation, extreme poverty, and sparse colonization. Indians checked Spain's expansion northward. Subjected to enforced labor and demands for tribute, Indians resisted Spanish domination, and this resistance culminated in the Pueblo Revolts of 1680 and 1696 in the New Mexico province.

For two centuries the integration, exploitation, and destruction of Indian populations—the latter often achieved through a scorched-earth policy—were key to the economic development of the northern frontier society. The mission was the bulwark of California settlement. Missionaries made concerted efforts to make Indians loyal and obedient Christians. The mission system, with Indians serving as colonists, overall proved unsuccessful in the face of serious foreign threats. The presidios required tough frontier forces to confront Indian raids and garrisons to deter foreign invasions. The presidio became the core of the internal discord that pitted missionaries against civilians and military authorities over land distribution and the exploitation of Indian labor.

As the eighteenth century closed, a relative peace existed with the Indians on the Spanish northern frontier. The Indians had forced the Spanish to negotiate peace and gained more gifts, open and fair trading arrangements, and a dependable alliance. The halt in Indian hostilities spurred economic growth and the expansion of trade routes. Despite Apache raiding on convoys, travel made possible routes opening between Tucson, Santa Fe, and San Antonio. Two decades of relative prosperity were ushered in for Spanish merchants and artisans, as well as for the expansion of stock raising and farming. The impetus was the demand for grain, livestock, and textiles in the revived mining districts of Chihuahua and Sonora.[100]

Spanish North America never moved beyond the frontier stage because it remained linked to a declining Spain swimming in a sea of debt and now vulnerable to its modernizing and predatory neighbor—the new American republic, the United States.[101] Having been an ally of the Americans for much of the Revolutionary War, after 1783 Spain became concerned about the territorial ambitions of the United States. Spain's fears were justified as American settlement crossed the Appalachians and spilled into the Ohio and Mississippi Valleys and into the fertile province of Texas. However, Spanish power on its northern frontier and elsewhere was crumbling.

In 1821, the Spanish era ended on the northern frontier, with independent Mexico taking control of the region. Although culture and unity remained relatively intact, local customs and conditions shaped these traditions that eventually resulted in distinctive forms. Despite claims to whiteness by its ruling elite, the settler population was overwhelmingly a racial amalgam, with mestizos predominating. These dark-hued Spanish-speaking residents stood as minor obstacles to United States expansion until 1836, when Anglo-Texans, who cared little for Mexico and its government, and their Tejano allies won their revolt for independence.[102]

# NOTES

1. Thomas D. Hall, *Social Change in the Southwest, 1350–1880* (Lawrence: University Press of Kansas, 1989), 5, 75; Virginia Maria Bouvier, *Women in the Conquest of California, 1542–1840* (Tucson: University of Arizona Press, 2001), 33.

2. J. H. Elliott, *Empires of the Atlantic World: Britain and Spain in America, 1492–1830* (New Haven, CT: Yale University Press, 2006), 269; Bouvier, *Women in the Conquest of California*, 36, 46–48.

3. Charles L. Kenner, *The Comanchero Frontier: A History of New Mexican–Plains Indian Relations* (Norman: University of Oklahoma Press, 1969), 17–18; France V. Scholes, "Troublous Times in New Mexico, 1659–1620," *New Mexico Historical Review* 12 (July 1937): 396–397.

4. Brian De Lay, *War of a Thousand Deserts: Indian Raids and the U.S.–Mexican War* (New Haven, CT: Yale University Press, 2008), 10, 233; Hall, *Social Change in the Southwest*, 76; Ida Altman, Sarah Cline, and Juan Javier Pescador, *The Early History of Greater Mexico* (Upper Saddle River, NJ: Prentice Hall, 2003), 195; Oakah L. Jones, *Los Paisanos: Spanish Settlers on the Northern Frontier of New Spain* (Norman: University of Oklahoma Press, 1979), 253.

5. David J. Weber, *Bárbaros: Spaniards and Their Savages in the Age of Enlightenment* (New Haven, CT: Yale University Press, 2005), 6; Bouvier, *Women in the Conquest of California*, 34.

6. Steven W. Hackel, *Children of Coyote, Missionaries of Saint Francis: Indian–Spanish Relations in Colonial California, 1769–1850* (Chapel Hill: University of North Carolina Press, 2005), 142, 321.

7. David J. Weber, *The Spanish Frontier in North America* (New Haven, CT: Yale University Press, 1992), 107, 212; Altman et al., *Early History of Greater Mexico*, 196; Samuel Truett, *Fugitive Landscapes: The Forgotten History of the U.S.–Mexico Borderlands* (New Haven, CT: Yale University Press, 2006), 27; Charles W. Polzer and Thomas E. Sheridan, eds., *The Presidio and Militia on the Northern Frontier of New Spain: A Documentary History*, vol. 2, part 1, *The Californias and Sinaloa-Sonora, 1700–1765* (Tucson: University of Arizona Press, 1997), 254–255.

8. Elliott, *Empires of the Atlantic World*, 301, 353–355.

9. Ibid., 61–62, 270, 274; Weber, *The Spanish Frontier in North America*, 225–226.

10. Max L. Moorehead, *The Presidio: Bastion of the Spanish Borderlands* (Norman: University of Oklahoma Press, 1975), 268–269; Weber, *Bárbaros*, 160.

11. Truett, *Fugitive Landscapes*, 27; Polzer and Sheridan, *Presidio and Militia*, 254–255; Bouvier, *Women in the Conquest of California*, 37.

12. Weber, *Spanish Frontier in North America*, 233; Moorehead, *Presidio*, 268–269.

13. Moorehead, *Presidio*, 269–270; Weber, *Bárbaros*, 160.

14. Hackel, *Children of Coyote,* 57; Weber, *Spanish Frontier in North America,* 323–324.

15. Weber, *Spanish Frontier in North America,* 325; Truett, *Fugitive Landscapes,* 26.

16. Weber, *Spanish Frontier in North America,* 223.

17. Hackel, *Children of Coyote,* 57.

18. Elliott, *Empires of the Atlantic World,* 170–171. For a brilliant discussion of *mestizaje* in America, see Gary B. Nash, "The Hidden History of Mestizo America," *Journal of American History* 82, no. 3 (1995): 941–962.

19. Elliott, *Empires of the Atlantic World,* 275; Weber, *Spanish Frontier in North America,* 326–327. The cost of these certificates of whiteness ranged from five hundred to eight hundred reales. Bouvier, *Women in the Conquest of California,* 75.

20. Weber, *Spanish Frontier in North America,* 308, 313–317.

21. Ibid, 323, 326.

22. Ramón Gutíerrez, *When Jesus Came, the Corn Mothers Went Away: Marriage, Sexuality, and Power in New Mexico, 1500–1846* (Stanford, CA: Stanford University Press, 1991), 55–94; Weber, *Spanish Frontier in North America,* 78–79; Hall, *Social Change in the Southwest,* 74–76, 81; George Hammond and Agapito Rey, eds. and trans., *The Rediscovery of New Mexico, 1580–1594: The Explorations of Chumascado, Espejo, Castero de Sosa, Morlete, Leyva de Bonilla and Humaña* (Albuquerque: University of New Mexico Press, 1966), 6, 15–28, 66–114.

23. Hall, *Social Change in the Southwest,* 76.

24. George Hammond and Agapito Rey, eds. and trans., *Don Juan de Oñate, Colonizer of New Mexico, 1575–1628,* 2 vols. (Albuquerque: University of New Mexico Press, 1953), 7, 57; Weber, *Spanish Frontier in North America,* 81. In 1540, the expedition of Francisco Vazquez de Coronado, consisting of three hundred Spanish soldiers and eight hundred Tlaxcala Indian auxiliaries, first entered the high plateau area of New Mexico in search of Cabeza de Vaca's fabled seven cities of Cibola. The Coronado expedition spent nearly two years exploring the area between the Grand Canyon and present Kansas. It encountered large Indian communities living in multistoried pueblos or towns with well-developed political and religious systems. Weber, *Spanish Frontier in North America,* 48–49.

25. Weber, *Spanish Frontier in North America,* 81; Hall, *Social Change in the Southwest,* 81; Hammond and Rey, *Don Juan de Oñate,* 68, 392; Mark Simmons, *The Last Conquistador: Juan de Oñate and the Settlement of the Far Southwest* (Norman: University of Oklahoma Press, 1991), 93–97.

26. Weber, *Spanish Frontier in North America,* 77; Hammond and Rey, *Don Juan de Oñate,* 390.

27. Elliott, *Empires of the Atlantic World,* 98; Gutíerrez, *When Jesus Came,* 150–151; Weber, *Spanish Frontier in North America,* 85–87; Hall, *Social Change in the Southwest,* 82–83; Hammond and Rey, *Don Juan de Oñate,* 426, 461, 473; Andrew L. Knaut, *The Pueblo Revolt of 1680: Conquest and Resistance in Seventeenth-Century Mexico* (Norman: University of Oklahoma Press, 1995), 45–46; Ned Blackhawk, *Violence over the Land: Indians and Empires in the Early American West* (Cambridge, MA: Harvard University Press, 2006), 23–24.

28. Simmons, *Last Conquistador,* 183–185.

29. Elliott, *Empires of the Atlantic World,* 275; James F. Brooks, *Captives and Cousins: Slavery, Kinship, and Community in the Southwest Borderlands* (Chapel Hill: University of North Carolina Press, 2002), 103–104.

30. Elliott, *Empires of the Atlantic World,* 274; Gutíerrez, *When Jesus Came,* 92, 172; Weber, *Spanish Frontier in North America,* 77–78, 90; Hall, *Social Change in the Southwest,* 82; Blackhawk, *Violence over the Land,* 24.

31. Weber, *Spanish Frontier in North America,* 133–134; Hall, *Social Change in the Southwest,* 86, 88; Fray Angelico Chavez, "Pohé Yemo as Representative and the Pueblo Revolt of 1680," *New Mexico Historical Review* 42, no. 2 (April 1967): 89.

32. Weber, *Spanish Frontier in North America,* 134–135. The chief priest was unable to unite all the Pueblos because several communities resisted the rebellion. Knaut, *Pueblo Revolt,* 167.

33. Knaut, *Pueblo Revolt,* 169; José Sando, "The Pueblo Revolt," in *Handbook of North American Indians,* ed. Alfonso Ortíz (Washington, DC: Smithsonian Institution, 1979), 195; Gutíerrez, *When Jesus Came,* 132.

34. Weber, *Spanish Frontier in North America,* 135; Hall, *Social Change in the Southwest,* 88; Knaut, *Pueblo Revolt,* 170.

35. Weber, *Spanish Frontier in North America,* 135.

36. Ibid., 135–136.

37. Ibid., 91–137; Gilbert R. Cruz, *Let There Be Towns: Spanish Municipal Origins in the Southwest, 1610–1810* (College Station: Texas A & M University Press, 1988), 36–41; Hall, *Social Change in the Southwest,* 88; Knaut, *Pueblo Revolt,* 172. In 1659, Fray García de San Francisco founded Nuestra Señora de Guadalupe Mission south of the Río Grande. The four settlements of San Lorenzo, Senecú, Ysleta, and Socorro were founded in 1682 in the area of El Paso del Norte as a result of the Pueblo Revolt. For decades the towns remained under a virtual state of siege by Indian rebels.

38. Elliott, *Empires of the Atlantic World,* 272; Knaut, *Pueblo Revolt,* 127; María Elena Galaviz de Copdevielle, *Rebeliones indigenas en el norte del Reino de la Nueva Espana, Siglos XVI y XVII* (Mexico, DF: Editorial Campesina, 1967), 133–140.

39. Weber, *Spanish Frontier in North America,* 137–139; Hall, *Social Change in the Southwest,* 90, 92.

40. Weber, *Spanish Frontier in North America,* 139–140. Released from prison in Mexico City after defending himself from false charges, Diego de Vargas was reappointed governor of New Mexico from 1700 to 1703. Vargas would protect the Pueblos from each other and from raids of Apaches and Navajos. He died in 1704 while leading a military expedition against the Apaches.

41. Ibid., 141; Hall, *Social Change in the Southwest,* 92.

42. Weber, *Spanish Frontier in North America,* 90; Hall, *Social Change in the Southwest,* 96. In 1695, a new seat of government was established at Santa Cruz de La Canada, north of the capital of Santa Fe.

43. Hall, *Social Change in the Southwest,* 96–97.

44. Weber, *Spanish Frontier in North America,* 309.

45. Ibid., 197; Hall, *Social Change in the Southwest,* 93–94; De Lay, *War of a Thousand Deserts,* 59.

46. Weber, *Spanish Frontier in North America,* 307–308; Brooks, *Captives and Cousins,* 123–125; Gutíerrez, *When Jesus Came,* 152; Blackhawk, *Violence over the Land,* 76–77. The fund was also used to resolve quarrels with the Indians who participated in the trade fair; the Indians would attack people they bartered with or steal back the horses and other livestock they had traded. To ensure harmony, the governor of New Mexico and priests attended these fairs. By 1750, genízaros constituted over 10 percent of New Mexico's population.

47. Weber, *Spanish Frontier in North America,* 197; Hall, *Social Change in the Southwest,* 94–95; Henri Folmer, "Contraband Trade Between Louisiana and New Mexico in the Eighteenth Century," *New Mexico Historical Review* 16 (1941), 265–266. A mercy fund

was authorized for the purchase of slaves as some captives were Spanish colonists taken from distant settlements.

48. Weber, *Spanish Frontier in North America*, 196; Max L. Moorehead, *New Mexico's Royal Road: Trade and Travel on the Chihuahua Trail* (Norman: University of Oklahoma Press, 1954), 49–54.

49. Weber, *Spanish Frontier in North America*, 196; Hall, *Social Change in the Southwest*, 93.

50. Weber, *Spanish Frontier in North America*, 308.

51. Ibid.; Blackhawk, *Violence over the Land*, 46–47, 78–79.

52. De Lay, *War of a Thousand Deserts*, 11; Weber, *Spanish Frontier in North America*, 221–223.

53. Weber, *Bárbaros*, 72, 75. The Apache tribes occupied an area extending from the Arkansas River to northern Mexico and from Central Texas to Central Arizona.

54. Ibid., 71–72; Pekka Hämäläinen, *The Comanche Empire* (New Haven, CT: Yale University Press, 2008), 22, 27; Weber, *Spanish Frontier in North America*, 189–191.

55. De Lay, *War of a Thousand Deserts*, 12–13, 199; Hämäläinen, *Comanche Empire*, 109; Weber, *Bárbaros*, 193; Kenner, *Comanchero Frontier*, 49–51; Alfred B. Thomas, *Forgotten Frontiers: A Study of the Spanish Indian Policy of Don Juan Bautista de Anza, 1777–1787* (Norman: University of Oklahoma Press, 1937), 119–142.

56. Hämäläinen, *Comanche Empire*, 120.

57. De Lay, *War of a Thousand Deserts*, 13, 20; Weber, *Spanish Frontier in North America*, 230–231; Kenner, *Comanchero Frontier*, 53–54; Bernardo de Gálvez, *Instructions for Governing the Interior Provinces of New Spain, 1786*, ed. and trans. Donald E. Worcester (Berkeley, CA: Quivera Society, 1951), 40–43; Blackhawk, *Violence over the Land*, 117.

58. Elliot, *Empires of the Atlantic World*, 272; Weber, *Bárbaros*, 105; Weber, *Spanish Frontier in North America*, 161; John Francis Bannon, *The Spanish Borderlands Frontier, 1513-1821* (Albuquerque: University of New Mexico Press, 1974), 115.

59. Raúl A. Ramos, *Beyond the Alamo: Forging Mexican Ethnicity in San Antonio, 1821–1861* (Chapel Hill: University of North Carolina Press, 2008), 17–18. For a discussion of the establishment and growth of the five missions in the Río San Antonio area of Texas, see Félix D. Almaráz, Jr., "Harmony, Discord, and Compromise in Spanish Colonial Texas: The Rio San Antonio Experience, 1691–1741," *New Mexico Historical Review* 67, no. 4 (1992): 329–356. The buildings and grounds of Mission San Antonio de Valero one hundred years later would become the scene of one of the most famous battles in American history, the Battle of the Alamo.

60. Donald E. Chipman, *Spanish Texas, 1519–1821* (Austin: University of Texas Press, 1992), 123–128. Captain Domingo Ramón was in charge of the presidio, and the mission was under the supervision of Fray Augustín Patrón y Guzmán. The settlers of La Bahía began to experience problems with Indians owing to the incompetence and corruption of Captain Ramón. A disgruntled Indian later killed the inept Spanish officer.

61. Ibid., 129, 168; Weber, *Spanish Frontier in North America*, 211–212.

62. Patricia Osante, *Orígenes del Nuevo Santandar, 1748–1772* (Ciudad Victoria, Mexico: UNAM/University of Tamaulipas, 1997), 146–151.

63. Chipman, *Spanish Texas, 1519–1821*, 121, 193, 204–205; Andres Tijerina, *Tejanos and Texas Under the Mexican Flag, 1821–1836* (College Station: Texas A & M University Press, 1994), 16, 19, 22–23; De Lay, *War of a Thousand Deserts*, 56.

64. Weber, *Spanish Frontier in North America*, 192, 194; Chipman, *Spanish Texas, 1519–1821*, 248.

65. Jack Jackson, *Los Mesteños: Spanish Ranching in Texas, 1721–1821* (College Station: Texas A&M University Press, 1986), 4–5; Chipman, *Spanish Texas, 1519–1821*, 121, 140–141, 168; Tijerina, *Tejanos and Texas, 1821–1836*, 167–168.

66. Ramos, *Beyond the Alamo*, 18, 20; Weber, *Spanish Frontier in North America*, 192–194; Chipman, *Spanish Texas, 1519–1821*, 131–133, 135–136, 184; Weber, *Bárbaros*, 249; Jesús F. de la Teja, *San Antonio de Béxar: A Community on New Spain's Northern Frontier* (Albuquerque: University of New Mexico Press, 1995), 123.

67. Weber, *Spanish Frontier in North America*, 194; Chipman, *Spanish Texas, 1519–1821*, 188, 193.

68. Ramos, *Beyond the Alamo*, 18, 22; Chipman, *Spanish Texas, 1519–1821*, 206. Two years later, in 1779, the census of Texas noted six racial castes: Spanish, mulatto, Indian, mestizo, *lobo*, and *coyote*. (The latter two terms refer to offspring of Indian, mulatto, or mestizo parents.) According to the census, only 150 persons were "Spanish"-born, either in Texas or in other places in northern Mexico. Mulattos made up 29 percent of the population, and the remaining groups were listed as mestizos, lobos, and coyotes. Slaves were not listed in the census, though other documents noted small numbers of both mulatto and Indian slaves. Chipman, *Spanish Texas, 1519–1821*, 206–207.

69. Weber, *Bárbaros*, 72, 151.

70. Chipman, *Spanish Texas, 1519–1821*, 130–131; Weber, *Spanish Frontier in North America*, 188, 214.

71. Chipman, *Spanish Texas, 1519–1821*, 181; De Lay, *War of a Thousand Deserts*, 12–13; Weber, *Spanish Frontier in North America*, 204–212, 221.

72. Chipman, *Spanish Texas, 1519–1821*, 156, 160–161, 171, 177; Weber, *Spanish Frontier in North America*, 188–189.

73. Hämäläinen, *Comanche Empire*, 95; Weber, *Spanish Frontier in North America*, 198; Weber, *Bárbaros*, 148–149. Spain continued to administer Texas from Mexico City, whereas Louisiana was placed under the control of the viceroy of Havana. Odie B. Faulk, *The Last Years of Spanish Texas, 1778–1821* (The Hague: Mouton, 1964), 63–64.

74. Hämäläinen, *Comanche Empire*, 118; Weber, *Bárbaros*, 244; Chipman, *Spanish Texas, 1519–1821*, 198–199, 227; Faulk, *Last Years of Spanish Texas*, 64–65. See also Carol A. Lipscomb, "Burying That War Hatchet: Spanish-Comanche Relations in Colonial Texas, 1743–1821" (Ph.D. diss., University of North Texas, 2003).

75. De Lay, *War of a Thousand Deserts*, 13; Chipman, *Spanish Texas, 1519–1821*, 198–200, 292.

76. Chipman, *Spanish Texas, 1519–1821*, 205. The total population of the Interior Provinces of New Spain averaged six inhabitants per square league, and Texas averaged fewer than two per league.

77. Ibid, 210. Phillip Nolan of Kentucky headed the first American filibustering expedition into Texas. Nolan was interested in the vast herds of horses for export to Louisiana to work the growing cattle industry. In late 1800, Nolan and his party of filibusters crossed into Texas north of Nacogdoches and built a corral for mustangs. The next year Texas governor Juan Bautista de Elguezábal ordered commander Manuel Múzquiz to capture and arrest Nolan. Nolan was killed, and his men surrendered. Although promised safe passage back to the United States, the American prisoners were transported to Chihuahua, where eight were executed. The others died in prison. Ibid, 213–215; Maurine T. Wilson and Jack Jackson, *Philip Nolan and Texas: Expeditions to the Unknown Land* (Waco: Texian Press, 1987), 1–2, 13–15, 35–36, 47–73.

78. To contain the American westward-moving juggernaut at the Mississippi River, Spain conceded Louisiana to France in 1800 through the Treaty of San Ildefonso. Three years later, in October 1803, Emperor Napoleon Bonaparte of France sold the Louisiana Territory to the United States, once again making Texas the northern frontier of New Spain. American expansionists believed that Texas was part of the Louisiana Purchase and that the Río Grande was its western boundary. De Lay, *War of a Thousand Deserts,* 14; Chipman, *Spanish Texas, 1519–1821,* 215, 223; Weber, *Spanish Frontier in North America,* 291–292. See also Philip Coolidge Brooks, "Spain's Farewell to Louisiana, 1803–1821," *Journal of American History* 27 (June 1940): 29–42.

79. De Lay, *War of a Thousand Deserts,* 14–15; Chipman, *Spanish Texas, 1519–1821,* 224–225. See also J. Villesana Haggard, "The Neutral Ground Between Louisiana and Texas, 1806–1821," *Louisiana Historical Quarterly* 28 (October 1945): 1001–1128; Jack D. L. Holmes, "Showdown on the Sabine: General James Wilkinson vs. Lieutenant-Colonel Simon de Herrera," *Louisiana Studies* 3 (Spring 1964): 46–76. Spanish and American forces launched joint military operations against the outlaws of the Neutral Ground.

80. Chipman, *Spanish Texas, 1519–1821,* 229–232; Félix D. Almaraz, Jr., *Tragic Cavalier: Governor Manuel Salcedo of Texas: 1808–1813* (Austin: University of Texas Press, 1971), 55–59.

81. Bannon, *Spanish Borderlands Frontier,* 153–154.

82. Ibid.; Elliot, *Empires of the Atlantic World,* 304, 353; Weber, *Spanish Frontier in North America,* 238–239; Douglas Monroy, *Thrown Among Strangers: The Making of Mexican Culture in Frontier California* (Berkeley: University of California Press, 1993), 21.

83. Weber, *Spanish Frontier in North America,* 242–246.

84. Miroslavo Chávez-García, *Negotiating Conquest: Gender and Power in California, 1770s to 1880s* (Tucson: University of Arizona Press, 2004), 8; Bannon, *Spanish Borderlands,* 155; Hackel, *Children of Coyote,* 42–43, 56–57; Chapman, *History of California,* 221–224; Bouvier, *Women in the Conquest of California,* 37.

85. Chávez-García, *Negotiating Conquest,* 16; Bouvier, *Women in the Conquest of California,* 58–62.

86. Chávez-García, *Negotiating Conquest,* 17–18; Bouvier, *Women in the Conquest of California,* 70.

87. Hackel, *Children of Coyote,* 56–57; Weber, *Spanish Frontier in North America,* 164, 258–259; Theodore E. Treatlein, *San Francisco Bay: Discovery and Colonization, 1769–1776* (San Francisco: California Historical Society, 1968), 88–100; Daniel J. Gorr, "A Frontier Agrarian Settlement: San José de Guadalupe, 1777–1850," *San Jose Studies* 2 (November 1976): 93–94.

88. Weber, *Spanish Frontier in North America,* 259; Monroy, *Thrown Among Strangers,* 99–100; Harry Kelsey, "A New Look at the Founding of Old Los Angeles," *California Historical Society* 55, no. 4 (Winter 1976): 327–337; Bouvier, *Women in the Conquest of California,* 70.

89. Chávez-García, *Negotiating Conquest,* 7–8, 14, 16, 20–21; Haskel, *Children of Coyote,* 56–60; Weber, *Spanish Frontier in North America,* 265; William Marvin Mason, *The Census of 1790: A Demographic History of Colonial California* (Menlo Park, CA: Ballena Press, 1998), 19–20, 22, 28–29, 67, 69; Bouvier, *Women in the Conquest of California,* 74–77.

90. Chávez-García, *Negotiating Conquest,* 19–20. None of the colonists in Los Angeles were able to sign their names to land grants awarded to them, and only one of nine

family heads in San Jose could read or write. The same situation held true for the presidios. Only fourteen of the fifty soldiers at the Monterey presidio and seven of the thirty soldiers in San Francisco were literate.

91. Chávez-García, *Negotiating Conquest,* 6; Haskel, *Children of Coyote,* 65; Weber, *Spanish Frontier in North America,* 263; Monroy, *Thrown Among Strangers,* 1–18; Bouvier, *Women in the Conquest of California,* 80–81.

92. Chávez-García, *Negotiating Conquest,* 11–12, 15, 21.

93. Haskel, *Children of Coyote,* 160–161, 319; Weber, *Spanish Frontier in North America,* 263; Bouvier, *Women in the Conquest of California,* 81.

94. Weber, *Spanish Frontier in North America,* 285–286; Warren L. Cook, *Flood Tide of Empire: Spain and the Pacific Northwest, 1543–1819* (New Haven, CT: Yale University Press, 1973), 200–249.

95. For example, nearly half of Santa Barbara's 850 residents lived on ranches. This area of Alta California grew at the expense of the province's northern and southern regions.

96. Weber, *Spanish Frontier in North America,* 235.

97. Elliott, *Empires of the Atlantic World,* 381; De Lay, *War of a Thousand Deserts,* 15; Chipman, *Spanish Texas, 1519–1821,* 232–236.

98. Chipman, *Spanish Texas, 1519–1821,* 236–237.

99. Elliot, *Empires of the Atlantic World,* 399–400.

100. Truett, *Fugitive Landscapes,* 40.

101. Elliot, *Empires of the Atlantic World,* 406; Weber, *Spanish Frontier in North America,* 334.

102. Elliot, *Empires of the Atlantic World,* 275; Weber, *Spanish Frontier in North America,* 234–235, 339.

CHAPTER 2

⋆⟋

# Life and Society in Mexico's Northern Borderlands

## 1821–1846

Newly independent Mexico faced an uncertain future. This nation's lack of a consensus government was the cause of the political instability that between 1833 and 1855 saw the presidency change thirty-six times. The country's fragile control over its vast northern territories stretching from Texas to California was made weaker by depression due to the destruction of its mining and other economic sectors during its war of independence. Money was not the only worry in Mexico. Its independence came as American settlers pushed into Texas and American traders seeped into the West reaching the Plains Indian tribes. All of these Americans carried with them their own principals of law, liberty, and religion that would soon clash with the region's inhabitants, whose laws, religion, and language were unfamiliar and considered inferior to those of the Americans.[1]

Mexico regarded its northern territories as a unified region with a common set of purposes and problems. In addition to being financially exhausted, Mexico saw its military strength on its northern frontier erode with the demise of the neglected presidios. This left settled parts of the region to be ravaged and depopulated by Comanches, Kiowas, Apaches, Navajos, and other Indians who in the early 1830s abandoned the peace treaties agreed on in the late eighteenth century. The vast lands also became vulnerable to encroachment by western-moving Americans, who traded with and armed the Indians and made them a more formidable foe to the Spanish-speaking residents.[2]

Regional autonomy increased for the northern frontier inhabitants who viewed Mexico with growing ambivalence. Though sentiment varied from region to region, disputes on a host of issues drove a deepening wedge between the frontier residents and Mexico. From 1825 to 1835 small revolts broke out in California, Texas, and northern Sonora (parts of present Arizona) over the issues of the right of home rule and local control of economic development. In 1835 Mexico's centralized regime transformed states into departments, further limiting the control of its citizens over their own affairs. The Mexicans in California and New Mexico resented what they viewed as the high-handed tactics of officials sent from Mexico to rule them. There were no acts of defiance in New Mexico until 1837, when Mexico assigned Albino Pérez as the territorial governor, and he threatened local autonomy. Conflict with the Navajo Indians frequently led to violence and the loss of life among vecinos. Pérez imposed centralized control and taxation, in addition to mandatory service in the militia to fight in campaigns against marauding Navajos, an important political issue at this time. The 1836 revolt in Texas was likewise indicative of the overall desire for home rule on the northern frontier.[3]

Mexicans in the northern frontier lived along the Río Grande, with most of the settlement on the river's upper reaches in New Mexico. New Mexico's population exceeded that of northern Sonora, Texas, and Baja and Alta California. Most of the approximately thirty thousand settlers were mestizos who lived in or near the villages and towns of Socorro, Albuquerque, Santa Fe, and Taos along the Río Grande. This frontier society was stratified into *ricos* and *pobres* (rich and poor); large landowners and government officials and the larger population of New Mexican vecinos. With deep ties to their lands, the latter had a strong belief that it was their right to choose their own local officials and pay no taxes. Farming and sheep ranching, supplemented by weaving and other female-operated handicrafts reflecting a barter economy, and fighting off the hostile raids by nomadic Indians were the principal activities of New Mexicans. Maintaining a standing volunteer militia rested heavily on the local inhabitants, who had learned to fight like Indians. They were isolated and under constant harassment by fierce and determined Ute, Navajo, and Apache Indians. The most noteworthy change in New Mexico was the termination of Spanish policies prohibiting contact and trade with foreigners. Enjoying relatively peaceful relations with the Comanches, the increasing demand for wool in southern and eastern markets led to the development of sheep ranching east of the Río Grande into Texas, northward into Colorado, and westward toward Arizona in the 1830s and 1840s. For the majority of settlers economic resources remained extremely limited, and they remained hard pressed. New Mexican traders, called *comancheros,* left their villages in eastern New Mexico at the head of mule trains loaded with bread, cornmeal, blankets, tobacco, and iron and traveled to the camps of Plains Indians to trade for horses and buffalo hides and robes. Later, comancheros traded guns, powder, and lead for stolen Texas cattle. New Mexico authorities were unable to control this exchange in the huge trading area called la Comanchería, which continued into the 1870s. With the decline of the trade fairs in the eighteenth century, the Chihuahua Trail was New Mexico's only link with the outside world until the arrival of the American trade caravans from Missouri in 1821.[4] Yet commerce in New Mexico continued to suffer from official Mexican tyranny, competition, and exaction, even though authorities knew that the trade was necessary for the well-being of the New Mexicans.

In the area of present-day Arizona, the town of Tucson had four hundred residents, and south of Tucson, six hundred Mexicans were scattered on farms and ranches throughout the Santa Cruz Valley. Many settlers were former residents of Tubac and Tumacácori further south but had been run off by the powerful Apaches. Following the Apache peace of the 1790s, nearly five hundred farmers, ranchers, and miners, along with their families, lived in Tubac-Tumacácori and Santa María located in the San Luis Valley. Living as they did on the remote and isolated Arizona frontier, the repeated Indian raids multiplied their problems. Here, single, married, and widowed women, whose menfolk had been killed by Indians, and their children often worked on farms on former mission lands, taking over all farm work.[5]

Texas remained sparsely settled, with most Mexicans concentrated around Béxar, Goliad, Nacogdoches, and along the Río Grande. The Béxar-Goliad (formerly La Bahía) region contained a combined population of 2,500, of which 1,500 lived in Béxar. Nacogdoches in northeast Texas was less populated. El Paso had a population of about 5,000 residents in 1830 engaged in horse, mule, goat, and sheep ranching. As elsewhere in New Mexico's northern regions, the Texas ranchers were dependent on the labor of their women and children for the survival of the family. The frontier between the Río Grande and the Nueces River in South Texas contained a string of farming and ranching communities in which fighting marauding Indians was a matter of survival, as it was in Arizona and New Mexico. The elite Tejano ranching families, because they concluded that prosperity would come by attracting foreign colonists, promoted Anglo colonization of Texas. Many of the Anglos arriving in Texas were from the slave South. They entered the rich and open land of Texas illegally settling as squatters. Others, hoping to find economic opportunity in Texas, were arriving from the United States accompanied by their black slaves. Anglo dissenters, joined by like-minded Tejanos, soon aimed to return Mexico to its 1824 constitution. The Texians (as Anglo-Texans called themselves) were also united in their attempts to expand the domain of slavery into Texas and succeeded in wresting Texas from Mexico.[6]

In California the small population of Mexicans, numbering 3,200, mostly lived along the five-hundred-mile coastline extending from San Diego to San Francisco. California's presidios and mission system had declined steadily during the final years of the Spanish colonial period through mismanagement and internal turmoil, namely the removal of the Indians from the control of the missionaries. Those who favored secularization of the missions caused a shift in California's economy, namely in livestock production, to the powerfully connected elite Californios. The Californios welcomed Russian, English, and American traders and smugglers (chiefly American). At first the latter had traded with the missions for hides but now took advantage of Mexico's weakness to bring manufactured goods to trade. At this time, American fur trappers employed by St. Louis companies came into California over the mountains. The Californios welcomed them because they believed the Americans would benefit California. Like New Mexico and Texas, the new arrivals had no intention of becoming Mexican citizens.

Centralism, clericalism, militarism, and soon American imperialism were debilitating Mexico. Chaos in the wake of revolution, combined with unfolding change in the north, led to loss of control by Mexico over its frontier. The present Southwest became a new frontier for American settlement enthused over the prospects the place seemed to offer. Though they entertained a strong admiration for American institutions, the Spanish-speaking inhabitants at the same time feared the advancing American frontier. Nonetheless, the Americans brought much-needed aid. Mexico's northern frontier became commercially oriented and linked to the United States markets as more and more Americans entered the area after 1821. A fretful Mexico could not regulate trade nor stop the smuggling of contraband because northern officials put local and regional interests first over those of

Mexico. Mexico's inability to satisfy these demands increased the gulf between it and the northern region. The recent citizens of Mexico in the northern borderlands learned too late that the acquisitive North Americans now in their midst were as contemptuous of Mexicans as they were of Indians and blacks. The Americans were also conniving and untrustworthy. Reflecting the racial prejudice already deeply embedded in the United States, anti-Mexican sentiment in the region grew among the Americans, who did not regard Mexicans as their social equals and who believed their own interests were more important than those of the Mexicans. The Americans would soon affirm their dominant position.

## INDIAN RELATIONS ON THE NORTHERN FRONTIER AFTER MEXICAN INDEPENDENCE

Because of Spain's Indian policy, the Indians on Mexico's northern frontier had been made even more reliant on raiding and trading. Moreover, the powerful Indian forces would not accept Mexican rule; most had not heard nor cared that Mexico had gained its independence from Spain. A main reason for the resumption of Indian raiding was that Mexican authorities were unable to provide them with desirable trade goods and gifts. Relations between the northern frontier settlers and Indians deteriorated and fractured the fragile peace between them. Raiding was widespread and renewed the cycle of fighting. Newly independent and weak, Mexico understood that the numerous Indian tribes could not be defeated. Mexico had granted citizenship to the Indians in 1811 and signed peace treaties with both the Lipan Apaches and the Comanches in 1822, but this did not stop Indian depredations. Indians fought tenaciously to preserve their way of life based on raiding.[7]

Surrounding the rural village settlements of northern New Mexico were plains and mountains inhabited by hostile Indians who attacked Mexicans and sometimes other Indians. Mexico could provide no security for New Mexico; the few federal soldiers assigned to the territory were poorly equipped, undisciplined, and easily harried. Responsibility for defense of New Mexico thus remained with its citizenry. However, the settlers had few guns and little ammunition because New Mexico had no public arsenal, and, to avoid the potential for armed insurrection, laws prohibited the introduction of guns and ammunition into the territory. Along with endemic warfare with the Navajos and Apaches, accommodation existed with the Plains Indian tribes. Indian slaving was an accepted way of life for many poor New Mexican communities; they were wholly dependent on contraband trade with the Indians in the form of horses and hides, as well as captives. Some of the latter were Mexicans. However, Comanches, Kiowas, and Kickapoos who captured Mexican women and children Indianized them and sold them to other Indians, though they rarely ransomed their captives to their families. In 1834, a confrontation between Indians and Mexicans occurred when the Ute Indians declared war on the Department of New Mexico. Furthermore, the Navajo Indians, breaking eight years of peace, renewed their warfare with New Mexico's Spanish-speaking settlements.[8]

Warfare with the Navajos became an accepted feature of life on the New Mexico frontier. Sweeping down from northwest New Mexico, the Navajo Indians mounted incursions and retaliatory raids on settlements of the upper Río Grande Valley and acquired horses, mules, sheep, and goats from the villages. Although contending that the punitive campaigns against the Navajos were intended only to protect the rico sheep farmers, vecinos and their Pueblo Indian allies launched violent counterforays and kidnapped Navajo children and stole Navajo sheep and horses as booty. Stealing Navajo children to sell was the principal occupation of groups of New Mexicans known as *cebolleños*. Navajo hatred of the Spanish-speaking settlers was bitterly intense because of the latter's practice of selling Navajo captives as slaves. The cycle was perpetuated when Navajo Indians retaliated and raided New Mexican villages for captives for ransom and revenge.[9] Accustomed to slave raiding, native New Mexicans fueled the hostilities by staging additional raids to acquire Navajo captives. Although illegal, the custom flourished openly.

More numerous and better armed, Comanches succumbed to the forces of trade and maintained a precarious peace with native New Mexican traders. At times allied with their former enemies, Kiowa and Kiowa Apache warriors, and having assimilated numerous Indian and Mexican captives, Comanches came down from the Great Plains into Texas on the Great Comanche War Trail that traversed west Texas, the Chihuahua-Coahuila boundary, and present Maverick County, Texas, and plundered the Spanish-speaking ranches and towns, taking thousands of head of livestock and hundreds of captives. Mixed-blood Indian warriors, such as the Comanche-Spanish His-oo-sán chees, had to display more bravery and tenacity in battles to balance their tainted heritage in the tribal hierarchy. The motive that triggered the Comanche raids into Texas was revenge for their displacement resulting from the quickening of Texas settlement. The hostilities between Texas and the Plains Indians improved the frontier situation in New Mexico; the Indians needed this frontier for trading and the Texas frontier for raiding. While New Mexicans promoted trade with the Indians, Texas-Coahuila and Chihuahua caught the brunt of Indian marauding. The anarchy of the Texas rebellion for independence further triggered Comanche raids on cattle ranches and settlements along the lower Río Grande between Laredo and Matamoros and south into Mexico.[10] So did the growing penetration of U.S. market forces into the trans-Mississippi west.

The greatest Indian threat was in Arizona, owing to Apache and Mexican population increases. The Mexican pioneers constantly faced the ever-present threat of Indian attacks. Lurking everywhere and using terror and guerilla-war tactics, the raiding Apaches forced their long-time enemies the Mexicans to live inside armed, walled stockades with their livestock or to move to safer areas near Tubac and Tucson. Spanish policy had replaced Apache extermination with a strategy to reduce these Indians by pitting them against each other and by forming alliances with Apache bands and tribes that sought peace and using these against hostile Apaches. To gain control over the Apaches, Governor José María Irigoyen now followed a policy of creating dissension among the tribes and offered rewards for the taking of scalps. Mexican officials employed American scalp hunter James Kirker and his motley band of Mexicans, Anglos, and Delaware and Shawnee Indians to hunt Apaches. This extermination policy resulted in

**His-oo-sán chees, Little Spaniard, a Warrior, 1834.**
CREDIT: Gift of Mrs. Joseph Harrison, Jr. Courtesy of the Smithsonian American Art Museum.

retaliatory raiding by the Apaches. From staging areas in Arizona, New Mexico, and west Texas, Apaches pushed southward into Chihuahua, Sonora, and Durango, the raiding parties slaughtering or stealing livestock, destroying crops, taking weapons, murdering settlers, and kidnapping terrified Mexican women and children to sell as slaves.[11]

In the context of the relative prosperity and the western land boom of the early 1830s, the influx of Americans was disrupting many Indian tribes and forcing them across the Mississippi River, where they came into contact with other Indian groups. The rapid influx of Americans in turn increased Indian depredations against Mexicans because they upset the balance of power and weakened Mexican-Indian trade alliances. Mexico's weak military presence in the region exacerbated the problem. Indians raided Mexican settlements for livestock and captives to trade with Americans, who furnished them with more efficient weapons and alcohol. This trade extended as far east as Louisiana. The opening of the Santa Fe Trail and the building of trading forts in Colorado outside Mexican jurisdiction furthered the trade in guns and ammunition of the Americans with the Apaches, Comanches, and other Indian tribes and shifted the balance of power between Mexicans and Indians to the latter's advantage. The removal of the Cherokee and other Indian tribes west of the Mississippi River by the United States placed additional pressure on Indian and Mexican relations as far west as

California. Moreover, the United States believed that it had a right to expand its borders westward through purchase and negotiation. Manifest Destiny would soon underline the United States' nationalist expansionist credo.[12]

New Mexico's expanding population steadily increased buffalo hunting. Large numbers of New Mexican vecinos ventured out onto the Plains, and from New Mexico's frontier villages comancheros traveled to the Plains to trade with the Comanches.

## MEN OF THE PLAINS: NEW MEXICAN CIBOLEROS AND COMANCHEROS

Pacts of economic interdependence were forged between the New Mexicans and the southern Plains Indians. Although Mexico was at war with the Indians, many New Mexican settlers continued their trade with them. Comancheros from eastern New Mexico pushed out into the vast reaches of the Plains with pack animals and wooden carts to trade with the Comanches and Kiowas. Contact between New Mexicans and the Comanches included negotiating peace with these Indian buffalo hunters. For almost two centuries the lives of the settlers on New Mexico's eastern plains revolved around the buffalo. The New Mexicans who hunted this majestic animal were called *ciboleros*. Having mastered the Plains Indians' buffalo-hunting techniques, the ciboleros were renowned for their hunting prowess.[13]

Twice a year the ciboleros traveled in groups of more than one hundred men to hunt the buffalo through eastern New Mexico and into the barren *llano estacado* (Staked Plains) of west Texas. To avoid trouble with the buffalo-hunting Plains Indians, the ciboleros brought onions, dried pumpkin seeds, flour, sugar, coffee, hard bread, beads, saddles, lances, tomahawks, iron for blades and arrow points, arms and ammunition, and other items as barter and as a sign of friendship.[14]

The buffalo hunts took place after the spring planting and fall harvest seasons. Borrowing methods learned from Plains Indians, the ciboleros trapped the buffalo in long, deep trenches, where they killed the animals using lances. Other times the ciboleros rode their ponies alongside the fattest cows and speared the animals on the run, quickly dismounting to pull out the lance and then remounting to continue the chase. The cibolero's primary objective was to kill as many buffalo as possible. A skilled lancer could slaughter twenty-five buffalo during a single chase, covering two or three miles in the pursuit.[15]

Once the killing was completed, other hunting party members went to work and skinned the buffalo, loaded the meat onto horses, pack mules, and wooden carts, and hauled it back to the campsite, where they dressed the meat. The fat was rendered in large copper kettles and made into tallow for cooking, candles, and a soap called *jabón de lejía*. Stretched out in the sun to dry, the hides were tanned to make clothing, moccasins, robes, rugs, and harnesses. Horns were made into utensils and decorative objects, and the long hair from the bison's neck and shoulders was made into coarse cloth or was used as mattress stuffing.[16] The ciboleros sold most of these bison by-products but kept the dried buffalo meat for themselves and shared it with the village members. There was enough meat to last the winter.

The ciboleros became prolific buffalo hunters. By 1832, these hunters were killing between ten thousand to twelve thousand bison annually. This buffalo hunting antagonized Mexican officials and the southern Plains Indian tribes. The former complained that buffalo hunting and trade with the Indians took New Mexicans away from tax-generating farming and manufacturing, whereas the Indians wanted to protect their main source of livelihood. By the time of the American Civil War, Indians who traded the hides at American trading posts had overhunted the buffalo. The New Mexican ciboleros depleted the buffalo herds even more. The ciboleros continued their hunting activities until the late 1870s, when American hide hunters armed with long-range rifles decimated the buffalo herds.[17]

The cibolero hunting parties were an essential economic element in New Mexico, supplying meat to the settlements and buffalo hides and other by-products for the rich Santa Fe–Chihuahua trade. The Spanish-speaking buffalo hunters acquired a thorough knowledge of the llano estecado and inspired the Comancheros to begin their lucrative trading expeditions to the region. Mexican military officials closed the area to all native New Mexicans in an effort to curb the burgeoning though illicit Comanchero trade, which finally came to an end with the destruction of the South Plains Indians. As the settlement of northern New Mexico expanded, trade became increasingly important. Annual trade fairs brought Indians into New Mexico's commercial orbit. The most important trade fair occurred at Taos. New Mexicans developed new trade routes as a reorientation of New Mexico's trade from Mexico to American markets took place through the Santa Fe Trail to Missouri and the Old Spanish Trail to California.

## THE OPENING OF COMMERCIAL MARKETS: THE TAOS TRADE FAIR AND THE SANTA FE TRAIL

At first limited to Indians and local settlers, Mexico opened New Mexico's trade fairs to outsiders shortly after Mexico became independent in 1821. This ended nearly two centuries of isolation for New Mexico, shifting its economy from one based on barter to one based on money. Following Mexico's easing of its restrictions on commerce, a group of New Mexican merchants traveled north to seek trade with their American counterparts, who were beginning to filter into New Mexico offering low-priced trade goods in exchange for silver and furs. The Santa Fe trade began with the establishment of a federal road from present Missouri, the famous Santa Fe Trail. To facilitate New Mexico's trade with the United States, New Mexican officials began to develop the areas north and east of the territory along the trading route with Missouri. They did this by making huge land grants to Anglo and French commercial enterprises. The comparatively inexpensive, mass-produced goods from the United States had only trickled into New Mexico before Mexican independence. Now they increased, and so did much-needed tariff revenues for Mexico.[18]

The Santa Fe trade multiplied six times between 1822 and 1826. The first American traders started out for New Mexico with about $5,000 worth of

**March of the Caravan, n.d. (covered wagons on the Santa Fe Trail).**
CREDIT: LC-USZ62-69027. Courtesy of the Library of Congress.

merchandise carried on pack horses. By 1824, traders were using wagons to carry merchandise valued at almost $30,000, with a return trade value of $180,000. Nearly a decade later, American trading commodities sent to Santa Fe were worth $450,000. On the eve of the Mexican War, the Santa Fe trade was valued at about $1 million annually.[19]

American commerce entering New Mexico via the Santa Fe Trail transformed the New Mexico economy, reorienting trade away from Chihuahua toward Missouri. Residents who could afford to began buying more manufactured goods from Missouri of higher quality and lower price than those from Chihuahua, where enterprising New Mexican traders resold their surplus trade goods. New Mexican officials began charging custom duties of 25 percent for goods entering New Mexico from the United States. They also negotiated with American authorities to protect this trade from Indian attacks.[20]

The fact that New Mexicans' dependence on Chihuahua was reversed raised concern for the Mexican government; particularly troubling were the growing numbers of Americans moving into Mexican territory. Mexican authorities stopped supporting American efforts to build a road from Missouri to Santa Fe, as it would further encourage trade and migration. The officials subjected American traders to repeated customs inspections at the Mexican border and again at other towns along the trail inside the territory. In 1843, Mexico's president, Antonio López de Santa Anna, outlawed trade between New Mexicans and Americans. However, Santa Anna rescinded the law the following year as a result of protests by New Mexicans now heavily dependent on American merchandise from the north.[21]

Trade with the United States raised the New Mexicans' living standard, but unevenly, because it did not extend beyond the ricos who monopolized it.

The profit-hungry ricos, the upper classes who ruled New Mexico as quasi-feudal lords, in essence achieved power and prestige at the expense of the lower classes, because they profited from the wealth the latter produced. The local political bosses readily ingratiated themselves with the American merchants. Presenting themselves to the Americans as loyal and dutiful subordinates, the ricos reduced New Mexico's lower classes to poverty. The end result of this control, reflecting the apparent inequities of wealth and power within New Mexico, was debt peonage. The ricos used their new wealth to increase their land holdings and blocked all attempts to introduce changes in New Mexico's economy, politics, and class relations. The Santa Fe trade as a result came to be dominated by fewer merchants with larger investments. There was more trouble in store for New Mexico with Mexico regarding local autonomy and tax levies.[22]

## CONFLICT IN NEW MEXICO: THE 1837 REVOLT

The vecinos and genízaros subsisted on agriculture, trade with Indians, and the home manufacture of goods for the Santa Fe trade. Kept in various degrees of dependency, the lower-class New Mexicans had become disillusioned with the ricos, who controlled a large portion of the Santa Fe trade and much of the land. The settlers did not regard themselves as the social inferiors of the ricos, and they were just as passionately opposed to Mexico's interference in New Mexico. An important facet of conflict with the government of Mexico was that it exacted taxes and duties unfairly and enforced laws in New Mexico that had been previously ignored.[23]

In 1835, Mexico appointed Albino Pérez as governor and military commander of New Mexico. Pérez was one of the right-wing army officers with whom Mexico's President Antonio López de Santa Anna was establishing ties. This group drafted a centralist constitution, imposed strict property qualifications on political participation, implemented taxation, and greatly reduced local autonomy throughout Mexico. The following year New Mexico was relegated to the status of a territorial department and made part of the state of Chihuahua. This departmental plan had already been challenged in Texas and California.[24] The New Mexicans disliked Governor Pérez because he was an outsider; he was not a native New Mexican.

In July 1837, Pérez adopted a strict timetable for restructuring the regional political system. The new governor greatly expanded the war with the Navajos. He ordered a campaign in the winter of 1836–1837 and forced conscription on the vecinos to fight a war against their will. The governor's vision of a swift victory proved disastrous for the vecinos. Deployed in the extreme cold made worse by gusts of subzero winds, hundreds of the militia's animals froze to death, and 140 men got frostbite. Denied spoils as a result of the botched campaign, many hard-pressed vecinos were financially ruined because they lost their farms, some of which had been in the family for generations. The Apaches all the while continued their depredations along the extended frontiers of New Mexico. Governor Pérez's centralized departmental control, heavy taxation, and compulsory militia service eventually met opposition from both ricos and pobres in New Mexico. Without financial support from either Mexico or the ricos, Pérez could not maintain a militia in New Mexico, and he was thus blamed for the increase in Indian depredations. Because of the growing resentment, the ricos incited the vecinos from Santa Cruz de la Cañada on the Santa Cruz River to revolt against Pérez. The latter issued a proclamation protesting the neglect of New Mexico by Mexico. Taking the law into their own hands, the dissidents encouraged the local Pueblo Indians to join them in destroying the despotic Pérez. Pérez's compulsory militia service also weighed heavily on the Pueblo Indian population, given that Indians, along with poor vicenos, made up the militias.[25]

Manuel Armijo offered himself as the provisional head of New Mexico's government. The son of a wealthy and prominent ranching family and a militia lieutenant and former mayor of Albuquerque, Armijo was appointed governor of New Mexico in 1827. Prone to intrigue and bribery, Armijo wanted to regain power, and he did so after putting down the Río Arriba rebellion.[26]

In early August 1837, enraged vecinos from Santa Cruz de la Cañada issued a proclamation denouncing centralism and Governor Pérez for imposing new taxes. The call for restoring self-rule by the rebels stoked the fires of protest that soon escalated into a full-scale rebellion. Believing the uprising could lead to anarchy, Pérez attempted to suppress it with force. With their Pueblo Indian allies, the rebels numbered more than two thousand and quickly overtook the governor and his force of one hundred fifty men near Black Mesa south of present-day Española. The rebels captured Pérez and sixteen of his men and executed them as a warning to other Mexican officials. They decapitated Pérez while he was still alive. A dozen other henchmen of Pérez were also killed, the hapless victims done in by the federalist-centralist revolts sweeping northern Mexico.[27]

The rebels elected a cibolero from Rancho de Taos, José Gonzales, as the new governor and set out to establish an independent government. Some of Gonzales's faction, averse to rule by Mexico, called for the annexation of New Mexico to the United States. Meanwhile, Manuel Armijo, who was in Albuquerque, gathered support to oppose the vecino Gonzales. Under the Plan de Tomé, Armijo and his co-conspirators called upon Río Arriba's residents to fight against Gonzales and his large rebel army. In late September 1837, Armijo's forces captured Santa Fe. However, Armijo's plan was disrupted because a squadron of Mexican dragoons from Zacatecas, Mexico, arrived in Santa Fe in January 1838 to police New Mexico. The federal troops defeated the rebels in a skirmish east of Santa Cruz de la Cañada, thus ending the revolt against Antonio López de Santa Anna's centralist policies. Captured in the battle, José Gonzales was swiftly put to death. New Mexico was again in the hands of Mexico, with Manuel Armijo confirmed as its departmental governor.[28]

Convinced Americans had been behind the 1837 revolt known as the Chimáyo Rebellion, Mexico in retaliation placed a tariff of $500 on each wagonload of merchandise that came down the Santa Fe Trail from the United States. The New Mexicans suffered most because prices rose on goods entering New Mexico. Manuel Armijo ruled New Mexico with an iron fist. Once more, compulsory militia service was imposed on the New Mexican masses, and preexisting inequalities became entrenched.[29]

In the meantime, the United States pursued western expansion in order to make the nation a world power. Texas was especially appealing to land-hungry Americans, who could get land more cheaply in Texas than they could from the U.S. public domain.

## TEJANO LIFE ON THE TEXAS FRONTIER
## UNDER MEXICO

Unavoidably enmeshed in Mexico's war of independence, the Spanish-speaking population of Texas, the Tejanos, declined by half, from approximately four thousand in 1810 to two thousand in 1820. Along with the devastation of war, drought and a long series of Indian raids had led to the heavy loss of cattle and horses. Most of the Tejano population lived in the present South Texas region extending south and southwest from the San Antonio River to the Río Grande and subdivided by the Nueces River. South of the Nueces River, small Tejano settlements were situated along the Río Grande. In the lower Río Grande more than three million head of livestock grazed on ranch lands by 1830. The Tejanos living north of the Nueces River were concentrated in the Béxar district and survived by exporting hides and pelts obtained through trade with Indians. By the late 1830s, the South Texas region's Tejano population increased through land settlement under the new headright programs of the Texas Republic.[30]

Tejano society was characterized by a three-tiered social structure, reflecting the northern frontier's extant race and class divisions. The top tier was made up of the small Tejano elite. Many were soldiers who had come to the Texas region from Tamaulipas as *cuidadanos armadas* (armed citizens) to provide a line of defense for Mexico. The elites' wealth came from the new commercial and political opportunities in Texas. They owned the large ranches, formerly the colonial haciendas that were almost wiped out by Indian raiding and the turmoil caused by Mexico's war of independence. Although some Tejano cattle ranchers sold their cattle in Mexico and Louisiana, most were not large commercial ranchers. Nonetheless, the Tejano gentry enjoyed wealth and prestige. On the eve of the Texas Revolution, there were about eighty ranches in the Béxar-Goliad area and more than four times this number in South Texas. Through clan loyalties and their status, the Tejano ranchers exacted considerable power in the region, though less than their wealthy and politically connected counterparts in Tamaulipas, Nuevo León, Coahuila, Chihuahua, and Durango south of the Río Grande.[31]

Small- and medium-sized landowning ranchers composed of a handful of families made up the second and largest tier of Tejano society. Typically each family held 8,856 acres of pasture or grazing land. Vaqueros, cartmen, and *peónes* (indebted workers) made up the bottom tier. The concentration of wealth and the demand for labor on the Texas frontier strengthened the institutionalized practice of debt peonage. Owning no property, peónes provided the Tejano landowner elite with a dependable and continuing supply of labor. The *patrónes* (employers) enjoyed all the benefits of peonage; they gave their underlings permission to travel, marry, and engage in other activities, and they served as judge and jury when the peónes broke the law. Through these patriarchal relations, the peónes received favors and material benefits. Vaqueros herded cattle, work that both the elite ranch owners and mission priests considered below their station. Though poor and with little social status, vaqueros had more independence than the peónes; they were not bound to the land as debtors and could acquire property. Carting was the most profitable line of work open to poor Tejanos. Most of the *fleteros* (cart drivers) lived in San Antonio or along the route to the Texas Gulf Coast.[32]

The Tejanos were resourceful and self-reliant, traditions passed down from generation to generation, and most had a relatively strong sense of community. The Tejanos were also staunch federalists; they mistrusted and resented Mexico's interference in their affairs. Notwithstanding their social position, all of the Tejanos faced aggressive nomadic enemies, the Comanches and Lipan Apaches. Together with the advancing Anglos, the Indians forced the Tejanos into a two-front war by the time of the Texas Revolt of 1835–1836.[33]

## THE NEVER-ENDING INDIAN MENACE: COMANCHE RAIDS IN TEXAS

Tejano settlements happened to lie in the path of the Comanches' frequent forays into Texas, and by 1825 war with the nomadic warriors raged along the entire Río Grande. Raids by Comanches and by Lipan Apaches on Tejano communities and livestock were precipitated by the shifting Indian populations on the Plains. Some Texas officials believed assimilation of the Indians was an alternative to their annihilation or removal. Other officials with a military background favored peace through treaties, trade, and agriculture. One of these military officers who attempted to arrange a truce with the Comanche Indians in 1822 was Tejano José Francisco Ruiz. Educated in Spain, Ruiz had been a teacher in Texas until 1813, when he joined the insurgents and fought against the Spanish royalists. Ruiz seemed to be on good terms with the Indians, because he lived by trading with them. The Tejano helped the Comanche representative Guonique sign a treaty of friendship in Mexico City. However, Mexico lacked the money to pay for the gifts it had promised to the Comanches, and thus the latter resumed their raiding. The treaties Mexico signed with the Comanche Indians at Chihuahua in 1826 and at El Paso in 1834 were ineffectual and did not stop the marauding in the region.[34]

The Comanches stepped up their raids southward into Texas to obtain booty and captives. Some of the forays extended all the way to the lower Texas Gulf Coast, and others expanded south into Mexico. Moving silently and unobserved through familiar natural terrain, the Comanches attacked isolated Mexican ranches and other small settlements of the Nueces River strip, killing the herders and taking women and children captive. The Comanche and Kiowa Indians also stole cattle from newly arrived Americans who called themselves Texians, and they traded the cattle to New Mexican comancheros for guns and ammunition and for foodstuffs. Comanche reprisals against Texians continued as the bitter hatred of the Anglo interlopers from Texas intensified. The fact that the Texians were appropriating substantial portions of the range through land grants awarded to them by Mexico only further inflamed the hatred of the Comanches.[35]

Failing to establish military settlements in Texas and to adequately colonize the region, Mexico, through its policy of continual immigration to thwart filibustering—private armed interventions—opened Texas to foreign colonization. In the last years of Spanish rule, Spain had initiated the *empresario* (enterpriser) system, a new version of its buffer strategy to bring Americans to the sparsely settled Texas province. This occurred at the same time as an economic depression in the United States triggered by the Panic of 1819 and the passage of the Land Act of 1820 by the U.S. Congress. The latter lowered the price of land in the public domain from $2.00 to $1.25 per acre but removed the credit allowance. Spain's actions were a godsend to landless Americans, many of whom were deep in debt and facing imprisonment. The influx of Americans into Texas soon became an invasion; it would render the Tejano population a social and political minority and lead to difficulties in the relations between the two groups.[36]

## THE GROWING CONFLICT IN TEXAS
## WITH MEXICO

Whereas Mexico's provinces became states in the Mexican republic, Texas was made part of the new state of Coahuila. Mexico did not specify a boundary between Coahuila and Texas, and it gave power to the individual states versus the central government. Desiring settlement of thinly populated Texas, Mexico's 1824 national colonization law made Anglo settlement of Texas possible. Although Mexico added stringent conditions to its colonization law, Coahuila-Texas government representatives received exceptions to the restrictive federal code.[37]

Mexico's colonization of Coahuila-Texas began in earnest. In its first stage, from 1821 to 1828, elite Tejanos and Anglo migrants cooperated in empresario colonization of Texas. Its purpose in settling a specified number of families in designated areas of Texas on six-year land contracts was to fortify and retain hold of the region, thus creating a buffer zone free of foreign influence and possible intervention. In 1820, Moses Austin of Missouri obtained a charter from Texas governor Antonio Martínez to settle three hundred Catholic families from Louisiana on the Brazos River. The Missourian was granted two hundred thousand acres of land. Following the sudden death of Moses Austin, his son Stephen F. Austin persevered with plans for the Texas colony.[38]

Tejano Erasmo Seguín cordially received Moses Austin at Nacogdoches in July 1821 with news that Mexico, in the process of securing its independence from Spain, had approved his colonization proposal. Seguín escorted Austin and his slave from Nacogdoches to San Antonio de Béxar. The head of a politically important Tejano family who represented Texas in Mexico's National Congress, Seguín worked judiciously to advance American colonization as a way to promote economic expansion into Texas and northern Mexico. A warm friendship developed between the Seguín family and Austin. Tejanos José Antonio de la Garza; Juan Ángel Seguín, the son of Erasmo Seguín; José Francisco Ruiz; and José Antonio Navarro likewise lobbied to continue American immigration to Texas. All of these Tejanos would champion Texas's independence from Mexico but then found themselves in the dilemma of fighting for the rights of Tejanos.[39]

The Coahuila-Texas colonization measure passed on March 25, 1825, and, up to 1836, it greatly facilitated American immigration to Texas. The liberal law offered settlers who were family men one league of grazing land and 177 acres of farming land for less than $100 in fees that could be paid over six years. The American settlers had to become naturalized Mexican citizens, adopt the Catholic faith, and observe all Mexican laws, including the prohibition of the slave trade. Single men received one-fourth league of land and had to meet the same requirements. Additional lands were granted to colonists who married Mexican women, a policy Mexico adopted to encourage assimilation of the American colonists. No payment was due the first four years, and tax exemptions were offered for six years, including exemptions on imported goods used by the settlers. For their part in advancing colonization, empresarios received five leagues (22,000 acres) of grazing land and 885 additional acres of land for every one hundred families they brought to Texas.[40]

The younger Austin advertised in local papers about Mexico's generous and nominally priced land grants offered on easy terms and numerous concessions. He recruited in New Orleans and Nashville, and American settlers from Louisiana, Tennessee, Missouri, Arkansas, Alabama, and Mississippi immigrated to Texas. Most were deeply in debt or escaping imprisonment for indebtedness. None in this first wave of immigrants owned slaves. Austin sold land at twelve and a half cents an acre, which settlers could resell at a profit. Farmers and stock raisers were eligible to receive 4,438 acres of land. The families had to take possession of the land in two years.

Approximately 297 land titles were initially issued; five years later, there were land contracts outstanding for seven thousand American families. The Mexican colonization law more than achieved its purpose. American migration to Texas accelerated. By the mid-1820s, the Americans outnumbered the Tejanos, and many outside the empresario system who entered East Texas as squatters had no intentions of obeying the laws of Mexico. Moreover, the Anglo colonies in Texas became commercial outposts of Louisiana.[41]

Mexico originally wanted Americans to settle around San Antonio de Béxar so that colonists could be absorbed into the local population and also to help defend against Comanche raids. By concentrating the settlers in Béxar, contact with the United States would be broken by a wide swath of unsettled Texas territory. Mexico remained distrustful of the United States; its government officials believed the United States had advanced its boundaries by dubious means. By establishing a colony in the direct line of this advance, Mexico could avoid further American encroachment into its northern territory. However, the American colonists scorned the company of Tejanos. Ignoring Mexico's colonization regulations, the Americans established enclaves separate from Béxar and Goliad and on lands close to the U.S. border and along the Texas coast. Meanwhile, more and more Americans were drifting into east Texas and squatting on land. By 1823, squatters numbered three thousand. Many of these unauthorized migrants in advance of the tide of actual settlement were fugitives from justice and escaped criminals.[42]

Because of Mexico's underlying fear of losing Texas, it implemented several measures to check immigration from the United States. No foreigners could settle within twenty leagues of Mexico's national boundary and, so as not to jeopardize Mexico's trade with New Orleans, ten leagues from the Texas coast. No colonizer could own more than forty-nine thousand acres of land, immigration could be stopped by Mexico at any time, and Texas's southern boundary was at the Nueces River, which separated Texas from the Mexican province of Tamaulipas. To the southwest, Texas was joined to Coahuila as a single Mexican state, and to the west Texas was bounded by New Mexico.

Mexico's apprehension about the safety of Texas was well founded. The aggressive Americans wanted Texas. In 1825, American emissary Joel R. Poinsett made an unofficial visit to Mexico to buy Texas from the Mexicans and to ask Mexico's president for revision of the international boundary to the Río Grande. Two years later, Secretary of State Henry Clay, who had Poinsett's instructions, offered Mexico $1 million to recognize the Río Grande as the border with the United States. As American interest in Texas increased, the United States raised its offer to $5 million. When Andrew Jackson became president, he asserted that the Louisiana Purchase of 1803 carried the boundary of the United States to the Río Grande. Meanwhile, in Congress, Senator Thomas Hart Benton of Missouri, another ardent advocate of western expansion, proposed acquiring all of Texas.[43]

## THE DRIVE FOR TEXAS INDEPENDENCE

Coveting more virgin land in Texas, their newfound Eden, the American settlers early on became involved in conspiracy to wrest the territory from Mexico. Many were slaveholders or those who supported slavery, so they wanted to open Texas to the slave market. Mexico united its individual states under a central authority. In May 1824, Mexico gave its province Nuevo León statehood. The Anglo-Texan colonists wanted the same for Texas. They believed the Texas territory as far south as the Río Grande should be separated from Coahuila as a Mexican state. A handful of Tejanos also wanted this political change.[44]

Settlement increased land values and expanded markets for Tejano merchants and ranchers, but it also produced problems. Advertisements in American newspapers intentionally misled prospective buyers on land sales in Texas. Thousands of buyers purchased property only to discover that most of the advertisers had no claim to the land they fraudulently sold. Land speculators often purchased grants from Mexicans who had petitioned the government for the grants. Many Americans had come to Texas illegally and settled on lands that Mexico had set aside as part of its national domain and that were closed to colonization. Mexican officials, furthermore, were unable to drive off Americans of less than "good character," individuals who were either escaping debts or were fugitives from justice. The situation got worse as some Americans staged filibustering expeditions and seized lands owned by Tejanos, whom they forced off their land. As a result, Mexico set up military garrisons in Texas to defend against further filibustering activities. American empresario Haden Edwards led one filibustering expedition in late 1826 to take Texas away from Mexico.[45]

In 1825, Mexico granted Haden Edwards a contract to settle eight hundred families on land in east Texas near Nacogdoches. The contract required Edwards to respect the rights of the Anglo and Tejano landowners already living within the territory of the grant. However, the empresario immediately issued a decree that all these people required proof of titles to their grants. Those without proof had to leave or else purchase the land they claimed to own from Edwards. As Edwards expected, almost none of the Anglo settlers owned their land, and very few Tejanos possessed land titles.[46]

Edwards reasoned that the only way he could bolster his forces and carry out his rebellion was with the aid of Indian allies. In late 1826, he persuaded neighboring Cherokee Indians to negotiate a treaty of friendship and alliance through a mixed-blood Cherokee trader, calling for war to claim land from Mexico. Resentful of Mexican authorities, Edwards easily convinced the Cherokees that by uniting with him in this effort they could gain lands that they did not receive from Mexico via its colonization law. Through this alliance the Cherokees would get title to all the land extending from Louisiana to New Mexico north of an east-west line from Nacogdoches. Edwards would take all the land south of the line. Haden Edwards thus established the "Republic of Fredonia" extending from the Sabine River south to the Río Grande.[47]

The aggrieved settlers turned to the government of Coahuila-Texas for military help against Edwards's extravagant scheme. Mexico, which decided to cut back immigration to Texas, revoked his colonization contract. Austin denounced Edwards and ordered his militia to join Mexican forces to put down the Fredonia Rebellion. Lasting less than a month, the Republic of Fredonia collapsed, and Edwards and his settlers were expelled from Texas.[48]

The Fredonia Rebellion was a portent of things to come. The potential for a full-scale rebellion, combined with growing American interest in Texas, raised further problems for Mexico. Erasmo Seguín and other Tejanos, who preferred the liberalism of the Texians to autocratic centralist rule by Mexico, soon found themselves increasingly pulled toward opposing Mexican rule by declaring independence for Texas.[49]

Anglo Texian colonists, with their Tejano allies, began to build an independent republic. The Mexican government interpreted the separation of Texas from Mexico as treasonous and actively suppressed the effort. The conflict with the Mexican government evolved because Coahuila controlled government rule in Texas. The main grievance was that Texas did not have final jurisdiction in important civil and criminal cases. Moreover, the Americans did not respect the Mexican constitution. Slavery existed in Texas, and nearly every Anglo colonist benefited from it.[50]

Slaveholders such as Stephen F. Austin believed that the rapid development of Texas was dependent on the right of the colonists to introduce slaves or contract servants to make Texas a land based on a plantation economy. Insisting that the slave system benefited all of Texas, Austin continued to work to allow immigrants to bring slaves to Texas. On July 13, 1824, the Mexican Congress had passed a law prohibiting the purchase and sale of slaves in the Mexican Republic. However, neither Mexico's constitution nor its colonization law contained anything on the matter of slavery. Erasmo Seguín was a deputy to the Mexican Congress that passed the colonization law. The Tejano deplored the law but was unable to prevent its passage.[51] His passion on this issue helped explain his arguments to his friend Austin. On July 24, 1825, Seguín wrote:

> I agree with you that the great development of your colony, and of the other colonies of Texas, depends . . . upon permitting their inhabitants to introduce slaves . . . But, my friend . . . it was resolved that commerce and traffic in slaves should be forever extinguished in our republic and that the introduction of slaves into our territory should not be permitted under any pretext.[52]

Texas was fast inheriting the slave economy of the South. Mexico's manumission of slaves in 1829 was a defense measure to halt the further weakening of Mexico in Texas by discouraging the immigration of Americans from southern states. Ignorant or else contemptuous of Mexico's laws, American colonists in Texas were unhappy with Mexico's emancipation of slaves, even though the law did not apply to Texas. The disloyal Texians, described by the Mexican boundary commission's draftsman as "a lazy people of vicious character," saw themselves in danger of becoming the alien subjects of Mexico, a people to whom they believed themselves to be morally, intellectually, and politically superior. Their arrogant and dismissive attitude toward all things Mexican was alienating to their Tejano allies, who tolerated this kind of talk because as federalists they wanted trade to grow in Texas and also wanted autonomy from the national government of Mexico.[53]

Mexico imposed tighter controls on the Texians; it passed the Law of April 16, 1830, criminalizing further American settlement in Texas and issued new taxes and stricter laws on American trading interests operating on the Río Grande. In addition, the new law promoted the colonization of Mexican and European families in Texas to counterbalance the Americans already in the province, and it specified that Mexico would stop the further importation of slaves. The Texians and their Tejano friends disagreed with the law and began advocating for secession from Mexico. Austin obtained permission for himself and for Green DeWitt to continue the settlement of American immigrants in their established colonies until their empresario contracts expired. Mexican General Manuel de Mier y Terán was ordered by Mexico into Texas to expel the colony and establish military posts.[54] The Texians and their Tejano followers were soon pitted against what they believed was an ever-encroaching centralist Mexican government. The Texan colonists participated in the revolt as federalists. From the beginning, however, the Anglo-Texans led and controlled the insurgency.

The Texan rebels rallied to their cause enthusiastically. They built up a supply of weapons and a fleet of river schooners and in late June 1832 attacked the Mexican garrison at Velasco Fort at Galveston Bay; the garrison surrendered. The attack by both land and water marked the first instance of anti-Mexican government violence since the Fredonia Rebellion. In October, the Texans called a convention and passed a number of resolutions addressed to Mexico. Among these: nullify the ban on further immigration into Texas, return de facto free trade, reopen Texas to settlers (squatters), and separate Texas from Coahuila. This convention was held in defiance of an 1824 law denying the right of assembly. Only one Tejano, Rafael Antonio Mediola, was among the fifty-five delegates representing every Texas municipality except San Antonio de Béxar. Mexico further tightened its control over Texas, an action that stirred up more discontent among the Texan colonists.[55]

The 1827 Coahuila-Texas state constitution outlawed slavery in Texas. However, Austin, the ever-consummate diplomat, had cleverly procured a special provincial law permitting slavery to operate in Texas under a different name— "permanent indentured servitude." Slaves would first be freed, then brought into Texas and held indefinitely as indentured servants who would work to pay for their freedom. Tejano civic leader José Antonio Navarro introduced a defense of plantation slavery in the demands for statehood, and it was adopted on May 5, 1828, thereby ensuring the growth of slavery in Texas. The fact that Americans could enter Texas freely, coupled with rumors that the United States was to purchase Texas, triggered a wave of land speculation. By the summer of 1832, there were over six thousand American settlers in Texas. In contrast, there were about three thousand Tejanos in Texas. Moreover, there were one thousand slaves, reflecting the expansion of cotton production in east Texas that in 1834 produced seven thousand bales of exported cotton.[56]

The Texans called another convention on April 1, 1833, and it reenacted the resolutions of the preceding 1832 convention: to lift the ban on immigration from the United States, to extend the tariff exemption to Texas, and to establish a state government in Texas and allow its separation from Coahuila. The delegates drafted a provisional state constitution. Tejanos Juan Nepomuceno Seguín, José Antonio Navarro, and José Francisco Ruiz forged a pact with Austin and with the recently arrived Sam Houston, both of whom favored Texas independence. Elected to present petitions to the Mexican government, Austin traveled to Béxar to persuade the Tejanos to endorse the petitions and to send a representative to Mexico. Meanwhile, revolution had broken out in Mexico and brought Antonio López de Santa Anna to power. The Texans supported Santa Anna by expelling Mexican officials from Texas; they believed that, as a federalist, Santa Anna would support their cause. The federalists in Coahuila fled to Monclova and nervously began to put up lands in Texas for sale to pay for men and weapons, overlooking the prior claims of empresarios who no longer recognized Coahuila's federalist elite.[57]

Austin arrived in Mexico City in July 1833 with a petition that Texas be made a separate state of Mexico. Santa Anna told Austin that Texas did not have the population to justify Mexican statehood. The Mexican president promised Austin he would use his influence with the Coahuila-Texas legislature to gain more rights and privileges in local administration. Believing that Austin advocated rebellion, the Mexicans arrested him at Saltillo for recommending Texas statehood without approval by Mexico. The Mexican Congress in the fall removed the restriction against American colonists, scheduled to go into effect in six months. Austin languished in jail in Mexico City for a year before he was released in December 1834 and returned to Texas. On March 2, 1835, the Texas Convention formally severed its connections with Mexico. By this time a confrontation between the Texas colonists and Mexico was imminent.[58]

In the summer of 1835, at the end of the two-year grace period on tariffs, thirty Texans, led by William Travis, a lawyer who had entered Texas illegally in 1831 after killing a man in Alabama, captured the customhouse and military garrison at Anáhuac. In October, at the village of Gonzales, the Texans defeated a

Mexican force led by General Martín Perfecto de Cos that had sailed up the Río Grande from Matamoros. On October 4, 1835, the Anglo-Texans then hurriedly formed a "Texas Army of the Republic," chose Stephen F. Austin as commander in chief, and declared war on the Mexican government. Although plagued by poor logistical support, disciplinary problems, and desertions, the insurgents seized the garrison at Goliad. The Texans met again as a convention to form a state government and once more pledged loyalty to a centralist Mexico. They declared they were fighting against the policies of the Mexican government and to restore the 1824 Republican Constitution. The Tejanos joined the Anglo-Texans in the cause of independence by enlisting in the Texas volunteer army.[59]

Mexican forces were on the move in Texas. On November 11, 1835, Austin sent a detachment of Tejano volunteers led by Lieutenant Salvador Flores, brother-in-law of Juan N. Seguín, on a scouting mission between the Medina and Nueces Rivers. In December, 1,200 Mexican soldiers led by General Cos took control of Béxar.[60] On the 5th, the Texans laid siege to this town. A company of thirty Tejano volunteers, organized and led by Juan N. Seguín and Placido Benavides, the latter mayor of Victoria, participated in the assault. Against heavy odds in terms of both men and artillery, the Texans fought the Mexican forces for four days. On the 9th, Cos signed a truce with the Texans agreeing to all their demands. In exchange for the release of General Cos and his men and their safe return to Mexico, the Texans were given San Antonio de Béxar.[61]

The small Texas volunteer force had driven the Mexicans out of Texas. Angered by the Texans' action, Santa Anna raised an army to attack Texas. His troops were made up largely of raw recruits—vagabonds, Indians, and criminals, a ragged group devoid of military equipment, medical care, and food. Santa Anna force-marched his exhausted army into Texas. All but a few of the Texas rebels were withdrawn from the Alamo garrison near San Antonio de Béxar just before Santa Anna launched his assault. On March 2, 1836, fifty-eight Texan delegates met at Washington-on-the-Brazos and declared Texas an independent republic. José Francisco Ruiz and his nephew José Antonio Navarro, their sympathies with the Texans, were the only Tejanos to sign the Texas Declaration of Independence, thereby making the cause of Anglo-Texans their own. Ruiz, the mayor of San Antonio de Béxar, always favored annexation of Texas by the United States. Elected to serve as deputy to the National Congress in 1835, Navarro resigned his post to help lead the revolutionary movement in Texas. The Texas patriot later served as a senator to the Congress of the Republic of Texas and held that office until Texas was annexed to the United States.[62]

An angry Santa Anna, at the head of his ragtag army of six thousand soldiers, pressed north to suppress the Texan rebels, who were reinforced with newly arrived volunteers from the United States. Leaving part of his troops under José Urrea to fight the insurgents near the coast, Santa Anna marched on the other Texan insurgents farther inland. Rumors flourished that Santa Anna would free all the slaves in Texas and loot it, as he had with Zacatecas. Taking advantage of the vulnerable situation in Texas, Santa Anna called on slaves to rise up against their masters and support him, assuring them that his army had come to procure their freedom, and many did in their quest to gain freedom.[63] The Mexicans marched against the treasonous Texans at the Alamo.

Following a nearly two-week siege of the Alamo, Santa Ana's Mexican forces stormed the old mission compound from four directions before dawn on March 6, 1836, and within an hour the Mexicans killed nearly 250 Texans barricaded behind the mission walls. Many of the Alamo defenders were summarily executed afterward, including thirty-two men and boys from Gonzales. Six hundred Mexican soldiers died in combat. Badly mauled in the battle, the surviving members of the Texas Army of Independence were forced by Santa Anna's men to withdraw. Panicked, the Texans fled in a massive exodus, which they called their great "runaway scrape." At this time, slaves on the Brazos River made a desperate but unsuccessful attempt at insurrection. Nearly one hundred were later whipped to death, and some of the ringleaders were hanged. Other slaves managed to flee to Mexican lines, along with many Tejanos who had not renounced their loyalty to Mexico. The Mexicans, through the capture of the Alamo, became momentary masters of Texas. The seven survivors of the battle, including the legendary Tennessee Congressman Davy Crockett, were all summarily shot under orders by the ruthless Santa Anna. The fall of the Alamo and the atrocities committed there by Santa Anna's army, acting under the general's blanket no-quarter policy, united Anglo-Texans against a common enemy, and they soon redirected hatred of their defeat at the Tejanos. The Anglos could not restrain their vengeance; they had learned that 342 of their fellow Texians, caught in open country, had surrendered to Mexican forces and had been executed, their bodies set on fire and burned at the presidio at Goliad. The aura of pride that surrounded the Tejano rebels began to wear off as their Anglo-Texan comrades had their revenge at the Battle of San Jacinto.[64]

The victorious Santa Anna withdrew from San Antonio and was now in pursuit of General Sam Houston. Confident, Santa Anna rested his troops by the San

**Dawn at the Alamo, 1905.**
CREDIT: Courtesy of the State Preservation Board, Austin, Texas. Accession ID: CHA 1989.81; Photographer: Perry Huston 8/3/1994; postconservation.

Jacinto River near present Galveston. The Mexican camp was one thousand yards from Houston's position. Here the tide of fortune turned in favor of the Texans. Santa Anna delayed his attack on the Texans, who, in a surprise attack lasting all of eighteen minutes, quickly routed his army. The army suffered a disastrous defeat at the hands of the Texans in their decisive victory. Sam Houston's soldiers pursued the Mexicans into the swamps and bayous and killed six hundred of them while losing only nine men. Santa Anna escaped, but the Texans captured the general the next day, took him prisoner, and forced him to sign the Treaties of Velasco recognizing the independence of Texas. Santa Anna ordered his commander to cease hostilities and withdraw the troops below the Río Grande. The Texas victory over the Mexican army at San Jacinto on April 21, 1836, was a key turning point, for it marked the end of the actual fighting for Texas independence. Mexico secured Santa Anna's release and withdrew its armies from the Texas frontier. One of the peace treaties the Mexican general signed was secret; it included the provision that claimed the Río Grande as Texas's southern boundary. This treaty made the area between the Nueces River and the Río Grande a source of contention between the United States and Mexico that in ten years would spark war between the two countries. The triumphant Texans basked in glory. However, Mexico denied the legitimacy of the new Republic of Texas, for it refused to sign the Treaties of Velasco.[65]

Many Tejanos fought alongside Texans against General Santa Anna. These Tejanos included Ambrosio Rodríguez, Manuel Flores, Placido Benavides, Salvador Flores, and Antonio Menchaca, all of them lieutenants and captains. The Mexican Lorenzo de Zavala, Jr., an aide to Sam Houston, held the rank of major. Juan N. Seguín was a colonel in Houston's army. At the onset of the Texas Revolt, Stephen F. Austin had commissioned Seguín as captain in the Texas army after he organized several dozen Tejano ranchers into the Ninth Company. Seguín's cavalry unit provided invaluable service as scouts and messengers in five Texas battles, including the Alamo and San Jacinto. The seven Tejanos killed inside the Alamo fighting alongside Travis were all from Seguín's Ninth Company. Juan N. Seguín himself escaped death at the Alamo because Travis had sent him to Goliad for reinforcements. The Tejano was part of the rear guard of Houston's army as it retreated eastward. Later, it was Seguín's duty as commander of the military garrison in San Antonio to bury the remains of the Texans who died defending the Alamo.[66]

Following his military service, Juan N. Seguín was elected to and served in the Texas Senate, the only Tejano to do so during the Texas Republic era, but he resigned to become mayor of San Antonio. In addition to Seguín, José Antonio Navarro, José Francisco Ruiz, and Rafael de la Garza were elected to the Texas Congress. Ruiz also served as one of five Indian commissioners in San Antonio's first municipal election in 1837. Manuel Martínez, Francisco Bustillos, Rafael Herrera, Francisco Antonio Ruiz, Ramón Treviño, Pedro Morales, and Francisco Granado won office as well. Erasmo Seguín was elected to serve as Béxar county judge, and José Antonio Navarro and Ignacio Chávez were elected as associate justices. Tejanos made up the majority of San Antonio's city council through 1844. Anglo-Texans held most of the political offices in Goliad, Victoria, Nacogdoches, and elsewhere.[67]

By now Tejanos were an isolated minority, because Anglos were the dominant population in the new Republic of Texas. There were more than thirty thousand Americans in Texas, ten times the Mexican population. Consequently, the number of Tejano elected officials and of Tejanos in the military soon declined. The right of Tejanos to the franchise was hotly debated and contested at the Texas Convention of 1845. Anglos disliked the incorporation of Tejanos as fellow Texas citizens. Their representation in politics was undermined by racial and national prejudice, language differences, and the overall unsettled conditions in Texas. Although Tejanos had joined Anglo-Texans in the call for Texas independence, conflict spread rapidly between them as a result of festering resentment developing toward one another. The Anglo-Texans viewed Tejanos as lazy, cowardly, and backward, "a race of mongrels . . . of Spanish, Indian, and negro blood." Tejanos saw Anglo-Texans as arrogant, rude, aggressive, and dishonest. Along with the disregard of their civil rights, Tejanos soon experienced extensive land loss. The Tejanos in essence became the victims of the freedoms they won.[68]

Between 1837 and 1838, intense land speculation spurred the influx of Anglos into Texas, and they placed more pressure on landowning Tejanos. From San Antonio to the Gulf Coast, Anglo-Texans threatened Tejanos with forced expulsion from their homes and farms. Hundreds of Tejano landowners sold their land, totaling more than one million acres, at greatly reduced prices and left Texas for New Orleans or Mexico, the Texans claiming the cattle and other abandoned livestock. Those Tejanos from Victoria, Goliad, Nacogdoches, and other towns were warned to leave lest they be "put to the knife" and to not return for a mandated ten years. Juan N. Seguín—longtime friend to the Anglo-Texans, one of the loudest champions of Texas independence who had fought against Santa Anna and was mayor of San Antonio—fled with his family to Mexico. Cheated and mistreated, Seguín's life had been threatened. The Texas revolutionary hero returned to the service of Mexico in 1842, the year the Mexican government attempted to reconquer the Republic of Texas by occupying San Antonio. Now seen as enemies, Anglo-Texans forced more and more Tejanos from their homes. The latter fled to South Texas and Mexico to seek shelter, and Anglo-Texans took over their abandoned ranches and cattle.[69]

The Texas war for independence, which lasted from September 1835 to April 1836, was largely a revolt by Anglo-Texans directed against a government they did not respect. Its significance was that the fragmentation of Mexico's northern territory began with the loss of Texas. The new leaders of the Republic of Texas quickly sought American statehood. However, the annexation of Texas was delayed because of northern congressional resistance to another slave state and problems with Mexico over the southern boundary of Texas.

The era of the Texas republic saw the demise of the Tejano communities north of the Nueces River. The Tejanos of the Río Grande region escaped this, as well as the Mexican war that made their region a part of the new state of Texas. Feelings of injustice gave rise to a lingering resentment among Tejanos that focused on revenge against Anglos, who were also despised by the Comanches, for they, too, saw Anglos for what they were: treacherous and murderous land-grabbers.[70]

Dedicated to empire building and facing an accumulated debt of $7 million, Texas President Mirabeau B. Lamar (1838–1843) wanted to divert the commercial benefits of the $5-million-dollar-a-year Santa Fe trade to Texas and to establish the republic's claim to more than half of the New Mexico area as its boundary. Lamar appointed commissioners to travel to the region to win over the native New Mexicans—who in 1837 had renounced and revolted (like the Texans) against the central government of Mexico—with promises of governmental representation and other benefits. Lamar's intentions were less than sincere; the Georgia-born Anglo-Texan despised Mexicans as he detested Negroes and Indians. The New Mexicans' longtime hatred of Texans began in earnest at this point.[71]

Without approval, Lamar solicited volunteers for his proposed expedition to Santa Fe to promote trade. Promised transportation and protection for their goods, William G. Cooke, Richard F. Brenham, George Van Ness, and José Antonio Navarro joined the three-hundred-man expedition as commissioners. Navarro was selected for his knowledge of Mexican law and the Spanish language. Moreover, Lamar reasoned that by involving Tejanos he could persuade New Mexicans of the benefits of Texas sovereignty. Despite his reluctance, Navarro agreed to be part of the expedition to prevent trouble between Anglos and Tejanos. The trading caravan carrying merchandise worth $200,000 set out for New Mexico on June 19, 1841. It was actually an undercover military expedition.[72]

The Mexican government deemed the Texas–Santa Fe expedition a hostile incursion into its territory. New Mexico Governor Manuel Armijo assembled an army of regulars and civilian militia to repel the invasion. Not all New Mexicans supported Governor Armijo's decision. With their allegiance to Mexico eroding, many New Mexicans believed conditions for them would improve if the Texans took over the area.[73]

In early September 1841, a small New Mexican patrol intercepted the Texans outside Santa Fe. The captured Texan scouts disclosed that the expedition was in disarray owing to heat, thirst, and starvation; it became lost and repeatedly harassed and attacked by Kiowa Indians. Needing to find food and safety, the Texas–Santa Fe expedition had broken up into small groups. The New Mexicans took the Texans prisoner and marched them more than two thousand miles to Mexico City. After considerable diplomatic negotiating between Mexico and the United States, most of the Texans were released.[74]

Texan reprisals in the form of attacks on the New Mexican militia interrupted the trade between New Mexico and Missouri. The ill-advised and failed Texas–Santa Fe expedition was one of several confrontations between Texas and Mexico that followed and that eventually culminated in the annexation of Texas by the United States and war with Mexico.[75]

Tejano settlers, especially those who had relocated or had been forced to relocate by Anglo-Texans following the Texas Rebellion, were once again plagued by the threat of unfriendly tribal Indians. With Mexican rule no longer present in Texas, the focal point of Comanche and Kiowa raiding shifted from devastating isolated settlements and ranches in eastern Chihuahua to surprise raids on Tejano settlements along the lower Río Grande. The Indian attacks on the settlements wreaked havoc as they ran off thousands of horses, mules, and sheep from the area ranches. Tensions remained high with the Indians. In surprise raids, Indian parties attacked, plundered, and burned all dwellings in the settlements located between the Nueces River and the Río Grande. Tejano families caught in the throes of the murderous campaign were forced to flee for their lives across the Río Grande to Mexico. The Indian depredations thus reversed the economic and demographic growth of the region to pre-1820 levels.[76] California was also on the agenda as the acquisitive United States set on its course of empire building.

## MAKING CALIFORNIA MEXICAN

The combination of good climate, abundant land, and indentured Indian labor underlay the growth of the cattle ranching areas of California. The Americans filtering into California remarked on this economic system and the social relations it had fostered. These accounts of native California life had a veiled motive—the desire to convince Americans elsewhere that California wanted annexation.

The Californios for their part had an insular view of the Americans and remained ambivalent toward the foreigners. However, others thought more highly of the American government than they did of its citizenry. A unifying nationalistic sentiment among the Californios was largely absent. The Mexican War and the subsequent political and economic dispossession later provoked a strong sense of identity in the Californios.

In contrast, a fervent nationalism was in full force among Americans. The desire for more territory coincided with a belief that Mexico, weak and internally divided, would easily surrender territory to its more powerful northern neighbor the United States. California and the Pacific Coast was the ultimate goal of American expansionists.

After winning its independence in 1821, Mexico opened California's ports to foreign trade. British monopoly of the California hide and tallow trade and its ports ended in 1827 when England's trade agreement with Mexico expired. This opened up trade for New England merchants, especially the Boston firm of Bryant, Sturgis, and Company, which was involved in trade with Mexico via the Chihuahua Trail. Over a twenty-year period, this New England firm exported a half million hides from California. Other New England merchants joined in this highly profitable trade. Some of the Americans married the daughters of the California province's ruling families, accepted the Catholic faith, became Mexican citizens, and assimilated into Mexican society.[77] These Mexicanized Americans served as a fifth column; they would aid the United States in taking possession of California.

By the early nineteenth century American fur trappers were hunting in the mountains of eastern California. These trappers established routes across the mountains that were later followed by American settlers. Overland trade with the fledgling Mexican settlements in California actually began with the opening of the so-called Old Spanish Trail, used for generations as a route by Ute Indian slave raiders who sortied against other Indians for women and children and horses. The pack-train trade extended from the old established settlements of Santa Fe and Taos in New Mexico, crossed present Colorado and Utah to the Little Salt Lake, and then turned southwest to the Colorado River in Nevada and Arizona. The Old Spanish Trail would link with American trade outlets east along the Mississippi River and with the Camino Real trail south to Mexico City. In 1829, New Mexican Antonio Armijo, at the head of sixty Spanish-speaking traders and one hundred mules and horses laden with woolen blankets and other trade goods, left Abiquiú on the Old Spanish Trail and opened up the annual trade between New Mexico and California, where demand for trade goods was huge and which was rich in cattle, horses, and mules for trade. Armijo and his trade caravan heavily laden with goods made their way from Abiquiú through Cajón Pass to Mission San Gabriel in southern California in eighty-six days. They traded goods with the Californios in exchange for livestock, which they drove back to New Mexico to replenish the herds chased off in Indian raids and to supply traders traveling east on the Santa Fe Trail. Armijo, with other New Mexicans and American and Ute Indians, also used the Old Spanish Trail regularly to search for Paiute Indian slaves, seizing women and children in raids. Paiute males from ten to fifteen years of age sold for $50 to $100 in the slave markets, whereas young Paiute females, who were in great demand as domestic servants, sold from $150 to $200. Although Mexico banned the Indian slave trade in New Mexico in 1812 and in California in 1824 for fear that the practice would incite intertribal warfare, lax enforcement and high profits kept the trade in human cargo going throughout the first half of the nineteenth century.[78]

**Dress of Wealthy Californians, 1826–1839.**

CREDIT: "Costume de Haute Californie and Dame de Monterey, 1841," from Abel du Petit-Thouars, *Voyage autour du monde sur la frégate la Vénus pendant les années 1836–1839: Atlas pittoresque, 1841.* Courtesy of the Bancroft Library, University of California, Berkeley, California.

There were about 4,700 Mexicans in Alta California, originally from Sinaloa and Sonora, most living in small pueblos near presidios on the coast. The California Mexicans shared common lands for raising crops and grazing cattle and horses. There were only fifty private ranches owned by the Spanish-speaking rich in all of California, because the Franciscans controlled most of the land; twelve million acres were held by Franciscan missionaries in trust for the Indians in accord with Spanish law and custom. The California missions owned a combined total of one and a half million head of cattle, three hundred thousand sheep, and five thousand horses.[79]

## THE CALIFORNIA MISSIONS: MAKING INDIANS FAITHFUL AND INDUSTRIOUS CHRISTIANS

In 1823, the twenty-one missions in California spanned an area from San Diego Bay in the south to Sonoma, north of San Francisco Bay. The Franciscan priests quickly went to work converting the Indians into faithful Christians and industrious subjects. Despite the decline of the mission population after 1824 through the ravages of disease, over twenty-one thousand Indians were assigned to these missions. Under harsh treatment that underlined enforced servitude, Indian labor produced almost all the food and other products for California.[80]

The rapacious priests resolved to claim for their own property as many of the California Indians as possible. The paternalistic Franciscans, who viewed their Indian subjects as children, opposed secularization because their whole mission economy depended on the efforts of mission Indians. According to the Catholic Church, California Indians were not prepared to become citizens, because once freed they would revert to pagan ways. Indian labor, enforced through humiliation, floggings, and incarceration, had made the missions profitable; therefore, these slaves of Christ needed protection against possible exploitation by others. This fact was also well understood by the Mexican government and the Californio ricos. By monopolizing Indian labor, the mission system had retarded the growth of ranching and farming in California. The Indians themselves indirectly contributed to the decline of the missions by refusing to work or by running away. The mission industries—blanket making, tanning, the making of wine, soap, candles, and so forth—as a result went unattended. What was more, the Indian mission population was declining because it was dying of disease, taking its greatest toll among Indian women and young children.[81]

The California Indians were always on the lookout to rebel against or escape their subjugation and exploitation. In most instances, cruelty and corporal punishment triggered Indian resistance. The deteriorating conditions at the missions caused the runaway-Indian problem to worsen. These Europeanized Indian runaways formed guerilla bands and provided other rebellious California Indians with excellent leadership.[82]

At first, the Indians did not strongly resist the military expeditions that scoured the countryside in search of them, but this changed when Indian children were stolen from the missions and soldiers sexually abused Indian women. Other

Indians resisted after they heard the horror stories of the inhumane mission life from the fugitive Indians. Horses made California Indians extremely mobile; the Indians hit-and-run tactics created chaos among the Spanish-speaking ranchers and farmers and had a contagious effect on other mission Indians, for it raised their morale and assertiveness and led to consequent rebellion. These military raids, in which male Indians either escaped or were killed, increased in intensity because the militia, accompanied by priests, set off in hunt of recruits to replace the dying mission populations. To stabilize the sex ratios at the missions, the raids especially targeted Indian women.[83]

One of the largest and most explosive Indian rebellions occurred in 1824 on La Purísima and the Santa Barbara missions in central California, two of the five missions that, along with a presidio, were constructed with forced Indian labor. The cruel flogging of a La Purísima neophyte at Santa Ynez triggered the uprising. Nearly two thousand Indians captured mission La Purísima and burned many of the mission buildings. Hundreds of presidio soldiers armed with artillery pieces attacked the Indian rebels at La Purísima and captured the leaders of the rebellion. Seven Indians were summarily executed, and the others were imprisoned and forced to do hard labor. Notwithstanding, disease had a much greater effect on Indians than any act of violence. The missions were pestholes and a haven for diseases. Smallpox and scarlet fever sickened and killed thousands of domiciled Indians during this period. And the epidemic of venereal diseases accounted for the massive death rates of mission Indians.[84]

The missions in time became outmoded. This development was spurred by the declared equality of Indians with Mexicans as a result of the 1824 constitutional affirmation of equality to "all persons." Indians were no longer wards of the Catholic Church but parishioners and taxpayers. Their land, which had been held in trust by the missionaries, was returned to them. The Franciscans had paved the way for exploitation of the Indians by the Californio elite. The latter subjected the Indians to forced labor on their immense land holdings. Exploitation of Indian labor was the principal cause of revolt.

On August 17, 1833, Mexico resumed colonization of its northern frontier. Mexico's president Valentín Gomez Farias, who wanted less clerical influence in Mexico, enacted legislation calling for the secularization of the missions. In the same year, José Figueroa became governor of California, and he began the formal change from religious to civil use of the missions. However, other legislation yet to be approved by the Mexican Congress called for the distribution of mission lands to various foreign and domestic groups. This vague and badly communicated law produced the Cosmopolitan Company, created by Californios Juan Bandini, José María Híjar, and José María Padrés, all of whom supported both secularization and colonization to "develop California agriculture and manufacturing and export its products to world markets." The so-called Híjar-Padrés colonization set out to distribute lands belonging to the missions.[85]

The Híjar-Padrés colonization expedition left Mexico City for California in April 1834 with 239 colonists made up of 105 men, 55 women, and 79 children. The colonists, including families, received public land to raise crops and livestock for themselves. However, because of Mexico's political turmoil, including the return of Santa Anna, the colony was disbanded after it reached present Sonoma, California. Moreover, Alta California's leaders were reluctant to share secularized mission lands or political power with the settlers who stayed on after the dissolution of the colony.[86]

The purpose of Mexico's plan to nationalize the Church's vast land holdings was to undermine the Church's economic power, lessen its political influence, and free capital for investment. As the emphasis of Mexico's government changed from a mission approach to private enterprise, huge land grants for cattle ranching were awarded to Mexican citizens.

Secularization led to the division of immense areas of mission land among the Californio landowners and to closer contacts between American foreigners and the Mexicans of California. A host of Californios, including the Peraltas, Sepulvedas, Picos, Yorbas, Figueroas, Castros, Carrillos, and Vallejos, drew their wealth, as well as their social ascendency, from desirable land holdings totaling fourteen million acres. As in Texas, New Mexico, and Arizona, a highly developed and structured patrón-client relationship existed in California through which the rich Californios exerted their power. Mexico's colonization laws of 1824 and 1828, which made naturalized citizens eligible for land grants, allowed John Marsh, John Sutter, John Bidwell, and other foreign adventurers to become large landowners in California.[87]

## THE GOLDEN AGE OF CALIFORNIA RANCHING

The period between the 1830s and the start of the Mexican-American War in 1846 was the golden age of the California ranches. The Mexican Colony Law of 1824 set up rules for petitioning for a land grant, and in 1828 these rules were codified in the *Mexican Reglamento*. Native-born or naturalized Mexican citizens such as John Sutter and others could make an application for a land grant. A non-Mexican settler could petition for citizenship, pledge his loyalty to both Mexico and the Roman Catholic Church, and after one year of probation receive Mexican citizenship and a petition for a land grant.[88]

The laws placed no limit on family land holdings or on land holdings from inheritance or purchase. The Mexican government could revoke land grants if conditions were not satisfactorily met. For the first time private land acquisition was made possible in California. Land was now open to be passed across generations.[89]

However, the ruling Californio elite blocked the acquisition of mission lands by lower-class California Mexicans, foreigners, and immigrants from Mexico. The entire economy of Mexican California as a result shifted from the missions to the landed estates of the Californios through devious means and swindle. The one constant was that Indian labor kept the ranches and the farms in California operating.[90]

Because of their incessant drive for gain and strong belief that physical work was below their station in life, the Californio ranchers forced labor from the Indians. They accomplished this through their appointments as *mayordo-mos* (overseers) of mission property. The California mission overseers sold off cattle, grain, and land belonging to the Indians. They also made pacts with one Indian group to bring in other Indians to serve as laborers, who were then sent off to work on the ranches, where they became indentured servants. An unfree labor system developed in California based on free, enslaved, or convict Indian labor. The Indians ended up either trapped in a cycle of debt and forced labor or as free laborers encouraged to work on the ranches by material incentives and liquor.[91]

On the typical Californio ranch, huge herds of cattle, mules, and horses, the primary source of commerce, ranged over the land. Cattle raising for hides and tallow became extremely profitable. The Californios were not taxed on their income. Aping Spanish aristocracy, the Californios' comfortable ranch lifestyle dedicated to family and tradition, all of which were needed to satisfy their social vanities, was based on Indian and later Mexican ranch hands doing all the mundane physical work. Ranching was the basis of California's social and political system; it was this prosperous and seemingly idyllic lifestyle, observed by the Americans, that fueled the great myth of California wealth and ease. Elsewhere in California, Indians were treated very harshly by California Mexicans.

**Vaqueros Lassoing a Steer, 1849–1850.**
CREDIT: Courtesy of the Bancroft Library, University of California, Berkeley, California.

During the Mexican period, the Indian population of California living in the interior experienced considerable violence at the hands of Californio land barons. Landowner José María Amador exemplified the extreme form of this barbarity. In 1837, Amador led an unauthorized warfare expedition against the Indians who had stolen livestock from his Rancho San Ramón. According to Amador, his party:

> invited the wild Indians and their Christian companions to come and have a feast of pinole and dried meat . . . the troops, the civilians, and the auxiliaries surrounded them and tied them up . . . we separated 100 Christians. At every half-mile or mile we put six of them on their knees to say their prayers, making them understand that they were about to die. Each one was shot with four arrows. . . . Those who refused to die immediately were killed with spears . . . We baptized all the Indians (non-Christians) and afterward they were shot in the back.[92]

The violence against the Indians by Mexican Californios and their Indian auxiliaries provoked more Indian individual and group resistance. The Indians warred against the Mexicans, killing settlers and, because their food supply was dwindling, taking large numbers of horses and cattle. As noted, contact with California Mexicans triggered changes in the Indian way of life. Beef and horse meat had become staple food items for some Indians, and the only way they could obtain these food items was by raiding. Another factor contributing to this turmoil was that, following the secularization of the missions, former California mission Indians took control of many of the feral horse herds in the California Central Valley. Because these wild horses were hard to break, tame, and drive to markets located in New Mexico, horse raiders began attacking southern California ranches to steal highly prized domesticated horses and mules. The raids were sometimes coordinated with California Indians working on the ranches.[93]

The Yokuts and the Miwok Indians crossed Cholam Pass, Panoche Pass, Pacheco Pass, and Tejón Pass to raid Californio Mexican ranches. In 1838, Indians killed several Californio ranchers near Monterey; in the next year, Indians attacked the grain storehouse at Santa Clara; and in 1841, Indians seized the San Juan Bautista mission. In one attack at San Luis Obispo in 1840 Indians took more than a thousand head of stock. The San Luis Obispo raid was part of the largest Indian horse raid, in which they simultaneously attacked the San Gabriel, San Juan Capistrano, and San Luis Obispo areas and plundered three thousand horses, driving them over Cajon Pass into the Mojave Desert and then into southwestern Utah. The government official of Los Angeles, Tiburcio Tapia, organized parties to pursue the horse raiders, even freeing prisoners from jail to augment his forces.[94]

Californio authorities met the Indian threat with their own warring expeditions. To stop the dramatic increase in thefts of livestock from the missions and ranches, Governor Figueroa ordered that "from every presidio a military expedition shall set out each month and scout those places where the robbers shelter themselves." Later, Governor Alvarado ordered military patrols to police the mountain passes to prevent the Indians from using them to stage attacks. So widespread were the Indian depredations in California that in 1843 official policy shifted from the offensive to the defensive in dealing with the Indian threat. By

**Northern Valley Yukut Indians Hunting on San Francisco Bay, California, 1822.**
(Note: variation in spelling for Yokut Indians.)
CREDIT: Courtesy of the Bancroft Library, University of California, Berkeley, California.

this time, California could not handle Indian problems because it was embroiled in political turmoil.

## THE CALIFORNIO ERA REVOLTS
## AGAINST MEXICAN RULE

California lacked a strong presence of Mexican authority. The Californio merchants and ranchers had developed a system of aristocratic government in California in alliance with the Catholic Church. Unlike New Mexico, and except for Indians and the small mixed-race bandit groups that roamed the mountains and valleys, few of the lower classes in California contested the power of their elites. Authority and control was wielded by shifting alliances among the Californio elite families, who enjoyed relative wealth in land and livestock and considered themselves racially and economically distinct from the other Mexicans. Even the Americans in California believed that the elite Californios as a "race" were better than the common Mexican. The Californios' strong local ties led to a north-south regionalism centered on the towns of Monterey, Los Angeles, and Santa Barbara. The existing north-south rivalries were further complicated by family feuds of long standing. Disunity thus marked relations between the northern and southern Californio factions who feared seizure by foreign powers, especially by the Americans. Gradually the Californios were pitted against an ever-encroaching Mexican government. Although at odds with one another, the Californios carried out a series of open rebellions against Mexico in 1828, 1829, and 1831. In 1831, the Californios united and rebelled against Manuel Victoria, whom Mexico had sent to govern California. A despotic ruler, Victoria opposed the secularization of mission land owned by the Catholic Church.[95]

Californios Pío Pico and José María Echeandia raised an army and fought Governor Victoria's Mexican forces outside of Los Angeles. Mexico recalled Victoria, who was wounded in the conflict, and installed Nicolas Gutiérrez as governor. In 1835, a "decade of revolution" began in California in which corrupt or incompetent officials from Mexico were sent to California, where they vied with Californios for the right to rule. In one thirteen-month period the governorship of California changed four times.[96]

The Californios wanted sovereignty for California, to control tariffs and trade, to eliminate the practice of importing convicts as settlers to California, and to gain access to civil and military government posts. In 1836, Californios led by Juan B. Alvarado marched on the capitol of Monterey, forced Governor Gutiérrez to surrender, and ordered him and other Mexican officials to leave California. In 1837, Mexico declared California a "free and sovereign state" within the Mexican Republic and appointed Alvarado the governor. For the next five years, Mexico did not meddle in California's internal affairs.[97] Americans in California played a minor role in these insurrections.

In 1842, Mexico again attempted to take control over California. It sent Manuel Micheltorena to California and declared him governor. Micheltorena marched to Monterey, where his soldiers pillaged the town, abused and raped its residents, and forced Governor Alvarado to surrender. Three years later, in 1845, Californios led by Alvarado and José Castro fought with Micheltorena's soldiers and defeated them, forcing Micheltorena and his army to flee back to Mexico. José Castro became military commander of California, and Pío Pico became governor.

Californios remained fearful that the Americans wanted to take California. There were only several hundred Americans in California, representing less than 10 percent of the population. Yet, beginning in 1841, more land-hungry Americans in organized groups were pushing at the borders of California. Each year saw the arrival of Americans adding to the numbers already living there. The growing presence of Yankees raised increasing concern among the Californios. However, the full-scale American invasion of California would not take place until after the end of the Mexican War.[98]

## CONCLUSION

Mexico's northern frontier was marginally incorporated into Mexico. Both the political and judicial systems were weak or nonexistent, population growth rested with foreign immigration, and trade was poorly regulated and oriented to the United States. Indian hostilities could not be contained. The northern frontiers' weak integration with Mexico produced unique social, cultural, and economic conditions in the region.

New Mexico was little affected by Mexico's independence. Farming, ranching, and warring with hostile Indians were principal activities. In New Mexico, the contact and interaction between the Spanish-speaking settlements and the opposing economy extended across a longer time period. The Santa Fe Trail reoriented New Mexico's trade from Chihuahua to the United States. Unlike in Texas, the migration of Americans into New Mexico was not as sudden or massive. A chasm existed between the poor and the wealthy. As subordinates in a rural society, the poor resented the ricos as too manipulative and, eventually, too firmly aligned with the Americans. Mexican Albino Pérez was an accidental governor; he did not understand local New Mexican customs, and his graft made him a symbol of oppression. The ambivalent loyalty to Mexico was due to the reliance of the New Mexicans on foreigners for trade and for money in the form of taxes.

Democratic ideals and beliefs were taking root among the masses living in Mexico's northern territories. In Texas, the case of local autonomy diminished the Tejano period of community-oriented politics. A small group of wealthy, self-serving Tejanos, seeking a federalist form of government because it resembled the government of the United States, fought side by side with Anglo-Texans for independence. However, behind the popular talk of liberty by the Texians lurked the reality of plantation slavery. The Anglo-Texans and their Tejano allies fought on behalf of the right to maintain the institution of slavery introduced into Texas. After the 1836 Texas Revolt for Independence, Tejanos quickly found themselves hated and distrusted by both Anglos and Mexicans. In California the residents likewise staged revolts against Mexico, and some endeared themselves to the Americans.[99]

The rebellions in New Mexico, Texas, and California against Mexican rule were the result of centuries-old problems that had plagued the northern frontier: little or no contact with Mexico, Mexican government officials who did not understand the needs of its distant citizens, and the lack of goods and services. These troubles brewed dissension and generated defiance among the inhabitants of Mexico's northern frontier.

The United States saw California, New Mexico, Texas, and the rest of the Mexican northern territory as promising economic fortune and the opportunity to establish empires. In light of the climate of nationalism in the United States, many Americans believed that they were not merely seekers of wealth but the founders of a new, enlightened, and powerful nation. Anglo-Texans took control of Texas in 1836 following a revolt. The New Mexicans were now integrated into a U.S. economy. Americans believed that they could easily win California from the Mexicans, whom they perceived as a shiftless people who would not bother defending their land. Mexico did not have the men to defend California; besides, by the 1840s Mexican authority had almost disappeared there. With northern and southern California at war with one another and thus divided, many Californios welcomed United States rule as a means of restoring order and protecting property rights.

Mexico faced a powerful American juggernaut that seemed to be advancing everywhere in its northern territories. The subsequent American invasion of Mexico's northern territories brought together peoples of different cultures, societies, and ways of life. Relationships between the Mexican people and the Americans were marred by cultural differences and, in Texas, by violence. American westward expansion into Mexico's northern territories, which took place between Mexico's independence in 1821 and the opening of the Santa Fe Trail, would result in domination by midcentury. Most important, attempts to expand the dominion of slavery in the West would lead to the annexation of Texas and the outbreak of full-scale war with Mexico in 1846. New Mexico, Texas, and California had become a breeding ground for a conflict of cultures and eventual war.

## NOTES

1. John H. Coatsworth, "Obstacles to Economic Growth in Nineteenth-Century Mexico," *American Historical Review* 83, no. 1 (February 1978): 80–100.
2. Weber, *Bárbaros*, 269; De Lay, *War of a Thousand Deserts*, xv, xvii
3. Hall, *Social Change in the Southwest*, 162, 184; De Lay, *War of a Thousand Deserts*, 165, 166–168.
4. Hall, *Social Change in the Southwest*, 144; Jones, *Los Paisanos*, 129; De Lay, *War of a Thousand Deserts*, 51, 58–59, 109.
5. Truett, *Fugitive Landscapes*, 39–40; James E. Officer, *Hispanic Arizona, 1536–1856* (Tucson: University of Arizona Press, 1987), 36–50.
6. Andrés Reséndez, *Changing National Identities at the Frontier: Texas and New Mexico, 1800–1850* (Cambridge: Cambridge University Press, 2005), 60; Tijerina, *Tejanos and Texas Under the Mexican Flag, 1821–1836*, 12–18; De Lay, *War of a Thousand Deserts*, 50–51.
7. Reséndez, *Changing National Identities*, 47–55; Ross Frank, *From Settler to Citizen: New Mexican Economic Development and the Creation of Vecino Society, 1750–1820* (Berkeley: University of California Press, 2000), 31–33; Weber, *Bárbaros*, 268; De Lay, *War of a Thousand Deserts*, 59.
8. Reséndez, *Changing National Identities*, 181; Hall, *Social Change in the Southwest*, 147; Frances Leon Swadesh, *Los Primeros Pobladores: Hispanic Americans of the Ute Frontier* (Notre Dame, IN: University of Notre Dame Press, 1974), 148; De Lay, *War of a Thousand Deserts*, 214.
9. Reséndez, *Changing National Identities*, 181–182; Swadesh, *Los Primeros Pobladores*, 125–126; Marc Simmons, *The Little Lion of the Southwest: A Life of Manuel Antonio Chaves* (Chicago: Swallow Press, 1973), 135; De Lay, *War of a Thousand Deserts*, 167, 202. Enslaved Navajos made up 5 percent of the Navajo population. In the wealthy Mexican communities, Indian slaves made up as much as 38 percent of the residents. So great was Navajo raiding for captives that a Mexican clan developed made up of the descendents of New Mexican women.
10. Reséndez, *Changing National Identities*, 21; Hall, *Social Change in the Southwest*, 224; De Lay, *War of a Thousand Deserts*, 38–40.
11. Hall, *Social Change in the Southwest*, 163; Ana María Alonzo, *Thread of Blood: Colonialism, Revolution, and Gender on Mexico's Northern Frontier* (Tucson: University of Arizona Press, 1997), 26; Ralph Smith, "Indians in American-Mexican Relations Before

the War of 1846," *Hispanic American Historical Review* 43 (1963): 41; Odie B. Faulk, "Presidio: Fortress or Farce" in *New Spain's Far Northern Frontier*, ed. David J. Weber (Albuquerque: University of New Mexico Press, 1979), 42; De Lay, *War of a Thousand Deserts*, 160.

12. Weber, *Bárbaros*, 269; Weber, *Mexican Frontier*, 83–105; Thomas W. Kavanaugh, *Comanche Political History: An Ethnohistorical Perspective, 1706–1875* (Lincoln: University of Nebraska Press, 1996), 286–291.

13. Brooks, *Captives and Cousins*, 218.

14. De Lay, *War of a Thousand Deserts*, 110. The New Mexican buffalo hunters sometimes gave provisions to the Indian hunting parties who called on the cibolero camps. Brooks, *Captives and Cousins*, 314.

15. Brooks, *Captives and Cousins*, 218. In the 1840s, the American trader Josiah Gregg described in detail the cibolero's colorful manner of life. Writing in *The Commerce of the Prairies*, Gregg remarked: "As we were proceeding on our march, we observed a horseman approaching, who excited at first considerable curiosity. His picturesque costume, and peculiarity of deportment, however, soon showed him to be a Mexican Cibolero or buffalo-hunter. These hardy devotees of the chase usually wear leathern trousers and jackets, and flat straw hats; while, swung upon the shoulder of each hangs his carcage or quiver of bow and arrows. The long handle of their lance being set in a case, and suspended by the side with a strap from the pommel of the saddle, leaves the point waving high over the head, with a tassel of gay parti-colored stuffs dangling at the tip of the scabbard." Joshua Gregg, *The Commerce of the Prairies: The Journal of a Santa Fe Trader* (Whitefish, MT: Kessinger Publishing, LLC, 2006), 53.

16. Brooks, *Captives and Cousins*, 314.

17. Ibid., 315, 319; Weber, *Mexican Frontier*, 98. In southeastern Colorado the Cheyenne Indians and the ciboleros skirmished over buffalo hunting. The Cheyenne eventually forced the ciboleros to limit their buffalo hunts to the Comanchería in the Texas Panhandle. The spread of bovine disease from domesticated cattle, overgrazing, timber cutting, and water pollution further contributed to the demise of the bison.

18. Reséndez, *Changing National Identities*, 34–37; Hall, *Social Change in the Southwest*, 150–151. The Santa Fe Trail passed through Kansas and then continued either through Colorado over the mountain trail branch or over the Cimarron cutoff in northeastern New Mexico. The latter route was shorter and therefore became the major route.

19. Hall, *Social Change in the Southwest*, 150; Moorehead, *New Mexico's Royal Road*, 187. In 1826, the U.S. government began surveying a road from Missouri to Santa Fe.

20. Hall, *Social Change in the Southwest*, 151; Moorehead, *New Mexico's Royal Road*, 18.

2. Hall, *Social Change in the Southwest*, 154.

22. Ibid., 154–159, 160; Nancy L. Gonzales, *The Spanish Americans of New Mexico: A Heritage of Pride* (Albuquerque: University of New Mexico Press, 1967), 45.

23. Hall, *Social Change in the Southwest*, 190.

24. Reséndez, *Changing National Identities*, 171–172, 174; Weber, *Mexican Frontier*, 33, 261.

25. Reséndez, *Changing National Identities*, 173, 175–177, 180, 182; Weber, *Mexican Frontier*, 262; Hall, *Social Change in the Southwest*, 190–191.

26. Reséndez, *Changing National Identities*, 185; Janet Lecompte, *Rebellion in Río Arriba, 1837* (Albuquerque: University of New Mexico Press, 1985), 42–43; Janet Lecompte, "Manuel Armijo's Family History," *New Mexico Historical Review* 48 (July 1973):

252–256. Armijo rejected a demand from General Mariano Arista in 1841 to join a military campaign against the Comanches with whom New Mexicans traded.

27. Reséndez, *Changing National Identities*, 173; Lecompte, *Rebellion in Río Arriba, 1837*, 110; Hall, *Social Change in the Southwest*, 191; Weber, *Mexican Frontier*, 262; De Lay, *War of a Thousand Deserts*, 166, 169.

28. Reséndez, *Changing National Identities*, 183, 186, 196; Lecompte, *Rebellion in Río Arriba, 1837*, 19–34, 115–116; Weber, *Mexican Frontier*, 262–263.

29. Reséndez, *Changing National Identities*, 176, 190; Weber, *Mexican Frontier*, 265.

30. Timothy J. Henderson, *A Glorious Defeat: Mexico and Its War with the United States* (New York: Hill & Wang, 2007), 37; Jesús F. de la Teja, "The Colonization and Independence of Texas: A Tejano Perspective," in *Myths, Misdeeds, and Misunderstandings: The Roots of Conflict in U.S.–Mexican Relations,* ed. Jaime E. Rodríguez O. and Kathryn Vincent (Wilmington, DE: Scholarly Resources, 1997), 81; De Lay, *War of a Thousand Deserts*, 52, 59; Randolph B. Campbell, *Gone to Texas: A History of the Lone Star State* (New York: Oxford University Press, 2003), 189–190; Tijerina, *Tejanos and Texas Under the Mexican Flag, 1821–1836*, 6–7, 21; Hall, *Social Change in the Southwest*, 210.

31. Campbell, *Gone to Texas*, 190; Weber, *Mexican Frontier*, 209; Tijerina, *Tejanos and Texas Under the Mexican Flag, 1821–1836*, 7, 21; De Lay, *War of a Thousand Deserts*, 52.

32. Henderson, *Glorious Defeat*, 53; Campbell, *Gone to Texas*, 190–191; Weber, *Mexican Frontier*, 211–212; Arnoldo DeLeon, *The Tejano Community, 1836–1900* (Albuquerque: University of New Mexico Press, 1982), 50–86; De Lay, *War of a Thousand Deserts*, 52.

33. Henderson, *Glorious Defeat*, 54; Jack Jackson, *Texas by Terán: The Diary Kept by General Meir E. Terán on His 1828 Inspection of Texas* (Austin: University of Texas Press, 2000), 94; De Lay, *War of a Thousand Deserts*, 21–22; Walter Nugent, *Habits of Empire: A History of American Expansion* (New York: Knopf, 2008), 131.

34. Weber, *Mexican Frontier*, 104–105; De Lay, *War of a Thousand Deserts*, 17; Hämäläinen, *Comanche Empire*, 191–192, 229–230.

35. Hall, *Social Change in the Southwest*, 224.

36. Mark E. Nackman, "Anglo-American Migrants to the West: Men of Broken Fortunes? The Case of Texas, 1821–46," *Western Historical Quarterly* 5, no. 4 (October 1974): 446–448; Nugent, *Habits of Empire*, 132.

37. Josefina Zoraida Vásquez, "The Colonization and Loss of Texas: A Mexican Perspective," in *Myths, Misdeeds, and Misunderstandings,* ed. Rodríguez O. and Vincent, 47, 51; Campbell, *Gone to Texas*, 101–102, 105–106.

38. Henderson, *Glorious Defeat*, 36; Zoraida Vásquez, "Colonization and Loss of Texas," 49; Campbell, *Gone to Texas*, 101; Ramos, *Beyond the Alamo*, 86.

39. Jesús F. de la Teja, ed., *A Revolution Remembered: The Memoirs and Selected Correspondence of Juan N. Seguín* (Austin, TX: State House Press, 1991), 6–7; de la Teja, "Colonization and Independence of Texas," 84–85; Ramos, *Beyond the Alamo*, 84.

40. Nackman, "Anglo-American Migrants to the West," 447; Henderson, *Glorious Defeat*, 38; Zoraida Vásquez, "Colonization and Loss of Texas," 48–51; Campbell, *Gone to Texas*, 107.

41. Nackman, "Anglo-American Migrants to the West," 448; Henderson, *Glorious Defeat*, 38, 40; Reséndez, *Changing National Identities*, 38; Campbell, *Gone to Texas*, 105, 108; Ramos, *Beyond the Alamo*, 91; Nugent, *Habits of Empire*, 138–139.

42. de la Teja, "Colonization and Independence of Texas," 98; De Lay, *War of a Thousand Deserts*, 27; Nugent, *Habits of Empire*, 139.

43. Henderson, *Glorious Defeat*, 37, 42; Zoraida Vásquez, "Colonization and Loss of Texas," 55; Campbell, *Gone to Texas*, 185–187.

44. Henderson, *Glorious Defeat*, 58.

45. Ibid., 49–50; Zoraida Vásquez, "Colonization and Loss of Texas," 70; Andreas Reichstein, *Rise of the Lone Star State: The Making of Texas* (College Station: Texas A&M University Press, 1989), 190; de la Teja, "Colonization and Independence of Texas," 90.

46. Zoraida Vásquez, "Colonization and Loss of Texas," 54–55; Eugene C. Barker, *The Life of Stephen F. Austin* (New York: AMS Press, 1970), 152.

47. Henderson, *Glorious Defeat*, 50–51; Zoraida Vásquez, "Colonization and Loss of Texas," 55; Campbell, *Gone to Texas*, 108–109; De Lay, *War of a Thousand Deserts*, 5.

48. Henderson, *Glorious Defeat*, 51; Zoraida Vásquez, "Colonization and Loss of Texas," 55; Campbell, *Gone to Texas*, 109–110; De Lay, *War of a Thousand Deserts*, 5–6; Nugent, *Habits of Empire*, 144.

49. Henderson, *Glorious Defeat*, 54; Zoraida Vásquez, "Colonization and Loss of Texas," 55.

50. Henderson, *Glorious Defeat*, 57–58.

51. Ibid., 58; Zoraida Vásquez, "Colonization and Loss of Texas," 56; Campbell, *Gone to Texas*, 111–112.

52. Eugene C. Barker, ed., *Austin Papers* (Washington, DC: American Historical Association, 1924), 1:1157.

53. Zoraida Vásquez, "Colonization and Loss of Texas," 57–59; de la Teja, "Colonization and Independence of Texas," 90; De Lay, *War of a Thousand Deserts*, 27.

54. Henderson, *Glorious Defeat*, 68–69; Zoraida Vásquez, "Colonization and Loss of Texas," 61; de la Teja, "Colonization and Independence of Texas," 90–91; Vito Alessio Robles, *Coahuila y Texas de la consumación de la independencia hasta el trado de paz de Guadalupe Hidalgo*, 2 vols. (Mexico City, Mexico: Editorial Porrúa, 1979), 383–386; Campbell, *Gone to Texas*, 117–118; De Lay, *War of a Thousand Deserts*, 72.

55. Henderson, *Glorious Defeat*, 72–73, 86; Zoraida Vásquez, "Colonization and Loss of Texas," 66–67; Campbell, *Gone to Texas*, 121–122.

56. Zoraida Vásquez, "Colonization and Loss of Texas," 53, 70; de la Teja, "Colonization and Independence of Texas," 91–92; Lester G. Bugbee, "Slavery in East Texas," *Political Science Quarterly* 13, no. 3 (1898): 409; De Lay, *War of a Thousand Deserts*, 27; Campbell, *Gone to Texas*, 112; Hall, *Social Change in the Southwest,* 187.

57. Henderson, *Glorious Defeat*, 85–87; Zoraida Vásquez, "Colonization and Loss of Texas," 67; de la Teja, *Revolution Remembered*, 11; de la Teja, "Colonization and Independence of Texas," 72; Campbell, *Gone to Texas*, 123–125; De Lay, *War of a Thousand Deserts*, 72–73. San Antonio did not send delegates to the convention despite neglect by the state government.

58. Zoraida Vásquez, "Colonization and Loss of Texas," 68; Campbell, *Gone to Texas*, 125–126.

59. Henderson, *Glorious Defeat*, 92–94; Zoraida Vásquez, "Colonization and Loss of Texas," 71–73; de la Teja, "Colonization and Independence of Texas," 94; Campbell, *Gone to Texas*, 128–134.

60. Henderson, *Glorious Defeat*, 93; Campbell, *Gone to Texas*, 138–139.

61. Henderson, *Glorious Defeat*, 94; Zoraida Vásquez, "Colonization and Loss of Texas," 73; Campbell, *Gone to Texas*, 139.

62. Zoraida Vásquez, "Colonization and Loss of Texas," 73–74; Campbell, *Gone to Texas*, 141, 148.

63. Campbell, *Gone to Texas*, 114; De Lay, *War of a Thousand Deserts*, 73.

64. Wendell G. Addington, "Slave Insurrections in Texas," *Journal of Negro History* 35, no. 4 (October 1950): 412; Henderson, *Glorious Defeat*, 96–97; de la Teja, "Colonization and Independence of Texas," 94; Campbell, *Gone to Texas*, 142–146; De Lay, *War of a Thousand Deserts*, 73.

65. Reichstein, *Rise of the Lone Star State*, 194; Henderson, *Glorious Defeat*, 98–99; Zoraida Vásquez, "Colonization and Loss of Texas," 76–77; Campbell, *Gone to Texas*, 148–156.

66. de la Teja, *Revolution Remembered*, 24–25, 32; de la Teja, "Colonization and Independence of Texas," 94; Rubén Rendón Lozano, *Viva Tejas: The Story of the Mexican-Born Patriots of the Republic of Texas* (San Antonio, TX: Southern Literary Institute, 1936), 37–38.

67. de la Teja, *Revolution Remembered*, 33–34; Joseph M. Nance, *After San Jacinto: The Texas Mexican Frontier, 1836–1841* (Austin: University of Texas Press, 1963), 281.

68. Reséndez, *Changing National Identities*, 207–209; de la Teja, "Colonization and Independence of Texas," 95; Joseph Eve, "A Letterbook of Joseph Eve, United States Charge d' Affairs to Texas," *Southwest Historical Quarterly* 43, no. 4 (1940): 494; William R. Hogan, *The Texas Republic: A Social and Economic History* (Austin: University of Texas Press, 1968), 269; De Lay, *War of a Thousand Deserts*, 75.

69. de la Teja, *Revolution Remembered*, 12, 35–36; Campbell, *Gone to Texas*, 191–192; Tijerina, *Tejanos and Texas Under the Mexican Flag*, 131–138; De León, *Tejano Community*, 14-15.

70. After Texas gained its independence from Mexico, it signed a treaty of peace and friendship with the Comanches. However, the treaty did not address the Comanches' main concern, their call for a boundary between the Comanchería and the white settlements. In 1839, Texas expelled the Cherokee, Shawnee, and Delaware Indian tribes that the Mexican government had encouraged to settle in eastern Texas to keep the Americans out. Without resources for a standing army, Texas created small horse-mounted volunteer companies to pursue and fight the Comanches. These *companias volantes,* or flying squadrons, consisting of mounted groups of up to seventy armed men, enforced the Tejano system of frontier justice. The companias volantes that launched punitive expeditions against the Comanches became the Texas Rangers. Campbell, *Gone to Texas*, 117.

71. Henderson, *Glorious Defeat*, 123–124; Reséndez, *Changing National Identities*, 197; Dorman A. Winfrey, "Mirabeau B. Lamar and Texas Nationalism," *Southwestern Historical Quarterly* 59 (1955): 191; Campbell, *Gone to Texas*, 174.

72. Henderson, *Glorious Defeat*, 124; Reséndez, *Changing National Identities*, 195, 205–206, 208; Simmons, *Little Lion of the Southwest*, 70; Campbell, *Gone to Texas*, 174.

73. Simmons, *Little Lion of the Southwest*, 70.

74. Henderson, *Glorious Defeat*, 125; Reséndez, *Changing National Identities*, 199–200; Campbell, *Gone to Texas*, 174–175; Stephen G. Hyslop, *Bound for Santa Fe: The Road to New Mexico and the American Conquest, 1806–1848* (Norman: University of Oklahoma Press, 2002), 277–290.

75. Henderson, *Glorious Defeat*, 125; Campbell, *Gone to Texas*, 179–181; Hyslop, *Bound for Santa Fe*, 290–293; Seymour V. Connor and Jimmy M. Skaggs, *Broadcloth and Britches: The Santa Fe Trade* (College Station: Texas A & M University Press, 1977), 107–114.

76. De Lay, *War of a Thousand Deserts*, 75.

77. Hall, *Social Change in the Southwest,* 174; Monroy, *Thrown Among Strangers*, 156.

78. Richard Rice, William Bullough, and Richard Orsi, *The Elusive Eden: A New History of California* (Boston: McGraw-Hill, 2002), 129: Hall, *Social Change in the Southwest,* 193; Blackhawk, *Violence over the Land*, 120, 133–136, 141–143.

79. Hall, *Social Change in the Southwest*, 60; Monroy, *Thrown Among Strangers*, 66–67.

80. Monroy, *Thrown Among Strangers*, 79.

81. Weber, *Mexican Frontier*, 66, 102; Monroy, *Thrown Among Strangers*, 125; Bouvier, *Women in the Conquest of California*, 97–98.

82. Monroy, *Thrown Among Strangers*, 36.

83. Bouvier, *Women in the Conquest of California*, 97–98.

84. Monroy, *Thrown Among Strangers*, 94–95; Bouvier, *Women in the Conquest of California*, 98.

85. Monroy, *Thrown Among Strangers*, 122–123; Weber, *Mexican Frontier*, 185–186; Bouvier, *Women in the Conquest of California*, 77. The Cosmopolitan Company provided a ship used in this colonization effort.

86. Bouvier, *Women in the Conquest of California*, 77–79.

87. Leonard Pitt, *The Decline of the Californios* (Berkeley: University of California Press, 1966), 86; Rice et al., *Elusive Eden*, 151; Weber, *Mexican Frontier*, 135–146. John Sutter petitioned California Governor Juan Bautista Alvarado for a settlement in the Sacramento Valley. Governor Alvarado saw Sutter's proposal as a way to create a buffer colony that would protect the coastal settlements from American colonists. In 1841, Alvarado granted John Sutter fifty thousand acres of land for his settlement, which Sutter named New Helvetia. Sutter later received twenty-two more square leagues of land from Governor Micheltorena in exchange for military aid to the governor. Weber, *Mexican Frontier*, 198–199, 204–205.

88. Weber, *Mexican Frontier*, 162.

89. Herbert Howe Bancroft, *California Pastoral* (San Francisco: History Company, 1888), 257.

90. Weber, *Mexican Frontier*, 66. Governor Figueroa's policies held the mission economy intact. One half of the mission property would go to the Indians, and the other half would go to support the priests and other officials. The Indians could not sell their plots of land.

91. Alberto Hurtado, *Indian Survival on the California Frontier* (New Haven, CT: Yale University Press, 1988), 69.

92. Robert F. Heizer and Alan M. Almquist, *The Other Californians: Prejudice and Discrimination Under Spain, Mexico, and the United States to 1920* (Berkeley: University of California Press, 1978), 105–106.

93. Pitt, *Decline of the Californios*, 24, 28; Blackhawk, *Violence over the Land*, 138.

94. Monroy, *Thrown Among Strangers*, 118–119; Blackhawk, *Violence over the Land*, 139.

95. Pitt, *Decline of the Californios*, 139.

96. Ibid.

97. Hall, *Social Change in the Southwest*, 194; Weber, *Mexican Frontier*, 243, 255–260.

98. Hall, *Social Change in the Southwest*, 194; Weber, *Mexican Frontier*, 269.

99. Weber, *Mexican Frontier*, 282; Hall, *Social Change in the Southwest*, 199.

⁂

# CHAPTER 3

# Mexican Americans
# in the Era of War
# and American Westward Expansion

The dispute over the boundary separating Mexico and the newly annexed Republic of Texas was the main issue that drove Mexico and the United States to war in 1846. The United States claimed as its territory the land between the Nueces River and the Río Grande by virtue of prior claim to the Río Grande as its border with Mexico. By 1841, more than twenty-one thousand Americans were living in Texas, and they outnumbered the Tejanos five to one. However, Mexico refused to recognize Texas independence, and although the United States was obligated to defend Texas, it asserted that the annexation of Texas gave the new republic title to what is now the eastern half of present-day New Mexico. Mexico protested this claim, but it was politically divided and militarily ill prepared to endure a protracted struggle with the United States. Despite its defiance, Mexico's internal divisions condemned it to face the United States in the inevitable war to come.[1] America had a booming economy; in contrast, Mexico had a stagnant economy and was a debtor nation, owing England nearly fifty million pesos. Moreover, the United States was aggressive and land hungry, and it embraced racial superiority, notwithstanding the ongoing moral and political debate over slavery that resulted in sectionalism. Concerned over America's lust for its northern territories, Mexico chose to resist and fight a superior force rather than recognize the annexation of Texas and cede New Mexico and a portion of California to the United States. The loyalties of Mexico's citizenry on the northern frontier were split between centralist and liberal factions over the extent of their government's involvement in their local and state affairs. These factors served as a backdrop for the Texas Revolt of 1836, New Mexico's Chimáyo Rebellion, and now the Mexican War itself.[2]

In New Mexico, a privileged class of landholders ruled the department. Their ambivalent loyalties to Mexico were the result of their reliance on the United States for trade and money derived from tariffs, combined with the presence and influence of Americans in local society. The Santa Fe trade produced dramatic change in the region's economy and politics and had brought wealth to the ricos, many of whom had been co-opted by the Americans. In contrast, although poor and largely illiterate, much of New Mexico's Spanish-speaking and Indian population sided with Mexico. They were opposed to the United States conquest and in 1847 rose

**Map of the United States of Mexico on the Eve of the Mexican American War.**
CREDIT: "Mapa de los estados unidos de Mejico segun lo organizado y definido por las varias atas del congreso de dicha republica: y costruido porlos mejores autoridades." (Disturnell, John, 1949). Map Collection, University of California Los Angeles Library, Department of Special Collections.

up in rebellion in Taos. Abuse at the hands of the ruling elite, who feared the poorer classes and the American military invasion, was at the heart of the uprising that was put down by soldiers of Stephen Watts Kearny's Army of the West.

In California, the way of life of the 6,500 to 7,000 Californios was cattle ranching, now realigned and largely integrated into the market economy of the United States. The wealth of the Spanish-speaking cattle barons was based on the exploitation of their Indian and Mexican workers in a way that gave the ranches the feel of a plantation. As was the case for Texas and New Mexico, those Californios dependent on the United States cash economy grew more wealthy and forged alliances with the Americans. There was much infighting among the ruling Californios owing to factionalism, and Mexico was unable to govern California. When war between the United States and Mexico broke out, the Californios lacked weapons and an army to battle the American invaders who took possession of California. In the summer of 1846, American forces encountered no resistance in taking California. However, a revolt broke out among the Mexican Californio rancheros against the U.S. occupation. The fighting was confined to guerilla attacks by poorly armed militias and volunteers against better armed Americans. The Californios fought heroically and well, but in vain. The Mexican American War (1846–1848) resulted in the defeat of Mexico and the loss of its northern territories, ceded to the United States by the Treaty of Guadalupe Hidalgo.

# THE SOUTHWEST ON THE EVE OF THE MEXICAN WAR

In New Mexico the ricos prospered and retained their elite legitimacy while life was hard for the majority of New Mexico's poor. There was an obvious rift between class and national interest. The centralists defended Mexico and would instigate the lower classes to oppose the American invasion. Because of their preferential access to trade, some ricos would eventually aid the American war effort. Those who were liberals were disappointed at their state's mismanagement and neglect by Mexico. On May 15, 1844, showing his cowardice in a citizens' campaign against Texans, Manuel Armijo was replaced as New Mexico's governor by General Mariano Martínez de Lejanza, who tried but failed to enforce taxation on the New Mexicans. Martínez left New Mexico in 1846 after finishing his term, and Manuel Armijo again became governor. The ambitious Armijo manipulated his fellow citizens for his own interests, namely remaining dependent on trade with the United States. New Mexico's confidence in Mexico was further weakened by rumors that it had agreed to sell the territory to the United States. A group of New Mexicans drafted a protest against Mexico's right to sell New Mexico and called for independence.[3] Nothing came of this plan.

Separatist sentiment was similarly present in California. The landowning class was the principal social base from which California's rulers emerged. The entrenched landowning and military elites were all interrelated through family networks and looked after one another's interests. Those who were liberals struggled against the autocratic rule of Mexican-appointed governors. They organized themselves behind the banner of autonomy for California, for they wanted independence from Mexico. A small minority even favored American annexation. In August 1844, they held a secret meeting in Monterey with the British counsel. They told him they were ready to drive Governor Micheltorena out of California, declare independence, and ask for British protection.[4]

The Californios resented General Micheltorena, California's new governor and friend of Santa Anna, and his army of convict soldiers. Though at odds, northern and southern Californios joined forces in November 1844 and initiated a revolt. Led by José Castro, the northern rebels captured San Juan mission and its ammunition cache. Micheltorena forced the insurgents to withdraw to San Jose, where his soldiers defeated them. The Californios persevered. Micheltorena at the head of four hundred soldiers marched south to Los Angeles, where several hundred Californios led by Juan Bautista Alvarado, representing the southern faction, waited. In February 1845, the Californios defeated Micheltorena in a bloodless battle at Cahuenga and forced him to leave California, taking his army with him.[5]

Mexico's hold on California ended. It did not appoint another governor to replace Micheltorena. Instead, the mulatto Pío de Jesús Pico, soldier, rancher, and senior member of the California legislature, was named governor and made Los Angeles the capital. José Castro became military governor of the territory. He remained in the north at Monterey, where he controlled the customhouse. Californios wanted to maintain their autonomy in the face of pressure from the United States. They remained fearful that Mexico would sell California to Britain, America's main rival for the Asian trade. California's ports, particularly the choice harbor of San Francisco, would help increase America's share of the Pacific trade.

San Diego was likewise desirable because of its harbor, in addition to its central role in the lucrative hide and tallow trade. California's fertile valleys were also attractive, as was other Mexican territory.[6]

The vast Mexican lands between newly annexed Texas and the Pacific coast showed great promise for the United States. Believing they should fulfill their Manifest Destiny, many Americans thought their country should settle lands west of the Mississippi claimed by Mexico, England, and the array of Indian nations. Newspapers supported the idea of Manifest Destiny. In 1842, John L. O'Sullivan, Jacksonian editor of the Washington, DC, monthly the *United States Magazine and Democratic Review,* coined the term Manifest Destiny in articulating the prevailing national sentiment for United States territorial expansion from the Atlantic to the Pacific into Texas, Oregon, and Mexico. O'Sullivan's publication was a staunch defender of Democratic Party positions on slavery, states' rights, Indian removal, and soon the Mexican War. The Texas rebellion set a pattern of racist attitudes toward Mexicans that later drew on cordial relationships between Anglos and Mexicans in New Mexico and California to denigrate Mexicans. Political publicists started to describe Mexicans as racially inferior to Anglo Saxons, an idle people incapable of self-government.[7] Other aggressive American nationalists added their voices to that of O'Sullivan.

Territorial expansion was a contentious issue for the United States. A sectional confrontation between the North and South occurred through all of the West. Proslavery forces demanded the acquisition of new territory and had vilified Mexico during the 1830s debate over annexing Texas. The opponents of slavery, on the other hand, were strongly against expansionism because they believed it would add new slaveholding states to the Union, thereby upsetting the balance of power between North and South.

In the wake of the Oregon territorial boundary dispute with Great Britain, the American national debate over westward expansion settled on the Texas Republic. With its government and citizens committed to slavery, Texas continued to seek annexation. Through annexation, Texas would enter the Union as a slave state and give proslavery forces an advantage in the House and the Senate. Vigorous opposition by northern antislavery forces, combined with the desire to avoid conflict with Mexico, led the United States to delay the request for Texas annexation. However, as abolitionist power increased, it became imperative for the South to bring Texas into the Union as a slave state, for it represented a deterrent to any congressional vote to abolish slavery. For Mexico, the annexation of Texas constituted another brazen act of American aggression against its sovereignty.[8]

An embittered Mexico still claimed Texas; it refused to recognize Texas independence. Moreover, the pretext for war between Mexico and the United States was the long-standing dispute over the international boundary between the two nations. The United States supported Texas's claim of the Río Grande as the boundary, but Mexico raised heated objections to America's presumptuous claims, steadfastly maintaining that the boundary was the Nueces River. The United States wanted the Río Grande as the border because it would place Santa Fe with its profitable trade inside the United States. The Nueces strip, the one-hundred-mile area between the Nueces River and the Río Grande extending from the Texas Gulf coast to eastern Colorado, was claimed by both Texas and Mexico. Texas declared that its border encompassed the Nueces area, reaching to the Río Grande, whereas Mexico wanted all of Texas to the Sabine River.[9]

Annexation of Texas became the central campaign issue of the 1844 presidential election. The election of the expansionist candidate James K. Polk, a westerner and a devotee of agrarianism, was a victory for the American expansionists who coveted Texas and California. In Mexico, the nation's liberal wing considered the United States a model for Mexico's development, whereas Mexican conservatives feared American Manifest Destiny and expansionism. Tensions rose among liberals and conservatives alike in Mexico after Polk's election in 1844 because of his apparent intent to make the acquisition of Mexico the primary objective of war. Mexico's acting president General José Joaquín de Herrera faced a daunting challenge. Herrera wanted conciliation with the United States. Though fearing that Mexico's loss of Texas would precipitate loss of its northern provinces, and aware that Mexico could not risk war with the United States, Herrera's short-lived liberal government proposed a peaceful settlement to the issue of Texas annexation. Britain advised Herrera to recognize the independence of the Republic of Texas on condition that Texas agreed not to be annexed by any country. However, to appease Mexico's ruling military elite, who considered him weak-willed, Herrera declared that any attempt to annex Texas would be considered an act of war. On February 27, 1845, the U.S. Senate voted to annex the Republic of Texas, and a few days later the U.S. Senate voted in favor of statehood for Texas. Texas entered the Union as the twenty-eighth state. Mexico City learned of this in mid-March, and the response in Mexico was immediate hostility toward the United States and a call for war. Mexico promptly ordered its foreign minister to tell the American ambassador that relations between the two nations were terminated.[10] Interpreting American annexation of Texas as a violation of Mexico's 1828 border treaty, Herrera went before the Mexican Congress to request mortgaging one-fourth of Catholic Church property to raise four million pesos to defend Mexico's territorial integrity.[11]

President Polk was intent on defending the boundary claims made by Texas and on precluding a possible invasion by Mexico before annexation of Texas could be completed. America's military intrusion onto contested Mexican soil furnished perfect evidence of a continued American political plot aimed at provoking Mexico into war and taking possession of the region. On July 1, 1845, the President ordered 1,500 American soldiers deployed to Texas near Corpus Christi. The next month, Polk doubled the number of American troops in Texas, and he sent newly appointed minister to Mexico John Slidell to Mexico City. Slidell was instructed to settle the Texas-Mexico boundary dispute, negotiate outstanding debts of United States citizens against Mexico, and offer Mexico four boundary adjustments in lieu of cash payments of $50 million for California and New Mexico. Slidell arrived in Mexico City in December. Herrera refused to accept the American minister's credentials for fear that receiving the American diplomat would lead to a popular uprising.[12]

Mexican President Herrera was assailed by his nation's archconservatives, as well as by the liberals led by Valentín Gómez Farías, for his lack of political leadership. Disunity provided opportunity for Mexico's archconservatives. On January 2, 1846, General Mariano Paredes y Arrillaga and his Army of the North, the largest in Mexico, entered Mexico City and ousted Herrera from office, claiming that Herrera was compromising Mexico's honor by "conspiring with the enemy" concerning Texas. Paredes called his like-minded generals together, and the junta selected him as president of Mexico. This abrupt change in government ended work in the Mexican Congress on the proposal to mortgage Church property to defend the nation's northern territories. The armed demonstrations and further diplomatic bickering between Mexico and the United States that preceded open hostilities ended as Paredes plunged Mexico into war.[13]

## THE OUTBREAK OF WAR

On January 13, 1846, President Polk, after months of negotiations with Mexico to buy Texas, ordered General Zachary Taylor to advance to the Río Grande. Taylor, who had fought with distinction in the War of 1812, ordered his three-thousand-strong army of occupation encamped near Corpus Christi to assert American sovereignty over the disputed Nueces strip at Laredo, near to present-day Brownsville opposite Matamoros, Mexico. On March 27, Taylor set his troops to building an earthen fortress named Fort Texas. The news of the American invasion of Mexico set off an intense nationalist response among Mexico's liberals and conservatives. They saw this action as an invasion of Mexican territory. President Paredes refused to meet Slidell, who was asked to leave Mexico. The Mexican president then ordered five thousand Mexican soldiers commanded by General Mariano Arista north to Matamoros.[14]

On April 23, Paredes announced that Mexico had begun a defensive war against the United States. Two days later, on the twenty-fifth, General Arista dispatched 1,600 Mexican soldiers on patrol across the Río Grande. The Mexicans encountered a company of U.S. dragoons led by Captain Seth Thornton. A firefight broke out in which American soldiers rode into an ambush and were cut to pieces. Sixteen Americans were killed. Greatly outnumbered by the Mexicans, the remainder of the Americans surrendered, including Captain Thornton. The Mexicans took the American officer and his men prisoner and held them in Matamoros. The subsequent Thornton Affair, or Thornton Skirmish, became the primary reason that President Polk asked for a state of war against Mexico. Taylor sent a message to Washington that war with Mexico had begun. Mexico had not invaded American territory; rather, the United States had provoked an attack in territory it claimed.[15] Once on the battlefield the Americans would deliver heavy volumes of lethal artillery fire and every time outmaneuver the numerically superior Mexican forces.

On the morning of May 3, Mexican artillery batteries in Matamoros began bombarding Fort Texas. The subsequent battles of Palo Alto north of Brownsville and Resaca de la Palma opposite of Matamoros were the first real challenges of the Americans and were easily won by them. At Palo Alto Taylor's huge cannons tore at the Mexican lines, causing numerous casualties, and at the Battle of Resaca American troops engaged Mexican soldiers in furious hand-to-hand combat and cavalry charges. More important, the two battles took place before the United States officially declared war on May 13. Mexican authority was expelled from Texas by the victorious Americans.[16]

In politically tumultuous Mexico, dissensions stirred against Paredes. On May 7 at the Mexican Pacific port of Mazatlán, an expeditionary force scheduled for duty in California had been swept up in the anti-Paredes rebellion led by liberals calling for a return of Santa Anna, who was in Cuba. On May 20, the proliberal military commander at Guadalajara joined the rebellion. Liberals also organized against Paredes in the states of Guanajuato, Zacatecas, Durango, and Puebla.[17]

Mexico broke off diplomatic relations with the United States, and President Polk used this snub as a cause for war. On May 7, one day after meeting with John Slidell, the president received General Taylor's report that American soldiers had been killed by Mexican troops near Matamoros. Polk now had his reason for war. On the eleventh, the president's message asked for a declaration of war in response to Mexico's initiation of hostilities. "Mexico has invaded our territory and shed American blood on the American soil," the president asserted. Two days later, on May 13, the U.S. Congress declared war on Mexico. Antiexpansionists were outraged at the turn of events; they believed the United States was bullying a weak neighbor and making a blatant land grab.[18] Their voices were quickly drowned out by the overwhelming support from Americans who rallied behind Polk's war of conquest.

## THE AMERICAN OCCUPATION OF NEW MEXICO

The territorial claim of the United States to New Mexico was strategic; trade with Mexico's interior provinces passed through it, and New Mexico also provided an overland connection to California's Pacific ports. Unlike California and Texas, New Mexico had large Mexican and Indian populations. Political factionalism along conservative and liberal lines also characterized New Mexico. Because of its dependence on American trade, money, and arms in fighting nomadic Indians, the pro-American faction at first offered little resistance to the American armies when they arrived in New Mexico in 1846. On the other hand, mostly poor Spanish-speaking and Indian residents made up the conservative faction who wanted no foreign intervention in New Mexico's internal affairs. This anti-American group produced the only organized resistance in Mexico's northern territories against the American army of occupation.[19]

New Mexico's sixty-five thousand Spanish-speaking and Indian population was concentrated along the Río Grande. The Río Abajo, New Mexico's southern region, was home to the ricos. These elites controlled most of the land, the livestock, and a considerable portion of the Santa Fe trade. The inhabitants of the Río Arriba, New Mexico's northern region, were poor subsistence farmers and ciboleros—the vecinos, who traded with various Indian groups. Unlike California, the division of the more populous New Mexico into the Río Arriba and Río Abajo and the disparities between rich and poor were based essentially on distinct class differences and on a cash nexus. In any case, the Americans, as did their national leaders, looked down on and despised all the Mexicans as an inferior race, because the whole concept of Manifest Destiny rested on a foundation of racism.[20]

Many New Mexico ricos had become less dependent on Mexico than on Americans for trade, of which they controlled over one-third. Their wealth was derived from tax revenues totaling more than 70 percent of New Mexico's budget, assessed on the annual half-million-dollar Santa Fe trade, or else came from the production of trade goods. American traders complained to Washington about the import duties on goods, as well as the special taxes and forced loans. They filed claims against the Mexican government despite the fact that some averted taxes because they had become Mexican citizens, formed partnerships with New Mexico's ricos, or married into the rico families. The ricos profited from the growth of American trade, but that trade had eroded the economic standing of the vecinos. Beaten down by poverty, the vecinos produced market goods and traded with the Indians while their women worked for wealthy New Mexicans and American households as servants, laundresses, and seamstresses.[21] Moreover, although lacking weapons and horses, the vecinos were the main offense against Indian raids. They were alienated by the elite, who could not be entirely trusted, and bitter at their treatment by these privileged members of New Mexican society. Pueblo Indian resentment had likewise been growing.

Upon the initiation of hostilities with Mexico, President Polk assigned General Stephen Watts Kearny to command the newly created Army of the West. Kearny's orders were clear: march to Santa Fe, secure the territory and establish a garrison and civil government, and then march on to California, where he was to follow the same process. The Americans in California were "well disposed towards the United States," claimed Secretary of War William L. Marcy and other officials in Washington. Their assertions were based on the fact that the United States helped the Americans in California to revolt (the Bear Flag Rebellion) and proclaim themselves a republic, as the Americans had done in Texas. And, like the Americans in Texas, many in the California territory were there illegally, did not partake in California's social and political life, and as a white race believed they were inherently superior to the California Mexicans and Indians, who soon became targets of escalating Anglo racism.[22]

James W. Magoffin, Kearny's civilian agent, was sent to New Mexico one week ahead of the American troops to arrange a treaty with the ruling New Mexicans. Magoffin was accompanied by Lieutenant Phillip St. George Cook and a small dragoon escort. A successful Santa Fe merchant and close friend of Governor Manuel Armijo, Magoffin had been instructed to convince Armijo, Diego Archuleta, and other New Mexican officials to surrender. Merchant Manuel Alvarez, American consul and commercial agent, also spoke with Armijo to persuade him to surrender. American newspapers had started a black propaganda campaign against Governor Armijo aimed at persuading the American public that he was the typical dishonest, depraved, gutless Mexican. Magoffin offered the governor a large sum of money as an incentive to hand over New Mexico to the United States. Armijo, waiting for Mexican reinforcements from Durango and Chihuahua, balked.[23]

The American occupation of New Mexico met immediate resistance from the New Mexicans, as they rose up when American forces arrived. Up to four thousand Spanish-speaking and Indian volunteers, draftees, and professional soldiers had converged on Santa Fe to fight the Yankee invaders but then suddenly dispersed. The reason was that Governor Armijo stifled resistance, even though he had publicly declared he would meet and battle the Army of the West at Apache Canyon, east of the capital at Santa Fe. Armijo assembled his militia, presidial troops, and a squadron from Veracruz, but he lost the will to fight the Americans, claiming that they were too powerful and that it would be futile to engage them. Armijo then fled to Albuquerque and from there to El Paso and on to Mexico City. Prior to his departure, the shrewd and greedy coward sold all his business interests and confiscated the Church's treasury funds. General Kearny took possession of Santa Fe without firing a shot.[24]

The Army of the West under Kearny's command marched into New Mexico unopposed and raised the stars and stripes. Kearny established a military command and promised the New Mexicans to honor their civil and religious rights. The general proclaimed, "It is enjoined on the citizens of New Mexico to . . . pursue uninterruptedly their peaceful avocations. So long as they continue in such pursuits they . . . will be protected . . . in their property, their persons, and their religion." The United States easily took possession of territory it had wanted to buy from Mexico. All ties between Mexico and New Mexico were now severed. Many contemporary observers complained that the American soldiers from Missouri did not make a good impression on the New Mexicans because of their public drunkenness and violent behavior. Unruly drunken soldiers roamed the streets of Santa Fe terrorizing the panic-stricken residents.[25] These experiences were not very reassuring to the New Mexicans who had just come under American occupation.

So as to diminish hostility to United States rule, Kearny toured New Mexico announcing to local authorities that the Army of the West had not come as conquerors but to protect and liberate their new subjects. Kearny, however, had to exert control over his men; many remembered the outrages committed five years earlier on the Texans who were part of the disastrous Santa Fe expedition and contemplated inflicting vengeance on the New Mexicans. Kearny promised United States citizenship to all New Mexicans but sternly warned that whosoever took up arms would be hanged. On September 22, 1846, the American general instituted the Kearny Code to govern New Mexico and retained local New Mexicans who swore loyalty to the United States to administer these laws. From this pro-American faction, he appointed American trader Charles Bent as governor, Diego Archuleta as lieutenant governor, Antonio José Otero as chief justice, and Donaciano Vigil as territorial secretary. To protect the New Mexicans from Indian attacks, Kearny sent troops to the Apache, Navajo, and Ute tribes to negotiate peace. He then divided his command into three groups: one under Colonel Sterling Price to occupy New Mexico, a second under Colonel Alexander William Doniphan to take Chihuahua, and the third under his own command headed for California.[26]

In October 1846, Doniphan's forces headed south to link up with General John E. Wool in Chihuahua, along the way fighting both Indians and Mexicans.

On reaching Brazito on Christmas Day 1846, Doniphan's Missouri troops engaged a Mexican battalion and militia sent from El Paso del Norte to stop their advance. Although outnumbered, the Americans soundly defeated the Mexicans. The half-hour battle won by the Americans gave the United States legal claim to New Mexico. Doniphan's troops took El Paso del Norte and the rest of Chihuahua and then joined forces with General Wool.[27]

Kearny set out for California, leaving Colonel Doniphan in charge in New Mexico to maintain the peace until the arrival of Colonel Price. On October 6, 1846, Kearny met up with Kit Carson, who informed the general that California had already fallen with little opposition to American forces commanded by Robert F. Stockton and aided by John C. Frémont's Volunteer Battalion. Ordering two hundred of his men back to Santa Fe, Kearny pushed on to California. On November 23, he learned that a revolt had broken out in California in which Los Angeles, Santa Barbara, San Diego, Santa Inés, and San Luis Obispo had fallen to the Mexican Californio rebels, who once more were in control of the whole of southern California. Unfazed by the news, Kearny pushed on. He believed the Californios not to be determined adversaries but poor fighters.[28]

## THE 1847 TAOS REVOLT AGAINST AMERICAN OCCUPATION OF NEW MEXICO

Despite their apparent apathy, native New Mexicans and Indians of the Río Arriba area, resentful of the American occupation and the loss of sovereignty and contact with Mexico, began holding secret meetings to resist the invaders through a general uprising that took shape on December 12, 1846. The conspirators were led by Pablo Montoya and the Indian Tomás Romero. These northern New Mexicans, many who had fought nine years earlier against Mexican governor Albino Pérez to maintain their autonomy, regretted that nothing had been done to stop the American advance. At the core of the unrest was the fear of the insurgents that the registration of land titles would result in further taxation and eventual confiscation of their lands. Moreover, the American merchants Charles Bent and Carlos Beaubien had antagonized the Taos Pueblo Indians with the settlement and development of the Pueblos' communal grazing and hunting lands along the Santa Fe Trail—the Beaubien-Miranda grant—and by trading with the Pueblos' enemies, the Utes, who raided the Pueblos for plunder. Believing the two foreigners, who had purchased large parcels of land, would check their power and privileges, the Catholic clergy urged the rebels to carry out their revolt. December 19 was set as the date to kill Charles Bent and Colonel Sterling Price and drive the Americans from New Mexico. Seizing the artillery at Santa Fe would be the signal for the general revolt. Delays in communication to the outlying areas pushed the day of the revolt to Christmas Eve.[29]

However, New Mexico Secretary Donaciano Vigil, a pro-American, foiled this plan to kill Governor Bent. Conservatives Diego Archuleta and Tomás Ortiz were discovered as the plotters of the murder plan. Archuleta was a military officer and son of Juan Andrés Archuleta, the former military commander of New Mexico;

Ortiz was the brother of the vicar of Santa Fe, Father Juan Felipe Ortiz, and a former mayor of the town. Both men escaped, but the Pino brothers and Manuel Chavez, part of the anti-American cabal, were arrested and later released. On January 5, 1847, Governor Bent issued a proclamation condemning Archuleta and Ortiz and warned residents against further treasonous acts. Bent carefully explained to New Mexicans that private lands were not going to be taxed, stressing that the land registration was intended to make titles more secure, not to rob owners of their property. To emphasize that resistance was futile, the governor announced that Colonel Doniphan had defeated Mexican troops at Brazito. The plotters had been counting on rumors of Mexican victories in Chihuahua, which they thought would bring a sizable force of Mexican soldiers north to New Mexico.[30]

Though Bent quelled the initial revolt, he ignored the growing anti-American sentiment. Unaccompanied by American soldiers, the governor left for Taos, where he met resistance that soon proved fatal to him. Area New Mexicans organized a secret revolt on January 19, 1847, to kill Americans and anyone who collaborated with the occupying forces. The previous night the rebels had murdered and then scalped sheriff Stephen Luis Lee, judge Cornelio Vigil, attorney James W. Leal, and Carlos Beaubien's son Narciso. "It appeared," wrote Colonel Price, "to be the object of the insurrectionists to put to death every American and every Mexican who had accepted office under the American government." The rebels then came after Governor Bent. Lead by Tomás Romero, they went to the governor's house and pounded on the door. Bent asked the angry men what they wanted. They responded: "We want your head, gringo. We do not want for any of you gringos to govern us, as we have come to kill you." Bent begged the insurgents to leave but they ignored his pleas. The rebels wounded Bent, threw him to the floor, scalped him alive in front of his wife and children, and then cut off his head. By ringing the mission church bell at the Taos pueblo, the revolutionists without knowing alerted the Americans to their location.[31]

The four-day open revolt against American occupation spread to longtime resident Simon Turley's distillery near Arroyo Hondo, twelve miles north of Taos, and it would eventually engulf all of northern New Mexico. Violence between the contending groups of vecinos and Indians and the Americans turned the countryside into a war zone. Fighting commenced on January 20, when the rebels seized the distillery and killed several Americans, including Turley. Terrified, the survivors of the massacre fled and took refuge at the house of the Catholic priest Antonio José Martínez.[32] The report that 1,500 armed New Mexicans and Indians, determined to force a showdown, were advancing on Santa Fe triggered a call to action by the American army and its sympathizers. However, very few American troops were in Santa Fe. Colonel Price, in command of Santa Fe, sent for reinforcements from Albuquerque, calling on Captain Witham Angney's Missouri battalion and a company of New Mexico volunteers led by Colonel Ceran St. Vrain.[33]

By now, Colonel Price had information on the insurgents' movements. Price quickly left Santa Fe with four howitzers, the 1st U. S. Dragoons, the 2nd Missouri Infantry, and the company of New Mexico volunteers to attack Taos. Only the volunteers had mounts. Eighty American troops under the command of Captain Israel R. Hendley defeated two hundred of the popular insurrectionists, led by local vecino Manuel Cortez at Mora. Hendley was killed in the three-hour battle that claimed the lives of twenty-five insurgents. About two hundred American soldiers, armed with two howitzers under Captain Jesse I. Morin's command, returned to Mora on February 1. In retaliation for rebelling against the new government, the American officer ordered his troops to destroy the village of Mora and burn the surrounding wheat fields. According to the *Niles' National Register*, "Capt. Mor[n] . . . burnt to ashes every house town, and rancho in his path. The inhabitants fled to the mountains. . . ." Another battle took place at La Cañada, where American soldiers killed thirty-six rebels and drove the rest before them to Embudo, twenty-three miles south of Taos. At Embudo the insurgents made another stand but were driven out, sustaining many casualties, including the death of one of their leaders. Between six hundred and seven hundred rebels were concentrated at Taos Pueblo in the mission church, where they fortified themselves against attack.[34]

Meanwhile, the reinforced American assault force arrived at Taos and immediately launched an attack to break the siege. The American troops cornered the rebels in the Mission Church of San Gerónimo. On February 3, nearly two weeks into the rebellion, artillery pieces opened fire on the mission. The New Mexicans pushed the Americans back. After two hours of shelling, taunted and jeered at by the rebels, the Americans rested and regrouped. Early the next morning, they advanced again.[35]

Colonel Price posted Captain John Burgwin's dragoons about 260 yards from the western flank of the church. Next, Price ordered the New Mexican volunteers to the opposite side of Taos to prevent the rebels from escaping. The rest of the American troops took positions about three hundred yards from the north wall of the church.[36] The artillery batteries pounded away at the enemy. Price ordered the men commanded by Captains Burgwin and Samuel H. McMillan to storm the building. Advancing against heavy fire, the American soldiers climbed onto the church roof and set it on fire. Leading a small team of soldiers, Captain Burgwin entered the corral in front of the church, attempted to force the door open, and was mortally wounded.[37]

In the meantime, the Americans cut small holes in the western wall of the church and rolled in bombs. Undaunted, the rebels kept up their fire on the Americans. Following an artillery barrage, American soldiers stormed into the smoke-filled building. The rebels were gone. Fifty insurgents who tried to escape capture were shot dead.[38]

The fighting was constant for a day and a half. Finally on February 5 the guerrilla force broke up and scattered in all directions. One hundred and fifty rebels lay dead and an untold number had been wounded. Fifty-one rebels who attempted to escape were run down and killed by Ceran St. Vrain's "emergency brigade" in fierce, hand-to-hand combat. Price's troops suffered fifty-two casualties. Of the rebel leaders, Tomás Romero and Pablo Montoya were later tried by the American military court for bearing arms against the United States. They were found guilty of treason and received the sentence of death by hanging in accordance with martial law. One of the defendants, Antonio María Trujillo, argued at trial that Colonel Sterling Price had no right to prosecute the insurgents for treason because they did not consider themselves citizens of the United States but Mexican patriots defending their homeland. In the following weeks, at least twenty-eight accused New Mexican and Indian insurgents were hanged in the Taos Plaza for treason. American officials later ordered that "no house [be] permitted to retain arms, or other munitions of war."[39]

The defeat of the Taos revolt broke the resistance to American rule in New Mexico and put an end to rebellion in that territory. It was now in the control of the Americans. Donaciano Vigil became acting governor of New Mexico, but United States military rule prevailed for the next several years.[40] The focus of the war on Mexico's northern territory now shifted to the West Coast.

## THE AMERICAN OCCUPATION OF CALIFORNIA

The United States had long been interested in acquiring California. This attention took the form of a diplomatic campaign to negotiate purchase of the territory from Mexico to prevent it from selling California to Britain. The sea otter trade, whaling, fine ocean ports, and fertile land generated much American interest in California. In addition, there was the lucrative hide and tallow industry. The years between 1826 and 1848 were exceptionally profitable ones. Six million hides and seven thousand tons of tallow were shipped from California to Boston. The hide trade was centered at San Diego, so its choice harbor was particularly desirable. American interest in California thus rested in its potential to help American merchants gain a greater foothold in the Asian Pacific trade, and this became a primary impetus for California's contribution to the start of the Mexican War. Settlement of California by Americans was key to its conquest by the United States. These American arrivals began calling for United States intervention to take California away from the indolent Mexicans.

On September 5, 1842, U.S. Naval Captain Thomas C. Jones, stationed offshore at Callao, Peru, received a false message that war with Mexico over Texas had broken out. Jones learned that Mexico had ceded California to England for $7 million, in violation of the Monroe Doctrine, to keep it out of American hands. Concerned that the British would occupy Mexico if rumors about war proved true, Jones sailed for Monterey to stop such an incident. The U.S. naval officer took his fleet north to California, sailing into Monterey Harbor on October 19. Marching to the tunes of "Yankee Doodle" and "The Star Spangled Banner," the men under Jones's command seized the presidio and customhouse and took occupation of Monterey, summoning acting civil governor José Alvarado to surrender. Jones's capture of Monterey was the first action taken to apply the Monroe Doctrine. The next day, Thomas Oliver Larkin, a longtime American resident of Monterey and a future U.S. agent, convinced Captain Jones that the United States and Mexico were not at war. Jones hauled down the U.S. flag, apologized to Mexican authorities, and departed.[41] The fiasco broke up talks between Mexico, the United States, and England concerning California's international boundaries.

Larkin was under orders from President Polk to encourage the Californios to look to the United States rather than to England and France to best serve their interests. The Yankee merchant and former American consul in California easily won

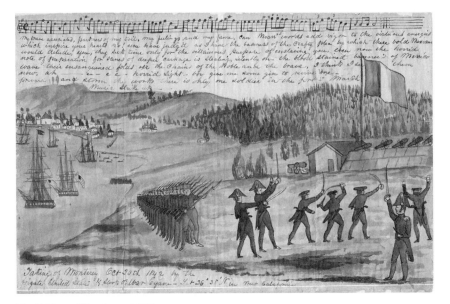

**The Taking of Monterey, 1842.**
CREDIT: Courtesy of the Bancroft Library, University of California, Berkeley, California.

over Mariano Vallejo and General José María Castro to his cause of making California an American protectorate. California's ranching aristocracy concurred that their future rested with the United States, and together they plotted to make California an independent republic managed by it. This change in Californio sentiment came in response to the activities of John C. Frémont, who was leading an armed topographical corps into California, and to the short-lived Bear Flag Rebellion. Frémont's father-in-law was the powerful senator Thomas Hart Benton of Indiana, an outspoken western expansionist. Frémont had been instructed by President Polk that if war broke out with Mexico he was supposed to secure California for the United States.[42]

News that the United States had declared war with Mexico arrived late in California, but already there was apprehension that open armed conflict was imminent. In April 1846 a rumor spread among Americans in the Sacramento Valley that several hundred Mexican soldiers were pushing through the area, laying waste to homes, destroying crops, and scattering cattle. On June 10, American settlers from Sutter's Fort revolted against the Mexican government of California. The Bear Flag Rebellion was an attempt to repeat the 1836 Texas revolt and subsequently gain American annexation. Frémont, who had returned to California from Oregon, had organized the rebellion. The Americans invaded the home of Mariano Vallejo, the commandant at Sonoma. The wealthy grantee of the Petaluma and Suscol ranches that took up much of the land between the San Francisco Bay and Sonoma, General Vallejo wanted to break with Mexico. He immediately offered his services to the Americans, but they took him and three other Californio officials to Sutter's Fort, where they were imprisoned for several months under very poor conditions. The rampaging Americans then seized 150 horses from General Castro and proceeded to the town of Sonoma. Joined by additional Americans, the rebels took more than a dozen inhabitants prisoner and confiscated 18 can-nons, 750 arms, and 250 horses, all the while ransacking the homes of California Mexicans and killing some of them. Then, hoisting their makeshift flag with a crudely drawn bear and a star, the Americans proclaimed the "Bear Flag Republic of Independent California."[43]

Desperately needing money to finance the war against the United States, Mexico authorized Governor Pío de Jesús Pico to borrow $14,000 from the Spaniard Eulo-gio de Célis of Los Angeles. Although Californios such as Mariano Vallejo actively supported the Americans, many Californios considered themselves patriotic Mexicans and cast their lot with Mexico. One of these patriots was Andrés Pico, who would lead the fight against the Americans in California. In July 1846, Pico asked the California deputy chamber to give him permission to take command of forces to fight the American invaders. The chamber refused. Issuing orders from Santa Barbara that all citizens in the territory take up arms, Pico raised almost one hundred men and met Castro and his army north of San Luis Obispo. Putting their regional differences aside, the Californios, most notably José María Flores and Andrés Pico, led the resistance against superior American forces.[44]

**Pablo de la Guerra, Salvador Vallejo, and Andrés Pico, n.d.**
CREDIT: Original daguerreotype in possession of Mrs. McGethigan, S.F.  Courtesy of the Bancroft Library, University of California, Berkeley, California.

After Mexico broke off diplomatic relations with the United States, several American naval ships under the command of Commodore John D. Sloat arrived off the coast of California, ending Frémont's Bear Flag Revolt. Sloat's orders were to seize and blockade California's ports once war between Mexico and the United States commenced. On July 2, Sloat led his five warships into Monterey Bay. Learning that the Bear Flag Republic had been declared with likely authority from Washington, on July 6 Sloat ordered sailors and Marines from his warships to land onshore at Monterey. Meeting no resistance, the landing party raised the American flag over the customhouse. In declaring the American occupation of California, Sloat promised protection for the rights of the Californios. Two days later, seventy Marines and sailors from the *U.S.S. Portsmouth* marched north to Sonoma and declared the annexation of California. The men raised the American flag and then hiked to Sutter's Fort. Sloat sent a message to Governor Pío Pico in Los Angeles. Describing himself as "the best friend of California," Sloat invited "his Excellency" to meet him in Monterey.[45]

Taking over command from Sloat, Commodore Stockton's naval squadron dropped anchor at other locations off California's coast. On August 17, after receiving news of war between the United States and Mexico, Stockton claimed the towns of San Diego, Los Angeles, and Santa Barbara for the United States.[46]

## THE BATTLES AT MONTERREY AND BUENA VISTA

On July 6 and 7, 1846, as American forces landed in California, U.S. Agent Alexander MacKenzie met with Antonio López Santa Anna in Cuba. MacKenzie told the Mexican general that the United States wanted to buy New Mexico and California. Santa Anna, the consummate dealmaker, said he wanted peace but added that if the United States helped him return to power in Mexico he would agree to the sale. President Polk ordered the U.S. Navy to allow Santa Anna, aboard the British steamer *Arab,* to cross the blockade and enter Mexico. Veracruz received Santa Anna as a hero, and the savior of the nation proceeded to Mexico City.[47]

Meanwhile, as American troops were advancing on Monterrey, Mexico, political chaos broke out once more in Mexico City. In August 1846, President Paredes was overthrown and replaced by a coalition of liberals and moderates awaiting Santa Anna's arrival.[48]

On September 14, 1846, Santa Anna entered Mexico City. One week later, General Zachary Taylor's army of occupation took control of Monterrey. The taking of this Mexican city resounded with the evil of massacre as Texas Rangers systematically slaughtered its Mexicans. Following the American army's victory, volunteer Texas Rangers went through the city and murdered more than one hundred innocent civilians in cold blood. On the heels of this serial massacre and terror, more Ranger atrocities took place. A group of Texans rode into Rancho de San Francisco and selected and bound thirty-six men, and the killing squads executed them with shots through their heads. The Texans enjoyed the violence that they would never consider doing to whites because racism played an integral part in these actions. Notwithstanding this ruthless Texas Ranger conduct, Taylor now held Monterrey and Saltillo, and Mexico's northern region was under American control.[49] When Mexico did not sue for peace after the American victory at Monterrey, Polk responded with a plan for an invasion of Mexico to be led by General Winfield Scott, the great strategist and field commander who had been general in chief of the U.S. Army in 1841. In contrast, although commanding numerically superior forces, Santa Anna was no military strategist and ignored the advice of others. The Mexican general consequently would be outmaneuvered and outfought by the Americans. Santa Anna organized an army, and on September 28 he led 2,500 troops on a 327-mile forced march to San Luis Potosí, where four thousand other Mexican troops were staged. The poorly trained Mexican soldiers had no uniforms, possessed inferior weapons, and had little food. Nearly one-fourth of the Mexican troops had died of hunger, thirst, and exhaustion during their march to Saltillo. Santa Anna's starving and bedraggled army reached San Luis Potosí on October 8 to face Taylor's 5,000-man army that arrived nine days later near Saltillo. Santa Anna's plan was to confront Taylor's force near Saltillo.[50]

Additional Mexican troops arrived at San Luis Potosí as part of Santa Anna's plan to capture Taylor's army provisions. On February 22 the Battle of Buena Vista began, and by the end of the second day of intense fighting, Taylor had annihilated Santa Anna's army, forcing them to withdraw in defeat after losing about 2,100 men. Taylor lost 678 men and had 1,500 desertions. In the march back to San Luis Potosí, Santa Anna lost most of his army of 20,000 troops. A Mexican victory at Buena Vista would have allowed the Mexican general to push on to the Río Grande and perhaps even to the Nueces River, thereby nullifying all American gains of the war. Northern Mexico was now in the possession of American forces.[51]

On August 7, 1846, Mexican commandant José Castro wrote Commodore Stockton expressing his desire to hold a conference to end hostilities in California. Stockton agreed on the condition that Castro raise the American flag over Los Angeles, declaring the territory under American protection and thus independent of Mexico. Castro refused and ordered the evacuation of the pueblo. Then, on the tenth, Castro and Pío Pico fled for Mexico to get money, reinforcements, and weapons to return California to Mexico. Los Angeles was in the hands of the Americans. Stockton declared martial law and appointed Captain Archibald H. Gillespie military commandant of Los Angeles. Gillespie did not like the Californios; the American officer, who had been with Frémont in northern California, deemed them inferior and cowardly. Gillespie conducted house searches, seized goods, detained residents, and arrested many others for minor offenses. The town's Mexicans quickly grew to dislike Gillespie's harsh measures in carrying out martial law in the region. Frémont's California Battalion of Volunteers' pillaging as they made their way down to southern California also outraged the Californios.[52]

The United States had committed only a few men to the occupation of southern California; a forty-eight-man American garrison was stationed at Los Angeles, and there were nineteen American soldiers at San Diego. On September 23, a small force of twenty California Mexicans attacked the American barracks at Los

Angeles. The Mexicans were driven off, but the attack inspired other Mexicans at ranches away from the towns to join the patriotic cause with some fighting on its behalf. The next day a proclamation was issued and signed in Los Angeles by three hundred residents charging that Americans subjugated and oppressed them "worse than slaves." The proclamation was a call for Californios to take up arms, which they did; they chose Sérbulo Varela and Captain José María Flores as their leaders. The Californios rebelled in the last week of September, forcing Gillespie's troops to surrender and abandon Los Angeles. A group of Mexican women who had witnessed their families and community repeatedly humiliated by the American soldiers presented the departing and defeated Gillespie with a basket of peaches rolled in cactus needles. The women not only hurled insults at the Americans but also showered them with rage at being abused by the intruders. As commander in chief and governor of California, Flores issued a proclamation calling on all male citizens between the ages of fifteen and sixty to appear for military duty. For their part, women hid Californio soldiers or refused to give information to the American enemy about the whereabouts of others.[53]

In San Pedro, Gillespie, with a combined force of sailors, Marines, and volunteers, marched back to retake Los Angeles. The Mexican Californios under José María Flores and José Antonio Carrillo constantly harassed the American forces. They killed four Americans and wounded several others in what became known as the Battle of San Pedro. The Americans gave way to the Californios. Meanwhile in Santa Barbara, a band of California Mexicans drove a nine-man American force out of the town.[54]

The Battle of Dominguez Ranch took place on October 8–9, 1846, when a small force of Californio troops led by José María Flores held off the invasion of Los Angeles by American Marines commanded by Captain William Mervine. The American forces were without artillery or horses and lacked the means for resupply. By running horses across the dusty hills out of gun range and dragging a single small cannon to various sites, Flores and his troops fooled the Americans into thinking they had encountered a large enemy force. The Californios engaged the Americans and killed four and wounded ten others.[55]

On November 16, American and Mexican forces clashed near Salinas ten miles inland from Monterey Bay, and other small battles broke out elsewhere in northern California. All were won by the Americans. Meanwhile, Kearny's forces, guided by Kit Carson, arrived in California and took command of the territory.[56]

The United States had so far encountered relatively little opposition in California. However, the badly outmanned California Mexicans were bent on defending their homeland. On December 6, Andrés Pico's Presidial Lancers fought Kearny's tired, unprepared First Dragoons at the Indian village of San Pasqual. The Californios had a small number of firearms acquired from the British; however, it was their famed skills as lancers and their superior horsemanship that helped them defeat the Americans in hand-to-hand combat in the biggest battle of the war in California.[57]

Kearny dispatched three dragoons to scout Pico's position in an Indian village in the San Pasqual Valley, led by Lieutenant Thomas C. Hammond and Gillespie's guide Rafael Machado, a Californio deserter. An Indian approached the

Americans and told them the whereabouts of Andrés Pico and his men. Alerted to the Americans' presence by an Indian sentry, Pico mobilized his Presidial Lancers for battle. The next day, Kearny headed for the San Pasqual Valley to engage the Californios, who by now numbered 160 men.[58]

Moving his men to the valley's south rim and aligned with Captain Benjamin D. Moore's squad, Gillespie engaged the Californios. The latter pushed back the American dragoons, captured one of the American artillery pieces, and defeated the Americans in the Battle of San Pasqual. They killed seventeen American soldiers, officers Moore and Hammond, and wounded eighteen others, including Kearny and Gillespie. The Californios suffered eleven wounded and no dead. Realizing that more Americans would soon arrive, Pico quickly moved his men to the western end of the Pasqual Valley.[59]

The next day, Kearny led his men west along the hillsides to avoid attack by the Californios. In the afternoon the Americans came upon several Indians, who told Kearny that the Californios had just left with their wounded. As Kearny and his men rode away, between thirty and forty of Andrés Pico's men attacked them, but the Americans escaped. On December 8, the Californios agreed on a truce. Pico wanted to exchange an American prisoner for a captured Californian, Pablo Vejar, and Kearny agreed.[60]

With the Californios cutting off Kearny's path from Stockton's forces at San Diego, Kit Carson and another American volunteered to go to San Diego for aid. Meanwhile, Kearny was in a standoff with the Californios and planned to shoot his way out. As the haggard Americans prepared for battle, they heard Stockton's army approaching and shouting "Americans!" The Californios also heard the reinforcements arrive, and, firing one last shot, they disappeared. This symbolized the end

**Night at San Pascual.**
CREDIT: William Meyers, "Night at San Pasqual." Courtesy of the Franklin D. Roosevelt Presidential Library.

of the battle, the worst defeat for American forces during the Mexican-American War. Kearny, in his report to the army adjutant general in Washington, praised the Californios as "well mounted and among the best horsemen in the world. . . ." Kearny and his troops marched to San Diego and entered the town on December 12, 1846. Without delay, Kearny and Stockton began planning the reconquest of California.[61]

American forces left San Diego on December 29, 1846, and marched on Los Angeles to end the revolt. U.S. naval vessels blockaded Mexican ports. On January 8 and 9, 1847, Commodore Stockton, with six hundred sailors, Marines, and volunteers that included General Kearny's men, fought five hundred California Mexicans at the San Gabriel River twelve miles south of Los Angeles. After ninety minutes of ineffective artillery fire and several unsuccessful cavalry attacks against lethal American artillery, Flores conceded the battle and withdrew. The Californios had killed or wounded sixty Americans while losing only seven men.[62]

On January 9, California Mexicans led by Flores fought the Americans in the Battle of La Mesa. The Mexicans, armed only with lances, almost managed to surround the American force; however, Flores's cavalry attacks and artillery once again could not stop the advance, and he gave up Los Angeles. Stockton's combined force of soldiers, Marines, and sailors entered Los Angeles on January 10. Aware of the outcome, a deputation of California Mexicans from Los Angeles approached Stockton's camp the next morning. The group told Stockton that they would surrender the town to the Americans if Californio property and persons would be respected.[63]

Flores learned that American forces commanded by Frémont were marching southward to link up with Stockton and Kearny. On January 11, the Americans arrived in the San Fernando Valley and occupied Mission San Fernando. Frémont dispatched Jesús Pico, a cousin of Andrés Pico, to persuade Flores and Manuel Castro to surrender. The two Mexicans responded by turning over command of about one hundred men to Andrés Pico and fleeing to Sonora, Mexico.[64] The Americans were now in control of California and all of northern Mexico.

On January 13, Andrés Pico met with Frémont at a ranch in Cahuenga Pass, discussed the terms for surrender, and signed the Articles of Capitulation. The Treaty of Cahuenga ended the war in California, surrendered all of California to the United States, and promised to protect the property rights of the California Mexicans. The treaty forgave past hostilities and allowed all the Mexicans to return home on surrendering their arms. It also bestowed American citizenship on the California Mexicans once a treaty of peace was signed by both countries and granted permission to leave to those who wished to go to Mexico. Kearny established a provisional government in California. The Americans were now in possession of all its vital bays and harbors.[65]

In December 1846, Alexander Doniphan and over eight hundred soldiers left Santa Fe for Chihuahua, Mexico. On February 28, 1847, Doniphan's soldiers fought and defeated a Mexican force of eight hundred men and the next day marched into Chihuahua unopposed and formally took over the city. In late May, Doniphan's men joined General Taylor's forces. Fighting was unduly brutal because of the criminal conduct of the Texas Rangers, who also hit at the city's inhabitants and torched and plundered their homes. The pillaging had no purpose other than punishment and terror; it afforded Texans the opportunity to avenge the Alamo and Goliad and to release other strong feelings of resentment against Mexico. Contemptuous of the Mexicans, the Texas Rangers, called *los diablos tejanos* (Texas devils) by the Mexicans, used vicious guerrilla tactics that showed little regard for civilian lives or property. Commenting on the relentless butchery committed by the Texas Rangers, a contemporary observer noted: "the bushes, skirting the road from Monterrey southward, are strewed with the skeletons of Mexicans sacrificed by these desperadoes."[66]

Desperately short of money, Mexico could not continue the war effort without financial help from the Catholic Church. Amid protests from priests and lay people, the Mexican Congress passed two laws to seize Church property. With the support of the Church, creole regiments revolted in what became known as the Polka Rebellion, which was put down by acting president Valentín Gómez Farías. The Polkas refused orders to go to Veracruz to prepare for its defense against a United States invasion. Moderates joined the opposition, but the government imprisoned its leader, Gómez Pedraza. Santa Anna, who had returned to Mexico City, ordered an end to the hostilities. Farías resigned, and Pedro Anaya, one of Santa Ana's henchmen, replaced him as Mexico's provisional president. The Catholic Church gave Santa Anna twenty million pesos in exchange for the repeal of the two anticlerical laws.[67]

By now the storm center of the war had shifted from Mexico's northern provinces to an invasion of Mexico from the east at Veracruz. On March 9, twelve thousand American troops commanded by General Winfield Scott landed south of Veracruz City unopposed. The United States pulverized Veracruz with four days of artillery barrages, and on March 29 the Mexicans surrendered the battered city to the Americans. Mexico gave no sign of a desire for peace, however. News of the American invasion reached Mexico City and triggered a wave of patriotism and calls for national unity. The focus of the war was now on Mexico City and entered its final phase. Santa Anna, the self-styled Napoleon of the West, massed his forces for the defense of the capital.[68]

Skillfully executing his Mexico City campaign, General Scott marched his army toward the capital. On April 17, the Americans met the careless and overconfident Santa Anna and his sick and exhausted army at a narrow pass by the town of Cerro Gordo. The Battle of Cerro Gordo, the quick but messy finale of Santa Anna's ignominious defeat, saw some of the most destructive fighting of the war. The Americans delivered withering fire into the ranks of the Mexicans, who sustained heavy casualties; Scott's army killed or wounded about one thousand Mexicans and took three thousand others prisoner. The remainder of Santa Anna's mauled army fled in disorder, abandoning the dead and wounded. Sixty-three Americans were killed and 353 were wounded. Returning to Mexico City, Santa Ana learned that Mexican forces had been soundly defeated at the Battle of Buena Vista. The Americans tightened the noose on Santa Anna. As the U.S. Army marched toward Mexico City, its residents grew alarmed at the government's failure to protect the city.[69]

In June, a British delegation arrived at General Scott's headquarters and announced that Santa Anna agreed to surrender and bring an end to the war on the condition that the United States halt its advance on Mexico City and send him $10,000 to bribe members of the Mexican government. Santa Anna decided to dupe the Americans; the opportunist and wily Mexican general received the money but had other plans.[70]

On August 7, General Scott started for Mexico City with 10,700 men, half of whom were untrained volunteers. Santa Anna, leading a tattered army of 7,000 soldiers and volunteers, marched to a fortified hill seven miles east of Mexico City. On August 20, a major battle unfolded. Scott launched his attack, and the victorious Americans inflicted heavy losses on the Mexicans; they killed 700 and took more than 800 prisoners, including four generals, while losing only 60 dead or wounded.[71]

Flush with victory, General Scott's army reached Chapultepec Castle two miles southwest of Mexico City on September 12 and began shelling it. The next day the fierce artillery bombardment resumed, followed by an assault to drive the Mexicans from the summit. The Americans poured fire into the Castle. More than eight hundred Mexican soldiers, joined by forty-three young academy cadets, made a valiant stand. Rather than surrender, the cadets, in hand-to-hand combat, fought to their deaths. This disastrous defeat put Mexico firmly under American control. The Mexico City Council summoned General Scott to parlay for the safety of the city's residents. After Mexico surrendered on September 13, the people staged a popular uprising against the American occupiers. Outraged Mexicans armed mostly with stones attacked American forces as they entered the city, which was captured on September 15. Sixteen months after the United States declared war on Mexico, the American army occupied Mexico City. The army remained there for nine months during the peace negotiations between the United States and Mexico. In a final act of defiance, General Santa Anna opened all the jails upon leaving Mexico City, resulting in total chaos and pillaging. Following the government's abandonment of Mexico City, many of its populace began to see the American occupation force as a protector. Some Mexicans cursed Santa Anna with almost as much vehemence as they had damned the Americans with.[72]

Santa Anna, at the head of an army of around 5,700 men, fled Mexico City. His exhausted and frightened army disintegrated before he reached Puebla, and Santa Anna took up residence in the town of Tehuacán. On January 23, 1848, Texas Rangers arrived to capture the Mexican general, but he had slipped away two hours earlier. The United States gave Santa Anna safe passage to Jamaica and exile. The two-year war between the United States and Mexico was over. Mexico suffered tremendous casualties, an estimated 20,000 soldiers killed. The United States lost 1,721 men killed in combat and tallied 11,550 deaths from other causes, mainly disease. A peace treaty was signed by Nicolas P. Trist with Mexican officials at the town of Guadalupe Hidalgo outside Mexico City on February 2, 1848. However, the last confrontation between American and Mexican forces took place on March 16, 1848. Disregarding reports of the signing of the Treaty of Guadalupe Hidalgo as insufficient evidence that the Mexican War had ended, General Sterling Price moved his Missouri Volunteers to Santa Cruz de Rosales in Chihuahua,

Mexico. Here, American soldiers disobeyed Price's order to cease their fire and, driven by racism, savaged the Mexicans.[73]

## THE ENDURING PARADOX: THE TREATY OF GUADALUPE HIDALGO

With the war ended, Mexico established a provisional government at Querétaro. Many Mexicans wanted to continue fighting the United States so as to destroy the Mexican army, discredit the Catholic Church, and thereby institute social reforms. In November, Mexico's government had enough support to establish its legitimacy. Receiving word that the United States was proposing a total annexation of Mexico, the Mexican nation's newly elected president, Pedro María Anaya, commenced negotiations with the United States.[74]

Since the summer of 1847, the debate in the United States had centered on how much of Mexico to annex. An unbounded jingoism by journalists and politicians underscored a strong "all Mexico" movement, demanding the annexation of all of Mexico. Abolitionists fought for the exclusion of slavery from any territory. The Wilmot Proviso stipulated that none of the territory acquired from Mexico should be open to slavery or involuntary servitude. A late attempt to add the Wilmot Proviso to the Treaty of Guadalupe Hidalgo was blocked, however. American racism saved Mexico. Senate members responded to aroused racist passions: the United States should not admit more Indians or mixed-race Mexican Catholics into the American body politic. "Ours is the government of the White man," John C. Calhoun told the Congress. Calhoun, a state's-rights champion and ardent expansionist who as U.S. Secretary of State in 1845 helped secure the annexation of Texas, added that to place nonwhites on an equal footing with white Americans would be a "fatal error." Congress backed the call for the United States to take over Mexico's northern territories because of their sparse population of nonwhites. The Treaty of Guadalupe Hidalgo would be ratified without calling for the annexation of additional Mexican territory populated by people deemed a mongrel race.[75]

Negotiations between the United States and Mexico took place from February 1847 to February 1848. The two countries agreed that the international boundary would follow the course of the Río Grande from the Gulf of Mexico to present El Paso. From El Paso the boundary would go up to the Gila River and then to the Colorado River. From that point the international boundary ran straight across to the Pacific Ocean at the thirty-second parallel.[76] The United States agreed to pay Mexico $15 million for New Mexico and California, to assume responsibility for $3 million dollars in claims by U.S. citizens against Mexico, and to relieve Mexico's debt to the United States. Mexico turned over 55 percent of its land and was given a guarantee of rights for its citizens who had been living in these areas and assured that the United States would prevent Indian attacks across the new border into Mexico. It was the largest land grab since the Louisiana Purchase of 1803. President Polk received the treaty on February 19, 1848, which the U.S. Senate ratified on March 10 after considerable contentious debate. Mexico's Congress ratified the treaty on March 30, though after much deliberation; no Mexican official wanted to be held responsible for the loss of so much of Mexico's territory through war. The United States had fulfilled its Manifest Destiny.[77]

The Treaty of Guadalupe Hidalgo stipulated that all the estimated one hundred thousand non-Indian inhabitants who did not leave Mexico's former northern territory within one year would become American citizens. Although some Mexicans returned to Mexico, most chose to remain in the United States. Articles 8 and 9 of the treaty obliged the United States to protect these new American citizens and guarantee their civil rights, including their right to retain their language, religion, and culture.[78]

The Mexican War and the impact of the Treaty of Guadalupe Hidalgo resulted in further losses of land and civil rights by Tejanos. Things proved much worse for New Mexicans, though the treaty clearly guaranteed that all of the land rights enjoyed by its Spanish-speaking inhabitants under Mexican rule would be respected by the United States. Much of the land in New Mexico was reserved as commons. Through the U.S. Senate's elimination of Article 10, related to the validity of Mexican land grants, many inhabitants of the newly acquired territory lost their lands held in common. Moreover, neither the territorial courts of New Mexico nor the U.S. Supreme Court upheld the common property rights of New Mexicans under the treaty.[79] The American system of land ownership involved accurate surveys and detailed titles and deeds of transfer. In contrast, the Mexican land system was imperfect or unsubstantiated by legal documents, and land grant titles were deposited and recorded in Mexico or in Spain.[80] Consequently, many Mexican Americans could not produce legal title to the lands they owned. The United States established a land claims court, but much of the lands owned by Mexican Americans passed into the public domain for lack of adequate documentation of ownership. The story was the same throughout the Southwest. Utilizing both legal and illegal means, Americans soon dispossessed Mexican Americans of their land. Furthermore, disputed land claims were tied up in the courts for decades and were often decided in favor of Anglo ranching and mining interests.[81]

The Treaty of Guadalupe Hidalgo officially ended the war, but it failed to protect Californio property rights as the Treaty of Cahuenga had promised. Moreover, California beckoned: several weeks before Mexico relinquished California to the United States, gold was discovered at John Sutter's mill in the foothills of the Sierra Nevada. The gold discovery brought thousands of Americans and Mexicans, in addition to interlopers from around the world, to northern California. Racist mob violence broke out as Yankee gold seekers descended on the diggings. The California gold rush produced a decade of turbulence and bloodshed. Anglo-American xenophobia, nativism, and racism were a result of the recent war with Mexico, widespread anti-Catholicism, and competition between American miners and the more experienced polyglot mixture of South American, Mexican, and Chinese miners. Vigilante justice was meted out through hangings, floggings, ear cropping, head shaving, branding, and banishment. The gold rush coincided with industrialization and the formation of the working class in the United States. Anglo-American resentment against slavery as unfair competition with free labor was played out in campaigns against the Mexican miners, whose servitude to their creditors was associated with the master-slave relation. Despite protests by

Mexican officials, there was no protection under the Treaty of Guadalupe Hidalgo for those Mexican gold diggers who were American citizens. The Chinese, who did heavy labor for little pay, similarly became a target for American racism because their wage labor likewise contradicted the ideology of free labor.[82] Violent antipathies heightened as mining fortunes decreased and poisoned relations between Mexican Americans and Anglo-Americans.

By their sheer force of numbers, a tidal wave of American settlers and gold-hungry foreigners transformed California and triggered a process of disenfranchisement. It bore heavily on the Mexican Americans of northern California when frustrated wealth seekers left the gold fields and took over plots of land as squatters. Only in southern California, where they outnumbered the Anglos until the 1870s, did Mexican Californians manage to maintain a degree of social and political dominance, albeit temporary.[83]

In September 1850, California was admitted into the Union as a free state under the Compromise of 1850, which allowed the new American territory of New Mexico to either introduce or ban slavery when its citizenry sought statehood. The deluge of Americans immigrating to California had hastened the call for statehood. National issues also contributed to the situation because the U.S. Congress was deadlocked over the question of the expansion of slavery in the new territories.[84]

Mexican War hero Zachary Taylor took office as President of the United States in March 1849. Taylor supported statehood for California, as well as New Mexico, and told Californians to create a constitution and apply for admission as a free state. Taylor's refusal to oppose the Wilmot Proviso banning slavery from the territory acquired from Mexico infuriated southerners, already angry at attempts to abolish the slave trade in the District of Columbia. From the American takeover of California on July 7, 1846, to 1849, a succession of military governors ruled California. General Bennet Riley became governor of California in April 1849. On June 3 Riley called for a constitutional convention in Monterey to create a government and to organize California as a state. Mariano Vallejo was one of six California Mexican delegates to the constitutional convention. Vallejo, along with delegates José Antonio Carillo and Manuel Domínguez, attempted to protect the interests of the outnumbered California Mexicans—but at the expense of siding with their Anglo colleagues to exclude citizenship rights to Negroes and Indians. California's constitution was drafted using the laws of both Mexico and the United States to accommodate the Mexicans who chose to stay in California. In February 1850, California established a court system that replaced the one the military government had set up based on the Mexican judicial system of alcaldes and prefects (chief judicial officer and chief magistrate). In April 1850, English common law became the judicial basis.[85]

On September 9, 1850, after a long debate on the issue of admitting California as a free state, President Millard Fillmore, who succeeded Taylor following the latter's unexpected death in 1850, signed the bill admitting California to the Union as the thirty-first state. The opposition of southerners in Congress to California's admission to statehood led the Mexican Americans in California to accept the voting system favoring recently arrived Americans.[86]

In April 1851, under the Compromise of 1850, the New Mexico and Utah territories were formed from the rest of the Mexican cession. Because the Spanish-speaking New Mexicans were residents of a United States territory, they were denied full citizenship rights: they could not vote for their governor or for the President of the United States, decisions by the elected officials required federal approval, and they lacked an independent judiciary. Texas gained thirty-three thousand square miles of New Mexico territory and gave up its claims to New Mexico in exchange for the payment of its national debt by the United States government.[87]

A mapping error resulted in a dispute between the United States and Mexico over the location of the border between New Mexico and Mexico. President Franklin Pierce, an expansionist who favored southern interests, had secretly instructed U.S. Minister to Mexico James Gadsden, a South Carolina railroad president, to buy enough territory from Mexico for a railroad to the Gulf of California. Under the treaty provisions a joint Mexican-American commission undertook the task of establishing an international boundary for the two nations. John B. Weller was chief U.S. delegate to the boundary commission. Before meeting with Mexican boundary officials in San Diego, Weller collected information on the metals and flora and fauna in the disputed territory. He had also been instructed to map and recommend future sites for a railroad, road, or canal. United States topographical engineers advised Gadsden that the most direct route for a transcontinental railroad line would be south of the United States boundary. Gadsden began to plan to have the federal government acquire title to the necessary territory from Mexico.[88]

After the war the Mexicans of the Southwest experienced an increase in violence as Comanches, Kiowas, Apaches, and other Indians attacked Mexican settlements in cross-border raids. For example, in 1850, eight hundred Comanches raided Laredo, Texas. Raids claimed thousands of lives and depopulated much of the countryside. Despite diplomacy and the stationing of two thousand American soldiers in the Southwest, Indian marauding could not be controlled. Texas eventually drove all the Indians into the Oklahoma Indian Territory. In New Mexico and Arizona, the Navajo, Apache, and other Indian groups survived, whereas in California, disease, battles, and genocide eliminated most of the Indian population. Those California Indians who survived faced virtual enslavement because they were bound to compulsory labor through the 1850 Act for the Government and Protection of Indians. Contributing to the instability of Indian–Mexican American relations was the migration to Indian lands of Americans, many of them avowed Indian haters.[89]

The difficult task of regulating the hostile Indian frontier was a matter of importance. Many Mexicans in the north had favored annexation to the United States because American forces were protecting their properties from the incursion of Apaches, Comanches, and Navajos. Long and bloody warfare between New Mexicans and Indians in the territory marked the nineteenth century. The Indians had taken advantage of the chaos caused by the Mexican War and the transfer afterward of New Mexico territory to the United States to once more savage their old enemies and enjoy the spoils of raiding. Despite U.S. protection, native New Mexicans succumbed to the increased Indian raiding that extended into Mexico.

Competition over land and livestock grazing versus buffalo hunting placed pressure on many nomadic Indian tribes, forcing them to raid or starve. The use of volunteer forces to carry out U.S. Indian extermination policy worsened conditions further. These volunteers were paid with Indian captives, which only prolonged the fighting. Native New Mexicans in the territorial militia did most of the fighting against the Ute and Jicarilla Apache Indians in the north, the Navajos to the west, and the Gila Apaches in the south. A similar situation existed in the territory of present-day Arizona. The United States asked Mexico to participate in the pacification of the Indians because some of the tribes used Mexico as a safe haven to run raids across the borders.[90] The Indian threat strained relations between the two nations until the 1870s.

Mexico remained in political turmoil. Its army destroyed, the nation suffered from economic deprivation and was wracked by widespread Indian attacks, banditry, raids by American fortune seekers, racial warfare in the Yucatán, and more rebellions and threats of secession. Conservatives in Mexico called for General Antonio López Santa Anna, still viewed by many Mexicans as a hero, to return and restore order. In 1853, Santa Anna became President of Mexico for the eleventh time, but his stay in office would be short.[91]

War-torn Mexico urgently needed money and wanted a settlement of its Indian claims against the United States. In 1853, James Gadsden paid Santa Anna $10 million for a narrow strip of land south of the Gila River in what is now southwestern New Mexico and southern Arizona. It included the rich Santa Rita mines. By a narrow margin, the Senate ratified the Gadsden Purchase in June 1854. The United States acquired nearly thirty million acres for about thirty-three cents an acre. The deal was so unpopular in Mexico that it forced Santa Anna into exile.[92]

## CONCLUSION

In the 1840s, sectionalism between slave and free states dominated American politics, as did an overriding ideology of expansionism. The United States claimed to be destined by divine Providence itself. The presumption of Manifest Destiny was the orienting principle of American foreign policy. The United States would employ military aggression against Mexico, a nation of darker breeds that dared oppose its territorial imperial design. As one historian noted, the Mexican War "provided America with a venue to confront their own internal conflicts as they fought a war . . . in the name of white, Anglo-Saxon supremacy."[93]

Mexico did not enthusiastically support the war because its citizenry seemed more concerned with state versus national citizenship. Lacking a sense of nationalism made it difficult to raise military troops. Mexicans eventually fought for a nation that was weak and whose government was riven by factional intrigue. Moreover, regions most distant from Mexico City, such as Alta California and New Mexico, offered little opposition to the American invading forces during the war. Some lost faith that Mexico's leadership would ever be able to govern and believed that the United States was stronger and hence more likely to provide security. The reason was that regional economies by now were dependent on international trade. New Mexico was a by-product of a quarter century of trade with Americans. Local elites such as New Mexico's Manuel Armijo sought to maintain trade with United States markets. Armijo and other ricos collaborated with the Americans and rejected attempts at popular resistance.[94]

American immigration accounted for population growth in the newly acquired territory. The military conquest of sparsely settled New Mexico and California was easily accomplished. In California, there was little resistance to American conquest and eventual annexation, because the general belief was that nothing would be lost in severing ties with Mexico. Moreover, many Californio elites thought positively of the American democratic form of government. Ultimately, the Californios failed to stop American immigration to California, to take control of the Indians, or to secure money, arms, and troops from Mexico to fight the war against the United States. The gold rush was the first real contest for California. A northern and southern phase of land dispossession took place in the breakup of the California ranches. The Mexicans of California were brought under the heel of Yankee power, prejudice, and vigilantism and ultimately fell into "legislative and political decline."[95] Texas withdrew its claims to the Río Grande as its western boundary in return for the United States assuming its $10 million debt.

The end of the Mexican War and implementation of the Treaty of Guadalupe Hidalgo in 1848 ended the era of the Spanish and Mexican frontier. The American conquest of the Southwest produced local, regional, and national patterns of change and development, but it took the United States a long time to consolidate its victory. Control over Texas and California had to be affirmed; there was the question of settling the deepening sectional controversy; and the numerous warring Indian nations had to be subdued. California was admitted as a free state to offset the earlier annexation of Texas, a slave state, whereas the New Mexico Territory soon became embroiled in the sectional controversy.[96]

California and Texas developed rapidly, whereas New Mexico and Arizona would remain territories for a longer period owing to the large Mexican American and Indian populations deemed unfit for American citizenship. New forms of government were put in place in the former Mexican territories, and new patterns of commerce replaced the older ones. The Southwest was remade in profound ways after the Mexican War's end. The war had disrupted old ways of life and replaced them with new social relationships. One thing was certain. The Mexican Americans of the Southwest found themselves strangers in a strange land, a minority struggling for social acceptance in a sea of Americans.

## NOTES

1. Richard V. Francaviglia and Douglas W. Richmond, eds., *Dueling Eagles: Reinterpreting the U.S.–Mexican War, 1846–1848* (Forth Worth: Texas Christian University Press, 2000), 60.
2. Reséndez, *Changing National Identities, 265–267.*
3. Ibid., 243–244, 249; Weber, *Mexican Frontier,* 272. The secessionists named their separate nation *La republica mexicana del norte* (the Mexican Republic of the North). Its

boundaries would be northward from Chihuahua to the Arkansas River and to Oregon and westward to the Colorado River.

4. Weber, *Mexican Frontier*, 269–270. The new centralist government in Mexico had appointed General Manuel Micheltorena governor of California in 1842.

5. Lizabeth Haas, "War in California, 1846–1848," *California History* 76, nos. 2–3 (1997): 337; Weber, *Mexican Frontier*, 270; Monroy, *Thrown Among Strangers*, 175.

6. Haas, "War in California," 336–337, 341; Weber, *Mexican Frontier*, 270. Pico owned several ranches that he had acquired after the secularization of the missions. Pico's smallest property was his four-thousand-acre Rancho Paso de Bartola. Monroy, *Thrown Among Strangers*, 175–176; Hall, *Social Change in the Southwest*, 193.

7. Henderson, *Glorious Defeat*, 137.

8. Ibid., 137–138.

9. Ibid., 148; John S. D. Eisenhower, *So Far from God: The U.S. War With Mexico, 1846–1848* (Norman: University of Oklahoma Press, 2000), 196, 198; Campbell, *Gone to Texas, 187.*

10. Henderson, *Glorious Defeat*, 138–140, 143–144; Eisenhower, *So Far from God*, 20–22, 24–25; Campbell, *Gone to Texas*, 185. On June 4, Herrera issued the following declaration: "The Mexican nation calls upon all her children to the defense of her national independence, threatened by the usurpation of Texas, which is intended to be realized by the decree of annexation passed by the congress, and sanctioned by the president, of the United States of the north. In consequence, the government will call to arms all the forces of the army . . . for the support of her institutions." Steven R. Butler, ed., *A Documentary History of the Mexican War* (Richardson, TX: Descendants of Mexican War Veterans, 1995), 5.

11. Henderson, *Glorious Defeat*, 150.

12. Eisenhower, *So Far from God*, 45–47; Campbell, *Gone to Texas*, 187–188.

13. Henderson, *Glorious Defeat*, 152–153; Reséndez, *Changing National Identities*, 245; Pedro Santoni, *Mexico at Arms: Puro Federalists and the Politics of War, 1845–1848* (Fort Worth: Texas Christian University Press, 1996), 141–150.

14. Henderson, *Glorious Defeat*, 153–154; Eisenhower, *So Far from God*, 65; Campbell, *Gone to Texas*, 188.

15. Henderson, *Glorious Defeat*, 155; Campbell, *Gone to Texas*, 183.

16. Henderson, *Glorious Defeat*, 155–156; Eisenhower, *So Far from God*, 75–84; Campbell, *Gone to Texas*, 188.

17. Henderson, *Glorious Defeat*, 158–159; Eisenhower, *So Far from God*, 114.

18. The House voted 173 to 14 and the Senate voted 40 to 2 in favor. This vote for war took place despite Mexico's protests that Captain Thornton had crossed its international border, which it asserted began at the Nueces River. Eisenhower, *So Far from God*, 66–68.

19. Reséndez, *Changing National Identities*, 244–246.

20. Deena J. González, *Refusing the Favor: The Spanish-Mexican Women of Santa Fe, 1820–1880* (New York: Oxford University Press, 2001), 6; De Lay, *War of a Thousand Deserts*, 288–289.

21. Reséndez, *Changing National Identities*, 248–249; Stella Drumm, ed., *The Diary of Susan Shelby Magoffin, 1846–1847: Down the Santa Fe Trail and into Mexico* (Lincoln: University of Nebraska Press, 1982), 131–132. Some of these women were whipped by their employers for poor work. González, *Refusing the Favor*, 43–45.

22. Haas, "War in California," 336; U.S. Congress, *Messages to the President of the United States with the correspondence. Therewith Communicated Between the Secretary of War*

*and other Officers of the Government: The Mexican War*, 30th Cong., 1st sess., House Executive Document 60 (Washington, DC: Wendell and Van Benthusyen, 1848), 154; Eisenhower, *So Far from God*, 105; Howard R. Lamar, *The Far Southwest, 1846–1912: A Territorial History* (New Haven, CT: Yale University Press, 1966), 51–52, 55.

23. Reséndez, *Changing National Identities*, 249–251; Eisenhower, *So Far from God*, 208; Lamar, *Far Southwest, 1846–1912*, 53–55; De Lay, *War of a Thousand Deserts*, 255.

24. Reséndez, *Changing National Identities*, 239, 251–252; Richard Bruce Winders, *Crisis in the Southwest: The United States, Mexico, and the Struggle over Texas* (Wilmington, DE: Scholarly Resources, 2002), 102; Eisenhower, *So Far from God*, 209; Lamar, *Far Southwest*, 1846–1912, 54–55; Simmons, *Little Lion of the Southwest*, 91–93.

25. Reséndez, *Changing National Identities*, 238, 253; González, *Refusing the Favor*, 20; Drumm, *The Diary of Susan Shelby Magoffin*, 114; Bernard De Voto, *The Year of Decision, 1846* (Boston: Little, Brown, 1943), 17; Eisenhower, *So Far from God*, 207–208; Lamar, *Far Southwest*, 1846–1912, 53–55.

26. Haas, "War in California," 344; Reséndez, *Changing National Identities*, 250; Winders, *Crisis in the Southwest*, 102; Eisenhower, *So Far from God*, 209–210, 233–234; Lamar, *The Far Southwest, 1846–1912*, 56–58.

27. Eisenhower, *So Far from God*, 234–235; De Lay, *War of a Thousand Deserts*, 257. On the battle of Brazito, see Neil C. Mangum, "The Battle of Brazito: Reappraising a Lost and Forgotten Episode in the Mexican American War," *New Mexico Historical Review* 72, no. 3 (1997): 217–228.

28. Haas, "War in California," 333, 342–343; Eisenhower, *So Far from God*, 219–221; Neal Harlow, *California Conquered: The Annexation of a Mexican Province, 1840–1850* (Berkeley: University of California Press, 1982), 175–177.

29. Reséndez, *Changing National Identities*, 239, 254–257; Lamar, *Far Southwest, 1846–1912*, 59; Simmons, *Little Lion of the Southwest*, 97. See also E. Bennett Burton, "The Taos Rebellion," *Old Santa Fe Journal* 1, no. 2 (1913): 176–192.

30. Reséndez, *Changing National Identities*, 255–256; Lamar, *Far Southwest, 1846–1912*, 59; Simmons, *Little Lion of the Southwest*, 98, 101.

31. Reséndez, *Changing National Identities*, 239; Burton, "The Taos Rebellion," 176–202; Lamar, *The Far Southwest, 1846–1912*, 60.

32. Reséndez, *Changing National Identities*, 254; Eisenhower, *So Far from God*, 237; Lamar, *Far Southwest, 1846–1912*, 60.

33. Eisenhower, *So Far from God*, 237; U.S. Congress, *Message from the President of the United States to the Two Houses of Congress. With Accompanying Documents*, 30th Cong., 2d sess., House Executive Document 1 (Washington, DC: Wendell and Van Benthusyen, 1848), 521; Lamar, *Far Southwest, 1846–1912*, 60; Simmons, *Little Lion of the Southwest*, 101–102.

34. *Niles' National Register*, April 10, 1847; Eisenhower, *So Far from God*, 231–238; U.S. Congress. *Message from the President of the United States to the Two Houses of Congress*, 521–522; Lamar, *Far Southwest, 1846–1912*, 60; Simmons, *Little Lion of the Southwest*, 104–105.

35. Eisenhower, *So Far from God*, 238; Simmons, *Little Lion of the Southwest*, 105.

36. Eisenhower, *So Far from God*, 238.

37. Ibid., 238–239; Simmons, *Little Lion of the Southwest*, 105.

38. Eisenhower, *So Far from God*, 239.

39. Reséndez, *Changing National Identities*, 39–40; Eisenhower, *So Far from God*, 239–240; Michael McNierey, *Taos, 1847: The Revolt in Contemporary Accounts* (Boulder, CO:

Johnson, 1980), 5; Lamar, *Far Southwest, 1846–1912*, 60–61; De Lay, *War of a Thousand Deserts*, 279.

40. Lamar, *Far Southwest, 1846–1912*, 60; Eisenhower, *So Far from God*, 240; Simmons, *Little Lion of the Southwest*, 108.

41. Haas, "War in California," 334–336; Eisenhower, *So Far from God*, 203; Harlow, *California Conquered*, 4–9; Pitt, *Decline of the Californios*, 4, 21.

42. Eisenhower, *So Far from God*, 203–204; Harlow, *California Conquered*, 30; Pitt, *Decline of the Californios*, 4, 21.

43. Haas, "War in California," 338–340; Eisenhower, *So Far from God*, 213–214; Harlow, *California Conquered*, 96, 97–114. The rebels marched under a flag with a single red star and the crude figure of a bear that gave the incident its name.

44. Haas, "War in California," 341–342; Monroy, *Thrown Among Strangers*, 177; Harlow, *California Conquered*, 143. The previous year, Andrés Pico and Juan Manso had been granted a nine-year lease for the San Fernando Valley. Harlow, *California Conquered*, 143–144.

45. Eisenhower, *So Far from God*, 214–215; Harlow, *California Conquered*, 121–126.

46. Eisenhower, *So Far from God*, 215–216.

47. Ibid., 115.

48. Ibid., 114.

49. Henderson, *Glorious Defeat*, 163; Eisenhower, *So Far from God*, 116, 131; De Lay, *War of a Thousand Deserts*, 280.

50. Henderson, *Glorious Defeat*, p.164; Eisenhower, *So Far from God*, 153.

51. Henderson, *Glorious Defeat*, 164–165; Eisenhower, *So Far from God*, 179–191.

52. Haas, "War in California," 333, 342; Eisenhower, *So Far from God*, 216–217; Harlow, *California Conquered*, 147, 159–161; Monroy, *Thrown Among Strangers*, 177–178; Albert Hurtado, *Indian Survival on the California Frontier* (New Haven, CT: Yale University Press, 1988), 82.

53. Haas, "War in California," 343; William David Estrada, *The Los Angeles Plaza: Sacred and Contested Space* (Austin: University of Texas Press, 2008), 53; Eisenhower, *So Far from God*, 217; Harlow, *California Conquered*, 161–163; Monroy, *Thrown Among Strangers*, 178–179.

54. Eisenhower, *So Far from God*, 218; Harlow, *California Conquered*, 162, 167–168, 170.

55. Eisenhower, *So Far from God*, 218.

56. Ibid., 222; Harlow, *California Conquered*, 179, 225.

57. Haas, "War in California," 344; Eisenhower, *So Far from God*, 223; Harlow, *California Conquered*, 185.

58. Eisenhower, *So Far from God*, 223; Harlow, *California Conquered*, 182–185.

59. Haas, "War in California," 344; Eisenhower, *So Far from God*, 223–224; Harlow, *California Conquered*, 187.

60. Eisenhower, *So Far from God*, 224–225; Harlow, *California Conquered*, 188–189.

61. Eisenhower, *So Far from God*, 225–226; Harlow, *California Conquered*, 185, 189–191, 227–228.

62. Haas, "War in California," 344; Eisenhower, *So Far from God*, 228; Harlow, *California Conquered*, 211–213.

63. Haas, "War in California," 344; Eisenhower, *So Far from God*, 228–229; Harlow, *California Conquered*, 215–217.

64. Haas, "War in California," 345; Eisenhower, *So Far from God*, 229–230; Harlow, *California Conquered*, 231.

65. Haas, "War in California," 334, 345; Eisenhower, *So Far from God,* 230; Harlow, *California Conquered,* 232.

66. Frank S. Edwards, *A Campaign in New Mexico with Col. Doniphan* (Philadelphia: Carey and Hart, 1847), 154–156; Eisenhower, *So Far from God,* 246–247. The Texans were "too licentious to do much good," complained General Taylor, and they needed discipline. Robert Walter Johannsen, *To the Halls of the Montezumas: The Mexican War in the American Imagination* (New York: Oxford University Press, 1988), 38. See also Stephen B. Oates, "Los Diablos Tejanos: The Texas Rangers," in *The Mexican War: Changing Interpretations,* 2nd ed., ed. Odie B. Faulk and Joseph A. Stout, Jr. (Chicago: Swallow Press, 1973), 120–136.

67. Henderson, *Glorious Defeat,* 162; Eisenhower, *So Far from God,* 270–271.

68. Henderson, *Glorious Defeat,* 115; Eisenhower, *So Far from God,* 259, 271–272. Mexico issued a decree that any Mexican who sought peace with American forces would be charged with treason. Douglas W. Richmond, ed., *Essays on the Mexican War* (College Station: Texas A & M University Press, 1986), 97–99.

69. Henderson, *Glorious Defeat,* 166–167; Eisenhower, *So Far from God,* 272–283.

70. Henderson, *Glorious Defeat,* 169.

71. Ibid., 165–170. With Santa Anna's forces were 204 deserters from the U.S. army. The deserters were mostly Irish Catholics who had decided that the war with Mexico was in part a religious war of Catholics against Protestants. The Irish formed the Batallón San Patricio (Saint Patrick's Battalion). Among the prisoners taken at the Battle of Chapultepec were men of the St. Patrick's Battalion. Military trials were held, and fifty of them were sentenced to death. General Scott pardoned five of the Irish recruits and reduced the sentences of fifteen others to fifty lashes and the letter D (for desertion) branded on the cheek. The remaining thirty were hanged on September 12. Eisenhower, *So Far from God,* 341–342.

72. Henderson, *Glorious Defeat,* 171; Eisenhower, *So Far from God,* 339–342, 345–346.

73. Henderson, *Glorious Defeat,* 171, 177, 179; Eisenhower, *So Far from God,* 347, 363, 368. Negotiations for peace actually began before the last battles of the Mexican War were fought. See William Gorenfeld, "The Cowpen Slaughter: Was There a Massacre of Mexican Soldiers at the Battle of Santa Cruz de Rosales?," *New Mexico Historical Review* 81, no. 4 (2006): 413–440.

74. Henderson, *Glorious Defeat,* 175; Zoraida Vásquez, "The Colonization and Loss of Texas," 121; Eisenhower, *So Far from God,* 359–360.

75. Henderson, *Glorious Defeat,* 175–176; Zoraida Vásquez, "Colonization and Loss of Texas," 119–120; Eisenhower, *So Far from God,* 286–287.

76. Henderson, *Glorious Defeat,* 177; Manuel Ceballos-Ramírez and Oscar J. Martínez, "Conflict and Accommodation on the U.S. Mexican Border, 1848–1911," in *Myths, Misdeeds, and Misunderstandings: The Roots of Conflict in U.S.–Mexican Relations,* ed. Jaime E. Rodríguez O. and Kathryn Vincent (Wilmington, DE: Scholarly Resources, 1997), 136, 138; Eisenhower, *So Far from God,* 363.

77. Henderson, *Glorious Defeat,* 177–178; Eisenhower, *So Far from God,* 363, 367, 369.

78. Henderson, *Glorious Defeat,* 182; Ceballos-Ramírez and Martínez, "Conflict and Accommodation," 147.

79. Zoraida Vásquez, "Colonization and Loss of Texas," 122.

80. Henderson, *Glorious Defeat,* 182; Richard Griswold del Castillo, *The Treaty of Guadalupe Hidalgo: A Legacy of Conflict* (Norman: University of Oklahoma Press, 1990), 73. In 1869, New Mexico territorial governor William Pile sold a large portion of the Spanish colonial and Mexican archival records as wastepaper.

81. Henderson, *Glorious Defeat,* 182. In 1904, the Court of Private Land Claims approved only 2 million of the more than 35 million acres of land Mexicans claimed under land titles.

82. Henderson, *Glorious Defeat,* 182; Griswold del Castillo, *Treaty of Guadalupe Hidalgo,* 67–68; Pitt, *Decline of the Californios,* 50; Harlow, *California Conquered,* 281; John Boessenecker, *Gold Dust and Gunsmoke* (Hoboken, NJ: Wiley, 1999), 22. In 1849, seven hundred Chinese were in California. By 1850 this number had grown to three thousand, and to ten thousand two years later.

83. Griswold del Castillo, *Treaty of Guadalupe Hidalgo,* 73–75; Monroy, *Thrown Among Strangers,* 180.

84. The U.S. Congress failed to provide a civil government for California following the end of the Mexican War. A longer period of military government ensued in California before a civil administration could assume control.

85. Henderson, *Glorious Defeat,* 180; Griswold del Castillo, *Treaty of Guadalupe Hidalgo,* 66–67; Harlow, *California Conquered,* 317–318, 338, 342, 351; Lamar, *Far Southwest, 1846–1912,* 69; Robert J. Chandler, "An Uncertain Future: The Role of the Federal Government in California, 1846–1880," *California History* 81, nos. 3–4 (2003): 224–271.

86. Harlow, *California Conquered,* 318.

87. Griswold del Castillo, *Treaty of Guadalupe Hidalgo,* 70–71; Robert W. Larson, *New Mexico's Quest for Statehood, 1846–1912* (Albuquerque: University of New Mexico Press, 1968), 19.

88. Ceballos-Ramírez and Martínez, "Conflict and Accommodation," 138–139; Lamar, *Far Southwest, 1846–1912,* 98.

89. Michael Magliari, "Free Soil, Unfree Labor: Cave Johnson Couts and the Binding of Indian Workers in California, 1850–1867," *Pacific Historical Review* 73, no. 3 (August 2004): 349; De Lay, *War of a Thousand Deserts,* 301–302.

90. Ceballos-Ramírez and Martínez, "Conflict and Accommodation," 143; Truett, *Fugitive Landscapes,* 47–48; Hall, *Social Change in the Southwest,* 215, 217; Simmons, *Little Lion of the Southwest,* 111–112. Americans didn't like Article XI of the Treaty of Guadalupe Hidalgo, which held the United States financially liable for Indian raids in Mexico.

91. Henderson, *Glorious Defeat,* 173–174.

92. Ceballos-Ramírez and Martínez, "Conflict and Accommodation," 139; Paul Neff Garber, *The Gadsden Treaty* (Philadelphia: University of Pennsylvania Press, 1923), chapters 4 and 5.

93. Paul Foos, *A Short, Offhand, Killing Affair: Soldiers and Social Conflict during the Mexican-American War* (Chapel Hill: University of North Carolina Press, 2001), 4.

94. Francaviglia and Richmond, *Dueling Eagles,* 99.

95. Haas, "War in California," 341, 344; Pitt, *Decline of the Californios,* 197.

96. Pitt, *Decline of the Californios,* 66–67.

# CHAPTER 4

꙳

# Mexican Americans from the 1850s to the End of the Civil War

A fter the Mexican War, the estimated one hundred thousand Mexicans in the Southwest recently granted U.S. citizenship soon became a dispossessed minority in both numbers and power, as they fell victim to the deep-seated prejudice against nonwhite peoples brought by the arriving Americans. The ruling Democratic Party of the United States was the party of white supremacy and racism. The belief that blacks, Indians, Mexicans, and Chinese were backward races inferior to whites took root. Racist ideas about Mexicans, which served to legitimate the Mexican American War, only grew more virulent after the war. Nativism made itself felt as Anglos lashed out at Mexicans for their indolence, moral laxity, and criminality. Eyeing the new territories in Texas and the West and embracing the mandate of the "right of manifest destiny," land-hungry Americans dispossessed Mexicans of their lands through subtle and extralegal fraud, pressure through tax forfeiture, and squatting, often accompanied by force. This Yankee xenophobia profoundly affected the Mexicans struggling to define themselves as U.S. citizens.[1]

Hostilities broke out from California to the Texas border region as a war of "gringo against greaser" ensued, whereby the latter surrendered their labor and land to the former. The outbreak of disorder in California can be attributed to the rapid pace of social change. Although a free state, California was flooded by Anglos with proslavery views. There was a near absence of civil and legal authority, and, as a result, considerable tension arose between Mexican and Anglo. Equating wage labor with free labor and free men, the latter charged that Mexicans were taking away the work of the white man. Choosing between cowardice and violence, some resentful Mexicans chose violence expressed as robbery and banditry. Lawlessness broke out in the mining camps and along the highways. In this chaotic situation Anglo vigilantes attacked and terrorized Mexicans, associating them with criminality. In the suppression that followed, whites detained and executed Mexicans, many of whom had no involvement in the robberies and killings. These actions served as justification for the activities of the Mexican outlaws: they adopted and applied the same principles of frontier justice used on them.

In Texas, the increasing concentration of land in Anglo hands brought penury to many more Tejanos than ever before. Texas, like the rest of the Southwest, was a frontier region in which there was one standard of justice for the Anglos and another for the Mexicans. Many Anglo-Texans came from the slave South, a region predisposed to extralegal violence and justice. Others had spent time in the California gold fields and had participated in the vigilante justice that targeted Mexicans with floggings and lynchings. The escalating violent conflicts between Anglo-Texans and Tejanos over land highlighted cultural differences and glorified racism.[2]

In South Texas, Tejanos were pitted against Anglo land grabbers as the lives of Tejanos worsened. Anglo-Texans turned to repression and persecution as a means of disciplining Tejanos, even to the point of murdering them. The abuse of Tejanos generated resentment and a desire for retribution. Juan Nepomuceno Cortina enforced their vision of justice; he urged Tejanos to rise up against the Anglos who attacked them and seized their lands. War between Tejanos and Anglos soon seared the South Texas landscape as the full force of the Texas Rangers and the U.S. military concentrated against Cortina and his followers, the *Cortinistas*.

The Civil War divided Mexican Americans between those who saw the conflict as a crusade to preserve the Union and secessionists who believed in state's rights and condemned abolitionists and the Republican Party. Nearly ten thousand Mexican Americans volunteered for military service in both the Confederate and the Union armies. There was Anglo opposition to their recruitment, and racism against Mexican American soldiers was widespread. Anglo officers and soldiers questioned the bravery of the Spanish-speaking troops. Disciplined fighting men, Mexican Americans played decisive roles in the Southwest and held fast in the southern campaigns, in which they experienced horrific carnage and savagery in some of the Civil War's most famous battles. Regular Army soldiers taken out of the Southwest for service in the Union and Confederate armies left local settlements exposed to renewed Indian attacks. Following the end of the Civil War, Mexican American soldiers in the New Mexico and Arizona territories fought the Indians, often alongside African Americans of the Tenth Cavalry.[3]

American racism became even more pronounced after the Civil War, and by 1870 violence once again was on the upswing in the Southwest region. Anglos, many of them southern whites loyal to the defeated Confederacy, fled to the Southwest and subjected Mexican Americans to new extremes of racism, thereby stoking the fires of future conflicts. In the midst of growing hostility a new society developed in the Southwest. It matured with the building and consolidation of an American economic empire in the region.[4]

## MEXICAN AMERICANS
## IN THE POSTCONQUEST SOUTHWEST

The Territory of New Mexico was created on September 9, 1850, and consisted of present-day New Mexico, Arizona, and parts of present-day southern Colorado, southern Utah, and southern Nevada. In 1863, New Mexico was divided in half, and the western portion became the Arizona Territory. New Mexico and Arizona remained territories until 1912 because the majority of the inhabitants were Mexican or Indian and thus considered inassimilable and unqualified for citizenship.[5]

Arizona was a military outpost first under Mexico and then under the United States. Arizona's Santa Cruz Valley grew and became a prosperous center of trade, farming, and ranching. The Apaches and Mexicans were longtime enemies. The Apache Indians raided regularly and kept the Santa Cruz Valley in a virtual state of siege. The Apaches especially hated the professional scalp hunters among the Mexicans, paid by the governors of Mexican states of Sonora and Chihuahua starting in 1835 to bring in scalps of warriors, women, and children in a systematic attempt to exterminate them. Because of Apache depredations, the Spanish-speaking settlers deserted Tubac and abandoned the ranches on the San Pedro River and Babocómari Creek located on the San Ignacio Babocómari land grant. Fewer than a thousand Mexicans lived in the Tucson area.[6]

The United States acquired that portion of Arizona in which Tucson was located from Mexico through the Gadsden Purchase, which transferred more Mexicans to the United States. On January 1, 1856, the U.S. Army took possession of the Tucson presidio as Mexico's Adjutant Inspector Ignacio Pesqueíra directed the transfer of the Mexican residents to Imuris, Sonora, one hundred miles to the south. The residents could choose to stay and become U.S. citizens. Less than half left, but many returned to Tucson. With the arrival of large numbers of Anglos in Arizona, the Apaches began to raid more vigorously and ventured as far as Mexico. In addition to relentless Indian attacks, the Mexicans in Arizona now experienced Anglo racism.[7]

New Mexico changed during the American territorial period. The Old Spanish Trail provided an important connection to California, and the construction of forts resulted in an economic boom. New settlements were started along the Río Hondo, in the Valley of the Río San Francisco close to Arizona, and in the San Juan Basin in the northwest area of the territory.[8]

Anglo racism became pronounced in New Mexico. Native New Mexicans remained the dominant population, with some ricos holding positions of power; the basis for this racism was competition for local trade, land, and other resources.[9] Authorities connived with speculators and, abetted by New Mexico's ricos, seized more than 75 percent of the land owned by native New Mexicans. The land grab included community grants and communal holdings. New Mexicans forfeited their lands owing to their inability to document ownership or pay the steep taxes. The Surveyor General Claims Office could not process claims fast enough to prevent the takeover. Even the U.S. government seized the opportunity to acquire land for the public domain.[10]

The gold rush did much to mold California society, for it fueled the postwar immigration of eighty thousand Americans to California. Many of the arrivals were Mexican War veterans and southerners with proslavery views who deemed Mexicans a conquered people, a despised race with no equality before the law. Immigration to California continued at a fast pace, so that by 1852 the state census counted two hundred sixty thousand non-Indian residents. Northern California received most of the migration, whereas southern California remained Mexican. This reality factored into the debate over dividing the state in half, as happened with the New Mexico territory.[11] California's Indian population was the first to feel the sting of Anglo wrath.

Indians were hunted down like animals and shot under American rule as a "veritable slaughter of Indians occurred all over California. . . ." Of the remaining one hundred thousand Indians, fifty thousand would die of disease, starvation, and murder. Violence against Mexicans likewise simmered. Having decimated the Indian populations near the gold fields, Americans resented the Spanish-speaking miners in the diggings. The Mexicans were considered undesirables, for California was now "American," obtained through the rite of conquest, and thus the profits from its gold fields belonged to them. Ignoring posted threatening notices and unwilling to give up their claims and the mines they had developed, the Mexicans and other Spanish-speaking people came under attack by armed militias. Anglos roamed the countryside targeting the Mexicans, because killing a greaser risked little punishment.[12]

The rapidly established Anglo majority in California, backed by the new Democratic state legislature, passed laws imposing restrictions on Mexicans. To limit Mexican access to the mines, the state legislature in 1850 enacted a $20-per-month Foreign Miners Tax. Counties with large numbers of Spanish-speaking people were taxed at a rate five times higher than other parts of the state. Violence against Mexicans, Indians, and the Chinese accompanied the racist tax because local Anglo militias enforced it. Thousands of Mexicans fled from the

**"Hounds" Attacking Chilean Miners, 1849.**
CREDIT: "'Hounds of San Francisco' attacking Chileans, 1849." Courtesy of the Bancroft Library, University of California, Berkeley, California.

growing chaos in the gold fields. They headed south to Los Angeles or else crossed into Mexico, all of them carrying bitter hatred of the Americans.[13]

Some Mexicans put up resistance to the new Foreign Miners Tax imposed on them and on the Chinese miners. On May 19, 1850, in the town of Sonora, a large gathering of Spanish-speaking miners protested the tax enacted to deport them from the gold fields. Outnumbering the protestors, angry whites retaliated with violence. They lynched scores of Mexicans and placed additional barriers against those who remained in the mother lode. Many Mexicans turned to violence to avenge the Anglo racist violence. Local and state authorities quickly responded in kind.[14]

Through additional legal racialization, Anglos consolidated their control over Mexicans in California. The state legislature enacted laws prohibiting such amusements as bull- and bear-baiting and cockfighting. The right to assemble and associate peacefully was denied or severely curtailed. Most brutal were the antivagrancy provisions. In 1855, a law known as the "Greaser Law" was passed. The disparagements "greaser," "yellow-bellied greaser," and "half-bred greaser" came into use during the Mexican War. The law stated "persons commonly known as 'greasers' who are vagrants and who go armed may be punished." The antivagrancy law provided one more justification for expropriating lands belonging to Mexicans in northern California. Another repressive law overturned the requirement that California state laws be translated into Spanish. These popular forms of justice further stirred deep anti-Anglo sentiment among Mexicans. Finally, there was growing vigilantism and squatter violence against Spanish-speaking landowners.[15]

The land on the California coast and in the interior valleys was owned by about two hundred Californio families and totaled fourteen million acres in parcels averaging 45,000 acres to 49,500 acres.[16] The land grants to a large extent lacked surveyed boundaries and were closed to preemption or to free homestead. Anglos who had come to California tried farming when their quest for gold proved fruitless. Learning about the 160-acre preemption and homestead rights settlers were using elsewhere in the West, the ex-gold seekers rushed to stake out their claims in California by direct occupation and working of the land through squatting. Squatter violence was rampant in these early years. Many squatters banded together or formed associations for aggressive action on behalf of their interests. Ignoring or expressing indifference to the property and civil rights provisions of the Treaty of Guadalupe Hidalgo and emboldened by the Federal Land Grant Act of 1851 that violated the specific provisions of the Treaty of Guadalupe Hidalgo, the squatters did not distinguish public lands from those included in the Mexican grants. Overlapping land claims erupted into a series of ongoing disputes that clogged the legal system.[17]

Most of the Spanish and Mexican land grants were vaguely described, seldom recorded on paper, and split by inheritance. Already burdened by heavy taxes and lacking capital, Californio landowners now had to legally confirm their claims. Verifying a land claim was a long and stringent process and, because either side could appeal a court decision, very expensive. Lawyers' fees averaged between 25 and 40 percent of the land grant's value. Cases were argued before U.S. judges and a Board of Land Commissioners established through the Federal Land Grant Act of 1851. The act ordered that all land titles held under Spanish or Mexican grants were invalid and must be submitted for verification. The act mandated that either side could appeal to the U.S. District Court and the U.S. Supreme Court. It further stated that land claims not submitted within two years would be automatically forfeited. Californio land was the chief target of this federal act. Poorly trained government lawyers were unfamiliar with Spanish and Mexican legal principles and the land tenure system on which grants were based. Precedents were set that hampered efforts to distinguish between legal, fraudulent, and undocumented land titles. Some questionable land claims were confirmed, and other claims had their boundaries extended. Many Californios could not speak English; moreover, they were ignorant of American law and had to take out high-interest loans to cover the legal costs or else pay their legal fees with land. As a result, those who verified their land titles were ruined by the expense of adjudication; the land often fell into the hands of their lawyers as payment for their services. Landownership as a result became concentrated in the hands of speculators who took 40 percent of the great estates the old-line Californio families had owned prior to 1846.[18]

Between 1852 and 1857, the Board of Land Commissioners reviewed more than 800 Spanish and Mexican land titles, involving about twelve million acres of land. Of these claims, 549 were appealed, some claims as many as six times. Because of multiple appeals, litigation of land cases dragged on for an average time of seventeen years. The remaining land claims were either rejected or withdrawn and became the property of the federal government, which sold the land at auction. The Americans' lust for land, believed to be rightfully theirs through preemption, and the Californios failure to understand the American legal system led to the latter's wholesale dispossession.[19] The self-aggrandizing Californios were essentially knocked off their lofty perch.

On the other hand, the enormous food needs of the northern California gold fields proved an economic boon to many cattle ranchers in southern California. Spanish-speaking ranchers driving their cattle north to the lucrative markets could demand from $30 to $40 a head, or a price ten times greater than that of the previous hide-and-tallow era.[20]

However, the southern phase in the decline of the Californio ranches set in. As cattle ranching spread westward, Spanish-speaking ranchers faced competition from stockmen in Texas, New Mexico, and the Plains States who began to drive cattle and sheep to California. This new source of meat was of better quality and less expensive. Soon the demand for local beef fell off sharply. Moreover, during the record-breaking floods in the winter of 1861–1862 in California, the so-called "Noachian Deluge of California Floods," hundreds of thousands of Californio-owned livestock died. This deluge-induced die-off of livestock was followed by two years of severe drought in which immense swarms of locusts devastated the water-stressed cattle pastures, resulting in nearly three million cattle dying through starvation, or approximately half of California's cattle. This succession of natural catastrophes, along with overexpansion, poor investments, and unregulated and high interest rates, sounded the death knell for Californio ranchers. Many of them, already in debt and laden with unpaid property taxes, went bankrupt. The breakup of the huge Mexican land grants quickened through sale and subdivision to a host of speculators. By 1871, livestock grazing ceased to be an important economic factor in southern California. It had succumbed to overgrazing, the rise of the sheep industry, and the conversion of range land to agricultural uses.[21] With large tracts of pasturelands turned into farms, Mexican vaqueros and sheepshearers no longer could find work, and they moved to cities and towns. They were confined to itinerant work because white union workers who refused to work with them excluded Mexicans from the skilled work.

As Anglos gained dominance in California, the elite Californios lost their social, racial, and political standing. Their land taken away, their wealth lost, and their political power on the decline, the dispossessed Californios responded by embracing their whiteness and emulating the aristocratic cultivation of Spanish hidalgos. That is, they claimed the privileges of whiteness by emphasizing their "blue Spanish blood" (*sangre azul*). They took great pains to distinguish themselves from the thousands of Sonoran Mexican mestizos or "cholos" emigrating from Mexico, whom they disdained as inferior, deprived, and below their station. However, to Anglos caught up in the derogatory dogma about inferior races, Californios and Mexicans were a vanquished race, all one and the same: "greasers" and "greaseritas." Whites further charged that "as a hybrid race Mexicans represented the worst nightmare of what might become of the white race if they let down their racial guard." A mestizo, but mistaken as an Indian, Manuel Domínguez in April 1857 was barred from giving testimony for the defense because of prohibitions against testimony from Indians. Domínguez was a wealthy landowner, a Los Angeles County Supervisor, and a delegate to the State constitutional convention and signer of the constitution.[22] In Los Angeles, Mexican American journalist Francisco Ramírez, with his ally José Elias González, lashed out at American racism that now deeply marred the California landscape. Through the columns of his newspaper *El Clamor Publico*, Ramírez condemned lynchings, supported reforms, opposed slavery and squatters, and spoke out vigorously against the courts, one of the key instruments of racist power, trying Mexican land claims. His articles on growing discrimination proved powerful in arousing moral indignation among California's Mexican Americans.

Francisco Ramírez quickly established a reputation among California Mexicans as a defender of their rights. The young Mexican American journalist launched his newspaper in July 1855. The first statewide Spanish-language newspaper of the post-Mexican War era, *El Clamor Publico* published weekly until August 1859. Born in Los Angeles in 1837, Ramírez was a printer and former editor for *La Estrella*, the Spanish edition that occupied two pages of the weekly tabloid the *Los Angeles Star*. Ramírez was a strong admirer of the democratic principles of both Benito Juárez and Abraham Lincoln, and he became the unofficial voice of the Mexican people of California. The principal subjects engaging editorial opinion in *El Clamor Publico* were strong views against lynchings and the public floggings introduced at the Los Angeles Plaza in 1850 by a local vigilante committee.[23]

*El Clamor Publico* at first urged cooperation between Mexicans and Anglos because Ramírez endorsed the American ideals of "popular government, economic progress, civil rights, and . . . peace." However, the mounting number of lynchings and murders of Mexicans by Anglo mobs deeply angered Ramírez. For example, in February 1857 a justice of the peace assembled the local Mexicans outside the San Gabriel Mission to watch as he sliced off the head of the recently killed robber Miguel Soto and then stabbed repeatedly at the corpse. It prompted the Mexican American journalist to exclaim in his newspaper's editorial pages that American democracy and law was hypocritical. "Why trouble to publish California's laws in Spanish and English?" Ramírez asked. "What language they may be published in does not matter much—in Kanaka or Chinese it is the same if we are always to be governed by Lynch Law. Everyone understands perfectly the words 'hang! hang!'" *El Clamor Publico* disparaged the new American government for failing to protect the rights of Mexicans. Ramírez exhorted the Spanish-speaking community to unite against these prejudices.[24]

Journalist Francisco Ramírez was one of the few Mexican Americans in the mid-nineteenth century aware of the scale of Mexican American subjugation to Anglos. Through his newspaper, Ramírez defended the rights of Mexicans, promoted public education for them, instructed its readership in American civics, and advocated for their assimilation. Ramírez told Mexicans "like it or not, we are under the American flag . . . let us divest ourselves of all bygone traditions, and become Americanized all over—in language, in manners, in customs and habits." Distributed throughout California as far north as San Francisco, *El Clamor Publico* was an important source of information about local, state, and national politics and international news and remained committed to improving the lot of the mass of Mexicans. The cause of Ramírez's downfall and the demise of his newspaper was his outspoken opposition to the expansion of slavery, one of the issues embraced by the newly emerged Republican Party, opposed to slavery. Ramírez's views were opposed by the state's proslavery Democrats.[25] Nonetheless, Francisco Ramírez began a tradition of social and political commentary in articulating the concerns and the dilemmas faced by Mexican Americans in the 1850s. In what many Californians called acts of crime, a handful of Mexican bandits meted out their own brand of justice on their enemies for vengeance.

## THE CALIFORNIO BANDITTI JOAQUÍN MURIETA AND TIBURCIO VASQUEZ

In the years following the Mexican War, murder, robbery, and intimidation were frequent occurrences in nearly every town and were meted out universally. Most of this social disorder was attributed to Mexicans, though the bands of thieves included Anglo drifters, ex-convicts, fugitives from the law, and Army deserters. In California, mobs of nativist roughnecks such as the El Monte Boys of Los Angeles took justice into their own hands. Suspected malefactors were searched for, apprehended, and brought before impromptu citizens' courts, which pronounced sentences. The vigilante committees lynched some Mexicans, jailed or flogged others, and exiled still others as the crime of murder was generally equated with other crimes such as cattle and horse theft and robbery.[26]

Mexicans and Anglos both shared the responsibility for the mayhem that plagued the Southwest. In California, years of distrust and animosity between Anglo and Mexican erupted into violence and lawlessness. Joaquín Murieta, Juan García, Tiburcio Vásquez, and lesser lights who engaged in highway murder and robbery for personal gain became the embodiment of Mexican criminality.

The most famous of the California outlaw-heroes in legend of the early 1850s was Joaquín Murieta. Murieta's myth grew; he captured the rage that California's Mexican people felt toward Anglo injustice. Joaquín Murieta was born in Sonora, Mexico. As a young man, Murieta was one of the thousands of Mexicans from Sonora who left for California between 1848 and 1850. From 1850 to 1851 Murieta panned the rivers for gold in the Stanislaus mining district. He was soon caught up in the anti-Mexican climate created by the heightened racial tensions that exploded in violence. According to the story of Murieta, he had been a peaceful miner in the California gold fields until Anglos jumped his claim, killed his father and brother, and drove his mother out of the family ranch. These actions forced the young Murieta to avenge himself on all whites. As a hunted Mexican, he went into hiding and became a thief and a bandit in order to survive. So began the notorious career of Joaquín Murieta. A wave of highway robberies plagued much of northern and southern California's valleys and mountains and served to keep tensions high; almost every crime committed was blamed on Murieta, and the price on his head grew. With Bernardino García (Three-Fingered Jack) and his other partners in crime, Murieta raided ranches and towns until he was allegedly captured and killed in an ambush. The Mexican robbers enjoyed widespread support from Spanish-speaking lower classes, which did not regard them as bandits but as heroes who had righted wrongs even though by illegal actions. Unfortunately, the bandit activity brought retribution to all Mexicans.[27]

Using the mountains to hide and protect themselves, the bands of brigands began robbing and murdering travelers, stealing cattle and horses, and looting stores and saloons. As the disorder spread across California, Anglos attributed all the crimes to Mexicans, even though many of the crimes were committed by Anglos. The Spanish-speaking highwaymen who terrorized the California countryside all seemed to be named Joaquín, with the surnames Botilleras, Ocomorenia, Valenzuela, Carrillo, and Murieta.[28]

The growing accounts of Joaquín Murieta's exploits, combined with pressure from the Anglo population and from Californios such as Andrés Píco, forced the state of California to take action. On May 17, 1853, it passed a bill authorizing the formation of the California Rangers, hired mercenaries modeled after the Texas Rangers, to reduce lawlessness in the region. The mounted rangers were under the leadership of Los Angeles County deputy sheriff Harry Love. The "well armed and equipped" California Rangers, some of them gunfighters and Indian hunters, were ordered to capture the "party or gang of robbers commanded by the five Joaquíns, Muriati, Ocomorenia, Valenzuela, Botellier, and Carillo." Californio legislator Antonio María de la Guerra insisted on adding these specific surnames to the bill given that its original language made every Mexican in California named Joaquín suspect. Governor John Bigler then posted a $1,000 reward for any of the Joaquíns captured or killed.[29]

On July 25, 1853, the California Rangers came upon a group of Mexicans near Panoche Pass west of Tulare Lake. The peace officers cornered the "Murieta gang" and, in the ensuing gunfight, fatally wounded Joaquín Valenzuela, killed Three-Fingered Jack, and two other bandits. The California Rangers cut off Three-Fingered Jack's head and hand, and an Army surgeon at Fort Miller preserved the severed head in a jar of whiskey. The same was done to the head of Joaquín Valenzuela. These acts were carried out for the reward and as a token of the defeat of the Mexicans. The California state legislature accepted the grisly evidence and awarded Captain Harry Love and his California Rangers their blood money.[30]

However, it became difficult to sort out fact from fiction as to the details of what actually occurred during the shootout. The editor of the *San Francisco Alta California* charged that the California state legislature created the fictive Murieta to justify the money appropriated to fight the "Joaquín War."[31] The editor put the story of the capture of Joaquín Murieta this way:

> A few weeks ago a party of native Californians and Sonorans started for the Tulare Valley for the . . . purpose of running mustangs. Three of the party have returned and report that they were attacked by a party of Americans, and that the balance of their party, four in number, had been killed; that Joaquín Valenzuela . . . was killed . . . and that his head was cut off by his captors and held as a trophy. It is too well known that Joaquín Murieta was not the person killed by Captain Harry Love's party at the Panoche Pass.[32]

Murieta's alleged pickled head was the prize trophy of the struggle with Mexican bandits. The severed head was displayed in San Francisco at John King's Saloon on Sansome Street and could be seen for the price of a dollar. In 1856, the head was taken on a world tour by its owner as a money-making scheme. It remained a popular museum piece at Dr. Jordan's Museum of Anatomy and Natural Science in San Francisco for young and old alike until the 1906 earthquake. The legend of Joaquín Murieta, a wronged man who sought vengeance on society, was pieced together from conflicting, contradictory, and fraudulent evidence. It grew and endured as a result of the 1854 publication of *The Life and Adventures of Joaquín Murieta, Celebrated California Bandit* by John Rollins Ridge. To many Americans fed on racism, the fictional Joaquín Murieta symbolized the violent nature and lawlessness of Mexicans of 1850s California in general. For Mexicans, angered by Anglo nativism, the myth of the good-bad man Murieta filled their need for heroic villains. Joaquín Murieta's folklore image as an unvanquished hero endured.[33]

After Joaquín Murieta, the most notorious of the California bandits was Tiburcio Vásquez. Like other Mexicans who had been jailed, flogged, or chased back into Mexico, Vásquez was a product of the particularly violent clashes between Anglos and Mexicans in California. The highway robbers and cattle rustlers either were emigrants from Mexico, came from old-line California families as did Simón Píco or, like Tiburcio Vásquez, were from the lower classes. These men committed crimes because they were motivated by personal aggrandizement or revenge.[34]

Tiburcio Vásquez was born in Monterey in 1835. The native Californian attended school and could speak, read, and write English. He nurtured an intense hatred of Anglos and the institutions dominated by them. As a sixteen-year-old in 1851, Vásquez and several other Mexicans were falsely accused of taking part in the murder of a local constable during a fandango in Monterey. From this time forth, Vásquez embarked on a life of cattle rustling, stage robbing, and other crimes until he was caught. He joined a gang of outlaws and eventually led his own group of highwaymen that ranged up and down central and southern California.[35]

In 1857, Tiburcio Vásquez was caught horse stealing in Los Angeles, convicted, and sentenced to San Quentin prison for his crime. Two years later, on June 25, 1859, Vásquez, along with forty-one other men, escaped from prison; but he was recaptured on August 17. After serving his full prison term, Vásquez was released on August 13, 1863, and endeavored to lead a peaceful and honest life. However, he resumed his life as a brigand and was sent to San Quentin again from January 1867 until June 4, 1870. Vásquez had spent almost ten years of his life in San Quentin and the rest as a bandit and gambler. He and his men committed robberies and murders over a four-year period in the San Benito County area and made their way to southern California. Once again, Vásquez was a fugitive from the law but no longer an unknown bandit; he had a dual price on his head, $3,000 alive and $2,000 dead, for robbing and killing three men at Snyder's Store in Tres Pinos on August 26, 1873. For several months, Vásquez managed to elude law enforcement officers and vigilante committees of three counties by hiding in the canyons around the Tejón Pass. He would be betrayed by one of his own men, Abdon Leyva.[36]

Following a quarrel with Tiburcio Vásquez, Abdon Leyva surrendered to the authorities and, to save his own neck, agreed to turn state's evidence against Vásquez. Leyva revealed that the wanted highwayman was hiding out at a shack in the Arroyo Seco area ten miles north of Los Angeles. On the morning of May 14, 1874, Los Angeles County Sheriff William Richard Rowland and a posse left Los Angeles to apprehend and arrest Vásquez. Six armed peace officers charged the cabin, but Vásquez dove out the window and ran. He was hit by a shotgun blast as he fled. "Don't shoot me," exclaimed the wounded Vásquez, throwing up his hands. "You've got me." The posse closed in on the Mexican, blood running from his wounded arms and leg. "You boys have got me," repeated Vásquez. "My name is Alejandro Martínez." "I have had your photograph for years," countered Undersheriff Albert Johnson, "and know you to be Tiburcio Vásquez."[37]

Why did Vásquez choose a life of crime? After his capture, Vásquez told a *Los Angeles Star* reporter in an interview on May 16, 1874: "A spirit of revenge took possession of me. I had numerous fights in defense of what I believed to be my rights and those of my countrymen." Nine days after his capture, Vásquez was transported from Los Angeles on the steamer *Senator* up the California coast to San Jose to stand trial for the two murders he allegedly committed at Tres Pinos. Thousands came to visit or catch a glimpse of Tiburcio Vásquez, who became a major tourist draw, and many of the outlaw's visitors supported him. Convicted of two murders on January 9, 1875, Vásquez was sentenced to death on January 23. Despite rumors that the Mexican government was sending troops to his rescue, as well as an unsuccessful appeal, Tiburcio Vásquez was hanged on March 19, 1875. Allowed to make a short speech, the only word Vásquez spoke from the gallows was "Pronto." His final capture and execution brought to an end the rash of banditry by Mexicans in California.[38] Not all outlawry was political protest against social injustice, for, as the example of Tiburcio Vásquez illustrates, many Mexican bandits often fell far short of their heroic images. Nevertheless, such legends die hard.

The worst outbreaks of violence in the Southwest occurred in Texas as a result of the ongoing conflict between Mexicans and Anglos. The discontent was aggravated by land disputes. The Nueces strip that extended to the border region became particularly fraught with violence as Tejano landowners and Anglo-Texan ranchers and land speculators began to face off against each other. Sporadic fighting between ranchers, irregular militia, and army troops from both sides of the Río Grande dated to the Texas Revolution. The Texas Constitution aided Anglos in taking property from the Tejanos. It allowed confiscation of land if the owner had left the land vacant, had refused to participate in the Texas Revolution, or had aided Mexico in the struggle. By 1854, the twenty-five thousand Tejanos who lived in Texas formed the majority of the population in the South Texas region. They had lost much of their land and had no political power.[39] Of the fifty thousand Anglos living in Texas, one of every four was a slave owner, and 80 percent had come from slave-holding states. Texas teemed with racism because of the growing sectional conflict. Anglo-Texans embraced the mantle of white supremacy.

## JUAN CORTINA: CHAMPION AND HATED VILLAIN OF THE TEXAS BORDER REGION

The Texas Revolution had been a slaveholder's conspiracy. Proslavery Texans held that Tejanos did not have the same rights as "white folk" because they were "yaller niggers," a cut above the black slaves with whom Tejanos sympathized. Abolition was an attack on property rights, and it encouraged slave uprisings. Despite threats and violence against antislavery advocates, Tejanos took part in the struggle to end slavery and risked their lives in the process. They rescued runaway slaves, hid them, fed them, and at great risk guided them to safe passage across the Río Grande at Laredo and Eagle Pass. When the Texas Rangers captured Tejano abolitionists, they immediately executed them. Racist passions in Texas were further enflamed when the Know-Nothing Party appeared in 1854. Several Texas counties had organized vigilance committees to investigate threats of slave insurrections and to punish lawbreakers. In September 1854, Anglo-Texans in the South Texas town of Seguín drafted a resolution prohibiting Mexican "peons" from residing in or entering Texas and associating with black slaves. Similar resolutions were passed by Anglos representing eight South Texas counties who met in Gonzales to discuss actions against Tejanos who helped runaway slaves escape to Mexico via an underground railroad. In Austin, a citizen's committee threatened violence against the "half-negro, half-Indian greasers" if they did not leave town within ten days. Two years later, authorities aided by white mobs ran out all the Tejanos from Colorado and Matagorda counties, concluding that Mexicans had aided a slave insurrection. In Uvalde County west of San Antonio, officials prohibited Tejanos from passing through the area without a passport. Meanwhile, in the area of Goliad and Karnes counties, southeast of San Antonio, tensions between Tejanos and Anglo-Texans culminated in the so-called cart war. Sparked by racism and economic competition, the cart war was a terrorist campaign against Tejano *carreteros* (cart men) by rival Anglo-Texan freighters determined to take over the relatively lucrative freight trade.[40]

Tejanos and Mexican fleteros hauled freight from the Texas port of Indianola to San Antonio and to other towns in the Texas interior, charging less than Anglo freighters. On July 3, 1857, at Manauila Creek in Goliad County, Anglo-Texans attacked carreteros and wounded some of them. For more than a year, bands of heavily armed Anglo-Texans wearing masks intercepted and destroyed the carts, stole the freight, shot and killed scores of Mexican freighters, and generally disrupted the cart traffic. Because public sentiment weighed heavily against the carreteros, whom area Anglo-Texans regarded as "greasers" and a "nuisance" and who helped slaves to escape, nothing was done by local authorities to stop the crimes or apprehend the criminals. Mexico protested the hostilities that had thus resulted in the willful killing of seventy-five Tejano freight men to U.S. Secretary of State Lewis Cass. The Mexican Embassy in Washington, DC, reported that posses of armed Texans "have been organized for the exclusive purpose of hunting down Mexicans on the highway, despoiling them of their property, and putting them to death." Cass urged Texas Governor Elisha M. Pease to take action in the matter. The Texas Legislature approved setting aside monies for the protection of the carreteros, but no law was passed to guarantee their safety. In fact, Goliad County's citizens warned Tejanos that any Mexican caught committing a crime would be swept "from the face of the earth." For many Tejanos the cart wars remained a potent metaphor for Anglo-Texan racism.[41]

The general disorder in the South Texas border region over Tejano lands escalated into a confrontation between Anglos and Tejanos. Through adverse court rulings, swindling, and coercion, Anglo speculators and Mexican War veterans were consolidating land ownership and water rights in the Río Grande Valley. Unlike California and New Mexico, the federal government played no role in the land issue in Texas because Texas entered the Union with control over all its public lands. Anglo-Texans challenged the claims of the original heirs to the Espíritu Santo grant and turned on the Tejanos, sowing the seeds of the Cortina War. The border region's Tejanos did not yield their land without a fight. Their resistance was considered an "uprising" that needed to be savagely suppressed.[42]

Juan Nepomuceno Cortina became the self-appointed champion of the border region Tejanos. He was born in Camargo, Tamaulipas, Mexico, on May 16, 1824, into a prominent landowning family who for three generations had lived along the Río Grande. During the Mexican War, Cortina enlisted in the National Guard of Tamaulipas, served as a scout, and fought against General Zachary Taylor's troops at the battles of Palo Alto and Resaca de la Palma. Following the end of the war, the Cortina family became American citizens under the provisions of the Treaty of Guadalupe Hidalgo. Juan Cortina worked briefly for a contractor in the U.S. Quartermaster Corps, ironically assisting the army he had previously fought against. In 1850, the Tejano was involved in several filibustering expeditions financed by local Anglo-Texan merchants wanting to form the "Republic of the Sierra Madre" out of the Río Grande region south of New Mexico. On the death of his father in 1855, Cortina's family moved to the Espíritu Santo grant located in the southern Nueces strip near Brownsville, Texas. Juan Cortina became a cattle rancher and endeared himself to the local vaqueros, who nicknamed him "Cheno." Active in politics, he gained some power in the local Democratic Party as leader of the Tejano vote. Texas governor Sam Houston counted on Cortina (who had opposed Houston's election to governor) to prevent Texas from seceding from the Union. Like Houston, Cortina opposed slavery. The elite Tejano rancher won over the poor Tejanos of South Texas because he responded to their strongly felt antipathies toward Anglos who abused them because of their race.[43]

Cortina acquired his reputation as a defender of the rights of poor Tejanos on July 13, 1859, after witnessing Brownsville marshal Bob Spears, an ex-Texas Ranger, humiliate an old vaquero who formerly worked on the Cortina ranch, then brutally pistol-whip him until he was bloody and nearly unconscious. Cortina chose to avenge the assault. The Tejano shot Spears, carried the injured vaquero to his mother's ranch, and then slipped across the border into Mexico. Two months later, Cortina, at the head of over seventy Tejanos, two-thirds of them from Cameron County, attacked Brownsville. They freed a dozen jailed Tejanos, killed three Anglos, and then rode out of town shouting "*Mueran los gringos!*" ("death to the gringos"). In a *pronunciamiento* (proclamation) written by Cortinista Miguel Peña and issued at his mother's ranch, Juan Cortina cited his reasons for avenging the injustices Tejanos suffered at the hands of Anglo-Texans. Cortina vowed that he and his men would continue their fight for justice and commenced a campaign of harassment of the isolated settlements and towns along the Río Grande from Brownsville to as far as Eagle Pass, Texas. The Cortina War that would rage for ten years had begun.[44]

On November 23, 1859, Cortina issued another proclamation. In it he again outlined the wrongs committed against Tejanos and vowed to protect their rights guaranteed by the Treaty of Guadalupe Hidalgo. After a brief lull, Cortina renewed his attacks and defeated a group of Texas Rangers pursuing him. Cortina expanded his border war. Despite protests by the state of Texas that Mexico shielded Cortina and his followers, Mexico did not pursue and prosecute Cortina because he was an American citizen. Cortina's army mushroomed to four hundred men as additional Tejanos joined his movement. Settling personal scores contributed to the ascending level of violence in the Río Grande Valley as Tejanos united solidly behind his insurgency. Juan Cortina's support from the Tejano population grew. Cortina "was received as the champion of his race—as the man who would right the wrongs the Mexicans had received; that he would drive the hated [Americans] to the Nueces. . . ." The Cortinista sympathizers provided supplies, offered refuge, and refused to help officials in capturing the elusive rebel and putting a stop to the hit-and-run warfare. The violence mounted. On December 27, near Río Grande City, Cortina and his men fought American troops under Major S. P. Heintzelman and a force of Texas Rangers led by John "Rip" Ford. The Tejanos lost this skirmish and escaped to Mexico. This clash further fueled the Cortina War that shook the lower

Río Grande Valley for a decade as Juan Cortina staged raids from Río Grande City to Brownsville. Federal troops and Texas Rangers found Cortina impossible to capture; the elusive Tejano succeeded in antagonizing his pursuers, including an expedition led by Lieutenant Colonel Robert E. Lee. In retaliation, the Texas Rangers cracked down on the Tejano insurgency by unleashing a reign of terror against Mexicans. All along the Río Grande and up to central Texas, the Rangers burned ranches and farms and shot Tejanos believed to be Cortinistas or Cortina sympathizers. Heintzelman reported "The whole country from Brownsville to Río Grande City, 120 miles and back to the Arroyo Colorado, has been laid waste." Fighting the Cortinistas with the Texas Rangers were members of the Knights of the Golden Circle, whose goal was the destruction of the Union and the perpetuation of slavery.[45]

Cortina rode away from the Texas border and into Mexico once the Mexican military began cooperating with the U.S. military in his capture. Chaotic conditions prevailed in Mexico. The country was wracked by civil war and then by foreign intervention and occupation by France. Emperor Ferdinand Maximilian Joseph ruled Mexico until he was executed in 1867. Juan Cortina had sympathized with Mexico's conservatives in the War of the Reform, but in 1860 he joined the liberal army supporting President Benito Juárez. Cortina quickly rose through the military ranks, becoming Juárez's military commander. Campaigning against the French, Cortina helped defend Tamaulipas and settled there, serving as its military governor and as mayor of Matamoros. However, Cortina turned against republican leaders in Mexico and went over to Maximilian's side.[46] Cortina soon lapsed into banditry as his political fortunes collapsed.

Cattle raids by Cortinistas ravaged the Río Grande Valley. In 1876, under pressure from the United States, the Mexican government arrested Cortina for transporting stolen cattle and imprisoned him in Mexico City. He was branded a bandit and a cattle thief, and, because he was a Union sympathizer during the American Civil War, efforts were delayed to gain a pardon for Cortina from the state of Texas. Cortina escaped from prison, but as he made his way to the Texas-Mexico border, Mexican forces captured him. The Tejano was court-martialed and ordered executed. However, Mexico's president Porfirio Díaz intervened and ordered that "the Robin Hood of the Río Grande," now an old man plagued by rheumatism, be kept under house arrest for the remainder of his life.[47] On October 30, 1894, Juan Cortina died at his residence at Azcapotzalco, Mexico. His death was noted by only a few newspapers on either side of the border. Cortina nevertheless left a powerful legacy for decades in South Texas. Great numbers of Tejanos joined him in common cause against Anglo-Texans who stole their land and hated all Mexicans.[48]

The secession movement took power in the Deep South and began occupying federal military installations, soon triggering a civil war in the United States. In the Southwest, Mexican Americans mobilized to fight for both the North and the South. Nearly ten thousand Mexican Americans fought in the American Civil War in both the Union and the Confederate armies. Anglos questioned the loyalty and fighting spirit of the Mexican American soldiers and officers despite their numerous acts of courage and sacrifices.

**Cattle Raid on the Texas Border—Cortinistas, 1874.**
CREDIT: *Harpers Weekly*, January 31, 1874.  Provided courtesy of HarpWeek, LLC.

## MEXICAN AMERICANS IN THE AMERICAN CIVIL WAR

In 1861, as civil war loomed, Mexican Americans in California, New Mexico, and Texas responded to President Lincoln's call for seventy-five thousand volunteers. The loyalty of the state of California to the Union cause was in doubt. Forty percent of the recently established Anglo population had origins in the South or were sympathetic to the confederate cause. Other Anglos were Democrats from the Midwest or Northeast who disliked both abolitionists and blacks. Notwithstanding, Californians believed strongly in popular sovereignty and wanted the Pacific states to remain neutral regarding the slavery issue.[49]

On May 17, 1861, the state legislature of California unanimously passed a resolution declaring the state's loyalty to the Union and its readiness to defend the United States. Volunteers in the state replaced regular Army soldiers. Native Californians firmly supported the Union. They had rallied to the Republican cause in 1860 when Abraham Lincoln became the party's nominee. In 1863, the United States government established four companies that made up the First Battalion of the Native Cavalry of California. The companies were made up mostly of Californios but included California and Yaqui Indians, Sonorans, and Germans recruited by Mexican American officers such as Captain José Ramón Pico of Company A, who traveled throughout the state calling for Spanish-speaking volunteers. Pico advanced the cause of the Union. Passing through San Jose on a recruiting mission, Captain Pico addressed an assembly of Mexican Americans. To inspire them to join the Union cause, Pico proclaimed:

Sons of California! Our country calls and we must obey. This unholy rebellion of the Southern States must be crushed; they must come back to the Union, and pay obedience to the Stars and Stripes. United we will by force of circumstances become the first and mightiest republic on earth![50]

Mexican Americans in San Juan Bautista, San Francisco, and elsewhere also answered Pico's call and enlisted, so that by September the Mexican American officer had formed a full company of cavalry soldiers. Antonio María de la Guerra of Santa Barbara formed other companies from the volunteers recruited by José Antonio Sánchez in Monterey and Watsonville. One hundred and sixty-three Spanish-speaking recruits from Los Angeles joined the Union army. Serving as brigadier general of the First Brigade of the California militia, Mexican War veteran Andrés Pico was commissioned major of the First Battalion of the Native Cavalry, but due to sickness he declined the commission. Major Salvador Vallejo of Napa replaced Pico as the First Battalion's commander.[51]

The California Unionists regretted that they were not sent east to serve. Instead, the 470 Mexican Americans who made up the four companies of the First Battalion of the Native Cavalry, with the rest of the California volunteers, served throughout California and in the New Mexico and Arizona Territory, where they helped to defeat a Confederate invasion. In May, the First Battalion of Native Cavalry was assigned to patrol the Colorado River region of southern Arizona and east to Texas. The men guarded telegraph lines, settlements, and travelers and captured Army deserters. The later assignment took Captain Pico and his men into Sonora, Mexico. In April 1866, the First Battalion returned to California and was mustered out.[52]

Because of the continued Indian raiding in northern California and the deployment of Union army units for duty in the East, a mounted company of native Californians joined the California Mountaineers Battalion and the Sixth California Infantry. These units were engaged in brutal military campaigns against California Indians to secure the area for Anglos, some of whom had been murdering Indians and stealing their lands. The fighting against the Indians, many of the California tribes already on the verge of extinction, did not stop until the surrender of the South that ended the Civil War.[53]

The Confederacy's plan of campaign in the Southwest involved capturing the strategically important gold fields of Colorado and California, as well as the valuable Santa Fe Trail. In July 1861, three hundred Texans, led by Lieutenant Colonel John R. Baylor, took the southern New Mexico settlement of Mesilla and proclaimed the area the Confederate Territory of Arizona. Baylor's forces were later reinforced by three Texas regiments led by General Henry H. Sibley in preparation for an invasion of New Mexico. New Mexico was to serve as a springboard for securing the gold fields of Colorado and California for the Confederate States of America. In early February 1862, the Confederates launched an attack on Fort Craig, located south of Socorro, New Mexico. The Confederates planned to capture supplies at the fort and then move north and take Albuquerque, Santa Fe, and the military supply depot at Fort Union and then seize Colorado, Utah, and California.[54]

Washington officials at first expressed little interest in the military problems of the New Mexico Territory. The Territory's non-Indian population numbered about ninety-five thousand and was made up mostly of Mexicans who only thirteen years earlier had been citizens of Mexico. Washington dismissed the Mexicans as troublesome citizens who contributed nothing to the United States and whose need for protection from Indian depredations was costly and burdensome. The United States nevertheless asked the New Mexico Territorial Governor to raise units of volunteers to serve for three years. The racist regular army officers and soldiers believed the native New Mexicans were by nature cowardly and doubted their fighting ability.[55] That the Spanish-speaking New Mexicans made good soldiers was soon proven in the face of enemy fire.

In July of 1861, the First New Mexico Infantry was organized in response to the invasion of the southern New Mexican territory by Baylor's Texas Confederate forces. The enlistments of New Mexicans increased through appeals to their patriotism, the offer of bounties and higher pay, and, for some, an end to their peonage. However, it was the news of the arrival of the much-hated Texas forces that had captured Fort Fillmore and occupied Mesilla that spurred more New Mexicans to enlist. New Mexico Governor Henry Connelly exploited the threat of the Texan invasion. Declaring a state of emergency, the governor visited towns and addressed crowds of native New Mexicans. He played on their longtime hatred of Texans as he called for volunteers to oppose the Confederate invasion. Connelly exhorted: "Do you want them to take away your lands? Didn't your fathers repulse the invaders . . . ? Were not these enemies not [sic] taken in chains to Mexico? You are a fighting race. Fight for your rights and repel the invaders."[56]

As in California, New Mexicans awarded officer commissions signed up entire communities of relatives, friends, and fellow townsmen. By August 13, 1861, two regiments of New Mexico volunteers had been raised to pit against the Confederates. The First New Mexico Infantry Regiment was a 1,100-man unit of ten companies, four of which were mounted at their own expense. Native New Mexicans made up the majority of the soldiers and officers commanded by Colonel Christopher "Kit" Carson. Carson's son-in-law, Major J. Francisco Chaves, was second in command. Colonel Miguel Pino was in charge of the Second Regiment, and the Third Regiment of Volunteers was led by Colonel José Guadalupe Gallegos. By December, 3,500 New Mexican volunteers, excluding the militia and independent companies, were in active service.[57]

The First New Mexico Regiment suffered from poor equipment and lack of other supplies; it was originally equipped with Mexican War surplus ordnance. Other regiments had few government-issued weapons. The New Mexican volunteers bought their own uniforms from a clothing allowance. This circumstance had an impact on the already low level of morale among the men because of widespread racism by Anglo officers and soldiers toward them. The latter displayed condescension and contempt for the Spanish-speaking volunteers; the Anglos insisted the Mexicans were cowardly and incompetent, treated them as inferiors, and referred to them disparagingly as "greaser soldiers." Despite the racism, lack of pay, and substandard weapons, the First New Mexico regiment performed well in the field. The men of the Second and Fourth New Mexico Regiments soon proved indispensable in the Battles of Valverde and Glorietta Pass.[58]

Colonels Carson and Pino and Lieutenant Colonel Manuel Chaves set out to stop General Sibley's Confederate troops' attempt to take control of the New Mexico territory. Chaves, who had declined a Confederate commission, was a veteran Indian fighter, as were many of the Spanish-speaking soldiers under his command. The New Mexicans were aided by Major John Chivington's Colorado Volunteers, who were led over rugged terrain behind the Confederates by Colonel Chaves.

In February 1862, 4,500 battle-hardened rebel soldiers, including the Texan Mounted Volunteers, were moving into northern New Mexico with several artillery pieces. Union troops, reinforced by several battalions of New Mexico militia led by Colonel Edward S. Canby, clashed with the Texans north of Fort Craig at a ford on the Río Grande known as Valverde. Valverde was a turning point in the Confederate effort to conquer the West. Many of the New Mexicans were brave and skillful Indian fighters such as Captain Rafael Chacón, but none had prior experience with large-scale military confrontations. Verbally insulted and physically abused by scornful Anglo officers and soldiers, the New Mexicans demonstrated loyalty and courage at Valverde. The New Mexicans performed well under fire and in hand-to-hand combat, inflicting great losses on the Confederate soldiers, but also sustaining heavy casualties. The New Mexicans were humiliating the Texans on their front when they were abruptly ordered to fall back to Fort Craig. Unable to seize Fort Craig from the New Mexicans, the rebel troops instead continued their march north. The New Mexicans pursued the fleeing Confederates, who were fast running out of supplies. Despite the conspicuous bravery of the New Mexicans in combat, Canby's report of the battle of Valverde accused them of cowardice and blamed them for losing the battle.[59]

The Confederate troops approached Santa Fe in early March, forcing Union soldiers from Fort Marcy to evacuate Governor Connelly to safety. The soldiers also moved military supplies and equipment from Fort Marcy to Fort Union to keep them from falling into enemy hands. Confederate forces entered Santa Fe on March 10 and occupied the capital for more than two weeks.

The Battle of Glorieta Pass was the pivotal battle of the Civil War in New Mexico. It began on March 26, 1862, when 1,342 Union troops from Fort Union, including New Mexico militia and volunteer infantry and cavalry from Colorado, fought the 3,500-strong Confederate army at Apache Canyon east of Santa Fe. For three days each side vied for control of this strategic pass. A Union raiding party led by Colonel Chavez attacked the Confederate rear positions and destroyed their train of provisions and ammunition. The loss of the supply train weakened the rebels; they had underestimated Union forces and were forced to retreat. The First New Mexico Volunteers Regiment harassed the exhausted rebel troops as they fled to Texas. Five hundred Texans died in combat or succumbed to smallpox and pneumonia, and an additional five hundred were reported missing or captured. The Confederates' threat to New Mexico ended, and the rebels were forced to abandon the campaign. The Battle of Glorieta Pass became known as the "Gettysburg of the West," the turning point of Civil War hostilities in New Mexico. By midsummer 1862, the Civil War in New Mexico was over. But in the East bitter fighting continued.[60]

**Rafael Chacón, 1880.**
CREDIT: "Rafael Chacón (1833–1925) veteran of the civil war in New Mexico, 1880." Courtesy of the Palace of the Governors Photo Archives (NMHM/DCA), 148455.

The Confederacy's 1862 Conscription Act in many instances was unenforceable in parts of the South, and many Confederate governors refused to share supplies or soldiers with Confederate armies not defending their own states. Many Tejanos were reluctant to become involved in the Civil War. Tejanos either joined Texas militia units, as they feared being sent away from their families, or avoided conscription by claiming to be Mexican citizens. The Tejanos also faced accusations of subversion and disloyalty because they were suspected of participating in the ongoing Cortina War along the border. All the South Texas counties with large Tejano populations voted for secession, though they were either misled or had been forced to do so by political bosses. Some Tejanos refused this call for help against the Union because they remembered all too well how the Texans had mistreated them. On April 12, 1861, one day before the surrender of Fort Sumter, Tejano rancher Antonio Ochoa with forty armed Tejanos took control of the third precinct of Zapata County. Most of the Tejanos were either Cortina sympathizers or veterans of the first Cortina War. Ochoa threatened to kill all the gringos in Zapata County and hang the sheriff if county officials swore allegiance to the Confederacy. Ochoa's brief insurrection reflected the strong anti-Anglo sentiment in South Texas against the large landowners who ruled over them.[61]

Most Texas Confederate soldiers did not participate in campaigns east of the Mississippi River, but those who did engaged in some of the worst fighting of the Civil War. The four thousand Texans in the First, Fourth, and Fifth Volunteer Infantry regiments were organized into the Texas Brigade under the command of

Major General John Bell Hood. The Tejanos in Hood's Texas Brigade participated in thirty-eight battles and skirmishes that included action in Virginia in the battles of Gaines' Mill, Second Bull Run, and Antietam (fought and lost at a cost of 60 percent casualties); the defensive victory at Fredericksburg; and the Gettysburg and Wilderness campaigns. Those Texans who saw combat in the latter battle suffered 70 percent casualties. By October 1864, of the original four thousand Texans only three hundred remained to take part in the Appomattox Court House campaign. Tejanos from San Antonio, Eagle Pass, and the Fort Clark area served with John R. Baylor's Second Texas Mounted Rifles that marched to the Mesilla Valley on the Río Grande created as the Confederate Territory of Arizona. These units were incorporated into three regiments organized at San Antonio and became the Army of New Mexico commanded by General Sibley. The Tejanos fought at Valverde, occupied Albuquerque and Santa Fe, and battled again at Glorieta Pass.[62]

By the summer of 1863, the Confederacy lost its military momentum to the Union forces. Tejanos from San Antonio who served in the Sixth Texas Infantry were involved in several of the extremely bloody eastern campaigns. They saw action at Chattanooga and Chickamauga, in the devastating defeats at Atlanta, and in the suicidal assault mounted against the Federal Army at Franklin; and they were obliterated at the Battle of Nashville in John Bell Hood's invasion of Tennessee. Tejano officers who served the Confederacy included Captain Manuel Yturri in the Third Texas Infantry and Lieutenant Joseph de la Garza from San Antonio. De la Garza reenlisted in the Confederate Army in 1864 and was killed in the De Soto Parish in Louisiana in the same year in the Battle of Mansfield during the bloody Red River campaign in which both Confederate and Union armies sustained heavy casualties. More than three hundred Tejanos from Webb, Refugio, and Béxar counties served in the Eighth Texas Infantry. Joseph M. Peñaloza and José Ángel Navarro commanded the Eighth's two all-Tejano companies. In mid-August 1862, these Tejano Confederate soldiers helped defeat a Union army in the Battle of Corpus Christi. Tejanos also served the Confederacy in the Tenth Texas Cavalry, the Fifty-fifth Alabama Infantry, and the Sixth Missouri Infantry.[63]

Tejanos and Mexicans made up most of the First Texas Cavalry, the first Confederate regiment organized in Texas. Among the Tejanos in the unit was Adrián J. Vidal, the adopted son of Anglo-Texan land baron Mifflin Kenedy. Vidal was born in Monterrey, Mexico, in 1840. After the death of his father, Adrián's mother Petra Vela de Vidal took him to Meir, Texas, where she met Mifflin Kenedy, whom she married in 1852. Adrián Vidal joined the Confederacy in San Antonio in October 1862 as a private in James Duff's Partisan Rangers. Promoted to lieutenant and then to captain, Vidal was assigned to an all-Tejano Confederate cavalry militia unit and ordered to guard the Río Grande. Tejanos fought effectively against the invading Union forces. In July 1863, Vidal was recognized for bravery for capturing a Union gunboat.[64]

Captain Vidal's Tejano unit undertook reconnaissance missions, harassed the enemy, fought small-scale skirmishes, and was constantly on the move despite inadequate equipment and supplies. The Tejanos also endured flagrant discrimination from Confederate soldiers. Frustrated, Captain Vidal complained to his commanders but got no reply. General Hamilton P. Bee sent two soldiers to recall

Captain Vidal and his militia to Brownsville. Fed up with the racism, Vidal and his men mutinied in October 1863 and crossed enemy lines to join the First Texas Union Calvary commanded by Colonel Edmund J. Davis, killing one rebel soldier and wounding another. The latter reported to Bee's unit that Vidal and his men were going to launch a nighttime attack on Brownsville. Following a short skirmish with Vidal and his men, Bee's troops retreated to Brownsville to wait for Vidal's attack, but it never came. The Tejanos instead passed within a mile of Brownsville, plundering the ranches upriver, and killing several Confederate sympathizers.[65]

The Union army took occupation of Brownsville on November 6, 1863. Captain Adrían Vidal and his men were formed into the unit Vidal's Independent Partisan Rangers, which was attached to the Second Texas Union Calvary. The unit scouted for the Union Army along the Río Grande Valley and north to the Nueces River. On May 30, 1864, Vidal resigned his commission. However, Union army officials cancelled Vidal's discharge, classified him as a deserter, and issued orders for him to be shot on sight. Vidal and his men had fled to Mexico and joined up with Juan Cortina and the Juáristas. In June 1865, Vidal was captured by Mexican forces at Camargo on the border. Although Mifflin Kenedy offered a sizable ransom for the release of his adopted son, Vidal was summarily executed. Kenedy recovered his body and buried it at the family ranch in Texas. Discrimination led to Vidal's changing allegiance and his last alliance with Juan Cortina.[66]

The most recognized Tejano participant in the Civil War was Laredo rancher-merchant Santos Benavides. Benavides was the highest-ranking Tejano to serve the Confederacy, rising to the rank of colonel and commander of the Thirty-third Texas Cavalry Regiment. With his two brothers Refugio and Cristóbal, both captains in the regiment, Colonel Benavides compiled a distinguished record of border defense against Union forces. Though ill equipped, frequently without food, and forced to march across vast expanses of land, the Thirty-third Texas Cavalry never lost a battle.[67]

Born in Laredo on November 1, 1823, Santos Benavides was the great-great-grandson of Tomás Sánchez de la Barrera y Garza, the founder of Laredo. Like other prominent Mexican Americans, Benavides used political institutions to advance his private ends. His prominence in Laredo politics resulted from the influence of his uncle Basilio Benavides, who served three times as mayor of Laredo under Mexican rule and then as mayor and state representative after Texas annexation. Tejanos controlled Laredo city government, whereas Anglos dominated newly created Webb County. Santos Benavides was elected mayor of Laredo in 1856 and chief justice of Webb County in 1859. He joined a coalition of wealthy Laredo Tejanos and Anglos that pitted their privilege against the poor. The Tejano rancher-merchant also gained distinction as an Indian fighter by leading several campaigns against the Lipan Apaches. Santos Benavides fought for the Federalists during the Federalist-Centralist wars that swept the Río Grande frontier in the 1830s and 1840s. During the Mexican War, the Tejano cooperated with Mirabeau B. Lamar, whose forces occupied Laredo. After the Mexican War, Santos Benavides joined his uncle in opposing the annexation of the Laredo area by the United States. When Texas seceded from the Union, Benavides with his brothers supported the Confederacy. A pro-Confederate and slave owner, Santos Benavides and his brothers defeated a band of Tejanos led by Juan Cortina in the border battle of Carrizo on May 22, 1861.[68]

Commissioned a captain in the Thirty-third Texas Cavalry Regiment and assigned to the Río Grande Military District, Santos Benavides quickly gained a reputation for bravery. Benavides and his unit invaded northern Mexico several times in retaliation for Union guerilla raids into Texas. In November 1863, Benavides was promoted to colonel and authorized to raise his own regiment of partisan rangers. Benavides's greatest achievement was his defense of Laredo on March 19, 1864. With just forty-two troops, the Benavides brothers drove off two hundred Union soldiers from the First Texas Union Cavalry commanded by Colonel Edmund J. Davis. Davis had earlier offered Benavides a Union generalship. During the Union occupation of Brownsville, Benavides's regiment guarded the safe passage of Texas cotton to Matamoros and drove Union forces back from Brownsville in March 1864.[69]

Two thousand Texans opposed to the Confederacy joined the United States Army, and Tejanos made up over half of these Texan Unionists. In addition to opposing slavery, these Tejano Unionists saw military service as an opportunity to strike a blow against Anglo landowners, attorneys, and politicians who defrauded them of their land. Tejanos and Mexicans recruited by Anglo-Texan and Tejano union officers from towns and villages along the lower Río Grande made up the Second Texas Cavalry, commanded by Colonel John L. Haynes. Many of the Tejano recruits had enlisted while living in Mexico after being driven there by the Confederate occupation of the Río Grande Valley. A significant number had fought with Cortina or were sympathetic to his cause. The Second Texas Cavalry saw duty along the Río Grande and later in Louisiana. Tejano company commanders included George Treviño, Clemente Zapata, Cesario Falcón, and Mónico de Abrego. A number of Tejano Union soldiers provided invaluable service as guerillas on the Nueces Strip. The most famous soldiers of these defensive forces were Cecilio Balerio and his son Juan, who single-handedly fought Confederates at Los Patricios, fifty miles southwest of Banquete in March 1864.[70]

Nearly one-fourth of the soldiers from Texas who fought in the Civil War died, half succumbing to their wounds and to disease. Tejanos proved their worth as military men. However, their wartime sacrifices got them little after the war; they did not receive land under the headright system. They returned to their homes, where most lived out their lives in poverty among the unfolding economic and political oppression of Tejanos.[71] There were still Indians to subdue. Mexican Americans would be sent into the Southwest to deal with the Indian problem that was delaying settlement of some areas of the region.

## MEXICAN AMERICANS FIGHT IN THE INDIAN WARS

Mexican Americans and the U.S. Army turned once more to halting the problem of Indian attacks. In New Mexico, the new Indian threat was an outbreak of warfare by Navajo, Apache, and Plains Indians. It fell on the New Mexicans of the First New Mexico Cavalry to undertake the task of rounding up and placing the territory's Indian tribes on reservations.

In 1863, after fifteen years of intermittent warfare, four hundred Mescalero Apache Indians were relocated to Bosque Redondo reservation at Fort Sumner on the Pecos River in eastern New Mexico. In 1865, the Mescalero Apaches left Bosque Redondo and returned to their home in the mountains of southern New Mexico. Another long period of warfare followed. Led by Chief Victorio, Mescaleros with other Apaches raided, plundered, and killed on both sides of the border and into Texas.[72]

The Navajos resumed their generations-old practice of raiding the Mexican population of New Mexico. The Mexicans retaliated as they always had—by killing Navajos and taking women and children as captives. The First New Mexico Cavalry under General James H. Carleton was sent to pacify the Navajos and, in a brutal scorched-earth policy, destroyed their homeland. In the summer of 1864, nine thousand Navajos were force-marched from their ancestral lands on the Arizona border to the Bosque Redondo reservation.[73]

The First New Mexico Volunteers saw duty against Kiowa, Comanche, Cheyenne, and Arapaho Indian war parties throughout New Mexico, Arizona, and Texas, as well as Oklahoma and Colorado. They were aided by three thousand African American troops, the famous Buffalo Soldiers, stationed at eleven of the sixteen forts of the New Mexico territory. Enduring long forced marches through blizzards, heat, and drought, the New Mexicans kept open the Santa Fe Trail, the Cimarron cutoff, El Camino Real, and the California Trail (the Butterfield Stagecoach route), byways prone to Indian attack. United States soldiers gained new respect for the New Mexicans after witnessing their accomplishments on the battlefield.[74]

The Mexican population in Arizona grew as the social and economic links between the United States and Mexico evolved. Shortly after the end of the Civil War, 4,187 non-Indians lived in Arizona; most of them were Mexicans newly arrived from Sonora. The region was quickly repopulated as American investors developed the mines near Tubac. Mining would be the foundation of Arizona's economy, and it was based on the labor of Mexicans from both sides of the border. Former residents returned to work in the mines and smelter owned by the Sonora Exploring and Mining Company and later for the railroads. Within a few years the population of the Tucson-Tubac area grew from three hundred to almost two thousand residents. On April 30, 1871, Mexican Americans would plot and execute the massacre of defenseless Aravipa Apache women and children camped outside Camp Grant.[75]

Previously denied the vote in the 1850s, some Arizona Mexicans began to participate in politics after Arizona qualified for statehood. Ties of marriage and business between an emerging Anglo and an old-line Mexican elite characterized political and economic order in Arizona. This included fighting Indians. Jesús María Elias was a leading member of a prominent Mexican family that owned more than two hundred thousand acres of land. He served three terms in the Arizona House Legislature, and, with another veteran Indian fighter, William S. Oury, helped form the Committee of Public Safety.

Because Apache raids placed sharp restrictions on farming, ranching, and mining activity, Indian killing was the main occupation of Elias, who earned the moniker "the boss of all wars." Apaches had recently attacked the Elias ranch, stealing cattle and killing two of Elias's brothers, Ramón and Cornelio, and a relative, Luis Elias. The most active promoter of the Committee of Public Safety, Jesús María Elias was elected as the commander of the committee that was made up of sixty Anglos, forty-eight Mexicans, and ninety-four Papago Indians. In the predawn hours of April 30, they assaulted Aravaipas Apaches camped on the San Pedro River. The men opened fire on the camp. The wounded, unable to escape, had their brains beaten out with clubs or were knifed or hatcheted to death in what became known as the Camp Grant Massacre of April 1871. It was all over in thirty minutes. Almost all of the 118 Apaches killed in the wanton slaughter were women and children. In addition, the assailants kidnapped more than two dozen Aravaipas Apache babies, who were sold into slavery in Mexico. The Camp Grant Massacre outraged the nation. More than one hundred of the men who participated in the massacre were put on trial. After less than twenty minutes of deliberation, the jury ruled for the release of the killers. The celebration of the not-guilty verdict lasted for days. The next month, Oury was elected alderman, and Elias, a leading figure in the murders, was elected town dog catcher.[76]

When the railroad arrived in 1880, Anglos increasingly became dominant in Arizona. However, the development of a mining economy dependent on a reserve of cheap labor is what subordinated Mexicans in Arizona and elsewhere in the Southwest.

**Camp Grant Massacre Trial, 1871.**
CREDIT: "'Not Guilty': Camp Grant Massacre trial participants outside Pima County Court House in December 1871." Courtesy of the Arizona Historical Society/Tucson, AHS # 654.

## CONCLUSION

Following the end of the Mexican War, American authority in the Southwest rested on the claim that Anglos were representatives of a superior civilization. Anglos were violently prejudiced against the hated Mexicans, a conquered people, losers in America's war of national destiny. The myth of the Alamo, combined with Anglo-Texan participation in the Mexican War, further increased the vicious racism found in Texas. Anglos empowered some Mexican Americans, and these individuals, such as Santos Benavides of Laredo and Tucson's Jesús María Elías, accommodated themselves to the new social order arising from the rapidly growing Anglo population. The Mexicans' decline was the result of numerical domination, racism, and Anglo control of political and economic institutions. Mexicans also experienced an American legal system as an instrument of injustice and oppression. Throughout the Southwest the ranchero tradition was all but extinguished. Land dispossession was accompanied by an immense amount of fraud, as well as violence. Anglos ended up owning almost all the land in the new Southwest region. Mexican Americans found themselves pushed into urban settlements as the foundation of their economic life was torn away.

Without recourse to local or state authorities or the law, Mexican Americans at times met force with force to defend their rights against armed vigilante groups incited by local politicians. The tensions exploded into the violence of ethnic cleansing. Mexicans in California such as Tiburcio Vásquez turned to banditry, whereas in Texas Tejanos such as Juan Cortina and Antonio Ochoa resorted to rebellion as a means of expressing grievances and frustrations with Anglo mistreatment. In their own way, the latter fought for justice, and their struggles had racism as their basis. Yet choosing violence as a response to violence usually generated more violence. Moreover, despite calls for revenge, most of these bandits and rebels could not see beyond their own individual needs. There were other memories of insurgency in the Southwest as Mexicans heroized rebels against law and property. In the end, none were able to escape the grasp of authorities.

Many Mexican Americans opposed slavery and secession, but others supported the Confederacy. About ten thousand Mexican Americans joined Union and Confederate armed forces and, despite various forms of discrimination, participated in dozens of military campaigns during the American Civil War. Mexican American officers and soldiers in the Confederate and Union armies met the test of combat and exhibited bravery under fire.

Victims of hard times and limited opportunities, Mexican Americans were condemned to a lifetime of menial labor. With the eventual expansion of commercial agriculture in California and the passage of the Chinese Exclusion Act in 1883, most of the displaced Mexican Americans became farm laborers. Their fate was sealed. They faced growing employment restrictions. As Mexican American men found themselves occupationally disadvantaged, more and more women began to work regularly outside the home as domestics, laundresses, and seamstresses. Children were also introduced to the world of work and, like the women, were more vulnerable to exploitation. Mexican Americans with wealth, social status, light skins, and a presumed Spanish identity did not escape the racism.

Along with employment discrimination came residential segregation. Traditional Mexican towns were transformed into segregated barrios or were enveloped by expanding cities. Extended households were very common. Mexican American community and family life nonetheless flourished. Where not outlawed, there were bullfights, rodeos, horse races, and various fiestas, including the celebration of Mexican and American national holidays. Mexican Americans founded mutual aid societies and fraternal orders and political and labor organizations. Spanish-language newspapers such as *El Clamor Publico* of Los Angeles protested against the injustices and strengthened community cohesion.

The coming of the transcontinental railroad in the 1870s spurred a land boom in the Southwest and another major population explosion in the region. The immigrants who arrived from Mexico in the Southwest adapted to the new way of life. By the end of the nineteenth century, Anglos were more numerically, politically, and economically dominant, whereas Mexican Americans declined further in their status as a defenseless, oppressed minority. The modernization of the Southwest economy was based on capitalist forms of production, and the expansion of railroads, mining, and agriculture intensified the demand for Mexican labor. Their productivity fueled this expansion of American capitalism.

## NOTES

1. Ceballos-Ramírez and Martínez, "Conflict and Accommodation," 136, 146–147; David J. Weber, *Foreigners in Their Native Land* (Albuquerque: University of New Mexico Press, 1973), 140, 143. In 1850, Mexicans made up less than 10 percent of the total population of Texas and California but over 90 percent of the population of New Mexico.
2. William D. Corrigan, *The Making of a Lynching Culture: Violence and Vigilantism in Central Texas, 1836–1916* (Urbana: University of Illinois Press, 2005), 24, 26.
3. Hall, *Social Change in the Southwest,* 208; Robert M. Utley, *The Indian Frontier of the American West, 1846–1890* (Albuquerque: University of New Mexico Press, 1984), 67–70; Jerry Don Thompson, *Vaqueros in Blue and Grey* (Austin, TX: Presidial Press, 1976), 5–6.
4. Hall, *Social Change in the Southwest,* 205.
5. Ibid., 211, 216. In 1861, the northeastern portion of the New Mexico territory was attached to Colorado.
6. Truett, *Fugitive Landscapes,* 40; Reséndez, *Changing National Identities,* 99; Hall, *Social Change in the Southwest,* 228; Odie B. Faulk, *Crimson Desert: Indian Wars of the American Southwest* (New York: Oxford University Press, 1974), 142–145; Officer, *Hispanic Arizona,* 109, 150–151; Thomas E. Sheridan, *Los Tucsonenses: The Mexican Community in Tucson 1854–1941* (Tucson: University of Arizona Press, 1986), 18, 22. For example, the legislature of Chihuahua made "blood contracts" with bands of American adventurers and outlaws to kill Indians at so much a head. The price scale took into account age and sex.
7. Truett, *Fugitive Landscapes,* 41; Weber, *Foreigners in Their Native Land,* 143; Officer, *Hispanic Arizona,* 229–232, 281–283, 310; Sheridan, *Los Tucsonenses,* 35; Joseph F. Park, "The Apaches in Mexican-Indian Relations, 1848–1861: A Footnote to the Gadsden Treaty," *Arizona and the West* 3 (Summer 1961): 139–141.
8. Lamar, *The Far Southwest, 1846–1912,* 362, 416–417; Hall, *Social Change in the Southwest,* 207.

9. Hall, *Social Change in the Southwest*, 211, 216; Weber, *Foreigners in Their Native Land*, 143–144. Some Americans claimed the United States had made a bad bargain by annexing New Mexico, the most heavily populated of Mexico's former territories. For example, Connecticut congressman Truman Smith remarked that it was a mistake to bring New Mexicans into the Union because of their low morals. South Carolina's Senator John C. Calhoun was appalled at the idea of making New Mexicans citizens of the United States because he claimed they were a "colored race" and that the Union was "a white race."

10. Hall, *Social Change in the Southwest*, 210, 213–214; María E. Montoya, *Translating Property: The Maxwell Land Grant and the Conflict over Land in the American West, 1840–1900* (Berkeley: University of California Press, 2002), 148–151; Weber, *Foreigners in Their Native Land*, 156–157.

11. Pitt, *The Decline of the Californios*, 52–53; Monroy, *Thrown Among Strangers*, 180; Weber, *Foreigners in Their Native Land*, 148–150; Estrada, *Los Angeles Plaza*, 58. Eight thousand Mexicans from Sonora had migrated to California, as well as five thousand Chileans, Peruvians, and Basques from Latin America and Europe. California's Spanish-speaking population composed 15 percent of the state's population in 1850 but just 4 percent twenty years later.

12. Heizer and Almquist, *The Other Californians*, 196; Weber, *Foreigners in Their Native Land*, 151; Lisbeth Haas, *Conquest and Historical Identities in California, 1769–1936* (Berkeley: University of California Press, 1995), 56–63; Hurtado, *Indian Survival on the California Frontier*, 1.

13. Heizer and Almquist, *The Other Californians*, 196; Pitt, *Decline of the Californios*, 53, 60, 68; Monroy, *Thrown Among Strangers*, 201–203.

14. Pitt, *Decline of the Californios*, 61–64.

15. Ibid., 97–98; Act of April 30, 1855, ch. 175, § 2, 1855, Cal. Stat., 217 ; Weber, *Foreigners in Their Native Land*, 149.

16. Pitt, *Decline of the Californios*, 86; W. W. Robinson, *Land in California* (Berkeley: University of California Press, 1948), 63–64.

17. Pitt, *Decline of the Californios*, 103.

18. Ibid., 85–86, 91, 97, 100; Monroy, *Thrown Among Strangers*, 203–204; Haas, *Conquest and Historical Identities*, 63–64; Weber, *Foreigners in Their Native Land*, 156, 159; Donald J. Pisani, "Squatter Law in California, 1850–1858," *Western Historical Quarterly* 25, no. 3 (Autumn 1994): 302.

19. Haas, *Conquest and Historical Identities*, 65–66; Monroy, *Thrown Among Strangers*, 204–205; Weber, *Foreigners in Their Native Land*, 156, 159. Land tenure for California Indians changed considerably after the Mexican War. When California became a state in 1850, land officially not in private hands became public domain. The state set up a Land Claims Commission in 1851 to adjudicate disputes, but because Indian people did not know of the Commission and the state of California did not enter a claim in their behalf, no one represented Indian claims. Throughout the state Indian leaders agreed to cede their traditional lands, comprising 7,488,000 acres, for reservations. California officials objected. U.S. Representative Joseph Walker McCorkle from San Francisco argued in Congress on March 26, 1852, that in some cases the land set aside for Indian people comprised "the most valuable agricultural and mineral lands in the state." California Governor John Bigler concurred. He wrote to Redick McKee on July 18, 1852, that not only are the lands included within the reservations valuable but that "I have the assurance of the united opposition of our delegation in Congress to ratification of the

treaties, and that their rejection by the United States may be regarded as beyond doubt." He was right. The Senate refused to ratify the treaties.

20. Estrada, *Los Angeles Plaza*, 58; Haas, *Conquest and Historical Identities*, 52; Pitt, *Decline of the Californios*, 108–110; Monroy, *Thrown Among Strangers*, 180–183; Richard Griswold del Castillo, *Los Angeles Barrio, 1850–1890: A Social History* (Berkeley: University of California Press, 1975), 42.

21. Haas, *Conquest and Historical Identities*, 66–67; Robert Cleland, *The Cattle on a Thousand Hills* (San Marino, CA: Huntington Library, 1951), 110; Carey McWilliams, *North from Mexico: The Spanish Speaking People of the United States* (New York: Greenwood Press, 1948), 91; Monroy, *Thrown Among Strangers*, 230–231.

22. Pitt, *Decline of the Californios*, 201–202; Monroy, *Thrown Among Strangers*, 223–224; Weber, *Foreigners in Their Native Land*, 151–152.

23. Kirsten Silva Gruesz, *Ambassadors of Culture: The Transamerican Origins of Latino Writing* (Princeton, NJ: Princeton University Press, 2001), 101–102; Estrada, *Los Angeles Plaza*, 64, 68; Pitt, *Decline of the Californios*, 181–182; Monroy, *Thrown Among Strangers*, 221.

24. Pitt, *Decline of the Californios*, 182–183; Monroy, *Thrown Among Strangers*, 219–220.; Weber, *Foreigners in Their Native Land*, 152.

25. Pitt, *Decline of the Californios*, 187, 194.

26. Estrada, *Los Angeles Plaza*, 60; Pitt, *Decline of the Californios*, 70; Shelley Streeby, *American Sensations: Class, Empire, and the Production of Popular Culture* (Berkeley: University of California Press, 2002), 277–278.

27. Bruce Thornton, *Searching for Joaquín: Myth, Murieta and History in California* (San Francisco: Encounter Books, 2003), 12–17; Monroy, *Thrown Among Strangers*, 212.

28. Monroy, *Thrown Among Strangers*, 212.

29. Pitt, *Decline of the Californios*, 79–80; James Varley, *The Legend of Joaquin Murieta: California's Gold Rush Bandit* (Twin Falls, ID: Big Los River, 1995), 75–76; Susan Lee Johnson, *Roaring Camp: The Social World of the California Gold Rush* (New York: Norton, 2000), 38. Harry Love first came to California as a seaman in 1839. He served in the Mexican War and later as an army express rider and an explorer of the Río Grande. Love returned to California. He arrived in San Francisco in December 1850 and took up residence in Mariposa County. On May 28, 1853, Love was commissioned captain of the California Rangers.

30. Thornton, *Searching for Joaquín*, 8; Pitt, *Decline of the Californios*, 80.

31. Thornton, *Searching for Joaquín*, 23–24.

32 Ibid., 25. See also Joseph Henry Jackson, *Bad Company: The Story of California's Legendary and Actual Stage-Robbers, Bandits, Highwaymen and Outlaws from the Fifties to the Eighties* (New York: Harcourt, Brace, 1949).

33. Thornton, *Searching for Joaquín*, 30, 88; Monroy, *Thrown Among Strangers*, 213. The legend of Murieta achieved notoriety in 1854 with the publication of John Rollin Ridge's *Joaquin Murieta: The Celebrated California Bandit*. In the book, Ridge describes Murieta as a peaceful miner who turned into an outlaw after Americans stole his claim and attacked his family. Chilean poet Pablo Neruda would later write a poem about Murieta. Pitt, *Decline of the Californios*, 82.

34. Pitt, *Decline of the Californios*, 256–257, 262.

35. Ibid., 215–216; Ernest R. May, "Tiburcio Vásquez," *Historical Society of Southern California Quarterly* 29, nos. 3–4 (September-December 1947): 123–134.

36. Pitt, *Decline of the Californios*, 216; Weber, *Foreigners in Their Native Land*, 226; Robert J. Rosenbaum, *Mexicano Resistance in the Southwest* (Dallas, TX: Southern Methodist University Press, 1998), 56.

37. Pitt, *Decline of the Californios*, 216; Rosenbaum, *Mexicano Resistance in the Southwest*, 56.
38. Pitt, *Decline of the Californios*, 75–76, 262. See also George Beers, *California Outlaw: Tiburcio Vásquez* (Los Gatos, CA: Talisman Press, 1960); John Rollin Ridge, *California's Age of Terror: Murieta and Vásquez* (Hollister, CA: Evening Free Lance, 1927); Rosenbaum, *Mexicano Resistance in the Southwest*, 55.
39. Jerry Thompson, *Cortina: Defending the Mexican Name in Texas* (College Station: Texas A & M University Press, 2007), 20, 30, 34; Rosenbaum, *Mexicano Resistance in the Southwest*, 41, 63; Weber, *Foreigners in Their Native Land*, 146.
40. Sean Kelley, "'Mexico in His Head': Slavery and the Texas-Mexico Border, 1810–1860," *Journal of Social History* 37, no. 3 (2004): 17; Thompson, *Cortina*, 35; Mike Cox, *The Texas Rangers: Wearing the Cinco Peso, 1821–1900* (New York: Doherty, 2008), 97, 142; Arnoldo De Leon, *The Tejano Community, 1836–1900* (Albuquerque: University of New Mexico Press, 1982), 15, 28–29; Weber, *Foreigners in Their Native Land*, 152–153; Corrigan, *Making of a Lynching Culture*, 29.
41. George P. Garrison, *Texas: A Contest of Civilizations* (Boston and New York: Houghton Mifflin, 1973), 274; Thompson, *Cortina*, 35; Cox, *Texas Rangers*, 142–143; De Leon, *The Tejano Community, 1836–1840*, 15–16; Weber, *Foreigners in Their Native Land*, 153; John J. Linn, *Reminiscences of Fifty Years in Texas* (Austin: University of Texas Press, 1935), 352–354; Corrigan, *Making of a Lynching Culture*, 29. See also Ellen Scheider and Paul H. Carson, "Gunnysacks, Carreteros and Teamsters: The South Texas Cart War of 1857," *Journal of South Texas* 1 (Spring 1988), 1–9.
42. Thompson, *Cortina*, 20, 32; De Leon, *Tejano Community*, 17; Rosenbaum, *Mexicano Resistance in the Southwest*, 41; Weber, *Foreigners in Their Native Land*, 155–156.
43. Thompson, *Cortina*, Chapter 1; Rosenbaum, *Mexicano Resistance in the Southwest*, 42; Charles W. Goldfinch, *Juan N. Cortina, 1824–1892: A Reappraisal* (Brownsville, TX: Bishop's Print Shop, 1950), 17–24; Marquis Jones, *The Raven: A Biography of Sam Houston* (New York: Grosset & Dunlap, 1929), 394; Weber, *Foreigners in Their Native Land*, 231.
44. Thompson, *Cortina*, 36–47; De Leon, *Tejano Community*, 17–18; Rosenbaum, *Mexicano Resistance in the Southwest*, 42; Weber, *Foreigners in Their Native Land*, 232. Cortina later moved his family to Mexico and gained a commission as captain and commander of a Mexican cavalry unit in Matamoros.
45. Geoffrey C. Ward, *The West: An Illustrated History* (New York: Back Bay Books, 2003), 180; Thompson, *Cortina*, 72–88; Cox, *Texas Rangers*, 153–156, 160–161; Rosenbaum, *Mexicano Resistance in the Southwest*, 42–43. On the Knights of the Golden Circle in Texas, see Roy Sylvan Dunn, "The KGC in Texas, 1860–1861," *Southern Historical Quarterly* 70 (April 1967): 543–569.
46. Thompson, *Cortina*, 95, 104–106; Rosenbaum, *Mexicano Resistance in the Southwest*, 45; Weber, *Foreigners in Their Native Land*, 232; Robert Ryal Miller, "Arms Across the Border: United States Aid to Juarez during the French Intervention in Mexico," *Transactions of the American Philosophical Society* 63, no. 6 (1973): 48.
47. Thompson, *Cortina*, 202–204, 238–241; Rosenbaum, *Mexicano Resistance in the Southwest*, 45.
48. Thompson, *Cortina*, 245–252.
49. Alvin M. Josephy, Jr., *The Civil War in the American West* (New York: Knopf, 1991), 232–233, 236.
50. Pitt, *Decline of the Californios*, 230–231; Aurora Hunt, "California Volunteers on Border Patrol, Texas and Mexico, 1862–1866," *Historical Society of California Quarterly* 30 (1948), 266.

51. Pitt, *Decline of the Californios*, 230–231.
52. Ibid., 232; Brigadier General Richard H. Orton *Records of California Men in the War of the Rebellion, 1861 to 1867* (Sacramento, California: Adjutant General's Office, 1890), 304–306. In February 1865, Vallejo resigned his commission and was replaced by Major John C. Cremony.
53. Josephy, *Civil War in the American West*, 243.
54. Ibid., 39, 52; Simmons, *Little Lion of the Southwest*, 176–178.
55. Josephy, *Civil War in the American West*, 41, 390, fn 20; Thompson, *Vaqueros in Blue and Grey*, 6. In a letter to the assistant adjutant general of the Western Department at St. Louis, Colonel Canby said about the New Mexicans: "I place no reliance on any volunteer force that can be raised unless strongly supported by Regular troops." Josephy, *The Civil War in the American West*, 41.
56. Josephy, *Civil War in the American West*, 42; Jacqueline Dorgan Meketa, ed., *Legacy of Honor: The Life of Rafael Chacón, A Nineteenth-Century New Mexican* (Albuquerque: University of New Mexico Press, 1986), 121–122.
57. Josephy, *Civil War in the American West*, 42; Meketa, *Legacy of Honor*, 118–119, 122, 125–126; Simmons, *Little Lion of the Southwest*, 178. Several New Mexican captains who could afford the financial outlay paid for the horses for their men but never received reimbursement from territorial officials.
58. Josephy, *Civil War in the American West*, 63.
59. Meketa, *Legacy of Honor*, 164–165, 178–179; Simmons, *Little Lion of the Southwest*, 179–180.
60. Josephy, *Civil War in the American West*, 78–92; Meketa, *Legacy of Honor*, 183; Simmons, *Little Lion of the Southwest*, 182–186.
61. Campbell, *Gone to Texas*, 241–246; Jerry D. Thompson, *Mexican Texans in the Union Army* (El Paso, TX: Texas Western Press, 1986), 1–5.
62. Campbell, *Gone to Texas*, 247, 251–252; Thompson, *Vaqueros in Blue and Gray*, 26–27.
63. Campbell, *Gone to Texas*, 249, 253, 257–258; Thompson, *Vaqueros in Blue and Gray*, 26–27.
64. Thompson, *Vaqueros in Blue and Gray*, 71–72; Thompson, *Mexican Texans in the Union Army*, 19.
65. Thompson, *Vaqueros in Blue and Gray*, 72–74; Thompson, *Mexican Texans in the Union Army*, 19. A judge from the lower Río Grande Valley, Davis had opposed Texas secession.
66. Thompson, *Vaqueros in Blue and Gray*, 75–79; Thompson, *Mexican Texans in the Union Army*, 19.
67. Thompson, *Vaqueros in Blue and Gray*, 8.
68. Ibid., 12; Thompson, *Mexican Texans in the Union Army*, 5–6; Gilberto M. Hinojosa, *A Border Town in Transition: Laredo, 1755–1870* (College Station, TX: Texas A & M University Press, 1983), 68.
69. Campbell, *Gone to Texas*, 180, 223; Thompson, *Vaqueros in Blue and Gray*, 60. At the end of the Civil War, Benavides twice served as an alderman of Laredo and three times in the Texas state legislature. His leadership built Democratic support among Tejanos in Webb County. Because of Benavides's friendship with the followers of Benito Juárez, Porfirio Díaz selected him as an envoy to the United States. With the coming of the railroads to Laredo in the 1880s, Anglos challenged the power of Laredo's political elite such as Santos Benavides.
70. Campbell, *Gone to Texas*, 264–265; Thompson, *Vaqueros in Blue and Gray*, 85–96.

71. Campbell, *Gone to Texas,* 261; Thompson, *Vaqueros in Blue and Grey,* 96.

72. Josephy, *Civil War in the American West,* 277.

73 Ibid., 286; De Lay, *War of a Thousand Deserts,* 308.

74. Josephy, *Civil War in the American West,* 277, 284–286, 287–291; Simmons, *Little Lion of the Southwest,* 191, 195; Meketa, *Legacy of Honor,* 248.

75. Truett, *Fugitive Landscapes,* 41–42.

76. Ibid., 47–48, 95; Hall, *Social Change in the Southwest,* 209; Sheridan, *Los Tucsonenses,* 69; Officer, *Hispanic Arizona,* 214. On the Camp Grant Massacre see James R. Hastings, "The Tragedy at Camp Grant in 1871," *Arizona and the West* 1, no. 2 (1959): 146–160, and especially Karl Jacoby, *Shadows at Dawn: An Apache Massacre and the Violence of History* (New York: Penguin, 2008).

# CHAPTER 5

✦

# Mexican Americans in the Southwest
## 1870 to the Early Twentieth Century

The years between 1870 and the turn of the twentieth century were marked by animosity and violence between Mexican Americans and Anglos focused on land. Clashes occurred from the lower Río Grande in Texas to Arizona and involved Texas Rangers, outlaws, Kickapoo and Apache Indians, and Mexicans. In the former confederate state of Texas, friction between Anglo-Texans and Tejanos remained intense and continuous because of the long-standing hatred between them. Anglo-Texan ranchers, aided by the Texas Rangers, were intent on driving Tejanos from the border region claimed by the ranchers. In the New Mexico territory, the contest over land produced the Santa Fe Ring and the Lincoln County War and, combined with racism, caused delays in achieving statehood. This domination did not take place without a struggle. The abusive power of the land monopolies and the railroads prompted aggrieved New Mexicans to join Las Gorras Blancas (White Caps), the Holy Order of the Knights of Labor, and the Populist Party. In the Southwest the lives of Mexican Americans were undergoing great change because industrial capitalism was establishing its historical presence in the region. Mexicans were being driven off their lands and transformed into landless wage workers for the new industrial economy of the West.[1]

Triggering this process of "creative destruction" in the Southwest was the development of an American economy dependent on natural resources and finished products moving between regions. Railroads helped to effect this transition to industrial capitalism by linking western resources with eastern markets. In the 1880s, a boom in railroad construction rapidly expanded track mileage, much of it railroad feeder lines that connected the western region's hinterlands. Cattle and grain production on huge farms and ranches financed by foreign investment soon dominated the West.[2]

The American West's extractive agriculture and industrial economy needed great numbers of workers. Between 1870 and 1910, the number of workers in the region engaged in railroad work, agriculture, and mining increased 84 percent. The railroads were responsible for the flood tide of Mexicans entering the labor force as U.S.-financed railroads connected Mexico's interior with its northern rail lines. Migration to the Southwest from Mexico was linked to the demand for labor during this period of economic growth. Race, more than any other factor, deter-mined work opportunities in the region. Because of racism, Mexican Americans and the immigrants from Mexico were incorporated into the low-wage jobs and experienced both poor working and living conditions. By the late nineteenth century, immigration from Mexico and economic growth in the Southwest became integrally related. Likewise, racial conflict became interwoven with class and economic conflict.[3]

## THE MEXICAN AMERICANS OF CALIFORNIA

In California, landownership patterns established by force and fraud in the ten-year period from 1860 to 1870 became fixed, creating the basis for the capitalist transformation and displacement of the state's remaining Spanish-speaking land-owners. Whereas in 1860 29 percent of California's Mexican population owned land consisting of small parcels, ten years later 5 to 10 percent were landowners. The railroads would dominate California's expanding economy; they ushered in large-scale agriculture as the key to the state's economic development. During the 1870s the huge cattle, horse, and sheep ranches of southern California were subdi-vided into small land tracts on which grain, wool, grapes, and citrus were grown. The remaining Mexican vaqueros and sheepherders saw their work vanish as the area ranchers shifted from ranching to more profitable cereal grain production and then to fruit and vegetable production.[4]

Mexicans first replaced Indians and then the Chinese in California's agricul-tural fields, vineyards, and citrus orchards. Three-fourths of the Mexicans entered southern California's labor market as itinerant wage workers. By the 1890s Mexicans made up the majority of unskilled day laborers in Los Angeles, as skilled and semi-skilled jobs were the preserve of white labor. Most engaged in building and street construction and supplemented this with farmwork. In light of the existing restricted opportunities for Mexican wage workers, women entered the workforce, some as domestics and others as seasonal harvest and cannery workers.[5]

Organized violence became a method of punishment for the region's non-white population, and there were frequent calls for the formation of vigilante com-mittees to enforce swift punishment through lynchings and hangings. Lynching found expression in lawless Los Angeles as wanton killers, bandits, thugs, and common drunks roamed the streets near the downtown Plaza. Vigilance commit-tees maintained order with the dangling rope. The lynching bees were public spec-tacles and an amusing pastime. Between 1850 and 1870, Los Angeles witnessed seventy-seven hangings by Anglo mobs, and most of their victims were Indians or Mexicans rightly or wrongly convicted of killing whites. The lynching of Mexicans continued into the late nineteenth and early twentieth centuries; the practice became so common that Spanish-speaking people cynically referred to American democracy as "linchocracia."[6]

As the overall population of Los Angeles rose to 17,400 in 1872, the town's Mexican population remained constant at about 2,100 residents. In 1876, the Southern Pacific Railroad arrived in Los Angeles bringing industry, commerce, and people. Ten years later the Santa Fe Railroad completed a line to Los Angeles, transporting 120,000 people to the city and to other parts of southern California. By 1890, the population of the region had increased by 200 percent and totaled 201,000. At the turn of the century, as a result of the region's real estate boom, the population of Los Angeles nearly doubled from 50,395 to 100,479 residents. As the Anglo population of Los Angeles grew, residential segregation by race and class accelerated. It confined the city's Mexicans to Sonora Town and excluded them from the city's booming economy and culture. Moreover, perceptions of Mexicans were distorted to fit the negative stereotype about them.[7]

Tens of thousands of immigrants from Mexico brought in by the railroads and commercial growers eventually supplemented California's native Spanish-speaking labor force so that by 1900 it stood at over 119,000.[8] This signaled the end of California's Spanish era. This bygone era now existed only in myths and fantasies celebrated up and down the California coastal towns as "Spanish Heritage Days." These romanticized celebrations that ignored the contributions of Indian and Mexican culture were concocted by Anglo urban boosters to appeal to tourists, especially to the prospective real estate investors and developers among them.[9] In South Texas, Anglo-Texans were driving Tejanos off the land, often at the point of a gun. The Anglos stole the Tejanos' livestock, destroyed their property, and killed them.

## THE TEJANOS AND MEXICANS OF TEXAS

Two-thirds of the Mexican population of the United States resided in Texas. The cattle drives and the arrival of the railroads in the post-Civil War era were features of the rapid change unfolding in the Lone Star State. The massive transfer in land titles from Tejanos to Anglo-Texans was accomplished through fraud and violence. Frequent acts of racial violence, particularly the surge in lynching, were fairly common in Texas during the 1860s and 1870s. One cause of the disorder was Reconstruction. To preserve their privileged sense of superiority, Texas Democrats who regained power called for the disfranchisement of Mexicans to deprive them of their rights and to continue their exploitation. Governor Richard Coke proposed resolving the border issue by the wanton killing of Mexicans and mandated state violence that included use of the Texas Rangers to carry it out.[10]

The ongoing strife between Tejanos and Anglo-Texans extended from central Texas down to the border and arose over land, water rights, and cattle ownership. Cattle rustling was especially rampant in Texas; observers estimated that one hundred thousand head of cattle were stolen each year. So great was cattle theft along the Texas border that American officials believed it would lead to open warfare between the United States and Mexico. Within the context of the racialized Mexican as inherently predisposed to thievery, Tejanos bore the brunt of the vendettas and consequently came under constant attack. Considering Tejanos as creatures somehow less than human made it easy for Anglo-Texans to perpetrate a slaughter of this population.[11]

In the area around San Antonio, a race war between Tejano and Anglo-Texans raged over unbranded livestock. Vigilantes killed seven Tejanos near the town of Boerne, and around San Marcos observers noted that the trees were "bearing a new kind of fruit"—alleged Tejano cattle rustlers hung by vigilance committees. Tejanos elsewhere were similarly mistreated and murdered. In west Texas, lynchings of Mexicans were commonplace. In fact, many local Anglo-Texans wanted the hangings to continue; they were calling for complete extermination. In 1877, the Salt War broke out in this region of Texas where Tejanos worked the salt lodes to gather the mineral for their use. However, ownership of the salt deposits changed hands; the new owners now made the Tejanos pay for the salt. Violence flared, resulting in four deaths and several thousand dollars' worth of damage. Texas Rangers and militia from New Mexico were called in to restore order, and in the bloody melee that ensued Tejanos were killed indiscriminately.[12]

The boom in smuggling contraband from South Texas into Mexico and the movement of Mexicans to the Texas side of the Río Grande prompted the governor of Tamaulipas to institute a *zona libre*, or free zone, in 1858. Stretching from the mouth of the Río Grande and twelve miles inland, the free zone exempted towns south of the Río Grande from paying high tariff duties. Frustrated, Texas merchants began agitating for the abolishment of the free zone because it further increased smuggling and cattle rustling.[13]

The revolutionary upheaval that plagued Mexico's northern states after 1867 added to the violence along the Río Grande border. Mexican insurgents crossed and recrossed into Texas to obtain weapons and supplies. Cattle rustling, a practice initiated by the United States Army during the Civil War, intensified as well. Juan Cortina again became the arch villain of the border region. All the crimes committed "under the control of armed thieves" were attributed to him or his followers, the Cortinistas. Predictably, the constant unrest caused by the general rebellion along the border provoked another wave of indiscriminate violence against the area Tejanos.[14]

Disputes over raids escalated and triggered a literal reign of terror on the Tejanos of South Texas. The killing of Tejanos soon took on a momentum of its own, becoming a kind of blood sport. The murders prompted the Texas adjutant general to note that in the Nueces Strip, "A considerable element . . . thought the killing of a Mexican no crime." Mexicans, the San Antonio *Express* reported, "were no longer safe along the highways, or outside of towns; they were shot . . . just because they were Mexicans."[15]

In 1875, more than two dozen Anglo-Texan raiders plundered and burned Nuecestown outside Corpus Christi in retaliation for a Mexican raid, creating terror in the Spanish-speaking settlements all the way south to Brownsville. Anglo-Texans killed every Tejano they could find. Mexicans were shot on sight and their bodies pitched into the local lakes and creeks, and others were hung from trees. Neither life nor property was safe in the Texas border region extending from the mouth of the Río Grande to El Paso. Over one hundred murders were reported to have been committed on the border, though untold numbers very likely went unreported. Great numbers of horses and cattle were stolen and all the thefts blamed on Tejanos. Killing squads of Anglo-Texan vigilantes roamed the South Texas countryside sowing panic as they hanged Tejano vaqueros and burned the homes and crops of others in retaliation for the cattle raids.[16]

To curb the raids, the state of Texas mobilized fourteen Texas Ranger companies to patrol the rural countryside from the Red River down to the Río Grande. Fearing that the manhunting Texas Rangers and their acts of bloodshed would provoke further violence, the Texas Legislature mustered twenty-two militia companies to replace the Rangers. These efforts failed to suppress the raiding that plagued the border region. Many local ranchers held meetings for the purpose of protecting themselves against the marauders as tensions among Anglo-Texans increased. The attacks on ranches had convinced them that Juan Cortina, "the terror of the Texas frontier," was responsible for the problems. Caving into pressure from the United States government, Mexico ordered his arrest.[17]

Vengeance raged through the Anglo-Texan community, and its response was swift and brutal retribution against Tejanos. Anglo mobs hanged Tejanos in San Patricio, Refugio, and Goliad counties. In Corpus Christi, a Committee of Public Safety was formed and ordered the registration of all males over eighteen years of age, giving name, age, occupation, color, birthplace, and nationality. Anglo-Texans were demanding an invasion of Mexico as a final solution to the mayhem they helped produce. As news of the terror spread, Tejanos fled their farms and towns and crossed into Mexico.[18]

Hostility between Anglo-Texans and Tejanos remained intense as the nineteenth century came to a close. Banding together, the former demanded subordination and insisted on preserving their dominance over the latter through violent means. Tejano resistance of any kind was fatal. In the summer of 1901, in an act of self-defense, Tejano Gregorio Cortez made the unfortunate mistake of killing two Anglo sheriffs, an act that transformed him into the most hunted fugitive in Texas history. His brave struggle had an enormous appeal for Tejanos, also the victims of racist treatment.

Gregorio Cortez was born on June 22, 1875, near the Mexican border town of Matamoros. In 1887, the Cortez family moved to Manor, Texas, north of Austin, where the young Gregorio learned his trade as a vaquero and farmer. Going to Karnes County in central Texas, Gregorio Cortez settled on the W. A. Thulmeyer Ranch, about ten miles west of Kenedy. Here he and his brother Romaldo rented land as tenant farmers and raised corn. The Tejanos also did itinerant ranch work in Gonzales County and in several other central Texas counties.

Gregorio Cortez's troubles began on June 12, 1901, when the sheriff of Atascosa County requested help from Karnes County Sheriff W. T. "Brack" Morris in locating a horse thief identified as a "medium-sized Mexican." Gregorio Cortez fit that vague description, but so did many other Tejanos in the area. To the Texans all Mexicans looked alike. One witness told Sheriff Morris that he had recently traded a horse to Gregorio Cortez for a mare. The law officer suspected that the mare was stolen.[19]

Lawmen Morris and D. P. Choate rode to the Cortez farm and confronted Gregorio Cortez at his home. Serving as interpreter, Deputy Choate told the Tejano he was under arrest. When Gregorio Cortez protested in Spanish to the law officers that they had no reason to arrest him, Choate told Morris that the Tejano said, "No white man can arrest me." Angered, Sheriff Morris drew his gun and fired. The sheriff wounded Romaldo and barely missed hitting Gregorio Cortez, who then shot and killed Morris only to save his own life. Fear of an unfair trial or mob violence most likely caused Gregorio Cortez to flee, and he became a "wanted man." As Cortez made his escape, his wife, children, and mother were taken into custody. The Texas Rangers and a posse numbering more than three hundred men soon began the pursuit of Gregorio Cortez, who was determined not to be taken back.

A hunted man and on the run for more than five hundred miles, Gregorio Cortez made his way to Belmont in Gonzales County. Here, Cortez hid at the home of his friends Martín and Refugia Robledo on land owned by a Mr. Schnabel. A posse led by Gonzales County Sheriff Robert M. Glover tracked Gregorio Cortez to the Robledo home. A gunfight soon broke out in which Glover and Schnabel were killed. Cortez escaped capture and once more was in flight, much of it now on foot.[20]

Gregorio Cortez walked one hundred miles to the home of another friend, Ceferino Flores, who gave him a horse, saddle, and provisions. Cortez then decided to head for Laredo. He was captured on June 22 about eight miles from the Mexican border after being on the run for ten days. A mob of several hundred people threatened to lynch the Tejano, but peace officers turned them away.[21]

A Gonzales County jury found Gregorio Cortez guilty of the murder of Mr. Schnabel, and the court sentenced him to fifty years in prison. On January 15, 1902, the Texas Court of Criminal Appeals reversed the Gonzales County verdict and gave the Tejano life in prison for the murder of Sheriff Glover.

Gregorio Cortez had spent time in eleven jails in eleven counties and was now in prison. A model prisoner, he received much support from both Tejanos and Anglos to obtain a pardon. Cortez became a source of inspiration for the poor

**Gregorio Cortez, 1901.**
(Cortez is first row, center.)
CREDIT: 068-0478. Copy courtesy of the University of Texas, San Antonio, Institute of Texan Cultures; Primary Repository: University of Texas, Austin.

Tejanos of the state of Texas, their hero, a legend commemorated in a well-known *corrido* (ballad). In 1913, Texas Governor Oscar B. Colquitt granted Cortez a conditional pardon.[22]

Anglo dominance transformed Tejano life in South Texas, where Tejano land claims became a dominant issue. The cattle drives, along with the introduction of barbed wire in the 1870s, led to the enclosure of rangeland in the region by the mid-1880s. By 1892 in Cameron County, forty-six Anglo-Texans controlled over 1,200,000 acres of land, equaling four times the acreage owned by Tejanos. In Hidalgo County, only a third of the land was left in Tejano hands. However, devoid of credit, many of the remaining Tejano ranchers went bankrupt during the drought-induced "die-ups" of range cattle in the 1890s.[23]

The number of Mexicans in Texas increased from 43,161 in 1880 to 71,062 in 1900. Tejanos now formed a minority in central Texas, but they constituted 92 percent of the population in the region below San Antonio and along the Río Grande. The Tejano's numerical dominance served only one purpose—as the principal source of rural labor—for the influx of Anglos into South Texas who were transforming the region into a major center of commercial agriculture.[24] More and more Tejanos fell into the ranks of low-wage workers as cotton garment manufacturing, the 1902 Reclamation Act, and the construction of the St. Louis, Brownsville and Mexican Railways in 1904 further stimulated commercial agriculture in South Texas. The railroad's financial backers included a handful of well-to-do Tejano ranchers, bankers, and merchants such as Francisco Yturria and J. A. Fernández. These wealthy Tejanos served as intermediaries between Anglo-Texans and their Tejano workers. Some did not escape the outbreak of violence ten years later triggered by *El Plan de San Diego* (Plan of San Diego) that would see the lower Río Grande Valley once again awash with bloodshed and violence.[25]

The influx of Anglo newcomers led to further Tejano land displacement through taxes, fraud, legal costs to validate land claims, enclosure of water, fluctuating cattle prices, and the inability to compete with Anglo land companies. The sharp rise in land prices in anticipation of the railroad's arrival proved ruinous to the last visage of Tejano landowners. Once the railroad line was constructed, Anglo-controlled towns such as Mercedes, San Benito, Chapin, Raymondville, and Mission rose in the lower Río Grande alongside the railroad. Dozens of irrigation companies increased the arable acreage in South Texas. Hidalgo County as a result soon boasted of being the nation's highest producing agricultural county. The railroads and real estate promoters of the Río Grande Valley advertised to prospective Anglo investors that Mexicans would perform the labor in the region. They also promised that Mexicans would be excluded from sharing in their society. Peonage in South Texas meant Tejanos and Mexicans working for Anglo-Texan *patrones* and *patronas.* A Laredo newspaper would later observe: "The lands which mainly belonged to Mexicans [passed] to the hands of Americans . . . the old proprietors work as laborers on the same lands that used to belong to them." Tejanos and immigrants from Mexico made up the floating population utilized in railroad construction and farmwork. The long-time Tejano residents and the newcomers from Mexico were indistinguishable to the Anglos.[26] The next stage was the disenfranchisement of Tejanos.

## DISENFRANCHISING TEJANO VOTERS
## AS POLITICAL STRATEGY

The Democratic Party, the self-described "party of the white man," dominated Texas politics after Reconstruction. Political disenfranchisement of Tejanos set in as Anglo-Texan Democrats used voter fraud and election-law trickery and racism to retain power over them, just as they did with blacks and poor whites. Voter fraud was rampant in the Río Grande Valley counties and in those precincts with large Spanish-speaking populations. Entrenched South Texas political bosses such as James B. Wells, the products of Democratic political machines appearing throughout the Texas border region, had large numbers of aliens from Mexico brought in just before elections, naturalized, and declared legal residents; the new residents were then expected to vote for the bosses. Certain precincts voted more than the entire population combined. In a failed attempt to stop this political boss-ism, the State of Texas passed a law in 1895 requiring six months' residency before a person could vote. Some Tejano Democrats had access to public office. Unreconstructed Confederate Army veteran and banker-merchant Thomas A. Rodríguez of Brownsville served three terms in the Texas state legislature representing parts of Atascosa, Karnes, and San Patricio counties. Confederate Army veteran and Laredo businessman Santos Benavides held the most terms in the Texas House of Representatives, serving from 1879 to 1884. However, owing to increased disenfranchisement, Thomas A. Rodríguez was the sole Tejano in the Texas House of Representatives by the end of the nineteenth century.[27]

Relying on Jim Crow techniques, Anglo-Texans retained full control of the Tejano vote via the poll tax. Between 1879 and 1899 six attempts were made to pass poll-tax legislation in Texas. All failed because of opposition from blacks and Tejanos, labor groups, and Populists. In 1901, the Texas Legislature finally passed the poll tax, which state voters approved the following year by a two-to-one margin. Requiring Texas residents to pay $1.75 to vote, the poll tax effectively created a barrier to keep Tejanos from voting. Because of greatly restricted district electorates, Texas Democrats dominated political leadership. In addition to the poll tax, gerrymandering weakened voter strength. Finally, the white primaries undercut manipulation of the Tejano vote by prohibiting Tejanos from joining the Democratic Party or participating in primary elections.[28]

The efforts of Anglo-Texans to further consolidate their political power took a strange turn in 1896. In the same year in which the U.S. Supreme Court upheld racial segregation in public accommodations in *Plessy v. Ferguson*, Ricardo Rodríguez appeared in federal district court in San Antonio, Texas. The Tejano, a five-year resident of San Antonio employed as a street cleaner, made an application for United States citizenship that would grant him the right to vote. His actions initiated concerted legal maneuvers by Anglos to disallow Tejanos the right to vote in the state of Texas.[29]

The Rodríguez case involved the right of naturalization. It focused attention on the fact that Tejanos born in Mexico could not vote unless they applied for naturalization. At the center of the debate was an 1872 federal statute that ruled that only Caucasians and Africans could become U.S. citizens. Under this law and reflecting nineteenth-century color designations of black, white, red (American Indian), and yellow (Asian), Ricardo Rodríguez did not qualify for American citizenship because the state of Texas considered him neither "a white person, nor an African, nor of African descent."[30]

At issue was the question of racial and educational qualification for achieving U.S. citizenship. Interest in the Rodríguez case was high among Tejanos who were facing desperate times in Texas during which what remained of their political rights were being threatened. They rallied to condemn the "effort being made in Federal Court to prevent Mexicans from becoming voting citizens of the United States." In his court testimony, Rodríguez claimed his cultural heritage to be "pureblooded Mexican," but the Tejano stated to the court he was not a descendant of any of the aboriginal peoples of Mexico (American Indian), nor was he of Spanish (white) or African descent (black).[31]

Defense lawyers for Ricardo Rodríguez and witnesses who testified on his behalf asserted that he had the right to become an American citizen. They argued that since 1836 both "the Republic of Texas and the United States had by various collective acts of naturalization conferred upon Mexicans the rights and privileges of American citizenship." The defense further observed that the U.S. Congress in 1845 had extended citizenship to Mexicans after Texas annexation. The defense noted that Article VIII of the Treaty of Guadalupe Hidalgo automatically conferred American citizenship on Mexicans who did not leave the territory after one year as long as they did not declare their desire to become Mexican citizens. On May 3, 1897, the federal court ruled in favor of Rodríguez. *Re Rodriguez* declared that the Fourteenth Amendment granted citizenship to all people born or naturalized in the United States regardless of color or race. What was more, the Rodríguez decision upheld the legal right of Mexicans as "white," legally affirmed the rights of Tejanos to vote, and prevented further attempts by Anglo-Texans to use the courts to deprive them of their voting rights.[32]

## THE MEXICANS OF ARIZONA AND NEW MEXICO

Arizona's residents of Mexican descent made up the majority population. Most were common laborers who cleared land, built irrigation canals, and worked in agriculture, on the railroads, and in the copper mines in the southern part of the territory. Another segment of the population were farmers, ranchers, and businessmen, mainly in Tucson, a commercial center for the surrounding agriculture and mining industries. The small elite class of Mexicans affiliated with the wealthy Americans served as liaisons and go-betweens for the Anglos and Mexicans. As a reward for their patronage, this group of Mexicans obtained special favors in the form of government contracts. Many were merchants; therefore, they profited handsomely from the large American military presence in the Arizona territory. Very few of these leaders participated in Arizona's territorial affairs because Mexicans had been excluded from Arizona politics beginning in the 1870s. No Mexican served as a congressional delegate from the Arizona territory, which was controlled by mining interests. In fact, the Organic Bill excluded representation for Mexican areas in Arizona, and as a result Mexicans were disenfranchised and fell victim to a dual wage scale and other forms of racial inequality.[33]

Mexicans made up half the population of Arizona's Salt River Valley and were primarily small farmers who raised wheat and barley for the U.S. Army. They were originally from Tucson and Tubac, whereas others had come from Sonora's Altar Valley, having fled that region of northern Mexico because of political turmoil and raiding and taking of captives by Chiracahua Apaches. Due to U.S. federal pacification or extermination policies, the Chiracahua Apaches no longer upset daily life in the Arizona territory. The Mexican homesteaders had built the San Francisco Canal to irrigate their fields with loans from Prescott merchant Michael Wormser, a speculator in water rights. These were loans that benefited only the lender, because Mexicans eventually lost their lands to Wormser through foreclosures. Other Mexicans fell victim to Anglo business interests that were consolidating power in the territory. They became wage laborers on the commercial farms. Additional numbers of Mexicans were hired by Arizona's commercial farms with the arrival of the railroads, which opened up larger markets for agricultural products. In addition to encouraging the expansion of livestock raising, the railroads promoted private investment in mining by large eastern companies.[34]

Mining in Arizona was dependent on Mexican labor. The mine operators significantly reduced labor costs, because, under the racially based Mexican scale, Mexican workers earned about a third less than Anglo miners for the same work. Anglo miners disliked Mexicans because they undermined the wage structure. The "whites-only" policy of the mining unions, occupational discrimination whereby whites held the higher paying and higher status jobs, relegated Mexicans

**Family and Friends in a Corral, 1910–1918.**
CREDIT: "Family & Friends in a corral w/ocatillo fence, 1910–18." MP SPC 173: 648. Chicano Research Collection: "Friends of Francisca R. Ocampo. ca. 1910–1918." Courtesy of the Ocampo Family Photograph Collection, Arizona State University Libraries, Department of Archives and Special Collections, Arizona State University, Tempe.

**Coyotero Apache with a Mexican Captive, 1870, p.**
CREDIT: "Coyotero Apache Warrior and a Mexican Captive, 1870." LC-USZC4-5673. Courtesy of the Library of Congress.

to the bottom ranks of mine work. Management justified the wage differential by citing improved production. Mexican miners increasingly sought to adjust this unequal wage system on both sides of the U.S.-Mexico border by joining the Magónistas, the anarcho-syndicalist *Partido Liberal Mexicano* (or PLM) of the brothers Enrique and Ricardo Flores Magón. The Magónistas played an important role in radicalizing Mexican workers in the Southwest, as did the militant industrial unionism of the Western Federation of Miners and later the Industrial Workers of the World. These organizations led the strike in Cananea, Mexico, in 1906 that was eventually crushed by the combined forces of American mine managers, the Mexican government, American troops, and the Arizona Rangers.[35] Nevertheless, such repression further radicalized Mexican miners.

New Mexico retained the significant features of the political and social structure ruled over by the small group of wealthy Spanish-speaking ricos and Anglos whose power rested in the Republican Party. Through the Republican Party patronage system, this coterie of ricos held local and legislative offices and served as territorial delegates in the U.S. Congress. As members of the powerful and corrupt Santa Fe Ring, the Spanish-speaking ruling class took part in the greedy land grabbing and corruption that marked New Mexico's late territorial period, in addition to competing for federal contracts to supply U.S. Army forts and Indian reservations.[36]

The majority of New Mexico's Spanish-speaking population remained concentrated in northern New Mexico. They were communal landholders dependent on agriculture and sheep ranching for their livelihood. Northern New Mexico's subsistence economy was disappearing because capitalist market-oriented agriculture and stock raising had taken hold in the region. Furthermore, the U.S. Court of Private Land Claims refused to grant the small landholders title to their land. The coming of the railroad served as the catalyst for this transformation that ushered in marked changes to other parts of the territory. Growing numbers of Spanish-speaking villagers were migrating seasonally to work for the mines, ranches, and farms in the New Mexico territory and in Colorado. Entire New Mexican families eventually became itinerant workers.[37] The coming of the railroads quickened this large-scale displacement of New Mexicans from their land and their further integration into a wage-labor market.

Seeking a route west, the Atchison, Topeka, and Santa Fe Railroad arrived at Raton Pass, New Mexico, on January 1, 1879, and by July had extended a rail line to Las Vegas. Two years later, railroad service came to Santa Fe—ending more than a century of commerce on the Santa Fe Trail—then to Albuquerque, and it later joined the Southern Pacific Railroad at Deming. The Atchison, Topeka, and Santa Fe was the world's largest railroad system. Along with its main competitor, the Denver and Río Grande and other railroad companies, it had lines throughout the New Mexico territory servicing the growing agriculture, livestock, mining, and timber industries. The railroads led to the growth of towns such as Raton and Springer in the northwest, Las Cruces in the south, Deming and Silver City in the southwest, and Gallup in the west. As in California, Texas, and elsewhere, the railroads caused property values in New Mexico to jump dramatically. Property valued at $41 million in 1880 increased almost six times to $231 million in 1890. In the same ten-year period, railroad cattle shipments from New Mexico increased almost fivefold from 347,000 to 1,630,000. What one contemporary observer noted about the arrival of the Santa Fe Railroad held true for the arrival of other railroad lines to New Mexico: The railroads "heralded the replacement of mercantile capitalism by . . . industrial capitalism."[38]

Commercial and political rivalries over land intensified the widespread disorder and unrest in New Mexico. Ranchers hungry for pastures waged bloody campaigns against New Mexican land grantees. This period witnessed the Colfax (1875–1878) and the Lincoln County (1878–1881) shooting wars. The native New Mexicans would fight against the land fraud that was driving them off their lands. Racism became intertwined with class and economic conflict.

Economic growth brought additional problems to the Spanish-speaking residents of the New Mexico territory. After 1870, a different breed of Anglo came to New Mexico. Most were ex-soldiers who had fought in the Indian campaigns or were Civil War veterans left jobless by the 1873–1879 depression. These rootless men drifted from one mining and cattle ranch to another in search of work. Many became outlaws and livestock rustlers, such as William Bonney—also known as Billy the Kid—and formed the criminal element that gained notoriety for the lawlessness and violence that scarred the New Mexico territory. They did not like Mexicans.[39]

Beginning in 1869, native New Mexicans migrated to southeastern New Mexico in present-day Lincoln County and established small farms and sheep ranches. They came under mounting pressure from invading cattlemen and rustlers from Texas. Lincoln County became known as "Little Texas" as Anglo ranchers killed or drove out the Spanish-speaking population from the range country. "Native inhabitants" are being "ousted from their homes" by ranchers, wrote Territorial Governor Edmond Ross to a rancher. "I understand very well . . . what a cow-boy or a cattle herder with a brace of pistols . . . and a Winchester in his hands means when he 'asks' a sheepherder to leave a given range." The Lincoln County Stock Growers Association first warned Spanish-speaking sheepherders out of the area; then hired guns killed their animals in attempts to drive them out after the threats were ignored.[40] Salman's Scouts attacked local communities, looting and destroying property, raping women, and killing unarmed men and boys. Sheepherders also lived in fear of raids by outlaws, who attacked and killed them and stole their flocks. Spanish-speaking sheepmen likewise battled with cattlemen from northern Arizona. The town of Trinidad in southern Colorado gained a reputation for violence following the so-called Trinidad War in the winter of 1867–1868 during which Anglos and Mexicans fought each other in a series of pitched gun battles that required intervention by federal troops from Fort Lyon to restore peace.[41]

The cattle industry in the Southwest reached its zenith in the 1880s, then declined as overgrazing and drought severely damaged the pastures. This put an end to the open-range system and the yearly cattle roundups. The demise of the cattle industry opened up opportunities again for sheepherders; however, legislation curtailed the use of the public lands for sheep raising. Stock raising was now linked by a railroad network to a national American economy versus a local one. Land had also become a commodity in the New Mexico territory, stolen through legal and illegal means by land speculators looking to make huge profits.[42]

## THE UNITED STATES AND THE NEW MEXICO LAND GRANTS QUESTION

During the New Mexico territorial period the land held by native New Mexicans rapidly changed ownership. Numerous factors accounted for this development, the primary reason being that the land grantees did not have any control of the adjudication of land. Land claims were not surveyed prior to the confirmation hearing. For example, the Maxwell and Sangre de Cristo land grants were confirmed first, then the claimants disclosed their size. The Maxwell Grant was the largest tract of privately owned land in the western hemisphere, totaling 1,714,764 acres. The Sangre de Cristo Grant totaled 2,713,545 acres, though under the 1824 Mexican Colonization Law (48,500 acres for each grantee), these grants together should have been limited to 97,000 acres. Both grants were challenged before the U.S. Supreme Court, and the Court validated the confirmations. It ruled that Mexican law had never granted such large holdings; rather, the U.S. Congress had granted the land. On January 28, 1870, Lucien B. Maxwell sold the Maxwell Land Grant to foreign investors for $1,350,000.[43]

The Office of the Surveyor General was ill prepared to adjudicate land grants. None of the members knew Spanish, nor were they familiar with Spanish and Mexican law. None were lawyers. The Office of the Surveyor General did not provide for due process; thus the rights of the land grantees as American citizens were violated. In adjudicating disputed land claims, the Office of the Surveyor General opted to simply rule in favor of the claimant who brought up the claim. In this way, large grants that overlapped several smaller grants were confirmed. When claimants of the smaller land grants sought confirmation, they were informed that the federal government had already confirmed the land to someone else.[44] Through the auspices of the Office of the Surveyor General, individual speculators profited at the expense of the Spanish-speaking land grantees. In a conflict of interest, these speculators included those appointed to the Office of the Surveyor General. Henry Atkinson and T. Rush Spencer each opportunely held land grants while serving in this federal branch of government. The president of the New Mexico Land and Livestock Company, Atkinson made decisions on the Antón Chico community land grant as he participated in legal proceedings, claiming that he owned the grant. Such conflicts of interest, combined with the defects of the federal Surveyor General system, guaranteed that land grant adjudications remained patently unfair.[45]

According to Spanish and Mexican law, a land grant was issued to a person representing the entire community, and that person was named on the grant. Speculators purchased the land grant from this person even though the land belonged to an entire community. In this way, community land grants were legally wrested away as private land grants. The new land grantee then petitioned the U.S. government to get the grant ratified.[46]

Another method by which land was taken away from native New Mexicans was through "partitioning," the subdividing of land as had been done in California according to an 1876 law. A lawyer agreed to represent a community land grant with the understanding that a portion of the grant was given as payment for services. Those who had no money lost in court. Thomas B. Catron obtained the Tierra Amarilla community land grant on the border of northern New Mexico and southern Colorado through this procedure. Catron was involved in sixty-three land grant cases that gained the future senator from New Mexico about three million acres, in addition to his holdings in six states and Mexico. After the Tierra Amarilla grant was confirmed to the heirs, Catron purchased all their interests for $200,000 and obtained a court decree stating that he now owned the grant. The Tierra Amarilla grant heirs went to court to regain their common lands but lost their case. In 1909, Catron sold the Tierra Amarilla grant for $850,000.[47]

The most notorious of the New Mexico land swindlers was the Santa Fe Ring, involved in land, cattle, mining, lumber, and freight speculation. This cabal of judges, lawyers, territorial officials, businessmen, and newspaper editors engaged in widespread fraud, bribery, and corruption. Up to the 1880s, all of New Mexico's governors were members of the Santa Fe Ring. Several New Mexican ricos collaborated with the Santa Fe Ring to acquire land grants. The Santa Fe Ring manipulated or exploited legal loopholes to gain control of vast Spanish and Mexican land grants to become the most powerful force in the New Mexico territory.

In 1875, the *Grant County Herald* reported that "fraud and corruption are freely employed by the [Santa Fe] Ring which now controls the Territory in order to further their designs."[48]

The native New Mexican landowners banded together to challenge the Santa Fe Ring. Those on the Maxwell Land Grant resisted the Ring's attempts to displace them, and New Mexico's congressional delegate from San Miguel County, Trinidad Romero, indicted the Ring in a report to Washington. Expressing the idea of an ethnic homeland and a right to equality that cut across class lines, Spanish-speaking New Mexicans stood up to encroachment by an Anglo-dominated modern society and growing racism.[49] In 1884, the Santa Fe Ring became the target of protest in Las Vegas, New Mexico. At a meeting held at Baca Hall angry citizens denounced the Ring, indicting it for its control of the territorial legislature, for real estate investments, and for jury tampering. Singled out were Thomas Catron, territorial secretary William G. Ritch, and Governor Lionel Sheldon. Indignant New Mexicans rallied against the fraud and corruption and helped bring about the demise of the Santa Fe Ring. In 1885, a court of land claims was established to settle the disputed land grants and to prosecute land fraud in the New Mexico territory.[50]

Spanish-speaking villagers could not stop the tide of Anglo invasion that accompanied the incorporation of the New Mexico territory into the American national economy. Anglos seized millions of acres of communally held pasture-lands that were protected under the Treaty of Guadalupe Hidalgo despite federal legal intervention. Additional land was being lost to lawyers as payment for legal fees, and competition with the new Anglo stock raisers forced additional numbers of New Mexicans to sell their lands. Like the Mexicans of California and Texas, more and more native New Mexicans were driven from their land and forced into wage labor. They wound up on the large cattle and sheep ranches, as miners or loggers, or on railroad construction projects, earning less money and working harder than their Anglo counterparts. The desperate though proud New Mexicans experienced a systematic dispossession, the main grievance that spurred resistance.[51]

Poor Spanish-speaking herders and ranchers turned to self-help through secret societies. The Gorras Blancas undertook retributive justice that was necessary during these trying times. The society became a staging ground for Mexicans to become members of the Holy Order of the Knights of Labor, who were proclaiming the identity of interests between the capitalists and the working classes. The Knights of Labor had become the preserve of rural labor and small-town mechanics. The Knights viewed land speculators and large landholders as it did lawyers and bankers—as monopolists who prospered at the cost of workers and poor people.[52]

## LAS GORRAS BLANCAS AND THE STRUGGLE
## TO PROTECT LAND GRANTS

San Miguel County was leading New Mexico in the transition to a modern capitalist economy with the feature of wage work in railroad and commercial agriculture and ranching. Land loss and low wages owing to a growing labor surplus were developments of the troublesome times in San Miguel County, the largest county in the northeastern section of the New Mexico territory. The county extended from the eastern flank of the Sangre de Cristo Mountains to the Texas Panhandle border. It contained 24,204 of the New Mexico Territory's 153,593 inhabitants, and almost 90 percent were Mexicans. Several thousand Anglos lived in San Miguel County; most were recent arrivals and consisted of wealthy ranchers or those with links to the railroads. The independent farms run by Spanish-speaking New Mexicans that had flourished since the antebellum period began to compete with the Anglo stock raisers for land, water, and timber. Las Vegas was the county seat, the largest town, and a force in territorial politics. The formation of the Anglo enclave "New Town" in Las Vegas, several miles east of Old Town near the Las Vegas plaza, indicated the growing racial divisions in New Mexico. Unlike the Anglos who arrived before the Mexican War, this new group refused to acculturate to the ways of the New Mexicans, including learning their native language.[53]

The Anglos enlisted the ricos on their side because the latter served the ranchers' interests and because they benefited economically from regional enterprise. The bitter conflict in San Miguel County was related to the issue of community land grants. In their fight against a common enemy, the native New Mexicans banded together to demand their rights to land grants, equitable tax laws, education, labor, and statehood. Agricultural misery, as represented by land displacement, was the goad to action. The aptly named weekly newspaper *La Voz del Pueblo* (The Voice of the People) showed sympathy toward New Mexico's victimized rural poor. In its pages, it defended native New Mexicans against the "capitalists, monopolists and land grabbers."[54]

The 1887 civil suit won by landowner José Leon Padilla (*Phillip Millhiser et al. v. José Leon Padilla*) against the Las Vegas Land and Cattle Company over the legality of recent land acquisitions by speculators boosted the morale of the aggrieved native New Mexicans and helped to hasten the collective struggle unfolding over the issue of land. The Las Vegas Grant, a community grant, was one of the largest in the territory, encompassing almost half a million acres. A few wealthy Anglos and Spanish-speaking New Mexican speculators purchased the tracts illegally and established large cattle and sheep companies. Disputes took place between New Mexican farmers and the large stock companies over boundaries, water, and fencing. The unsettled legal status of the Las Vegas grant allowed the land speculators to continue fencing. The Spanish-speaking farmers wanted the land to remain open to them for grazing, water, wood, and other common needs until the dispute over land was settled in the courts. As industrial capitalism burst through in northern New Mexico, hidden avengers struck in defense of the common people to challenge it. In 1889, the clandestine organization Las Gorras Blancas began organizing the poor Spanish-speaking ranchers and farmers threatened by the partitioning off of the Las Vegas Grant into separate ranches by promoters and profiteers of the new order. The Gorras Blancas increased its membership, and it began to openly challenge corporate power in San Miguel County. The county, and much of northern New Mexico, would soon become the site of an uprising by this secret organization that united the local Spanish-speaking population in demanding equal rights as American citizens.[55]

Las Gorras Blancas had a local indigenous character and confirmed the presence in northern New Mexico of individuals with radical leanings. Juan José Herrera and his brothers Pablo and Nicanor, all of whom were from San Miguel County, organized the group in 1888. A former mayor of Las Vegas, a captain in the New Mexico territorial militia who fought in the Civil War, Juan Herrera belonged to the labor organization the Holy Order of the Knights of Labor. The Knights had catapulted to national fame and power in 1885 following their victory in the Southwestern railroad strike. The Knights were opposed to land speculation. Living on a ranch near San Geronimo, Juan Herrera founded Las Gorras Blancas because local Anglo ranchers had fenced land that prevented Spanish-speaking farmers from grazing their livestock. To his advantage, Herrera had knowledge not only of labor unionism but also of American law, and he spoke Spanish, English, French, and several Indian languages. In the same year he organized Las Gorras Blancas, Juan Herrera became a "sojourner," that is, a recruiter for the Knights of Labor in New Mexico. The class-conscious native New Mexican established twenty local assemblies of the Knights in San Miguel County and recruited new members in Santa Fe, San Miguel, Mora, Taos, and Colfax counties in northern New Mexico and in counties in southern Colorado with Spanish-speaking populations. These new Knights pledged to "defend the life, interests, and reputation, and family of all true members." Seven hundred people in the area of El Salitre, El Burro, Ojitos Frios, and San Geronimo within the boundaries of the Las Vegas grant joined Las Gorras Blancas in warning Anglos to stay away from their land. Starting in the summer of 1889, and convinced justice was with them, Las Gorras Blancas began cutting fences and destroying other property. Striking at night, the masked riders began settling old scores; they cut several miles of barbed wire fence belonging to two unpopular ranchers near San Geronimo who had claimed common lands. Then Las Gorras wrecked the farm and sawmill of José Ignacio Luján outside the village of San Ignacio. Anonymous warnings soon turned up in localities troubled by the rural rebellion, cautioning that dire consequences would follow if fencing did not stop. Homes and barns on grant lands were also burned. Throughout the winter, going from one place to another in a circuit of destruction, Las Gorras Blancas kept up their nighttime raids on other fenced-in ranches within the Las Vegas grant, demolishing fences, crops, farm equipment, and other rural property. Las Gorras Blancas committed few acts of vigilance against persons. Rural agitation continued throughout much of northern New Mexico. Alarmed by this rise in clandestine activity, San Miguel County officials urged New Mexico Governor LeBaron Bradford Prince to organize a militia to stop the growing terror.[56]

Las Gorras Blancas increased in size and determination and extended their attacks on land grabbers to stolen land grants adjoining the Las Vegas grant and to those in Mora and Santa Fe counties. In March 1890, several hundred armed Gorras Blancas boldly rode into Las Vegas in a show of force. Members posted leaflets throughout town declaring their motives and intentions. The leaflets were signed "The White Caps, 1,500 Strong and Growing Daily." The fence cutters made common cause with the area land grantees who were now wage workers or tenant farmers. In another notice posted along roads, Las Gorras Blancas told land grant members not to cut and sell lumber or crossbeams to the railroads unless it was for the price approved by their organization and not to work for anyone unless the Gorras approved the work and the pay. "White Caps, Fence Cutters, and Death" was prominently appended to this threatening notice. Claiming full employment at a decent wage was a just cause, Las Gorras Blancas stopped wagon teams hauling railroad ties for the Atchison, Topeka, and Santa Fe Railroad and unloaded and destroyed the ties if the drivers were not charging enough for their hauls. The masked riders also exhorted railroad workers to strike for higher wages and compelled employers to meet their terms. Because of this defiant intrusion by Las Gorras Blancas, the Atchison, Topeka, and Santa Fe Railroad stopped purchasing railroad ties in the Las Vegas area. Las Gorras Blancas began destroying and burning railroad bridges and tracks. By the summer of 1890, there were dozens of reports of violence. Hundreds of miles of fence had been destroyed, homes ransacked and burned, and agricultural implements smashed, all of this handiwork attributed to Las Gorras Blancas.[57]

Organizing by the fence cutters continued as residents on land grants in northern New Mexico and southern Colorado came into its fold. Las Gorras Blancas also infiltrated the Knights of Labor, and the contingent of Spanish-speaking Knights named themselves *Los Caballeros de Labor*. The fifty Knights' local assemblies joined native New Mexicans in resisting land grabbers by organizing into the Las Vegas Land Grant Defense Association. Los Caballeros de Labor expanded its enlistment of native New Mexican wage earners, declaring to them that it was their right to organize to protect their jobs and families. Tapping the membership of the Knights' local assemblies, Juan Herrera recruited them into Las Gorras Blancas. On the night of July 3, Los Caballeros de Labor once again rode into Las Vegas. During the next day's July 4th celebration, a thousand Caballeros de Labor from San Miguel County, led by a twenty-five piece band playing "John Brown's Body," joined a daytime procession through the town in a show of strength and support of the right of the people to own the land and to protect them against monopolists. Some members carried banners with slogans proclaiming in Spanish their organization's principles and objectives—free schools for their children, popular election of those who held public office, and protection of the workers against the monopolists, among others. In an indication of the populist leanings of Las Gorras Blancas, other men marching in the procession chanted: "*El pueblo es rey, y los oficiales publicos son sus sirvientes humildes que deben obedecer sus mandados*." ("The people are king, and the public officials are her humble servants who must obey her mandates.") On July 12, Knights' leader Terrence Powderly granted the San Miguel Caballeros de Labor a charter.[58] There was dissension, however, among the Caballeros de Labor regarding the tactics of Las Gorras Blancas.

Membership in Los Caballeros de Labor increased, and so did the night riding by Las Gorras Blancas. Tensions were running high in San Miguel County as a result of the rural rebellion. Aware of the growing threat to established order posed by Las Gorras Blancas, Governor Prince was in Washington, DC, lobbying for statehood for New Mexico, and could do nothing. Upon his return to Santa Fe, Prince contemplated using American soldiers stationed in the territory to patrol areas in which Las Gorras Blancas was active. On August 16, the governor paid a visit to Las Vegas. With over half the population of Las Vegas endorsing the fence cutting and other disturbances on the Las Vegas Land Grant, the meeting turned into a loud protest against the land grabbers. The Caballeros de Labor sent a committee headed by Nestor Montoya, the leader of San Miguel's Knights of Labor in Santa Fe who was also part owner of the newspaper *La Voz del Pueblo*, to speak with the governor. Angry that the public associated the Knights with the outbreak of violence, Montoya told the governor that Los Caballeros de Labor would help him quell the fence cutting and other destruction of rural property.[59]

The influence of Las Gorras Blancas waned as a result of Governor Prince's intervention, but more so because few fences remained standing in northern New Mexico. Another factor leading to Las Gorras Blancas' demise was that those who were members of the Knights of Labor became involved in politics. Native New Mexicans in Los Caballeros de Labor and in the Knights of Labor turned to the Populist Party. San Miguel County emerged as a bastion of *El Partido del Pueblo Unido* (the United People's Party). Composed of dissident factions from the Democratic and Republican parties, El Partido del Pueblo Unido was opposed to placing corporate and financial interests above the general welfare of New Mexico's mechanics, laborers, farmers, and ranchmen.[60]

Las Gorras Blancas, Los Caballeros de Labor, and the United People's Party were consequences of a long process of economic and social deterioration in the situation of the Spanish-speaking people of northern New Mexico. Organized resistance on such a large scale against the ruthless and greedy Anglo and Spanish-speaking ruling classes in the territory had not been seen since the Taos Revolt of 1847. It would not occur again until the early 1960s with the rise of the alianza movement of Reies López Tijerina. The loss of village lands in northern New Mexico continued and pushed more and more rural New Mexicans into the ranks of seasonal work. Some fled to Colorado while others remained in the countryside, landless, and further depressing rural wages by their competition. Racism played a role in the opposition by Congress to block statehood for New Mexico, whereas in Arizona many Anglos believed Mexicans were not ready for statehood.

## STATEHOOD FOR NEW MEXICO AND ARIZONA?

New Mexico had been seeking statehood for over half a century. In 1850, the year of President Zachary Taylor's death, and in the midst of the debate over slavery, the U.S. Congress nullified statehood for New Mexico when it passed the Compromise Bill granting New Mexico territorial status. In light of the era's racism, many officials were reluctant to admit large numbers of Mexicans, who were considered inferior. Other attempts to implement a state constitution followed. In 1871, the House failed to pass the Enabling Act to adopt a constitution in preparation for being admitted as a state, despite a passionate speech by House U.S. congressional delegate J. Francisco Chaves in support of the bill. In the following year, New Mexico voters rejected a proposed constitution for statehood because of a provision for public schools and another provision that was unfavorable to the territory's largely Catholic population.

The majority of native New Mexicans joined the call for statehood out of their fear of being further disenfranchised by the growing Anglo presence. Mining interests, merchants, railroads, and large landowners, on the other hand, lined up to oppose New Mexico's becoming a state because they feared it would increase taxes. The main obstacle to New Mexico's gaining statehood was prejudice against the territory's native New Mexicans. Nativists believed the large Spanish-speaking population was too Catholic, too foreign, and unable to govern themselves. Some questioned their loyalty, even though thousands of native New Mexicans fought for the Union in the Civil War. Nevertheless, a movement for statehood took hold. Blocking this effort would be members of the U.S. Congress who championed imperialism and articulated a belief in white dominance. In the wake of late-nineteenth-century xenophobia, they deemed the New Mexico territory undeveloped and "too Mexican."[61]

In 1888, a bill before Congress proposed statehood for several western territories, including New Mexico. The congressional Committee on Territories favored statehood for the Anglo territories of the Dakotas, Montana, and Washington but not for the New Mexico Territory because it lacked a public school system. Despite efforts of New Mexico's Republican political machine to amend a public school system proviso, the statehood bill was defeated. Racial prejudice remained a factor in denying the territory statehood. According to the subcommittee, "about two-thirds of the population is of the mongrel breed known as Mexicans and harbored anti-American sentiment." The Mexicans of New Mexico were "illiterate, superstitious, morally decadent, and indifferent to statehood." Native New Mexicans protested to their delegate to Congress, Antonio Joseph, who was working to pass the Enabling Act before Congress adjourned. Still, the U.S. Congress denied New Mexico statehood.[62]

Eight years later, in 1902, the "omnibus bill" called for statehood for the Oklahoma territory and for the Arizona and New Mexico Southwest territories. The chair of the Committee on Territories was Indiana Senator Albert J. Beveridge, and he refused to act. Beveridge opposed admitting any more western states, as this would weaken Indiana's voice in the Senate, but more so because he was an ardent racist and imperialist. The Indiana senator was determined to keep "Mexican" New Mexico and "frontier" Arizona out of the Union. A subcommittee toured the three western territories marked for statehood. The subcommittee held sessions and heard testimony in Las Vegas, Santa Fe, Albuquerque, Las Cruces, and Carlsbad. Only one witness gave unfavorable testimony regarding the fitness of the territory's Mexicans for statehood. This was sufficient evidence for Senator Beveridge to conclude that the people of New Mexico did not want statehood. The subsequent Beveridge Committee report recommended that New Mexico and Arizona be left as territories. Besides listing economic conditions, statehood for New Mexico was rejected because of the "condition" of the Spanish-speaking residents—specifically their "education, moral and other elements of citizenship were underlined as unfavorable qualities."[63]

To Senator Beveridge, New Mexicans were at most second-class citizens. The Senator casually dismissed the fact that the New Mexicans had voted for statehood by noting that ignorant people could be convinced to vote for anything, if told that it would help them. The Beveridge Report triggered indignation among Spanish-speaking New Mexicans. Finally, in 1910, Congress and President William Howard Taft approved an Enabling Act permitting New Mexicans to draft a constitution for statehood. Special language, voting, and educational guarantees were drawn up for the citizens of "Spanish descent."[64]

Although native New Mexicans volunteered to fight in the Spanish American War, the stereotype of the foreign-leaning Hispano persisted. Eastern newspapers accused New Mexico of siding with Madrid against Washington. Spanish flags reportedly were seen flying in Taos and Santa Fe, and it was feared that the territory's Spanish-speaking population was set to revolt against the United States. New Mexicans reacted strongly to these newspaper reports of disloyalty by holding mass protest meetings in Santa Fe and Albuquerque. The 17,000 American soldiers who landed on the southeastern tip of Cuba in June 1898 included 1,200 men of the First U.S. Volunteer Cavalry commanded by Lieutenant Colonel Theodore Roosevelt. Known as the "Rough Riders," this unit featured a contingent of New Mexicans, led by Captains Maximiliano Luna and George Washington Armijo, who were in the forefront of the fighting. Educated at Georgetown University and a member of the New Mexico legislature, Luna was commissioned captain of Troop F, First U.S. Volunteer Calvary. He served in Cuba and then was sent to the Philippines, where he died. Many more New Mexicans had volunteered for service in the Spanish American War, but Governor Miguel A. Otero, Jr., kept them out. The governor feared that racial conflict between native New Mexicans and their Anglo comrades-in-arms would erupt and forestall efforts to gain statehood for New Mexico.[65]

In 1906, the U.S. Congress passed a joint statehood bill for both the Arizona and New Mexico territories. New Mexico's population was about 50 percent Spanish-speaking, whereas Arizona's combined Indian and Mexican population was a little over 12 percent. The bill stipulated that rejection of joint statehood by the voters of either territory would prevent both Arizona and New Mexico from becoming states. Socially conservative members of the Arizona legislature passed a resolution protesting joint statehood, declaring that it "would subject us to the domination of another commonwealth of different traditions, customs and aspirations." Arizona's nativist residents assailed the territory's Mexican Americans as "un-American." Their opinions were summarized in a protest presented to the U.S. Congress on February 12, 1906. It stated that "the people of Arizona, 95 percent of whom are Americans, [object] to the probability of the control of public affairs by people of a different race, many of whom do not speak the English language. . . ."[66]

Finally, on June 20, 1910, President Taft signed the Enabling Act authorizing the New Mexico territory to call a constitutional convention. Three provisions were proposed to protect the rights of the Spanish-speaking population to vote and to have access to education and to preserve all rights granted to native New Mexicans under the Treaty of Guadalupe Hidalgo. On October 3, one hundred delegates convened at Santa Fe and drafted a constitution that voters confirmed on January 21, 1911.[67] President Taft approved the constitution on February 24, 1911. Arizona also ratified its constitution, but President Taft rejected it. Congress asked New Mexico to resubmit a less restrictive provision for constitutional

**Captain Maximiliano Luna, 1898.**
CREDIT: "He was the most distinguished of the Hispanic 'Rough Riders' during the Spanish-American War."
000-742, William A. Kelleher Collection, Center for Southwest Research, University Libraries, University of New Mexico.

amendments and asked Arizona to resubmit an amendment on the recall of officers. As the nineteenth century ended, the long-term territorial status of New Mexico and Arizona remained unresolved. With manual labor scarce in the Southwest, great numbers of workers from Mexico were recruited under labor contracts to fill this gap.

## THE NEW SOUTHWEST ECONOMY AND THE FIRST MODERN PHASE OF MEXICAN IMMIGRATION TO THE UNITED STATES

An expanding American economy produced an extractive industry and agriculture economy in the Southwest that became the hallmark of the late-nineteenth-century American West. Mexico was also on the verge of modern economic development. This unfolding structural transformation continued to concentrate wealth and power in the hands of the rich and to impoverish workers on both sides of the border to further enrich the wealthy. Rapid expansion of the railroads initiated this process by linking rural areas abundant in natural resources to national and international markets. The railroads employed labor on a mass scale, transforming once isolated workers into an industrial proletariat. American-owned railroads recruited and transported large numbers of workers from Mexico's

Central Plateau to northern Mexico, where the emigrants easily crossed the border to earn even higher wages. Trains allowed the workers to ride great distances free, or American employers paid the transportation. The latter hired Mexican workers through newly opened recruiting centers in El Paso, Eagle Pass, and Laredo, Texas, and spread this labor throughout the Southwest and West.[68]

Work in the American West was unsteady at best, as the cyclical fluctuations of the economy periodically threw large numbers of people out of work. Another characteristic of the West was that unskilled low-paid work became the domain of nonwhite workers. Employers argued that nonwhite workers were racially suited for this work because they, unlike white workers, lacked the necessary innate qualities such as ambition, skill, and intelligence for the better jobs. The debasement of work resulted in the emergence of a dual-wage labor system in the Southwest. Its long-range consequence was that it reinforced fragmentation on the basis of race among workers and led to their disunity.[69]

Under President Porfirio Díaz, railroads spurred the modernization of Mexico. Mexico's national railroad system was based on heavy foreign capital investment and tied to the American Southwest, a region undergoing vigorous expansion and relative prosperity. The construction of Mexico's north-south railroad lines permitted the economic development of its northern border by drawing tens of thousands of Mexicans to the region as economic pressures in Mexico mounted.[70] Mexican and foreign investors who already had large properties in that country took possession of more of Mexico's land. With unemployment already severe in Mexico, both living costs and population growth increased significantly, and wages stagnated. Almost 90 percent of Mexico's workers earned between twenty and twenty-five cents per day, as the price of basic foodstuffs more than doubled.

The migration from remote districts in Mexico by this country's poor to the newly developed industries in northern Mexico in search of work was one stage in the general movement of Mexicans to the United States. Although freight traffic—usually in boxcars with no accommodations—was far more important than passenger traffic, Mexico's trains played an essential role in increasing Mexican immigration to the United States.

In 1877, one year after the United States celebrated its centennial, Mexico's President Díaz initiated the building of a national rail network. The construction program more than doubled Mexico's track mileage from seven hundred miles in 1880 to more than fifteen thousand miles by 1910. The Mexican Central and the Mexican National Railroads became the major north-south conduits of goods and people. Both roads made possible the opening of important American markets, which in turn advanced the growth of agriculture, ranching, and mining in Mexico's northern region and made it easier for thousands of Mexicans to ride the freight lines long distances to search for work.[71]

The Mexican Central Railway provided a direct link between Mexico City and Mexico's northern border with the United States. Controlled by the Atchison, Topeka, and Santa Fe Railroad, the Mexican Central Railroad ran through the Mexican states of Aguascalientes, Zacatecas, and Chihuahua to the twin border towns of Ciudad Juárez-El Paso. The Ciudad Juárez Railroad provided another link between central Mexico and Mexico's northern border.[72]

The arrival of the railroad in El Paso, Texas, spurred rapid population increases in this border town, turning it into a major railroad, mining, ranching, and labor hub. El Paso was a strategic point between the American railroad network of the Southern Pacific Railroad from the west, the Atchison, Topeka, and Santa Fe Railroad from the north, the Texas and Pacific and the Galveston, Harrisburg, and San Antonio railroads from the east, and the Mexican Central Railroad originating in central Mexico. In 1881, the Southern Pacific Railroad, laying lines east from Los Angeles, met the Texas and Pacific Railroad at El Paso, and the Santa Fe Railroad arrived at this American border town from Santa Fe. Connecting with the Santa Fe Railroad at Ciudad Juárez across from El Paso, the Mexican Central Railroad was an extension of this American rail line into Mexico. As a result of this railroad network covering a large area, El Paso became the quintessential entry point into the United States for Mexican immigrants seeking to cross the U.S. border. In 1887, the Kansas City Consolidated Smelting and Refining Company (ASARCO) built a copper and lead smelter near the El Paso railroad yards. The community of "Smeltertown" came into existence as ASARCO's Mexican employees began building houses for themselves and their families.[73]

Constructed in 1881 and initially called the Texas Mexican Railway, the Mexican National Railroad ran through Saltillo and Monterrey to Nuevo Laredo, Tamaulipas. Across the Río Grande from Nuevo Laredo was Laredo, Texas. In 1883, the International Mexican Railroad reached Piedras Negras, Coahuila, located across the border from Eagle Pass, Texas. The twin border towns of Piedras Negras and Eagle Pass served as a departure point for Mexicans immigrating to Houston and other cities in eastern Texas. In the same year, the Mexican National Railroad reached the city of Matamoros, Tamaulipas. Brownsville, Texas, was located across the border from Matamoros. There, the Mexican National Railroad linked up with the St. Louis and Mexico Railroad into the interior of Texas.[74]

Agua Prieta, Sonora, became an important link for minerals and for labor to extract these minerals for American mining interests in the Sonora area. The Nacozari Railroad Company, owned by the Phelps Dodge Corporation's El Paso and Southwestern Railroad, reached Agua Prieta in 1901. This Mexican rail line served as the conduit for Mexican labor to Douglas, Tucson, and Phoenix, Arizona, and to El Paso. In 1882, the Sonora Railroad Company Limited, owned by the Atchison, Topeka, and Santa Fe Railroad, arrived in Nogales, Arizona, across the border from Nogales, Sonora.[75]

Characterized by an abundant supply of unskilled labor, the Porfiriato, the more than thirty-three years in which Porfirio Díaz ruled Mexico, contributed to the growth of a labor market in the northern states of Mexico. Drawn by work opportunities at relatively high wages, 270,900 Mexicans from central Mexico settled in the Mexican and U.S. border states. The employment of Mexicans by American railroad companies expanded greatly between 1880 and 1890. In 1908, 16,000 Mexicans were recruited by labor agents in El Paso for railroad work; two years later, 2,000 Mexicans were being hired each month for track work. Some Mexicans on their own sought out labor recruiters or tapped kinship networks to obtain jobs. Making up from 60 to 75 percent of some of the track crews, thousands of Mexicans employed on six-month contracts as graders, track layers, and "spikers" constructed track lines and branch lines. Using handcars and in gangs of four to six workers, they inspected, maintained, and repaired worn rail arteries in southern California, Arizona, New Mexico, and Nevada and north to the Canadian border and east to Chicago.[76]

Mexican labor built, maintained, and repaired the railroads that forged the links between the Southwest and the urban markets of the Midwest and the East. Over 70 percent of the track laborers had lived in the United States less than five years, and 98 percent were aliens. Most had been recruited in El Paso. Mexican track hands earned between $1.00 and $1.25 per day, less than other workers doing similar kinds of work but six times greater than the amount earned by workers in Mexico. Many worked as laborers and as helpers in the railroad shops and powerhouses.

Commenting on the influx of Mexicans, the U.S. Commissioner-General of Immigration pinpointed their appeal as railroad workers:

> Mexican labor met an economic condition demanding laborers who could stand the heat and other discomforts of that particular section. The peon makes a satisfactory track hand, for the reasons that he is docile, ignorant, and non-clannish to an extent which makes it possible that one or more men shall quit or be discharged and others remain at work; moreover he is willing to work for a low wage.[77]

Mexican labor also made agricultural expansion in the Southwest possible. Cotton began to supplement ranching throughout Texas. In 1900, Texas cotton farmers expanded production into central and southwestern Texas. Unlike east Texas, these regions lacked black and white tenant farmers and sharecroppers to harvest the cotton. Therefore, Mexicans were recruited to fill the labor demand. Before the great Texas cotton harvests became possible, Mexicans performed the backbreaking work of "grubbing" the land. Grubbing consisted of clearing the land of mesquite brush and thorny undergrowth to make it fit for cultivation. The wages for Mexican workers almost doubled as they became vital to agricultural production. In 1903, Mexican agricultural workers earned 50 to 75 cents per day; in 1907, they were earning between $1.00 and $1.25 per day.

Mexicans met the increased demand for labor in the planting and harvesting of sugar beets. In 1897, the U.S. Congress imposed a 75 percent tax on foreign sugar imports. This tariff encouraged the development of American sugar beet production, and by 1906 domestic sugar beet production more than tripled from the 135,000 acres planted in 1900. Within two decades, land dedicated to sugar beets would increase to 872,000 acres, with the Great Plains region producing two-thirds of the nation's total crop.[78]

Railroad transportation to eastern markets stimulated expansion of the California citrus industry. The refrigerated railroad car and technical innovations in canning and food preservation increased perishable fruit and vegetable crop production. Between 1900 and 1920, California orange production quadrupled, and lemon production increased fivefold. In 1909, more than fifteen million boxes of California citrus, harvested with Mexican labor, were shipped by rail to the East.

By 1925, California was harvesting about twenty-four million boxes of citrus wholly through the use of Mexican labor. Mexican workers also aided in the growth of cotton in the Imperial Valley.[79]

The Southwest produced 40 percent of America's fruits and vegetables, production that was accomplished with Mexican labor. The mines and smelters, sugar beet farms, government irrigation projects, road construction, cement factories, and municipal street railway work all depended on Mexican labor. In all instances of employment, Mexicans were given the worst jobs at the lowest pay. Working conditions were brutal. Mexicans were isolated from Anglo workers by laws, custom, and the dictates of society. American labor unions disliked and complained about Mexicans because they were used by employers to break strikes, destroy unions, and depress wages. However, the unions placed no restrictions on non-skilled employment opportunities for Mexicans. The workers were subjected to a barrage of racial slurs and insults and became the targets of Anglo working-class frustration during economic depressions.[80]

U.S. immigration officials reported that many of the immigrants from Mexico were married and had their families with them but were mobile and moved readily to places that needed their labor. Widespread discrimination against Mexicans was a recurring fact of life in the American West. Anglos ensured that Mexicans remained not only in low-wage jobs but also relegated to the worst living conditions. The daily life of mining families was harsh. Segregated by race and ethnicity, the mining camps had a higher turnover of workers. Mexican workers and their families occupied adobe huts or hovels outside of the town limits. Railroad section hands lived in freight cars fitted with windows and bunks or in shacks along the roads. Housing for the Mexicans who lived in the region's urban centers was likewise deplorable, marked by poor sewage, dilapidated housing, and rampant disease. In all these instances, Anglos showed no compassion but instead blamed Mexicans for their own lamentable conditions as the result of poor morals, laziness, or their alleged backward culture. Mexicans nonetheless established a sense of community and common interests in the United States. Restaurants, grocery stores, barbershops, tailor shops, and other services catered to the community. The desire of Mexicans to locate near kin and friends resulted in residential clustering. In these insular environments circumscribed by prejudice and discrimination, Mexicans maintained their social, cultural, and family customs and language, and their newspapers stressed Mexican pride and the importance of Mexico as the homeland. Along with churches, mutual aid societies were the first social institutions created by Mexican immigrants in the United States.

Mexicans banded together in mutual aid societies to defend themselves and to maintain old customs in the new environment. The orientation and goals of the mutual-aid societies and fraternal organizations varied from welfare and relief to Masonic and social pursuits. All produced camaraderie and advocated ethnic consciousness already strong among the immigrants. Most of the self-help organizations were local in nature, whereas others became national in scope. Founded in 1894, the *Alianza Hispano-Americana* (Hispanic American Alliance) had chapters in Arizona, California, Colorado, New Mexico, and Texas. The tendency of

Mexicans toward trade unionization derived in part from the mutual-aid societies among them.

As wages began fluctuating in response to industrial development, Mexicans found the need to organize for decent wages and better working conditions. In 1883, Tejano vaqueros in west Texas were among the several hundred cowboys who went on strike against the cattle companies. Thousands of Mexicans from Texas to California joined the Holy Order of the Knights of Labor. The expansion of mining in Arizona, New Mexico, and Colorado led to prounionism. Mexican farmworkers likewise fought to improve wages and working conditions. In 1903, more than one thousand Mexican and Japanese sugar beet workers on area farms near Oxnard, California, waged a successful two-month-long strike.[81] Even though they were unwelcome in the predominantly white unions because they were imported at times to break strikes, more and more Mexicans in the early twentieth century turned to labor unions for help.

## CONCLUSION

Following the end of the Civil War, the twin practices of paternalism and patronage in the Southwest gave way to a virulent strain of racism with regard to Anglo relations with Mexicans. By the late nineteenth century, racial divisions defined one's place in the region. The forces of oppression were marshaled against Mexicans to deny them their rights and drive them off their land. This was done at times in collusion with the elite Mexicans. However, the wealth, status, and education of the elite Mexicans mattered little to Anglos, many of the latter newcomers to the Southwest. Assimilating racist instincts, they did not draw distinctions between the landowning and merchant elite and the Mexicans employed as ranchers and tenant farmers, for they now regarded all Mexicans much as they did blacks and foreign immigrants—a "servile people . . . beaten men of a beaten race."[82]

Land-hungry Anglo migrants and speculators from the East flooded southern California with the arrival of the railroads. Racism was quickly picked up by these new arrivals, who remained isolated from the Mexicans on whose labor they depended. Segregated by race into Sonora towns, Mexicans dug ditches, harvested crops, and performed other wage work considered unfit for Anglos. In South Texas, Tejanos lost their land through fraud and coercion. Texas Rangers' hatred and brutality toward the Mexicans was extreme; the Rangers acted as hired guns to Anglo-Texan ranchers who dispossessed and proletarianized Tejano ranchers and vaqueros. The eventual violent collapse of Tejano ranching society took place in the early twentieth century, when the Texas Rangers, intermediaries in the transition to capitalism, cleaned out the remaining Tejano landowners, summarily executing more than three hundred "suspected Mexicans."[83] The railroads' arrival in Texas led to economic penetration. In addition to population shifts and the Americanization of cities, commercial agriculture underscored the taking away of land from Tejano farmers and ranchers and increased their use as low-wage itinerant workers. As the nineteenth century came to a close, Tejanos and growing numbers of Mexican immigrants now made up the large labor force in South Texas.[84]

Those in power in the New Mexico territory followed a policy of keeping the Spanish-speaking population subjugated. The transition to wage work for New Mexicans came as they lost control of their lands to growing market forces. The antimonopoly outrage briefly brought down the wrath of the native New Mexicans. Seeking to halt their dispossession and exploitation and to protect themselves against the monopolists, they formed Las Gorras Blancas, the Holy Order of the Knights of Labor, and the Populist Party. This movement, which included fence cutting, began in 1888 and was spent by 1890. It succumbed to the power pressures of the industrial capitalism that ushered in proletarianization. The Spanish-speaking farmers, small ranchers, and craftsmen were transformed into a migratory labor force in mining and agriculture.

Because of xenophobia that witnessed a rebirth of nativism, the U.S. Congress objected to statehood for the New Mexico territory, claiming language difficulties, illiteracy, and the lack of desire for statehood on the part of its Spanish-speaking residents. Racism was also an underlying factor in the Arizona Territory. Here, Anglos deemed the Mexicans as un-American and an obstacle to America's progress and development.

At the dawn of the twentieth century, the extractive economy of the American West was firmly fixed to the larger national and world economies. The railroads and their feeder lines created the infrastructure for its development and added enormously to power and wealth for a few and to proletarianization for masses of Mexicans as they moved into the labor force as racialized wage workers.[85] Railroads, mines, corporate ranches, and farms came to depend on the labor of Mexicans, both U.S. citizens and, increasingly, nationals from Mexico.[86] Powerful economic forces governed the streams of Mexican immigration to the United States.

As the development of the Southwest economy opened up in railroad, mining, and agricultural work, similar economic expansion in northern Mexico drew Mexicans to the border region in search of work. Employment agencies advanced board, lodging, and transportation to the job-hungry Mexicans. U.S. immigration officials looked the other way, as they did not think the Mexicans would become a public charge.[87] In fact, U.S. immigration policy was being shaped to favor the labor demands of American employers always in need of cheap labor. The U.S. Departments of Labor, Agriculture, and the State began to work closely with American businesses in shaping labor migration patterns on the U.S.-Mexico border.

Mexican immigration followed certain cyclical trends related to the social and economic situation in Mexico and the labor needs of the Southwest economy. By 1890, more than 75,000 Mexicans had immigrated to the United States. Almost two-thirds crossed into Texas, whereas the remainder went to California, New Mexico, and elsewhere. In 1908, following a short recession, between 60,000 and 100,000 Mexicans entered the United States each year. In 1910, the Mexican population of the United States was estimated at between 381,000 and 562,000.[88] The continual arrival of immigrants from Mexico soon became the most compelling drama that unfolded in the Southwest.

# NOTES

1. Robert W. Larson, "The White Caps of New Mexico: A Study of Ethnic Militancy in the Southwest," *Pacific Historical Review* 44, no. 2 (May 1975): 173.

2. Richard White, *It's Your Misfortune and None of My Own: A New History of the American West* (Norman: University of Oklahoma Press, 1991), 252; William G. Robbins, *Colony and Empire: The Capitalist Transformation of the American West* (Lawrence: University Press of Kansas, 1994), 31.

3. White, *It's Your Misfortune*, 243, 334–335; Jorge Durand, Douglas S. Massey, and Rene M. Zenteno, "Mexican Immigrants to the United States: Continuities and Changes," *Latin American Research Review* 36, no. 1 (2001): 109; Sarah Deutsch, "Landscape of Enclaves: Race Relations in the West, 1865–1990," in *Under an Open Sky: Rethinking America's Western Past*, ed. William Cronon, George Miles, and Jay Gitlin (New York: Norton 1994), 120.

4. White, *It's Your Misfortune*, 232, 240; Tomás Almaguer, *Racial Fault Lines: The Historical Origins of White Supremacy in California* (Berkeley: University of California Press, 1994), 30–31.

5. Almaguer, *Racial Fault Lines*, 32; White, *It's Your Misfortune*, 324; Carey McWilliams, *Factories in the Fields: The Story of Migratory Farm Labor in California* (Boston: Little, Brown, 1935), 21; Monroy, *Thrown Among Strangers*, 271–272. For example, only 10 percent of the Spanish-speaking population of Los Angeles were permanent residents in 1870. Ten years later, in 1880, census records showed that over 90 percent of the town's Mexicans had arrived after 1848.

6. Estrada, *Los Angeles Plaza*, 71. Between 1850 and 1851, forty-four homicides were committed in Los Angeles County. No one was convicted of these murders. Griswold del Castillo, *The Los Angeles Barrio*, 106–107; White, *It's Your Misfortune*, 332–333; Robbins, *Colony and Empire*, 30.

7. Estrada, *Los Angeles Plaza*, 85; White, *It's Your Misfortune*, 240; Monroy, *Thrown Among Strangers*, 235–237, 252, 274–276.

8. Almaguer, *Racial Fault Lines*, 31. The remaining Chinese in California worked as farm hands and ranch hands. They made up half the workforce in the southern California citrus industry and over 90 percent of the truck gardeners and vegetable vendors in Los Angeles. White, *It's Your Misfortune*, 323. In Santa Barbara, 80 percent of the Mexican wage earners were unskilled workers but did not hold full-time employment. Monroy, *Thrown Among Strangers*, 245–250, 252.

9. Carey McWilliams, *North from Mexico: The Spanish-Speaking People of the United States* (New York: Greenwood Press, 1949), 35–47; Miguel P. Servín, "California's Hispanic Heritage: A View into the Spanish Myth," in *New Spain's Far Northern Frontier*, ed. David J. Weber (Albuquerque: University of New Mexico Press, 1979), 117–133; Joseph A. Rodríguez, "Becoming Latinos: Mexican Americans, Chicanos, and the Spanish Myth in the Urban Southwest," *Western Historical Quarterly* 29, no. 2 (Summer 1998): 167.

10. Michael G. Webster, "Texan Manifest Destiny and the Mexican Border Conflict, 1865–1880" (Ph.D. dissertation, Indiana University, 1972), 67; Robbins, *Colony and Empire*, p. 29; Teresa Palomo Acosta and Ruthe Winegarten, *Las Tejanas: 300 Years of History* (Austin: University of Texas Press, 2003), 66.

11. David Montejano, *Anglos and Mexicans in the Making of Texas, 1836–1986* (Austin: University of Texas Press, 1987), 86; White, *It's Your Misfortune*, 334–336; Webster, "Texan Manifest Destiny," 68–69.

12. Cox, *Texas Rangers,* 284–290. See also *Relations of the United States with Mexico,* 45th Cong., 2d sess., House Executive Document 701. (Washington, DC, 1878).

13. Thompson, *Cortina,* 22–23. See also Samuel E. Bell and James M. Smallwood, *The Zona Libre, 1858–1905: A Problem in American Diplomacy* (El Paso: Texas Western Press, 1982). In 1861, Benito Juárez approved establishing these free ports along Mexico's northern frontier. Texas commercial interests remained unapparent because of the Civil War and the struggle in Mexico against French intervention. Webster, "Texan Manifest Destiny," 74–76.

14. Thompson, *Cortina,* 200–204, 207; Webster, "Texan Manifest Destiny," 70–73.

15. U.S. Consul Thomas F. Wilson testified that along the border no concern was raised over killing a Mexican. De Leon, *Tejano Community,* 18–19.

16. Webster, "Texan Manifest Destiny," 136–137, 140–144; J. Frank Dobie, *A Vaquero of the Brush Country* (Austin: University of Texas Press, 1981), 62.

17. Thompson, *Cortina,* 207–209; Webster, "Texan Manifest Destiny," 79–80, 83.

18. Webster, "Texan Manifest Destiny," 131–134. A battle of attrition was also taking place against Indians that followed the swelling Anglo settlement onto Indian lands.

19. Benjamin Heber Johnson, *Revolution in Texas: How a Forgotten Rebellion and Its Bloody Suppression Turned Mexicans into Americans* (New Haven, CT: Yale University Press, 2003), 21.

20. Ibid.

21. Meanwhile, Gregorio's brother Romaldo died in the Karnes County Jail from his gunshot wound.

22. Following his release from prison, Gregorio Cortez moved to Nuevo Laredo, Mexico, and fought in the Mexican Revolution. The Tejano died of pneumonia on February 28, 1916. Johnson, *Revolution in Texas,* 21.

23. Ibid., 18–20.

24. White, *It's Your Misfortune,* 241.

25. Johnson, *Revolution in Texas,* 28.

26. Ibid., 29–32, 34; White, *It's Your Misfortune,* 323–324.

27. Gregg Cantrell and D. Scott Barton, "Texas Populists and the Failure of Biracial Politics," *Journal of Southern History* 55, no. 4 (November 1989): 671, fn 31.

28. Campbell, *Gone to Texas,* 227–228; Chandler Davidson, *Race and Class in Texas Politics* (Princeton, NJ: Princeton University Press, 1990), 21–24; Johnson, *Revolution in Texas,* 36.

29. Steven H. Wilson, "Brown over 'Other White': Mexican Americans' Legal Arguments and Litigation Strategy in School Desegregation Lawsuits," *Law and History Review* 21, no. 1 (Spring 2003): 152.

30. Ibid.; Victoria Hattam, "Ethnicity and the Boundaries of Race: Rereading Directive 15," *Daedalus* 134, no. 1 (Winter 2005): 63. San Antonio politician T. J. McMinn, who had raised the issue previously, and another politician, Jack Evans, likewise approved Rodríguez's quest for citizenship. De León, *Tejano Community,* 25.

31. Wilson, "Brown over 'Other White,'" 152–153. Rodríguez also stated that he was unacquainted with the American form of government.

32. Ibid., 152; De León, *Tejano Community,* 33. See also Arnoldo De León, *In Re Ricardo Rodríguez: An Attempt at Chicano Disenfranchisement in San Antonio, 1896–1897* (San Antonio, TX: Caravel Press, 1979) and Fernando Padilla, "Early Chicano Legal Recognition: 1846–1897," *Journal of Popular Culture* 13 (Spring 1980), 564–574.

33. Truett, *Fugitive Landscapes,* 57; Marcy G. Goldstein, "Americanization and Mechanization: The Mexican Elite and Anglo American in the Gadsden Purchase Lands,

1853–1880" (Ph.D. dissertation, Case Western University, 1972), 120, 123–124, 126. Tucson had been slated to become the future capital of Arizona.

34. Truett, *Fugitive Landscapes,* 58; White, *It's Your Misfortune,* 213, 228, 307.

35. Truett, *Fugitive Landscapes,* 144, 157–158; Goldstein, "Americanization and Mechanization," 129, 182–185, 192.

36. White, *It's Your Misfortune,* 240.

37. Laura E. Gomez, "Race, Colonialism and Criminal Law: Mexicans and the American Criminal Justice System in Territorial New Mexico," *Law and Society Review* 34, no. 4 (2000): 1137; Robbins, *Colony and Empire,* 26–27; White, *It's Your Misfortune,* 240. The passage of the Alien Land Law in 1887 and similar earlier legislation in Texas in 1882 banned ownership of land in the western territories by foreign corporations and those who did not intend to become U.S. citizens. American officials overlooked the laws in most instances. Robbins, *Colony and Empire,* 262. Extended kinship patterns remained strong in the villages of the Upper Río Grande Valley, and women took over the responsibility for maintaining them. White, *It's Your Misfortune,* 324.

38. White, *It's Your Misfortune,* 255; Lamar, *The Far Southwest, 1846–1912,* 153–154; Gomez, "Race, Colonialism and Criminal Law," 1137.

39. Gomez, "Race, Colonialism and Criminal Law," 1161–1163. For more information on Billy the Kid, see Robert M. Utley, *High Noon in Lincoln: Violence on the Western Frontier* (Albuquerque: University of New Mexico Press, 1987).

40. White, *It's Your Misfortune,* 334–335.

41. John Mack Faragher and Robert V. Hine, *The American West: A New Interpretive History* (New Haven: Yale University Press, 2000), 323; Robert K. DeArment, *Bravo of the Brazos: John Larn of Fort Griffin, Texas* (Norman, OK: University of Oklahoma Press, 2002), 24, 160; Goldstein, "Americanization and Mechanization," 268; Philip B. Gonzales, "Struggle for Survival: The Hispanic Land Grants of New Mexico, 1848–2001," *Agricultural History* 77, no. 2 (Spring 2003): 306; Howard Roberts Lamar, "Land Policy in the Spanish Southwest, 1846–1891," *Journal of Economic History* 22 (December 1962): 498–515.

42. White, *It's Your Misfortune,* 227, 241; Goldstein, "Americanization and Mechanization," 260.

43. Gonzales, "Struggle for Survival," 301; Malcolm Ebright, "The Embudo Grant: A Case Study of Justice and the Court of Private Land Claims," *Journal of the West* 19, no. 3 (July 1980): 36. The U.S. Constitution mandates that no one be deprived of property without a judicial determination that meets the requirements of due process of law. Due process requires that there be a hearing at which interested parties can present evidence and cross-examine opposing witnesses. The failure to require a hearing meant that most land claims were decided solely on the affidavits of the claimant and their witnesses. Claimants were usually not even notified of the proceedings.

44. Gonzales, "Struggle for Survival," 301.

45. Ebright, "The Embudo Grant," 37.

46. Ibid., 38; Gonzales, "Struggle for Survival," 302.

47. Gonzales, "Struggle for Survival," 302.

48. Ebright, "The Embudo Grant," 40; Lamar, *The Far Southwest, 1846–1912,* 121–146.

49. For example, Governor William Pile and his librarian were accused of selling or destroying Spanish and Mexican archive records. In its report to President Ulysses S. Grant, an investigative committee recommended removing Governor Pile from office. Phillip B. Gonzales, "'La Junta de Indignación': Hispano Repertoire of Collective Protest in New Mexico, 1884–1933," *Western Historical Quarterly* 31, no. 2 (Summer 2000): 166–167.

50. Ibid., 167–168.

51. Johnson, *Revolution in Texas*, 19.

52. Bruce Laurie, *Artisans into Workers: Labor in Nineteenth-Century America* (New York: Hill and Wang, 1989), 160, 175.

53. Gomez, "Race, Colonialism and Criminal Law," 1134, 1136–1137, 1169.

54. Rosenbaum, *Mexicano Resistance in the Southwest*, 118–119.

55. Ibid., 101–102; Robert W. Larson, *New Mexico Populism: A Study of Radical Protest in a Western Territory* (Boulder, CO: Associated University Press, 1974), 35–36; Larson, "The White Caps of New Mexico," 176.

56. Laurie, *Artisans into Workers*, 154; Rosenbaum, *Mexicano Resistance in the Southwest*, 119–121; Larson, *New Mexico Populism*, 36, 40; Larson, "The White Caps of New Mexico," 175, 178, 181.

57. Larson, *New Mexico Populism*, 36, 40; Larson, "The White Caps of New Mexico," 176, 179.

58. Rosenbaum, *Mexicano Resistance in the Southwest*, 102, 123; Larson, *New Mexico Populism*, 40–41, 43; Larson, "The White Caps of New Mexico," 178.

59. Rosenbaum, *Mexicano Resistance in the Southwest*, 109–110; Larson, *New Mexico Populism*, 38–39; Larson, "The White Caps of New Mexico," 177, 188.

60. Laurie, *Artisans into Workers*, 175; Rosenbaum, *Mexicano Resistance in the Southwest*, 126; Larson, *New Mexico Populism*, 67; Larson, "The White Caps of New Mexico," 182. In one nighttime procession, five hundred masked men on horseback rode through Las Vegas, carrying torches and flags and shouting, "*Que viva el Partido del Pueblo Unido en el Condado de San Miguel!*" ("Long Live the United People's Party in San Miguel County!").

61. Gonzales, "'La Junta de Indignación,'" 168; Robert W. Larson, *New Mexico's Quest for Statehood, 1846–1912* (Albuquerque: University of New Mexico Press, 1968), 154–155, 202; Larson, "The White Caps of New Mexico," 185.

62. Gonzales, "'La Junta de Indignación,'" 168–169; Larsen, *New Mexico's Quest for Statehood*, 148–151; Lamar, *The Far Southwest, 1846–1912*, 162.

63. Gonzales, "'La Junta de Indignación,'" 169–170; Lamar, *The Far Southwest, 1846–1912*, 426–427.

64. Gonzales, "'La Junta de Indignación,'" 175; Lamar, *The Far Southwest, 1846–1912*, 427, 431.

65. Richard Melzer, "Governor Miguel Otero's War: Statehood and New Mexican Loyalty in the Spanish-American War," *Colonial Latin American Historical Review* 8 (Winter 1999), 79–103; Lamar, *The Far Southwest, 1846–1912*, 430.

66. The Arizona Territorial Teachers Association passed a resolution opposing joint statehood. It noted that whereas Arizona schools taught all classes in English, New Mexico schools used interpreters. It warned that the union of Arizona with New Mexico would disrupt Arizona's school system. U.S. Senate Document 216, 59th Cong., 1st Sess. (Feb. 12, 1906), 1–2. This section is from *The Excluded Student: Educational Practices Affecting Mexican Americans in the Southwest*, Mexican American Education Study, Report III (Washington, DC: U.S. Government Printing Office, 1972), 76–82.

67. "The rights, privileges and immunities, civil, political and religious, granted to the people of New Mexico by the Treaty of Guadalupe Hidalgo shall be preserved inviolate." See N. Mex. Const. art. VII § 3, art. XII §§ 8, 10, 1912.

68. Victor S. Clark, "Mexican Labor in the United States," *Bulletin of the U.S. Bureau of Labor* 78 (September 1908): 470.

69. White, *It's Your Misfortune*, 282–284.

70. Truett, *Fugitive Landscapes,* 59; Sarah Deutsch, *No Separate Refuge: Culture, Class, and Gender on an Anglo-Hispanic Frontier in the American Southwest, 1880–1940* (New York: Oxford University Press, 1987), 15.

71. Truett, *Fugitive Landscapes,* 59.

72. Ibid.

73. Ibid., 60; Montejano, *Anglos and Mexicans in the Making of Texas,* p. 94; Robbins, *Colony and Empire,* 31–32; White, *It's Your Misfortune and None of My Own,* 255.

74. Truett, *Fugitive Landscapes,* 60; Montejano, *Anglos and Mexicans in the Making of Texas,* 95, 98.

75. Truett, *Fugitive Landscapes,* 59, 82–83; Miguel Tinker Salas, *In the Shadow of the Eagles: Sonora and the Transformation of the Border During the Porfiriato* (Berkeley: University of California Press, 1997), 131–132. In 1927, the Southern Pacific of Mexico Railroad linked Guadalajara with Nogales, Arizona. This rail link altered the dynamics of immigration from Mexico because prior to this most immigrants from the Mexican state of Jalisco entered the United States through El Paso.

76. Juan Mora-Torrez, *The Making of the Mexican Border: The State, Capitalism, and Society in Nuevo Leon, 1848–1910* (Austin: University of Texas Press, 2001), 127–133. For example, Mexicans were introduced into sugar beet work in central California to undercut the wages of Japanese and German-Russian workers.

77. Mark Reisler, *By the Sweat of Their Brow: Mexican Immigrant Labor in the United States, 1900–1940* (Westport, CT: Greenwood Press, 1976), 6.

78. From 1923 to 1932 Nebraska ranked second behind Colorado in annual sugar beet acreage (74,000 acres) and first in the nation in yield per acre (12.7 tons).

79. Matt García, *A World of Its Own: Race, Labor, and the Citrus Industry in the Making of Greater Los Angeles, 1900–1970* (Chapel Hill: University of North Carolina Press, 2000), 23.

80. Three-fourths of the street railway workers earned $1.75 per day. Mexicans performed almost all of the construction and maintenance work on southern California's urban street railway systems.

81. Montejano, *Anglos and Mexicans in the Making of Texas,* 87–88; White, *It's Your Misfortune,* 289. Founded in 1911 in Texas, the Mexican Protective Association was one of the earliest Mexican agricultural unions.

82. Montejano, *Anglos and Mexicans in the Making of Texas,* 94.

83. Don E. Coerver and Linda B. Hall, eds., *Texas and the Mexican Revolution: A Study in State and National Border Policy, 1910–1920* (College Station: Texas A&M University Press, 1984), 107.

84. Montejano, *Anglos and Mexicans in the Making of Texas,* 89, 92.

85. White, *It's Your Misfortune,* 257, 267, 323.

86. Arthur F. Corwin, "Mexican Immigration History, 1900–1970: Literature and Research," *Latin American Research Review* 8, no. 2 (Summer 1973): 7.

87. Ibid.

88. For example, many of the Mexicans employed as railroad section hands took advantage of the free transportation furnished by the railroad companies and returned to their homeland.

CHAPTER 6

Mexican Immigration, Work,
Urbanization, and Americanization
1910–1929

The first three decades of the twentieth century witnessed the rapid growth of
the Mexican population in the United States. Between 1910 and 1920, an estimated two hundred nineteen thousand Mexican immigrants entered the country,
doubling the Spanish-speaking population in Arizona, New Mexico, and Texas
and quadrupling it in California. World War I shut off immigration from Europe
and, along with the mobilization of the armed forces in 1917, exacerbated labor
shortages. Tens of thousands of Mexicans were allowed into the United States as a
war emergency measure. The demand for labor due to the economic boom in the
Southwest facilitated the entrance of additional Mexicans into the United States.[1]
Immigration from Mexico also gained momentum because of unfolding events in
Mexico, namely the spread of violence and the disruption of Mexico's economy
by revolution. The United States offered the newcomers—overwhelmingly young,
single, and of working age—not only freedom from revolutionary upheaval but
work at wages almost six times higher than in their homeland.[2]

By the summer of 1920 the economic boom in the United States ended,
triggering the highest rates of joblessness in America's history. Thousands of
Mexicans who lost their jobs left for Mexico; others were repatriated. Following
the 1920–1921 depression, Mexican immigration to the United States quadrupled,
increasing to 486,408 in the peak decade of the 1920s.[3]

Mexicans had little difficulty crossing into the United States because border
restrictions were minimal. Moreover, the United States government had not yet
distinguished the beginnings of a major immigration influx from Mexico. It was
an unusual range of movement involving temporary workers contracted by
employers, undocumented border crossers, legal immigrants with visas, and
commuters. That is, the Mexicans were both sojourners and settlers; some made
multiple trips back and forth across the border, whereas others established
themselves and sent for family members whom they had left behind until they
could afford to bring them north. Most who settled in America did not intend to
sever their connections with their homeland. The majority of Anglos who came
into contact with Mexicans perceived them in racial terms, regardless of their
backgrounds.

Mexicans became another group of workers exploited by employers. They were not only paid less than any other workers with the exception of blacks but also their wages never increased, irrespective of work experience. During these years when waves of strikes swept the United States, the workers responded to their exploitation, abuse, and discrepancy in wages by striking. There was much want and suffering among the coal miners and their families of southern Colorado. In 1914, no longer wanting to endure their exploitation and suffering, the coal miners struck the coalfields of southern Colorado. Mexican American miners were involved in this prolonged and violent dispute that climaxed as the Ludlow Massacre. Insisting that the capitalist system was at fault for their oppression, labor radicals rallied Mexicans against their employers. Some Mexicans such as Primo Tapia brought their radical ideologies to "Yankeeland" (the United States) and played important roles in strikes led notably by the Industrial Workers of the World. There were scenes of violence as employers put down the worker actions that they denounced.[4]

One of the worst atrocities in American history occurred in 1915 in the lower Río Grande Valley of Texas. Here, the Anglo influx was changing the social and economic balance of the region. The rapid collapse of Tejano ranch society under an expanding commercial agriculture that had a disastrous impact on Tejanos was accompanied by great racial violence against them. Tejanos resorted to the same form of violence by declaring war on the Anglo invaders with the Plan of San Diego. The Texas Rangers were called out to quell the mounting retaliatory violence, turning the revolt into a war of atrocities against the Tejanos.

Immigration from Mexico continued at a relatively high level. Migration chains drew on the mechanisms of family and kinship networks and linked the United States and Mexico. Information about work and where to live traveled back and forth between Mexico and the United States among relatives and friends. These contacts eventually replaced recruitment so that the movement of Mexicans became self-perpetuating. Family and ethnic ties were connected to the workplace because new arrivals secured their first jobs through these liaisons. Women played an important role in reconstituting families in America and in seeking opportunities for family betterment. Many women, before marriage and afterward, worked out of necessity. The sporadic and seasonal employment of male breadwinners required even children to contribute to the family economy. The immigrants lessened language barriers, their unfamiliarity with American customs, and discrimination by forming internal support networks among kin and neighbors. The strength of the Mexican communities was built not just on extended family and kinship support but also on voluntary organizations. Soon after arriving, the immigrants helped organize a variety of mutual benefit societies committed to social and cultural advancement that contributed to a rich array of community institutions. Mexican organizations urged their members to take pride in their heritage and culture. Mexican American organizations in Texas agitated for integration and equality in response to the different standard of justice for Mexicans. Following a policy of racial acquiescence, the League of United Latin American Citizens was concerned first and foremost with respectability, though it worked to improve inferior and inadequate schooling for Mexican American children.

## MEXICAN LABOR STRIFE AND STRUGGLE

In the first decades of the twentieth century, Mexicans did many of the low-wage jobs performed in the Southwest as single men or as gangs of families. They lived in rural areas and in isolated labor camps, with minimal contact with the larger Anglo community.[5] Struggling for security for themselves and their families, Mexicans participated in organizing efforts for higher wages and better living conditions. They faced immediate responses from employers who, on the local and national levels, moved to put down labor unrest and eradicate unions.

Mexicans were paid extremely low wages compared with white workers even in the same jobs, because since the nineteenth century much of the Southwest region had been under the so-called Mexican scale. Employers regularly used Mexican labor to hold down wages and also to break strikes and weaken unions. Along with being hostile to radical influences, the American Federation of Labor (AFL) restricted membership to skilled white workers. AFL union affiliates such as the railroad brotherhoods refused to accept Mexican skilled workers or else confined them to separate, albeit powerless, union locals. Defining class in racial terms, Anglo workers rarely felt solidarity with Mexican workers. As a result, Mexicans predisposed to unionism often pursued their goal of equality alone. Their demands were better pay and an end to job discrimination. They later added the demand of restricting the number of workers emigrating from Mexico so as not to undermine their union efforts.

The Magónista movement gave a political dimension to collective action on the part of Mexican workers to better their conditions and to protect themselves against oppression. The Socialist Party likewise imbued Mexicans with a conviction that their interests could be defended and advanced by a struggle against the "class enemy."[6] The Industrial Workers of the World (IWW or Wobblies) was the most militant labor organization that made a concerted effort to recruit Mexicans into its ranks on both sides of the border.

With industrial unionism as its foundation, the IWW introduced untold numbers of Mexicans such as Jesús González-Monroy of Los Angeles to the influence of its radical ideas regarding the unfair distribution of wealth and income. By 1908 the IWW was endeavoring to organize Mexicans into "One Big Union" with the objective of maintaining their wages. In 1910, the Wobblies came to the support of Mexican railroad and construction migratory workers in Fresno, California, and of the Mexican workers in Los Angeles who struck the Los Angeles Gas Works for higher wages. The IWW's anarcho-syndicalist orientation of direct action—of "meeting force with force"—aroused the furor and hatred of employers, however. In 1913, in the Wheatland Strike, the IWW bridged ethnic and racial differences by stressing cooperation to advance common interests. On the huge Durst Ranch outside Wheatland, California, the workers were striking against intolerable living conditions; they were camping out in tattered makeshift tents and shanties alongside highly polluted drainage ditches. The Wheatland Strike became the largest farmworker strike in California. The IWW sent organizers to Wheatland to lead the strikers, and in one of the confrontations several people were killed. The California National Guard was called in and the strike ended. The so-called Hop-Fields Riot attracted national attention to the awful living and working conditions of the workers on the Durst Ranch, leading to the creation of the California Commission on Immigration and Housing. The Commission made recommendations for regulation of the state's farm labor camps, but few improvements actually came about. Having carried out more than 150 strikes on the West Coast and in the Rocky Mountain and plains states, the IWW gained fame from their free-speech fights, for the Wobblies were outspoken in opposing America's involvement in World War I. This and the subsequent "red scare" contributed to the IWW's eventual demise.[7]

Mining dominated the economies of New Mexico, Arizona, and Colorado. Reflecting the location of mineral deposits, most of the region's Mexican miners lived in rural isolation and endured harsh living and working conditions.[8] Beginning in the 1870s, coal extraction took on importance in bringing industrialization to the Rocky Mountain region. The production techniques and other changes in coal production affected both working conditions and wages for the miners. Paid by the amount of coal they loaded, the coal diggers also had to reinforce the shafts with timber, lay track, and perform other tasks inside the mines. This was dead work, all of it unpaid. The men lived with the constant threat of death because of poor ventilation, rock falls, gas and coal-dust explosions, and fires underground. On October 22, 1913, an explosion at a coal mine outside Dawson in northern New Mexico owned by the Phelps Dodge Corporation killed more than 230 workers. The cause of the deadly explosion in the worst mining disaster in the western coalfields was methane gas ignited by a miner's lamp.

Wage scales were too low to feed a family. The frequent wage cuts, coupled with bouts of unemployment lasting two to four months per year, brought the coal miners and their families to the verge of starvation. These wretched working and living conditions fueled discontent. Miners formed organizations, but mining companies refused to consider any demands.[9]

In Colorado's coal districts, miners were separated along lines of occupation, race, and ethnicity. In Las Animas and Huerfano counties in southern Colorado, Mexicans made up one of thirty-two different nationalities struggling in a hostile environment. The mining companies enforced their own regulations through county sheriffs and deputies and company guards. Racism ran high against the miners and their families, "drawn from the lower classes of immigrants," and their "primitive ideas of living and ignorance of hygienic laws." The ethnically diverse coal diggers were mixed together in work units to hinder communication, and immigrants were brought in to be used as scabs. A stream of Mexicans were brought up to the Colorado coalfields from El Paso for this purpose. This did not curb the determination of the miners—they belonged to socialist-organized lodges and their strong bonds inside the coal pits, combined with the solidarity of the mining camp women's committees and the presence of the United Mine Workers of America (UMWA) strengthened their resolve.[10]

Coal miners employed by the Rockefeller-owned Colorado Fuel and Iron Company (CFI) once more set out to gain some control over their work lives. In September 1913, the miners walked out to gain recognition for the UMWA. Negotiations turned increasingly hostile; the CFI rejected meetings even after the union waived its key demands. The men and women of the tent colonies staged parades, circulated petitions, and, anticipating a confrontation, dug slit trenches and dugouts to protect themselves from the armed clashes that had become routine with Colorado National Guard troop and company guards. The subsequent "Great Coalfield War" through the harsh, long winter of 1913–1914 pitted the UMWA against the CFI. The sides had been drawn, and what resulted was the infamous Ludlow Massacre.[11]

On April 20, 1914, National Guard troops and company guards waging a war against striking coal miners attacked them and their families at the tent colony they established near Trinidad, Colorado, following their eviction from CFI's coalfields. The soldiers raked the camp with rifle and machine-gun fire, killing twenty miners, two women, and twelve children, among them Mexican Americans. Three strikers were seized and executed on the spot. The troops then entered the tent colony, burning tents, shooting more people, and destroying the miners' property. The senseless carnage of the Ludlow Massacre infuriated the miners and incited a full-scale miners' war as the UMWA, the Colorado Federation of Miners, and the WFM leadership called their members to arms. The miner's ranks were reinforced by the arrival of fellow miners from as far away as Thurber, Texas. The United States Army was later summoned to the southern Colorado coalfields. Disorganization and infighting diffused the protracted labor dispute, and it was called off on December 10, 1914. The UMWA gained no concessions from the coal operators. With their morale depleted, the miners wearily returned to the coalfields, where they came under a procompany representation plan.[12]

At this time, Mexican copper workers made attempts to organize in Arizona, New Mexico, Nevada, Utah, and El Paso, Texas. The men were subjected to harsh and dangerous working conditions and were poorly paid because of the notorious and humiliating Mexican wage scale. Moving from mining camp to mining camp, the state of the miners and their families was wretched; with no local alternatives, and as a condition of their employment, they lived in company-owned housing with exorbitant rents, and the high prices charged at company stores made living conditions more intolerable. Misery, poverty, and degradation were manifest everywhere in the copper mining region. In September 1915, copper mine workers at Clifton and Morenci, Arizona, went on strike as they had in earlier years against the mine companies.

The sixteen-week-long copper strike involved doing away with the Mexican pay scale and job discrimination. The miners requested help from the WFM, formerly unfriendly to Mexicans and a leading advocate of the anti-Mexican "80 Percent Law." The latter stated that 80 percent of all of Arizona's mining companies' employees must be U.S. citizens. The WFM agreed to help organize the miners against the copper companies.[13] Unlike most of the strikes during this time, the Clifton-Morenci walkout was not marred by violence and property destruction because organizers kept the miners in check. Furthermore, Arizona governor G. W. P. Hunt prevented the importation of strikebreakers by deploying the National Guard to Clifton-Morenci. The strike ended when the miners accepted the company's commitment to pay the same wage rate to both Anglo and Mexican workers.

In 1917, the mostly Mexican copper miners of the IWW at Bisbee in the Clifton-Morenci mining region walked out after the mine owners refused their

**Morenci-Clifton Strike, 1916.**
CREDIT: CP MCC-78. Arizona Collection: "Morenci Strike. 1916." Courtesy of the Henry Stanley McCluskey Photograph Collection, Arizona Collection, Arizona State University Libraries, Arizona State University, Tempe.

demands for higher wages, bringing production to a standstill. Mine owners vowed they would not give in to the miners. When the miners ignored patriotic appeals to increase production and not walk out, President Woodrow Wilson called in federal troops to quell the strikes. The strikes were broken by the Citizen's Protective League and the Workmen's Loyalty League through an antilabor offensive of propaganda, vigilantism, and expulsions, the so-called "Bisbee Deportations." The strikebreakers manipulated the psychology of wartime hysteria by branding strikers as saboteurs and traitors ("yellow bellies"); 1,876 IWW strikers were arrested, put on El Paso and Southwest Railroad cattle cars, dumped in the desert outside the town of Hermanos, New Mexico, and told not to return. The strike was lost.[14] A few months later, the massive nationwide arrests and show trials of IWW members charged with obstructing the war effort unfolded and led to the Palmer raids. Its energies absorbed in defending itself, the IWW never regained its prewar strength.

The spread of anarcho-syndicalism among Mexican workers and the unsettling effects on the Southwest labor market pushed President Wilson to support initiatives by the AFL and the Pan American Federation of Labor to restrain immigration from Mexico. One positive result of this action was that the Arizona and the Texas State Federations of Labor opened their union affiliates to Mexican workers.[15]

Meanwhile, Tejanos in the lower Río Grande Valley vented their rage and hostility at Anglos through a general uprising known as the Plan de San Diego. Anglos, as well as property, fell victim to the violent mayhem that unfolded as a series of reprisals and counterreprisals in this region.

## TEJANO FREEDOM FIGHTERS:
## THE PLAN DE SAN DIEGO

Mexicans were accepted by Anglos on terms that Anglos defined, and nowhere else were race relations so tense between Mexicans and Anglos than in Texas. In the lower Río Grande Valley Anglos rapidly reordered power and property in the region. Land ownership was equated with power and combined with racial status, increasingly relegating Tejanos to a permanently displaced class. Land grabbing, in combination with the racial violence of the Texas Rangers, once more ignited the long-standing animosities, triggering a brutal rampage against the Mexican population.[16]

Tejanos greatly feared Anglos but did not talk about it because they would be subject to Anglo violence if they spoke out. One Tejano civic leader who bravely raised his voice against the discrimination and organized violence against Tejanos was Nicasio Idar. The Tejano newspaperman was dedicated to Tejano civil rights and racial uplift and unity.

Born in Point Isabel, Texas, in 1855, Nicasio Idar moved to Laredo in 1880, where he quickly emerged as an influential activist and advocate of Tejano rights. He and his wife Jovita raised eight children. Three of them, Jovita, Clemente, and Eduardo, later helped their father publish *La Crónica* (*The Chronicle*) in the late 1890s. *La Crónica* became the mouthpiece of *La Gran Concilio de la Orden Caballeros de Honor* (Knights of Honor) founded by Nicasio Idar in 1910. The Idar family championed progressive national and local issues and were devoted to achieving social justice for Tejanos.[17]

Through their newspaper, the Idar family sounded off against separate and inferior housing and schools, the abysmal conditions faced by Tejano workers that took on the visage of peonage, and the gross violations of Tejano civil rights. Physical abuse, floggings, mutilations, and lynchings remained popular means of Tejano subjugation. In 1910, the Idar family took up the cause of twenty-one-year-old cowboy Antonio Rodríguez, one more victim of mob-led Anglo-Texan justice meted out to "bad Mexicans." Unjustly accused of murdering an Anglo woman near Rock Springs, the Anglo horde took Rodríguez a mile out of town, tied him to a mesquite tree, doused him in kerosene, and burned him alive. There were immediate protests by Mexicans, but it provoked additional Anglo attacks on those displaying an "impudent attitude" rather than the Mexicans' proper submissive attitude toward their Anglo patróns. In Webb, Duval, LaSalle, Dimmitt, and Stark counties, Anglos attacked Mexicans who showed any reactions to the brutal lynching of Rodríguez that the Anglos considered threatening.[18]

Violence meted out to Mexicans in the lower Río Grande Valley increased as Anglos drove them off their land and confiscated their property. The Texas Rangers lent organizational effectiveness to the sporadic terrorism and violence. Between 1907 and 1912, Texas Rangers, along with local peace officers, acting as "trial judge, jury, and executioners" killed more than a dozen Mexicans. In response to this increasing violence against Tejanos, in September 1911, Nicasio Idar and his family, assisted by other Tejanos, organized the conference *El Primer Congreso Mexicanista* (The First Mexican Congress) in Laredo. The Congress drafted a plan of action to protect the lives and land rights of Tejanos. Through *La Crónica* Idar appealed to mutual aid societies, fraternal lodges, and other organizations to send representatives to the landmark conference in Laredo. Four hundred Tejanos of various political persuasions took up the call. The conference participants established *La Gran Liga Mexicanista de Benefinenica y Protección* (The Mexican League of Beneficence and Protection) whose motto was *"por la raza y para la raza"* (by the race, for the race). The assembly denounced the extralegal lynchings of Tejanos and exhorted them not to sell their lands to Anglos despite the tremendous pressure placed on them.[19]

Many Tejanas in attendance were labor radicals, anarchists, and free thinkers in orientation. Those who identified themselves as feminists spoke for the rights of women, an end to educational discrimination, and other progressive reforms. Others who took an anarchist perspective believed in both women's liberation and revolutionary struggle. In order to gain mutual support, the women created networks of women anarchists. In October, these Tejanas formed the women's auxiliary *La Liga Femeníl Mexicanista* (the Mexican Feminist League). Promoting equal education for women, La Liga responded to the widespread illiteracy among Mexicans in South Texas by opening their own schools. They also distributed food and collected clothing for poor Tejanos and raised funds for charities and other projects. Jovita Idar, Nicasio's daughter, served as the league's first president.[20]

Born in Laredo in 1885, Jovita Idar attended Laredo's Methodist Holding Institute, earned a teaching certificate in 1903, and began teaching at a small school in Ojuelos, Texas. However, the poor conditions at the school forced Jovita to resign. She returned to Laredo and became a writer for *La Crónica*, adopting the pen name Astraea, the Greek goddess of justice and indignation.[21]

Tejanos supported the revolution in Mexico against Porfirio Díaz and gave money, weapons, and other assistance to the rebels. Jovita Idar, a member of the Laredo chapter of *La Junta Femeníl Pacifista* (Feminist Pacifist Group), joined *La Cruz Blanca* (White Cross) and, as a nurse, traveled with revolutionary forces in northern Mexico giving comfort to sick and wounded soldiers. The young Tejana returned to Laredo and joined the staff of the newspaper *El Progreso* (Progress). She wrote editorials lambasting President Woodrow Wilson's dispatch of American army troops to the border. The Texas Rangers tried to shut down *El Progreso's* offices, but a defiant Jovita Idar blocked the doorway and prevented the Rangers from entering. When the Rangers finally closed down *El Progreso*, Jovita Idar

**Jovita Idar and the Members of the Union of Stone Masons and Bricklayers, Laredo, Texas, ca. 1915.**
On the platform are (l. to r.): Jovita Idar, Professor Simon Dominguez, and his daughter.
CREDIT: Loaned by A. Ike Idar.  University of Texas, San Antonio, Institute of Texan Cultures, 084-0599.

returned to *La Crónica*. She took charge of the paper in 1914 on the death of her father, Nicasio. Jovita Idar later moved to San Antonio, where she established a free nursery school and worked as an interpreter at a county hospital and as an editor. She became active in the Democratic Party, working on behalf of the drive to gain women the vote in Texas primary elections.[22]

In 1915, Jovita Idar witnessed the collision between Anglos and Tejanos in the lower Río Grande Valley break out in open war. Bound together by sentiments of self-interest and by common perceptions of themselves as Tejanos, the brave insurrectionists paid for their convictions with their lives in the ensuing reign of terror, counterterror, assassination, robbery, and arson.[23]

## THE KILLING FIELDS OF SOUTH TEXAS

Between July and November of 1915, a bloody episode of racial violence broke out in the lower Río Grande Valley. It was triggered by El Plan de San Diego, a manifesto announcing a revolution by Tejanos in the town of San Diego in Duval County. Led by Aniceto Pizaña to overcome the "Yankee tyranny" of race, the Plan's insurgents called for a "Liberating Army for Races and Peoples" to reclaim Texas, New Mexico, Arizona, Colorado, and California, lost from Mexico in 1848, and create an independent republic. All Anglo males over the age of sixteen were to be executed, including prisoners.[24] The subsequent massacre of Tejanos put a stop to these efforts.

Tejanos and an untold number of African American and Indian sympathizers, in guerrilla bands of from twenty-five to one hundred men, began attacking

**Las Norias Bandit Raid, 1915.**
CREDIT: "Las Norias Bandit Raid: Dead Bandits, October 8, 1915." Runyon (Robert) Photograph Collection, RUN00099. Courtesy of the Dolph Briscoe Center for American History, University of Texas, Austin.

area Anglo-Texans. The rebels, in more than two dozen raids in the lower Río Grande Valley, ran off livestock, robbed stores, burned train trestles, destroyed irrigation pumping plants, and killed several dozen Anglos. The Plan de San Diego provoked the governor of Texas to take a war footing. He ordered in the U.S. Army, but it was the Texas Rangers who did the actual fighting.[25]

Sixty Tejano raiders flying a red flag with the inscription: *"igualdad e indepencia"* (equality and independence) assaulted a symbol of Anglo power: the King Ranch. This triggered retaliation by Texas Rangers. Aided by local peace officers and vigilantes, the Rangers launched a counteroffensive and killed three hundred Tejanos. Executions became commonplace, and many Tejanos were shot in the back while allegedly trying to "escape." The Plan de San Diego served as an excuse for wholesale murder, and the Tejano death toll rose precipitously. Raising the cry "We have to make this a white man's country," the Texas Rangers, some with reputations as Angels of Death because they had the power of life and death over many Tejanos, scorched the earth, massacring hundreds, perhaps as many as five thousand Tejano men, women, and children in reprisals against the insurrection. The Rangers took possession of Tejano land by forcing Tejanos to sign bills of sale "at the point of a gun." The Mexicans were disarmed and moved into town so they could be better controlled. Many of the Tejanos whom the blood-crazed Rangers hunted down and shot were innocent victims. More than thirty-five thousand residents fled the lower Río Grande Valley to avoid the retaliations. About fifty thousand men, members of militias from ten states, were ordered to combat duty along the Río Grande River.[26]

Contemporary observers speculated that the Plan de San Diego was invented by Germany to distract the United States from the world war raging in Europe. Another speculation was that Mexico may have also devised the Plan to create a border crisis so that President Venustiano Carranza could offer support in exchange for recognition by the United States. Nevertheless, the Plan de San Diego would generate controversy for years to come.[27]

Clashes between Anglo-Texans and Tejanos continued. White lynch mobs routinely victimized Tejanos in reprisals for attacks by Mexican "bandits" on Anglos or their property. However, many of the instances of violence continued to be over land. In 1918, news came out of Presidio County in West Texas of the murder of fifteen unarmed Mexicans by Texas Rangers. It became known as the Porvenir Massacre, and Anglos would attempt to suppress inquiry into the atrocity.[28]

There were bad feelings between local Anglo sheep and cattle ranchers and the Mexican subsistence farmers of Porvenir. In November 1917, Texas Ranger Captain J. M. Fox reported an outbreak of cattle and horse rustling raids in northwest Presidio County, fifteen miles from the U.S.-Mexico border. Fox suspected it was the work of Mexican thieves. The Ranger captain focused on the Mexicans who lived in Porvenir, who had a "bad reputation." On Christmas Day outlaws raided the huge Brite Ranch near the town of Porvenir, killing several men. Several days later, Captain Fox, at the head of Company B of the Texas Rangers, and local Anglo ranchers rode onto the ranch of Manuel Morales and brandished firearms. The Anglos seized fifteen Mexicans, who were then marched barefoot to a small rock bluff a half mile from Porvenir. The captives were ordered to kneel down and on Fox's orders all of them were shot so many times they were nearly unrecognizable. The youngest victim was sixteen years old. The dead included two landowners in possession of deeds to their land.

Captain Fox waited almost two months to report what had taken place at Porvenir to the adjutant general of Texas. According to Fox, the Texas Rangers found property from the Brite Ranch on the dead Mexicans, implicating them in the raid. One of them told Fox before he was killed that he had "sent word" nine months earlier that a raid would be made on "Texas gringos" and would involve looting and burning. The testimony of other witnesses revealed another story: around 1:00 a.m. on January 24, 1918, forty Anglos surrounded Porvenir and rounded up the residents at gunpoint, while Rangers searched their houses. The Rangers took fifteen Mexican men into custody and then executed them in cold blood. The Brite Ranch had been raided for livestock by an Anglo rancher, who later told the Texas Rangers that "Mexican bandits" had raided the ranch, hoping that the subsequent killings would cover up his own crime.[29]

In 1919, Texas state representative José Tomas Canales, great-nephew of Juan Cortina, called hearings to investigate the Texas Rangers' role in the Porvenir massacre and in other acts of crime committed against Tejanos. Federal authorities also launched an investigation.[30] Despite threats to his life by Texas Rangers, Canales completed his inquiries, resulting in Texas Governor William P. Hobby disbanding Company B and dismissing five Rangers for gross misconduct. Fearing for their lives, Porvenir's residents abandoned their homes and fled to Mexico. The community of Porvenir ceased to exist.[31]

By now the immigration of Mexicans to the United States had increased rapidly and generated its own momentum. Seeking opportunities better than they had in Mexico, the immigrants poured across the border to wherever jobs could be found.

## IMMIGRATION FROM MEXICO
## DURING THE YEARS 1910–1920

The Mexican Revolution, the subsequent labor shortages caused by World War I, and the cutoff of immigration from Europe brought another wave of large-scale immigration from Mexico to the United States. Chain migration and chain occupations directed the immigrants to specific places in the United States. Once Mexicans were settled and secured employment, family members and friends followed. The immigrants often married people from their villages and towns, as loyalty to the same region in Mexico was strong. Many Mexicans immigrated to the United States intent on accumulating money to send or take back to Mexico. Others came to seek change in their own lives and stayed. Three-fourths of the Mexican population was concentrated in the southwestern states of Texas, Colorado, New Mexico, Arizona, and California, with the remainder of the population scattered throughout the Midwest and the plains states.

Among the cities offering new employment opportunities, El Paso, Texas, represented the premier point of entry and destination for Mexican immigrants. The development of railroad transportation around 1888 had transformed El Paso into a bustling trading center and border metropolis that attracted agricultural supply, smeltering, and other mining support services. Easily accessible via the Mexican rail connection that stretched southward into Mexico, El Paso made possible a plentiful flow of immigrants into the United States. The Mexican immigrants used the border city as a base from which they undertook seasonal work. Labor contracting in El Paso became an important service industry as the economic development of the Southwest stimulated the constant demand for labor.[32]

After San Antonio and Los Angeles, El Paso had the nation's third largest Mexican population, and most were immigrants. They were segregated and restricted to unskilled jobs as day laborers and became the targets of anti-alien sentiment prevalent in working-class circles. Mexicans were concentrated in El Paso's Eastside and Southside, where the overcrowding was a serious problem, made worse by the lack of municipal services, poor sanitation, severe poverty, and high mortality rates from disease. Because of economic hardship, Mexican women worked in commercial laundries, though private household work became the mainstay of their employment. A host of mutual-aid societies and fraternal organizations sprang into existence, providing insurance benefits and vitalizing community life, while Spanish-language newspapers, stores, and clubs expanded and bonded the unity of interests of the Mexican enclaves.[33]

Mexicans made up almost half the population of San Antonio. The city's Spanish-speaking residents had arrived in the United States between 1911 and 1930. The men were employed on a seasonal basis in manufacturing, trade, and transportation as unskilled labor. Nearly three-fourths of the city's Mexican women worked to support their families as domestics and cigar and garment factory operatives or took jobs in pecan shelling. Like the Mexicans of El Paso, those of San Antonio became targets of anti-alien campaigns by Anglo trade unions. The lower Río Grande Valley had the largest Mexican population in Texas. They worked picking cotton throughout the state, and many harvested fruit and vegetable crops out of state.[34]

## MEXICANS, WORLD WAR I,
## AND THE 1920–1921 DEPRESSION

From World War I until early 1920, railroad, mining, and grower interest prodded the U.S. Secretary of Labor to waive the head tax, literacy tests, and the prohibition on contract labor to admit alien labor from Mexico into the United States. This brought tremendous employment opportunity for Mexicans. Mexican track workers helped modernize America's railroad system, and increased northern employer demand for labor allowed the entrance of Mexicans into steel and auto manufacturing and meatpacking production, jobs in which they enjoyed a minimum wage and an eight-hour day.[35]

Despite the great demand for labor during the World War I years, thousands of Mexicans fled to Mexico because they feared military conscription for duty overseas. The exodus was the result of widespread misunderstanding regarding the 1917 Selective Service legislation expanding the size of the U.S. armed forces from one hundred thousand to five million within a year. As one scholar observed, "this legislation required all men, including aliens, between twenty-one and thirty-one years of age to register for military service. Mexicans in Texas could not understand why they were required to register for military service if they were not subject to the draft."[36] Most Mexican Americans patriotically backed World War I and served overseas as volunteers or draftees. They viewed the war as an opportunity to improve their status by demonstrating their loyalty and thereby gain full equality.

Owing to the patriotism of "One Hundred Percent Americanism" sweeping the country, Mexican Americans were organized by the federal government into Loyalty Leagues. The leagues selected "Four-Minute Men" to make brief speeches at churches, labor union halls, movie theatres, and public gatherings as a way to encourage voluntary enlistments and home-front participation in agencies such as the Councils of Defense and the Red Cross, the purchase of Liberty Bonds, and patriotic commitment by men and women to the war effort.[37]

The U.S. military was strictly segregated and rife with discrimination. Soldiers with Spanish surnames were often the objects of ridicule and abject scorn by Anglo officers and enlisted men and, like black soldiers, were relegated to menial positions. Mexican Americans who could not speak English were separated by Spanish-language group and sent to Camp Cody in New Mexico or to Camp Gordon in Georgia to improve their English proficiency with bilingual officers as their instructors. Mexican American soldiers served on the front lines with the American Expeditionary Force in France, Belgium, and Germany and fought bravely and effectively. About ten thousand Spanish-speaking New Mexicans volunteered for

**María Delgado, Red Cross Worker During World War I.**
CREDIT: [n.d.] MP SPC 173: 813. Courtesy of the Ocampo Family Photograph Collection, Chicano Research Collection, Arizona State University Libraries, Department of Archives and Special Collections, Arizona State University, Tempe.

service in the war. In southern Colorado the Mexican American volunteer rates exceeded that of Anglos. Many Mexican Americans were cited for their valor and bravery on the battlefields of Europe.[38]

A member of Company B of the 355th Infantry Regiment, Private Marcelino Serna of Albuquerque, New Mexico, single-handedly charged and captured twenty-four Germans on September 12, 1918. For this and other acts of bravery and courage under fire, Serna was awarded the Distinguished Service Cross, the French Croix de Guerre, the Victory Medal with three bars, and two Purple Hearts. David B. Cantú of Laredo enlisted in the U.S. Army using his Anglo father's name Barkley to avoid being segregated into a noncombat unit. Barkley-Cantú served with Company A, 356th Infantry, 89th Division, in France. In November 1918, his unit was engaged in pushing the Germans out of the Argonne Forest and across the Meuse River. The Tejano drowned crossing the river after going behind German lines to gather information about troop strength and deployments. For his actions, Barkley-Cantú was awarded the Medal of Honor, the French Croix de Guerre, and the Italian Croce al Merito di Guerra. Fellow native Texan José de la Luz Sáenz served with the 360th Regiment Infantry of the 90th Division in France and Germany. Sáenz kept a diary, which was published in 1933. In recounting his wartime service, Sáenz linked the American World War I "rhetoric of democracy" with the Mexican American struggle for civil rights. On his return from the war, Sáenz translated his sacrifices and those of the many other American soldiers of Mexican descent fighting for democracy into a movement for civil rights in Texas.[39]

The labor strife of 1919, the Red Scare after the war, and the brief economic recession of 1920–1921 contributed to the revival of immigration restriction in the United States. As the economic depression set in, Mexicans experienced more unemployment, because they were discharged in favor of U.S. citizens. As an unemployed Mexican worker noted: "The good work lasted about a year and a half. Then came 'la crisis' and I was laid off. So were many, many Mexicans . . . but they kept the Americans. It made some of us mad but what could we do? Nothing."[40] Tens of thousands of Mexicans found themselves on their way home to their own country because of government expulsions.

Countless Mexicans had crossed into the United States surreptitiously without paying the visa fee. As a result, the U.S. Immigration Bureau began apprehending and deporting Mexicans suspected of breaking their 1917 labor contracts or those who could not prove legal entry prior to 1921. The nationwide dragnet began in New York City and Chicago. The male detainees were first sent to New Orleans and then to the Mexican border for deportation. Federal agents continued apprehending Mexicans along the border, swinging up to San Francisco and then back again to the border. Overall, more than one hundred fifty thousand Mexicans were repatriated to Mexico.[41]

The expulsions caused an atmosphere of fear among Mexicans but won favor from nativists and labor unions. The latter hated Mexicans because they were used as strikebreakers and brought down wages for all American workers. Moreover, the 1920–1921 national economic crisis wiped out the limited advances Mexicans had made up to 1920, hindering as well overall opportunities for assimilation and citizenship by this immigrant group.[42] The campaign of repatriation did not entirely set back the flow of Mexicans to the United States as jobs once more beckoned them north. In fact, Mexican immigration to America reached major proportions at this time.

## MEXICAN IMMIGRATION FROM 1920 TO 1929

About half a million Mexicans entered the United States in the 1920s, representing 11 percent of total immigration. Mexicans became more distributed throughout the country, though most remained concentrated in the Southwest. Most areas of this rapidly developing region had become heavily dependent on Mexicans for low-wage and often dirty and dangerous jobs in agriculture, railroad, construction, mines, and factory work. Despite the strengthening of border controls in 1924, unauthorized immigration reached large dimensions through the work of "coyotes," or professional alien smugglers. American employers willingly hired the aliens, knowing they were illegal, because they coveted the cheap labor.[43]

Reflecting the growing dependence on Mexican labor by employers, Mexicans made up three-fourths of the workforce of the six major western railroads; three-fourths of construction workers and 80 percent of migrant farm workers in Texas; three-fourths of the agricultural workforce in California, and nearly two-thirds of the workers in this state's construction, food processing, textiles, automobile and steel production, and utilities industries. In the industrial heartland of the Midwest, railroads and steel, meatpacking, and auto manufacturing firms with their standardized working conditions and wages came to rely increasingly on Mexican labor along with that of blacks.[44] Most Mexicans struggled to survive on their wages; therefore, women and even children worked to make ends meet. Women operated boardinghouses or procured work as domestics, waitresses, cooks, hotel maids, nannies, and factory workers. In addition to their paid labor, which made a significant difference to their families' survival, women ran the households and raised children.

The railroad industry was a significant source of employment for Mexicans. As previously noted, Mexicans constructed many of the trunk lines of the southwestern railroads in the late nineteenth century. Once these were completed, and with incentives such as free transportation and housing, the railroads hired tens of thousands of Mexicans to build auxiliary lines and to maintain and repair the tracks.[45]

Gangs of Mexican workers under Spanish-speaking straw bosses unloaded rails; prepared roadbeds; laid switches, ties and tracks; and tramped, lined, and later replaced ties for the railroads.[46] Mexicans were restricted to unskilled tasks; the railroad companies hired them as general laborers in shops, engine houses, and power plants. Construction and maintenance drew Mexicans to the street railway systems of southern California and Texas cities.[47]

As the pace of recruitment by the railroads accelerated, Mexican boxcar communities situated on almost all the railroad lines began to dot the American landscape from California to the Canadian border. With the pull of higher paying jobs and expectations for a better life, with such advantages as running water and electricity and school for their children, families made collective decisions to head for urban centers. The desire for economic betterment and a generally increased standard of living likewise motivated Mexican farm workers to search for work in the cities.[48]

Mexican migration continued flowing to San Antonio, Los Angeles, Chicago, Detroit, and other large cities because of the availability of work and the newcomers' collective desire for material betterment. Those in Mexico contemplating immigration gained a wealth of information from family members or friends already in the United States. Chain migration linked specific towns and villages in Mexico with settlements in the United States. Males who came north without families continued to dominate the migration.

The migrants formed new colonies adjacent to agricultural, railroad, and mining camps, as newly arrived families tended to live near their places of employment and moved together whenever possible. Fellow Mexicans were next in importance in the support networks. The dramatic increase in Mexican immigration affected residential patterns. Thousands settled in older and established Spanish-speaking working-class communities, adding to the overcrowding and generating construction of cheap housing to meet the increased demand.

Immigrants from Mexico outnumbered Mexican Americans by two to one, and the result was a layering of generations in which identity took on many distinct forms. This was reflected in the workplace, schools, churches, neighborhoods, and community organizations. As Ruth D. Tuck noted of the Mexicans of San Bernardino, California, in her book *Not with the Fist:* "There is a street . . . on which three families live side by side. The head of one family is a naturalized citizen, who arrived eighteen years ago; the head of the second is an alien who came . . . in 1905; the head of the third is the descendant of people who came . . . in 1843. All of them, with their families, live in poor housing; earn approximately $150 a month as unskilled laborers; send their children to 'Mexican' schools; and encounter the same sort of discriminatory practices."[49]

## MEXICAN LOS ANGELES

From the 1920s on, Los Angeles was a magnet for Mexican immigrants. The 134,300 Mexicans who peopled and energized Los Angeles in 1928 represented 10 percent of the city's total population and its largest single minority group. Mexican Los Angeles was an aggregate of numerous subcommunities, all of which helped define the city. Some of the city's Mexican colonies dated from the ranches of the Spanish and Mexican periods, whereas others grew out of the boxcar camps, company towns, and agricultural sites established in the late nineteenth and early twentieth centuries. The neighborhood and housing patterns of the Mexican colonies were marked by social problems. Racial discrimination confined the Mexicans to the city's polyglot working-class zones, though most lived in the "Mexican" sections with the highest rents and the poorest and most unhealthful homes. Infant mortality rates here were three times higher than for Anglos, and the areas contributed a third of the city's tuberculosis cases. Regarded unfavorably by Anglos, the city's Mexicans likewise experienced discrimination in public services and recreational facilities, and children generally received a poor education.[50]

Mexicans settled in the Plaza area located downtown, where housing was affordable but overcrowded due to the constant arrival of great numbers of immigrants from Mexico. Many escaped the overcrowded downtown by moving to areas east of the Los Angeles River, settling around Stephenson Avenue, in the South Boyle Heights section, and in the Belvedere area. Rail service provided by Los Angeles Pacific Electric Railway enabled Mexican community formation in this section that became known as East Los Angeles. These working-class colonies were not singularly Mexican but ethnically mixed from the onset. The growing Mexican colonies fostered the expansion of merchants and other businesses such as grocery and dry goods stores, restaurants, barbershops, tailor shops, and other small commercial enterprises. These thriving businesses, like the five restaurant-bakeries owned by Rudy and Guadalupe Moreno, were owned and operated by a small middle class oriented toward serving the surrounding Spanish-speaking population. Other Mexican-owned businesses reached out to a wider clientele. In 1930, the U.S. Census noted that the Mexican and Mexican American population of Los Angeles had surpassed San Antonio as the largest in the United States.[51]

For Los Angeles Mexicans, familial interdependence was the key to economic survival. Kinship networks formed an integral part of work life and contributed to a collective identity shaped by the respective work culture. Los Angeles County remained a major agricultural producing and processing center. Drawing on networks of family and kin, employers recruited Mexican women to work in clothing and needle trades, other light industries, and the commercial laundries. Many women operated boardinghouses, where they prepared meals for boarders and washed their clothing. Others worked as domestics.[52]

Paralleling the growth of Mexican Los Angeles, newcomers who were citrus workers settled in "citrus villages" in Orange County and in the Inland Empire of southern California. These outlying Mexican colonies, such as Arbol Verde, with their own cultural and institutional life, were plagued by discrimination. In addition to inadequate housing and schooling, Mexicans who settled in rural areas in many instances were expelled from local communities at the end of the harvest season.[53]

By the second half of the 1920s, California contained more than a third of all large-scale farms in the western states. With the proximity of the border ensuring a steady infusion of workers, Mexicans became the foundation of the industrialized labor relations in California crop production. Of the two hundred thousand farm laborers in California, three-fourths were Mexican. In addition, employers recruited Mexican women, some of them young girls, to do piecework in the canneries and packing sheds. Employers believed the Mexican females were cheaper to hire and easier to control than native-born women.[54]

The climate of labor unrest spread in agriculture, triggered by worsening working and living conditions. Discontented Mexicans organized against grower exploitation and substandard housing and, soon, competition with fellow Mexicans crossing the border. Burdened by poverty and racism, the farm workers organized themselves into unions that dealt with a specific labor issue. Once the issue was resolved, workers abandoned the organization, and it ceased to exist. Solidarity was weakened by the constant wandering of Mexican farmworkers from city to countryside and back again. Moreover, the strike actions were quickly put down by violent grower repression, with the aid of sheriffs and vigilante groups. Because of the farmworkers' desperate condition, California's farms remained hotbeds of unrest.

## MEXICANS IN THE ROCKY MOUNTAIN AND PLAINS STATES

With sugar beet work wages rising by 50 percent, Mexican Americans and Mexicans replaced Russian Germans in the beet farms of Colorado and the plains states. Reliance on Mexican farmworkers became great. In Colorado, Mexicans made up

90 percent of the labor used in planting and harvesting sugar beets. Using dozens of labor recruiters and Spanish-language advertisements, Great Western Sugar by 1920 was recruiting thirteen thousand Mexicans annually to work in the beet fields in Colorado, Wyoming, Montana, and Nebraska. Seven years later, the sweat labor of about fifty-eight thousand Mexicans provided for the continued expansion of beet acreage as far as Ohio. Defined by family and kin, Mexicans formed a virtual army of field hands that harvested 7.5 million tons of sugar beets worth between 60 and 65 million dollars. A large number of the beet workers were children. Believing Mexican children did not need an education, locally governed school systems removed Mexican children from school to help farmers harvest their beet crops.[55]

The Mexican workers in Colorado's South Platte and Arkansas River Valleys had been recruited by labor agencies in Eagle Pass, Texas. The remainder were from New Mexico's upper Río Grande Valley. Immigration had doubled New Mexico's Spanish-speaking population and increased that of Colorado fivefold. Eight thousand Mexicans lived in Denver, and three-fourths left this city each spring for the beet fields. Owing to widespread discrimination, the Mexicans of Colorado organized to defend themselves. Those with IWW affiliation formed *La Liga Obrera de Habla Español* (Spanish-Speaking Workers' League) and its influence extended throughout Colorado and New Mexico.[56]

Migration took Mexicans to railroad construction and maintenance jobs in Nebraska with the Union Pacific, Burlington Northern, and the Santa Fe Railroads. Many went to Omaha for the stockyard and meatpacking jobs. One thousand lived in South Omaha in mixed ethnic neighborhoods adjoining the foul-smelling slaughterhouses and meatpacking plants. A Mexican community developed in the city of Scottsbluff near the Great Western Sugar refinery on land families purchased from the factory.

The burgeoning presence of Mexicans in Kansas occurred because significant numbers got jobs with the railroads and sugar beet growers. Kansas was a major transfer point and railroad hub for the Midwest and the eastern states. Kansas Mexicans worked for the Atchison, Topeka, and Santa Fe Railroad and in the state's meat processing plants, salt mines, and sugar beet fields. Some Mexicans left their families in Mexico while they worked from spring to fall and returned home in the winter months. Those in Topeka formed a camp in the Santa Fe rail yards, crowded housing that was a mix of dismounted boxcars and hand-built shacks.[57]

Because of hostility against Mexican immigrants, the Spanish-speaking communities of Kansas remained separate from the larger Anglo society in every town and city. Mexicans were unwelcome in movie theaters and in parks and other public facilities, in the schools, and in Catholic churches, all reserved for whites. Kansas's Mexican population was large enough to support a broad range of institutions that assisted them in their adaptation to American society. The Benito Juárez Mutual Aid Society was the largest, with chapters throughout the state. Topeka's Mexicans sponsored baseball and football teams, held dances, and instituted classes in English, Spanish, and arithmetic. Other Mexicans in the state founded their own parishes and organized church-centered social events. To combat discrimination, in 1915 Mexicans in Kansas City founded the Spanish-language newspaper *El Cosmopolita* (*The Cosmopolitan*) that catered to their needs and worked to keep the public informed about Mexicans.[58]

Kansas's Mexican population in 1920 totaled 13,770. More and more new arrivals brought their families with them, leading to the formation of permanent communities. Because the men were confined to low-wage work, women sought jobs outside the home to supplement family incomes. On the eve of the Great Depression, Mexicans constituted the second largest immigrant group in Kansas, with the most colonies established in Kansas City, Topeka, Emporia, Wichita, and Garden City.[59] In their quest for greater job opportunities, Mexican migration shifted in direction as they began hearing about new openings in the North.

## MEXICANS IN THE URBAN INDUSTRIAL HEARTLAND OF THE MIDWEST

Sugar beet work initially spurred the Mexican migration to the Midwest. More than fifty-eight thousand Mexicans started life in the industrial and manufacturing cities of America's heartland. Their importance in the Midwest was their transformation into the first Mexican industrial working class, as blue-collar jobs beckoned in railroads, meat packinghouses, steel mills, foundries, and auto factories. These early arrivals provided assistance to immigrants who came later. Information about jobs and where to live traveled through family and friendship networks that extended to the Southwest and into Mexico. These networks determined the migration paths, as well as decisions about work and settlement patterns in the urban manufacturing environment of the Midwest. Discrimination, which shaped work and housing, was heightened by employment fluctuations, job competition, and housing shortages. Anti-immigrant sentiment and the racism produced by the Great Black Migration contributed to the hostile reception of Mexicans.[60]

Chicago was a favorite destination for immigrants from Mexico. Mexicans went to Chicago to work in the rail yards, mills, and packinghouses. By 1920, more than five thousand Mexicans were employed by twenty railroads with terminals in Chicago and composed 21 percent of the track workforce, which doubled to 42 percent eight years later. Along with blacks, Mexicans took "dirty work" that most white workers shunned in the unhealthy and dangerous meatpacking plants of Wilson and Company, Swift and Company, and Armour, Hammond, and Omaha.[61]

The massive worker unrest at the end of World War I brought Mexicans, many as strikebreakers, north to Chicago's big, noisy steel mills, where they encountered unsafe work environments. After the 1920–1921 depression, the steel companies expanded their recruiting efforts as the mills shifted to the eight-hour, three-shift schedule. Mexicans constituted 14 percent of the overall workforce in steel production.[62]

The United States Steel Corporation became the largest employer of Mexicans, hiring thousands for its plants in Wisconsin, Illinois, Indiana, Ohio, and New York. Mexicans also worked for the Carnegie Steel Corporation, Bethlehem Steel, Jones and Laughlin, and National Tube. In Indiana Harbor, Indiana, more than two thousand Mexicans accounted for a fourth of Inland Steel's hourly employees.

In nearby Gary, more than one thousand Mexicans found jobs at the Illinois Steel plant, constituting almost 8 percent of the workforce. Mexicans readily accepted the hard, low-paying work and embraced the factory regimen, becoming efficient steelworkers who worked according to an enforced routine. As one observer noted, "the men showed great endurance at work, sometimes working continuously without a day off in a year . . . where others would not stay a month."[63]

The high rents and living costs in the northern cities made it necessary for Mexican women to work in order to supplement the family's income. The men opposed entrance of women into the labor force but grudgingly accepted it because additional income was needed. Providing lodging permitted many women to earn money while remaining home with their children. Others did domestic work in private homes or broadened their job options by turning to the city's factories, all of it low-wage work. As with the men, opportunities for Mexican women varied in each city.[64] Elsewhere, small numbers of Mexican women gained access to nonindustrial occupations as office clerks or secretaries or in retailing. Unmarried women remained in the labor force because of their wish for both personal and financial independence. Taking jobs open to females, the women embraced the emerging mass consumer culture of the 1920s that contributed to shaping their identity. Others adopted the ideal of American domesticity because of their exposure to corporate welfare programs that provided various amenities such as medical care and profit-sharing plans by which employers fostered and gained the loyalty of their immigrant and black workers.[65]

Overcrowded working-class tenements underscored life for Mexicans in industrial Chicago. Mexicans rented houses, apartments, and flats in the city's deteriorated neighborhoods, where nearly half the households took in lodgers to help meet payments. The noise from the rail yards, the noxious fumes from the steel mills, and the foul air of the stockyards was constant and unbearable. A Mexican woman from Back of the Yards, a neighborhood adjoining the meatpacking plants, told an observer: "the smell and stench here are bad . . . it makes me sick and it makes me vomit at times. . . . Some of the other Mexican women around here feel the same way. It is very bad but what can we do? Our husbands work near here, the rent is cheaper, and we have to live." Living conditions for Gary's 2,500 Mexicans were no better. Overcrowding endured by Mexicans in the United States was particularly acute in Indiana Harbor, where the housing was deplorable. The nearly 5,000 Mexicans clustered in this mill town lived in ramshackle houses concentrated in less than a square mile abutting the Inland Steel plant.[66]

By the end of the 1920s, approximately twenty thousand Mexicans were in Chicago, representing the greatest concentration of Mexicans outside the Southwest. Women and children made up a third of the newcomer population. Many of the city's industrial firms turned to Mexican labor. Over 80 percent of the men toiled in freight yards, steel mills and iron foundries, and the meatpacking plants. They endured frequent layoffs and dangerous working conditions. Washing, cooking, and cleaning for boarders, as well as jobs open to females in the Windy City, allowed women to earn extra cash. Mexicans experienced a limited supply of working-class housing, but kin and community helped them with the problem of finding shelter. Taking in relatives, friends, and former townsmen as lodgers strengthened kinship and community ties. Mexicans established colonies near their place of employment. Religious and settlement house reformers aided adjustment to the new environment by offering Mexicans educational and cultural programs and material assistance. Political, religious, and cultural institutions developed by Chicago's Mexican colonies enlivened community life and nourished working-class culture. The settlements took on unique identities that embraced the urban and industrial ethos of the Windy City. Like other immigrants, Chicago Mexicans maintained strong ties to their homeland, conveyed in newspapers, political rallies, and through celebrations of Mexican holidays.[67]

Thousands of Mexicans were drawn to Michigan because of the growth of jobs in the auto industry. During World War I Mexicans began working in the auto factories of Detroit, Pontiac, Flint, and Saginaw, Michigan. Most came to Detroit, the nation's fastest growing metropolitan area because of the high wages offered by the Ford Motor Company, the world's largest car, truck, and tractor manufacturer. By the mid-1920s, four thousand Mexicans worked for Ford Motors at its Highland Park, Fordson, and River Rouge plants, and two hundred were enrolled in the Henry Ford Service School. In the Ford auto plants, Mexicans encountered standardization and division of work tasks, strict shop floor supervision, and bureaucratic personnel policies. Fifteen thousand Mexicans eventually settled in Detroit, representing the second largest population of Mexicans in the Midwest. Most lived on the city's southwest side and contributed to the distinct ethnic character of the Motor City's highly diverse working-class districts. Kinship and community were

**Mexican Auto Workers with Henry Ford, 1919.**
(Henry Ford is first row center, sixth from right.)
CREDIT: "Henry Ford with Mexican Employees, 9/8/19, (Highland Park Employees)," (P.833.27439/THF63258), from the Collections of the Henry Ford Museum.

vital to the newcomers' adjustment to life in Detroit. They provided an essential link to family members who made the trek north and settled in the Motor City and who now helped them secure jobs and find housing.[68]

The urban and industrial Midwest became a magnet of opportunity for Mexicans seeking a new way of life. In 1927, the U.S. Department of Labor reported that almost thirty-one thousand Mexicans held industrial employment in northern urban centers extending from St. Paul, Minnesota, to Pennsylvania's Monongahela Valley.[69] Midwestern Mexicans came together as self-identifiable communities centered on immigrant institutions. Mutual aid and fraternal organizations shaped by ethnicity and class fostered group identity and solidarity. Moreover, based on the new circumstances, Mexicans built their communities as members of the industrial working classes with specific identities, lifestyles, and aspirations.

Mexicans in the industrial heartland were exposed to an industrial form of time that demanded adaptation to a faster work pace and strict work rules to enforce discipline. As industrial employers expanded their vast power of domination over workers, Mexicans were influenced as well by various components of corporate welfare capitalism's efforts to inculcate worker loyalty, tractability, and efficiency. Through wage incentives, insurance and pension plans, and recreational programs, industry sought to undercut the Mexicans' reliance on both unions and community-based services. Included in this corporate scheme for the loyalties of Mexican workers were religious institutions, most of them antiunion, which helped the newcomers from Mexico adjust to new conditions in the United States. Faced with the rise of nativist sentiment, the Mexican immigrant working classes retreated to the sanctuary of their ethnic communities.

## MEXICANS AND SOCIAL AND CULTURAL CHANGE AND AMERICANIZATION

The Catholic Church was the principal church of Mexican immigrants. Church-sponsored social events brought cohesion to the Mexican communities, and the Church played an important role as a community center. For some women, church services were one of the few acceptable social outings. The Church's assistance to the Mexicans was plagued by a shortage of funds and Spanish-speaking priests. After 1926, Mexican immigrants entered the United States from west central Mexico, the site of the Cristero Revolution, an uprising by persecuted Catholics against the Mexican government's anti-clericalism. Dissension flared in the Mexican colonies as pro-Cristeros and anti-Cristeros clashed over ideological differences originating in the homeland. A larger threat than the pro-Cristeros were the missionary efforts of evangelical Protestant ministers, who proselytized among the immigrants to get them to convert and join Christian churches. Many won new church members; other immigrants had either converted to or been exposed to Protestant sects in Mexico.[70]

Revivalism was a way evangelical churches gained many converts to "born-again Christianity." Along with settlement house workers, Protestant missionaries felt it was their duty to protect Mexican newcomers against atheistic,

radical influences as an important goal. "The thousands of Mexican immigrants . . . are . . . in a state of transition, and the forces of evil are at work among
them. The question . . . is whether they are to be won over to . . . Bolshevism or to
Democracy; to Trotsky or to Christ." Doing their best to battle against the "new
religion" of Bolshevism, various Americanization programs aided in the socialization of Mexican immigrants into "100 percent Americans" through civic classes,
language instruction, and home economics.[71]

Nativist anxieties about the nation's "alien problem" and the fear of the worldwide conspiracy of Bolshevism fueled the public and private drive for Americanization work among immigrants. U.S. government agencies conducted nationwide
surveys of immigrants, and state and local governments, religious groups, and
private social service organizations collaborated in a program of Americanization.
These efforts targeted the men to become U.S. citizens. Women were seen as the
ones who would pass on American culture to their families, so programs for
women focused on birth control, child rearing, and domesticity. Settlement houses
Americanized Mexicans by encouraging political conformity and a single set of
domestic habits. Americanization projects for Mexicans such as those run by the
YMCA grew throughout the Southwest and Midwest, promoting literacy and
instruction in the English language, American culture, and job skills training.[72]

The Americanization movement involved employer participation. Manufacturing companies required their immigrant employees to attend English and

**YMCA Boy's Club, Miami, Arizona, 1928.**
CREDIT: MP CM-74. Courtesy of Christine Marin Photograph Collection, Chicano Research Collection, Arizona
State University Libraries, Department of Archives and Special Collections, Arizona State University, Tempe.

citizenship classes to instill American values and habits and, more so, to acquaint them with factory discipline. More important, employers saw Americanization as an effective antiunion device, just as employers maintained an ethnic mix in the workplace to perpetuate mutual distrust among their workers.

Public education was a training ground for U.S. citizenship. Educational theories emphasized English usage, American values, and work as vehicles for acculturation to American language and society. However, these theories also embraced the prevailing racist stereotypes of the Mexican's innate intellectual inferiority. Bolstered by biased tests and surveys, Anglo teachers and administrators believed that Mexican students, because of their intellectual limitations, had few aspirations and limited abilities beyond manual or domestic work. Consequently, the vocational curricula in "Mexican" schools served to funnel youth into low-wage work. Schooling for Mexicans essentially trained them for the menial roles they would play in American society.[73]

The efforts to Americanize Mexicans were thwarted because of Mexico's proximity, which made visits and permanent return possible. This homeward orientation resulted in low naturalization rates. In addition, the Mexicans' relative isolation at railroad, mining, agricultural, and similar work campsites enabled them to retain their native culture and language while limiting opportunities to gain familiarity with American society. Moreover, the everyday reality of racism made the Mexicans resist Americanization.[74]

Various conservative groups loyal to Americanization worked hard politically to curb Mexican immigration. They condemned the immutable foreignness and "inferiority" of Mexican life and deemed this alien menace a threat to the health and morals of the nation. Various forms of outright racial discrimination set Mexicans apart. These included limited job advancement, restrictive housing covenants, separate days in churches, inferior "Mexican schools," separate entrances and Mexican sections in theaters, and special "colored" days in public swimming pools.[75]

## MEXICAN MUTUALISM AND FRATERNALISM

Mexicans created numerous mutual aid and fraternal organizations in the United States. Membership in each varied, reflecting a cross-section of occupations and wealth. Some Mexicans engaged in political activities related to Mexico, whereas labor issues were a matter of concern for many others because of their working-class composition that reflected the backgrounds of the Mexican population as a whole.[76] Individuals to whom members could go for help emerged as leaders and became spokesmen for the Mexican community without a public voice.

The mutual aid and fraternal organizations assisted their members in time of need with small emergency loans; medical, life, and burial insurance; and legal services. Some voluntary associations reinforced the customs, language, and traditions of its members through a host of cultural activities, such as the commemoration of Mexican holidays. Others ran schools because of the inferior education Mexican children received in the segregated public schools. Mexican consuls often served as honorary members of the voluntary associations. In the cause of employer antiunionism, the consuls exerted significant effort in censoring or containing subversive ideas and social unrest and generally maintaining control over Mexican workers.

Few voluntary associations subscribed to American assimilation. Instead, they promoted Mexican nationalism and encouraged members to maintain close ties to their homeland. Other organizations, open to the wider issues of class consciousness, encouraged labor activism among its membership. For example, in 1928, numerous Mexican working-class organizations joined millions of people in the United States and around the world protesting on behalf of the ordeal of Nicola Sacco and Bartolomeo Vanzetti, the two Italian immigrants and anarchists convicted of murder in 1921 in an atmosphere poisoned by antiradical and racial hysteria. Class solidarity, however, was sometimes impeded by the ethnic chauvinism of members.

In the years following World War I, Mexican labor activism increased and became a recognizable fixture in the Southwest. Overall, Mexicans recognized the benefits of involvement in unions for protection at a time when great numbers of them were unorganized. In November 1927, the Federation of Mexican Societies in Los Angeles persuaded a number of Mexican local unions to organize into the *Confederación de Uniones Campesinos y Obreros Mexicanos* or CUOM (Confederation of Mexican Workers and Peasants Unions). With its three thousand members organized into twenty affiliated locals, CUOM's goals included wage and job equality and protecting the members against unjust deportation practices. CUOM understood that it would fail so long as growers had a surplus labor pool; therefore, it called for the United States and Mexico to restrict immigration from Mexico. CUOM declined, but its objective of organizing Mexican workers to strengthen and improve their position was important in establishing the roots of Mexican trade unionism in southern California.[77]

In the following year, during the Imperial Valley cantaloupe strike, a high-profile work stoppage by Mexican farmworkers that was marred by vigilantism and strikebreaking, *La Unión de Trabajadores del Valle Imperial* (Imperial Valley Workers Union) was formed from two mutual-aid societies. Changing its name to the Mexican Mutual Aid Society of the Imperial Valley (MMAS), its members demanded recognition of their union and better housing conditions for workers.[78]

The *Liga Protectora Latina* (Latin Protective League) was founded in Phoenix, Arizona, in 1914. With its motto, "One for all. All for one," it protected the interests of its working-class membership, including their civil rights. Although anti-IWW, it fought against House Bill 54, the Claypool-Kinney Bill, restricting the employment of aliens (Mexicans) in mine work, and it later fought Law No. 23 that called for the exclusion of Mexicans from skilled railroad and mining work.[79] The *Sociedad Proteción Mutual de Trabajadores Unidos* (the Mutual Protection Society of Mexican Workers) similarly advanced the interests of Mexican workers in the Rocky Mountain states against discrimination. It was founded in 1900 in Antoñito, Colorado, as an alternative to the exclusive and racist American Federation of Labor (AFL) that declared that Mexicans were unorganizable and a threat to white workers. The Sociedad expanded; its members organized additional lodges in southern Colorado and northern New Mexico, and its influence was also felt in Utah.

Mexicans who were leaders and established members of their communities, with links to established groups and institutions, took on issues on its behalf. Tejano attorney Manuel C. Gonzales, through his law practice, was in contact with Mexican workers from San Antonio to the lower Río Grande Valley and understood the problems they encountered. In 1917, Gonzales created *La Liga Protectora Mexicana* (the Mexican Protective League) to provide Mexicans legal advice on such matters as alien residents' rights, workers' compensation, and tenant farmer contracts and due process.[80]

The Mexican Protective League lobbied the Texas State Legislature to halt the exploitation of Tejano tenant farmers by unscrupulous Anglo-Texan landowners who regularly defrauded them. In 1918, the league pushed for a state law requiring landlords to have a court order when law officials accompanied them onto a tenants' rented land. Maintaining Mexican labor in a cycle of indebtedness ensured worker stability. Two years later, in 1920, the league supported legislation to protect tenants' crops on shares. In addition, the league produced a bilingual handbook on landlord-tenant rights, workers' compensation, and on the penal code; it published a weekly legal-aid advice column in the San Antonio newspaper *El Imparcial de Texas* (*The Texas Impartial*); and it helped the Democratic Party defeat pro-Ku Klux Klan Republican gubernatorial candidate Joseph W. Bailey. In the same year, the Mexican Protective League founded *La Liga Instructiva Mexicana* (the Mexican Instructive League) to prepare Mexicans for U.S. citizenship. Mexican Protective League chapters were later established in many parts of the Southwest and in the Midwest.[81]

The *Alianza Hispano-Americana* (Hispanic-American Alliance) was the largest Mexican American fraternal organization in the Southwest. It was formed in 1894 in Tucson, Arizona, in response to the escalation of discrimination and racism against Mexicans. As an ally to Mexican workers in the copper mining region, Alianza founded chapters in Florence, Clifton, Bisbee, Globe, Tempe, Nogales, Yuma, and Metcalf. Alianza members expanded their organization into the Imperial Valley of California, Texas, and other parts of the Southwest. The Alianza spoke out on a wide range of issues, and the right to vote was an important message. Aware of the various ways Anglos kept Mexicans from voting, the Alianza supported the woman suffrage movement and expanded their membership to women in 1913.[82]

The League of United Latin American Citizens (LULAC) signaled the emergence of new leadership in the Mexican community of the United States. LULAC embraced a conservative point of view in matters of civil rights and race relations. Its goals were "to develop within the members of our race, the best . . . loyal citizens of the United States of America."[83]

On August 24, 1927, several dozen Mexican Americans convened a meeting in Harlingen, Texas, to form a new organization based on a coalition with the Sons of America, founded six years earlier in San Antonio. The Sons of America, promoters of loyalty to America, refused to participate as a group, though some members would join with the Tejanos to form the League of United Latin American Citizens.[84] World War I veteran, foreign service officer, and San Antonio attorney Alonzo Perales was one of LULAC's founders and an important figure. In its early

**LULAC–Sons of America Group, 1924–1929.**
CREDIT: "Grupo de miembros del Concilio no. 4 de Corpus Christi, Texas." Photograph of the Sons of America, LULAC Group Photo, 1924–1929, Ben Garza Collection, box 1, folder 1, album 1. Courtesy of the Benson Latin American Collection, University of Texas, Austin.

form, LULAC epitomized Mexican American middle-class concerns about maintaining respectability, as well as allaying the tensions and divisions within the Mexican American community over immigration.[85]

LULAC was an organization driven by the goal of creating a new Mexican American sense of self. It limited membership to American citizens and made English its official language. The founding of LULAC reflected the larger changes transforming Mexican American life in the United States, particularly the struggle to reverse the disenfranchisement that began in the late nineteenth century limiting Mexican Americans' rights as citizens with regard to the use of public facilities, voting, and serving on juries. A chief concern was the growing social restrictions placed on Mexican Americans resulting from the significant increase in the Spanish-speaking population through immigration from Mexico.[86]

Mexican immigrants in unprecedented numbers introduced new conflicts in American society already rife with racial unrest and embroiled in debates about immigrants. To many Mexican Americans, the Mexican immigrants who established enclaves in their communities accentuated differences between Mexican immigrants and Mexican Americans. Specifically, their presence challenged notions of identity.[87]

Much like northern African Americans responding to the Great Black Migration, LULAC's members feared that racial discrimination would force their social life inward toward the larger Mexican immigrant community rather than outward as they hoped. This is one important reason why LULAC's leadership strongly embraced an identity as Americans. They called attention to the contributions Mexican Americans had made to the United States. LULAC's constitution specified that English was its official language. The organization, moreover, encouraged cooperation with Anglos toward the goal of extolling and attaining the benefits of U.S. citizenship for Mexican Americans and, faced with the influx of laborers from Mexico, pushed for restrictive immigration legislation for that country.[88]

Through its national office and local branches, LULAC endeavored to be the voice of the Mexican American community. Education became a subject of urgent debate, and the organization took the lead in attempting to better schools for Mexican American children, many whom attended inferior Mexican schools. In many areas of the Southwest local primary schools were widely unavailable, or else Mexican American children were enrolled in school for only part of the year due to the demands of the job market on their parents and the need for children's labor. In its campaign for better education, LULAC formed the School Improvement League. Set in place by custom and local treatment rather than state statute, the school desegregation of Mexican children was left up to the discretion of local officials, the majority overwhelmingly Anglo. Seeking acceptance of Mexican Americans as Caucasian, LULAC began the unusual precedent of using the "legal whiteness" argument.[89]

Mexican American and Anglo attorneys worked on a pro bono basis to assist LULAC in its legal struggle to desegregate hundreds of local schools in Texas. In 1930, LULAC brought the first class-action lawsuit against segregation of Mexicans in Texas public schools. The *Salvatierra v. Del Rio Independent School District* case ended the designation of "Mexican schools" in Texas. However, mechanisms for enforcement of school integration were never realized beyond the demand on local school systems. In the same year, LULAC also campaigned for the U.S. Bureau of Census to reclassify persons of Mexican descent as "white." This was done so Anglos would distinguish them from blacks and to blur distinctions between Mexican Americans and Anglos.[90] Until the 1930s, when it was overshadowed by progressive class-based organizations, LULAC remained the most influential Mexican American organization in the United States.

## CONCLUSION

In the first two decades of the twentieth century, as World War I cut off the supply of immigrant labor from Europe, Mexican immigrants arrived daily in the United States in larger numbers. They found work wherever they could at whatever rate of pay was offered them. As the newest group of workers, Mexicans were often hired for the dirtiest jobs. Together with Mexican Americans, they organized to gain security as workers. Revolutionary politics reflected the era's global wars and revolutions. The IWW, with its inclusiveness and its tradition of leadership, spread industrial unionism among Mexican workers, and many embraced it. Countless Spanish-speaking workers were followers of anarcho-syndicalism or were sympathizers with the socialist movement. All faced repression by police, judicial, and military agencies as employers unleashed violent repression against them and used deportations to defeat them.

In the lower Río Grande Valley of Texas what remained of the old Tejano ranching society disappeared, destroyed by Anglos drawn to the region by new opportunities for profit. Tejanas, among them Laredo's Jovita Idar and sisters Andrea and Teresa Villarreal of San Antonio, eloquently addressed class, race, and gender inequities at this time in speeches and through newspapers they established for this purpose. In response to the explosion of race hatred in this region, local Tejanos rose up against the repression under the banner of the Plan de San Diego and were mercilessly defeated.

Immigration from Mexico proceeded apace during World War I as the first large wave of Mexican immigrants came to the United States. This immigration was a product of chain migration. Meanwhile, unauthorized immigration from Mexico was sustained by the recruiting efforts of greedy American employers and the pressure they placed on their congressional allies to relax border restrictions. Mexican immigration from this point on would present challenges to those concerned with the absorption, assimilation, and control of this group.[91]

Mexican Americans volunteered for service overseas with the American Expeditionary Force and fought in the Great War. To show their citizenship, and despite discrimination, Mexican American women volunteered for patriotic service at home, such as buying and selling Liberty Bonds and working for the Red Cross. Though their ability was doubted, Mexican American soldiers conducted themselves with bravery and courage. Little tribute was paid to the valor of Mexican American soldiers who fought for the flag of the United States in Europe.

The immigrants responded directly to the impact of industrialization and modern American values and adjusted to living in the United States, though they retained an attachment to their homeland. Women ran boardinghouses or procured work as domestics, waitresses, cooks, hotel maids, nannies, and factory workers. Mexicans recreated the familiar aspects of their home country in the United States. They lived and worked together, established their own Catholic parishes and other formal institutions, and possessed an elite, many of whom became community leaders. Mexicans, largely from the working classes, created the mutual-aid and fraternal organizations that gave voice to their myriad needs.

Anglos did not distinguish between the newcomers from Mexico and Mexican Americans. Both were perceived as foreigners, even though the latter's ancestors had been in the United States for generations or had become Americans with the Treaty of Guadalupe Hidalgo. Mexican immigration reinforced and intensified both the external Anglo hostility and the internal pressures within the Mexican communities. As evidenced by the rising tide of class and political polarization, Mexicans were divided between American-born citizens and immigrants. The persistent curse of racism dominated the lives of Mexicans and Mexican Americans alike, however. Some employers refused to hire Mexicans or utilized mandatory language tests to weed out non-English-speaking immigrants. State and municipal laws segregated the races. Whether as migratory farmworkers who moved their camps with the changing agricultural seasons or as factory workers who turned their efforts to a mechanized and subdivided process, Mexicans became the dregs of twentieth-century America.

The Great Depression forced Mexicans further into austerity and marginalization as their traditional institutions proved unable to give assistance and collapsed. As the economic crisis unfolded, controls were implemented on Mexican immigration. Nativist sentiment against them intensified, and additional numbers departed for their homelands.

Through the practice of mutual alliance that helped them develop their communities, Mexicans now turned to developing unions and methods of resisting employers. Leaders helped generate new forms of worker protest and association as Mexicans now turned to building an inclusive democratic union movement in the United States.

## NOTES

1. David Montgomery, *The Fall of the House of Labor: The Workplace, the State, and American Labor Activism, 1865–1925* (Cambridge: Cambridge University Press, 1987), 332.
2. Deutsch, *No Separate Refuge*, 15, 108.
3. Montgomery, *Fall of the House of Labor*, 332; Leo Grebler, Joan W. Moore, and Ralph C. Guzman, *The Mexican American People: The Nation's Second Largest Minority* (New York: Free Press, 1970), 64.
4. Montgomery, *Fall of the House of Labor*, 332.
5. Ibid., 36–37.
6. Juan Gómez-Quiñones, *Sembradores: Ricardo Flores Magón El Partido Liberal Mexicano: A Eulogy and Critique* (Los Angeles: University of California at Los Angeles, Chicano Studies Center and Aztlán Publications, 1973), 8; Philip J. Mellinger, *Race and Labor in Western Copper: The Fight for Equality, 1896–1918* (Tucson: University of Arizona Press, 1995), 62–65; Neil Foley, *The White Scourge: Mexicans, Blacks, and Poor Whites in Texas Cotton Culture* (Berkeley: University of California Press, 1997), 108.
7. An important document bearing on the subject of farm labor was Carleton H. Parker's *The Casual Laborer and Other Essays* (New York: Harcourt, Brace and Howe, 1920).
8. Grebler, Moore, and Guzman, *Mexican American People*, 10.
9. Montgomery, *Fall of the House of Labor*, 333, 335–337; Liping Zhu, "Claiming the Bloodiest Shaft: The 1913 Tragedy of the Stag Cañon Mine, Dawson, New Mexico," *Journal of the West* 35, no. 4 (1996): 58–64.
10. Montgomery, *Fall of the House of Labor*, 333, 344.
11. Ibid., 346.
12. Ibid., 346–351.
13. The United States Supreme Court declared the law unconstitutional in December 1915.
14. Truett, *Fugitive Landscapes*, 174–175; George Soule, "The Law of Necessity in Bisbee," *Nation* 113 (1921): 21–23; Colleen O'Neill, "Domesticity Deployed: Gender, Race, and the Construction of Class Struggle in the Bisbee Deportation," *Labor History* 34 (Spring 1993): 256–273. Columbus officials refused to take charge of the prisoners, and the Mexican strikers were taken out to the desert, where they were released and left to make their own way back home. McWilliams, *North from Mexico*, 197.
15. Gregory Andrews, *Shoulder to Shoulder?: The American Federation of Labor, the United States, and the Mexican Revolution, 1910–1924* (Berkeley: University of California Press,

1991), 15–16, 75–78; Ricardo Flores Magón, "Manifesto to Fellow Workers from the Organizing Junta of the Mexican Liberal Party," May 10, 1911, in *Investigation of Mexican Affairs*, 66th Cong., 2nd sess., 1920, S. Doc. 285, 2501; Mellinger, *Race and Labor in Western Copper*, 1.

16. Grebler, Moore, and Guzman, *Mexican American People*, 6.

17. *La Crónica*'s commitment to social justice was reflected in its masthead: "We work for the progress and the industrial, moral, and intellectual development of the Mexican inhabitants of Texas." Nicasio Idar also published *La Revista*. He helped found the Caballeros de Honor and the Sociedad Hijos de Juárez and was active in all of the Tejano fraternal organizations in Laredo. Nicasio Idar also served as a justice of the peace and as Laredo's assistant city marshal. Campbell, *Gone to Texas*, 328.

18. In Mexico, one newspaper demanded: "Where is the boasted Yankee Civilization?" *Philadelphia Public Ledger*, November 13, 1910.

19. Montejano, *Anglos and Mexicans in the Making of Texas*, 113, 116; Emilio Zamora, *The World of the Mexican Worker in Texas* (College Station: Texas A&M University Press, 1993), 61, 80–81, 97–98; Campbell, *Gone to Texas*, 328.

20. *La Crónica*, October, 19, November 2, December 7, 1911; Montejano, *Anglos and Mexicans in the Making of Texas*, 116; Zamora, *World of the Mexican Worker*, 99, 104–106.

21. Clara Lomas, "Transborder Discourse: The Articulation of Gender in the Borderlands in the Early Twentieth Century," *Frontiers: A Journal of Women Studies* 24, nos. 2 & 3 (2003), 57.

22. Zamora, *World of the Mexican Worker*, 77; Campbell, *Gone to Texas*, 347, 355–356.

23. Montejano, *Anglos and Mexicans in the Making of Texas*, 117; Zamora, *World of the Mexican Worker*, 81.

24. Montejano, *Anglos and Mexicans in the Making of Texas*, 117; Campbell, *Gone to Texas*, 328.

25. Campbell, *Gone to Texas*, 328.

26. Montejano, *Anglos and Mexicans in the Making of Texas*, 117–127; Campbell, *Gone to Texas*, 328.

27. Montejano, *Anglos and Mexicans in the Making of Texas*, 118. It was no coincidence that one day after Carranza cracked down on Mexican insurgents involved in the Plan of San Diego, President Woodrow Wilson extended official recognition to Carranza's government. James Sandos, *Rebellion in the Borderlands: Anarchism and the Plan of San Diego, 1904–1923* (Norman: University of Oklahoma Press), 208–209.

28. Montejano, *Anglos and Mexicans in the Making of Texas*, 125.

29. The Rangers spared the lives of several old Mexican men, women, and children and a lone Anglo.

30. A native of Nueces County and a graduate of the University of Michigan Law School, the Tejano Brownsville attorney and state legislator (1905–1910 and 1917–1920) was later influential in founding the League of United Latin American Citizens (LULAC). Canales helped write LULAC's first constitution and served as its president (1932–33).

31. *Proceedings of the Joint Committee of the Senate and House in the Investigation of the Texas State Ranger Force*, 36th Legislature, Regular Session, Legislative Papers, Texas State Archives, Austin, Texas; Henry Warren Papers, Archives of the Big Bend, Sul Ross State University. The father-in-law of one of the men killed by the Rangers owned a newspaper in Pilares, Chihuahua, Mexico. He asked the Mexican government for assistance, and Mexican ambassador Ygnacio Bonilla called for an official investigation.

32. Grebler, Moore, and Guzman, *Mexican American People,* 16; Mario T. Garcia, *Desert Immigrants: The Mexicans of El Paso, 1880–1920* (New Haven, CT: Yale University Press, 1981), 11–18, 51–58.

33. Zamora, *World of the Mexican Worker,* 26–29, 50; Mario T. García, *Mexican Americans: Leadership, Ideology, and Identity, 1930–1960* (New Haven, CT: Yale University Press, 1989), 63; Yolanda Chávez-Leyva, "'Faithful Hard-Working Mexican Hands,': Mexicana Workers During the Great Depression," in *Perspectives in Mexican American Studies 5—Mexican American Women: Changing Images,* ed. Juan R. García (Tucson: University of Arizona Press, 1995), 63, 65–70; Campbell, *Gone to Texas,* 364.

34. Zamora, *World of the Mexican Worker,* 50; Campbell, *Gone to Texas,* 364; Chávez-Leyva, "'Faithful Hard-Working Mexican Hands,'" 52–53.

35. Those employed as farmworkers helped American growers produce more than 5 billion dollars' worth of fruits and vegetables. Reisler, *By the Sweat of Their Brow,* 12.

36. George J. Sánchez, *Becoming Mexican American: Ethnicity, Culture and Identity in Chicano Los Angeles, 1900–1945* (New York: Oxford University Press, 1993), 234; Sheridan, *Los Tucsonenses,* 171–172.

37. Deutsch, *No Separate Refuge,* 111.

38. Ibid., 112, 114.

39. It was published as *Los méxico-americanos en la Gran Guerra y su contingente en pro de la democracia, la humanidad, y la justicia* (San Antonio, TX: Artes Graficas, 1933). See also Emilio Zamora, "Fighting on Two Fronts: José de la Luz Saenz and the Language of the Mexican American Civil Rights Movement," in *Recovering the U.S. Hispanic Literary Past,* Vol. 4, ed. José F Aranda Jr. and Silvio Torres-Saillant (Houston, TX: Arte Público Press, 2002).

40. Deutsch, *No Separate Refuge,* 124; Glenn C. Altschuler, *Race, Ethnicity, and Class in American Social Thought* (Arlington Heights, IL: Harlan Davidson, 1982), 70; Zaragosa Vargas, *Proletarians of the North: A History of Mexican Industrial Workers in Detroit and the Midwest, 1917–1933* (Berkeley: University of California Press, 1993), 79.

41. Vargas, *Proletarians of the North,* 83.

42. Deutsch, *No Separate Refuge,* 121–122; Grebler, Guzman, and Moore, *Mexican American People,* 85.

43. Grebler, Guzman, and Moore, *Mexican American People,* 66. The immigration was stimulated partly by the Cristero Revolution (1926–1929) in Mexico.

44. See California Mexican Fact-Finding Committee, *Mexicans in California: Report of Governor C. C. Young's Mexican Fact-Finding Committee* (San Francisco, CA: State Building, 1930; San Francisco: R. and E. Research Associates, 1970).

45. Vargas, *Proletarians of the North,* 35; Victor S. Clark, "Mexican Labor in the United States," *Bulletin of the Bureau of Labor* 78 (September 1908), 468–474; Lawrence A. Cordoso, *Mexican Immigration to the United States, 1897–1931* (Tucson: University of Arizona Press, 1980), 13–14. Railroad employment was synchronized with this industry's seasonal requirements in that hiring coincided with the beginning of track, bed maintenance, and construction in the spring.

46. Vargas, *Proletarians of the North,* 37–38.

47. Douglas Monroy, *Rebirth: Mexican Los Angeles from the Great Migration to the Great Depression* (Berkeley: University of California Press, 1999), 99–100.

48. Vargas, *Proletarians of the North,* 40.

49. Ruth D. Tuck, *Not with the Fist: Mexican-Americans in a Southwest City* (Harcourt, Brace and Company, 1946), 209–210.

50. Estrada, *Los Angeles Plaza*, 110; California Mexican Fact-Finding Committee, *Mexicans in California*, 175–176. Employment stability among Mexican workers determined their housing, which ranged from a shack in the infamous Hick's Camp in El Monte located east of Los Angeles to a four- or five-room bungalow in the city. In the 1930s, 18.6 percent of Mexican families in Los Angeles owned homes, as opposed to 4.8 percent and 8.6 percent of Japanese and Chinese families, respectively. Douglas Monroy, "An Essay on Understanding the Work Experience of Mexicans in Southern California, 1900–1939," *Aztlán* 12, no. 1 (Spring, 1981): 64–65; U.S. Bureau of the Census, *Fifteenth Census of the United States, 1930: Population, Special Report on Foreign Born White Families by Country of Birth of Head* (Washington, DC: Government Printing Office, 1933), 212.

51. Estrada, *Los Angeles Plaza*, 118, 129–131; Sánchez, *Becoming Mexican American*, 195.

52. Sánchez, *Becoming Mexican American*, 232; Monroy, *Rebirth*, 120–121; Monroy, "Understanding the Work Experience of Mexicans," 62–64; California Department of Industrial Relations, *Second Biennial Report, 1930–1932* (Sacramento, CA: California State Printing Office, 1932), 117.

53. García, *A World of Its Own*, 71.

54. Ibid., 164; Harry Schwartz, *Seasonal Farm Labor in the United States* (New York: Columbia University Press, 1945), 9, 53–59; Reisler, *By the Sweat of Their Brow*, 78–79; Almaguer, *Racial Fault Lines*, 30.

55. Deutsch, *No Separate Refuge*, 115–116, 119–120. The sugar beet industry lauded its boom years as the "Mexican Harvest." Vargas, *Proletarians of the North*, 30; Grebler, Moore, and Guzman, *Mexican American People*, 94.

56. Vargas, *Proletarians of the North*, 156–157; Deutsch, *No Separate Refuge*, 129, 133–134, 137–139; Schwartz, *Seasonal Farm Labor in the United States*, 115.

57. Vargas, *Proletarians of the North*, 50.

58. Robert Oppenheimer, "Acculturation or Assimilation: Mexican Immigrants in Kansas, 1900 to World War II," *Western Historical Quarterly* 16, no. 4 (October 1985): 431–432, 440, 445.

59. Arthur F. Corwin, ed., *Immigrants—and Immigrants: Perspectives on Mexican Labor Migration to the United States* (Westport, CT: Greenwood Press, 1978), 110, 116; Oppenheimer, "Acculturation or Assimilation," 431.

60. Vargas, *Proletarians of the North*, 1, 21, 29. Mexicans constituted a third of Michigan's sugar beet workers in 1922, and five years later about twenty thousand worked for sugar companies.

61. Mexicans constituted 5.8 percent of Chicago's meatpacking labor force. The Pennsylvania Railroad had three thousand Mexicans on its payroll as maintenance-of-way men in Pennsylvania and New York. Vargas, *Proletarians of the North*, 37–38.

62. Mexicans made up a third of the mill hands of Wisconsin Steel and Illinois Steel, representing 12.2 and 21.8 percent, respectively, of all the hourly employees. Ibid, 91.

63. Ibid., 92–94.

64. Mexican women in the Midwest earned money by cooking and taking in laundry, as boardinghouse operators, and as domestics. Those who held factory jobs worked as inspectors, packers, markers, sorters, box washers, candy dippers, or machine operators. Others worked as elevator operators, store cashiers, secretaries, office managers, and nurses. Ibid., 133–138.

65. Vicki L. Ruiz, *From Out of the Shadows: Mexican Women in Twentieth-Century America* (New York: Oxford University Press, 1998), 56–57.

66. Vargas, *Proletarians of the North*, 49, 64, 128; Paul S. Taylor, *Mexican Labor in the United States: Chicago and the Calumet Region.* University of California Publications in Economics, Vol. 7, no. 2. (Berkeley: University of California Press, 1932), 185.

67. Vargas, *Proletarians of the North,* 47.

68. Ibid., 50–51, 124, 126. In addition, nearly two thousand Mexicans worked for General Motors, Dodge Motors, Fisher Body, and Buick Motors and at Chevrolet's plants in Detroit, Pontiac, Flint, and Saginaw.

69. Over half (53.6 percent) of the Mexicans in the Midwest worked in manufacturing. Ibid., 86.

70. Ibid., 143–144; Manuel Gamio, *Mexican Immigration to the United States* (Chicago: University of Chicago Press, 1930), 117–118.

71. Monroy, *Rebirth,* 127–129; Vargas, *Proletarians of the North,* 147; R. Douglas Brackenridge and Francisco O. García-Treto, *Iglesia Presbiteriana: A History of Presbyterians and Mexicans in the Southwest* (San Antonio, TX: Trinity University Press, 1987), 128.

72. Monroy, *Rebirth,* 129; Ruiz, *From Out of the Shadows,* 33. The concept of Americanization dates back to the early twentieth century. The Americanization movement passed through three phases. The first phase began around the turn of the century and ran through 1914, the second during World War I, and the third covered the immediate post-World War I years.

73. Monroy, *Rebirth,* 132–133; James R. Grossman, *Land of Hope: Chicago Black Southerners and the Great Migration* (Chicago: University of Chicago Press, 1991), 257–258.

74. Monroy, *Rebirth,* 140–146; Vargas, *Proletarians of the North,* 85.

75. Sánchez, *Becoming Mexican American,* 71.

76. Monroy, *Rebirth,* 61–62. Coalitions of Mexican organizations were established, such as La Liga Protectora Latina (Latin Protective League) in Arizona and El Confederación de Sociedad Mexicanas (Confederation of Mexican Societies) of Los Angeles. Sánchez, *Becoming Mexican American,* 242; Corwin, *Immigrants—and Immigrants,* 235.

77. Monroy, *Rebirth,* 227–229. The Mexican consulate in Los Angeles had helped form CUOM to halt the influence of radical organizers among Mexican workers.

78. The two Mexican mutual-aid societies were La Sociedad Mutualista Benito Juárez El Centro and La Sociedad Mutualista Hidalgo El Brawley. Although the cantaloupe strike was broken, unionization efforts increased in the Imperial Valley. More important, the strike resulted in the formulation of the harvest contract by the California Department of Industrial Relations. The harvest contract recommended the elimination of abusive grower practices, made the growers rather than the labor contractors responsible for wages, and eliminated the withholding of a fourth of the workers' wages until the harvest season ended. A bonus served as an incentive to workers to complete the harvest. Charles Wollenberg, "Huelga, 1928 Style: The Imperial Valley Cantaloupe Workers' Strike," *Pacific Historical Review* 38, no. 1 (1969): 45.

79. Sheridan, *Los Tucsonenses,* 111–113, 167–171; James D. McBride, "The Liga Protectora Latina: A Mexican American Benevolent Society in Arizona," *Journal of the West* 14 (October 1975): 82–90.

80. Zamora, *World of the Mexican Worker,* 76; Campbell, *Gone to Texas,* 349.

81. Zamora, *World of the Mexican Worker,* 76; Campbell, *Gone to Texas,* 349.

82. José Amaro Hernández, *Mutual Aid for Survival: The Case of the Mexican American* (Malabar, FL: Robert E. Krieger, 1983), 75–83.

83. Craig A. Kaplowitz, *LULAC: Mexican Americans and National Policy* (College Station, TX: Texas A&M University Press, 2005), 20–21; Grossman, *Land of Hope,* 129.

84. Douglas O. Weeks, "The League of United Latin-American Citizens: A Texas-Mexican Civic Organization," *Southwestern Political and Social Science Quarterly* (December

1929): 260. See also Benjamin Marquez, *LULAC: The Evolution of a Mexican American Political Organization* (Austin, TX: University of Texas Press, 1993).

85. Kaplowitz, *LULAC*, 20–21; David G. Gutiérrez, *Walls and Mirrors: Mexican Americans, Mexican Immigrants, and the Politics of Ethnicity* (Berkeley: University of California Press, 1995), 75–77. During World War I, Perales served in the U.S. Army. Following his discharge, Perales moved to Washington, DC, where he worked for the U.S. Commerce Department. He earned a B.A. and received his law degree in 1926. Perales wrote the LULAC constitution with fellow Tejanos José Tomás Canales and Eduardo Idar. Perales rose rapidly within LULAC and won election as its second president. During his term Perales helped establish twenty-four new LULAC councils.

86. Kaplowitz, *LULAC*, 20–21; Gutiérrez, *Walls and Mirrors*, 74.

87. Gutiérrez, *Walls and Mirrors*, 79; Oscar J. Martínez, "On the Size of the Chicano Population: New Estimates 1850–1900," *Aztlán* 6, no. 1 (Spring, 1975): 56; Gutiérrez, *Walls and Mirrors*, 6.

88. Zamora, *World of the Mexican Worker*, 88–90, 207, 209; Monroy, *Rebirth*, 259. LULAC established the Four Hundred Clubs to teach English to Mexican American youths by having them master a four-hundred-word English vocabulary before entering school. Weeks, "The League of United Latin-American Citizens," 265.

89. Foley, *White Scourge*, 209; Neil Foley, "Becoming Hispanic: Mexican Americans and the Faustian Pact with Whiteness," in *New Directions in Mexican American Studies*, ed. Neil Foley (Austin, TX: Center for Mexican American Studies, 1999), 55–56.

90. Kaplowitz, *LULAC*, 33; Foley, *White Scourge*, 210.

91. Grebler, Moore, and Guzman, *Mexican American People*, 36.

# CHAPTER 7

⁂

# The Mexican American Struggle for Labor Rights in the Era of the Great Depression

Mexican Americans did not widely share in the economic prosperity of the 1920s, so the Great Depression that swept over the country for them was only a deepening of poverty and hardship. They remained apart from the larger American society, and as the Great Depression dragged on, it only intensified their lasting negative image in the public's mind.[1]

The worsening economic crisis seriously weakened and upset the traditional streams of migration from Mexico as the employment situation in the United States changed from one of constant labor shortages to one of acute surpluses. Mexicans faced greater hardships and different kinds of problems than Anglos, namely, racial discrimination and nativism. As a result Mexicans became victims of the practice "last hired, first fired."

A slashing of relief services followed on the heels of the near collapse of the economy. Because of local discrimination, Mexicans had to prove their legal status, as relief officials made no distinction between Mexican Americans and Mexican nationals. At the national level a repatriation campaign forced several hundred thousand Mexicans to leave the United States. The Mexican population suffered the humiliation of removal to Mexico because American society, in search of a scapegoat, blamed all segments of the Spanish-speaking population for the hard times. Individuals and families, the latter including pregnant women, young children, and the elderly, were picked up by government agents or local police and kept at assembly centers until transportation was arranged and paperwork had been completed for their removal. The repatriates were warned that if they returned to the United States they would be charged with a criminal offense. Those who remained were now forced to live in the shadows of society.

Because of family hardships, children assumed the responsibilities of supporting families by working even more. Children too young to work took care of younger siblings so their mothers could get jobs to sustain the household as Mexican women bore heavier economic responsibilities during the Depression. A number of industries had opened new jobs to women, yet most still found themselves in the worst jobs at the lowest wage and skill levels.[2] These women would be exhorted to political action by organizers recruiting for unions such as the International Ladies' Garment Workers Union.

The New Deal was a paradox for Mexican Americans. Those who were farmworkers were forgotten by the federal government. They could not appeal for protection from the Agriculture Adjustment Administration (AAA) because its purpose was to protect farmers and consumers. The National Recovery Act (NRA) was concerned with industrial workers and industry and not farm labor or domestic service. New Deal jobs were distributed on the basis of patronage rather than need, and because Mexicans had no political power they consequently gained less than whites from the New Deal. Nonetheless, Mexicans responded to President Franklin Delano Roosevelt and the New Deal enthusiastically. New Deal legislation expanded job training programs for Mexican Americans, improved housing conditions, and, in addition, provided many of them with public relief allowances to get them the food and the jobs they required to keep them from starving.

Through propaganda and publicity, government interest in the worker took hold with the passage of the National Industrial Recovery Act (NIRA). Mexican Americans were inspired that the New Deal labor law promised to protect workers' right to organize without interference or coercion, and they were emboldened when unions began organizing campaigns in 1933.

Traditional organizations such as LULAC experienced a decrease in membership and saw some of its chapters collapse. They were ineffective in achieving social change for Mexican Americans that would alleviate hunger and the need for adequate housing and health care and bring economic well-being. The Americanized LULAC, moreover, heartily advocated immigration restriction from Mexico, and Mexican workers did not have support from LULAC. Mexican workers realized that the only way they could protect their interests was by solidly standing together. In the first two decades of the twentieth century, Mexican workers had organized to demand their rights, and this same spirit fed into organizing movements in the 1930s. Unions were vehicles for social change, and Mexicans participated in the upsurge in unionization generated by the Great Depression. They heeded the call of labor organizers such as Refugio Martínez, Luz Salazar, Emma Tenayuca, and Armando Davila, who urged them to change existing conditions by organizing themselves to bring about this change.

In a climate of heightened collective activism, Mexicans in urban centers and from the deepest reaches of the agricultural and mining regions challenged the firmly entrenched race-based class system. Despite their heavy family involvement, Mexican women displayed a high degree of labor activism. The New Deal legislation discriminated against women, and few of the unions organized in the relatively unskilled occupations in which most Spanish-speaking females worked. There were exceptions. From the 1930s onward Mexican women organized themselves and actively participated in strikes in tobacco, garment, and food and cannery industries, demonstrating the power of class unity.

In the early 1930s mines shut down completely or cut hours and pay. Upheaval broke out in the coalfields, and the strike that erupted in 1933 in the mines around Gallup, New Mexico, continued for four long months. The desperate coal miners turned to outside unionizers from the National Miners Union (NMU), an avowed communist union. The miners committed themselves to the NMU, despite the pressure of the state of New Mexico and the mining company's hired thugs. However, the strategies and tactics of the NMU contributed to their defeat.

The aggressive organizing campaign by the Congress of Industrial Organizations (CIO), particularly its program of equality regardless of race that began in 1935, quickly gained the support of Mexican workers. Crucial in the unionization of the Southwest, the CIO opened up its ranks to Mexicans and in doing so broke down the barriers between them and the trade unions. Helping in the creation of a mass movement and pulling such campaigns together were talented Spanish-speaking organizers eager to forge an inclusive labor movement capable of remaking society. Their commitment, skill, and vision of social justice aroused their fellow Mexicans to organize into unions. Spanish-speaking women once more broke new ground in the struggles for job rights and wage justice. In unions such as the United Cannery, Agricultural, Packing and Allied Workers of America (UCAPAWA), its mostly female rank-and-file membership combined action on both economic and political issues with campaigns on community concerns. The latter included work on behalf of the Democratic Party for a Roosevelt victory.

The labor marches, demonstrations, boycotts, and strikes that took place in the 1930s represented the most extensive popular mobilization in the history of the Mexican American people and signaled a new consciousness among them. Unionization was the most important change Mexican American workers experienced during the Great Depression.

## THE PLIGHT OF MEXICANS IN THE EARLY YEARS OF THE GREAT DEPRESSION

Mexicans lived nearer the margins of economic security than Anglos, and consequently the Great Depression affected them more severely. Unemployment rates were considerably higher for them than for Anglos, who, desperate and unemployed, even sought "Mexican jobs." Mexicans with jobs faced the threat of wage cuts and discharge, and the jobless went hungry and soon became homeless.

The Great Depression increased the number of Mexican migrant workers. Perpetually cast adrift, entire families transported in open trucks crossed state lines to live in squalid camps consisting of shacks, tents, abandoned barns, and chicken coops, where hunger and disease ran rampant. Town officials made little effort to cope with migrant families. This restless labor force was always in debt to labor contractors. The facts that they were denied medical care, that child labor laws were ignored, and that they faced discrimination from the local population and unequal treatment from local law enforcement made conditions more intolerable. The half-starved migrant families were without access to relief because they seldom lived in one place long enough to meet residency requirements. As workers, they had no rights and no protection, as there were no federal government provisions for agricultural workers and minimal support from labor organizations.

Mexican migrant workers were vulnerable to shifting conditions in agriculture. In Texas, work in cotton declined significantly, causing a high state of joblessness among Tejanos in the border region. Texas cotton growers faced a mounting surplus and falling prices. As a result the state legislature, through the 1931 Cotton Acreage Control Law, cut cotton acreage by half. Though invalidated, this legislation pushed the jobless Mexican cotton pickers into the cities to search for work for any wage or to return to Mexico.[3]

In Colorado, a freeze destroyed most of the beet crop in 1929, leaving great numbers of Mexican farmworkers jobless and stranded. A five-year drought (1930–1935) that turned whole areas into a dust bowl left thousands more of Colorado's Mexicans without jobs or money. Displaced and without the benefit of housing, droves of Mexican beet workers flocked to Denver and other towns, adding to the unemployment and overcrowding and further straining relief rolls.[4] Congested, unsanitary shelter and malnutrition, in combination with cutbacks in public health funding, increased deaths and sickness among Mexicans from typhoid, pellagra, and other diseases. Taking advantage of the hostility toward Mexican aliens in the state, Colorado Governor Edwin C. Johnson in 1936 proclaimed martial law and ordered out the National Guard to Colorado's southern border to keep out Mexican farm laborers.

In southern California, joblessness among Mexican farmworkers soared as growers cut back on crop production. Except in Los Angeles, a large number of Mexican cannery workers were the first to be let go by companies. Mexican families who had never sought assistance before were forced to seek relief by the growing hard times and, failing this, left California. The Mexicans who remained could not find work or else competed for jobs with those pouring into the state in a futile search for work. California's excess supply of labor led to a significant fall in wages. Increasing demands for relief and assistance of all sorts outstripped the supply, prodding more than fifteen thousand Mexicans to leave the state.[5]

Having always known hardship, Mexicans still could not cope with the worst depression in American history. Yet they would not ask for relief until all their resources were exhausted. When they did receive assistance, it was inadequate, less than their needs warranted. Many Anglos began to ask why so many Mexicans, lauded by employers for their hard-work ethic, were on relief and falsely concluded that it was because they were lazy and irresponsible. Distinctions more and more were made between the deserving American and the undeserving Mexican, irrespective of the latter's U.S. citizenship or legal-resident status. That Anglos absolutely refused to provide for the Mexican and his family at public expense justified cutting off all public relief to them. Mounting anti-Mexican hostility culminated in calls for the removal of the Mexican from the United States.

Public officials and organized labor, feeling the effects of a labor surplus and long relief lines, lent their support to ban Mexicans from city- or state-sponsored employment programs. In 1930, the city of El Paso adopted an ordinance prohibiting the employment of Mexicans on city construction projects. The state of Texas enacted legislation restricting employment on public work projects to U.S. citizens.[6]

The Great Depression added to the misery and woes of New Mexico's Spanish-speaking rural poor. Mexican Americans made up half of the state's population but 80 percent of its relief load. Because of the influx of out-of-state transients, state agencies barred relief to Spanish-speaking seasonal migratory workers even though they were state residents. New Mexico's Anglo population vociferously charged that native New Mexican families were becoming permanently dependent on the dole because they were too lazy to work.

In Los Angeles, Mexican relief cases outnumbered those of Anglos, even though the latter were the city's predominant population. In 1931–1932, reductions in the Los Angeles County relief budget eliminated half the Mexican families on assistance. Similar reductions forced Catholic charities to cut their food allotments by one-fourth. Mexicans became the scapegoats for the economic problems. As a result, the exclusion of Mexicans from "white jobs" crystallized. Mexicans in California, like those in other states, were barred from public work projects, as this work now went to white American citizens who, reflecting prevailing racial attitudes, insisted they should have preference in employment. In 1931, the California Alien Labor Act eliminated the remaining Mexicans on state construction work gangs. Animosity against Mexicans in Los Angeles increased. Always against the inflow of labor from Mexico, organized labor openly endorsed the campaign to pressure Mexicans to repatriate to Mexico. Echoing the notion that jobs "belonged" to whites, the Los Angeles Labor Federation announced "Employ no Mexican while a white man is unemployed. . . . Get the Mexican back into Mexico regardless by what means."[7] Mexicans were blamed as the cause of the economic depression and high unemployment, and this garnered them greater attention by the federal government. The government initiated a massive repatriation campaign throughout the United States.

## THE REPATRIATION CAMPAIGN UNFOLDS

The Great Depression ended two decades of almost uninterrupted immigration from Mexico. Yet even before the economic collapse leaders of organized labor and other groups advocated restricting Mexican immigration and enforcement of the law by the U.S. Bureau of Immigration. Despite the clamor for restrictions, local chambers of commerce, supported by growers, blocked efforts to impose an immigration quota. Testifying before congressional committees, witness after witness observed that Mexicans performed the menial field labor indispensable to the region. Destroyed financially, county and local officials, on the other hand, maintained that they simply could not keep Mexicans on relief. A practical solution was reached at the behest of growers. A work program was designed to deny Mexican families public relief in the spring and fall and put them to work in the fields, thereby affecting a net savings in relief. Anyone who refused this conscription was cut off from the dole and was liable to be deported.[8]

Congress introduced legislation to curtail immigration from Mexico, passing the Immigration Act of 1929 making unlawful entry into the United States a felony. The immigration legislation authorized the United States to carry out a "federal deportation campaign" to remove foreign aliens. The repatriation movement gained national dimensions when President Herbert Hoover mobilized public opinion against the Mexican population. The president did this to deflect attention from his inability to deal with the deepening economic crisis and sharply mounting unemployment. Hoover made Mexicans the prime targets for government persecution, regardless of whether or not they were citizens of the United States.[9]

The American Federation of Labor placed itself at the forefront of the anti-Mexican campaign. Harboring anger that these foreign workers were taking jobs away from "real Americans," it pressured the Bureau of Immigration to impose a $1,000 bond regulation on immigrants seeking work in the United States. The Bureau also began to search for and stop Mexicans, who then had to prove their legal status. At the local level, there were county- and city-initiated sweeps of Spanish-speaking neighborhoods with high numbers of suspected deportable aliens.[10]

Relief agencies processed tens of thousands of indigent Mexicans for repatriation. They did this with monies from the Mexican government, which offered to pay for the transportation of its countrymen once they were inside Mexico. As a result, many Mexican families were unfairly deported. Some Mexicans very likely were exposed to dubious consultants providing costly legal advice, who exploited the fears of these individuals facing deportation. As an added insult, many American-born Mexican adults and children lacking proper identification but having dark skin and Spanish surnames were apprehended and removed to Mexico. Mexican families hid in their homes in alarm, even if they were American citizens, out of fear of being apprehended. Children saw one or both parents forcibly taken away in the neighborhood roundups and came face to face with disgrace and economic hardship.

There was no halt to the repatriations, as all over the United States the crackdown on Mexican aliens continued. In Arizona, the state legislature joined organized labor in scapegoating "alien" Mexicans for the hard times. From cities and small towns, thousands of Mexicans left voluntarily or were deported, often as the result of intimidation. In Tucson in 1930, the Southern Pacific Railroad discharged its Mexican blacksmith and car repair shop workers. In the Arizona copper mining district, Mexican miners, as the least skilled, were the first to be let go, and they and their families slid into poverty. Hundreds returned to Mexico. The depressed cotton market pushed Arizona growers to slash their workforce. Thousands of Mexicans were apprehended by federal agents, and these deportable aliens were returned to Mexico.[11]

In Los Angeles, one of every five Mexicans was out of work. To escape the extreme destitution, thousands sought voluntary repatriation to Mexico, but as they left, other Mexicans, fleeing the hard times in southern California, desperately made their way to the city in search of food and shelter. In order to scare Mexicans into leaving Los Angeles, in early January 1931 a press release warned that authorities were going to undertake a deportation campaign. Given the stressful time of heightened anxiety and vulnerability in the Mexican colonies, the scare tactic hastened the departure of more Mexicans from the city. In the fall of that year, Los Angeles celebrated its 150th anniversary with a romanticized pageant of old Spanish history, complete with Anglo officials on horseback dressed as Spanish dons. Local and federal officials made sweeps of the plaza aimed at Mexicans. Among the detained was the artist David Alfaro Siqueiros. Denied an extension on his visa, Siqueiros was forced to leave the United States in August 1932. The

Mexican artist had just painted a series of murals in the city, one of which was *La América Tropical* (*Tropical America*), a pictorial critique of racism and colonial domination in southern California. Deemed offensive, the mural was whitewashed in 1934. Growers, however, made sure enough Mexicans remained in southern California to harvest their commercial fruit and vegetable crops that were worth millions. The powerful growers, in their own interests, called on public and private officials to restore calm in the Mexican community. The impact of economic strife and terrorizing immigration raids had driven one-third of the Mexican population of Los Angeles back into Mexico.[12]

Mexicans residing in the cities of the North were concentrated in industries that significantly reduced output, resulting in massive layoffs. Labor unions began a campaign to remove Mexicans, arguing that they threatened American workers' jobs. The Detroit Federation of Labor warned of the dangers Mexicans posed to the city's workers. It declared that "most of the illegal entrants were undesirable . . . " and contended that "the result . . . is a rapid and alarming increase in numbers of unassimilable groups, and a gradual submersion of the class of citizenry upon which the nation must rely for maintenance of standards and life."[13]

Employers who had recruited Mexicans to come north now claimed no responsibility for their plight and asserted that Mexicans had only themselves to blame for their distress. Out of self-interest, a few came to the Mexicans' defense. Henry Ford discharged Mexican autoworkers and rehired them once car production resumed at his plants; however, extreme work speedup at reduced hours and pay became their lot. Other employers simply replaced Mexicans with Anglo workers. Meanwhile, in a parallel action, Detroit city officials kept Mexican families off public assistance or made it more difficult for them than for Anglos to obtain relief. Arriving in Detroit in April 1932, at Edsel Ford's invitation, to paint giant murals at the Detroit Institute of Arts, the Mexican muralist Diego Rivera and his wife, Frida Kahlo, aided and gave comfort to their Mexican countrymen. The main theme of Rivera's "Industrial Detroit" murals was to be a celebration of the new age of man and machine. Instead, his paintings' strong anti-Catholic and anticapitalist message wound up offending many of Detroit's wealthiest citizens. In August of that year, Rivera helped local Mexicans found *La Liga de Obreros y Campesinos* (League of Workers and Peasants). With the money he earned painting the Art Institute's murals, Rivera and La Liga helped organize the repatriation of Mexicans to farm cooperatives in Mexico.[14]

There was no halt to the removal campaign. The Mexicans departing for Mexico were permitted to carry with them only a few personal possessions. They were taken by train or truck and loaded by family groups. Special arrangements were made for invalid Mexicans taken out of hospitals for removal to Mexico. Advance lists expedited the processing of people and property at the assembly centers. Municipal officials eventually came to realize that repatriation actually generated additional relief need and was not cost effective. El Paso gained over six hundred new relief cases as a result of repatriation efforts. City officials estimated it would have to spend $90,000 to remove another 1,200 Mexican aliens. However, they would leave behind nearly 1,500 dependents who were U.S. citizens or legal residents and thus eligible for public relief in the amount of $147,000. Also, 80 percent of the aliens sent back qualified for nonquota preference for reentry because their dependents were United States residents.[15] Repatriation was flawed in large part because it proved so expensive.

A total of 345,839 Mexicans were repatriated or deported back to Mexico from 1930 to 1935. They constituted almost two-thirds of the Mexicans who had entered the United States in the 1920s. Los Angeles lost one-third of its Mexican population. Three-fourths of all the excluded aliens departed from Texas, reducing Texas's Mexican-born population by a third. The huge cuts in cotton production, the meager amounts of relief Texas doled out to its indigent residents, and the intense, universal hatred of Mexicans hastened their removal to Mexico. As previously noted, Mexican Americans were not excluded from the dragnets; in California over 80 percent of the repatriates were citizens or legal residents of the United States.[16] For the remainder of the Great Depression the Spanish-speaking community lived in a climate of fear and unease; no one was ever completely sure that they were safe. Mexicans became convenient scapegoats, blamed for job loss, strained relief services, housing congestion, and other social ills.

The deportation operations broke up many families. Untold numbers of American-born children were separated from their parents because federal officials did not properly screen immigrants to determine whether they were caring for young children or other dependents who might be at risk.

There were thousands of separated children in Mexico. Several years passed before the National Catholic Welfare Conference undertook a tracing program to reunite these lost children with their immediate families in the United States. Almost two decades passed before some of these children, now adults, saw their families and their homes. With the start of World War II, cohorts of these former repatriated children returned to the United States as contract laborers through the auspices of the Bracero Program or because they volunteered to serve in the U.S. Armed forces.

Some state and local agencies became centers for aid and contact for repatriated Mexicans searching for vital records. Blank birth certificates were sent to border cities in Mexico with instructions for the repatriates to find individuals who were in attendance at the birth of a child to fill out the certificates and stating their relationship to the child. In El Paso, Mexican American Cleofas Calleros worked tirelessly to reduce the number of Mexican repatriation cases. Calleros was Mexican border representative of the Bureau of Immigration Office, National Catholic Welfare Conference. Assigned to direct El Paso's relief and social services, Calleros convinced U.S. immigration authorities to accept a wider variety of proof of employment and residency from Mexicans, and he reduced verification of evidence in processing cases more than three years old. In addition, Calleros helped Mexicans with their applications for visas, legal residency, and petitions to become U.S. citizens.[17]

The repatriations made the fight by Mexican Americans for their civil rights in the 1930s imperative. The nation's Mexican American community undertook what would become the largest protests and demonstrations ever by this minority group for labor and civil rights.

# MEXICANS IN THE ERA
# OF THE NATIONAL RECOVERY ACT

Most Mexican workers were employed in agriculture, with high labor force participation as farmworkers. The newly created Agriculture Adjustment Administration Act (AAA) was of no help to them because it principally aided growers and because there were no provisions for agricultural workers in the National Industrial Recovery Act. However, Section 7a of the NIRA affirmed that workers had the right to join labor organizations of their own choosing and engage in collective bargaining without interference or coercion. This national policy prompted Mexican farmworkers to challenge the long-standing exploitive authority of the growers through a massive wave of strikes in their own defense. Sixty-one agricultural strikes unfolded involving 56,800 farmworkers, with most of the labor battles taking place in California. Their nemeses, the growers, fiercely resented the Mexicans' continued insistence on labor rights and opposed unions because communists promoted them. These factors led to the escalation of the ensuing conflicts in farm laborer relations.

Farmworkers were difficult to organize partly because of the mobility of the workforce and the seasonal and short duration of farmwork. A strike's success depended on timing it to coincide with peak periods of labor demand and on keeping away strikebreakers. The latter were workers allowed in from Mexico by U.S. Immigration and U.S. Border Patrol agents at the behest of growers. Most of these strikes were put down by police officers and goon squads, often with a great deal of bloodshed.

**Campsite of Striking Mexican Workers, Corcoran, California, 1933.**
CREDIT: LC-USF344-007487-ZB. Courtesy of the Library of Congress.

Forty percent of the nation's Mexicans resided in Texas. Nearly half worked as low-wage seasonal farmworkers and did not qualify for relief because they did not meet residency requirements and because of rampant racism. In addition to working in the fields and taking care of their families, women supplemented family incomes by seeking seasonal or part-time work at less than a living wage in the garment, cigar, and pecan shelling industries, where working conditions were generally poor.[18]

The amount paid to Mexican cotton pickers and their wretched working conditions in Texas motivated them to go out on strike in 1931. The cotton farmers responded with a well-coordinated terror campaign. Armed peace officers were dispatched, and vigilantes also entered the fray, beating Mexicans on sight to end their strike for higher wages. Mass arrests and roundups by immigration officers finally forced the cotton pickers back into the fields. The growers stopped union organization in the cotton fields outside El Paso by importing strikebreakers who included children. Two years later, the pickers walked out again. The strike spread, but farmers refused to cave in, and the workers called off their strike. The sporadic strike actions gained the cotton pickers a pay increase. More important, the Mexicans showed their employers they would fight for higher wages and better working conditions.[19] Cotton pickers in others states also began to resist. In 1933, near Tulare, California, a caravan of striking cotton pickers took to the road to voice their complaints.

Dissatisfaction among Mexican farmworkers was widespread. In the spring of 1932 in Colorado, Mexican beet workers, in reaction to low wages, launched a

**Caravan of Striking Cotton Pickers South of Tulare, California, 1933.**
CREDIT: LC-USF344-007484-ZB. Courtesy of the Library of Congress; and "Cotton Pickers on Strike," BE066882
© Bettmann/CORBIS.

strike under the leadership of the United Front Committee of Agricultural Workers Unions (UFC), a communist-led organization formed in Denver. Refusing to bargain with the workers who took orders from communists, the growers ordered local officials to cancel meetings and arrest and jail union leaders.[20]

Unflinching, the UFC went on the offensive and called a general strike for May 16 following a wage cut. The growers responded. They ordered relief agencies to deny assistance to those refusing to scab, and law enforcement officers were put at their disposal to force Mexicans to return to work. Deportations of the UFC's strike leaders followed. Fearing violence, the workers avoided a confrontation with the farmers by abandoning their strike. The workers returned to the beet fields without seeing their demands met, but they nevertheless established the idea in the minds of the growers that they as workers and Mexicans would not hesitate to take further action against exploitive practices.[21]

Displaying an extraordinary amount of labor militancy, Mexican women participated in the strikes that swept through tobacco, garment, and cannery factories. Domestic workers also organized to address their needs.

## MEXICAN WOMEN WORKERS BATTLE FOR EQUALITY

Mexican American domestic workers suffered exploitation. Anglo families paid them extremely low wages, arbitrarily fired them and rehired them on a part-time basis, then overworked them for the same low pay or gave them handouts of old clothes in place of wages. The domestic workers were expected to be grateful for these handouts. Even though the NRA legislation did not cover domestic work, it spurred El Paso's domestic workers to organize for higher wages. Competition for scarce work came from females from Mexico, who went door to door in the Anglo sections of El Paso offering to work as laundresses, cooks, and housemaids or to care for children at any wage that Anglo women offered to pay. These women's non-U.S.-citizen status made them readily exploitable. Launching their *Asociación de Trabajadoras Domésticas* (Association of Domestic Workers, or ADW), the women continued to organize.[22] Working against them were El Paso County officials, who cut off relief to any woman who refused to work.

In 1934, one of the first strikes by a mainly Mexican female workforce for higher wages and better working conditions unfolded in San Antonio, when Mexican female cigar workers employed by the Finck Cigar Company walked out. During the strike, the courageous women held firm despite facing down city police, who interfered with the peaceful picketing. Finally, the police drew their clubs and rushed the women pickets, knocking them to the pavement, clubbing and manhandling them, and then arresting the strikers. In jail, the women were threatened with deportation. These actions only heightened solidarity. Community support for the strike was strong, but neither the Mexican consul nor the League of United Latin American Citizens issued a statement in support of the women cigar workers. The cigar company finally yielded to the strikers' demand of improved working conditions.[23] Mexican women garment workers also struck to improve sweatshop conditions and demand labor rights.

The percentage of women workers in the garment trades increased from 64 percent in 1925 to 74 percent in 1935. The garment shops were labor-intensive industries that employed female labor. Many garment factories relocated to the South and Southwest, where labor was cheaper because of restrictions imposed on occupations in which Mexican women could find work and where unions were nonexistent. San Antonio's children's clothing industry employed between fifteen and twenty thousand Mexican women as needleworkers forced to work for low wages under awful conditions. Many performed work at home for upward of fifteen hours per day for meager wages. Heightened exploitation in the clothes shops provoked the women to organize. The International Ladies' Garment Workers Union (ILGWU) was at the height of power. Having organized women garment workers elsewhere, the ILGWU took up the cause of the Southwest's Mexican women garment workers. In 1934, the ILGWU chartered Locals 180 and 123 in San Antonio, and organizing by garment workers began at the A. B. Frank plant. The plant fought back by shutting down production. The Halff Company likewise fought the ILGWU. ILGWU Local 123 picketed Dorothy Frocks for six months amidst police violence. The company signed a contract in November 1936, but by then ILGWU Local 123 had ceased functioning. Nonetheless, the strike by San Antonio's garment workers showed that they were part of the nationwide struggles of working women to gain rights.[24] San Antonio's Mexican American and Mexican women garment workers were not the only ones to organize in the 1930s. Los Angeles garment workers waged one of the more celebrated strikes involving Mexican women over low wages and poor working conditions. In the fall of 1933, a wave of labor upheaval erupted in the garment shops of Los Angeles when dressmakers from eighty garment shops walked out under the ILGWU banner. Three thousand dressmakers toiled in the downtown garment district, a workforce that doubled during the height of the garment-making season. Three-fourths were Mexican.[25]

In the 1920s, Jewish and Mexican women made up the majority of garment workers on the West Coast. With the coming of the Great Depression, employers turned more and more to the larger pool of Mexican women desperate to find work at any wages or starve. The ILGWU maintained a nondiscrimination policy, but the union's more conservative leadership, which took over following the purge of radicals in the late 1920s, held tight control over the union. This action discouraged more aggressive organizing of minority women.

City officials, asserting a fear of violence from unruly women strikers, ordered the Los Angeles Police Department to deploy its Red Squad unit into the garment district. Strike discipline held. Meanwhile, the male cloak makers signed an agreement that won them union recognition. This labor agreement did not address the grievances of the women dressmakers, and they pressed on with their cause to unite. Through meetings, demonstrations, and marches the women took the knowledge and skills they had learned and applied them to promote their cause. Two thousand dressmakers honored the strike but under brutal conditions. Utility service was shut off at the homes of cash-starved strikers unable to pay their bills, many of whom had to resort to public relief. The ILGWU stepped in with food contributions, and funds poured in from across the Mexican community, which saw the women's fight as their fight. Despite their hardships, the temporary injunctions, and the numerous arrests, the dressmakers held the line in the mass picketing. The increased strikebreaking and the threat of violence throughout the strike prompted city officials to assign one hundred additional police officers to the garment district.[26]

An agreement was finally reached between the ILGWU and the employers that gained union recognition, wage increases, and benefits for the garment workers. Membership in the all-Mexican ILGWU Local 96 grew. However, the male leadership of the union kept the women out of the better paying skilled jobs and barred them from union leadership. No Mexican woman held a high decision-making post with the ILGWU. Nevertheless, the garment strike laid the foundation for the ILGWU in Los Angeles and drew attention to the contributions of Mexican women toward the larger goal of labor rights.[27] The push for equality for Mexican women workers had begun.

Strikes broke out in the coalfields for higher wages and better working conditions. The strike by Mexican coal miners in Gallup, New Mexico, combined labor organization with radical political activity against a propaganda campaign that characterized the labor upheaval as the work of communists.

## MEXICAN COAL MINERS' WAGE WAR IN GALLUP

Communists were central to the powerful strike wave that broke out in 1933–1934. They led militant protests to dramatize the common interests of all workers, regardless of race. Although most Mexicans had no real interest in communism, they came under its leadership and learned ideologies and techniques for how to agitate and organize the Mexican people. Moreover, the communist catechizers stressed the need for the sacrifice of one or the few for the many.

In New Mexico, Mexicans had been mining coal and fighting the coal bosses for nearly a half century. In the summer of 1933, the communist-led NMU was drawn to Gallup, New Mexico, when local coal miners took action against the coal operators. The NMU's fight against the coal operators was part of this union's national efforts. Though it failed, the 1933 Gallup coal strike took its place with other struggles by American workers against oppression and exploitation.

Discord in the coal mines outside Gallup grew out of the struggle to unionize the state's coalfields. The nearly four-month labor strike was part of the miner upsurge following the newly implemented NRA. Serious difficulties arose in the Southwest around NRA codes involving the coal mining industry sagging from overproduction and where wages for Mexicans were lower than those for Anglos because of the entrenched Mexican wage scale. In the face of national economic crisis, mine owners were forced to reduce operational costs by cutting hours and wages.

The situation in New Mexico's coal districts was now at a flashpoint not seen since the strike wave of 1922. The miners resisted the wage reductions the coal companies demanded because of the coal slump, and unsafe working conditions and repression by the mine guards were other points of contention. The embittered miners accepted the overtures of the NMU to organize, and the union mapped out a campaign of struggle. NMU organizers arrived and immediately organized rallies and distributed food and clothes to the destitute miners.

Mine work culture reinforced the cohesiveness of the mining communities. Ethnic identity also aided worker solidarity in building unionism. Organized into an auxiliary, the women of the mining camps helped build and sustain solidarity by providing food in the soup kitchens, ensuring that homes were heated, and giving children clothes. The coal operators rejected all the miners' demands and put up stiff resistance through martial law, evictions, and deportations. They and the people of Gallup and New Mexico rightly saw the coal strike as a communist undertaking.

The Gallup coal strike was part of the NMU's failed fight with the United Mine Workers of America. The NMU was vulnerable to UMWA tactics of red baiting and race baiting. Company guards hounded NMU members unmercifully. These thugs, aided by county sheriffs and the state militia, closed all meeting places and dispersed the miners and the women's auxiliary on the picket lines. The Gallup coal strike was doomed almost from the day it began.

The besieged coal miners called on the La Liga Obrera de Habla Español for help. With ten thousand members, La Liga had local branches throughout Colorado and New Mexico. It had secured injunctions against land evictions, defeated an antisyndicalism bill, and fought for relief aid for Spanish-speaking workers.[28] La Liga's presence infused the strike movement with a new spirit and determination. For its part, the NMU mobilized support across the United States for the striking Gallup miners and their families.

New Mexico state officials organized to oppose the strike, imposed martial law, and moved in militia units to Gallup. Strike leaders were arrested and tried by military tribunals. The coal company brought in strikebreakers. This array of forces eroded the coal miners' organizational efforts and ultimately brought the strike to an end, as prolonging the strike would have made the final terms of the settlement worse. The Gallup victory was short-lived.

The continued economic slump left many coal miners jobless. Other miners whom local officials discovered had participated in the strike were removed from New Deal relief work. The unemployed councils' inflammatory talk about hungry workers kept the town's focus on the NMU. A mob made up of members of the Veterans of Foreign Wars, the American Legion, and other patriotic groups committed themselves to getting the remaining coal miners off work relief and drive them out of town.

Three hundred Mexican miners and their families were evicted from the coal camp, their personal belongings dumped off company property. This action triggered a confrontation between the miners and Gallup city officials. This was a careless move on the part of the coal miners, because most of them could not read or write English, and they had overlooked a lease clause that allowed the coal company to evict them without notice.

The miners fought the evictions until the first warrant was served, but this did not stop two miners and a sympathizer from taking action against the evictions. All three were immediately arrested and jailed, spurring a group of protesters to march to the jailhouse to demand the release of the prisoners. Goaded and stoned by some of the protestors, the sheriff's men moved on the marchers, panicked, and opened fire. The sheriff was killed in the hail of gunfire. Gallup officials carried through with their plans to punish the miners, who essentially became hunted revolutionaries.[29] Served "John Doe" warrants, six hundred miners were rounded up for questioning, and two hundred of them were eventually jailed. With public feelings so high, it seemed clear that no jury in New Mexico would acquit the miners. In a mass trial, forty-eight men were tried for the murder of the sheriff, convicted, and sent to the New Mexico State Penitentiary. Federal immigration agents arrived from El Paso and began a deportation roundup with more than one hundred men, women, and children subsequently deported to Mexico.[30] The National Miners Union's days in New Mexico were over.

In the wake of this first wave of labor activism, New Deal labor legislation was passed that was favorable to workers and put the unemployed back to work through employment relief programs. Senator Dennis Chavez of New Mexico helped get work relief to Spanish-speaking communities. The only Mexican American in the U.S. Senate, Chavez made sure that Works Progress Administration (WPA) and Public Works Administration (PWA) money came home to his state. The WPA, PWA, the Civilian Conservation Corps (CCC), and other New Deal projects built hundreds of needed public structures and over a thousand miles of new roads in the state. Many New Mexican public buildings were erected during this era through Chavez's efforts. He worked to promote New Mexican artists, particularly Spanish-speaking and Indian artists, who were traditionally ignored. Chavez also supported the CCC and National Youth Administration (NYA). He helped ensure the employment of thousands of young Americans, both in New Mexico and nationwide, during the Great Depression years.[31]

The New Deal in New Mexico focused on vocational education programs to train native New Mexicans in the Spanish Colonial revival and artisan crafts. Experts flooded into northern New Mexican villages to instruct residents in traditional arts and crafts, as well as food canning, midwifery and health care, and agricultural techniques. The population that had combined migratory seasonal labor with village life shifted to work within the village. At the same time folklorists from the Federal Writers Project began to record and transcribe the last remnants of a fading past, the old Hispanic myths and legends, songs and musical rhythms, dances and ceremonies, folk customs, and folk medicine. These New Deal programs essentially imposed Anglo-American values, practices, and desires on northern New Mexico's Spanish-speaking villages, often in contradictory mixtures. The New Deal reformers on the one hand modernized the villages and on the other preserved the cooperative, communitarian values of a preindustrial lifestyle.[32]

Mexican Americans got WPA jobs building highways, bridges, parks, and schools. Public works of art provided work for artists, writers, actors, and musicians. Some Mexican American artists found jobs painting murals for public buildings. By 1935, more than half of New Mexico's population was involved in one or another of the WPA projects. Nevertheless, discriminatory federal policies excluded great numbers of Mexicans from participating in government programs and benefits. To be eligible for a job through the WPA and the other federal programs required applicants to be American citizens. Many Mexican Americans did

**Spanish American Woman Weaver on a WPA Project, New Mexico, 1939.**
CREDIT: "Spanish-American woman weaving a rag rug at WPA project, Costilla, New Mexico, 1939." LC-USF34-034227-D. Courtesy of the Library of Congress.

not qualify because, as migrant workers, they did not meet residency requirements. Consequently, Mexican Americans composed a very small percentage of people on New Deal projects.[33]

There were a number of strikes by Tejanos in Texas. Initially it was the Tejanos who were employed in agriculture who struck for higher wages, but they were soon joined by those employed in cigar, garment, and pecan shelling work.

## TEJANO STRUGGLES FOR UNIONISM IN SOUTH TEXAS

In the spring of 1935, three thousand Tejano onion pickers in South Texas, led by organizers from La Asociación de Jornaleros of Laredo, walked out over low wages. However, the growers united and moved quickly to break the strike and the union. They called in deputy sheriffs to escort several trucks of scabs across the strikers' cordon of the highway the governor of Texas had ordered kept open. A U.S. Labor Department conciliator was called in, but the workers refused to waver. This angered the growers, and they brought in the Texas Rangers—in fact, state-employed strikebreakers and custodians of Anglo supremacy—who arrested fifty-nine strikers but later released them. The strike was lost, and the onion pickers returned to work without union recognition.[34]

The onion strike signaled the entrance of the CIO into the South Texas agricultural fields. It also marked an attempt by Mexican Americans to develop cross-border labor solidarity with Mexico's *Confederación de Trabajadores Mexicanos,* or CTM, union.[35] The CTM began making contacts with Mexican American workers. In 1936, the CTM sent representatives to a national convention of Mexican American workers held in Dallas, and another CTM delegation visited Los Angeles.[36]

The Asociación de Jornaleros became Agricultural Worker's Union 20212 (AWU). Despite harassment by county sheriffs, the Texas Rangers, and the U.S. Immigration Bureau, the AWU in March 1936 met to plan for a major labor offensive. A similar meeting had been held by CIO union organizers in San Antonio.[37] The goal was to organize thirty thousand farmworkers in the lower Río Grande Valley. Unionists from Texas and Mexico met in Corpus Christi on January 23, 1937, and formed the Texas Agricultural Worker's Organizing Committee (TWOC). TWOC would spearhead the union drive.

In late June 1937, Tejanos, led by TWOC, walked out of the cotton fields. The growers' refusal to bargain sparked sympathy strikes throughout the South Texas cotton region. The walkouts gained a few wage increases in some cotton-growing areas. The UCAPAWA took over from TWOC and through another round of organizing brought five thousand workers into the CIO.[38] UCAPAWA's organizing campaigns in Texas and in the rest of the Southwest were called off as it turned to organizing packing and cannery workers. Despite a vigorous effort, neither the TWOC nor the UCAPAWA had much enduring success in breaking the antiunion tradition in Texas. Nevertheless, the CIO union movement had emboldened this region's Mexican Americans.[39]

The union drives in Texas shifted to San Antonio, a center for light industrial work with an entirely Mexican workforce. San Antonio became the site of the biggest labor upheaval by the nation's Spanish-speaking workers when more than eight thousand pecan workers went on strike.[40]

## EMMA TENAYUCA BRINGS SOCIAL JUSTICE TO SAN ANTONIO'S MEXICANS

In San Antonio, two-thirds of the city's one hundred thousand Mexicans were crammed into the Westside, a place of considerable human suffering. It had the nation's lowest health standards, as tuberculosis, diphtheria, and other infectious diseases swept through the impoverished shanty communities and posed a grave health threat. Poverty-worn migrant families from the lower Río Grande Valley trooped to San Antonio, and their constant arrival day in and day out worsened the problem of congestion and poor health.[41] A lifelong resident of San Antonio's all-Mexican West Side, Emma Tenayuca had grown up amidst this poverty, sickness, and malnutrition. She would bring the conditions in the Westside to the attention of the public. Emma Tenayuca is the best known of the Mexican American women who organized among the Mexicans in the 1930s. San Antonio's city bosses were determined to stop the Tejana, and they would use communism as the pretext to break the pecan shellers' strike that she led.

By the time she was sixteen, Emma Tenayuca had become involved in a strike by the city's cigar workers. The next year, Tenayuca helped the garment workers striking against the Dorothy Frocks Company. In 1935, the Tejana teenager became head of the Westside's unemployed council and a most effective public orator. Her fiery eloquence attracted large crowds to the open-air meetings she held to protest the removal of Mexican families from city relief. The following year Tenayuca set up chapters of the Workers' Alliance of America in San Antonio and eventually served as its main leader.[42]

The Works Progress Administration furnished jobs for many unemployed Mexican Americans. However, just as with blacks, the locally administered federal work relief program in San Antonio confined Tejanos to pick-and-shovel brigades, and in many instances Tejanos were passed over for Anglos for WPA work. The Civilian Conservation Corps likewise discriminated against Tejanos.[43]

As head of San Antonio's Workers Alliance of America and armed with a sense of determination, Emma Tenayuca held street meetings, organized mass demonstrations, picketed relief offices, and petitioned relief officials to raise WPA work relief pay for Tejanos equal to that of Anglos. Largely through Tenayuca's indefatigable efforts, San Antonio's Tejanos got jobs constructing the multilevel walks, steps, and bridges of San Antonio's River Walk. The pedestrian walkway was constructed as a WPA project between 1939 and 1941 and diverted the San Antonio River to run through the city's center. Emma Tenayuca also strongly protested the apprehension, arrest, and deportation of labor activists by city police and federal agents.[44]

With fifteen branches and three thousand members, San Antonio's Workers' Alliance was one of the nation's strongest. Emma Tenayuca's work did not go unrecognized. In 1937, she was elected to the National Executive Committee of the Workers' Alliance of America. This was the first time a national organization of any kind had chosen a Mexican American woman for a top position. In this year, Tenayuca joined the Communist Party and married Homer Brooks, the secretary of the Communist Party of Texas. The dynamic young Tejana leader of the Workers Alliance appealed for the organization of pecan shellers. The firebrand became a key figure in the subsequent pecan shellers' strike.

## THE 1938 STRIKE BY SAN ANTONIO'S PECAN SHELLERS

The Southern Pecan Company produced fifteen million pounds of shelled pecans annually from the sweat labor of twelve thousand Mexicans. Women made up a high proportion of the pecan-shelling workforce, over 90 percent; they depended on the pecan shelling plants for their family's livelihood. Pecan shellers earned the nation's lowest wages and were frequently paid with government food surpluses. In 1937, wage cuts, coupled with that year's economic recession, worsened the shellers' plight of poverty and near starvation. Out of desperation, in late January 1938, nearly eight thousand pecan shellers walked out under the leadership of Emma Tenayuca. City police quickly arrested her and several UCAPAWA organizers on charges of communist agitation.[45]

Released from jail, Emma Tenayuca resumed her work with the pecan shellers' strike. The charismatic leader devoted almost all of her waking hours to her work, even though she was ill with tuberculosis. The Tejana walked door to door in the Westside neighborhood urging Mexicans to support the pecan shellers by not taking the jobs of the strikers, and they respected her request, causing the strike to mushroom. LULAC and much of San Antonio's Mexican American middle class became the unwitting tools of the San Antonio Anglo establishment in neutralizing the strike. Emma Tenayuca also met with resistance to her role, as well as her message, from the UCAPAWA. Guilt by association with communists plagued the UCAPAWA. The UCAPAWA commended Emma Tenayuca for her work but asked her to step down as strike leader. The agitator reluctantly bowed to the UCAPAWA's pressure. Close to the life of the people whose cause she advocated, Tenayuca forged ahead. She continued to be a popular speaker on democracy and held daily open-air meetings, distributed strike pamphlets, and sent more Mexicans to picket lines. The strike expanded and put San Antonio on edge.[46]

The campaign of harassment against the pecan shellers increased. City police kept the shelling plants open and protected scabs that crossed the picket lines. The police teargassed and arrested the strikers, but they held firm. Federal immigration agents launched roundup raids but stopped after the Mexican consul intervened. The governor of Texas warned the striking pecan shellers that he would call in the Texas Rangers and the state militia to restore order in San Antonio. Calm returned once the Texas Industrial Commission, which had been holding public hearings of the strikers' grievances, announced that an agreement had been reached between the Southern Pecan Shelling Company and its employees.

The pecan shellers gained union recognition and wage increases; however, the Fair Labor Standards Act of 1938 nullified the pecan shellers' victory. The act exempted agricultural workers and set minimum wages at low levels. In San Antonio, this resulted in seven thousand pecan-shelling workers losing their jobs and being ineligible for state unemployment benefits.[47]

Emma Tenayuca pursued her campaign to educate Mexican workers in their struggle for democratic rights. The pecan shellers' strike impressed her deeply and undoubtedly contributed to her and Homer Brooks' writing the "The Mexican Question in the Southwest." According to Tenayuca and Brooks, the Southwest's Mexican American and Mexican population was one people, an oppressed working class whose common history, culture, and language were shaped by conquest as a result of the Mexican War (1846–1848). However, Tenayuca and Brooks noted that Mexican Americans and Mexicans historically had evolved separate communities in the Southwest. Emancipation could come for all Mexicans only by linking their struggle to "the labor and democratic forces in the Anglo-American population." This would require promoting the language and culture of this oppressed racial minority, eliminating the dual-wage labor system, preventing confiscation of small land holdings, and ending Jim Crow segregation and political repression by revising U.S. citizenship requirements.[48] Tenayuca and Brooks, moreover, noted that "the treatment accorded Mexicans is a carryover to the United States of Wall Street's imperialist exploitation of Latin America." The two asserted, "The task now is to build the democratic front among the Mexican masses through unifying . . . in support of the social and economic measures of the New Deal."[49]

A sole voice of dissent, Emma Tenayuca continued her Communist Party work on behalf of the Mexicans' struggle for a more just society. Mexican Americans remember her as a hero, the last to retreat and always ready to struggle for the cause.[50] Meanwhile, Colorado's Spanish-speaking beet workers were waging the struggle for labor unionism.

## THE UCAPAWA ORGANIZES COLORADO'S MEXICAN FARMWORKERS

In 1935, representatives from two dozen beet worker union locals representing the mountain and plains states met in Fort Lupton, Colorado, to form a national labor organization to address their problems. This meeting provoked the sugar companies to take action. Alerted about a potential union drive, the sugar companies' response was quick and forceful. They contacted the U.S. Immigration Bureau, which came in and launched a sweep of the farms and towns. Organizing by the beet workers continued. The workers held another meeting in Denver in July 1937, from which emerged the UCAPAWA. This CIO-allied organization would spearhead a broad campaign to organize harvest, cannery, and packinghouse workers into one big union to press for their rights.[51]

The UCAPAWA enrolled more than twelve thousand Colorado sugar-beet workers. A key impediment to labor unionism in Colorado was that growers brought out-of-state jobless workers to flood the beet fields with surplus labor. To prevent this, UCAPAWA called on the Workers' Alliance of America and La Liga Obrera de Habla Español to picket in New Mexico and Texas to dissuade workers from going to Colorado to scab. UCAPAWA also prepared to halt the discharge of WPA relief workers that took place at the start of the beet harvesting season.[52]

Only a handful of Colorado growers negotiated with UCAPAWA. The National Beet Growers Association refused to talk to the union. The 1937 Sugar Act required beet growers to pay their workers "fair and reasonable" wages set by the Agriculture Department following public hearings. As a result, UCAPAWA could only exert influence on wage rates by enforcing the new federal standards and by representing workers at the public hearings. The National Beet Growers Association remained uncooperative with UCAPAWA and put pressure on them by resorting to their high-handed methods. They ordered county sheriffs into the beet fields and deputized and armed farmers to fight the UCAPAWA. A last-minute settlement averted a violent confrontation.[53]

Organizing by sugar-beet workers was further hindered by southern congressional Democrats who, making effective use of their strength, voted against collective bargaining rights legislation intended to aid agricultural workers. The South's powerful congressional delegation was determined to keep farmworkers out of the Social Security old-age insurance plan, the Farm Security Administration, and other New Deal programs. The war in Europe halted congressional action on agriculture, leaving the plight of farmworkers unchanged.[54]

The labor struggles in the Southwest shifted once more to California, specifically to the city of Los Angeles. It now had the largest Mexican population and a very active progressive labor movement.

## MEXICAN AMERICAN CIO UNIONISTS ORGANIZE LOS ANGELES AND SOUTHERN CALIFORNIA

Despite opposition, California's farmworkers continued to press for unionization. In 1936, four thousand workers struck the orange orchards and packing plants in Orange County for higher wages. The defiant orange workers stayed out for seven weeks, but growers broke the strike with scabs. Strike militancy spread to Los Angeles. Mexican, Filipino, and Japanese American celery workers united and walked off the celery farms. Their strike was put down by 1,500 deputy sheriffs, hired thugs, and the infamous Red Squad, who branded the workers as criminals. In 1937, sixteen strikes took place in California. The next year, ten thousand pickers walked out of the San Joaquin Valley cotton district but lost their strike because the growers in their bloody antiunion campaign carried out violent attacks on them. UCAPAWA, sixty thousand members strong, was involved in a third of the strike upheavals that took place in 1938. Labor organizing increased in 1939 as determined union leaders, many of them Mexican Americans, pushed for labor rights. Strike actions by farmworkers had spread throughout the Southwest, and so did violent attacks aimed at destroying the worker movement. The farmworkers were unable to fight the mounting power of giant growers who denounced them and used every kind of tactic to defeat unionization, including bringing in children as strikebreakers, as had taken place on the Don Lucas Ranch outside of Ontario, California. The course of the farm labor movement thereby shifted in favor of the antiunion growers associations who thwarted these attempts to unionize field workers. The fact that agricultural workers were excluded from the collective bargaining and strike provisions of the National Labor Relations Act (NLRA) gave the expanded grower groups free rein to use antiunion schemes banned in other industries to put down radicalism in the fields. The AFL also began aligning local farm labor unions with the unionized allied processing industries, forcing the CIO to shift organizing to this labor sector.[55]

In 1939, the nation's attention focused on the plight of farmworkers with the publication of *Factories in the Field* by Carey McWilliams. This coincided with the appearance of *The Grapes of Wrath,* John Steinbeck's novel of Dust Bowl migrants. Aroused public interest in the grave plight of migrant workers promoted a federal investigation led by Senator Robert La Follette from the state of Wisconsin. The La Follette Civil Liberties Committee Hearings produced a damning report on farm labor repression.

The CIO union drives in Los Angeles brought the city's Spanish-speaking rank-and-file workers into the newly built and integrated union movement. Mexican American women cannery and food processing workers organized themselves and applied for membership in the UCAPAWA. Mexican women composed the main workforce of the California Sanitation Canning Company (Cal San) of Los Angeles but generally earned substantially less than the male employees. This changed when the new UCAPAWA Local 75 signed a contract with Cal San that gave the union a foothold in the Los Angeles fruit and vegetable canning industry.[56]

In 1941, UCAPAWA, seeing its chance to organize thousands of food processing workers in southern California, chose Luisa Moreno, its newly elected vice president, to spread democratic unionism. Emphasizing dignity and respect, Moreno used her organizing skills and helped build Local 92 at plants of the California Walnut Growers' Association. Moreno's positive contributions led to building Local 3, UCAPAWA's second largest union. In the Riverside-Redlands area and in San Diego, a 1942 National Labor Relations Board (NLRB) election brought the UCAPAWA to Val Vita workers. UCAPAWA Local 64 at San Diego's Van Camp Seafood Company emerged as a major California union. Mexican women once more proved fervent and dedicated labor activists. At this time Mexican Americans strengthened their attachment to the Democratic Party in response to the labor and social legislation of the New Deal and in their drive for equality. Mexican American cannery workers were heavily involved in the CIO's massive voter registration drive in support of President Roosevelt and the Democratic Party ticket.[57] This included voter education and getting out Mexican American qualified voters to the polling booths.

Because of the CIO's support of equality within labor and its clearly expressed position in favor of civil rights, more and more Mexican American workers joined the growing CIO union movement under way in Los Angeles. The International Longshoremen and Warehouseman's Union (ILWU) launched a major union drive. It fell on the mostly Mexican American ILWU Local 26, formed in 1937, to undertake to bring clothing, oil, auto, electrical, mining, and rubber workers into the CIO. Pledged to "absolute racial equality," the Steel Workers Organizing Committee (SWOC) became a major CIO voice. Mexican Americans were presidents of many SWOC union locals at steel plants in Los Angeles. The United Furniture Workers of America (UFWA) brought AFL-affiliated furniture workers into its fold and, together with ILWU Local 26, UFWA Local 576, and United Electrical Local 1421, was active in the Los Angeles CIO Industrial Union Council, which held the prospect of a movement for civil rights.[58]

The CIO organizing drive spread to other industries, and Mexican Americans joined in. There was more contact between Mexican Americans and white workers in the workplace and within specific unions in the urban industrial Midwest. Responding to the appeal for class solidarity, Mexican American autoworkers in Flint, Michigan, employed by General Motors participated in the spectacular sit-down strike of 1936–1937 to organize the giant corporation. The primary reason for the strike was speedups, as autoworkers were driven virtually nonstop to produce more car parts. Car sander Rafael Arcero and his coworkers met secretly to elude GM's spies, thugs, and sympathizers. Arcero pulled guard duty once a week to protect his fellow workers inside the huge Fisher Body Plant No. 1. The Mexican American won the respect of both his Mexican American and Anglo coworkers. The forty-four-day strike launched the new United Auto Workers union (UAW) as the bargaining agent for workers. In multiethnic and multiracial Chicago, a working-class "culture of unity" broke down ethnic divisions and animosities and made possible wide-scale industrial unionization. Labor union organizers Refugio Martínez and Joe Rodríguez were two CIO recruits who organized Mexican American packinghouse workers to secure better working conditions for them. Both individuals had been very active in the demonstrations led by the unemployed councils in the Back of the Yards neighborhood. Enthusiasm for the CIO among Mexican American industrial workers continued to grow. Thousands of Mexican American steelworkers imbued with the spirit of rank-and-file militancy were active in the SWOC organizing drive at East Chicago's Youngstown and Inland Steel plants and would make up 75 percent of the pickets. In 1937, picketing at Republic Steel in South Chicago culminated in the Memorial Day Massacre, in which Spanish-speaking steelworkers and their supporters were among the victims

**Lupe Marshall at the Memorial Day Massacre, 1937.**
CREDIT: "Woman walking/running through crowd with police in foreground at the Republic Steel strike, Chicago, Illinois, ca. 1937," ICHi-50126. Courtesy of the Chicago History Museum. www.newberry.org title: "Lupe Marshall Confronts Chicago Police During the Memorial Day Massacre, 1937."

assaulted with handguns and clubs by the Chicago police department. Lupe Marshall and two hundred other women were marching with the steelworkers on this day of tragedy. She attempted to intervene and beseeched the law officers to stop their senseless violence. Lupe, described by police as "a Mexican immigrant who worked at Hull House," was accused of "throwing a bag of pepper at the police" during the melee. "She was kicked, arrested, convicted and fined $12 for conspiracy to commit an illegal act."[59] Grassroots work by Mexican American steelworkers helped sustain the SWOC until the 1942 NLRB union election vote.

As the United States marched into war, Mexican Americans had forged a framework for labor solidarity and democratic action as CIO unionists. They especially responded to the CIO's message of workers' rights and equality.

## CONCLUSION

The Great Depression undercut whatever economic gains Mexicans had made. Many of the arrivals from Mexico, with long-time Mexican American residents, endured suffering as economic conditions worsened and they became targets of increasing hostility from Anglos. The unskilled labor that Mexicans were providing in agriculture and industry was no longer in demand.

Destitution among the Mexican population increased and became more widespread. The escalating impoverishment of the rural Spanish-speaking population triggered a rapid exodus to the cities. Men struggled to find jobs in the poverty-ridden urban centers. It fell to women to seek work in order to secure their families' survival. Mexican workers were usually the first to lose their jobs. The high incidence of unemployment was quite serious among Mexicans. Relief meant survival, but none came because many relief agencies turned against the Mexicans. Angry Anglos voiced concern that a disproportionate number of Mexicans were on relief and that relief would make chronic dependents of Mexicans. A concerted effort was made nationwide to induce or compel Mexicans to return to Mexico. Federal officials rounded up the idle and indigent Mexicans in the cities and countryside and deported them from assembly centers. The arbitrary enforcement of immigration laws by which all Mexicans were apprehended and detained was a stark awakening for Mexican Americans.

Federal work relief was highly prized given the hardships many Mexican Americans had to endure. Though discriminated against by nearly every New Deal agency, Mexican Americans were never entirely excluded from participation in federal work relief. In many instances, these jobs stood between them and complete impoverishment. Some federal programs specifically targeted Mexican communities, such as those in northern New Mexico that taught traditional crafts and the large-scale construction projects such as those in San Antonio that drew on Mexican labor. An estimated one hundred thousand Mexicans participated in New Deal work programs in the western states. More important, the New Deal introduced a new dynamic in the lives of Mexican Americans—the right to organize promised by Section 7a of the National Recovery Act. The New Deal rhetoric mobilized Mexican Americans. Many allied themselves with unions and engaged in strikes for higher wages, better working conditions, and union representation.

The Communist Party of the United States was the principal organization and voice for the unemployed in the Southwest region. In many instances, the party was the only group that concerned itself with the rights of Mexicans. It organized unions and demonstrations for relief, jobs, and an end to evictions. The leaders faced formidable obstacles: not only violent reprisals but also economic sanctions. In the coal mines outside Gallup, New Mexico, state and local governments and the coal operators collaborated to defeat the strike efforts of the NMU.

The CIO proceeded to organize hundreds of thousands of workers and included minorities and women in their ranks. Tens of thousands of Spanish-speaking workers joined the CIO. CIO unions led and followed by Mexican workers formed a distinct racial and ethnic identity in the broad stream of the American labor movement. Mexican American women participated in this union activism, with young women taking an especially active role in the struggle for labor and social justice. Many rose to leadership positions within the CIO unions and also in organizations that called for inclusion of Mexican Americans. Women such as Emma Tenayuca of San Antonio pushed for these progressive ideals. Seeking integration into American life, Mexican Americans understood that collective action brought higher wages and the promise of civil rights. They believed labor leaders who asserted that the labor movement stood "for equality of treatment, opportunity, and participation irrespective of creed, color, or nationality."[60] A new generation of Spanish-speaking leaders arose in response to the nationwide labor movement that was gathering force.

To achieve more victories, the Democratic Party needed the support of labor and Mexican Americans in the coalition that President Roosevelt built to amass his victories in 1932 and 1936. Mexican Americans helped establish the CIO as a powerhouse in Democratic politics. A main factor in this development was the belief that President Roosevelt's New Deal programs of relief and recovery were especially beneficial to them.

Important changes took place within the Mexican American community during the 1930s. These developments were a prelude to even larger changes and struggles that lay ahead for Mexican Americans. With Hitler's invasion of Russia in 1941, Mexican Americans subordinated their demands to address the problems in the labor force to aid the success of the war effort. World War II and the postwar struggle for equality became turning points in the history of Mexican Americans. The major events unfolding at home as America prepared for war and those in a Europe that was ravaged by war became transformative experiences. The composition of the nation's Spanish-speaking communities was shifting to American-born, as were conceptions of national identity and citizenship, because a new group consciousness had taken hold among Mexican Americans.[61]

## NOTES

1. Jacqueline Jones, *The Dispossessed: America's Underclasses from the Civil War to the Present* (New York: Basic Books, 1993), 170–171.
2. Robert McElvaine, *The Great Depression: America, 1929–1941* ( New York: Three Rivers Press, 1993), 185.

3. Zaragosa Vargas, *Labor Rights Are Civil Rights: Mexican American Workers in 20th Century America* (Princeton, NJ: Princeton University Press, 2005), 39–40; Bob McKay, "The Texas Cotton Acreage Control Law of 1931 and Mexican Repatriation," *West Texas Historical Association Yearbook* 59 (1983): 143, 148, 151.

4. Vargas, *Labor Rights Are Civil Rights*, 41–42; Suzanne Forrest, *The Preservation of the Village: New Mexico's Hispanics and the New Deal* (Albuquerque: University of New Mexico Press, 1989), 79–80, 99; Deutsch, *No Separate Refuge*, 163–165, 168.

5. Vargas, *Labor Rights Are Civil Rights*, 42–43; Reisler, *By the Sweat of Their Brow*, 229; Gilbert G. González, *Labor and Community: Mexican Citrus Worker Villages in a Southern California County, 1900–1950* (Urbana: University of Illinois Press, 1994), 72–74; McWilliams, *Factories in the Fields*, 285.

6. Vargas, *Labor Rights Are Civil Rights*, 44; Yolanda Chávez-Leyva, "'Faithful Hard-Working Mexican Hands': Mexicana Workers During the Great Depression," in *Perspectives in Mexican American Studies 5—Mexican American Women, Changing Images*, ed. Juan García (Tucson: University of Arizona Press, 1995), 69; Reisler, *By the Sweat of Their Brow*, 228; Sánchez, *Becoming Mexican American*, 211.

7. The $220 million bond issue for the construction of the Colorado River aqueduct was expected to provide employment for ten thousand men in Los Angeles. Vargas, *Labor Rights Are Civil Rights*, 45–46; Sánchez, *Becoming Mexican American*, 211.

8. Vargas, *Labor Rights Are Civil Rights*, 46–47; Reisler, *By the Sweat of Their Brow*, 209; Abraham Hoffman, *Unwanted Mexican Americans in the Great Depression, 1929–1939* (Tucson: University of Arizona Press, 1974), 35.

9. Vargas, *Labor Rights Are Civil Rights*, 47–48; Hoffman, *Unwanted Mexican Americans*, 33; Reisler, *By the Sweat of Their Brow*, 214–215.

10. The exceptions were immigrants who were skilled workers or professionals or married couples if either spouse was an American citizen. Vargas, *Labor Rights Are Civil Rights*, 48–49.

11. Ibid., 52. See also Eric V. Meeks, "Protecting the 'White Citizen Worker': Race, Labor, and Citizenship in South-Central Arizona, 1929–1945," *Journal of the Southwest* 48 (Spring 2006), 91–113.

12. Vargas, *Labor Rights Are Civil Rights*, 53; Hoffman, *Unwanted Mexican Americans*, 16; Sánchez, *Becoming Mexican American*, 210–213, 215–216, 221; Estrada, *Los Angeles Plaza*, 204–212.

13. For the position of the Detroit Federation Labor on the Mexican removal from the city, see: *Detroit Labor News*, March 24, 1933.

14. Vargas, *Labor Rights Are Civil Rights*, 54; Dionicio Nodín Valdés, *Barrios Norteños: St. Paul and Midwestern Mexican Communities in the Twentieth Century* (Austin: University of Texas Press, 2000), 87, 92–93, 95; Vargas, *Proletarians of the North*, 178, 186. The Santa Fe Railroad Company, in a move intended to benefit the railroad, protected its loyal Mexican workers and their families by claiming all were U.S. citizens. These instances of limited employer benevolence were rare. With the exception of religious groups and a few progressive secular organizations, no one defended the Mexicans singled out for removal.

15. Vargas, *Labor Rights Are Civil Rights*, 59; Francisco E. Balderrama and Raymond Rodriguez, *Decade of Betrayal: Mexican Repatriation in the 1930s* (Albuquerque: University of New Mexico Press, 1995), 60.

16. Gutiérrez, *Walls and Mirrors*, 72–73; Balderrama and Rodriguez, *Decade of Betrayal*, 53. There were further changes in federal policy. The $500 bond for violation of American

immigration laws and the $1,000 bond to procure work were each reduced to $150. Vargas, *Labor Rights Are Civil Rights,* 59–61.

17. Vargas, *Labor Rights Are Civil Rights,* 58–59. Calleros also served on the Board of Directors of El Paso's County Board of Welfare and Employment. It operated the El Paso Welfare Bureau and administered relief funds from the state of Texas and the Federal Emergency Relief Administration. Calleros later acted as notary public in the execution of citizen affidavits by Mexicans applying for WPA work, and he secured back pay for Mexicans repatriated to Mexico. Ibid.

18. Ibid., 126; Montejano, *Anglos and Mexicans in the Making of Texas,* 164–165; Farm Placement Service, *Origins and Problems of Texas Migratory Farm Labor* (Austin, TX: Texas State Employment Service, Texas Unemployment Compensation Commission, September 1940), 20, 42.

19. Vargas, *Labor Rights Are Civil Rights,* 67–70; Stuart Jamieson, *Labor Unionism in American Agriculture* (Washington, DC: U.S. Department of Labor Bureau of Labor Statistics, Bulletin No. 836, 1945), 271–272; Yolanda Chavez-Leyva, "Años de desperacíon: The Great Depression and the Mexican American Generation in El Paso, Texas, 1929– 1935" (Ph.D. diss., University of Texas, El Paso, 1989), 47–64; Zamora, *World of the Mexican Worker,* 133–139, 159–161, 200–202.

20. Vargas, *Labor Rights Are Civil Rights,* 70–73; Deutsch, *No Separate Refuge,* 154–158, 169, 170–172; Dubofsky, *We Shall be All: A History of the IWW* (New York: Quadrangle, 1973), 475–477; Jamieson, *Labor Unionism in American Agriculture,* 235–239.

21. Vargas, *Labor Rights Are Civil Rights,* 73; Deutsch, *No Separate Refuge,* 169, 172–173; Harvey Klehr, *The Heyday of American Communism* (New York: Basic Books, 1984), 149; Forrest, *Preservation of the Village,* 97–98; Gutiérrez, *Walls and Mirrors,* 106; Jamieson, *Labor Unionism in American Agriculture,* 240–241.

22. Vargas, *Labor Rights Are Civil Rights,* 76–78; Chávez-Leyva, "'Faithful Hard-Working Mexican Hands,'" 65–70; Chávez-Leyva, "Años de desperacíon," 17.

23. Vargas, *Labor Rights Are Civil Rights,* 81; Victor B. Nelson Cisneros, "La clase trabajadora en Tejas, 1920–1940," *Aztlán* 6, no. 2 (Summer 1975): 256–257.

24. Vargas, *Labor Rights Are Civil Rights,* 83; Melissa Hield, "Union-Minded: Women in the Texas ILGWU, 1933–1950," *Frontiers* 4 (1979), 61–64; Mary Sullivan and Bertha Blair, *Women in Texas Industries: Hours, Wages, and Working Conditions, and Home Work* (Washington, DC: U. S. Department of Labor. Women's Bureau Bulletin No. 126, 1936), 7; Nelson Cisneros, "La clase trabajadora en Tejas," 254–255.

25. Vargas, *Labor Rights Are Civil Rights,* 84–85; Clementina Durón, "Mexican Women and Labor Conflict in Los Angeles: The ILGWU Dressmakers' Strike of 1933," *Aztlán* 15, no. 1 (Spring 1984): 145, 149; Sánchez, *Becoming Mexican American,* 227–228, 232, 234; John Laslett and Mary Tyler, *The ILGWU in Los Angeles, 1907–1988* (Inglewood, CA: Ten Star Press, 1989), 30–31.

26. Vargas, *Labor Rights Are Civil Rights,* 87; Rose Pesotta, *Bread upon the Waters* (New York: Dodd, Mead, 1944), 58; Durón, "ILGWU Dressmakers' Strike," 154–155; Sánchez, *Becoming Mexican American,* 227; Monroy, *Rebirth,* 108, 236.

27. Vargas, *Labor Rights Are Civil Rights,* 88–89; Pesotta, *Bread upon the Waters,* 54; Monroy, *Rebirth,* 238; Durón, "ILGWU Dressmakers' Strike," 157–158; Sánchez, *Becoming Mexican American,* 234.

28. Vargas, *Labor Rights Are Civil Rights,* 93–94; Forrest, *Preservation of the Village,* 98; Deutsch, *No Separate Refuge,* 173.

29. Vargas, *Labor Rights Are Civil Rights,* 108–109; Erna Furgusson, *Murder and Mystery in New Mexico* (Albuquerque, NM: Merle Armitage Editions, 1948), 176–178.

30. Vargas, *Labor Rights Are Civil Rights,* 111–112.

31. On the career of Dennis Chavez during the New Deal years, see Joe Roy Luján, "Dennis Chavez and the Roosevelt Era, 1933–1945" (Ph.D. diss., University of New Mexico, 1987) and more recently Rosemary T. Díaz, "El senador, Dennis Chavez: New Mexico Native Son, American Senior Statesman, 1888–1962" (Ph.D. diss., Arizona State University, 2006).

32. Deutsch, *No Separate Refuge,* 163–164; Forrest, *Preservation of the Village,* 103–104.

33. See the *Wingspread Collector's Guide to Albuquerque and Central and Southern New Mexico,* Volume 12.

34. Ibid., 118–19; Jamieson, *Labor Unionism in American Agriculture,* 274–275; Nelson-Cisneros, "La clase trabajadora en Tejas," 248; Victor B. Nelson-Cisneros, "UCAPAWA Organizing Activities in Texas, 1935–50," *Aztlán* 9, no. 1 (1978): 73–74.

35. Vargas, *Labor Rights Are Civil Rights,* 119; Nelson-Cisneros, "La clase trabajadora en Tejas," 151–152; Gilbert G. Gonzalez, *Mexican Counsels and Labor Organizing: Imperial Politics in the American Southwest* (Austin: University of Texas Press, 1999), 201.

36. Vargas, *Labor Rights Are Civil Rights,* 119–120; Barry Carr, *Marxism and Communism in Twentieth Century Mexico* (Lincoln, NE: University of Nebraska Press, 1993), 97–98. The CTM also established El Colegio de Obreros in Mexico City to train Mexican Americans for union work in the United States.

37. The Agricultural Workers Union continued to organize Laredo's Tejano workers. Some joined the union every week. Although the AWU grew in membership, it lapsed for lack of leadership. The last full-time organizer was Clemente N. Idar. Nelson-Cisneros, "La clase trabajadora en Tejas," 252–253; Jamieson, *Labor Unionism in American Agriculture,* 275.

38. Vargas, *Labor Rights Are Civil Rights,* 121–122; Jamieson, *Labor Unionism in American Agriculture,* 276–278; Nelson-Cisneros, "La clase trabajadora en Tejas," 249–250; Nelson-Cisneros, "UCAPAWA Organizing Activities in Texas," 73–74.

39. Vargas, *Labor Rights Are Civil Rights,* 121–122; Jamieson, *Labor Unionism in American Agriculture,* 276–278; Nelson-Cisneros, "La clase trabajadora en Tejas," 249–250; Nelson-Cisneros, "UCAPAWA Organizing Activities in Texas," 73–74; Devra Weber, *Dark Sweat, White Gold: California Farmworkers, Cotton, and the New Deal* (Berkeley: University of California Press, 1994), 180.

40. Vargas, *Labor Rights Are Civil Rights,* 122; Jamieson, *Labor Unionism in American Agriculture,* 278.

41. Vargas, *Labor Rights Are Civil Rights,* 129; Green Peyton, *San Antonio: City in the Sun* (New York: McGraw-Hill, 1946), 147.

42. Vargas, *Labor Rights Are Civil Rights,* 127–130; Julia Kirk Blackwelder, *Women of the Depression: Caste and Culture in San Antonio, 1929–1939* (College Station: Texas A&M University Press, 1984), 103–104; Roberto Calderón and Emilio Zamora, *Chicana Voices: Intersections of Race, Class, and Gender* (Austin, TX: Center for Mexican American Studies, 1986), 33. In the spring of 1938, ILGWU Local 180 struck the Shirlee Frock Company. Three months later, the victorious garment workers signed a contract and gained increased wages. Another ILGWU strike followed, and it resulted in a favorable NLRB ruling.

43. Vargas, *Labor Rights Are Civil Rights,* 130. For the experience of New Mexico and Colorado Mexican Americans in the CCC, see Maria E. Montoya, "The Roots of Economic

and Ethnic Divisions in Northern New Mexico: The Case of the Civilian Conservation Corps," *Western Historical Quarterly* 26, no. 1 (Spring 1995): 14–34.

44. Vargas, *Labor Rights Are Civil Rights*, 130; Fraser M. Ottanelli, *The Communist Party of the United States: From the Depression to World War II* (New Brunswick, NJ: Rutgers University Press, 1991), 35–36.

45. Vargas, *Labor Rights Are Civil Rights*, 134–135; Jamieson, *Labor Unionism in American Agriculture*, 280; Blackwelder, *Women of the Depression*, 141, 148–149.

46. Vargas, *Labor Rights Are Civil Rights*, 140.

47. Ibid., 142–143; Nelson-Cisneros, "UCAPAWA Organizing Activities in Texas," 77–78; Jamieson, *Labor Unionism in American Agriculture*, 281.

48. Vargas, *Labor Rights Are Civil Rights*, 143–145; Emma Tenayuca and Homer Brooks, "The Mexican Question in the Southwest," *Communist* 18 (March 1939), 257–268; Calderón and Zamora, *Chicana Voices*, 34–35.

49. Vargas, *Labor Rights Are Civil Rights*, 145.

50. Ibid., 145–146; Richard B. Henderson, *Maury Maverick: A Political Biography* (Austin: University of Texas Press, 1970), 214–216. In August 1939, the Texas Communist Party convened a meeting in San Antonio, but the meeting was stopped abruptly by a rampaging mob of five thousand people.

51. Vargas, *Labor Rights Are Civil Rights*, 148; Deutsch, *No Separate Refuge*, 171. Sugar-beet workers in sugar crops were the only agricultural laborers who had their wages set by the federal government.

52. Vargas, *Labor Rights Are Civil Rights*, 148.

53. Ibid., 149. The Sugar Act raised the per-acre rate for beet workers, over half of them women, to $21, but this rate was $2 below the pre-Depression rate. In addition, the Sugar Act's restrictions on child labor cut a family's earnings by one-third.

54. Ibid., 149–150; Weber, *Dark Sweat, White Gold*, 189; Valdés, *Barrios Norteños*, 113–114.

55. Weber, *Dark Sweat, White Gold*, 190; Nelson-Cisneros, "UCAPAWA and Chicanos in California: The Farm Worker Period, 1937–1940," *Aztlán* 7, no. 3 (Fall 1976): 457, 466; Jamieson, *Labor Unionism in American Agriculture*, 124–126; Vargas, *Labor Rights Are Civil Rights*, 151; Weber, *Dark Sweat, White Gold*, 149; Cletus Daniel, *Bitter Harvest: A History of Southern California Farmworkers, 1870–1941* (Ithaca, NY: Cornell University Press, 1981), 272–273; García, *A World of Their Own*, 116.

56. Vargas, *Labor Rights Are Civil Rights*, 151–153; Vicki L. Ruiz, *Cannery Women, Cannery Lives: Mexican Women, Unionization, and the California Food Processing Industry, 1930–1950* (Albuquerque: University of New Mexico Press, 1987), 79–81.

57. Vargas, *Labor Rights Are Civil Rights*, 153–154 ; Sánchez, *Becoming Mexican American*, 243–244, 250; Nelson-Cisneros, "UCAPAWA and Chicanos in California," 463–464; Ruiz, *Cannery Women, Cannery Lives*, 76–77, 81–83.

58. Vargas, *Labor Rights Are Civil Rights*, 154–155; Bruce Nelson, *Divided We Stand: American Workers and the Struggle for Black Equality* (Princeton, NJ: Princeton University Press, 2001), 195.

59. Education Department of the International Union, UAW, *We Make Our Own History: A Portrait of the UAW* (Detroit: International Union, UAW, 1986), 7–8; Roger Horowitz, *"Negro and White, Unite and Fight!": A Social History of Industrial Unionism in Meatpacking, 1930–90* (Urbana: University of Illinois Press. 1997), 68; James B. Lane and Edward J. Escobar, eds., *Forging a Community: The Latino Experience in Northwest Indiana, 1915–1975* (Chicago: Cattails Press, 1987), 151–152; www.newberry.org. For a definition of a working-class "culture of unity," see Lizbeth Cohen, *Making a New Deal:*

*Industrial Workers in Chicago, 1919–1939* (Cambridge: Cambridge University Press, 1997), 333–349.

60. Vargas, *Labor Rights Are Civil Rights,* 155–156; Thomas Göbel, "Becoming American: Ethnic Workers and the Rise of the CIO," *Labor History* 29, no. 2 (Spring 1988): 195–196.

61. Vargas, *Labor Rights Are Civil Rights,* 156.

# CHAPTER 8

*ᴥ*

# The Mexican American People in the World War II Era

The nation's Mexican Americans made numerous gains through New Deal reform policies that raised their expectations for change as they entered the decade of the 1940s. Yet their social and economic status was hardly different from that of a decade before. The barriers of racial discrimination on many fronts remained, preventing them from fully entering the mainstream of American life. The start of World War II to preserve democracy abroad soon ushered in important changes in the life of the Mexican American population.

America's 2,690,000 Mexican Americans in the 1940s were full of hope that change would occur. Their optimism was nurtured in large part by the freedom and equality that the World War II effort promised. With unusual speed, the nation turned its energies to war production. By the end of 1942, the United States began to experience a shortage of workers, a condition that became increasingly more critical as the war unfolded. The manpower needs of America at war afforded Mexican Americans ample opportunities for work and drew hundreds of thousands of men into the armed services. Mexican American women not only worked in industry but also joined the armed forces, serving in traditional female assignments.

World War II created a new awareness of race throughout the world, yet rampant racism against America's minority groups produced vengeance at home. Flagrant violations of individual liberties marked this period, and the Mexican American population was deeply affected by the continued discrimination it experienced. Amidst a war for democracy, the American nation refused to extend the democratic principles of President Roosevelt's Four Freedoms to Mexican Americans.

The Second World War brought no letup in racial discrimination. War mobilization produced a volatile social climate on the home front as relocation, rationing, overcrowding, and long work weeks without recreation produced frustration. Specifically, the influx of newcomers into the nation's booming war production centers and the consequent competition for jobs and housing led to racial clashes. Employers in war industries prevented minority workers from making employment gains, and Anglos, who were favored for employment, were angry at the introduction of minorities and women into the workplace and subjected them to derision and racial discrimination. The result of this prejudice was that Mexican Americans found themselves the last hired in defense work, discriminated against in federal job training programs, and with few opportunities to secure much needed housing.[1] Yet Mexican Americans became more assertive because they were determined to fight for freedom not only abroad but also at home.

The Congress of Spanish-Speaking Peoples played a vital role in securing full social and economic rights for Mexican Americans. Much like the National Negro Congress, the Congress of Spanish-Speaking Peoples conducted a campaign to organize Mexican American workers, to defend their civil liberties, and to improve their overall status. The Mexican Americans' disadvantaged position lent itself readily to exploitation by the fascist *sinarquistas* and the Nazis, who employed a propaganda campaign about the conditions for America's minorities. The nationwide outbreak of racial conflict reached a zenith in 1943, when many American cities were wracked by explosive race riots that turned them into domestic battlegrounds. For Mexican Americans, the Los Angeles race riots became a symbol of wartime prejudice, as well as the championing of equal opportunity. Because of international considerations, namely the Good Neighbor Policy with Latin America and the overall relationship of the Spanish-speaking population to America's war effort, equality became a crucial matter of importance to the United States.[2] In light of the Los Angeles race riots and the fact that Mexican Americans suffered blatant discrimination, the federal government and private institutions began to take more interest in the plight of America's Spanish-speaking peoples. Within this context of ameliorating escalating racial turmoil, Mexican Americans persevered in demanding social and economic advancement.

The Mexican American population rallied to support the war effort with a flood of enlistments and a firm commitment to defeat the Axis powers. Concern over the threat of war had spurred President Roosevelt and Congress to approve the nation's first peacetime military draft in September 1940. By December 1941 America's military had grown to nearly 2.2 million soldiers, sailors, airmen, and Marines.

Economic deprivation among Mexican Americans made military service seem especially attractive. Drawn from all walks of life, poorly educated working-class Mexican Americans entered the armed forces in large numbers. However, inequitable draft deferment practices exposed more Mexican Americans to military service than Anglos. Kept off the local draft boards and denied deferments, Mexican Americans experienced high induction rates out of proportion to their numbers in the Selective Service registration. As a result, the number of Spanish-speaking draftees and voluntary enlistees rose precipitously. Notwithstanding the discrimination, for many Mexican Americans the military offered greater equality of opportunity than could be found in civilian life. More important, the war offered Mexican Americans an opportunity to demonstrate their patriotism. Mexican American soldiers, sailors, and Marines distinguished themselves in battle, risking death and maiming to prove their devotion to the United States and their right to be accepted as true equals.[3] Motivated by patriotism, as well as the opportunity for special job training, Mexican American women were enlisting in the various women's branches of the military services.

**Dora Ocampo Quesada, 1ˢᵗ Lt., A.A.F. Nurse Corps, 1944.**
CREDIT: "San Antonio Aviation Cadet Center, 1944." MP SPC 173: 621. Courtesy of the Ocampo Family Photograph Collection, Chicano Research Collection, Arizona State University Libraries, Department of Archives and Special Collections, Arizona State University, Tempe.

World War II contributed to the rapid rise of a Mexican American civil rights movement. It provided Mexican Americans with opportunities to realize the gap between the doctrine of democracy the United States advocated abroad and the racial practices maintained at home. The war heightened their assertiveness and desire to change their conditions. Increasingly dissatisfied with the barriers blocking their advancement, Mexican Americans began voicing their demands for equality more vigorously.

## MEXICAN AMERICANS ON THE EVE
## OF THE SECOND WORLD WAR

On the eve of World War II, a majority of Mexican Americans lived in rural areas. Incomes lagged well below national norms, and poverty was an enduring feature of life. Tens of thousands of Mexican Americans with their families continued to leave their homes to seek work as migratory farm laborers. The migrants moved from one crop to another, eking out an existence on cash incomes averaging between $350 to $400 per year, or about $1 a day. Constantly moving about following the crops, many migrants never had time or money to go to school. Their children did not attend school regularly and thus, like their parents, were caught in the trap of inadequate education and job skills.

Mexican Americans living in the central cities were concentrated in segregated, impoverished neighborhoods. The choice of residence for these low-skilled urban dwellers was limited by persistent housing discrimination. Inadequate health care and poor educational opportunities were also serious problems.

The need for labor and the call for men by the armed forces because of the national war emergency opened up opportunities for Mexican Americans. The nation's agricultural production increased between 1940 and 1943 through better utilization of farm workers, farm placement programs, longer hours of work, and mechanization. Owing to the absence of federal wage ceiling programs, as in other wage sectors, the earnings of farm workers increased fourfold. The labor of migratory workers was recognized as valuable to agriculture; indeed, along with black and white rural southerners, Mexican Americans fed America's armies, those of its allies, and a major portion of the world population. Soon, however, it was Mexican braceros, not Mexican Americans, who performed agricultural work. The federally sponsored contract labor program triggered the inflow of Mexicans into the United States. These foreign workers, in turn, pushed Mexican Americans out of farm work. The out-migration of thousands of Mexican Americans from rural areas to the cities, precipitated by the mobilization for war, continued.[4]

Texas remained the area of highest Mexican concentration in the nation with nearly one million. Race relations stayed virtually unchanged in both rural and urban areas, and the accompanying severe repression made life difficult for Tejanos. Spurred by the promise of job opportunities at Texas military installations, many migrated to San Antonio and Corpus Christi to seek war construction work. Yet despite the wartime job boom in Texas, less than 5 percent of the state's Mexicans held jobs in war-related industries because of labor market discrimination.[5]

By 1940, more than sixty thousand Tejanos migrated annually to urban northern industrial centers, drawn by the promise of well-paying jobs and the hope to wrest a better life from the cities. Anglo-Texan farmers deplored this migration but could do nothing to prevent the flight of Tejanos, who kept going northward. One in four Tejanos eventually left the migrant stream for the urban industrial north, where they were readily absorbed by the demand for war production work. Michigan's booming defense industries hired thousands of Mexican Americans, as did Chicago's meatpacking plants and steel mills. Job expansion in war production industries failed to reach more Mexican Americans because of skilled labor needs, racially exclusive defense contracts, and widespread discrimination in general. Spurred on by the possibility of employment, Mexican American migration to war production centers continued.[6]

Tejanos volunteered in great numbers for military service but also fell victim to the injustices of the all-Anglo local draft boards. Though the Tydings Amendment, passed in November 1942, exempted agricultural workers from the draft, it did not exempt Tejano farm laborers from military service. Nor could Tejanos claim deferment by reason of dependency. The discrimination practices had a cumulative effect. Soon complaints were being filed to the War Department from Texas that tens of thousands of the state's Spanish-speaking residents were unfairly being sent off to the war front at a higher rate than were Anglos. This was made clear by the disproportionate percentage of Tejano war casualties from South Texas, which, according to the reports, totaled nearly 75 percent.[7]

New Mexico's Spanish-speaking people made up over 40 percent of the state's population and, as Dr. George I. Sanchez wrote in his book *Forgotten People: A Study of New Mexicans,* which appeared in 1940, they suffered from widespread discrimination and economic deprivation. These factors had caused a host of social problems related to abject poverty. Migration continued to play an increasingly significant role in the lives of Spanish-speaking New Mexicans, as there were not enough jobs available. The acceleration of war production released over half of New Mexico's poor Spanish-speaking residents from agricultural serfdom, as did military service. One in four Spanish-speaking New Mexican males was serving in the military. Because of the unusually high jobless rates, the pace of migration of New Mexicans from rural communities to southwestern cities to work in vital war industries remained constant throughout the war years.[8]

Through the intervention of New Mexico's Democratic Senator Dennis Chavez, New Deal job training programs offered Mexican Americans many excellent opportunities and prepared them in numerous occupational fields previously closed to them. In New Mexico, thousands of Spanish-speaking New Mexicans entered war work as riveters, airplane mechanics, electric welders, and machinists and in airplane construction in defense plants in Arizona and California.[9] Still, the persistence of high unemployment remained the driving force behind high enlistment rates.

Spanish-speaking New Mexicans assumed a greater role in the war overseas because they were overrepresented as volunteer enlistees and draftees. As the lack of opportunities in the state forced many to volunteer for military service, Anglo-controlled draft boards kept the rate of Mexican American inductions high. The New Mexico National Guard provided money and training to New Mexicans. Prior to the war, to support their families, thousands of Spanish-speaking New Mexicans such as Miguel Encinias of Las Vegas joined the state's National Guard units; Encinias became a guardsman at age sixteen. The 200th Coast Artillery Regiment and the 120th Engineer Regiment were made up of local Spanish-speaking men from Las Vegas, Albuquerque, and Socorro. These state guard units were activated when the United States declared war on the Axis powers and were sent to defend the Philippine Islands. As a result, there were disproportionate numbers of Spanish-speaking New Mexicans at Bataan and Corregidor in the Philippines. The fighting at Bataan was fierce. Many soldiers were missing in action or were taken as prisoners of war.[10]

Despite their expressions of unity and patriotism, the Southwest's Mexican Americans were becoming extremely concerned about persistent racism and discrimination. Colorado's Mexican American population was concentrated in the San Luis and Arkansas River Valleys and in Denver. Many of Denver's thirty thousand Mexican Americans came to the city as part of the exodus of the state's Spanish-speaking residents from rural areas. All faced discrimination in employment, housing, and education. Less than 10 percent of the estimated five thousand Mexican Americans enrolled in Denver's public schools attended high school, as many dropped out to help their families or, ignored and neglected, were forced out before graduating. To offset the high dropout rate, federal programs prepared young Mexican Americans for employment in war industries. Lacking other economic opportunities, many Mexican American males joined the military prior to the national draft. Mexican Americans were likewise overrepresented among the draftees from Colorado.[11]

Because of anti-Mexican prejudice and resentment, Colorado's Mexican Americans experienced considerable difficulty in obtaining defense work; if they did get jobs, they were restricted to low-paid and unskilled work. Applicants with superior work experience or credentials were passed up in favor of less qualified Anglos for defense work. The state's Mexican Americans pushed the federal government into intervening on their behalf, but this brought about little improvement. At a time when fair employment laws were weak and unenforceable, employers followed a policy of token hiring of a few qualified Mexican Americans at entry-level positions to show their compliance with Executive Order 9346. The latter reiterated nondiscrimination policies in war industries and government. Issued on May 27, 1943, it established a new Fair Employment Practices Committee (FEPC) with broader jurisdiction than its predecessor, Executive Order 8002.[12]

Mexican Americans made up one-third of Arizona's population. Twelve thousand lived in Tucson and constituted nearly a fourth of its residents. Many worked for the Southern Pacific Railroad, Tucson's largest employer. They were keenly aware of the gap between the ideals of democracy generated by America's war effort and the flagrant discrimination of the railroads and the railway unions. Voluntary enlistments and the draft were drawing away thousands of railroad workers. With increasing transportation demands resulting from the movement of munitions and large numbers of American troops, the railroads suffered great manpower shortages. Yet in the midst of the critical labor shortage, the rail lines used the language barrier and faulty assumptions about incompetence as excuses to bar Mexicans (and blacks) from obtaining defense work. The employment demands ironically accounted for the entry of Mexican American women into railroad work. They filled jobs previously held by men now in uniform. Most of Arizona's Mexican Americans remained concentrated in agriculture or mining work.[13]

Copper was of critical need for bullets, artillery shells, and many other items. Therefore, mining, smelting, and refining facilities were expanded, and manpower needs increased. In southern Arizona's mining towns, Mexicans made up over half of the workforce. The CIO helped Mexican American copper miners obtain job parity and moved them out of dangerous blasting and loading jobs. Yet these copper miners failed to obtain full equal job opportunities above ground or underground. They filed hundreds of complaints about rampant discrimination directly with the FEPC and would have filed more charges of unequal treatment but feared retaliation. Mexicans in other Arizona war defense industries also complained of discrimination by employers and prejudice by white workers. As elsewhere in the Southwest, the federal government refused to hold hearings or make public the evidence of racial discrimination experienced by Mexican Americans, fearing it would jeopardize the Good Neighbor Policy. Specifically, the exposure of widespread discrimination would embarrass the

United States, a country based on the principles of democracy engaged in a fight against fascist racism. Mexican Americans were passed over in the military deferments issued to some miners, and they were drafted at higher rates because of the all-Anglo draft boards.[14]

In California, the war boom heightened Mexican American expectations about advancement in the workplace and in other areas of their lives. However, they first had to overcome the racial status quo. About 457,900 Mexicans resided in California, two-thirds of them American-born citizens, with the largest number in the southern part of the state. Regardless of U.S. citizenship status and class background, Mexicans experienced increasing discrimination. War work in aircraft and shipbuilding industries triggered the migration of Mexican Americans from the Southwest to the West Coast. They formed part of the huge migration to Los Angeles war industries that included more than fifty-four thousand blacks from the South. Hostility toward Mexican Americans and the increasing numbers of blacks aggravated the existing problem of segregation and discrimination in the city as the rising expectations of war work fueled racial tensions. These newcomers encountered stiff opposition from employers and some labor union local members, who vigorously opposed any kind of antidiscrimination measures in an effort to protect white privilege. Acute housing shortages, already severe before the war; a growing juvenile delinquency problem; and crime all contributed to the general social disorder.[15]

About 315,000 Mexicans lived in Los Angeles County, the highest concentration after Mexico City. Most were located in the metropolitan center, where they occupied substandard and overcrowded dwelling units. Discrimination, along with the city's race-based policies, substantially reduced their access to public and private housing. Builders shared in the blame for the city's housing problems. Along with real estate agents and banking institutions, they established and perpetuated segregated housing. The federal government encouraged this discrimination. The U.S. Housing Authority began building low-rent public housing units for defense workers. Some of this emergency housing was constructed in or near existing Mexican residential districts, but discriminatory housing allocations kept Mexicans and blacks out. Mexican American defense workers were moved out of their homes in residential areas that were targeted for federal housing programs but then were permitted into the newly built housing projects. This had come about through community pressure, mainly from the unions.[16] The main vehicle helping in this and other civil rights endeavors to eradicate bias against Mexican Americans was the *El Congreso del Pueblos de Habla Español,* or the Spanish-Speaking Peoples' Congress.

The Peoples' Congress was the idea of labor organizer Luisa Moreno so as to build progressive coalitions between Mexican American labor and civil rights organizations fighting for equality. To build as wide a front as possible, representatives of seventy-three organizations attended a meeting held in Los Angeles on December 4, 1938.[17] The following spring a broad coalition of more than 130 Spanish-speaking organizations were brought together to attend the first national convention of the Peoples' Congress in Los Angeles. Meetings addressed labor issues, education, health care, police violence, and citizenship and naturalization.

The resolutions adopted by the convention included support for the extension of the National Labor Relations Act to agricultural and domestic workers, relief to unemployed workers, minimum-wage revisions, affordable housing, and the defense of the Mexican immigrant from deportation and harassment by U.S. Immigration and the border patrol.[18]

A main concern of the Peoples' Congress was to spur the increase of Mexican membership in the CIO and to forge Mexican-CIO political ties. There was also a call for a Spanish-language newspaper to aid in organizing and lobbying Mexicans and to keep the CIO informed of incidents of discrimination against the Spanish-speaking population.[19] Because of the prominence of women in the Peoples' Congress, it cogently put forward the following resolution that addressed their concerns:

> Be it resolved: That the Congress carry out a program of organization and education of the Mexican women . . . that every Pro-Congress Club establish a Women's Committee . . . that it support and work for women's equality, so that she may receive equal wages, enjoy the same rights as men . . . and use her vote for the defense of the Mexican and Spanish American people, and of American democracy.[20]

The Peoples' Congress fully supported America's war effort against the Axis powers. In 1942, it organized a major rally in Los Angeles to show its support of national unity in the struggle to stop fascism.[21] In the same year, the Peoples' Congress became involved in combating police brutality against Mexican youths. With other community groups, it helped organize and raise money for the Sleepy Lagoon Defense Committee (SLDC) to help defend seventeen Mexican American youths wrongly convicted of murder.

The dramatic increase of the minority population of Los Angeles and heightened minority group assertiveness made Anglos feel threatened, and they acted to protect their advantages. The interplay of wartime tensions and racism would involve Mexican youths in the Sleepy Lagoon affair. The large number of defendants, the rush-to-judgment nature of the trials, and the prospect of multiple guilty verdicts transformed the case into one that attracted great public attention.

## JUSTICE DELAYED: THE SLEEPY LAGOON INCIDENT

In Los Angeles, young Mexican Americans were greatly affected by discrimination. Lawyer and civil rights activist Carey McWilliams observed that anywhere young Mexican Americans went outside of their neighborhoods they were faced with "signs, prohibitions, taboos, or restrictions. Learning of this 'iron curtain' [was] part of the education of every Mexican American boy in Los Angeles." Their unfair treatment at school made many bitter and rebellious. Police brutality and harassment that plagued Mexican youths had existed a very long time. The collective anger directed toward Mexican Americans erupted in the summer of 1942 as the Sleepy Lagoon murder case. Sleepy Lagoon was a popular Eastside reservoir used by young Mexican Americans who were barred because of race from using the city's public pools. On August 1, fighting broke out at a party at Sleepy Lagoon, where twenty-one-year-old José Diaz was killed. The legal consequences of this death would confirm that the Mexican Americans of the city of Los Angeles had no legal rights.[22]

The early 1940s was the "pachuco" era, marked by a distinctive style of dress with long coats, wide pants, and dangling watch chains that branded the zoot suiter. Los Angeles's newspapers presented an incredibly biased characterization of Mexicans by running a series of negative articles depicting pachuco gangs as a deviant subculture inclined toward crime and violence. Because the pachucos suffered from discrimination, their commonly shared experiences with overt hostility bound them together in nonconformity.[23] In light of discrimination and the anxiety over juvenile delinquency, the city's Anglos tended to judge all Mexican Americans by the lifestyle of the pachucos. In the minds of Anglos, all Mexicans were criminals. Public sentiment quickly turned against the pachucos following the Sleepy Lagoon case and its distorted depiction by the media. City police, in sweeps through the city's Spanish-speaking neighborhoods, arrested more than six hundred young men and shuttled them off to jail. A grand jury was impaneled to find out what had happened at Sleepy Lagoon. It indicted two dozen of these youths for conspiracy to commit murder and assault with a deadly weapon. Charges against two of the indicted Mexican Americans were dismissed for lack of evidence, though the remaining twenty-two defendants were tried en masse. During the court proceedings, the newspapers over and over again referred to the defendants disparagingly as "goons," and the prosecutors constantly portrayed them as bloodthirsty hoodlums. Openly biased testimony was admitted into the trial record. Access to justice became a central issue in the Sleepy Lagoon case, because only two of the defendants had attorneys.[24]

The SLDC stepped in and took up the fight for the defendants. Confident that justice would be served, the SLDC publicized the unfair trial, raised money to fund an appeal, and united activists from the Spanish Peoples' Congress, progressive unions, and others concerned with civil rights. In June 1943, hope turned to despair and then to anger when the all-white jury, in its "lynch verdict," found three of the Sleepy Lagoon defendants guilty of first-degree murder, nine others of second-degree murder, and five of assault. Five other defendants were acquitted. There was widespread outrage over the verdict, and the SLDC set out to vindicate the young men. In October 1944, all the convictions were reversed for lack of sufficient evidence. Sleepy Lagoon dramatized the social and economic injustices experienced by Mexican Americans. It energized the Mexican American civil rights movement in Los Angeles by bringing attention to these injustices. The Sleepy Lagoon trial marked the first time that Los Angeles Mexican Americans won a legal victory, yet it proved to be a harbinger of difficult days soon to follow. Overlapping the Sleepy Lagoon campaign was the fight to fend off printed, exaggerated rumors of a "Mexican crime wave" sweeping southern California. Steadily growing Anglo prejudice soon led to bitter racial clashes on the West Coast.[25]

Vivid testimony by a government representative to the Los Angeles Grand Jury investigating the Sleepy Lagoon murders reaffirmed arguments already made on behalf of the Sleepy Lagoon defendants: that it was destitution and congested slum conditions and not juvenile crime that set Mexican American youths apart.

**Sleepy Lagoon Murder Case Acquittal, 1944.**
CREDIT: uclamss_1387_b72_32252-2. Courtesy of UCLA Charles E. Young Research Library, Department of Special Collections.

The testimony further revealed that Spanish-speaking communities throughout the Southwest were complaining that right-wing groups in Mexico and Latin America were exploiting this collective sense of racial injustice, double standards, and subsequent demoralization of Mexicans to harm inter-American cooperation. In Los Angeles, increasing activity and agitation by the pro-Nazi sinarquistas exploited the long-standing bitter antagonisms to the hilt.[26]

## MEXICAN AMERICANS
## AND THE SINARQUISTA MENACE

The ranting of agitators from the *union nacional sinarquista* (USN) in Mexican communities in the Southwest and Midwest whipped up animosity against the United States, instigated provocations against the government of Mexico, and promoted civil disorder. The fascists paid special attention to the escalating racial discrimination against Mexicans.[27]

To achieve their goal of targeting Mexicans and Mexican Americans in the United States and recruiting them to its cause, the sinarquistas engendered Mexican pride to compensate for the intense discrimination they faced. The Mexican fascists established regional committees in Los Angeles and in El Paso and used these as propaganda agencies. Dating to 1937, the Los Angeles sinarquista regional committee had twenty municipal committees and planned to start others. Founded in 1938, the El Paso sinarquista regional committee had municipal committees in the lower Río Grande Valley, and other chapters were planned for Phoenix and Nogales, Arizona. The sinarquistas were also active in Indiana Harbor, Indiana; Chicago; and Milwaukee, Wisconsin.[28]

The sinarquistas attempted to sabotage Mexican American support of the war effort. Fascist agents told the Mexican people not to enlist in the Civilian Defense or the Red Cross nor purchase war bonds, because the "Mexican people have nothing to gain from an Allied victory."[29] Axis propaganda tried to turn World War II into a race war by stressing that Mexican Americans would be placed in the front lines to bear the brunt of the war, because the armies of Uncle Sam "are made up of colored peoples . . . considered as inferiors by the Anglo Saxons. . . . " This propaganda campaign was taking place at a time when the numbers of Mexican military inductees and enlistees was on the rise. The sinarquistas attacked the newly implemented Mexican contract labor program; as a way to undermine the morale and instill fear in the Mexican nationals, the sinarquistas told them they would be conscripted to serve in the U.S. Army.[30]

The sinarquista movement failed abysmally to sway Mexican Americans away from supporting the war because a rising spirit of American patriotism had taken hold in the Spanish-speaking community, and it was rallying behind the nation's war against the Axis powers. The sinarquistas underwent a quick decline in active membership owing to the decreasing number of native-born Mexicans but more because Mexican Americans showed strong antipathy for fascism. They recognized that Nazi doctrine preached the extermination not only of Jews but also of people of color.[31]

Still, long-standing prejudices continued to influence wartime treatment of Mexican Americans. Popular indignation, fueled by the war emergency and by negative media portrayals of Mexicans, created a climate ripe for conflict in Los Angeles. The city soon descended into chaos as Anglo soldiers and sailors, with civilians fighting alongside them, unleashed a wave of racial violence against the city's Spanish-speaking population—their target of hate.

## AMERICA'S WAR AT HOME:
## THE LOS ANGELES ZOOT SUIT RIOTS

Racial tensions in late spring 1943 exploded into violence with the war emergency in both military and civilian sectors of American society. The ten-day Los Angeles Zoot Suit Riot was one of these consequences of virulent wartime discrimination. Segments of the city's white population shared the belief that Mexican Americans somehow were not "true Americans" and thus could be physically attacked. From late May to early June 1943, several thousand Anglo servicemen and civilians in a violent free-for-all beat up Mexican American youths, creating mayhem in Los Angeles.

Police officers stationed downtown to maintain order did not stop the rampaging GIs' attack on Mexicans and blacks but watched and laughed. The police then roughed up these minority youths and arrested them on charges of rioting. The Los Angeles City Council did not actively attempt to stop the racial violence.

Rather, it ordered those Mexicans who had been beaten and rounded up arrested for vagrancy, and the Council later declared the wearing of zoot suits within the city limits a "public nuisance" and a misdemeanor.[32] For many Anglos who engaged in the rioting, it was a dress rehearsal for fighting the Japanese enemy in the Pacific.

The Zoot Suit Riot began after groups of white military personnel from the Chavez Ravine Training Base began engaging in a popular pastime: harassing and attacking Mexican Americans in the area. The ensuing violence was spawned by a media-driven climate of hate. Newspapers and radio broadcasts riled racist passions by depicting the city's Mexican Americans as a disloyal, criminal element. Prodding servicemen and civilians to attack Mexican Americans, the media perpetuated the ensuing bloody street battles between irate mobs of Anglo GIs and civilians and Mexicans defending themselves. Cars flooded into downtown Los Angeles filled with GIs who ran amuck attacking Mexicans. Roving mobs as large as one thousand swarmed the streets in search of Mexican American and African American zoot suiters to assault, dragging them off streetcars and out of movie theatres and beating them. Crowds quickly gathered to watch and whooped with approval as hapless Mexicans were beaten and had their clothes torn off. For six days the press demeaned the Mexican community by reporting the riots as scurrilous front-page news. Local authorities and military police finally made an effort to stop the fighting. Nonetheless, drunken soldiers and sailors continued to raid nightspots and movie theaters in their search for zoot suiters. The rioting reached a crescendo, and after another week of turmoil it stopped when the U.S. Navy declared the city of Los Angeles off limits to military personnel.[33] The riots had deeply angered and humiliated the city's Mexican community.

An investigation began into what sparked the rioting. Federal investigators reported that Los Angeles city officials could have prevented the local press from printing sensational news stories about Mexicans. They further stated that city police knew of the increasing friction between Anglos and Mexicans but did not move to quell the interracial discord. California governor Earl Warren launched his own investigation into the riots and found that lax police procedures had contributed to the racial outbreaks. Formed during the riots, the Los Angeles American Unity Committee issued a report stating that the riots were not caused by the alleged existence of a Mexican crime wave participated in by zoot suiters. It further blamed the city's newspapers in particular for criminalizing Mexicans and blacks and thus provoking a white backlash. This committee also pointed out that the city police department was complicit in the violence because it subjected both minority groups to a pattern of systematic repression.

By now, ugly and provocative stereotypes of Mexicans appeared regularly in the pages of the race-baiting newspapers: *The Examiner, The Herald Express,* and the *Los Angeles Times.* The articles instilled revulsion in Anglo readers by associating Mexican males and females with gang-related violence, sex crimes, and drugs. Media charged that this immoral and depraved behavior was at the root of the Mexican's high poverty rates, relief needs, and incarceration rates. The *Los Angeles Times* even attacked Mrs. Eleanor Roosevelt after she correctly "remarked in her column that the zoot suit riots were 'in the nature of race riots.'" The paper accused the president's wife of what they had already done: stirring racial discord by dubbing

Mexicans as "lazy, syphilitic, and tubercular." Los Angeles radio stations joined city newspapers in distorting information about Mexican juvenile delinquency. Concluding the opposite—that racial discrimination caused the rise of Mexican American juvenile delinquency—the Los Angeles American Unity Committee called for an interracial committee investigation of the Zoot Suit Riots.[34] This civil rights organization and others provided positive leadership and worked to improve police-Mexican relations. However, the Los Angeles Police Department refused to stop harassing and brutalizing Mexican Americans or locking them up as a means of social control. Poverty was the single greatest influence over Mexican Americans, and the armed services reduced this poverty by recruiting Mexican Americans to fight America's wars overseas.

Desperate to meet recruiting goals, local draft boards in Los Angeles became more lenient in assessing draft-age Mexican Americans, many of whom had been classified IV-F—unfit for service—and rejected by the army. As a result, this impoverished minority group soon came to constitute an unevenly balanced number of the city's draftees and suffered a greater number of casualties than their proportion of the population. By the final months of the war, Mexican Americans made up a fifth of the overseas casualties from Los Angeles, although they represented only 10 percent of its total population.[35]

Mexican Americans served with distinction overseas. Military service got them the status and prestige they were unable to acquire as civilians. However, they paid a tremendous price for it on the battlefield.

## MEXICAN AMERICAN GIS ON THE PACIFIC AND EUROPEAN WAR FRONTS

Upward of a half million Mexican Americans served in the armed forces, and they performed bravely in the military campaigns between 1941 and 1945 during World War II. They undertook difficult assignments because of the combination of patriotism, new opportunities, and pay. Texas contributed the greatest number of Mexican Americans to the war effort and to the high death and casualty tolls sustained overseas.

Mexican American GIs participated in bloody beach invasions in North Africa and on Sicily, and they took part in the Normandy invasion on D-day and subsequent land offenses that included the Battle of the Bulge and the final American drive into Germany. One of these GIs was Tejano migrant farm worker William R. Ornelas from Brownwood, Texas. He served as a medic with the 506th Parachute Infantry Regiment, 101st Airborne Division. Brothers Ralph and Philip Antuna of Chicago were also 101st paratroopers who engaged in fierce fighting in bitter cold weather with their outnumbered units at Noville, Foy, Neffe, Mageret, Longvilly, Fe'itsch, and other French villages. As soldiers and Marines, Mexican Americans took part in America's island-hopping campaign in the South Pacific in fighting against the Japanese Imperial Army.[36]

In 1940, the New Mexico National Guard units 200th and 515th Coast Artillery (antiaircraft) battalions were activated and sent to the Philippine Islands.

These two battalions were made up of Mexican American officers and enlisted men from New Mexico, Arizona, and Texas. The Japanese Imperial Navy's surprise attack on the American naval fleet at Pearl Harbor on December 7, 1941, forced America into war. Within days of this attack, Japanese forces struck and occupied American bases in the Philippines. General Douglas MacArthur moved the 200th and 515th Coast Artillery and the rest of his forces to the Bataan Peninsula west of Manila. Despite shortages of food and medical supplies, the outnumbered American units made a heroic three-month stand against the large, well-equipped invading Japanese forces.

The desperate fighting continued. Ammunition, rations, and medical supplies dwindled. Finally, on April 9, 1942, the half-starved Americans surrendered and became prisoners of war of the Japanese. These captured men were brutally mistreated in their twelve-day, sixty-five-mile "death march" from Bataan to the prison camps. Prisoners who collapsed during the march were shot or beaten to death. Others died of dysentery and starvation during their thirty-four-month captivity in the prison camps in Korea, China, and Japan. Many wound up in Japan as slave laborers in coal mines. Back home, the relatives and friends of the captured men formed the Bataan Relief Organization to get relief to the prisoners and flooded the federal government with letters demanding that it take responsibility for them. The Bataan death marchers were finally liberated.[37] As members of the U.S. Marine Corps, Mexican Americans participated in a pivotal event in the Pacific war—the Battle of Tarawa.

Part of the Gilbert Islands campaign, the Battle of Tarawa was one of the bloodiest battles of all time, one in which 1,056 Marines were killed and 2,292 Marines were wounded. It began on November 20, 1943, with heavy Japanese artillery and mortar bombardment of the landing boats filled with Marines. Then, in keeping with the Marine Corps' insistence on frontal attacks, thousands of Marines waded a thousand yards in chest-high water head on into the lethal Japanese machine gun and mortar fire. Marines in this first wave suffered 75 percent casualties. In the seventy-six hours of frontline battle, the Marines displayed tenacity and valor against the Japanese of the Seventh Special Landing Force who fought to their deaths. One of these brave Marines was gunnery sergeant Mike Valdez of California, who had served in the Corps since the 1930s. Before landing at Tarawa, Valdez had fought at Bougainville in the Solomon Islands. The battle-tested Marine next saw action at Iwo Jima, along with thirty thousand other Marines from the Third, Fourth, and Fifth Marine Divisions in February 1945. More than twenty-six thousand Marines were killed or wounded during the extremely fierce fighting, among them Sergeant Valdez, who received a serious leg wound. The Marines savaged the entrenched Japanese soldiers, and almost all of the twenty-one thousand enemy fighters were killed. Some died from ritual suicide. The 6,825 Marines killed in action were more than the total Allied casualties on D-day.[38]

Following two months in a hospital, Valdez landed with the Marines at Okinawa on April 1, 1945, in the largest amphibious landing of the Pacific war. Valdez won his second Purple Heart medal at Okinawa. "[Okinawa is] where their last stand was. It was kill or be killed. [The Japanese] put up a hell of a fight." The

**Marines Storm Tarawa, Gilbert Islands, 1943.**
CREDIT: WO Obie Newcomb, Jr., November 1943. National Archives Photo Number: 127-N-63458. (ww2_140.)

eighty-two-day battle saw ninety thousand Japanese killed and fifty thousand American casualties, twelve thousand of these men killed in action. Harold Gonsalves of Alameda, California, was one of the Marines killed at Okinawa. He dived on a grenade to save his fellow Marines. For this act of bravery, Gonsalves was awarded the Congressional Medal of Honor posthumously.[39] Mexican Americans soldiers in the Ninety-sixth and Twenty-seventh Infantry divisions also took part in the long, bloody Okinawa campaign. Alejandro R. Ruiz of Carlsbad, New Mexico, a member of the 165th Infantry Regiment, Twenty-seventh U.S. Infantry, was awarded the Congressional Medal of Honor for his bravery during a grenade and machine-gun-fire attack by the Japanese.[40]

The 158th Regimental Combat Team (RCT) of the U.S. Sixth Army Division, the Bushmasters, was an almost all Mexican American and Navajo Indian Arizona National Guard unit. During the Wakdi-Sarmi campaign in New Guinea (May 11–June 21, 1944) the GIs of the 158th RCT engaged in bitter jungle warfare against determined Japanese forces of the 223rd and 224th Infantry Regiments on Hill 225 and Lone Tree Hill. One of these Mexican American soldiers in the thick of the bloody fighting was William Todd of Nogales, Arizona. Todd later faced mass suicide attacks at the Battle of Slaughter Hill in Comifer, New Guinea, but survived to go and fight at Luzon in the Philippines. General MacArthur extolled the Bushmasters as "the greatest fighting combat team ever deployed for battle."[41]

The Twenty-fourth Infantry Division saw the most combat in World War II. This unit's Mexican American soldiers fought on the front lines against the Japanese in several crucial campaigns. Serving as a scout, Herman Saiz of Santa Rosa, New Mexico, took part in the landings at Hollandia, New Guinea, in the campaign to liberate Leyte and Luzon in the Philippine Islands. Saiz was wounded twice at Mindanao.[42]

The only all-Mexican American unit of World War II was Company E of the 141st Regiment of the Thirty-sixth Texas Infantry Division. It was made up of Tejanos from El Paso and the Southwest under the command of Captain Gabriel L. Navarrete. Company E engaged in almost a full year of combat in Italy, including the ill-planned and fatal Rapido River Crossing that was part of an Allied campaign to push the Germans out of the Italian peninsula and seize Rome. The Thirty-sixth Division came up directly against the strongly defended German Gustav Line overlooking the Rapido River from the north. German gunners rained shells with remarkable accuracy just outside the fast-shrinking American perimeter. After two desperate assaults, the Thirty-sixth Division was forced back. In forty-eight hours, the 141st and 143rd Infantry regiments suffered 2,128 casualties. One of the most bitter failures of the Allied forces during World War II, the attempted Rapido River Crossing became the subject of a Congressional inquiry.[43]

The 141st had been at Salerno, Alta Villa, San Pietro, and at the Rapido and had survived but suffered terrific casualties—1,126 dead, 5,000 wounded, and more than 500 missing in action. For their extended service and valor, the battered front-line infantrymen of the 141st earned thirty-one Distinguished Service Crosses, twelve Legion of Merits, 492 Silver Stars, eleven Soldier's Medals, and 1,685 Bronze Stars. Assigned to the Thirty-sixth's 143rd Infantry Regiment, Tony Aguilera of East Los Angeles, California, was part of the amphibious landing at Salerno, Italy, where he and his fellow soldiers were hit by German mortars, 88-mm cannon, and lethal machine gunfire. Aguilera was captured by the Germans and taken as a prisoner of war. He spent sixteen months at Stalag 2B in Germany.[44]

The Eighty-eighth Infantry Division, the Blue Devils, was a unit made up of draftees such as Tejano Jesús Leyva Armendaríz of El Paso, Texas, who served as a medic. The Eighty-eighth landed in North Africa in December 1943, entered into combat in Italy on March 4, 1944, and remained in combat longer than any other American division. The Eighty-eighth was the most effective division on the Italian front. The Thirtieth Infantry Regiment of the Third Infantry Division also had a large number of Mexican American soldiers, as did the 313th Infantry Regiment of the Seventy-ninth Infantry Division. On D-day, the latter unit landed at Utah Beach in Normandy and fought its way across France.[45]

Staff Sergeant Macario García of Sugarland, Texas, who served with the Fourth Infantry Division, was one of a dozen Mexican Americans who received the Medal of Honor for acts of bravery in World War II. The Tejano received the award for his actions on November 20, 1944, near Grosshau, Germany. Despite García's exemplary service fighting the Nazis in Europe, the Tejano returned to find that he faced the enemy of racism at home in Texas—the unchanging and callous discrimination of Anglo-Texans. In September 1945, shortly after returning from Washington, DC, where he was awarded the Medal of Honor by President Truman, García was refused service in a restaurant in Richmond, Texas, because he was Mexican. The reality of rampant discrimination likewise made life uncertain for the tens of thousands of returning Mexican American war veterans. Far from the integration that took place in foxholes, they found it difficult to obtain adequate health care or well-paying and meaningful work.[46]

As Mexican Americans fought and died in combat on the battlefields of Europe and the Pacific, Mexican Americans at home continued their struggle against the penalties of de facto second-class citizenship.

## MEXICAN AMERICANS FIGHT AGAINST DISCRIMINATION: THE CASE OF LOS ANGELES

On June 25, 1941, President Roosevelt issued his historic Executive Order 8803 banning discrimination in defense employment. The order established the President's Committee on Fair Employment Practices (FEPC) to deal with violations. Like African Americans, Mexican Americans had been the first fired during the Great Depression, and during the war years they were the last hired in defense work. Minorities found out that the wartime industries were an economic "white man's country." Many employers refused to hire Mexican workers, and Anglo workers resented Mexicans out of fear that they would potentially compete for their jobs, despite the major labor shortage caused by the war. The federal government had as its goal the elimination of racial discrimination in defense plants and the integration of minorities in war industries and industrial training programs. Federal officials soon realized that some means of local enforcement of antidiscrimination policies was necessary. Mexican Americans were being excluded from the drive to train skilled war workers. Other employers openly refused to hire Mexicans, using such excuses as that no trained Mexicans were available or that Mexicans were unable to perform skilled work. These were transparent excuses, for employers simply did not want to hire Mexicans. Insisting on a means of removing the barriers raised against their progress, Mexican Americans launched protests against employers who received government war contracts but refused to hire minorities, and they worked to tear down the racial order maintained in the workplace.

Early in the war, minorities were excluded from defense work, supposedly because labor shortages were not yet serious enough to make jobs available to them. Persistent and pervasive discrimination was the main factor in their exclusion from defense work, as employers and even organized labor repeatedly defied or circumvented the FEPC. Some industries made token hires to circumvent Executive Order 8802, which reaffirmed federal policies of full participation in the defense programs by all persons regardless of race, creed, color, or place of national origin. Employers feared that hiring minorities could disrupt war production by triggering hate strikes by Anglo workers increasingly made apprehensive about women playing a larger role in the war effort. Mexican American women defense workers, like their male counterparts, also faced prejudice. Those women who had taken government-sponsored job training courses were passed over in favor of less qualified Anglo women. Despite federal rules, Mexican American women defense workers were often placed in the worst job assignments as workplace racism continued throughout the war.[47]

Against staunch resistance by both employers and racist Anglo workers, the CIO, the progressive wing of the union movement, worked to open job training programs and jobs for minorities in war industries. As defense production peaked in 1943, minority placements increased two and a half times over the previous year in job training programs, in factory and military base construction, in steel production, and in aircraft and shipbuilding. Nearly fifty-eight thousand Mexican Americans were at work in war industries. Discrimination continued to dictate hiring policies; thousands of Mexicans could not find defense jobs, even though shortages were reported by many war industries. Labor unions and civil rights groups worked together to fully incorporate Mexican Americans into the war production effort; however, little of this effort lasted beyond the war years.[48]

## MEXICAN AMERICAN WOMEN WAR WORKERS

The war production boom provided new opportunities for Mexican American women. Although their take-home pay was less than what men received, their defense jobs paid at least twice as much as their previous jobs had. Many found employment in areas previously closed to them because of gender discrimination. Unlike Mexican American women prior to the war who were young, unmarried, and poor and procured employment as a temporary necessity, the majority of wartime women workers were middle-aged, married, came from middle class backgrounds, and took on employment as a patriotic act. Moreover, like other women, they had joined the job market before 1941. It was widely believed that Mexican American women didn't have the strength or aptitude for industrial work. They quickly demonstrated that they could effectively handle the job tasks in male-dominated industries. In the Midwest, thousands of Mexican women held jobs in defense plants in positions ranging from riveting to munitions. The government's failure to eliminate racial and gender discrimination in defense work caused Mexican American women war workers to endure much workplace discrimination; male workers regarded the presence of women as threats to their jobs, and many unions resisted the upgrading of women, just as they resisted the upgrading of minority males. Mexican American women were frequently assigned to work with black women, because Anglo women did not want to work with black females. Mexican American women were also hired in low-paying, dirty, and dangerous jobs in the place of African American women.[49]

In some munitions factories, Spanish-speaking female defense workers made up nearly 40 percent of the labor force producing bombs, fuses, bullets, shell casings, mines, grenades, rifles, machine guns, artillery, and rocket launchers for American soldiers, sailors, and Marines. They had been hired in lieu of African American women who were denied these dangerous job assignments. Those women in the steel mills performed the same jobs as the men in the rolling mills,

**Mexican Women Railroad Workers During World War II, 1944.**
CREDIT: "San Bernardino, California. Women suppliers who work at the Atchison, Topeka and Santa Fe Railroads." LC-USW3-022273-D. Courtesy of the Library of Congress.

the blast furnaces, and open hearths. Some were crane operators, welders, and riveters. Large numbers worked for the railroads. Chicago was a crossroads for transportation bringing military personnel for training and deployment overseas. The women held jobs as section hands and as roundhouse mechanics and train dispatchers; they loaded and unloaded war materials into and from boxcars and worked as waitresses in the railroad lunchrooms and as tellers in the ticket offices. During winter, women railroad workers cleared the tracks of snow and ice for the troop and supply trains. Mexican American women obtained jobs at meat companies as trimmers, butchers, and packers, in the production of C and K rations for the troops, and loading refrigeration cars.[50]

Women who had jobs in the shipyards were arc and gas welders, operated drill and punch presses, and made canvas tarpaulins and gun covers. Those employed in aircraft plants worked as riveters, sheet metal workers, machine operators, and assemblers. Most of the training Mexican American women war workers received occurred on the job. Others obtained vocational training through the War Manpower Commission's Bureau of Training.

Mexican American women put in 48-hour weeks as war production workers. The majority of this work required them to stand, and they were not given regular rest periods. They lacked hot food during hours on the job, sometimes having to eat out in the open, and lacked washroom and toilet facilities. Those with children had no day care. Twenty percent of the absentee rates was attributed to the demands made on working mothers with small children. After work they spent time waiting for transportation to get home and stood in long food lines. Rationing made shopping more time-consuming.[51]

Mexican American women's participation in civic and political affairs also increased. Tejana Concepción Alvarado of San Antonio, Texas, volunteered as an air raid warden and later served in the Women's Army Corps. Red Cross and civil defense branches were organized in practically every community in the country. Mexican women such as Julia Rodríguez of Laredo, Texas, rendered valuable services in their home communities by volunteering to do canteen work and providing entertainment and recreation for soldiers and sailors.[52] This service strengthened the morale of the women volunteers, as well as of the GIs. The women bonded together because many had husbands, fiancés, or other male relatives overseas fighting. They and their parents avidly followed news of Allied advances. Many dreaded the day when the fateful telegram arrived reporting that their loved one had been wounded or killed in combat overseas. Because of the high casualty rates among Mexican American servicemen, thousands of women were given a posthumous honor none aspired to—they became Gold Star Mothers.

One civilian war effort was the American Red Cross blood drive. The American Red Cross collected 13 million units of blood for use by the armed forces. War bond drives brought the government into movie theaters, schools, and factories. Americans could buy bonds on an installment plan through payroll deductions at their workplaces. An installment plan was also established for children. To conserve and produce more food, a Food for Victory campaign was launched. Mexican American female unionists took part in numerous war bond drives and other home-front activities. In southern California, Mexican American cannery workers raised over $21,000 for war bonds, increased their production in this industry's Food for Victory campaign, donated part of their wages to the Red Cross, and sponsored blood drives. In Texas, Spanish-speaking female war workers purchased war bonds and stamps, raised funds for the Red Cross, donated blood, took part in the United War Chest Campaign, and in campaigns by the CIO War Relief Committee. Mexican American women also plunged into political activism, namely voter registration, and enjoyed considerable success.[53]

California's Mexican American voting population greatly increased through wartime migration from other parts of the Southwest. Through the CIO Political Action Committee, Spanish-speaking workers mobilized into a broad coalition to reelect Franklin D. Roosevelt in 1944; Roosevelt's presidential campaign promoted economic and social security for Americans. Mexican Americans were being moved toward a more pluralistic understanding of goals in support of national unity. To halt prejudice against minorities and women was to insist on social equality and an expanded economy that provided well-paying jobs for all Americans. Mexican American women wanted jobs with good wages after the war, and this is the reason they joined the men in calling for a permanent FEPC. Women also wanted better housing, so they fought against exclusion from public housing. Eliminating police brutality was also a cause of concern and action.[54]

World War II might have provided new opportunities for work, but these were temporary; by the fall of 1944 signs appeared that the nation's booming war economy had crested. Many of the wartime gains in eliminating employment discrimination were lost as the nation moved closer to ending the war.[55] Following the war's conclusion, large numbers of Mexican American women stopped working and resumed their prewar routines.

## BRACEROS: THE MEXICAN CONTRACT LABOR PROGRAM BEGINS

In 1942, the need for men to fight overseas greatly reduced the number of farmworkers available for agriculture as American farmers expanded their production of crops for the war effort. The draft, voluntary enlistments, and defense work continued to draw away Mexican Americans from rural areas. Growers began seeking alternative sources of farm labor. Farm labor shortages led the United States to import contract labor from Mexico.[56]

In August 1942, Congress passed Public Law 45. Through an agreement with Mexico, the United States initiated a contract labor program that brought Mexican braceros as replacements for domestic migratory farmworkers. Under the bracero program, nearly a quarter million workers entered the United States to work mainly in the Southwest and Pacific Northwest. Intended as a temporary measure to fill a wartime labor shortage, the bracero program was extremely profitable for growers. Powerful farmers' associations took control of the bracero contracts and inflated labor needs, thwarted union efforts, and drove down wages for all farmworkers. Organized labor was reluctant to criticize the bracero program, though it recognized the program's potential impact on domestic farm workers. Mexican Americans added their voices to these protests. One of these was Ernesto Galarza, the articulate head of the Division of Labor and Social Information for the Pan American Union. Galarza and other Mexican American critics of the contract labor program were rightly concerned that discrimination against Mexican Americans would increase because of the added presence of Mexican nationals.[57]

The bracero program brought more than two hundred thousand Mexicans to the United States during the war. By the summer of 1945, braceros were working in agriculture or were assigned to work on railroads. Moreover, farmers continued to hire undocumented workers from Mexico. As predicted, the bracero agreement undermined the wages of domestic farm workers, who were fired and replaced by contract laborers from Mexico. The flood of contract laborers and undocumented workers would contribute to canceling almost all of the accomplishments of Mexican Americans on the labor and civil rights fronts.

## AMERICAN RACE RELATIONS AND MEXICAN AMERICANS

Fear and uncertainty gripped Mexican Americans as the United States committed itself to winning the war. Mass job openings and appeal to democratic ideals were contradicted by protracted discrimination against Mexican Americans. They could not count on the federal government to take an active hand in matters that concerned them. President Roosevelt had responded reluctantly to the FEPC, and even then the lack of enforcement criteria limited its effectiveness. To address the plight of Mexican Americans through government intervention not only would further expose persistent and pervasive racism in America but also jeopardize domestic and international relations. The latter included hemispheric solidarity with Latin America through the Good Neighbor Policy against the Axis powers and access to the region's raw materials, including bracero workers.

Achievement of the Good Neighbor Policy also depended on the success of the "good neighbor" policy at home with Mexican Americans. Despite progress, discrimination in employment, housing, education, recreation, and military service was widespread throughout the United States. Mexican American civil rights leaders expressed concern about the status of Mexican Americans in school, work, and labor unions; about residential restrictions made by law and housing covenants; about their limited access to organizations; and about the ordinary services frequently denied them. Discrimination against Mexican Americans in Texas remained virulent. According to the rules of racial etiquette in Texas, under no circumstances could a Mexican assume an air of equality with Anglos. Parks, entertainment centers, and other public places excluded Mexicans, if not by law then by custom. Signs posted that read "Mexicans and dogs not allowed" reminded Mexicans that their patronage was not wanted. In some communities Mexicans could not attend theaters and movie houses unless they sat upstairs. This segregation practice in her hometown of Stockton, Texas, vexed Elena Peña. The young Tejana went to the town movie theatre, bought her ticket, and sat in Anglo-designated seating. Movie theater ushers forcibly removed Peña from her seat. When she told her father what had happened to her, he loaded his gun and proceeded to the theater and at gunpoint forced the manager to shut down the theater. It remained closed for six months.[58]

Aware of the serious implications of racism for America's war effort and committed to multiracial democracy, Mexican American scholars George Sánchez, Arturo Campa, and Ernesto Galarza wrote on the conditions of the Spanish-speaking people, challenging the discrimination against them in education, employment, and political representation. Joining the campaign of national unity popularized through the slogan "Americans All," these three Mexican Americans called for cooperation and understanding between Anglo-Americans and Mexican Americans, in addition to recognition of the economic and cultural ties between Latin America and the United States. Elsewhere, Mexican American civil rights activists participated in national conferences to influence federal legislative action for civil rights for Mexican Americans.

San Antonio lawyer Alonso Perales and fellow attorney Manuel Gonzales, with other LULAC members, began to fight against job discrimination on behalf of "Latin Americans." This newly adapted term of self-identification was believed less pejorative than the label Mexican. Their efforts also focused on filing discrimination cases for the FEPC and advocating the creation of defense jobs in Texas. In addition to writing articles to bring national attention to racial injustice against Mexican Americans, Alonso Perales helped introduce a bill in the Texas State legislature prohibiting discrimination against "Caucasians." By reasserting their identities as white, Perales, along with other Tejanos, pursued a bill guaranteeing "Caucasians" equal access to public accommodations. The government of Mexico and organizations in both Mexico and Texas supported this plan. America's wartime demand for cheap labor from Mexico was also a factor that led to the passage of the Caucasian Race-Equal Privileges resolution in 1943. The Caucasian Race-Equal Privileges resolution did not have the force of law, but it demonstrated how the Good Neighbor Policy and American race relations shaped the Mexican American civil rights campaign in wartime Texas.[59]

Because of extensive prejudice, Mexican American servicemen in many situations were first Mexican, then American. Like African American and Japanese American GIs, Mexican American soldiers and sailors experienced maltreatment by civil authorities and Anglo townspeople, though especially in Texas by small businessmen who refused to extend them service. Mexican American GIs such as Macario García found out that "equal rights" in restaurants meant the right to refuse them service. To Anglo-Texans, violence and prejudice were appropriate responses to Mexican American GIs, who were overstepping acceptable social boundaries because they had had their horizons widened during their service in the U.S. military and expected more equitable treatment at home.

Draft officials routinely classified every Mexican American as "Mexican." A small group of Mexican Americans steadfastly refused to accept that designation. Their defiance sparked a controversy that involved state and national draft authorities and the War Department. The Mexican American challenge ultimately made the Selective Service System change this policy. Other recommendations included stationing Spanish-speaking noncommissioned officers at military centers with Spanish-speaking enlistees; recruiting Mexican Americans into the Red Cross, the United Service Organizations (USO), and other agencies working with Spanish-speaking servicemen; and producing bilingual information on issues of concern to Mexican American servicemen and their families. The Office of the Coordinator of Inter-American Affairs also published a pamphlet on the contribution of America's Spanish-speaking minorities to the war effort to bolster morale.[60]

## CONCLUSION

When America entered World War II, the Mexican American people of the United States still had pressing concerns about whether New Deal relief would bolster their standard of living. The war raised Mexican Americans' hopes and expectations, and the war emergency opened new opportunities for them. They got a boost from A. Phillip Randolph's march on Washington, intended to pressure federal action to secure employment opportunities for African Americans in defense industries. Mexican Americans wanted to show loyalty by full participation in the war effort, and tens of thousands entered the armed forces following Japan's attack on Pearl Harbor in 1941. Others left home for high-paying jobs in defense industries. The mass exodus by Mexican Americans to enlist in the war and engage in war work brought unprecedented changes in their lives. The workers' shortage led to emergency training programs, and American labor unions assumed responsibility for eliminating discriminatory barriers maintained by labor. Mexican Americans saw heavy combat in Europe and in the war in the Pacific. Both civilians and soldiers earned more than they were able to generally and had more contact with Anglos and African Americans than had been the case previously.

Yet there was a wide sense of dissatisfaction that war conditions had not brought equality. Mexican Americans were excluded from the high-paying defense jobs. In this regard, Executive Order 8802 spurred Mexican Americans to fight discrimination in employment. Although without any real influence, the FEPC did advance the employment of Mexican Americans in war industries. It was the unions, the Mexican Americans' only recourse against injustice, that secured good jobs for them.

Whether single or married, many Mexican American women went to work. A large number had been working before the war. Seeing this as an opportunity to make a claim on rights as American citizens long denied to them, women as working-class Mexican Americans exhibited greater militancy for civil rights than did Mexican Americans as a whole. Mexican American labor unionism became part of a wider campaign for civil rights after World War II. Discriminatory employment practices and housing shortages were addressed with the help of labor unions and the Congress of Spanish-Speaking Peoples. Mexican American women were not able to end workplace discrimination and housing problems during the war, and although they performed well in jobs traditionally held by men, they were forced to surrender their jobs to returning soldiers at war's end. The numerous contributions of Mexican American women to America's war effort included boosting the morale of Mexican American soldiers, sailors, and Marines on furlough through volunteer work for Red Cross chapters and the USO. Like their Anglo counterparts, they were concerned over family separations necessitated by war.

Widespread inequality remained a barrier to Mexican American citizens rallying to the defense of the nation. Mexican Americans demanded fair access to jobs in the nation's factories, decent housing, and an end to mistreatment by police. Poverty and the lack of job opportunities outside of agriculture pushed up military volunteer rates among Mexican Americans. Because all-Anglo local Selective Service boards made the decision on which men went into military service or were deferred for occupational reasons, draft rates for Mexican Americans remained very high. The vast majority of the Mexican American inductees and enlistees were poor, uneducated blue-collar workers or unemployed. The high percentage of Mexican American voluntary enlistments undeniably evidenced their patriotism and their desire to support the war effort. Most of these men were drafted or were induced to enlist by a lack of educational or economic options at home.[61]

The Sleepy Lagoon case demonstrated that Mexicans were denied equal protection under the law. The Zoot Suit Riots had a dramatic effect on the lives of the Mexican American people. Prodded by America's war against Nazism and its adherents' claim to racial superiority and by federal intervention in combating racial injustice at home, Mexican Americans demanded full rights as American citizens. Those who were most concerned with the ideas of equality were driven to increased militancy.

The federal government championed racial equality for Mexican Americans for the same reasons it championed it for African Americans. Mexican Americans were necessary for large-scale wartime economic and political mobilization. The nation's leaders were sensitive to international questioning of America's commitment to equality and democratic ideals and to foreign-inspired agitation among Mexican Americans and political mobilization by Mexican Americans who pressured leaders to push for reforms.

One of the reforms called for concerned the temporary importation of contract labor from Mexico, the bracero program. The Agriculture Department was in charge of the wartime program, and it helped to organize employer associations to handle the contract laborers. This government intervention had the effect of strengthening the power of growers and their voice in government at the expense of farmworkers, many of them Mexican Americans. The bracero program would be revived at the end of the war and expanded to the entire United States, displacing domestic farmworkers in its wake.

Whether they remained in the cities or returned to rural areas, the Mexican American ex-servicemen confronted an atmosphere of increased racial tensions. Some of these Mexican American war heroes were similarly beaten or thrown out of movie theaters and restaurants because Anglos did not like Mexicans. Rapid industrial reconversion and mobilization of the military forces at the war's end would not bode well for employment prospects. Along with African Americans, Mexican American war veterans quickly discovered that competition for too few jobs, too little housing, and scant food and clothing often became racial competition with Anglos, who claimed that minorities enjoyed better treatment and more rights than they did. Lack of legal protection against substandard wages, the virtual absence of unionization among farmworkers, and the continuation of the bracero program increased competition for farmwork and depressed wages as well.

The Mexican American community suffered from divided leadership until World War II dissolved acquiescence. Because exposure to a larger world transformed the Mexican American World War II veterans' understanding of their future, they would lead the fight for citizenship in the postwar years. Many war veterans used their military service as a basis to argue for further rights as American citizens. Although workplace discrimination and restrictive housing covenants existed, many Mexican Americans were active in breaking down barriers that compromised their quest for equality. Their work in securing access to and training for jobs in defense plants and fair housing opened opportunities for Mexican Americans and helped lay the groundwork for the postwar civil rights movement.

Profound changes had taken place in the lives of Mexican Americans during the World War II years and continued in the decade that followed. Encouraged by a new spirit of ethnic consciousness and hard-won patriotism, Mexican Americans began demanding more rights for the simple reason that they wanted to be treated as American citizens.

## NOTES

1. Richard Polenberg, *War and Society: The United States, 1941–1945* (New York: Lippincott, 1972), 99–100, 113; David Kryder, *Divided Arsenal: Race and the American State During World War II* (New York: Cambridge University Press, 2000), 208, 216,

256–257; Robert H. Zieger, *The CIO, 1935–1955* (Chapel Hill: University of North Carolina Press, 1995), 149; Valdés, *Barrios Norteños,* 134.

2. Memorandum on a proposal to coordinate activities and programs relating to Spanish-speaking minorities in the United States, November 20, 1942, box 47, Gardner Jackson Papers, Franklin Delano Roosevelt Library, Hyde Park, New York, 1–2.

3. Gerald Nash, *The American West Transformed: The Impact of the Second World War* (Bloomington: Indiana University Press, 1985), 107; "Fair Employment Practices Act Hearings," in *Are We Good Neighbors?* Alonso S. Perales, comp. (New York: Arno Press, 1974 [1948]), 93; Carey McWilliams, "The Forgotten Mexican," *Common Ground* 3 (Spring 1943): 65; Polenberg, *War and Society,* 129.

4. Jacob J. Kaufmann, "Farm Labor During World War II," *Journal of Economics* 13, no. 1, part I (February 1949): 132; Merl E. Reed, "The FEPC and the Federal Agencies in the South," *Journal of Negro History* 65, no. 1 (Winter 1980): 54.

5. McWilliams, "The Forgotten Mexican," 69; Malcolm Ross, *All Manner of Men* (New York: Greenwood Press, 1948), 269; "Statement of Dr. Carlos E. Castañeda, Regional Director, Fair Employment Practice Committee, Region 10, San Antonio, Texas," in Perales, *Are We Good Neighbors?,* 102.

6. Vargas, *Labor Rights Are Civil Rights,* 211–212; Montejano, *Anglos and Mexicans in the Making of Texas,* 219; Valdés, *Barrios Norteños,* 129–131, 136–137, 140–142, 149; Kryder, *Divided Arsenal,* 102–103, 107, 217.

7. Vargas, *Labor Rights Are Civil Rights,* 208, 210; David M. Kennedy, *Freedom from Fear: The American People in Depression and War, 1929–1945* (New York: Oxford University Press, 1999), 633–634; Julie Leininger Pycior, *LBJ and Mexican Americans: The Paradox of Power* (Austin: University of Texas Press, 1997), 53.

8. Vargas, *Labor Rights Are Civil Rights,* 214; Deutsch, *No Separate Refuge,* 205; McWilliams, "The Forgotten Mexican," 71–73, 75; Charles P. Loomis, "Wartime Migration from the Rural Spanish Speaking Villages of New Mexico," *Rural Sociology* 7 (December 1942): 386–390.

9. Vargas, *Labor Rights Are Civil Rights,* 216.

10. Ibid., 215; Judith Boyce, ed., *Essays in Twentieth Century New Mexican History* (Albuquerque: University of New Mexico Press, 1986), 8; Raúl Morín, *Among the Valiant: Mexican Americans in World War II and Korea* (Los Angeles: Borden, 1963), 23. Miguel Encinias later became a pilot and an officer. He was shot down over a German airbase in northern Italy and spent fifteen months in a German prisoner of war camp near the Polish border on the Baltic Sea. Interview with Miguel Encinias, U.S. Latino and Latina WWII Oral History Project, Nettie Lee Benson Latin American Collection, University of Texas at Austin.

11. Vargas, *Labor Rights Are Civil Rights,* 218; Barron B. Beshoar, "Report from the Mountain States," *Common Ground* 4 (Spring 1944): 24.

12. Vargas, *Labor Rights Are Civil Rights,* 219–220; Nash, *The American West Transformed,* 109; Beshoar, "Report from the Mountain States," 25–27; Polenberg, *War and Society,* 119; John Morton Blum, *V Was for Victory* (New York: Harcourt Brace Jovanovich, 1976), 212.

13. Vargas, *Labor Rights Are Civil Rights,* 220–223; Polenberg, *War and Society,* 115; Blum, *V Was for Victory,* 213; Clete Daniel, *Chicano Workers and the Politics of Fairness: The FEPC in the Southwest, 1941–1945* (Austin: University of Texas Press, 1992), 107–109; Christine Marín, "La Asociacion Hispano-Americana de Madres y Esposas: Tucson's Mexican American Women In World War II," in *Renato Rosaldo Lecture*

*Series 1: 1983–1984,* ed. Ignacio M. García et al. (Tucson: University of Arizona, 1985), 7, 11.

14. Vargas, *Labor Rights Are Civil Rights,* 222–223; Daniel, *Chicano Workers and the Politics of Fairness,* 63, 68–70, 96, 164; Ross, *All Manner of Men,* 265; Jonathan D. Rosenbaum, *Copper Crucible: How the Arizona Miners' Strike of 1983 Recast Labor-Management Relations in America* (New York: ILR Press, 1988), 31; "Statement of Dr. Carlos E. Castañeda," 99.

15. Vargas, *Labor Rights Are Civil Rights,* 224; Nash, *The American West Transformed,* 107–108; González, *Labor and Community,* 56; Zieger, *CIO, 1935–1955,* 149; Kryder, *Divided Arsenal,* 103, 106, 109.

16. Vargas, *Labor Rights Are Civil Rights,* 224–226; Nash, *The American West Transformed,* 107–109; Zieger, *CIO, 1935–1955,* 158; David Oberweiser, Jr., "The CIO: Vanguard for Civil Rights in Southern California, 1940–46," in *American Labor in the Era of World War II,* ed. Sally M. Miller and Daniel A. Cornford (Westport, CT: Praeger, 1995), 207; Luis Leobardo Arroyo, "Chicano Participation in Organized Labor: The CIO in Los Angeles, 1938–1950, An Extended Research Note," *Aztlán* 6, no. 2 (Summer 1975): 294.

17. García, *Mexican Americans,* 147–148; Sánchez, *Becoming Mexican American,* 245.

18. Mario T. García, *Memories of Chicano History: The Life and Narrative of Bert Corona* (Berkeley: University of California Press, 1994), 110–113; Sánchez, *Becoming Mexican American,* 245–246; Gutiérrez, *Walls and Mirrors,* 111–113; Albert Camarillo, *Chicanos in California: A History of Mexican Americans in California* (San Francisco: Boyd & Fisher, 1984), 63.

19. García, *Mexican Americans,* 151; García, *Memories of Chicano History,* 111–114; Camarillo, *Chicanos in California* 63.

20. Sánchez, *Becoming Mexican American,* 247–248; García, *Memories of Chicano History,* 111–112.

21. García, *Mexican Americans,* 151; García, *Memories of Chicano History,* 111, 115–116; Sánchez, *Becoming Mexican American,* 248.

22. Vargas, *Labor Rights Are Civil Rights,* 219; McWilliams, *North from Mexico,* 216; McWilliams, "The Forgotten Mexican," 70.

23. McWilliams, *North from Mexico,* 217.

24. Vargas, *Labor Rights Are Civil Rights,* 192–193.

25. Michael Denning, *The Cultural Front: The Laboring of American Culture in the Twentieth Century* (New York: Verso Books, 1997), 18; Frank P. Barajas, "The Defense Committees of Sleepy Lagoon: A Convergent Struggle Against Fascism, 1942–1944," *Aztlán* 31, no. 1 (2006): 33–62.

26. Vargas, *Labor Rights Are Civil Rights,* 193.

27. Allan Chase, *Falange: The Axis Secret Army in the Americas* (New York: Putnam, 1943), 167.

28. Vargas, *Labor Rights Are Civil Rights,* 188–189.

29. Ibid., 196.

30. Ibid.; Chase, *Falange,* 162, 174–175.

31. Vargas, *Labor Rights Are Civil Rights,* 197–198; Chase, *Falange,* 163; García, *Memories of Chicano History,* 116; Gutiérrez, *Walls and Mirrors,* 114; Camarillo, *Chicanos in California,* 64.

32. Vargas, *Labor Rights Are Civil Rights,* 193; Harvard Sitkoff, "Racial Militancy and Interracial Violence in the Second World War," *Journal of American History* 58, no. 3 (December 1971): 671.

33. Vargas, *Labor Rights Are Civil Rights,* 229; Kryder, *Divided Arsenal,* 229; Polenberg, *War and Society,* 129–130; Blum, *V Was for Victory,* 205; Sitkoff, "Racial Militancy and Interracial Violence," 671; Ruiz, *From Out of the Shadows,* 84.

34. Vargas, *Labor Rights Are Civil Rights,* 230; Blum, *V Was for Victory,* 205–206; Ruiz, *From Out of the Shadows,* 83; McWilliams, *North from Mexico,* 230.

35. Vargas, *Labor Rights Are Civil Rights,* 213–232; Camarillo, *Chicanos in California,* 72.

36. Interview with William R. Ornelas and Ralph and Philip Antuna, U.S. Latino and Latina WWII Oral History Project, Nettie Lee Benson Latin American Collection, University of Texas at Austin.

37. Gordon N. Hatch, *American Ex-Prisoners of War: 50-Year Commemorative History 3* (Paducah, KY: Turner, 1990), 9. J. L. Kunkle tells the story of Albuquerque native Carlos Montoya, a survivor of the infamous Bataan death march and years in Japanese prison camps, in his book *Carlos: A Tale of Survival* (Parker, CO: Outskirts Press, 2007).

38. John Wukovits, *One Square Mile of Hell: The Battle for Tarawa* (New York: NAL Caliber, 2006); Gary Warth, "Latinos Have Long Tradition of Service in U.S. Military," *North County Times,* May 26, 2007.

39. Warth, "Latinos Have Long Tradition of Service."

40. Scholars note that half of the Medals of Honor were for self-sacrifice on the part of soldiers and Marines in smothering enemy grenades. Craig Cameron, *American Samurai: Myth and Imagination in the Conduct of Battle in the First Marine Division 1941–1951* (New York: Cambridge University Press, 2002), 185.

41. Kevin C. Holzimmer, "Walter Krueger, Douglas MacArthur, and the Pacific War: The Wakdi-Sarmi Campaign as a Case Study," *Journal of Military History* 59, no. 4 (October 1995): 671–680; interview with William Todd, U.S. Latino and Latina WWII Oral History Project, Nettie Lee Benson Latin American Collection, University of Texas at Austin.

42. Interview with Herman Saiz, U.S. Latino and Latina WWII Oral History Project, Nettie Lee Benson Latin American Collection, University of Texas at Austin.

43. On the Rapido River crossing, see Martin Blumenson, *Bloody River: The Real Tragedy of the Rapido* (College Station: Texas A & M University Press, 1970), and Robert L. Wagner, *The Texas Army: A History of the 36th Division in the Italian Campaign* (Austin: University of Texas Press, 1972).

44. Interview with Tony Aguilera, U.S. Latino and Latina WWII Oral History Project, Nettie Lee Benson Latin American Collection, University of Texas at Austin.

45. Interview with Jesus Leyva Armendaríz, U.S. Latino and Latina WWII Oral History Project, Nettie Lee Benson Latin American Collection, University of Texas at Austin. On the history of the Eighty-eighth Infantry Division, see John Sloan, *Draftee Division: The 88th Infantry Division in World War II* (Lexington: University Press of Kentucky, 1986).

46. *Houston Post,* September 7, 1945; *New York Times,* August 9, 1945; Ignacio M. García, *Hector P. García: In Relentless Pursuit of Justice* (Houston, TX: Arte Publico Press, 2002), 76–86.

47. Vargas, *Labor Rights Are Civil Rights,* 232–233; Kryder, *Divided Arsenal,* 103; Ruiz, *Cannery Women, Cannery Lives,* 120; Polenberg, *War and Society,* 116; Camarillo, *Chicanos in California,* 72; Nash, *The American West Transformed,* 109.

48. Vargas, *Labor Rights Are Civil Rights,* 233; Kryder, *Divided Arsenal,* 108–109; Ruiz, *From Out of the Shadows,* 82.

49. Vargas, *Labor Rights Are Civil Rights,* 212–213; William H. Chafe, *The American Woman: Her Changing Social, Economic, and Political Role, 1920–1970* (New York: Oxford University Press, 1972), 195, 246; Richard A. Santillán, "Rosita the Riveter: Midwest Mexican

American Women During World War II," in *Perspectives in Mexican American Studies: 2–Mexicans in the Midwest,* ed. Juan Garcia (Tucson: The Department of Mexican American & Raza Studies, 1989), 115.

50. Vargas, *Labor Rights Are Civil Rights,* 213; Santillán, "Rosita the Riveter, 116.

51. Vargas, *Labor Rights Are Civil Rights,* 213–214.

52. Interview with Concepción Alvarado, U.S. Latino & Latina WWII Oral History Project, Nettie Lee Benson Latin American Collection, University of Texas at Austin; Interview with Julia Rodriguez, U.S. Latino & Latina WWII Oral History Project, Nettie Lee Benson Latin American Collection, University of Texas at Austin.

53. Vargas, *Labor Rights Are Civil Rights,* 214; Zieger, *CIO, 1935–1955,* 149; Nelson Lichtenstein, *Labor's War at Home: The CIO in World War II* (New York: Cambridge University Press, 1982), 74; Ruiz, *Cannery Women, Cannery Lives,* 81–82.

54. Zieger, *CIO, 1935–1955,* 181, 186; Arroyo, "Chicano Participation in Organized Labor," 296–297.

55. Vargas, *Labor Rights Are Civil Rights,* 233–234.

56. Ibid., 238; Cindy Hahamovitch, *The Fruits of Their Labor: Atlantic Coast Farmworkers and the Making of Migrant Poverty, 1870–1945* (Chapel Hill: University of North Carolina Press, 1997), 168–169.

57. Vargas, *Labor Rights Are Civil Rights,* 241–243; Kaplowitz, *LULAC,* 40–43; Ernesto Galarza, *Merchants of Labor: The Bracero Story* (Santa Barbara, CA: McNally & Loftin, 1964), 52; Ruiz, *Cannery Women, Cannery Lives,* 55–56.

58. Interview with Elena Peña Gallego, U.S. Latino and Latina WWII Oral History Project, Nettie Lee Benson Latin American Collection, University of Texas at Austin.

59. Thomas A. Guglielmo, "Fighting for Caucasian Rights: Mexicans, Mexican Americans and the Transnational Struggle for Civil Rights in World War II Texas," *Journal of American History* 92, no. 4 (2006): 1212–1237.

60. Vargas, *Labor Rights Are Civil Rights,* 250–251.

61. Ibid., 250.

## CHAPTER 9

# Mexican Americans in the Postwar Years

### 1946–1963

The Mexican American World War II veterans who returned home exhibited newfound dignity and expected to be treated with respect as full-fledged American citizens. They worked to gain access to decent jobs and educational opportunities and wanted the resources to purchase homes and life insurance. Demanding a just share of the benefits of equality, rights, and privileges, the willingness of Mexican Americans to stand up and fight not only for themselves but also for their communities helped define a new era of civil rights activism.[1]

The genesis of this process of change was in the late 1930s and 1940s, when Mexican Americans pushed unions and industry to be more inclusive and when they worked within their own groups and in coalition with other progressive organizations in fighting for civil rights more broadly.[2] From these experiences Mexican Americans gained a political voice, and they forged a movement that focused on economic rights rather than legalistic civil rights. The emergent cold war anti-Communism placed constraints on these Mexican Americans, some of whom fell victim to McCarthyism.

Labor organizer Ernesto Galarza waged an almost single-handed fight against California agribusiness and its supportive government regulatory agencies. The infinite supply of Mexican braceros and *mojados* (undocumented Mexican workers) provided growers with both cheap labor and an effective strikebreaking weapon. Though unsuccessful in his organizing drive, Galarza directed the nation's attention to the problems arising from the bracero program. Mexican American miners in southeastern New Mexico made a lasting impression on Mexican American civil rights at this time. In 1950, Local 890 of the International Union of Mine, Mill, and Smelters Workers (Mine Mill) waged a heroic struggle for over fifteen months to secure a satisfactory strike settlement despite the fierce red baiting used to scare the miners and destroy the strike. Women became the leaders of the strike because they saw the strike as their battle. They were going to go down fighting to the bitter end rather than submit to a compromise, for they saw themselves as defenders of their families and communities, as well as fighters for social justice.

As Mexican Americans used their collective strength as citizens and voters to fight for full equality at the local and national levels, others moved their politics and activism beyond the domestic struggle for civil rights to the international arena. They advanced their views through the National Association of Mexican Americans (ANMA), which set the example for the politically radical and racially nationalistic Chicano organizations that emerged twenty years later.[3]

McCarthyism brought ANMA and other Mexican American progressive political activism and its causes to an abrupt end. Moderate elements stepped in to fill the vacuum and reconfigured the Mexican American rights movement. Distancing themselves from fellow activists with Communist ties, they embraced a gradualist agenda in the matter of racial equality. The goal of the Community Service Organization (CSO) was to empower Mexican Americans as loyal American citizens through mass grassroots activism focused in neighborhoods. The CSO pressed for voter registration, open housing, and ending neighborhood displacement through urban development; it fought school segregation and protested police brutality. The idea of assimilation animated the conservative elements of the new movement that pursued legal equality and protection in the goal to gain recognition as American citizens. Race affected the criteria for membership in the Mexican American middle class. Some of these group leaders, in their rush for respectability, distanced themselves from the Mexican American lower classes.[4]

The Mexican American civil rights movement began as a coalition and alliance with labor, but it fell victim to the ravages of the unfolding Red Scare: McCarthyism. The most militant Mexican Americans became vulnerable for their political views and their associations, whereas moderate Mexican Americans were intimidated into silence and obedience.[5] Nor was this the end to the repression of the Mexican American community.

Periodic mass expulsions and roundups of Mexican residents have been the rule in modern United States history. In 1954 Mexican Americans were confronted with authenticating their American citizenship status in the face of intimidation and terror. Government officials used the anti-Communist hysteria fomented by them to launch a large-scale deportation raid code-named Operation Wetback. Because the threat was labeled "foreign," the raids fed racism by the deliberate targeting of all those considered "Mexican" regardless of their citizenship. Operation Wetback resulted in gross violations of civil and human rights—government agents conducted searches without warrants and denied detainees legal representation or hearings. Endorsed by the federal government as the name for a nationwide deportation drive, the demeaning power of the term *wetback* became a perennial weapon of discrimination. Mainstream Anglo society now lumped Mexican Americans, including many whose families went back generations to the division of land with the Treaty of Guadalupe Hidalgo, with undocumented Mexicans as "wetbacks."[6]

The heightening of the civil rights movement in the 1960s awakened a new generation of Mexican American freedom fighters. They once more launched grassroots campaigns in their workplaces and communities. Some activists began urging a more militant approach, for they realized that Mexican Americans must organize to achieve their own freedom because civil rights legislation did not end the structural realities of race and class in America. Others promoted nationalism and made alliances with the emergent black power struggle. The eventual transformation of the Mexican American civil rights movement to "Chicano power" redirected and reshaped the movement's political agenda in the cause of advancing both racial and economic justice.[7]

## FORGOTTEN: THE STATUS OF MEXICAN AMERICANS IN POSTWAR AMERICA

The postwar era witnessed a 50 percent increase in the Southwest's Spanish-speaking population, growing from 2.29 million in 1950 to 3.46 million in 1960. Sixty percent of this population expansion occurred in California, largely through the continued in-migration of Mexican Americans from across the Southwest in search of work and a better life. Texas had the highest density of Mexican Americans, with one and a half million (or 45 percent) of the nation's Mexican population residing in the state. Most remained concentrated in the agricultural counties of South Texas, one of America's poorest regions. Here, Mexican Americans lived meager lives in rural slums marked by high infant deaths, a tuberculosis rate seven times that of Anglos, a third-grade level of education, and segregation in public places. Moreover, many were denied the right to vote, to serve on juries, or to own real estate in certain areas by a hostile Anglo population.[8]

Mexican Americans elsewhere in the United States were likewise shut out of the postwar boom by racial and economic inequality; over a third (34.8 percent) lived in poverty. Annual incomes by 1960 for Mexican Americans averaged less than $3,000. For the small middle classes who took advantage of federal programs such as the GI Bill and the Federal Housing Authority loans to achieve advancement, the postwar years did bring prosperity and change, but discrimination limited social mobility.[9]

The movement of Mexican Americans from the countryside to the cities increased. Many of them were uprooted by the mechanization of agriculture and the double bind of cheap bracero labor and even cheaper mojado labor. By 1950, 80 percent lived in urban centers. The migrants headed to Los Angeles, one of the fastest growing cities in America, to begin their new lives. However, Los Angeles and other cities were no havens. Many companies located in the suburbs at the expense of jobs in the central cities. The newly arrived Mexican American migrants in Los Angeles entered the lowest rungs of the social ladder, for they had no jobs, no skills, and little education. Opportunity for the newcomers to the city was also limited by racial prejudice.[10]

Urban residential segregation in America was widespread and growing. Though restrictive covenants had been rendered illegal, Realtors and lending agencies found ways to keep minorities out of white neighborhoods. Anglo homeowners also put up resistance to the entrance of minorities into their enclaves. The belief promulgated was that African Americans and Mexicans only brought crime, property deterioration, and school troubles.[11]

Income and race confined Mexican Americans to overcrowded inner-city neighborhoods, where they paid high rents for substandard housing. These high rents and low incomes led to other social problems. Many neighborhoods were being destroyed through urban renewal and freeway construction projects.

Following the defeat of the Proposition 10 public housing referendum in 1950, the city of Los Angeles sanctioned the demolition of the working-class districts in Bunker Hill to make way for office buildings. Eminent domain proceedings focused on near-downtown Chavez Ravine, home to one of the city's oldest Mexican American neighborhoods. After outcry by its residents and futile attempts to save it, Chavez Ravine was razed to make way for the new Dodger Stadium. In Chicago, construction of the Dan Ryan and Eisenhower freeways displaced Mexicans from the city's Near West Side, the location of the Midwest's largest Spanish-speaking barrio. Southwest Detroit's Mexican Americans similarly lost their homes to urban renewal and the construction of the Fisher Freeway.[12]

Segregation in housing led to segregation and antagonism in the schools. Of thirty-six high schools in Los Angeles school districts, twenty-one had no African Americans or Mexican Americans enrolled, six had small percentages of African Americans and Mexicans, three were integrated, and six were entirely minority in

**Aurora Vargas During the Chavez Ravine Evictions, 1959.**
CREDIT: "Sheriff deputies carry Aurora Vargas from Chavez Ravine home (9 May 1959)," Uclamss_1429_
b382_116242-E.  Courtesy of UCLA Charles E.  Young Research Library, Department of Special Collections,
Los Angeles Times Photographic Archive, ©Regents of the University of California, UCLA Library.

composition. Segregation of school-age Mexican Americans was imposed by Anglo teachers and counselors, who tracked these students into vocational training classes because they shared the prevailing views on Mexican Americans' inherent intellectual inferiority. Those few Mexican Americans who did gain knowledge and skills did not get jobs, because the employment market blocked people with dark skins and limited English-language skills. The employability lessened for Mexican Americans with little education, so that by 1960 three-fourths of those in the Southwest were relegated to manual labor.[13]

Racial violence toward minorities by law enforcement officials remained a problem as police took a hard-line law-and-order stance against them. In Texas, police were so out of control when dealing with minorities that some community leaders called for intervention by the U.S. Department of Justice. For example, the sheriff of Bee County, in the performance of "his duty," gunned down eight Mexican Americans in cold blood over an eight-year period. After killing three of his victims, the Anglo peace officer assaulted their relatives, and he flogged his last victim with a chain before he shot him twice. In Taylor, Texas, a white policeman shot and killed two Mexican American brothers, both war veterans, after attempting to arrest them on a misdemeanor charge. Adding to the insult, the district attorney refused to take a complaint.[14] In Denver, Colorado, there were numerous instances of Anglo cops shooting unarmed Mexican Americans and beating them with batons while they were handcuffed and then setting police dogs on them.[15]

Los Angeles was a city increasingly hostile to minorities. The Los Angeles Police Department and the Los Angeles County Sheriffs had a long record of brutality against Mexican Americans and African Americans. Members of these two minority groups were arbitrarily stopped and searched without probable cause, punched, clubbed, kicked, called racist names, and pinned down at gunpoint and arrested. Others were simply shot. One of the worst incidents of racist law enforcement practices was the savage beating of seven jailed Mexican American youths on Christmas Eve 1951 by twenty-two Los Angeles Police Department officers during an all-night drinking party at the Lincoln Heights police substation.[16]

Supporters of Mexican American civil rights pushed the fight against police brutality and other large-scale deep-rooted injustices such as job and housing discrimination into the forefront. They first did this through their involvement in campaigns launched by racially progressive unions, most of which became the targets of unfolding postwar anti-Communist purges.

## MEXICAN AMERICANS IN THE EARLY POSTWAR AMERICAN LABOR MOVEMENT

The demand for full and fair employment was one of the leading arenas of early postwar civil rights protest. Senator Dennis Chavez of New Mexico helped pioneer the legislative battle for labor and civil rights. In 1945 the Mexican American Democratic senator introduced Bill S101 to establish a permanent FEPC. The Senate bill, which guaranteed "equality of economic opportunity," set off a national controversy over how much control the federal government should have in employment practices. It attracted the ire of antiblack and antilabor Southern Dixiecrats who upheld "states' rights" and opposed any kind of federal intervention. Viewing the bill as a step toward social equality of the races, these Southern politicians sought to sabotage the fight for the FEPC. Leading this opposition was arch-racist Senator Theodore G. Bilbo of Mississippi, who vowed he would beat the "damnable, un-American and unconstitutional" FEPC to death.[17]

The drive for the establishment of a permanent FEPC came under assault with the start of the cold war, as charges that Communists controlled organized labor grew louder and employers widened their assault on labor. Only a few unions were willing to support labor and civil rights legislation and other antidiscrimination measures. Anti-Communism and the passage of the Taft-Hartley Act in 1947 restricted and undermined trade unionism as a civil rights vehicle for minorities and women. Also, many states in the Southwest had passed right-to-work laws. These factors, combined with discrimination, confined Mexican Americans disproportionately to low-paid menial work with little promise for job advancement.[18]

Mexican Americans participated in the wave of strikes that marked the early postwar years. The near general strike in basic industry in 1946 produced a turnout of Mexican American unionists on the picket lines, as did the 1948 nationwide packinghouse strike two years later.[19] The struggle for labor rights was also about wages in the agricultural fields.

Mexican Americans composed the main labor force in domestic agriculture. Most toiled long, exhausting days as migrant workers. They lived a brutal existence excluded from minimum-wage and maximum-hour legislation and from workmen's compensation laws. Migrant farm workers averaged no more than 50 cents an hour in 1959. Those in Texas earned just 16 cents an hour. Over 100,000 Mexican America farm workers migrated within Texas and an additional 58,000 migrated out of state. About 70,000 Mexican Americans harvested crops in Colorado, Montana, and Wyoming; and they made up over 70 percent of the 150,000 field laborers in California. In California's Imperial Valley, the living conditions of farmworkers were appalling. They produced infant death rates from diarrhea and enteritis more than seven times the statewide average. The most extreme conditions were found in Hidalgo County in the lower Río Grande Valley of Texas, where migrant workers were concentrated. Half the migrant children went without medical care, milk, or meat. The living conditions of migrants were abysmal, prompting one observer to note that only a few migrant workers managed to obtain "a ramshackle shell, tent, or cabin" while others slept "on the ground, in a cave, under a tree, or in a chicken house." During the off-season these same workers lived in a shack town in shelters built from scrap wood and metal, burlap sacks, and pieces of cardboard.[20]

Mexican American migrant workers endured invisible lives of misery and despair as victims of malnutrition, disease, and squalor. The U.S. President's Commission on Migratory Labor issued its lengthy report in 1951, but the plight of Mexican American farm migrants would not receive national attention until 1962, with the publication of Michael Harrington's *The Other America: Poverty in the United States.*[21] As noted, many domestic farmworkers were being displaced by the mechanization of agriculture. However, growing numbers were being forced out by tens of thousands of workers imported from Mexico and by the ever greater numbers of mojados pouring across the border illegally.

Ernesto Galarza championed the cause of the farmworker and set the tone for the fight for their labor rights in California. A prominent community leader, scholar, and activist, Galarza helped establish the National Farm Labor Union (NFLU) in 1947 and organized strikes by this union; the best known was the confrontation with the DiGiorgio Fruit Company. It began in 1947 and lasted for thirty months before strikebreakers and congressional pressure forced the NFLU to back down.[22]

"[California] was flooded with braceros while we were on strike, and before and after [a] strike," recalled Ernesto Galarza. When growers pressured the U.S. Border Patrol not to apprehend mojados, NFLU unionists made citizen's arrests of these contraband workers and guarded California's border with Mexico to prevent their reentry. The growers countered by bringing in additional mojados, legalizing them ("dried them out"), and putting them to work. In 1952, growers used this tactic again to defeat the NFLU in the Los Baños strike.[23] Undeterred despite this setback, Galarza then focused on terminating the bracero program and bringing

**Ernesto Galarza at the Pan American Union, Washington, DC, 1943.**
CREDIT: "Ernesto Galarza at the Pan American Union, Washington, DC, with mural by Pietro Lizzorio in the background, 1943." From the personal collection of William D. Estrada, Curator and Chair of History, the Natural History Museum of Los Angeles County.

national attention to the magnitude of the wetback problem by documenting violations of the guest worker program and the pervasive corruption and scandals that accompanied it. Galarza also fought to repeal Public Law 78, which renewed the contract labor program.

Following the lead of Ernesto Galarza, two unions took up the cause of organizing domestic farmworkers. One was the Agricultural Workers Organizing Committee (AWOC) formed in 1959. It was an offshoot of a farmworker union started earlier by one of the nation's most ardent and successful organizers, Dolores Huerta. Rising from simple beginnings in rural New Mexico and taught by the examples of her father and mother, Huerta was a founding member of the Stockton, California, chapter of the CSO. As a highly committed CSO legislative advocate, Huerta successfully lobbied the state capital in 1961 for disability insurance for farmworkers, for pension and public assistance programs for legal U.S. residents, and for the right to vote in Spanish. The next year the seemingly tireless Dolores Huerta went to Washington, DC, to lobby to end the bracero program.[24] In this same year, Huerta started the National Farm Workers Association (NFWA) with César Chavez. Chavez was a World War II veteran and CSO member who had risen to become the CSO's national director, but he resigned from the CSO after it refused to organize farmworkers. Throughout farm growing areas in the Southwest and South, Dolores Huerta and César Chavez pushed for a minimum wage, social security coverage, and housing, health, and education benefits for domestic farmworkers. Victory would elude them, however, until 1973. The miner's strike in southeastern New Mexico became the most famous event of the Mexican American struggle for economic and social justice.

In the midst of the cold war, when America became embroiled in the Korean conflict, Mexican American leaders and members of the Mine Mill launched their strike for higher wages and better working conditions. Their struggle against an array of powerful interests resulted in a protracted labor battle that became known as the Salt of the Earth strike.

Mexican Americans constituted nearly half the workforce in the metal industries of the Southwest and Mountain states, though discrimination against these miners was long-standing. Most belonged to the Mine Mill union, with many serving as leaders of their locals. At a time when the trade union movement was retreating on racial issues, Mine Mill brought the fight for equality out of the mines and smelters and into the local communities; however, anti-Communists denounced Mine Mill, and it was expelled from the CIO. The mine operators and their supporters, some of the latter paid infiltrators or informers of the Federal Bureau of Investigation (FBI) and related law enforcement agencies, alleged that Mine Mill was planning to call a strike in order to hamper the Korean War effort. Miner discontent focused on the mining corporations that were trying to destroy their union and roll back what gains they had won during the 1940s. Union militants focused on southeastern New Mexico, and the ensuing strike against the Empire Zinc Company arose from both labor issues and political causes.[25] Women played a central role in sustaining the fight against the mine company that showed no respect or concern for its workers.

The miners of Mine Mill struck the Empire Zinc Company in September 1950 in the small town of Hanover, New Mexico. Organizational work began in earnest in the face of increased harassment, arrests, and dismissals of workers by police under instructions from mine management. In June 1951, Empire Zinc obtained a court injunction against the miners. Though they faced going to jail, the miners continued their strike, and it dragged on for fifteen months. New Mexican women felt great anger and bitterness at the attacks they and their families were subjected to and the misery that pervaded the mining camp. Virginia Chacón and Dorinda Moreno became central to the strike. They went on the picket line in place of the striking miners and added basic needs, such as housing, hot water, and indoor plumbing, to the list of demands. The women were humiliated, assaulted, and arrested by law enforcement officers and mine security forces, but they did not falter in maintaining their solidarity, which buoyed the striking miners' spirits. The women also gave speeches, raised money, and helped bolster morale. Some of the best public speakers during the strike were women who spoke pointedly about their cause and heaped scorn on the mining corporations.[26]

The overtly political film *Salt of the Earth* chronicled the protracted strike of these courageous Mexican American mine workers against the Empire Zinc Company. A monument of American film, *Salt of the Earth* was completed despite considerable harassment of the filmmakers and the real-life actors by the FBI and the Immigration and Naturalization Service (INS). Promoters of *Salt of the Earth* had difficulties showing the film, primarily resulting from concerted efforts by anti-Communist individuals and groups such as the American Legion. The most visible militant in the war against subversion, the American Legion claimed that the film was Communist propaganda. Despite threats to distributors and exhibitors with loss of business if they showed the film, *Salt of the Earth* attracted audiences. The success of the legendary strike film, however, focused attention on the blacklisted individuals who made the film and not on the struggle of the Mexican American mine workers striving for an improved standard of living.[27]

Elsewhere, other Mexican Americans were making efforts to eliminate de facto discrimination and the resulting social and economic inequality. In the Rocky Mountain states and California, the National Association of Mexican Americans was the leading advocate for labor rights and civil rights for Mexican Americans. Although vulnerable to the general prejudice at the time against politically progressive organizations, ANMA developed a campaign to educate and mobilize Mexican Americans against inequality.

## THE RADICALISM OF ANMA

The third-party presidential campaign of Henry A. Wallace of the Independent Progressive Party (IPP) gained the endorsement of many Mexican Americans who had joined the protests against the international and domestic cold war. Wallace appealed to Mexican Americans because he spoke out against racism and called for integrated housing and education and a permanent FEPC. Wallace also endorsed the Good Neighbor Policy in Latin America, backed the world peace movement, and opposed the Marshall Plan. Wallace's Spanish-speaking supporters organized grassroots campaigns in their communities for him and for state and local candidates running on the IPP ticket. Wallace lost the presidential election, but his campaign nevertheless politicized many Mexican Americans.[28]

The National Association of Mexican Americans lent considerable support to the IPP. ANMA demanded the same civil rights for Mexican Americans that other Americans enjoyed. Unlike the American GI Forum and LULAC, ANMA followed a radical path to attaining civil rights. Founded in 1948, ANMA at its peak in 1950 had four thousand members, made up mainly of male and female trade unionists concentrated in the Rocky Mountain states and California. Dedicated to advancing the cause of economic and civil rights, including women's equality, ANMA built coalitions and alliances with the American Committee for the Protection of the Foreign Born, the Progressive Citizens of America, the Civil Rights Congress, and other progressive organizations that wanted expansion of civil rights for minorities.[29]

ANMA defied organized labor's support of the cold war, and the radical group supported many causes. It joined the Civil Rights Congress in the drive for passage of an FEPC, provided funds and clothing to Mine Mill strikers in New Mexico, and backed a minimum wage for farmworkers and their right to form unions. Although critical of the bracero program, ANMA helped organize braceros, and in 1951 it appealed to the United Nations Commission on Human Rights on their behalf. ANMA protested the deportations by the McCarran-Walter Act of Mexicans who were permanent residents or American citizens.[30]

In matters of U.S. foreign policy, ANMA imagined a possible end to colonialism, desired peace, and called for international cooperation. It was an outspoken critic of U.S. support of dictatorships in Latin America and the Middle East. ANMA supported as well the Cuban revolutionary movement and the struggle for Puerto Rico's independence. It opposed the Korean War and worldwide nuclear proliferation through the Stockholm Peace Appeal. ANMA early on joined the battle for civil rights for African Americans because it recognized that African Americans were victimized by racism, just as Mexican Americans were. In fact, ANMA declared its commitment to interracialism in its founding document: "We have pledged ourselves to eradicating the force and violence so repeatedly used against Mexican, Negro, and other minority peoples by local police and lynch-minded racists."[31]

The United States, however, was tilting to the right, becoming more concerned about the subversive threats of radicalism. ANMA therefore came under increasing scrutiny owing to its stance on the issues of labor, racism, deportations, and the peace movement. The organization appeared on the U.S. Attorney General's list of subversive organizations. The House Un-American Activities Committee (HUAC) investigated ANMA for its alleged activities, which included criticizing American foreign policy overseas. Pressed into service, the FBI infiltrated ANMA, and paid informants provided the agency with membership lists and background information on its officers and members. Local and state authorities also harassed ANMA. Red-baited as a subversive organization, and with several leaders already threatened with deportation, ANMA's role diminished in the mid-1950s, and the group disintegrated.[32]

As anti-Communism neutralized or eliminated progressive organizations and individuals through purges of the Mexican American civil rights supporters, the CSO emerged as a major player in the struggle for equality for this minority group. By concentrating its efforts on community organizing, the CSO helped nurture a well-organized grassroots political movement among Mexican Americans in Los Angeles and in other parts of California.

## MEXICAN AMERICANS AND THE COMMUNITY SERVICE ORGANIZATION

An offshoot of Saul Alinsky's Back of the Yards Neighborhood Council, the CSO was founded in Los Angeles by Antonio Ríos, Edward B. Roybal, and Fred Ross, Sr. In 1948, Mexican Americans in East Los Angeles, working through the CSO and with strong support from several cold war liberal union locals with large Spanish-speaking memberships and the Catholic Church, undertook a mass voter registration campaign on behalf of Edward B. Roybal's candidacy for a seat on the Los Angeles City Council. Roybal pioneered multiethnic politics, advocating interracial cooperation between African Americans and Mexican Americans on the matter of civil rights. Pressed by African Americans from the city's South Central district for reasons that they should support his campaign, Roybal replied: "Our skin is brown—our battle is the same. Our victory cannot be but a victory for you, too." The Roybal campaign provided a crucial test of the impact of the larger Mexican American and African American vote that would bode well for the future.[33]

A World War II veteran, Edward R. Roybal was born in Albuquerque, New Mexico, to a family that traced its roots to the founding of Santa Fe. Roybal's parents moved to Los Angeles in 1922 and settled in Boyle Heights after his father lost his job following the nationwide railroad strike of that year. Roybal graduated from Roosevelt High School, participated in the Civilian Conservation Corps, and attended the University of California at Los Angeles. As a health worker for the Los Angeles County Tuberculosis and Health Association, Roybal labored to curb the high incidence of tuberculosis among the city's Mexican Americans.

Roybal lost his first run for a Los Angeles City Council seat by only three hundred votes. This close vote did not demoralize Roybal's precinct workers. In 1949, after launching a remarkable voter registration drive that gained fifteen thousand new voters, the CSO secured Roybal's second bid for a seat on the City Council.[34] Crucial to Roybal's success were the hundreds of Mexican American women who spearheaded the CSO's door-to-door organizing campaign strategy in the city of Los Angeles to register voters. Like African American women in the Deep South, Mexican American women canvassed more than the men did, attended more meetings and demonstrations, and served as major leaders, organizers, and strategists. ILGWU members María Durán and Hope Schecter Mendoza were leading figures in the Roybal campaign that also helped to put IPP presidential candidate Henry A. Wallace on the ballot against Harry S. Truman.

Even while holding down full-time jobs and caring for their families, women organized and spoke at public CSO meetings, made phone calls, distributed campaign literature, and performed other tasks to secure Roybal's victory.[35]

Once in office, Edward Roybal spoke out very strongly for civil rights and racial justice, as he had promised, and he was the only Los Angeles City Council member to do so. Moreover, the Mexican American councilman cast the lone vote against a controversial Communist registration ordinance, saying this about it: "The doctrine implicit in this ordinance . . . places every citizen and organization, whose word or act resembles at any time those of the Communists, at the mercy of any biased crack-pot who may decide to report the matter to the Police Department as subversive . . . " And he condemned the McCarran-Walter Act. In Roybal, both minorities and progressives had an example to admire. Over the next decade he would play a key role in the politics of Los Angeles and California, and his election helped the CSO reinforce its influence in the Mexican American community.[36]

By 1950, the CSO had more than five thousand members with chapters in thirty-five cities active in voter registration and electoral campaigns and other issues that affected Mexican Americans. The CSO was the dominant civil rights advocacy group in Los Angeles. Because many CSO leaders, like Hope Schecter Mendoza, María Durán, and Antonio Ríos, came from the labor movement, they pushed the CSO to promote the minimum wage, unionization, medical service for migrant workers, and other issues of importance to workers. Toward this end, the CSO established the Labor Relations Committee to educate the Spanish-speaking population about the importance of the labor movement, particularly the campaign for a permanent FEPC. Mexican Americans utilized their experiences gained from voter registration drives to engage in other civil rights struggles that included ending restrictive housing practices, neighborhood displacement through urban redevelopment, school segregation, jury exclusion, and police brutality.[37]

Working to obtain U.S. citizenship for Mexicans was an important CSO activity. By 1955, the CSO had established 450 citizenship classes in California and within five years had assisted more than forty thousand Mexicans to become U.S. citizens. Fred Ross had been the catalyst in founding the CSO, but the vanguard was made up of hundreds of Mexican Americans, many of them women, who through the CSO worked tirelessly to mobilize their communities for social change. In Los Angeles and in southern California's rural areas, Mexican Americans from the Unity Leagues launched voter registration drives to elect Mexican Americans to office. Newspaper editor Ignacio López formed the Unity Leagues with assistance from the American Committee on Race Relations. In New Mexico, coalitions of Mexican Americans helped to reelect U.S. Senator Dennis Chavez, while broad-based coalitions in Arizona likewise exercised their political power in several state campaigns.[38] Other Mexican American civil rights organizations emerged.

Texas had the highest density of Mexican Americans, and a priority was reversing their low voter participation in those South Texas counties in which they constituted large majorities. Rampant discrimination in the small towns and the poll tax voting requirement kept many potential Spanish-speaking voters away from the polls. The larger goal was overturning the entrenched Democratic Party structure.[39]

Dr. Hector P. García was a principal figure in the early struggle for civil rights for Mexican Americans. In 1948, the World War II veteran from Corpus Christi, Texas, held a meeting in his home town to form a new civic organization. The Mexican Americans in attendance chose the name American GI Forum. Constituted of locally run units, the nascent organization sought to employ mass participation in organizing and decision making and to involve Mexican Americans in public life. Thousands of Mexican Americans took up Dr. García's idea. Within five years, the GI Forum had grown to twenty thousand members in six hundred chapters that were engaged in various grassroots struggles around the issues of community need and welfare that included voter registration.

Averaging a weekly income of $19, Mexican Americans of Texas could ill afford the $1.75 poll tax, and thus their participation in the voting process was limited. The GI Forum, at times with LULAC and unions, launched local "pay your poll tax" drives to register Mexican American voters in Texas. In doing so the civil rights proponents from these two organizations challenged the long-standing history of political bossism in South Texas—the ability of area growers and businessmen to pay the poll taxes and deliver the Mexican American bloc vote. Women played an important role in the American GI Forum's success. They were this organization's backbone; in many instances women made up the majority at meetings and participated in all phases of activity. Because economic retaliation by Anglos was common, women often spoke at public meetings in lieu of their husbands, who feared losing their jobs.[40]

McCarthyism continued to stifle dissent. Owing to its ravages, activists of any kind provoked suspicion. Mexican American labor and civil rights advocates were forced to censure themselves for fear of being suspected of Communist activity. Banned and banished, they became victims of domestic anti-Communism.

## MEXICAN AMERICANS CAUGHT IN THE WEB OF THE RED SCARE

The crackdown on outspoken dissenters was a broad assault against civil liberties. Given the hostile anti-Communist climate, all persons who made an effort to ameliorate social problems and advocate or defend civil rights were put in a bad light. Political watchdogs did not fail to notice the leftward leanings of Mexican American activists. Their rights, as well as the rights of those who were aliens and naturalized citizens, were sacrificed because of cold war government practices. If they were aliens, they could be deported under the 1950 Internal Security Act. Those who were recently naturalized could be denaturalized if they were caught in the web of the McCarran-Walter Act and the attendant deportation frenzy the act created to deal with an unraveling Mexican guest worker program. The Mexican American civil rights movement was essentially stripped of its most capable activists through deportation procedures, which were far more menacing than criminal charges. The threat of deportation as an undesirable alien "served as a very effective weapon to keep the Mexican people as a whole in bondage. . . . As soon as a leader arises . . . deportation proceedings are immediately used to remove [the person] from leadership."[41]

The INS detained unionist Armando Davila of Los Angeles for deportation because of his political beliefs. Fortunately, Davila's union, the United Furniture Workers of America, came to his defense; it contacted the Civil Rights Congress to defend him. Long-time Spanish-speaking activist Refugio Martínez of Chicago came under investigation. Martínez was an organizer for the United Packinghouse Workers of America (UPWA) and an ANMA supporter. A twenty-seven-year resident of the United States, Martínez was deported under the McCarran Act because he had joined the Communist Party in 1932. The Martínez case went all the way to the U.S. Supreme Court, but Martínez lost.[42]

Another alien deportation case involved prominent labor and civil rights advocate Robert Galván of San Diego, California. Galván was a thirty-six-year resident of the United States with an American-born wife, four American-born children, and a stepson who had served in the Army overseas during World War II. In addition to his union work in southern California, Galván battled the Ku Klux Klan, an instrument of fear whose prime target of racial hatred and bigotry was Mexicans. The Klan captured Mexicans and hung and disemboweled them, buried others alive, cut the throats of those who "insulted" white women, and used gas torches on their victims to "see them dance." Though threatened and physically attacked by the Klan, the labor and civil rights activists refused to back down in fighting against the Klan's depraved acts toward Mexicans.[43] Galván was being deported because of his past membership in the Communist Party and the Communist affiliation of the organizations to which he had been linked. Galván disavowed any political agenda. Fortunately, fate smiled on him. Attorneys for the American Council of Spanish-Speaking People (ACSSP) finally won Galván's case when the federal judge ruled that he was "law-abiding . . . a steady worker and family man and loyal to the United States."[44] American-born Anna Correa-Bary of Denver, Colorado, was not so lucky.

Anna Correa-Bary was a member of the United Packinghouse Workers of America and had been recruited into the Communist Party of the United States. Anna Correa-Bary, her husband Arthur Bary, and four other Party members became prime targets of the anti-Communist campaigns. They were indicted in 1954 and tried for violation of the Smith Act. The Smith Act placed severe restrictions on any person alleged to have taught, published, or advocated or organized others in an attempt to overthrow the government of the United States.[45]

The Civil Rights Congress contacted more than one hundred lawyers to defend Anna Correa-Bary, but none wanted to take the case. In its indictments, the federal government relied on the testimony of four paid FBI agents hired to spy, make reports, and furnish other information to convict the defendants. After twenty long years of legal battles, including a final one before the U.S. Supreme Court, the indictment was withdrawn. Nevertheless, Anna Correa-Bary became a casualty of the abuses of civil liberties during the McCarthy era.[46]

The accusations of being a Communist were damaging, and Mexican Americans, many of them World War II and Korean War veterans, were not left unscathed by these charges. Closely associated in the public mind with Communists, Mexican American progressives could not get work and acquired an un-American aura that destroyed their political effectiveness, as well as their personal reputations. The singling out of Mexican Americans allied with the Left for punitive treatment was despairingly summed up by Anita Alvárez, a member of the American Committee for the Protection of the Foreign Born:

> In a land founded on freedom and justice, a mother of a war veteran is aroused in
> the morning and torn from her home. A father of a dead war hero is waylaid on
> his way home from work and snatched away from his family. . . . What is their
> crime? Where is the evidence? The accusation is "You believed—you thought—
> you spoke."[47]

Despite red baiting, police surveillance, and efforts to disrupt the organizing of Mexican Americans, activists such as Anita Alvárez fought for the rights of Mexican Americans against the government-sponsored deportations through the American Committee for the Protection of the Foreign Born, the Civil Rights Congress, and the American Civil Liberties Union. These progressive organizations tirelessly defended more than two hundred foreign-born and U.S.-born individuals charged under the McCarran-Walter law.

The American Communist Party was put on the road to disintegration because of the heightening of the cold war, the federal government's relentless pursuit and expulsion of Communists from society, and the Party's own internal shifts, weaknesses, and bitter factional disputes. The Red Scare drove away most of its Mexican American members. Others were deported or went underground. Many left the Party following Nikita Khrushchev's revelations about Stalin or became disillusioned with the Party's practice of addressing the issue of race only when it applied to Party strategy.[48]

In 1954, as Senator Joseph McCarthy's political fortunes were peaking, built largely on an assault on civil liberties, the United States government launched a massive deportation campaign targeting Mexicans. The paranoia over unauthorized Mexicans mirrored the witch hunts being conducted at the same time for suspected Communists. What began as a controlled, closely monitored deportation program to detain undocumented workers grew to encompass naturalized and American-born citizens.

## MEXICAN AMERICANS IN THE DRAGNETS
## OF OPERATION WETBACK
## AND OPERATION TERROR

The year 1954 was a time of economic recession in America in which unemployment doubled, imposing even greater hardship on minorities. The mood in the Southwest toward Mexican Americans was growing hostile and resentful. The highly publicized Operation Wetback launched in this year by the federal government was an effort to locate, seize, and deport undocumented Mexican aliens in the United States. Federal agents did not ask to see their documents or question them about their legal status. This indiscriminate roundup caused families to be separated and children left behind. As in the repatriations of the 1930s, the U.S. government made few attempts to distinguish between American citizens of Mexican descent and undocumented Mexican aliens. Many legal U.S.

residents as a result were shipped across the border without recourse to due process.

Pressured by labor unions, the U.S. Labor Department intervened to offset the massive flow of mojados into the United States by initiating a nationwide deportation drive on June 9, 1954, code-named Operation Wetback. Organized by the INS and with the full cooperation of county and state authorities, the United States deported more than one million unauthorized Mexican workers. Mass raids using low-flying airplanes, armed motorized patrols, and well-timed sweeps were carried out in agricultural fields and cities in northern and southern California. In California, 248,000 unauthorized Mexican aliens were deported between June 17 and July 8. An additional 83,000 men were removed from California through September. This was only the beginning of a vast deportation process that sent Mexicans back to Mexico. During the subsequent Operation Terror, the Mexican American community of Los Angeles was subjected to one of the most blatant violations of human rights.[49]

Operation Terror was a military-like operation launched on June 17, 1954, shortly after midnight; it focused primarily on the Mexican community of Los Angeles. Without search or arrest warrants, nearly a thousand immigration agents hunted down Mexicans. The federal government's offensive against the proclaimed illegal menace ferreted out Mexicans in business districts and places of entertainment, invaded residential areas, and burst into homes to search for them, in essence tracking down Mexicans wherever they might congregate to capture them. The Mexicans of Los Angeles could only watch fearfully as Operation Terror raged around them.[50]

Operation Terror meted out collective punishment to the entire Mexican population of Los Angeles. Thousands of Mexican immigrants and their American citizen families were processed for deportation without any hearings or legal counsel. Young American-born children were suddenly without their parents. Many of the parents wound up in Mexico penniless, having to beg for food and shelter. The actions drew public outcries and charges of civil and human rights violations. Outraged by the deportations, the Community Service Organization, the Civil Rights Congress, the American Committee for the Protection of the Foreign Born, and labor unions protested loudly. The Civil Rights Congress distributed an English-Spanish pamphlet, "Stop the Deportation Drive . . . Know your Rights." Trade unionists set up a picket line at a detention camp at Elysian Park near the Los Angeles Police Academy, prepared by INS agents to herd Mexicans for processing and shipment to Douglas, Arizona. Civil libertarians concluded that the Gestapolike method of government apprehension of Mexicans was the greatest mass movement of people in America's history. Operation Wetback and Operation Terror ensured the silencing of the nation's second largest minority group.

Failing to see the long-range impacts, the American GI Forum and LULAC, America's two principal conservative Mexican American organizations, endorsed the roundups. Although the GI Forum eventually protested the unfolding government repression, LULAC remained silent about the persecution of Mexican American citizens caught in the dragnet and about the misery suffered as a result. A symbol of the new attitude toward Mexican immigration at this time was the construction of a barbed wire fence along the border. American employers profited from the deportation campaign. They continued to import new crops of undocumented workers from Mexico and, under permanent threat of deportation, exploited this labor.[51]

Meanwhile, the task of acquiring legal equality and protection for Mexican Americans was taken up. Litigation would be through the ACSSP, which adopted an "other white" legal strategy. Part of a much larger campaign for civil rights, litigation ultimately failed to improve the position of Mexican Americans in American society.

## CIVIL RIGHTS LITIGATION BY MEXICAN AMERICANS

As the controversy over civil rights intensified, the spotlight shifted to the courts. Mexican Americans were profoundly affected by the legal civil rights battles being waged by African Americans, and they opened up legal offenses of their own. San Antonio attorney M. C. González conceived the litigation campaign in 1944. In this year he contacted the American Civil Liberties Union to seek advice on how to test the Good Neighbor Policy on the matter of race relations and jury discrimination for U.S.-born Mexicans. The two established Mexican American groups, the American GI Forum and LULAC, would take the lead in this endeavor.[52]

Equal educational opportunities for Mexican Americans were the key to improving their social condition. So long as Mexican Americans remained powerless, racism would take the form of unequal distribution of school dollars, gerrymandered school boundaries or clearly delineated "Mexican schools" that segregated Mexican American children, and prejudiced teachers and counselors who discouraged their aspirations. Eliminating segregation in the schools of the Southwest through the courts thus became a central activity of the established Mexican American organizations. It would be done by pursuing a legal strategy of whiteness but without embracing white racism or giving up common cause with African Americans.[53]

Assimilation and identification as whites were trumpeted by the conservative Mexican American leadership as a solution to the disparagement of Mexican Americans. They also distanced themselves from association with African Americans. With their attitudes shaped this way, Mexicans at this time "did not want to be white, neither did they want to be black." The hard legal fact was that, unlike the case of African Americans, most segregation of Mexican Americans in the 1940s and 1950s was de facto, set in place by custom rather than state statute and therefore not remedied by law. Because Mexican Americans occupied an ambiguous position in the nation's legal and social orders—they were considered legally "white" but treated as nonwhite—litigators used the conundrum term "other white" as a legal tool in their civil rights cases to desegregate schools. Attorneys argued before the courts that Mexicans should not be subject to Jim Crow because state law sanctioned only the segregation of "negroes" or "colored" people. However, this "other white" line of reasoning did little to dismantle segregation in the Southwest. Instead, it helped reluctant school districts in the region undermine post-Brown desegregation rulings by integrating African American students into so-called "Mexican schools." Officials, emboldened by their racist cohorts, claimed the latter were "white" schools, thus leaving the real white schools essentially unaffected under desegregation orders.[54]

Mexican American attorneys coordinated litigation to eliminate discrimination through the American Civil Liberties Union's Robert Marshall Civil Liberties Trust. It provided substantial financial assistance to the newly established ACSSP organization. Emulating the National Association for the Advancement of Colored People (NAACP) and the "ultra-progressive Negro-Americans," the ACSSP aided attorneys in gaining remedy through the courts for the civil rights violations of Mexican Americans and also assisted organizations attempting to create civil rights programs. The legal tactic evolved through several test trials, one of which was closely watched by the NAACP.[55]

The pioneering *Mendez v. Westminster* case against Mexican American segregation in California was litigated in 1947. The court ruled that because California's Jim Crow statutes did not expressly mention Mexican Americans, separation denied them due process and hence equal protection under the law. In Texas, most school districts prevented Mexican Americans from sharing public classrooms with Anglo students. Placing Mexican American students in separate classes based on language and academic ability undermined the ideal of equal educational opportunity. In 1948, Mexican American lawyers in *Delgado v. Bastrop ISD* succeeded in convincing a federal court to declare unconstitutional the segregation of Mexican Americans based on the presence of linguistically deficient students because it was arbitrary and discriminatory. However, this federal ruling was not enforced and resulted in continued legal challenges. In South Texas, approximately 90 percent of the public schools were segregated according to the "Anglo" or "Mexican" enrollment. Residential segregation also undercut educational opportunity in many Texas districts. In 1957, the ACSSP, in partnership with American GI Forum and LULAC attorneys, won a suit against the Driscoll, Texas, Independent School District. In this case, the federal court judge ruled that grouping Mexican American students as a separate class from Anglo students was arbitrary and unreasonable. Once again, subsequent legal challenges were made due to the slow process of school desegregation in light of weak civil rights legislation.[56]

Bound by a common cause, Mexican Americans and African Americans achieved a measure of victory in the drive for equal education in southern California. In 1950, the Alianza Hispano-Americana and the Spanish-American Alliance opted not to use the "other white" legal tool and filed a school segregation suit with the NAACP in El Centro, California. In the *Romero v. Weakley* case the parents of forty-four Mexican American children (including one white child falsely segregated) and twenty African American children alleged that the El Centro School District and the Imperial County Board of Supervisors illegally segregated their children into two separate and unequal schools while Anglos were bused to the "white" school. The plaintiffs were able to settle the case by forcing the defendants to agree by stipulation that the segregation would end.[57]

In addition to school segregation, there existed a long-standing, systematic, and arbitrary exclusion of qualified Mexican Americans from jury service, based solely on their race, in violation of the Fourteenth Amendment of the U.S. Constitution. For much of the twentieth century, courts pronounced Mexican Americans "white" in the courtroom, most often as a way of denying that they were victims of racial discrimination in jury selection.

In 1954, as Operation Wetback was initiated, beginning the process of sending undocumented Mexicans "back to Mexico," Gus García, with fellow attorney Carlos C. Cadena, won the United States Supreme Court case *Hernández v. the State of Texas.* Chief Justice Earl Warren wrote that Hernández was denied his rights to the equal-protection and due-process clauses of the Fourteenth Amendment because the county in which he lived did not allow Mexican Americans to serve on juries. The court accepted arguments of the plaintiff's attorneys that Anglos treated Mexicans as nonwhite despite the fact that they were actually white. To Anglo-Texans, southerners who cherished states' rights, however, the Supreme Court had rendered Mexican Americans "too white for their own good." Their hostile reaction predictably came in the form of mocking attacks, such as: "Why do you want Mexicans on juries? [Mexicans] claim to be white. Aren't we all white?" Two weeks later, challenges to state-mandated segregation culminated in *Brown v. Board of Education of Topeka,* when the Supreme Court unanimously ruled segregation in schools unconstitutional. Anglos immediately set out to sabotage the court's decision.[58]

To Southern Anglos, *Brown v. Board of Education* represented federal intervention in Southern race relations. Many Anglo communities evaded integration by redefining school district boundaries, appealing court desegregation orders or, as was the case in the Southwest, integrating African American students into the existing Mexican schools. Devoted to upholding white supremacy, the White Citizens' Councils began to appear first in Mississippi and then in Texas, where elected officials called integration a Communist plot to destroy the white race. Soon thereafter, one hundred and one racist legislators signed the "Southern Manifesto" endorsing segregation. Segregationists furthermore attempted to discredit civil rights organizations and activists by calling them subversive.[59]

Despite the succession of legal victories, the Mexican American community did not solve the problem of school segregation or win the constitutional struggle for civil rights. In 1959, the Marshall Trust assessed as a failure its nineteen-year venture, in which it spent nearly $300,000, to assist the Spanish-speaking people of the Southwest. It concluded that no organization existed to coordinate Mexican American civil rights on a national level. According to the trust's executive director, Roger Baldwin, "it became apparent that the major efforts in this field were localized ... the Trustees are disinclined to make grants for purely local enterprises ... " Marshall Trust liquidated its assets, the American Council of Spanish-Speaking People disappeared, and a national legal organization for Mexican Americans would have to wait nearly a decade, until the founding of the Mexican American Legal Defense Fund with Ford Foundation money. Nevertheless, the suits and arguments brought about by Mexican American civic organizations played a great part in broadening the legal rights of Mexican Americans. Lawyers like M. C. González and Gus C. García played important roles in achieving an awakening within the Mexican American civil rights movement.[60]

# DON'T BOW TO THE POWERS THAT BE: SHIFTS
# IN THE MEXICAN AMERICAN RIGHTS MOVEMENT

Texas had the highest density of Mexican Americans. One and a half million of the nation's Mexican people resided in this state where pervasive racism and legally mandated Jim Crow prevailed. They worked and lived under wretched conditions in both rural and urban areas extending from El Paso to San Antonio and southward to the Gulf of Mexico. Most remained concentrated in the agricultural counties of South Texas, one of America's poorest regions. Mired in poverty, the state's Mexican Americans had the shortest life expectancy, the highest infant death rate, the poorest housing, and the greatest rate of chronic unemployment and underemployment. They were segregated in schools and public places and were denied the right to vote, serve on juries, or own real estate in certain areas.[61]

Together, Mexican Americans and African Americans composed one-third of the population of Texas. And together they endured such indignities as attending movie houses built exclusively for "Negroes and Mexicans" and riding in segregated passenger buses. Although both minority groups suffered from discrimination, the mandated segregation of Mexican Americans was attributable to demography rather than law.[62] Segregationist legislation in the Texas House of Representatives in 1957 ultimately galvanized some Mexican American political leaders to more formally tie their civil rights efforts directly to those of African Americans by their effective opposition to proposed state segregation. These Mexican Americans rejected the skin-color politics of the GI Forum. A sense of common purpose with African Americans to undo racial injustice and remake American society explains one aspect of the Mexican American civil rights movement of the early postwar years.[63]

In May 1957, at the height of the Southern resistance to school desegregation, the Texas House of Representatives passed several bills designed to maintain the color line in the state's public schools. The bills had strong support in the Texas Senate, too—that is, before Mexican American state senator Henry B. González of San Antonio took the floor in opposition to a measure that allowed parents who objected to integration to withdraw their children from school.[64] The Mexican American was distinctly progressive by the standards of contemporary Texas politics; his support for civil rights was a striking departure from the views of the great majority of his Anglo colleagues who were fiercely determined to protect the state's established social order.

Unlike other Mexican American leaders in Texas, Henry B. González built coalitions with the African American community. With interracial support, González had been elected to the San Antonio City Council in 1953 and served as mayor pro tempore for part of his first term. González was neither a radical nor a conservative; rather, he was a multifaceted leader who followed an effective middle-course approach in an attempt to advance social justice. González spoke against legal segregation of San Antonio's public facilities, and he backed the city council's passage of desegregation ordinances. In 1956, González became the first Mexican American elected to the Texas State Senate in one hundred years. The following year González reacted bitterly to the legislature's resistance to integration, attracting national attention for holding the longest filibuster in the history of the Texas legislature. It lasted thirty-six hours and railed against the dangers posed by racists in the state legislature and their Southern Manifesto, the official white supremacist defiance of the civil rights movement. González, with State Senator Abraham Kazen of El Paso, stood his ground and succeeded in killing eight out of ten racial segregation bills aimed at circumventing the U.S. Supreme Court's decision in the *Brown v. Board of Education* case.[65] The Mexican American legislator stolidly told white Texans to abandon their racism, that it had no place in American society.

Steadfastly refusing to surrender their racial privilege and control, Anglo-Texan segregationists mobilized themselves in resistance to integration. With racial tensions already high, the task of desegregating public schools in Texas remained undone. By 1957 only seventy-five school districts in the state had been desegregated. Nor had segregation in privately owned places of public accommodation and in public facilities been eliminated. Signs in restaurant windows and posted at public swimming pools remained throughout the Southwest, stating: "No Dogs or Mexicans Allowed."[66]

The gap between the status of Mexican Americans and that of the dominant group continued to widen. Despite many legal victories and much hard work, the Mexican American people still suffered economic, educational, and social deprivation. Although Mexican American voters strengthened the Democratic Party, it failed to capitalize on this infusion of activism. Just as it did with African Americans, the Democratic Party defaulted on its promises to Mexican Americans for social reform because it remained beholden to white Southern Dixiecrats. The more than four million Mexican American people were without political representation at all levels of government—they had but two representatives in Congress, Henry B. González of San Antonio and Edward B. Roybal of Los Angeles.

## MEXICAN AMERICANS AND THE DEMOCRATIC PARTY

Then things began changing politically. In 1956, attorney Albert R. Peña became the first Mexican American in Texas elected to the Béxar County Commission. Peña spearheaded the efforts to desegregate local schools in San Antonio, championed the rights of the poor, and aggressively promoted putting into effect civil rights laws to challenge the discriminatory treatment of Mexican Americans. Raymond Telles won the mayor's office in El Paso in 1957. Two years later, in 1960, six Mexican Americans served in the Texas State Legislature, and nationwide the Mexican American electorate united in support of the presidential campaign of John F. Kennedy through Viva Kennedy Clubs and of other Democrats running for office.[67]

In 1959, Mexican Americans in California founded the Mexican American Political Association (MAPA). In Los Angeles, Edward B. Roybal and long-time activist Ralph Guzmán recruited MAPA volunteers to register voters and organized and oversaw the activities of MAPA campaign workers. In the following year, Mexican Americans formed the pro-Democrat Mexican Americans for Political Action and the Political Association of Spanish-Speaking Organizations

**Viva Kennedy Clubs, 1960.**
CREDIT: "Dr. Hector P. Garcia, Interview by Thomas H. Kreneck, Corpus Christi, Texas." Oral History Collection, Special Collections & Archives, Bell Library, Texas A&M University-Corpus Christi.

(PASSO) in Texas. PASSO was a counterpart of the California MAPA and an off-shoot of the Viva Kennedy Clubs. All of those in PASSO shared disaffection from mainstream Texas Democrats. Through MAPA and PASSO, Mexican Americans at last acquired effective agencies to help their assimilation into the mainstream of the American body politic. These organizations educated Mexican Americans on political issues, registered them to vote, and began pressuring the major political parties to nominate Mexican Americans for office or as advisors to elected officials.[68]

Many Mexican Americans looked to the liberal wing of the national Democratic Party for support. Having come of age during the New Deal, these activists believed that change would come under the watchful eye of a strong and active federal government. Mexican American political influence in national elections derived not so much from their numerical strength but from their diffusion in Texas, New Mexico, and California, where electoral votes were considered vital to the winning candidate. The Mexican American vote in 1960 proved to be decisive in determining the crucial margins that won many of the battleground states. The Democratic National Campaign Committee, supporting its presidential candidate, John F. Kennedy, made special efforts to draw the support of lower income and minority voters. Conceived by Texas Congressman González, New Mexico Senator Chavez, and Los Angeles City Council member Roybal, the "Viva Kennedy" campaign, along with the African American vote, contributed to Kennedy's narrow victory in Texas that helped win the national election. The Viva Kennedy Clubs successfully guided political changes that produced elected officials for local, state, and national offices. Mexican American voters strengthened the Democratic Party; however, the Party failed to capitalize on this infusion of activism. Just as it did with African Americans, the Democratic Party defaulted on its promises to Mexican Americans for social reform because it remained firmly beholden to its Southern wing. It was only in late 1963 that President Kennedy made civil rights and welfare central to his domestic programs. In Texas, Mexican Americans began to mount a serious challenge to the Democrats in the Río Grande border region, where they remained politically powerless and socially repressed.

The following summer of 1961 witnessed the heightening of the civil rights struggle, and Mexican Americans were caught up in the winds of change of that year. Union activist Francisco Medrano of Dallas, Texas, turned toward championing the civil rights movement. He joined the drive by African Americans to integrate lunch counters in politically conservative Dallas, where business elites maintained control of the city's segregated and repressed minorities. In addition to Medrano's civil rights work in Dallas, he joined the campaigns to challenge segregation in Mississippi and Arkansas. "When UAW leader Walter Reuther said we should help repeal the poll tax, I went into the Deep South," recalled Medrano. "I could understand the struggle of black people because my people [Mexican Americans] were experiencing the same sort of thing." Medrano later participated in the historic 1965 march on Selma, Alabama.[69]

With biracial support, Henry B. González of San Antonio was elected to the U.S. Congress. Congressman González worked for the passage of a number of legislative proposals benefiting both African Americans and Mexican Americans that included the 1964 Equal Opportunities Act, the Housing Act, and the Civil Rights Act.[70]

By 1963, the civil rights movement reached a crescendo of activity as demonstrations erupted in more than eight hundred cities and towns across America. One of these demonstrations took place in Phoenix, Arizona, in July when five thousand African American and Mexican American marchers angrily protested discrimination against minorities by the city's largest employers. At a civil rights meeting in Torrance, California, Mexican American and African American activists, bound by the common cause of demanding racial and economic justice, confronted angry racist hecklers from the right-wing John Birch Society and the fringe American Nazi Party that denounced the civil rights movement as a Communist plot to undermine America. In this year, despite intimidation by the Texas Rangers, Mexican Americans and Anglos from the Teamsters Union and PASSO mobilized the Mexican Americans of Crystal City, Texas, to elect five of their members to the city council and gained control of city hall for the first time in half a century.[71]

Mexican Americans made up over 80 percent of the population of the South Texas town of Crystal City. Crystal City's ill-educated and unskilled Spanish-speaking residents had slightly over one and one-half years of education and survived on an annual family income of less than $2,000 a year. Yet Mexican Americans constituted the majority of the electorate in Crystal City. Because of the growing local concern with fighting the Anglos who ruled Crystal City, success appeared possible, and the Teamsters Union therefore became interested. The labor organization reasoned that the Crystal City elections might turn out to be an opportunity to expand its influence into South Texas. A poll tax drive was launched in Crystal City, and Teamsters Carlos Moore and Henry Muñoz arrived from Fort Worth and San Antonio to help the voting drive. PASSO understood that political power was more easily achieved on the municipal and county levels because both were non-partisan and not just subject to the Democratic primary. Providing speakers, funds, and expertise, PASSO boosted the morale and enthusiasm of the whole campaign. Virginia Muzquiz, Enriqueta Palacios, Elvira de la Fuente, and other women in the PASSO chapter in Crystal City carried this campaign forward.[72]

Crystal City's Mexican Americans succeeded in electing an all-Mexican American slate to the city council. Virginia Muzquiz was one of the candidates who won, making her the first Mexican American woman ever to serve on the Crystal City Council. Muzquiz ran the next year for the Texas state senate, the first Mexican American woman in Texas to do so, but lost. "We have done the impossible," declared Albert Fuentes, one of the leaders of the voter registration campaign. "If we can do it in Crystal City, we can do it all over Texas. We can awaken the sleeping giant." The defeat by Mexican Americans of the old Anglo establishment that had run Crystal City since its inception in 1907 attracted national attention. The five Mexican American elected officials held office for only two years, but the Crystal City revolt was of symbolic importance; it was the starting point of what became known as the Chicano movement.

Mexican American civil rights organizations had a united record on civil rights but differed on how to achieve these goals. The more vocal activists were becoming frustrated at the slow pace of change. Some veered leftward, whereas assertive separatism appealed to those who had grown disillusioned with racism's dominance. Still others believed that cooperation and collaboration with African Americans was essential to progress in the struggle for equality. The rebellion in northern New Mexico that would be led by a fundamentalist preacher named Reies López Tijerina from Laredo, Texas, provided a preview of the impending insurgency.

On February 2, 1963, in northern New Mexico, López Tijerina founded the *Alianza Federal de Mercedes* (Federal Alliance of Land Grants). The Alianza was intent on securing the restoration of individual and communal land grants in New Mexico and the Southwest that had been guaranteed by the 1848 Treaty of Guadalupe Hidalgo but that Anglos had fraudulently acquired. The other goals of the Alianza were to gain respect and recognition for the Spanish language and culture. A spellbinding orator, Tijerina's voice evoked a sense of mission among thousands of Mexican Americans who seized hope and strength from his call to revolt. Tijerina tried to broaden his appeal beyond the circle in which it first won favor by including African Americans and American Indians. Five years earlier, in 1958, the interracialist Tijerina had gone to Chicago and met with Elijah Mohammed, the head of the Black Muslim movement. During his ten-day visit, Elijah Mohammed pointed out to the future proponent of Chicano nationalism that the Black Muslims identified racism as part of the basic nature of the white man, who was doomed to extinction, and emphasized black power and nationalism as opposed to integration. More important, the Messenger of Allah counseled Tijerina of the need for unity between the two minority groups.[73] Tijerina would contribute to the Chicano power movement that called on the Mexican American people to lead the struggle for their own liberation.

Already other Mexican American advocates of social change were moving into community positions. A broad array of strategies and tactics required to accomplish large-scale social change would all demand the simultaneous enlistment of organizations and leaders from different, sometimes competing, perspectives.

The new Mexican American organizations furnished the network to build solidarity and awaken consciousness in the struggle against racial inequality. Women, through their dedication and commitment to community issues, continued to participate as leaders and not merely as organizers in this next phase of the movement. Dolores Huerta's ingenuity and persistence greatly expanded the reach of the farmworkers' union movement throughout California and the Southwest and helped to create the grassroots network that provided a base for the Chicano movement in the following decades. As a trailblazer and an unsung hero of the early Mexican American civil rights movement, the Mexican American "Moses of her people," Dolores Huerta would inspire a range of political organizations and feminist groups.

**Dolores Huerta Registering Members at the NFWA's Founding Convention, 1962.**
CREDIT: Dolores Huerta, cofounder of the National Farm Workers Association, registering members at the NFWA's founding convention in 1962. Used with the permission of the Dolores Huerta Foundation and the photographer ©Joseph F. Gunterman. Dolores Huerta is currently president of the Dolores Huerta Foundation and continues her organizing work for social justice.

On August 28, 1963, the American public's attention centered on Dr. Martin Luther King, Jr.'s, March on Washington for Jobs and Freedom of two hundred thousand people, the largest demonstration in the nation's capital. Mexican Americans in Texas, California, and elsewhere with a vision of American society free from racial and economic injustice and who were unable to attend the big march in Washington joined locally held "freedom marches" in support of Dr. King's march. The demonstrators called for fair hiring practices, a minimum-wage increase, and the creation of new jobs through a federal public works program. In Los Angeles, there were Mexican Americans who supported a Mexican American–African American alliance, for they realized its full potential as a vehicle to attain equality. Those from the Mexican American Political Association, which had earlier sent members to work in the civil rights movement in the Deep South, carried the day for interracialist unity. To the five thousand demonstrators gathered in front of the Los Angeles City Hall, they proudly proclaimed in a spirit of mutuality and common cause: "On behalf of the Mexican-American community, we extend the hand of friendship and solidarity."[74]

In this year, an investigation was initiated by scholars at the University of California at Los Angeles, funded by the Ford Foundation, for "a comprehensive study of the social-economic position of Mexican Americans in selected urban areas in five southwestern states."[75] Relegated to the margins of American society, Mexican Americans came to realize that they lived in a country divided drastically between haves and have-nots and that they happened to constitute a large proportion of the have-nots. A rash of new leaders and organizations sprang up pledged to gaining not only racial justice but also economic justice for Mexican Americans.

## CONCLUSION

At the end of World War II, Mexican Americans experienced the stigma of social and economic oppression and political powerlessness. They were victimized by racism and poverty and lived in the dismal world of rural and urban slums. For the appallingly poor, undereducated, underclad, and underfed Mexican American farmworker and his children, working conditions were close to unendurable, and the labor camps they inhabited were primitive in the extreme.

Ernesto Galarza took charge of organizing domestic farmworkers against growers in California who regularly collaborated with the INS and the U.S. Border Patrol to break unionizing campaigns. Galarza was a tactical genius in dealing with the scourge of eager and hungry bracero and mojado workers. Dolores Huerta and César Chavez took up the torch borne by Ernesto Galarza and transformed their passion for social justice on behalf of America's farmworkers into a political movement. The activities of Hope Schecter Mendoza, María Durán, Virginia Muzquiz, and other Mexican American women demanded great respect and illustrate the pivotal role played by women in the Mexican American freedom movement.

The postwar environment shaped the politics of social change for Mexican Americans. Wartime service and sacrifices, the experience with racism at home and overseas, and the rising expectations for equality set the stage for a new era in

Mexican American civil rights. The National Association of Mexican Americans (ANMA) expressed, invoked, and gave meaning to the traditional fighting spirit and inherent radicalism of Mexican Americans. Remarkably outspoken about civil rights, this organization stated the obvious truths about America's disregard for international law and human rights. However, the domestic Red Scare destroyed or severely weakened progressive organizations such as ANMA and discredited radical Mexican Americans such as Robert Galván, Anna Correa-Bary, and others even though they fought back through the courts.

By 1954, more than a million workers from Mexico had crossed the Río Grande illegally. Faced with such competition, Mexican Americans were left with three options: to work for the same low wages as the Mexican aliens, to join the welfare roles, or to seek work elsewhere. It became an article of faith among many Mexican American activists that cheap labor displaced native workers, increased labor law violations and discrimination, and encouraged racist public discourse about unauthorized aliens and the rise in crime, disease, and other social ills. Mexican American organizational leaders united to oppose the bracero program and, when national concerns about undocumented workers rose, they supported immigration controls.

The Red Scare crackdown on dissenters led to a deportation frenzy while efforts to disrupt the organizing of Mexican Americans continued. Functioning under Operation Wetback and Operation Terror, U.S. Immigration, Border, and Customs agencies conducted search-and-seizure campaigns and committed innumerable human and civil rights violations.

In such a repressive climate, the Mexican American civil rights movement that emerged had a very different leadership with different methods. The anti-Communist Community Service Organization encouraged Mexican Americans to vote and to seize community power, in addition to developing multiple issues for grassroots action out of local concerns. LULAC rejected direct action as a means to affect change and avoided rhetoric that antagonized Anglos, choosing instead to work behind the scenes. In the context of anti-Communism's redefinition of the notions of Americanism, American loyalty, and American citizenship, these organizations advanced civil rights by replacing direct action through mass mobilization with litigation and cooperation.[76]

Mexican Americans wrestled with problems of racial classification. Some Mexican Americans expressed an urge to whiteness. For these individuals, the "Caucasian calculation"—the decision to fight for white rights for some, rather than equal rights for all—reflected a pragmatic albeit problematic political strategy. As Mexican Americans turned to the courts for redress, there were civil rights decisions in Texas, California, and Arizona against segregated schools that foreshadowed the 1954 Supreme Court ruling *Brown v. Board of Education*. The rights of Mexican Americans to serve on juries and to vote were no less hard won. The Hernández case demonstrates the pernicious nature of racism in Texas justice. The Hernández case attracted the attention of many Anglo-Texans, as well as civil rights groups, including the NAACP. Legal rights did not automatically produce equality for Mexican Americans because serious social and economic problems remained unsolved.

Both national political parties recognized the role of Mexican Americans as balance-of-power voters. Like John F. Kennedy before him, Lyndon Baines Johnson did not want to be abandoned by the Mexican constituency of the Democratic Party. Under President Johnson, the federal government would make the strongest commitment to equality for minorities. Through the use of federal power, President Johnson would provide the legal structure for the attainment of Mexican American civil rights. In 1964, President Johnson signed the Economic Opportunity Act to eliminate or alleviate the causes and roots of poverty. The domestic poverty programs for minorities and the poor ranged from education for preschool children to Model Cities, mobilizing unemployed youths, to employment for the aged. Although voting favorably as Democrats, Mexican Americans still had little to show for their party devotion in the way of political office or social reform.

The larger civil rights movement with its dual goal of attaining racial and economic uplift unquestionably provided the energy, inspiration, and model for the Mexican American struggle for equality as it did for every other social reform effort that emerged in the United States. Many Mexican Americans were strongly supportive of African American rights—not as a moral issue, as some historians contend, but because identification with the civil rights movement meant taking direct action against racial and economic inequality.[77]

The most visible change in the 1960s and 1970s would be the role of younger Mexican Americans in a broad-based movement for equality, more powerful than anything seen before. These young radicals shared their talents and energies with other movements spawned in the civil rights struggle: the farmworker's movement, educational reform, third-party politics, the antiwar movement, the Chicana women's movement, and the forging of a new social identity. The Chicano movement was better organized and more determined to bring down the final curtain on discrimination. It would be a poor people's revolt. Clearly, the even more far-reaching rights revolution that Mexican Americans launched was built on the foundation established by the activists of the early postwar years, who took a brave stand for meaningful change.

## NOTES

1. Nancy MacLean, *Freedom Is Not Enough: The Opening of the American Workplace* (Cambridge, MA: Harvard University Press, 2006), 163; Enrique R. Buelna, "The Mexican Question: Mexican Americans in the Communist Party, 1940–1957," Center for Research on Latinos in a Global Society, University of California, Irvine, 1999, http://repositories.cdlib.org/crlgs/WP14, 11.
2. MacLean, *Freedom Is Not Enough,* 163–164.
3. Ibid. The Los Angeles CRC provided free legal assistance and had a Bail Fund Committee and an outreach program in its defense against police brutality, job discrimination, and deportation. Buelna, "The Mexican Question," 21–22. In 1947 Party member Ralph Cuarón opened an office of the CRC near downtown Los Angeles where he referred cases to the CRC's main office. Ibid.
4. MacLean, *Freedom Is Not Enough,* 162–164.

5. Ibid., 164; Gerald Horne, *Black Liberation/Red Scare: Ben Davis and the Communist Party* (Newark: University of Delaware Press, 1994), 9.

6. MacLean, *Freedom Is Not Enough,* 159.

7. Martha Biondi, *To Stand and Fight: The Struggle for Civil Rights in Postwar New York City* (Cambridge, MA: Harvard University Press, 2003), 1–4; Ruth Needleman, *Black Freedom Fighters in Steel: The Struggle for Democratic Unionism* (Ithaca, NY: Cornell University Press, 2003), 142.

8. Mexicans accounted for 11 percent of the Southwest region's population in 1950 and 12 percent ten years later. In Texas border cities the Mexican American population increase averaged 75 percent. El Paso's Spanish-speaking population increased 112 percent, from 130,485 residents in 1950 to 276,687 in 1960. Grebler, Moore, and Guzmán, *Mexican American People,* 107.

9. Overall, Mexican Americans had the distinction of being "the only ethnic group for which a comparison of the characteristics of the first and second generations fails to show a substantial intergenerational rise in socioeconomic status." Richard Polenberg, *One Nation Divisible: Class, Race, and Ethnicity in the United States Since 1938* (New York: Penguin Books, 1980), 152. The postwar surge of industrialization in the Southwest took place in construction and service industries and in the creation of high-technical industries of aviation, electronics, and the atomic and space-related sectors. Mexican Americans were locked out of the new factory jobs because they lacked education and skills and because employers and unions blocked their entrance into training programs. Paul Bullock, "Employment Problems of the Mexican American," *Industrial Relations: A Journal of Economy and Society* 3, no. 3 (May 1964): 38.

10. Paul Bullock and Robert Singleton, "What to Do With a Drop Out," *New Republic* 147 (October 1962), 17–18. Between 1950 and 1960, Los Angeles County's Mexican population doubled from 287,614 to 576,716. Ibid.

11. Vargas, *Labor Rights Are Civil Rights,* 285–286.

12. Ibid., 286–287.

13. Ibid., 286.

14. American Council of Spanish-Speaking People, "Pistol Happy Texas Sheriff Gets Eighth Notch," *Civil Liberties Newsletter of the American Council of Spanish-Speaking People,* no. 4 (March 17, 1952): 3, Julian Zamora Papers, Special Collections, University of Texas, Austin; American Council of Spanish-Speaking People, "Taylor Cop Kills Latin Vets," *Civil Liberties Newsletter of the American Council of Spanish-Speaking People,* no. 6 (July 14, 1952), 1, Julian Zamora Papers, Special Collections, University of Texas, Austin.

15. Carl Abbott, "Plural Society in Colorado: Ethnic Relations in the Twentieth Century," *Phylon* 39, no. 3 (1978): 251; Rudolph "Corky" Gonzales, Los Voluntarios, et al., Denver, Colorado, to Governor John Love, Denver, Colorado, April 15, 1964, Dr. Hector P. García Collection, 27.6, Special Collections Library, University of Texas, Corpus Christi.

16. Kenneth C. Burt, "Tony Rios and Bloody Christmas: A Turning Point Between the Los Angeles Police Department and the Latino Community," *Western Legal History* 14, no. 2 (Summer/Fall 2001): 159–192; Vargas, *Labor Rights Are Civil Rights,* 261; Camarillo, *Chicanos in California,* 78. Julius Burns was beaten unconscious and collapsed over his dead brother's body. Seventeen-year-old Augustine Salcido was shot through the head by a Los Angeles police officer, while thirteen-year-old Eugene Montenegro, an honor student, was fatally shot in the back by a Los Angeles County deputy sheriff. Vargas, *Labor Rights Are Civil Rights,* 260–261.

17. Chicago Council Against Racial and Religious Discrimination, Chicago, Illinois, Senator Dennis Chavez Papers, Washington, DC, January 8, 1946, Papers, MSS 374 BC, box 79, folder 1, University of New Mexico Center for Southwest Research Collection, University of New Mexico, Albuquerque; Kevin M. Schultz, "The FEPC and the Legacy of the Labor-Based Civil Rights Movement of the 1940s," *Labor History* 49, no. 1 (February 2008): 79.

18. Camarillo, *Chicanos in California,* 78. The Landrum-Griffin Act helped to break the 1963 Tex Son Company strike, a prolonged and violence-marred action by Mexican American textile workers in San Antonio, Texas. Arizona and Texas passed right-to-work laws, and New Mexico was seeking similar legislation. The labor legislation in Texas was some of the most restrictive in the nation. Organized labor began to develop a campaign of political education and mobilizing to create a more favorable environment for labor. Michael K. Honey, *Southern Labor and Black Civil Rights: Organizing Memphis Workers* (Urbana: University of Illinois Press, 1993), 276.

19. Vargas, *Labor Rights Are Civil Rights,* 257–258.

20. Lawrence S. Wittner, *Cold War America: From Hiroshima to Watergate* (New York: Praeger, 1974), 136.

21. Juan Gómez-Quiñones, *Mexican Labor, 1790-1990* (Albuquerque: University of New Mexico Press, 1994), 234; Pauline R. Kibbe, *Latin Americans in Texas* (Albuquerque: University of New Mexico Press, 1946), 198–199; President's Commission on Migratory Labor, *Migratory Labor in American Agriculture. Report of the President's Commission on Migratory Labor* (Washington, DC: U.S. Government Printing Office, 1951), especially chapters 8 through 11; Michael Harrington, *The Other America: Poverty in the United States* (New York: Macmillan, 1963), especially chapter 3.

22. By 1950, the NFLU had recruited fifty thousand active members out of a half million domestic migrant farm workers; *New York Times,* January 14, 1950, 7. A detailed account of what transpired in the Di Giorgio strike can be found in Ernesto Galarza, *Spiders in the House and Workers in the Field* (Notre Dame, IN: University of Notre Dame Press, 1970).

23. *New York Times,* October 18, 1947, 19; Galarza, *Merchants of Labor,* 216.

24. Margaret Rose, "Gender and Civic Activism in Mexican American Barrios in California: The Community Service Organization, 1947–1962," in *Not June Cleaver: Women and Gender in Postwar America, 1945-1960,* ed. Joanne Meyerowitz (Philadelphia: Temple University Press, 1994), 183. The following year, Huerta helped to secure Aid for Dependent Families for the unemployed.

25. Jack Cargill, "Empire and Opposition: The 'Salt of the Earth' Strike," in *Labor in New Mexico: Unions, Strikes, and Social History Since 1881,* ed. Robert Kern (Albuquerque: University of New Mexico Press, 1983), 183–267.

26. Ruiz, *From Out of the Shadows,* 84–86; Larry R. Salomon, "It's Our Union, Too: Mexican American Women Rescue the 'Salt of the Earth' Strike," in *Roots of Justice: Stories of Organizing in Communities of Color,* ed. Larry R. Salomon (Hoboken, NJ: Jossey-Bass, 1998), 31–40.

27. Author's personal conversation with long-time labor activist Bert Corona in Santa Barbara, California, October 1995. For a history of the making of the film *Salt of the Earth* see James J. Lorence, *The Suppression of Salt of the Earth: How Hollywood, Big Labor, and Politicians Blacklisted a Movie in Cold War America* (Albuquerque: University of New Mexico Press, 1999).

28 Kenneth C. Burt, "Latino Empowerment in Los Angeles: Postwar Dreams and Cold War Fears, 1948–1952," *Labor's Heritage* 8, no. 1 (Summer 1996): 16; Vargas, *Labor Rights Are Civil Rights,* 275–276; Zaragosa Vargas, "In the Years of Darkness and Torment: The

Early Mexican American Struggle for Civil Rights, 1945–1963," *New Mexico Historical Review* 76 (October 2001): 399.

29. Vargas, *Labor Rights Are Civil Rights*, 276–277.

30. Ibid.

31. ANMA also protested the printing of racist news articles by the *Los Angeles Examiner* that, in associating crime with African Americans and Mexican Americans, blamed "rat-packs" and "pachucos" for a crime wave in that city. ANMA chronicled among its early activities "the first Mexican observance of Negro History Week" in the Maravilla Mexican community of East Los Angeles. Vargas, *Labor Rights Are Civil Rights*, 276–277; Vargas, "In the Years of Darkness and Torment," 400.

32. Organizations Designated Under Executive Order No. 10450. Compiled from Memoranda of the Attorney General. Consolidated List—November 1, 1955. Dr. Hector P. García Collection, 105.8, Special Collections Library, University of Texas, Corpus Christi, Texas; Vargas, *Labor Rights Are Civil Rights*, 277; Vargas, "In the Years of Darkness and Torment," 400–401; Ellen R. Baker, *On Strike and on Film: Mexican American Families and Blacklisted Filmmakers in Cold War America* (Chapel Hill: University of North Carolina Press, 2007), 106; Buelna, "The Mexican Question," 24.

33. Burt, "Latino Empowerment in Los Angeles," 8; Louis F. Weschler and John F. Gallagher, "Viva Kennedy," in *Cases in American National Government and Politics,* ed. Rocco J. Tresolini and Richard T. Frost (Englewood Cliffs, NJ: Prentice-Hall,1966), 53; Katherine Underwood, "Pioneering Minority Representation: Edward Roybal and the Los Angeles City Council, 1949–1962," *Pacific Historical Review* 66, no. 3 (August 1997): 409; Raphael J. Soneishien, *Politics in Black and White: Race and Power in Los Angeles* (Princeton, NJ: Princeton University Press, 1993), 26, 30; Sanford D. Horwitt, *Let Them Call Me Rebel: Saul Alinsky: His Life and Legacy* (New York: Knopf, 1989), 227–228.

34. Underwood, "Pioneering Minority Representation," 410.

35. Burt, "Latino Empowerment in Los Angeles," 13–15; Vargas, *Labor Rights Are Civil Rights*, 275; Rose, "Gender and Civic Activism," 186; Charles Payne, "Men Led, but Women Organized: Movement Participation of Women in the Mississippi Delta," in *Women in the Civil Rights Movement: Trailblazers and Torchbearers, 1941–1965,* ed. Vicki L. Crawford, Jacqueline Anne Rouse, and Barbara Woods (Brooklyn, NY: Carlson, 1990), 1–2; Underwood, "Pioneering Minority Representation," 407.

36. Underwood, "Pioneering Minority Representation," 402, 410, 413; Edward Ross Roybal, "Justification for Vote Against the Communist Registration Ordinance," box 8, 3, Edward Ross Roybal Papers, Department of Special Collections/UCLA Library.

37. By the early 1960s there were thirty-four CSO chapters in California with ten thousand dues- paying members. Underwood, "Pioneering Minority Representation," 406.

38. Vargas, "In the Years of Darkness and Torment," 397.

39. Pycior, *LBJ and Mexican Americans*, 61–62, 64–66.

40. Anglo-Texans paid the poll taxes of the local Spanish-speaking residents because they were the basis of their political power.

41. Patricia Morgan, *Shame of a Nation* (Los Angeles: Los Angeles Committee for the Protection of the Foreign Born, 1954), 39–48; Louise Pettibone Smith, *Torch of Liberty: Twenty-five Years in the Life of the Foreign Born in the U.S.A.* (New York: Dwight-King, 1959), 418–419; David Caute, *The Great Fear: The Anti-Communist Purge Under Truman and Eisenhower* (New York: Simon and Schuster, 1979), 215, 229.

42. Vargas, *Labor Rights Are Civil Rights*, 271; Vargas, "In the Years of Darkness and Torment," 392.

43. Carlos Larralde, "Roberto Galván: A Latino Leader of the 1940s," *Journal of San Diego History* 50, nos. 1–2 (2004): 154.

44. Carlos K. Blanton, "George I. Sánchez, Ideology, and Whiteness in the Making of the Mexican American Civil Rights Movement," *Journal of Southern History* 72, no. 3 (August 2006): 588; *Galvan v. Press*, Officer in Charge, Immigration and Naturalization Service, 201 F.2d 302 (10th Cir. 1954). Robert Galván joined the Party in 1944, but he ended his alliance with the Communists in 1947 after deciding that he no longer wanted to belong to the Party.

45. Although the Supreme Court upheld the Smith Act in 1951 in *Dennis v. United States*, the court later limited the operation of the act in *Yates v. United States* (1957). As a result, government prosecutors began abandoning its use in favor of administrative actions through the Subversive Activities Control Board, thereby avoiding the evidentiary and civil liberties problems posed by *Yates v. United States*. Yet such administrative actions did not last, as the government dropped the last case in 1964.

46. Gerald Horne, *Communist Front? The Civil Rights Congress, 1946–1956* (Rutherford, NJ: Fairleigh Dickinson University Press, 1988), 320; Susan J. Siggelakis, "Advocacy on Trial," *American Journal of Legal History* 36, no. 4 (October 1992): 502, 506; *Bary v. United States*, 248 F.2d 201; 292 F.2d 53 (10th Cir. 1961).

47 Ira Gollobin, *Winds of Change: An Immigrant Lawyer's Perspective of Fifty Years* (New York: Center for Immigration Rights, Inc., 1987), 9.

48. Vargas, *Labor Rights Are Civil Rights*, 146–147.

49. Morgan, *Shame of a Nation*, 35; Smith, *Torch of Liberty*, 423.

50. Ralph Guzmán, *Roots Without Rights: A Study of the Loss of United States Citizenship by Native Born Americans of Mexican Ancestry* (Los Angeles: American Civil Liberties Union, Los Angeles Chapter, 1957), 47–66. In the Midwest area, the INS established a "Chicago-to-Mexico airlift" to expedite the deportation drive in this region. Valdés, *Barrios Norteños*, 162–163.

51. Smith, *Torch of Liberty*, 421–422; Horne, *Communist Front?*, 329; Polenberg, *One Nation Divisible*, 181; Ralph Guzmán, "Politics of the Mexican-American Community," in *California Politics and Policies*, ed. Eugene P. Dvorin and Arthur J. Misner (Reading, MA: Addison-Wesley, 1966), 365; Henry A. J. Ramos, *The American GI Forum: In Pursuit of the Dream, 1948–1983* (Houston, TX: Arte Publico Press, 1998), 72.

52. Claire Sheridan, "'Another White Race': Mexican Americans and the Paradox of Whiteness in Jury Selection," *Law and History Review* 21, no. 1 (Spring 2003): 9. See also Thomas Guglielmo, "Fighting for Caucasian Rights: Mexicans, Mexican Americans, and the Transnational Struggle for Civil Rights in World War II Texas," *Journal of American History* 92, no. 4 (March 2006): 1212–1237.

53. Blanton, "George I. Sánchez, Ideology, and Whiteness," 592; Robert G. Newey and David B. Tyack, "Victims Without 'Crimes': Some Historical Perspectives on Black Education," *Journal of Negro Education* 40, no. 3 (Summer 1971): 199.

54. MacLean, *Freedom Is Not Enough*, 156–157; Ian Haney Lopez, *White by Law: The Legal Construction of Race* (New York: New York University Press, 1997), 212; James A. Ferg-Cadima, *Black, White and Brown: Latino School Desegregation Efforts in the Pre- and Post-Brown v. Board of Education* (Mexican American Legal Defense and Educational Fund, 2004), 12–13.

55. Blanton, "George I. Sánchez, Ideology, and Whiteness," 587–588; Sheridan, "'Another White Race,'" 9; Ferg-Cadima, *Black, White and Brown*, 35. In the 1950 *Gonzalez v. Sheely* case, Mexican Americans sued the board of trustees of the Tolleson Elementary School District of Maricopa County in federal court. The federal judge found that the

segregation of Mexican American schoolchildren violated the plaintiff's due process and equal protection rights under the Fourteenth Amendment. See *Gonzalez v. Sheely*, 96 F. Supp. 1004 (D. Ariz. 1951).

56. *Westminster School Dist. of Orange County et al. v. Mendez et al.*, 161 F.2d 774 (9th Cir. 1947); *Delgado v. Bastrop Independent School District* (No. 388 Civil, unreported: W. D. Texas 1948); Blanton, "George I. Sánchez, Ideology, and Whiteness," 589–590.

57. Though the Alianza and the NAACP intentionally filed separate suits on the same day, the court consolidated both. The outcome of these cases was positive for both the NAACP and Alianza. Blanton, "George I. Sánchez, Ideology, and Whiteness," 601; *Romero et al. v. Weakley et al.*, 131 F. Supp. 818 (9th Cir. 1955).

58. *Galvan v. Press*; Blanton, "George I. Sánchez, Ideology, and Whiteness," 590; Sheridan, "'Another White Race,'" 27–28; Ariela J. Gross, "Mexican Americans and the Politics of Whiteness," *Law and History Review* 21, no. 1 (Spring 2003): 15; Jake Rodriguez, Texas, to Senator Dennis Chavez, Washington, DC, July 26, 1957, Jacob Rodriguez File, General Correspondence, 1953–1959, box 1, folder 1, LULAC Papers, Nettie Lee Benson Latin American Collection, University of Texas, Austin.

59. Michael J. Klarman, *From Jim Crow to Civil Rights: The Supreme Court and the Struggle for Racial Equality* (New York: Oxford University Press, 2004), 301.

60. MacLean, *Freedom Is Not Enough*, 161; Blanton, "George I. Sánchez, Ideology, and Whiteness,"591.

61. MacLean, *Freedom Is Not Enough*, 160; Permanent Committee on Latin American Affairs, Texas AFL-CIO, *An Affair of Conscience: A Report and Some Recommendations to the Texas AFL-CIO of the Annual Convention*, Brownsville, Texas, August 17–20, 1964.

62. "Midland, Texas Theatre Discrimination," 1, Dr. Hector P. García Collection, 183.22, Special Collections Library, University of Texas, Corpus Christi, Texas; "Greyhound Bus Discrimination," 1–3, Dr. Hector P. García Collection, 181.52, Special Collections Library, University of Texas, Corpus Christi, Texas.

63. Robert A. Goldberg, "Racial Change on the Southern Periphery: The Case of San Antonio, Texas, 1960–1965," *Journal of Southern History* 49, no. 3 (August 1983): 362; Neil Foley, "Partly Colored or Other: Mexican Americans and Their Problems with the Color Line," in *Beyond Black and White: Race, Ethnicity, and Gender in the U.S. South and Southwest*, ed. Stephanie Cole, Alison M. Parker, and Laura F. Edwards (College Station: Texas A&M University Press, 2004), 137.

64. Blanton, "George I. Sánchez, Ideology, and Whiteness," 600.

65. Ronnie Dugger, "The Segregation Filibuster of 1957," *Texas Observer*, December 27, 1974; *Time*, May 13, 1957. In 1958, González unsuccessfully ran for governor of Texas; although an unlikely candidate, he wanted to offer an alternative to the race between Texas Governor Marion Price Daniel and former Governor W. Lee O'Daniel. González was reelected to the Texas State Legislature and served until 1961. In 1963, as a U.S. Representative, González once again received substantial publicity when he voted against additional appropriations for the House Committee on Un-American Activities.

66. Ricardo Romo, "George I. Sánchez and the Civil Rights Movement: 1940–1960," *La Raza Law Journal* 1 (Fall 1986): 342–344; Ramos, *American GI Forum*, 8, 60–61, 74, 82–83; Don E. Carleton, *Red Scare! Right-wing Hysteria, Fifties Fanaticism and Their Legacy in Texas* (Austin: Texas Monthly Press, 1985), 276, 284; Michael J. Klarman, "How Brown Changed Race Relations: The Backlash Thesis," *Journal of American History* 81, no. 1 (June 1994): 84, 90, 97, 102, 117.

67. Weschler and Gallagher, "Viva Kennedy," 56.

68. Ibid., 55–56. Much of this electoral politics initiative came about through the AFL-CIO's Committee on Political Education (COPE).

69. Oral history interview by José Angel Gutiérrez with Francisco Medrano, CMAS 37, Special Collections, University of Texas at Arlington Libraries, 63–67. In 1966, Medrano would participate in the march of Mexican American farmworkers from the Río Grande Valley to Austin, the so-called "Minimum Wage March" that contributed to the passage of the state's first minimum-wage law.

70. In 1962, Ernestine Tina Villanueva was elected judge in Jim Wells County and was later voted in as county commissioner through the help of her impoverished constituency. In the same year in California, Mexican Americans, aided by MAPA, helped secure Edward B. Roybal's election to the U.S. Congress and voted in two Mexican Americans to the California State Legislature. Ibid., 61.

71. Jack Languth, "March in Phoenix Is Met by Mayor," *New York Times*, July 26, 1963, A1; "Rights Parley Breakup Blamed on Hate Groups," *Los Angeles Times*, August 19, 1963, 20.

72. José Angel Gutiérrez and Rebecca E. Deen, "Chicanas in Texas Politics," (Occasional Paper No. 66, Julian Samora Research Institute, Michigan State University, East Lansing, Michigan, 2000), 9.

73. RE: Nation of Islam, University of New Mexico, Center for Southwest Research Collection, Reies López Tijerina Papers, MSS 654BC, FBI files, box 2, folder 13, 7–8; Reies López Tijerina to Dr. Alton A. Davis, September 7, 1963,University of New Mexico, Center for Southwest Research Collection, Reies López Tijerina Papers, MSS 654BC, box 41, folder 40; FBI District Office, San Diego, California, to Director, FBI, Washington, DC, January 27, 1964, University of New Mexico, Center for Southwest Research Collection, Reies López Tijerina Papers, MSS 654BC, box 41, folder 40; Frances Swadesh, "The Alianza Movement of New Mexico: The Interplay of Social Change and Public Commentary," in *Minorities and Politics,* ed. Henry Jack Tobias and Charles E. Woodhouse (Albuquerque: University of New Mexico Press, 1969), 53–84; Abbott, "Plural Society in Colorado," 259. The interracialist Tijerina would later meet with Dr. Martin Luther King, Jr., who chose him to coordinate the New Mexico section of the Poor Peoples' March and to lead the March's Southwest contingent.

74. On June 14, 1964, the MAPA at its state convention in Fresno, California, passed resolutions condemning the anti-Rumford Housing Act initiative and pledging "cooperation with Negroes in areas of common concern." Ruben Salazar, "Latin-Negro Unity Move Launched July 5, 1964," in *Ruben Salazar: Border Correspondent: Selected Writings, 1955–1970,* ed. Mario T. García (Berkeley: University of California Press, 1995), 144–146. Although there was growing sentiment on the part of progressive Mexican Americans to join the drive by African Americans for civil rights, a few conservative leaders expressed concern over the relation of Mexican Americans to the African American cause. One reason was economic, as employers were firing Mexican Americans workers from their jobs to make room for African Americans out of their fear of retaliation from African Americans if they did not hire them. Ruben Salazar, "Negro Drive Worries Mexican-Americans," *Los Angeles Times*, July 14, 1963, G10; *Los Angeles Times,* August 17, 1963; Gladwin Hill, "Mexican-Americans Now Back Negro Campaign in Los Angeles," *New York Times,* August 30, 1963, 11.

75. Grebler, Moore, and Guzmán, *Mexican-American People*, v.

76. Jenkins, *Cold War at Home*, 209.

77. MacLean, *Freedom Is Not Enough*, 169.

# CHAPTER 10

## Mexican Americans in the Protest Era

### 1964–1974

In 1960, the statistics for Mexican Americans seemed particularly disconcerting. The median income of a Mexican American family was just 62 percent of that of the general population. A third of all families subsisted on less than $3,000 a year, the federal poverty line. Unemployment was twice the rate of that for whites. Four-fifths of all Mexican American workers were concentrated in unskilled or semiskilled jobs, a third of these in agriculture.[1] In addition, the vast majority of Mexican Americans attended largely segregated public schools, and there were few Mexican American teachers. Seventy-five percent of Mexican American students dropped out before finishing high school to support their families, or they simply gave up. As a result, Mexican Americans nationwide averaged less than nine years of school and were thus not fully prepared for either further education or employment.[2]

The vote failed to protect the interests of Mexican Americans. Gerrymandered election districts, restrictive voting legislation, and other electoral arrangements still hindered political representation. In 1968, three years after the passage of the 1965 Voting Rights Act, the only Mexican American member of the U.S. Senate was Joseph M. Montoya of New Mexico, and just three Mexican Americans served in the U.S. House of Representatives: Edward R. Roybal of California and Henry B. González and Eligio de la Garza of Texas. No Mexican Americans served in the California State Legislature. Texas had ten Mexican Americans in the State Legislature, and a third of the members of New Mexico's state Senate and House were Mexican Americans. Mexican Americans had no representation on school boards, city councils, or other government offices, and they were underrepresented on juries or else excluded by English-language requirements. The situation was far worse in the small cities and rural areas of the Southwest, where racism remained a formidable barrier.[3]

The role Lyndon Baines Johnson assumed as president was as the nation's savior, the redeemer who would end decades of national division and advocate social change by forging a Great Society. The legislative outpouring of 1964–1965 that launched the Great Society brought aid and opportunity to America's poor and dispossessed. The landmark civil rights legislation guaranteed equal social and political rights, and the ambitious and broad agenda of the War on Poverty aimed to enhance economic opportunity. The federal aid for elementary and secondary education took the form of assistance for disadvantaged children. Depressed-area bills brought aid to the disadvantaged, and jobs and training programs helped the unemployed. Medicare benefited the sick and elderly.[4]

Mexican Americans joined Johnson's War on Poverty and participated in programs sponsored by the Office of Equal Opportunity (OEO). However, they soon learned it was very difficult to use federal monies for the needs of the poor. Moreover, OEO program officials did not like the demands of and methods utilized by Mexican Americans. Reflecting the growing disaffection of African Americans with the unfulfilled promises of the Great Society, a growing number of dissenting Mexican American voices argued that their people had still achieved little economic justice. They also became dissatisfied with the federal government's continuing inattention to civil rights matters. Drawing on the experiences, strategies, and rhetoric of the civil rights movement, Mexican Americans renewed their fight to alter their inferior status in American society and to secure a portion of the American Dream.

The war in Vietnam not only brought a new tone to America's role in world affairs but also created significant shifts on the domestic front, especially among racial minorities caught up in the throes of rising expectations for social change. These realities laid the groundwork for the new insurgent style of protest that followed. Mexican Americans came to an understanding of themselves as a people ostracized by an Anglo-dominated society, and this understanding became the basis of action. The Chicano movement provided its members with an ideological foundation of nationalism, with like-minded activists, and with a sense of empowerment. By the late 1960s, there was increasing militancy and a change in the rhetoric, tone, and goals of the Mexican American freedom struggle. It was a multifaceted struggle that had as its objectives labor rights for farm workers, the regaining of stolen lands, economic opportunity, the utilization of barrios as vehicles for the mobilization of political power, educational reform, antiwar activism, rights for women, and the formation of an independent political party. Mexican Americans and their organizations would play different roles in each cause.

César Chavez and Dolores Huerta were principal figures in the struggle to organize farmworkers. They awakened the Mexican American people to oppression and unified them against it. In 1965 in Delano, California, their union, the United Farm Workers of America, led its first strike. The enhanced stature of César Chavez and Dolores Huerta gave their union credibility and standing. Long before the call for Chicano power, Reies López Tijerina in northern New Mexico joined and led the fight to win compensation for the descendants of Spanish-speaking families whose lands had been seized illegally. Tijerina tapped a deeply rooted tradition of resistance within the Spanish-speaking New Mexican population as a whole. Rodolfo "Corky" Gonzales was another of the Chicano movement's guiding spirits. In Denver, Gonzales formed the Crusade for Justice to address and protest core urban problems in the city's barrio—the rising inequality of incomes, limited employment opportunities, and poor housing conditions common to many large metropolitan areas. Gonzales inveighed against Anglo oppression but also fostered awareness of Mexican Americans' cultural heritage and identity. Thousands of Mexican Americans were involved in furthering the spread of the movement in the local areas.

A new era known as the Chicano movement had begun with its own manifestos, leaders, newspapers, journals, and presses. Many Mexican American militants saw the Chicano movement as a revolution. These young idealists were determined to construct a new society, with Aztlán, a Chicano homeland within the United States, as its building block to help Mexican Americans organize to seek satisfaction of their needs. Chicano power figured in the shaping of the Chicana liberation movement and radical feminism, particularly the refusal of many pointedly sexist male leaders to consider women or women's interests.

Throughout America, wherever Mexican Americans lived a process of self-discovery was under way as a sweeping transformation took place. The Chicano movement linked education reform to wider social reform through an emerging brand of student activism and leadership. With other community-based organizations, the Brown Berets made an effort to effect community control over schools. Through walkouts and boycotts, Mexican American high school students in many parts of the Southwest expressed their discontent over the inferior quality of public schooling they were receiving. In 1968, fifteen thousand angry high school students in East Los Angeles, California, protested against abysmal schools and poor counseling. The walkout broadened into a general protest concerning educational policies. Experiencing the affirmativeness of Chicano power, high school and university students founded student organizations and established Mexican American studies programs whose curricula embraced the history, culture, and lives of Chicanos. Mexican American youths became the frontline troops of the Chicano movement. Another issue was opposition to the war raging in Vietnam.

Mexican Americans fought in the Vietnam War and protested against it. As in World War II and Korea, Mexican Americans trusted that if they defended democracy abroad they were likely to receive it at home. These expectations as a whole did not materialize. Outrage over the Vietnam War and over the disproportionate number of Mexican American GIs fighting and dying in Southeast Asia contributed significantly to the embrace of Chicano power. However, not all the Mexican Americans who took part in the antiwar movement were political or social radicals. Many Mexican American citizens were coming out in opposition to the war by 1970 because by this time public opinion had turned decisively against U.S. involvement in Vietnam. The National Chicano Moratorium Against the War in Vietnam was the largest antiwar demonstration by a racial minority. It created a broad-based antiwar campaign that also called for the mobilization against the unresolved issue of domestic inequality in the United States.

Mexican American activists adopted the term *La Raza* (the Race) to express the militant nationalism that became a response to their ambiguous status in America. Frustrated in their inability to achieve acceptable progress within the society through the major parties, Mexican Americans launched their own independent effort. They formed La Raza Unida Party (RUP). Its goal was effective political mobilization to run and elect Mexican American candidates responsible to their communities. Although all of the collective efforts of Mexican Americans exposed ideological and personal conflicts within the movement, they succeeded for the first time in arousing political awareness and heightened aspirations.

Farmworker union strength achieved between 1964 and 1973 was largely achieved through the heroic efforts of César Chavez and Dolores Huerta. These two Mexican Americans brought national attention to the plight of farmworkers and, moreover, challenged the power and control that growers in California and the rest of America had wielded over farmworkers for more than a century.

## VIVA LA HUELGA!: GAINING GROUND FOR FARMWORKERS

Farm labor conditions improved as a result of the building of the United Farm Workers of America. César Chavez and Dolores Huerta were the architects of this national farmworker movement. Born in Yuma, Arizona, in 1927, Chavez was one of five children of Mexican immigrants. Following their abrupt expulsion from their farm during the Great Depression, the Chavez family was forced into a life of migrant work. In 1944, Chavez joined the U.S. Navy and served two years in the Pacific. After the war, he got married and for a short period worked as a sharecropper, followed by stints as a farm and a lumber camp worker. Moving to San Jose, California, in 1952, Chavez met Fred Ross of the Community Service Organization, who recruited him into this group. Chavez joined the CSO and became a local organizer, establishing CSO chapters throughout California. He was appointed the CSO's statewide general director in 1958 but quit four years later because the CSO refused to organize farmworkers into a union. With his wife and their eight children, Chavez moved to Delano, California, the center of the nation's table grape industry. Here, he created a small social service organization for area farmworkers that he named the Farm Workers Association and that became the National Farm Workers Association (NFWA).

Meanwhile, in Stockton, California, Dolores Huerta quit her teaching job and joined Chavez in organizing farmworkers. "I couldn't stand seeing kids come to class hungry and needing shoes," Huerta later said. "I thought I could do more by organizing farmworkers than by trying to teach their hungry children." Dolores Huerta found her calling in the labor movement. The organizer's father and mother were formative in her childhood socialization. Her upbringing was based on an allegiance to family and a commitment to take care of the less fortunate within the community. Born in Dawson, New Mexico, Dolores Huerta's father was a coal miner and union activist who was elected state assemblyman for San Miguel County. He promoted a wage and hours bill and other legislation favorable to workers. Following the divorce of her parents, Dolores's mother took her children to Stockton, California, where she found a job as a cannery worker, then became the owner of a hotel. Dolores went to college and became a teacher to students who were poor migrant workers and who could not speak English. Building on and expanding her parents' social activism, Dolores left teaching in 1955 to start a chapter of the CSO in Stockton, serving as its lobbyist in the California State Legislature during the late 1950s and early 1960s.

**César Chavez (left) Outside the National Farm Workers' Association Headquarters, 1966.**
CREDIT: *uclamss_1387_b72_32252-2.  UCLA Charles E. Young Research Library, Department of Special Collections, Los Angeles Times Photographic Archive, ©Regents of The University of California, UCLA Library.*

Dolores Huerta brought years of experience to the fledgling farmworker struggle as an organizer, speaker, and writer and an unwavering belief that in group-centered leadership people collectively, through direct participation, could foster social change. Huerta and Chavez set themselves the task of transforming their union into a mass movement committed to the strike, boycott, and nonviolent direct action that drew its strength from farmworkers and their supporters. While fulfilling this mission of championing labor's cause, Huerta was arrested and jailed twenty times.

Two farmworker strikes took place in California in the spring of 1965. One was by workers on a rose farm in McFarland who asked the NFWA for help. The company called the police and brought in strikebreakers from Mexico. Ultimately, the company agreed to a wage increase but not union recognition. That fall, the Agricultural Workers Organizing Committee (AWOC), headed by veteran Filipino labor activist Larry Itliong, led a walkout of grape pickers in the Coachella Valley over low wages. The grape growers began bringing strikebreakers into the fields. AWOC asked the NFWA to join the strike, and it did on September 16. Five thousand grape workers from over thirty farms walked off their jobs.[5]

In December 1965, the NFWA began a nationwide boycott of grapes grown by Schenley Industries, DiGiorgio Fruit Corporation, and eighty-three other wine growers. UAW President Walter Reuther pledged five thousand dollars a month until the NFWA won the strike, and the great labor figure visited Delano and legitimized the farmworker struggle. To strengthen their position, the NFWA and the AWOC merged on August 22, 1966, as the United Farm Workers Organizing Committee (UFWOC). Cesar Chávez became UFWOC's director, Larry Itliong the assistant director, and Dolores Huerta the union's main negotiator. The strike against the grape growers would last five years.[6]

Unions, civil rights organizations, and church and faith groups came to the support of La Causa (the cause), as the farmworkers' movement became known. In many parts of the United States religious authorities were the UFW's most vocal supporters. A "Committee of Religious Concern" made up of Protestant, Catholic, and Jewish representatives visited Delano in December 1965. These religious leaders asked California Governor Edwin Brown to pass collective bargaining legislation for farmworkers, and they also urged President Johnson and the Congress "to enact federal legislation extending the provisions of the National Labor Relations Act so it includes agricultural workers."[7] Meanwhile, many Mexican Americans volunteered to work with La Causa; Chavez recruited them from churches and university campuses after asking them to come to Delano to join the farmworkers. One of these early recruits was Mexican American playwright and actor Luis Valdez.

Luis Valdez left the San Francisco Mime Troupe to join César Chavez in Delano where Valdez was born and, along with his brother Daniel, formed El Teatro Campesino (The Farmworkers Theater). The sons of migrant workers, the Valdez brothers wrote and performed in dynamic short skits on flatbed trucks and in union halls to popularize and raise funds for the grape boycott and farmworker strike. El Teatro became a well-known group that in 1967 began a national tour to publicize and drum up public support for the farmworker strike.

Chavez and Huerta brought the cause of the farmworkers to national attention. By painstaking work and campaigning at the grassroots level, Huerta raised support for the UFOWC. As more people saw La Causa as a just one, they joined in supporting it. Huerta directed UFWOC's national grape boycott and, with the help of the Citizens for Farm Labor, took the plight of the farmworkers to the consumer. Union volunteers, including women, were sent to major cities to publicize the boycott. The grape strike expanded to include all table grapes.

Following Chavez's decision that a march as a force would help dramatize the continued plight of the farmworkers and arouse support for their cause, the UFWOC organized a march from Delano to Sacramento on March 17, 1966. The participants walked nearly 340 miles in twenty-five days, picking up hundreds of supporters along the way. The mood was upbeat; the marchers exuded a general air of confidence, and thousands of people flocked to their rallies. As predicted, the march strengthened farmworker solidarity and gained media attention and public support. Meanwhile, Dolores Huerta successfully negotiated a UFWOC contract with Schenley. Arriving in Sacramento on Easter Sunday morning, César Chavez delivered a moving speech, the emotional high point of the march, to more than eight thousand supporters in front of the State Capitol building, declaring the nationwide grape boycott and adding that Schenley Industries had signed an agreement with the union. The grape strike continued, and nonviolence was accepted as official UFOWC policy. Dr. Martin Luther King, Jr., had given nonviolence legitimacy, so Chavez did not have to explain nonviolence to his followers.[8]

While Chavez spent time organizing workers in the fields, Huerta traveled the country organizing for the union. Huerta spearheaded the negotiating and lobbying for the UFWOC in Sacramento and Washington, DC, as well as directing UFWOC boycotts. In addition, the tireless unionist organized voter registration drives, led farmworker campaigns for political candidates, taught citizenship classes, and spoke out against toxic pesticides.

Within weeks, the DiGiorgio Corporation agreed to hold a representation election, but before the election could be held, the International Brotherhood of Teamsters offered itself to DiGiorgio as an alternative to the UFWOC. Chavez called for a boycott of the election, and Governor Brown appointed an arbitrator who ordered another election. This time the UFWOC beat the Teamsters.[9] Farmworker activism had also taken off in the Texas Río Grande Valley.

In the summer of 1966, Mexican American farmworkers in Starr County, Texas, went on strike. Mexican American high school and college students throughout South Texas supported the strike by staging walkouts, pickets, and boycotts, contributing money and food, and joining the farmworkers in their march from the Río Grande Valley to Austin, Texas. Support also came from PASSO, the GI Forum, and LULAC. The march was dubbed the "Minimum Wage March" and led to the passage of the first minimum-wage law in Texas. Meanwhile, in the Midwest, Baldemar Velásquez fresh out of the civil rights movement, launched the Farm Labor Organizing Committee, or FLOC, to unionize farmworkers in this region and elsewhere.[10]

Violence marred the California grape strike as it dragged on. To quell the escalating unrest, César Chavez began a twenty-five-day fast on February 14, 1968. Chavez ended his fast by taking Communion with New York Democratic senator and presidential candidate Robert F. Kennedy. Calling Chavez "a hero of our times," Kennedy supported him and the farmworkers. Mexican Americans proved exceptionally receptive to Kennedy's appeal as an outspoken champion of the disadvantaged. The senator had become an instant convert to La Causa two years earlier after participating in a Senate Subcommittee hearing on agricultural labor in Delano. In addition, Chavez got a message of support from Dr. Martin Luther King, Jr., one month before the great civil rights leader was assassinated in Memphis, Tennessee, where he had gone to support a black sanitation workers' strike.[11]

The bitter farmworker struggle that had attracted national attention dragged on. To further heighten public awareness and to pressure growers to come to the bargaining table, the UFWOC launched a boycott of table grapes. In 1969, Chavez organized a march from the Coachella and Imperial valleys to the California-Mexico border to protest growers' use of workers from Mexico as scabs. Following the assassination of Robert Kennedy and Dr. King, Dr. King's lieutenant in the civil rights struggle, Ralph Abernathy, joined this venture. And so did Senator Walter Mondale, who headed the Senate Committee on Labor and Public Welfare.

The next year two of the nation's largest grape growers agreed to settle with the union. Two-thirds of California grapes were now grown under contract with the fifty-thousand-member-strong UFWOC.

Following this victory, Chavez, on September 1, 1970, Labor Day, called a massive strike in the lettuce fields of Salinas, California, and declared a nationwide boycott of California- and Arizona-grown lettuce to protest grower contracts with the Teamsters. The boycott went into full swing, with flyers and leaflets urging customers not to buy nonunion lettuce and grapes. The UFWOC suffered a series of setbacks. Growers mounted a counterattack, putting the union on the defensive. Three months later, Chavez was jailed for defying a court injunction against boycotting. Coretta Scott King, the widow of Dr. King, visited Chavez in jail, as did Ethel Kennedy, the widow of Robert F. Kennedy. Following the media attention to Chavez's jailing, the California Supreme Court ordered the unionist released. Problems in the meantime beset the UFWOC: union membership declined, and so did public concern for the plight of migrant farmworkers. In 1972, the AFL–CIO chartered the UFWOC as the United Farm Workers of America (UFWA). The Teamsters immediately commenced a war with the struggling farmworker union.[12]

Both external pressures and UFWOC's failure to shift from a social movement to a functional labor movement finally signaled its demise. Nevertheless, César Chavez had plunged wholeheartedly into his life's work as he strove to attain the goals he and Dolores Huerta had set out earlier. Chavez and Huerta helped bring about a 70 percent increase in wages for farmworkers, as well as health care benefits, disability insurance, pension plans, and grievance procedures. The short hoe was eliminated, and the use of many pesticides, such as DDT and Parathyon, was banned. Chavez helped secure passage of the nation's first agricultural labor relations act. Like Dr. King, Chavez never wavered in urging a nonviolent revolution of the poor. More than anything, the movement that Chavez symbolized created a new Mexican American sense of self.

Dolores Huerta likewise displayed great courage and ingenuity in assisting farmworkers. In 1974, Huerta was instrumental in securing unemployment benefits for farmworkers. She lobbied against federal guest worker programs and spearheaded legislation granting amnesty to farmworkers who had lived, worked, and paid taxes in the United States but were denied the privileges of citizenship. Jessica López de la Cruz, María Elena Lucas, and other Mexican American women emerged as important farmworker and grassroots organizers within the farmworker struggles of the 1960s and 1970s.[13] For sheer drama, nothing could match the story of the United Farm Workers of America. The exploits of Reies López Tijerina in northern New Mexico had a special excitement of their own.

## THE PEOPLE'S CHOICE: REIES LÓPEZ TIJERINA AND THE NEW MEXICO LAND GRANTS MOVEMENT

The continuing influx of Anglos into northern New Mexico further exacerbated social and economic problems for the region's Spanish-speaking residents. Many had abandoned their villages and fled to Albuquerque or to cities outside the state to search for work. The severe depopulation reduced the state's Spanish-speaking population to below 30 percent, so that, by the 1960s, local communities were in the care of the elderly. Reacting to pressures that had been building for decades, the struggle over land brought discontented New Mexicans into conflict with established authority.[14]

For a hundred years, the land base of villages in northern New Mexico's poverty-stricken Río Arriba County had been eroding. What land remained could not provide for the population traditionally engaged in cooperative patterns of farming and stock raising. Of the county's twenty-three thousand residents, nineteen thousand were Spanish Americans, and eleven thousand of these were on welfare. Those forced onto relief assistance had to sell their land and spend the proceeds, because the existing welfare regulations denied assistance to families owning land.[15] The impoverished and demoralized Spanish-speaking inhabitants also experienced the added burden of racism. Anglo land grabbers and the federal government were convinced they would not put up much resistance.

The late 1950s saw the northern New Mexico countryside once more become the arena for insurgency. Activist stirrings among the disaffected native New Mexican farmers began in response to outside pressures that led to poverty as a result of their loss of land. Living standards had declined, malnutrition increased, and additional uprooted residents were forced to migrate or starve. A long line of lawyers and the courts had trodden on them. Law enforcement officials retaliated with suppression, jailings, killings, or exiling of insurgents until all that remained of leaders and organizations were folk songs and stories. Growing numbers of northern New Mexico farmers began again a course of unrest, and they now turned to the Alianza Federal de Mercedes, or the Federal Alliance of Land Grants, for relief. Their rallying cry became the Treaty of Guadalupe Hidalgo, which preserved their ancient right to their land. They stood up to the U.S. Forest Service because it banned their use of national forest lands while granting permits to Anglo ranchers. The insurgency was locally rooted, as were its goals. Battles soon erupted over land claims and water rights and were led by Reies López Tijerina, who was to become the era's most controversial Mexican American leader.[16]

Born in New Falls City, Texas, on September 21, 1923, the son of migrant workers, Tijerina began working in the fields at the age of seven. Marauding Texas Rangers hanged his great-grandfather as his family watched, and, consequently, his grandfather became a border raider, spreading panic by attacking Anglo ranchers and settlers along the Texas-Mexico border. Tijerina turned to God for salvation and guidance after attending an Assembly of God Bible School in Ysleta, Texas, outside El Paso. Ordained a fundamentalist preacher, Tijerina began his career of "soul winning" in Santa Fe, New Mexico. Traveling through northern New Mexico performing itinerant work, Tijerina settled in Tierra Amarilla and married a local resident. Tijerina with his wife and children left New Mexico and entered the migrant stream. It was while he was in California in 1957 that Tijerina was inspired by a dream that instructed him to lead the Mexican people out of poverty and bondage. Tijerina and a devoted following of seventeen families purchased land near Casa Grande, Arizona, and founded a community they called the

Valley of Peace. Hostile Anglo farmers and ranchers made that name a misnomer when they eventually ran them out of the area. Following a six-year stay in Mexico, where he studied the history of New Mexico's land grants and worked with militant peasants, Tijerina was deported back to the United States. His radicalization complete, Tijerina returned to Tierra Amarilla in 1962 and made common cause with the local people. Embracing the unresolved land issue on which he built a crusade, Tijerina warned the New Mexicans that diminishing lands and loss of community were leading to their demise as a people.[17]

A tireless proselytizer, Tijerina called for the restitution of the community land grants fraudulently usurped and dispersed when the U.S. government failed to protect them under the Treaty of Guadalupe Hidalgo. Recovery of lands was Tijerina's larger purpose, but he also sought to build an organization of Spanish-speaking New Mexicans united in pride of culture, language, and identity. The fiery orator spoke out on a wide range of issues: among these were obtaining via the courts equal rights in education and employment, which he claimed the federal and state governments had failed to provide, and fighting language discrimination.[18] His life was threatened because of his politics, so Tijerina moved to Albuquerque, where he continued his study of New Mexico land grants.

The next year, Tijerina founded the Alianza Federal de Mercedes to force the U.S. government to respect the 1848 Treaty of Guadalupe Hidalgo. Surrounded by his bodyguards, who called themselves Comancheros, Tijerina claimed, in his electrifying speeches, that the Alianza's poor, bankrupt members were the rightful heirs of 2 million acres of private land and 1.7 million acres of communal land illegally acquired by New Mexico, the federal government, and Anglo ranchers in collusion with their Spanish American accomplices. Large crowds gathered to hear Tijerina hold forth on the promise of this struggle. Within three years, twenty thousand New Mexicans had joined the Alianza.

Tijerina's ragged army lacked the funds to litigate the titles to privately held lands. To bring the issue of land rights before the U.S. Supreme Court, and without antagonizing local Anglos by attacking their private land holdings, Tijerina cleverly devised a legal strategy in which the Alianza would be the defendant. He would do this by acts of civil disobedience on confiscated grant lands to force the federal government into a legal confrontation. The U.S. Forest Service would be forced to prove its title to lands in northern New Mexico. The strategy of intentional mass arrests had been voted on by the Alianza membership.[19]

Alianza members embraced their organization with fervor as it continued its agitation. On the weekend of July 4, 1966, the Alianza staged a march from Albuquerque to Santa Fe to bring attention to its mission and to apply pressure on New Mexico governor Jack Campbell to look into the land grants issue. The Alianza movement grew more militant and staged mass meetings and protest marches. The tension began building. In October, determined to get the land grant issue into the courts, Tijerina and several hundred of his comrades-in-arms took over the Kit Carson National Forest, located northwest of the tiny community of Abiquiu, New Mexico.[20]

The Alianza occupied the Echo Amphitheater campground, and Tijerina proclaimed the establishment of a city-state, the Republic of San Joaquín del Cañón de

Río de Chama. The Alianza assumed all rights to land that was once part of the 1806 half-million-acre San Joaquín communal land grant. The Alianza staged an impromptu "camp-in" in the grant area, elected officers, and raised the blue and gold banner of their Republic of San Joaquín. The Alianza's next camp-in precipitated a reaction from the U.S. Forest Service. Two Forest Service rangers and five state police officers came in and arrested Alianza members for trespassing. To publicize the matter of land grants, Tijerina and several of his followers in turn arrested the rangers for trespassing and ordered them out of the camp. Several days later, the Alianza abandoned their campsite. Tijerina, his brother Cristobal, and several of their compatriots were subsequently arrested on federal charges of assault and battery and appropriation of government property. The charges were dismissed and replaced with new charges.[21]

The atmosphere in northern New Mexico became increasingly tense. Rumors were rampant that hordes of Alianza members were descending on northern New Mexico with vengeance on their minds. Anglo ranchers in the area came under virtual siege. Reminiscent of the Spanish-speaking night riders of the late nineteenth century, unidentified brigands cut miles of fence, poisoned wells, destroyed crops, killed cattle, and burned down ranch houses. Receiving anonymous warnings to abandon northern New Mexico, many Anglos moved their families out of the area. Tijerina declared that the Alianza was about to take direct action. At several meetings in Albuquerque, Tijerina attacked the federal and state government, the courts, and accommodationist native New Mexican political leaders who had gained the support of the Alianza. Fear spread throughout northern New Mexico. Deeply frightened Anglo ranchers who remained hired private gunmen to patrol their lands.[22]

Determined to maintain pressure on the Alianza and fearful that it was inciting violence, New Mexico State District Attorney Alfonso Sánchez and State Police Chief Joseph Black ordered the Alianza not to hold any further meetings. Moreover, Sánchez and Black denounced the Alianza as radical agitators and issued arrest warrants for them. Roadblocks were set up, and people were stopped and arrested. Feeling betrayed by the state government, Tijerina and the Alianza boldly sent a raiding party to attack the Tierra Amarilla Courthouse. The eventual courthouse confrontation was a desperate attempt by the Alianza to force authorities to release seven of their jailed members charged with illegal assembly and to make a citizens arrest of District Attorney Sánchez. Disturbing rumors soon spread in Santa Fe that Communist Cuban guerrillas were leading the Alianza, that urban Alianza cells were preparing to revolt, and that huge caches of weapons were hidden in the mountains.[23]

Nine months passed; then, on June 5, 1967, a score of armed Alianza members, including Tijerina's daughter Rosa, raided the Río Arriba County Courthouse to free jailed members and in response to a court summons issued to prevent the Alianza from holding a rally on the same day. Events got out of hand; in the ensuing melee, a state police officer and a deputy sheriff were shot and wounded, and a deputy sheriff and a news reporter were abducted and taken hostage. Suspected Alianza members, mostly women, children, and the elderly, were apprehended and held in a corral. The Alianza released their hostages and fled into the mountains. Acting in the absence of the governor, New Mexico's lieutenant governor called out the National Guard. Approximately 350 National Guardsmen, with 150 state police officers, dozens of state mounted patrolmen, and Apache tribal police on horseback, bolstered by tanks and helicopters, were deployed to pursue the Alianza members. The band of fugitives was the object of the largest manhunt in New Mexico's history. Sweeps through the native New Mexican villages and a house-to-house search were conducted for weapons and collaborators. Martial law was never declared, but a large part of northern New Mexico was under siege. Dodging an army of law enforcement officers and National Guardsmen, Alianza members eventually were identified and arrested, including Reies López Tijerina. The Tierra Amarilla Courthouse raid turned the Alianza protest into a high-profile struggle and front-page news. It quickly became the staple of Mexican American lore. The Alianza was a doomed campaign.[24]

On November 6, 1967, Tijerina and several of his followers were brought before a federal judge and found guilty of assaulting U.S. Forest Rangers and of conversion of government property for occupying the Kit Carson National Forest. All the defendants received lenient sentences. Tijerina was given two years in jail and five years' probation and was released on bail, pending appeal. Ordered by the court to produce a list of its members, the Alianza disbanded and reorganized as *La Confederación de Pueblos Libres* (Confederation of Free People). New Mexico state officials continued to pay close attention to the Alianza.[25]

The Tierra Amarilla Courthouse raid poisoned relations between Anglos and native New Mexicans. Most of the opposition came from affluent native New Mexicans embarrassed by the Alianza movement. Although Tijerina's gestures of defiance proved popular with New Mexico's poor and aggrieved Spanish-speaking inhabitants, the more affluent and conservative New Mexicans demonized and vilified Tijerina as a fanatic and accused him of being a Communist and a foreigner—a "wetback." Unmoved, Tijerina and some of his followers continued to speak out on behalf of La Alianza and the land struggle. Tijerina's movement got support from Elizabeth Martínez and Enriquita Vásquez y Longeaux. A long-time civil rights activist, Elizabeth Martínez was the former head of the New York office of the Student Nonviolent Coordinating Committee (SNCC) who had participated in the Mississippi Freedom Summer campaign. Enriquita Vásquez y Longeaux of Colorado was a former poverty program advocate and member of the Crusade for Justice in Denver. Martínez and Vásquez y Longeaux had founded the newspaper *El Grito del Norte* (*Cry of the North*). Both were joined by veteran SNCC activist María Varela, who had organized in the Deep South, and Valentina Valdez. Born in San Luis, Colorado, Valentina Valdez had grown up hearing her father talk repeatedly about lands stolen by the Anglos. Valdez headed to New Mexico to join La Alianza two months before the Tierra Amarilla Courthouse raid. Other La Alianza members appeared before the U.S. Civil Rights Commission but gained little sympathy. Awaiting trial, Tijerina tried to broaden his appeal. He conferred with César Chavez and met with Dr. Martin Luther King, Jr. In April 1968, just before he was assassinated, Dr. King chose Tijerina to coordinate the New Mexico section of the Poor People's March and to lead the March's Southwest contingent.[26]

In the fall of 1968, Tijerina was finally brought to trial, and he decided to conduct his own defense. The firebrand won acquittal but was tried again on charges stemming from the Echo Amphitheater incident. This time, Tijerina was convicted and sentenced to two years in Fort Leavenworth Federal Prison. He later served a short term in the New Mexico State Penitentiary.[27] In 1969, Tijerina was convicted of attempting a citizen's arrest of New Mexico's governor and Tenth Federal Circuit Judge Warren Burger (who later became Chief Justice of the U.S. Supreme Court). Tijerina's goal now was even more ambitious: creating a larger movement that would unite both American Indians and Mexican Americans. In 1971, Tijerina was released from prison under the condition that he make no contact with the former Alianza.

Tijerina's popularity in New Mexico dwindled further because the state's Spanish-speaking residents began seeking other solutions to their problems. Dubbed the "Appalachia of the Southwest," northern New Mexico remained plagued by poverty and land problems. Efforts to protect the land claims of poor Spanish-speaking New Mexicans continued. In 1975, New Mexico Senator Joseph Montoya and Congressman Manuel Luján again called for a study of violations of property rights guaranteed in the Treaty of Guadalupe Hidalgo and for restitution for those Mexican Americans whose rights had been violated. The bills sponsored by Montoya and Luján died in committee.

The actions of Reies López Tijerina sent shock waves throughout the Southwest because he provoked an uprising by rural and urban Spanish-speaking New Mexicans by making the land issue a focal point, a fact made clear by Elizabeth Martínez. The veteran activist and expert on African liberation movements wrote that the land grants movement had transcended the civil rights conflict, for it had "evolved within the framework of a long, popular struggle against U.S. colonization and for land . . . "[28] Moreover, Tijerina resolved to defy the law. His raid on the Tierra Amarilla Courthouse, which symbolized rectifying the wrongs inflicted by one people on another, and his self-defense in various state and federal trials made him a hero to many Mexican Americans.[29] Local Mexican American movements elsewhere were involved in direct action campaigns. In Denver, Rodolfo "Corky" Gonzales was at the forefront of a movement that was calling for self-determination.

## CULTURAL NATIONALISM AND COMMUNITY CONTROL: THE CRUSADE FOR JUSTICE

Brought up on the streets of Denver, the talented and energetic Corky Gonzales made his mark in Denver politics in the late 1950s by registering large numbers of Mexican American voters for the Democratic Party. Serving as the coordinator of Colorado's Viva Kennedy clubs in 1960, Gonzales orchestrated an unprecedented turnout of Mexican American votes in support of John F. Kennedy's bid for president of the United States. Denver's poor, minority urban neighborhoods reflected the industrial restructuring and rising inequality of many metropolitan areas. Large numbers of Denver's Mexican American residents did not have full-time work. Passionately devoted to ameliorating the suffering he saw in Denver,

Gonzales participated in Kennedy's ambitious plans for a national war on poverty. He served on the steering committees of the poverty programs for the Southwest, the national board of Jobs for Progress, and the community board of the Job Opportunity Center. When President Johnson launched his War on Poverty programs, Gonzales was appointed to several antipoverty community programs in Denver. In June 1965, Gonzales was named director of the city's Neighborhood Youth Corps, and four months later he was board chairman of Denver's War on Poverty.[30] Corky Gonzales had become the chief spokesman for his people; he did this by gaining influence over the antipoverty programs he was involved with, which he then used as a political base to challenge city government.

Gonzales was frustrated and embittered by the indifference of local government to the concerns of Mexican Americans. He concluded that Denver's Anglo political leaders could not solve the problems that beset the city's poverty-scarred Mexican American community, whose grievances and resentment against Anglos were strong. Particularly disconcerting was the continued violence and killings by police in their dealings with Mexican Americans. To Corky and the Spanish-speaking residents of Denver, the city police were seen as an occupying force. The murders they committed, which the city's Mexican Americans viewed as unjustified, set the tone for their interactions with City of Denver officials. Believing that forceful action was needed to bring about community reform, and having attracted a loyal following among Denver's working-class Mexican Americans, Gonzales formed *Los Voluntarios* (The Volunteers). In 1965, Rodolfo Gonzales founded the Crusade for Justice, which, like Los Voluntarios, was a kind of collective defense against Anglo oppression in Denver. It became the home base for the most militant Chicano activists, among them Enriquita Vásquez, who, like Gonzales, were staunch believers in self-determination and self-organization.[31]

Tensions erupted between Denver city officials and Gonzales because of the latter's unabashed political style of confrontation rather than conciliation and because of his provocative statements to the local press. Following his dismissal as the director of the Neighborhood Youth Corps, Gonzales led a protest and picketing of the mayor's office against the city's leadership that turned into a rally. Punctuating his speech with rhetorical attacks on both Republicans and Democrats, Gonzales drew large cheers when he declared the rally as "the beginning of political action of Spanish-named people." Denver's Anglos viewed this as a dangerous heresy. The association of community control with racial militancy eventually led to the Crusade for Justice's downfall.[32] As tensions mounted, city officials sought ways to squash the dissident group, as did the federal government. On May 14, 1968, J. Edgar Hoover of the FBI sent a memorandum to FBI field officers initiating a counterintelligence program to disrupt all leftist groups such as the Crusade for Justice. Full of determination, Gonzales thrust himself wholeheartedly into the center of the struggle.

For Corky Gonzales and other Mexican American leaders and their organizations, Chicano nationalism provided an ideological and symbolic foothold against the forces of Anglo racism and cultural diffusion. In March 1969, the Crusade for Justice hosted a Chicano Youth Liberation conference in Denver. Forthright about its ideological orientations, which called for a blanket rejection of Anglo culture, the conference issued the utopian *Plan Espiritual de Aztlán* (Spiritual Plan of Aztlán) that joined Mexican Americans together by ties of history and culture in the service of liberation. Corky Gonzales explained his vision of a new Mexican America. The intense nationalist declared that the liberation struggle would be a revolutionary one waged on two fronts: the development of a sense of Chicano identity and community and the destruction of the neocolonial relationship with the dominant Anglo society. Racial solidarity, cultural pride, and the desire for autonomy defined the calls to create Aztlán, a separate Chicano nation within the territorial United States. The ultranationalist poem "Yo Soy Joaquín/I Am Joaquín," allegedly written by Corky Gonzales, spoke buoyantly of this experience. Gonzales's appeal broadened, and his nationalism made him especially popular among Mexican American students and youths. However, this nationalism did not gain many adherents among Mexican American women, who were beginning their struggle against sexism in the Chicano movement. Enriquita Vásquez and other women of the Chicana Caucus were dismayed by the position adopted by the National Youth Conference—that ". . . the Chicana woman does not want to be liberated."[33]

Awareness grew among Mexican Americans that their fate was intertwined with the struggles of oppressed peoples worldwide, reflecting the keenly anti-imperialist themes of the Chicano movement. The Crusade for Justice protested broadly and loudly against the war in Vietnam early on, and by decade's end, as massive public opposition to U.S. policy in Vietnam arose, the antiwar movement had moved to the forefront of the crusade's activism. In addition, the Crusade for Justice helped organize La Raza Unida Party in Colorado, participated in the school walkouts in Denver, and had a contingent in the Poor People's March.[34] During the 1970s the Crusade for Justice came under more scrutiny by Denver police and by the federal government, as both began their war on the movement. The Denver police jailed crusade leaders and harassed members. The turning point occurred in March 1973, when the Crusade for Justice embraced the American Indian Movement (AIM), whose principal goal was militant Native American activism. A demonstration organized by the crusade and AIM in support of the siege of Wounded Knee, South Dakota, triggered further police aggression against the crusade. A gun battle broke out, followed by a deadly explosion at an apartment building owned by the Crusade for Justice. The explosion killed one person and injured seventeen people, a dozen of whom were city police officers. Gonzales alleged that police had thrown grenades in an assault on crusade headquarters, whereas the police accused the crusade of storing explosives inside its building. The bombing incident, along with a string of murders of key activists under suspicious circumstances, led to a gradual decline of the crusade's influence in Denver.[35]

For more than a decade the Crusade for Justice was a powerful and effective organization and a catalyst for broader social change. For Corky Gonzales, who symbolized the resistance of Mexican Americans to Anglo culture, the Mexican American community was a basis of organization to control political institutions in the community. But this concept also embodied problems. Chicano activists on the one hand called for greater control over the Mexican American community and on the other pressed for the destruction of existing institutions and replacing them with new forms. Moreover, in striving toward Mexican American unity, Corky Gonzales and other activists constantly grappled with the problems of cementing a movement marked by considerable regional and ideological differences.

## A SEARCH FOR IDENTITY:
## THE CHICANO STUDENT MOVEMENT

In Los Angeles, the Brown Berets represented a more militant phase of the Chicano movement. A revolutionary nationalist organization, the Brown Berets appealed to the most desperate segment of the urban Mexican American population— streetwise youths. Influenced by the revolutionary movements in Latin America and by the Black Panthers, the Puerto Rican Young Lords, and the AIM, the Brown Berets fought against police harassment, unemployment, and poor housing and education and called for Mexican American political representation and an end to the Vietnam War.[36]

The Brown Berets began as the Young Citizens for Community Action (YCA) in 1966. The following year the YCA worked on Dr. Julian Nava's campaign for a seat on the Los Angeles School Board. The group changed its name to Young Mexican Americans for Community Action and finally to the Brown Berets. Community issues were important elements of the organization's agenda. The Brown Berets operated free health clinics and free children's breakfast programs in East Los Angeles and brought awareness of the problems faced by barrio residents. The Brown Berets supported the United Farm Worker's struggle for union recognition and better working conditions and the land grant movement in New Mexico. They played a major role in the school walkouts in East Los Angeles and marched with the first Rainbow Coalition in the Poor People's Campaign in Washington, DC. A Brown Beret contingent was present at the Chicano Youth Liberation Conference in Denver, where the El Plan Espiritual de Aztlán was written, and the Berets organized the first Chicano Moratorium Against the Vietnam War that led to the National Chicano War Moratorium march and rally in East Los Angeles. With their main emphasis on Chicano nationalism, the Brown Berets by the mid-1970s were the leading revolutionary nationalist organization of the Chicano-power era. As the Brown Berets' rhetoric became more shrill and extreme, it came under more harassment and intimidation by the Los Angeles Police and County Sheriff's departments, which, along with the FBI, infiltrated the militant organization to destroy it. However, as with other segments of the Chicano movement, internecine battles eventually split the ranks of the Brown Berets.[37] The bitter disillusionment felt by many Mexican American students found political expression in the Chicano movement.

The schools became powder kegs of racial tension. For Mexican Americans in California, gaining an education was a nagging issue and a serious problem. The percentage of Spanish-speaking students in the state's elementary schools was 14.4 percent; it was 7.5 percent in junior colleges, 2.9 percent in state colleges, and 0.7 percent in the University of California system. As elsewhere, a significant number of California Mexican American college students entered what had recently been all-Anglo colleges and universities, and there they confronted racially insensitive Anglo students, faculty, and administrators. Moreover, cutbacks were made in federal spending for education, because the Vietnam War coincided with a period of retrenchment in state funding. In 1969, California was in its third year of austerity budgets.

The prevailing mood among Mexican Americans was that federal programs still had not brought any real change in the condition of most Mexican Americans' lives. The widespread feeling was that there was a need for a strong Mexican American community—a renewal in pride, culture, and power. Education was at the basis of this process.

Mexican American student activism was inspired by the protest activities in the larger community and by the participation of the students in the boycotts, demonstrations, rallies, and other forms of protest. Alienated by the dominant Anglo culture, Mexican American students were especially moved by the separatist ideology of Chicano leaders. The factors precipitating major changes in the Mexican American student movement were the failure of social institutions to implement civil rights legislation and emphasis on separatism versus integration.

Mexican American students issued demands and manifestos, and protests were staged in high schools and universities for the inclusion of Mexican American history courses in the curriculum, increases in the number of Mexican American instructors and administrators, and community and student involvement in decision making within the schools. In East Los Angeles, politically aware high school students and youths such as Harry Gamboa, Jr., were the first to enter the fray. Restless for change, students walked out of the public schools on March 3, 1968, refusing to be cowed by violence at the hands of the Los Angeles Police Department. Moved by the separatist ideology of Chicano power, they had had enough of attending schools that were anything but equal—that the federal government today would deem as "dropout factories." These walkouts drew the attention of Senator Robert F. Kennedy while he was campaigning in Los Angeles for the presidency of the United States. The walkouts spread to other schools in the Southwest.[38]

The all-Mexican schools in South Texas were similarly tinderboxes of student unrest. By 1968 there were thirty chapters of the Mexican American Youth Organization (MAYO) in Texas protesting the injustice against Mexican Americans. In the fall of 1969, José Angel Gutiérrez came from San Antonio to the small town of Crystal City to help direct the high school students led by Severita Lara and Diana Aguilera in their campaign against the all-Anglo-controlled school board. A native of Crystal City, Gutiérrez had been educated at Saint Mary's University in San Antonio, where he and four other Mexican American students founded MAYO. In November 1969, Crystal City experienced a second and wider revolt when discontented high school students, many of them MAYO members, and their parents took a list of grievances to the school board. Dissatisfied with discriminatory conditions in the schools, the students wanted more Mexican American teachers and a bilingual educational program. The school board's refusal to act on charges of discrimination forced a student strike with parental support.[39]

The student boycott spread to the entire Crystal City school system until the U.S. Justice Department intervened and negotiated a settlement. Losing a month of state funds owing to 65 percent absence rates, Crystal City school officials reluctantly caved in to the students' demands and granted most of their requests.[40] MAYO organized school walkouts in Edcouch, Elsa, Weslaco, and other towns in the Río Grande Valley. Another goal of MAYO was to build a grassroots political movement. In 1969, Mario Compeán ran as the MAYO mayoral candidate in the San Antonio City mayoral election. Although Compeán lost, MAYO helped increase voter registration among the city's Mexican Americans. In December 1969, MAYO held its first national conference in Mission, Texas, where participants endorsed the formation of La Raza Unida Party. MAYO spread to other parts of the Southwest.

The Mexican American student movement grew as dozens of student organizations appeared on high school, college, and university campuses. Mexican American teachers and administrators also banded together. In April 1969, *El Plan de Santa Barbara* (the Plan of Santa Barbara) was adopted at a symposium held at the University of California, Santa Barbara, where Mexican American students had gathered to discuss the problems and prospects of their movement. In May, all the student groups in California were organized as the *Movimiento Estudiantíl Chicano de Aztlán* (MECHA), which became the foundation of the burgeoning student movement.[41]

The founding document of MECHA outlined proposals for a curriculum in Mexican American studies, community control of schools, and other related work in regard to education. Guided by MECHA's vision, students and faculty together began to secure recruitment programs, financial aid, student support services, and Mexican American studies programs. The ideological orientation prevalent on college campuses included debates over assimilation and separation, Chicano arts and aesthetics, and invitations to campus speakers. All served as a catalyst for youths who rejected the integrationist attitudes of the early 1960s. MECHA's influence was also felt in the barrios, where the organization worked with other organizations on a variety of community-related projects that stressed empowerment, local control of antipoverty funds, and other social change.[42]

Third World liberation struggles, study groups, and political texts influenced Mexican American student radicalism. The Cuban Revolution made a significant mark in this radicalization. Dozens of Mexican Americans were in Cuba by late 1969 as Venceremos Brigade members chopping sugar cane. These radicals looked to Cuba's political and social structure and its development of the "new socialist man" as a goal the Chicano movement in America should work toward. Those who participated in the brigade's Third World seminars exchanged ideas with delegates from Vietnam, Africa, and Latin America.[43] Lenin, Stalin, and Mao likewise had appeal, and Marxism soon surfaced within the Mexican American student organizations as their members immersed themselves in elaborate theories concerning the plight of the oppressed. Predictably, as the question of Chicano authenticity became a matter of political orientation, endless discussion and conflict arose between Marxists and nationalists about the proper course for the Chicano movement. In the end, Mexican American students came to accept that class consciousness and the concept of self-determination were mutually exclusive.

As the rhetoric of Chicano identity became even more pointed, Mexican American women began to struggle with notions of race, gender, sexuality, and class, both in their activism and among the members of their groups. Many developed a collective identity as part of a Chicana women's liberation movement that transcended Chicano nationalism.

## RIGHTEOUS DISCONTENT:
## THE CHICANA WOMEN'S MOVEMENT

The rise of Chicana consciousness coincided with the redefinition of the goals of Mexican Americans toward a philosophy of Chicano power, and it evolved through hostile encounters with both the Chicano movement and the Anglo women's movement.

Mexican American women played a prominent role in the boycotts and mass demonstrations conducted by the UFWA, the student movement, and the antiwar movement between 1965 and the mid-1970s. Untold numbers of women were beaten and jailed but did not falter, for they maintained a high degree of commitment. Many were natural leaders, outspoken women who held positions of leadership in local, regional, or national organizations. However, hard feelings and misunderstandings disrupted the solidarity of the women, because the Chicano movement was overtly sexist. The ego militance of many Mexican American males marginalized and silenced female activists by accusing them of splitting the movement and not supporting its cause. The male leadership readily dismissed as irrelevant and divisive women's critiques of the movement—women's concerns such as abortion and reproductive rights were considered personal matters not worthy of political debate that diverted attention from more pressing issues, such as racism. Many male chauvinists embraced a conception of gender relations that privileged male authority. Mexican American women such as Anna Nieto Gomez, Corinne Sánchez, Mirta Vidal, and others increasingly united under the banner of *herminadad* (sisterhood) and spoke out militantly against male resistance to women's issues.[44] Mirta Vidal phrased the feminist baiting within the Chicano movement best:

> On the basis of the subordination of women, there can be no real unity . . . The only real unity between men and women is the unity forged in the course of struggle against their oppression. And it is by supporting, rather than opposing, the struggles of women, that Chicanos and Chicanas can genuinely unite.[45]

The growth of the mainstream women's movement was an important catalyst that at first aided Mexican American women by providing a basis on which to articulate their grievances. However, Mexican American women eventually denounced white feminism; they were reluctant to align themselves with Anglo women's groups because they could not embrace the ethnocentric perspective promoted by middle-class Anglo women. Many had identified men as the enemy, and not capitalism, racism, and imperialism. Owing to the inescapable problem of their own racism, Anglo women neglected the grievances of Mexican American women (as well as all women of color) about the peculiar conditions under which they lived because of poverty, classism, and racism. Mexican American women therefore defined their goals outside of the Anglo women's movement.[46]

To analyze their own subordinate position within the Mexican American community, women founded community and national women's organizations. The Mexican American National Issues Conference held in Sacramento included a women's workshop that became the *Comisión Feminíl Mexicana* (Mexican Feminine Commission). Women in MAPA formed a caucus, and in 1971 several women previously involved with MECHA formed the Chicana Service Action Center. More than six hundred Mexican American women met in Houston, Texas, at the end of May 1971 as *La Conferencia de Mujeres por la Raza* (Conference of Women for the Race), the first national Conference of Mexican American women. Martha P. Cortera, with other women who had helped found and were active in La Raza Unida Party, formed Mujeres por la Raza. Mexican American women were candidates on the Socialist Workers Party ticket. Other activists such as Elizabeth Martínez and Enriquita Vásquez y Longeaux, both of whom developed an international perspective on women's equality that required an end to violence and poverty worldwide, linked their agendas to those of women in other countries.[47] By the early 1970s, health care centers, child care centers, rape crisis centers, presses, and other alternative institutions evidenced a thriving Chicana feminism in service to women. The movement also saw participation of lesbians who viewed heterosexuality as an additional source of oppression.

Women contributed to the Chicano movement by addressing concerns previously neglected. They organized themselves as a direct result of blatant contradictions between the male leadership and women's secondary status within the movement. Due to conflicts arising over a developing feminist consciousness, the Chicano movement failed to fully tap a wellspring of energy and commitment among Mexican American women and thus lost a number of capable individuals. Mexican American women were not only leaders in a wide variety of struggles against racism while simultaneously fighting the cultural constraints on their lives but a large number also led the antiwar and antidraft struggles within the community.

## RAZA SÍ! GUERRA NO!: THE NATIONAL CHICANO WAR MORATORIUM

The late 1960s was a time of heightened racial antipathies. Richard M. Nixon won the 1968 presidential election mainly because the Democratic vote was split on the civil rights issue. In this same year, Governor George Wallace broke many white voters loose from the Democratic Party and gained 5 percent of the electoral votes as an independent candidate. Wallace, who appealed to whites who felt threatened by the civil rights movement of the 1960s, would win more than 3.3 million primary votes in 1972. Furthermore, there was waning support for the Vietnam War, a war the United States showed every sign of losing.

For many Mexican Americans, military service provided an opportunity for escape from poor economic and social conditions at home. Approximately eighty thousand Mexican Americans saw combat in all areas of Vietnam, from numerous small actions and civic action formats to major battles of the war. They fought from Con Tien on the demilitarized zone (DMZ) to the Mekong Delta, slugging it out with skilled and determined Viet Cong and North Vietnamese Army (NVA) soldiers in fighting holes, bunkers, and connecting trench positions, who willingly gave their lives for the cause of the revolution. Ambushes, booby traps, snipers, mines, and mortar and rocket attacks were the order of the day. The vast majority of Mexican Americans were in combat units that suffered high battlefield casualties.

In 1964, Navy Lieutenant Everett Alvarez of Salinas, California, became the first American pilot shot down over North Vietnam; he would spend almost eight and a half brutal years as a prisoner of war. Combat intensity grew each year from Alvarez's imprisonment in 1964 until the Tet Offensive in 1968. Mexican Americans were with elements of the First Cavalry Division (Airmobile) in

**Battle Scene, 101st Airborne, Vietnam War, 1961–1975.**
CREDIT: "Battle Scene in Vietnam, pulling back the wounded." CSMAT_106. 101st Airborne. Courtesy of the San Mateo Historical Photographs Collection, San Mateo Public Library, San Mateo, California.

the heroic and bloody Battle of the Ia Drang Valley against the 33rd, 320th, and 66th NVA Regiments and the Viet Cong H15 Battalion in November 1965. As members of the Third Marine Division, Mexican American Marine grunts were at the siege of the Khe Sahn combat base and its outposts (1967–1968), which three NVA Army divisions pounded each day with heavy mortars, artillery, and rockets. Mexican American Marines participated in the fierce house-to-house fighting with the First Marine Division to recapture the city of Hue from the communists in the 1968 Tet Offensive. The Tet Offensive eroded American support for the war despite the fact that U.S. forces inflicted significant losses on the Viet Cong. And as members of the F Division, Mexican American soldiers fought in one of the most brutal battles of the war, capturing Abi Mountain in the Au Shau Valley near the Laotian border, nicknamed Hamburger Hill. Thirteen Mexican American soldiers won the Medal of Honor by the time the bloodletting ended in Vietnam. However, the overwhelming goal of every Mexican American army rifleman and Marine grunt was to get out of Vietnam alive. More than several thousand brave Mexican American soldiers and Marines came back home from Vietnam in flag-draped coffins. Thousands of others came home painfully crippled, many with missing legs and arms, or with the lifelong psychic scars of war.

Mexican American GIs became increasingly disillusioned as the war dragged on in Vietnam. They grappled with the racial strife, fragging (attacking an officer with a grenade), and drug problems that affected U.S. military forces during the declining days of the war. They were also affected by many of the same racial and social conflicts that were tearing the United States apart. Additional numbers began to question the morality of the war once they began fighting. The United States did not lose the war on the battlefields of Vietnam, but it lost its national will to sustain the fight. The failure of many Mexican American war veterans to come to grips with the trauma of war resulted in untold misery—drug and alcohol addiction, unemployment, broken homes, and homelessness. Indeed, Mexican American soldiers and Marines, along with their families, were among the Americans who sacrificed most in the Vietnam conflict.

As the war raged on in Vietnam, Mexican Americans turned against a conflict they deemed morally unjustifiable. There were other reasons that they were sharply critical about Vietnam. The war's expense was more than the amount spent on Great Society reforms. By 1968, the Vietnam War was costing the United States $66 million dollars a day, and as a result President Johnson cut back on his War on Poverty programs.[48] Because Mexican Americans still suffered greatly from poverty, they were bitterly disturbed by this decision. Few attended college, so they did not qualify for student deferments, and due to discrimination in employment few could get occupational deferments. Mexican American critics of the war pointed out that granting student deferments, alternative military service in the National Guard and Army Reserves, and noncombatant roles for Anglo volunteers while assigning draftees to combat units and the tendency of Mexican Americans to choose combat resulted in high participation and casualty rates for minorities and the poor in Vietnam. In 1965, there were 23,000 U.S. servicemen in Vietnam, but as the war escalated the number expanded dramatically to 465,000 by the end of 1967. This was largely the result of Project 100,000 initiated by President Johnson in 1966. Project 100,000 lowered qualification standards for military service. For Mexican Americans this meant that those who had previously failed the draft owing to poor education or job deferrals were now eligible.[49] By the time Johnson left office in 1968, 30,000 Americans had been killed in Vietnam. The most disquieting issue was that Mexican American casualties proportionately far exceeded Anglo casualties in Vietnam. Mexican Americans made up nearly 20 percent of the American casualties from the Southwest, almost twice their proportion of the population.

Disturbing rumors flourished among Mexican Americans and African Americans that the U.S. government was pumping money into Vietnam instead of poor minority communities in America and that it was using the war as a form of genocide against America's minorities. Mexican Americans began making strong public statements against the war. Such antiwar activity was unprecedented in Mexican American history. Corky Gonzales made his own views clear on the specific question of the war in Southeast Asia as early as 1963. In Texas, Béxar County Commissioner Alberto Peña urged Mexican Americans to stay home and fight poverty and racism rather than serve in Vietnam. Reflecting the increased Mexican American antiwar activity, *El Grito del Norte* and other Mexican American newspapers that appeared began taking a stance against the war.[50] Political action shifted as more and more Mexican American activists became involved with community organization in relation to the war in Vietnam.

The idea to hold a national antiwar moratorium came out of the 1969 Denver Chicano Youth Conference. Angered over the inequities of the draft, the participants conferred and declared that the national antiwar movement was discriminatory— its purpose was to assist white middle-class youths in avoiding military service: "Up until now, the white peace movement has succeeded in teaching Anglo youth how and why to avoid the war which has resulted in the drafting of male Chicanos . . . " The conference participants approved a series of moratoriums to culminate in a national demonstration in Los Angeles on August 29, 1970, against a war deemed racist.

Demonstrations against the Vietnam War steadily grew in size. As a whole they became increasingly militant after Nixon expanded the war into Cambodia, which was being used by North Vietnam as a sanctuary and supply route for insurgent Vietnam guerrillas. The nation's college campuses became embroiled in protest over President Nixon's secret bombing campaign of Cambodia in early 1969 and his invasion of Cambodia the following year. During the first six days of the invasion of Cambodia, an average of twenty campuses went on strike each day; by mid-May, more than five hundred colleges and universities were on strike against the war in Vietnam. As public distrust of President Nixon increased, more and more Mexican Americans pushed for a new strategy to protest the war.[51] The Chicano War Moratorium was a defining moment for many Mexican Americans who had never openly declared their support for the dominant antiwar peace groups.

One immediate inspiration for growing Mexican American antiwar protest was the massive mobilization against the war that took place in thousands of localities around the country on October 15, 1969. Mexican Americans called for their own moratorium in Los Angeles. The Brown Berets and other major antiwar group organizers formed the National Chicano Moratorium Committee. Its antiwar agenda emphasized the "war at home" faced by working-class people of color that drew a close analogy between the plight of the Mexican American and that of the Vietnamese peasant. This is a point Elizabeth Martínez had made in her writings in *El Grito del Norte* following her return from visiting Vietnam.[52] Mexican Americans linked their struggles for liberation to the issue of anticolonialism and racism abroad. Some openly expressed their solidarity with the National Liberation Front, adding the name of Ho Chi Minh to their pantheon of nationalist liberation fighters that included Che Guevara and Malcolm X.

As the combat deaths of Mexican Americans mounted, and as more of them continued to leave for the war overseas, several protests were held in East Los Angeles to gather momentum for the national demonstration. The first took place at Obregón Park on December 20, 1969, and drew more than two thousand participants. Two months later, on February 28, 1970, this was followed by another rally at Obregón Park that attracted six thousand people despite rain. As the scheduled National Chicano Moratorium approached, support came from Spanish-speaking organizations across the nation.

On August 29, previous rallies culminated in the largest protest in Mexican American history as Mexican Americans from every segment of society converged in East Los Angeles to demonstrate their opposition to the Vietnam War, citing moral grounds and the high casualty rate for Mexican American servicemen. Overwhelming emotions marked the National Chicano War Moratorium, chaired by Chicano draft resister Rosalio Muñoz, as marchers expressed their collective grievances against a racist war largely fought by minorities and the poor. "Our War Is Not in Vietnam, It Is Here at Home!" ("¡Nuestra Guerra es Aquí!") and "Our Fight Is in the Barrio—Not in Vietnam" were major action slogans at the demonstration. Some of the marchers carried crosses to symbolize the large numbers Mexican American deaths in the war, and others carried banners of the Virgin of Guadalupe. Red and blue Viet Cong flags flew defiantly. Those protestors who carried flags of the National Liberation Front channeled their anger into louder and louder calls for freedom and self-determination for the Vietnamese people. Nonetheless, the demonstrators maintained their nonviolent discipline. The marchers, numbering thirty thousand and including many families, paraded peacefully to Laguna Park, where the speakers and entertainment were scheduled. An atmosphere of excitement prevailed. The speakers included César Chavez of the UFW, Crusade for Justice leader Corky Gonzales, MAYO chairman Mario Compeán, and David Sánchez of the Brown Berets. Unfortunately, the moratorium and rally deteriorated into a violent confrontation between Los Angeles county and city law enforcement officials and the demonstrators.

Early in the afternoon, scuffles took place between demonstrators and Los Angeles County deputy sheriffs deployed in force. Soon, more than 1,500 Los Angeles city and county peace officers in full riot gear were called out and began to attack the marchers indiscriminately. A phalanx of helmeted police with nightsticks and Mace and armed with gas masks, smoke grenades, and riot guns moved menacingly in the direction of the protestors and fired tear gas into the

**Chicano Moratorium, August 1970.**

CREDIT: "Chicano Moratorium Committee antiwar demonstrators ('Our Fight Is in the Barrio')," uclamss_1429_b662_265105-10. Courtesy of UCLA Charles E. Young Research Library, Department of Special Collections, Los Angeles Times Photographic Archive, ©Regents of the University of California, UCLA Library.

crowd to quell the disturbance. The deputies soon began beating the demonstrators, causing panic and starting a chaotic flight of the marchers. The law enforcement officials then called for reinforcements as they advanced toward Laguna Park, turning it into a war zone. More rioting broke out as the discipline of the bleeding and battered protestors began to break down. Several hundred marchers were arrested, including Corky Gonzales. When the smoke settled, two demonstrators lay dead and sixty others lay wounded. One of the tear gas projectiles struck *Los Angeles Times* journalist Ruben Salazar, an outspoken opponent of the war in Vietnam. He was killed instantly and immediately became a martyr, immortalized as a symbol of the Chicano antiwar movement. Whereas the images of middle-class Anglos protesting the war were emblazoned on America's collective memory, few Americans were aware that the largest protest against the Vietnam War by a racial minority group had taken place in Los Angeles.[53]

The attack on the antiwar demonstrators was widely condemned as a police riot. Organizers of the moratorium were quick to issue a statement blaming law enforcement officials, long known for their arbitrary brutality toward Mexican Americans, as the real perpetrators of the riot. Los Angeles Mayor Sam Yorty and the sheriff's department countered that militant radicals had infiltrated the demonstration. Five months later, on January 31, 1971, the Chicano War Moratorium Committee called for another march to protest the war, as well as police violence and misconduct. Once again, law enforcement officials brutally attacked the demonstrators, killing one person and wounding more than a dozen others. Following the huge antiwar protests in Washington, DC, four thousand Mexican Americans and other Latinos participated in the antiwar demonstration sponsored by the National Peace Action Coalition and the People's Coalition for Peace and Justice in San Francisco one day later, the largest protest in the history of the antiwar movement. On April 23, Mexican American Vietnam veterans had participated in Dewey Canyon III, the most highly publicized act of resistance. More than one thousand members of Vietnam Veterans Against the War converged on the steps of the U.S. Capitol in Washington, DC, to shout obscenities and throw down their medals and ribbons in protest against U.S. policies in Vietnam. Some of the veterans were silent witnesses and threw nothing at all. One year later, the American phase of the war began to end. Mexican Americans had paid a heavy cost in casualties and in further distrust of the United States government.

This period witnessed changes in the dynamics of resistance. Protest movements became more decentralized, and, increasingly, local and grassroots resistance tapped new constituencies. By the mid-1970s, the large, militant Third World movements had evaporated. Resistance was being subverted; Mexican American with African American, Puerto Rican, and Native American radicals were now burdened by increasing and devastating government attacks caused by COINTELPRO (counterintelligence program). The federal antisubversive program's main function was to crush the Left by breaking up meetings, launching a campaign of disinformation, and instigating violence against activists through false charges and frame-ups. Activists were portrayed as government agents, arrested, physically threatened or assaulted, and, if it was deemed necessary, killed in "shootouts" with police. For example, activist lawyer "Kiko" Martínez was indicted in Colorado in 1973 on trumped-up bombing charges; the work of the Crusade for Justice in the Spanish-speaking communities of Denver and northern New Mexico was disrupted; and the home of Brown Beret leader David Sánchez was firebombed.[54]

Mexican Americans seeking political office benefited from the social changes ushered in by the Chicano movement. Underrepresented at all levels of government, Mexican American political activists turned toward electoral strategies to challenge the Democratic Party because it no longer represented their interests. Their goal was to create a grassroots independent political party through which to consolidate their efforts to achieve community control over public institutions in urban and rural Mexican American working-class barrios.

## "PARDON MY ENGLISH": LA RAZA UNIDA PARTY

The majority of Mexican Americans remained faithful to the Democratic Party, though it seldom delivered on the promises it made to them. They held positions in local and state government, and several were members of Congress or were appointed to federal positions. However, few Mexican American office holders were in the decision-making positions necessary to bring about any substantial reforms. Mexican Americans as a result began to participate actively in gaining control of political and institutional decisions.

Mexican Americans had formed a number of organizations to register voters, endorse candidates, take stands on issues, increase political activity, and gain better political opportunities. Political organizations such as MAPA and PASSO continued to work within the Democratic Party on behalf of Mexican Americans. President Johnson rewarded those Mexican Americans who jumped onto the Democratic Party bandwagon. In 1964, the president appointed former GI Forum chairman Vicente Ximenes to head the new Inter-Agency Committee on Mexican American Affairs. The Office of Economic Opportunity coordinated local poverty programs such as the Neighborhood Youth Corps and Head Start. Through the community action programs, the OEO's highly controversial doctrine of "maximum feasible participation" urged social action and encouraged an alliance of poor people with the federal government in policy making in local programs of intervention. Mexican Americans assumed their communities would be one of the prime beneficiaries of the War on Poverty; moreover, they were led to believe the president would repay them for their support by addressing problems of the community through the War on Poverty by naming more Mexican Americans to antipoverty posts.[55] To the dismay of Mexican American leaders, Johnson failed to fulfill their hopes.

In 1966, fifty Mexican American leaders walked out of an OEO conference in Albuquerque, New Mexico, in protest, charging that the conference was biased. Formed under pressure by a contingent from PASSO, MAPA, and LULAC, who met with President Johnson to seek solutions to the crisis, the Cabinet Committee on Mexican American Affairs concerned itself with funding programs relevant to them. It scheduled a conference for El Paso in May 1967. Several Mexican Americans staged a boycott of the meeting, alleging that Mexican Americans were underrepresented in important government posts and that many of the conference attendees were accommodationist and thus subordinate to the Johnson administration. Their action led to a countermeeting out of which emerged La Raza Unida Committee. Frustrated by the seeming indifference to its concerns, the committee publicly accused the Johnson administration of backsliding over federal aid to Mexican Americans.[56]

Those attending the El Paso conference testified that Mexican Americans no longer trusted the federal government, that it was performing poorly in providing antipoverty programs, and that Mexican Americans were substantially underrepresented in federal agencies dealing with "jobs, welfare, health, housing, and similar services." Others called for extending the Fair Labor Standards and National Labor Relations laws to farmworkers and halting the commuter system that allowed Mexican nationals to cross the border to work in the United States.[57]

As in the case of African American activists, the president did not want to encourage or legitimize direct action by Mexican American activists who operated outside the bounds of political consensus. Needing the help of Mexican Americans for his renomination campaign, President Johnson appointed his longtime friend Dr. Hector P. García of the American GI Forum to serve on the U.S. Commission on Civil Rights. García was already an alternate ambassador to the United Nations. In addition, Johnson helped California Congressman Edward Roybal in passing into law an education bill to provide local school districts assistance with special bilingual teaching programs. But because of increased funding for the war in Vietnam, the $30 million dollars authorized for the Bilingual Education Act was reduced to $7.5 million. Due to electoral considerations, the president in 1968 aided Roybal in establishing a Cabinet Committee on Opportunities for Spanish-Speaking

People with the goal of improving education, housing, and employment.[58] Mexican Americans became disenchanted and frustrated by the all-too-frequent inaction of the Johnson administration in assisting them in attaining their goals. In South Texas, Mexican Americans made a calculated decision to take control of local political offices.

Led by MAYO's astute political strategist José Angel Gutiérrez, La Raza Unida Party (RUP) was formed in December 1969 to provide Mexican Americans with a vehicle to acquire power through local and state politics. Derived from a phrase coined by Juan Nepomuceno Cortina in 1848 that meant "the United People," La Raza Unida Party called for bilingual education in public schools, the education of migrant children, improved public services in Mexican American neighborhoods, hiring bilingual government employees, and an end to job discrimination.

The leaders of the fledgling RUP, a political party independent of both the Democratic and Republican parties, immediately began coordinating voter registration projects, collecting signatures, and performing other initiatives in South Texas. On April 4, 1970, RUP entered and swept the school board elections in Crystal City. Gutiérrez won a seat on the Crystal City School Board, and at a meeting of the reorganized school board he was elected its president. The Crystal City school system underwent a transformation: it hired Mexican Americans in administrative and teaching positions, started an early-grades bilingual education program, and introduced courses in Mexican American history and culture. RUP followed the Crystal City victory three days later by winning mayoral and city council elections in Crystal City, Carrizo Springs, and Cotulla, Texas. RUP spread to other Texas counties with large Spanish-speaking populations, empowering and energizing local Mexican American movements. When state courts denied the RUP access to the ballot, it conducted write-in campaigns in Texas and in Arizona, California, and Colorado. The political apathy that formerly marked the Southwest disappeared as RUP challenged the system to achieve representative government.[59]

In October 1971, the RUP held a convention in San Antonio at which the delegates discussed RUP philosophy and strategy. They voted to organize at the state level, although José Angel Gutiérrez wanted the RUP to concentrate on strengthening its presence in rural areas. Gutiérrez's views were overruled because support was finally gained for a state RUP organization to repeat RUP's success in Crystal City throughout Texas.

In 1972, Mario Compeán was elected RUP state chairman at the party's convention in El Paso. A third of the convention attendees were women. Like the men, the women were issue-oriented, cared about RUP's platforms and candidates and its policy views, and wanted power, too. That year the RUP conducted petition and voter registration drives and nominated and campaigned for six statewide candidates, including Ramsey Muñiz for governor of Texas, Alma Canales for lieutenant governor, and María Jimenez for attorney general. In November, RUP was certified for a place on the general election ballot. Organized in more than forty Texas counties, the RUP ran candidates for district, senatorial, state representative, and school board positions. All of the RUP candidates lost in the election. The Democratic Party of Texas placed pressure on the RUP to stop it from drawing away

**La Raza Unida Party Bumper Sticker.**
CREDIT: Raza Unida Party Collection, 1969–1979, OCLC Record No: 24005920, Courtesy of the Benson Latin American Collection, University of Texas, Austin.

Mexican American voters, especially in South and West Texas. These efforts succeeded.[60]

La Raza Unida Party became a symbol of Chicano power. RUP's appeal was easy to understand: it offered more radical remedies to Mexican Americans than its political rivals. Mexican Americans in South Texas had mobilized to fight for community and political control. Other Mexican Americans likewise swung to the RUP and initiated a powerful movement for social change throughout the Southwest. RUP essentially ushered in a new breed of Mexican American political activists who were young, highly educated, and politically pragmatic. Former RUP members joined other political activists in the new organizations: the Mexican American Legal Defense and Educational Fund (MALDEF), the Mexican American Unity Council, Communities Organized for Public Service, the Southwest Voter Registration Education Project, the Mexican American Democrats, and the Mexican American Legislative Caucus.[61]

State and federal court decisions furthered the cause of Mexican American political enfranchisement. Long-standing franchise restrictions were ruled unconstitutional, including the poll tax in 1966, annual voter registration in 1971, and at-large state legislative districts in 1974. The extension of the Voting Rights Act in 1975 to the Southwest was likewise pivotal. Reapportionment lawsuits became a basic staple of the MALDEF. The legal victories increased Mexican American voter registration, voter turnout, and representation at all levels. Whereas only seven Mexican Americans served in the Texas State Legislature in 1960, fifteen served in 1974.[62]

The Mexican American vote became of keen interest to the national political parties and their candidates as the 1972 presidential and congressional elections drew near. In a speech in the spring of 1971 before the California Democratic Council, presidential candidate Senator George McGovern warned that the Democratic Party had better start giving Mexican Americans more voice in the Party and more representation in government.[63] What was troubling not only McGovern but also President Nixon was the study released by LULAC and the Mexican American Bar Association. It revealed that, based on the 1960 and 1968 presidential election patterns, a shift of even 6 percent in the Mexican American vote in California, Texas, Illinois, and New Mexico could determine the outcome of the 1972 presidential elections.

# CONCLUSION

The 1960s and early 1970s represented an era of Mexican American causes. Their aspirations for equality were based on the fact that they were disenfranchised, poor, badly educated, and excluded from the national dialogue. Mexican Americans launched mass-based movements and stirred substantive reforms. All would come under attack by the early 1970s as the FBI and the U.S. Justice Department launched a dirty-tricks campaign to subvert the civil rights and antiwar movements through sabotage, falsified testimony, and the killing of leaders and organizers.[64]

Drawing on the tactics of the larger civil rights movement, a new cohort of Mexican Americans spoke more genuinely to the needs and aspirations of the larger community. In California, César Chavez synthesized the Catholic beliefs of Mexican American farmworkers with their protest traditions to build the United Farm Workers of America union. The UFWA brought organization and security to tens of thousands of farmworkers. It gained the support of the Catholic Church and such national figures as Robert F. Kennedy, Walter Reuther, and George Meany, as well as millions of American middle-class consumers who honored and supported the UFWA's boycott of California grapes and lettuce. Dolores Huerta was a highly visible UFWA spokesperson serving as the union's legislative advocate and political strategist. Contemporary observers noted that Huerta worked as hard as or harder than César Chavez, but as he did with other women in La Causa, he rarely mentioned her contributions. In contrast, Robert F. Kennedy openly acknowledged his debt to Huerta's tireless help in winning the 1968 California presidential primary.[65]

The famous rebellion that burst forth in northern New Mexico was led by the fiery Reies López Tijerina, one of the most enigmatic figures in Mexican American history. Through the sheer power of his personality, Tijerina convinced many of the region's Spanish-speaking people traumatized by land loss and rural poverty of the absolute rightness of his cause. Tijerina revealed himself to be the kind of leader many longed for. Nor were the federal government and wealthy Anglo landowners unimpressed by the rebellion Tijerina had sown in New Mexico.

Mexican Americans became frustrated and disillusioned with the shortcomings of the Great Society's reforms. In speeches punctuated with ultramilitant rhetoric, Rodolfo "Corky" Gonzales's blistering comments regarding racism in Denver and his measures to fight that racism stirred up raucous protests by the city's Mexican Americans. In the openly polemical poem, "Yo Soy Joaquin," attributed to him, Gonzales helped define Mexican American identity. Mexican American youths seemed eager for Gonzales's unifying message. Rejecting the premise of Anglo superiority, the Chicano nationalist from Denver called for the celebration of a particular historical experience and culture and emphasized the idea of a mestizo identity—la Raza. Chicano power contagion swept into the Southwest and became a symbol of Mexican American defiance. The long history of violence and domination against Mexican Americans contributed to the way the Denver police mobilized against the Crusade for Justice. The eventual open warfare between the Crusade for Justice and Denver city officials contributed greatly to racial conflict because of the association of community control with Chicano power. Gonzales's revolutionary fervor drew the attention of the FBI and led to the ruthless suppression of the Crusade for Justice in the early 1970s.

Student activism was an important element in itself and as part of the larger, unfolding Mexican American social reform movements. The inferior schooling that Mexican Americans received provoked a wave of indignation. The widespread student mobilization in 1968 in East Los Angeles was one of the high points in Mexican American student activism.[66]

The ideological base of Mexican American protest changed during the 1960s and 1970s, when the Chicano movement revealed an awakening consciousness and a newfound pride in Mexican identity. A range of ideologies influenced Chicano power advocates, but what bound the various tendencies within the movement was the ideology of dissent guided by nationalism. Chicano nationalists undeniably provided a powerful critique of American cultural imperialism and, through rousing mass meetings, demonstrations, picketing, and protests, played an invaluable role in organizing Mexican Americans in a manner heretofore impossible. Chicano nationalists gloried in the Chicano movement. However, they eroded Mexican American commitment to nonviolence and opened the way to the self-defeating tendencies of Chicano power. Nor did these activists provide Mexican Americans with tangible agendas for empowerment or programs for meaningful redress of grievances against American society. Although it did crystallize hostility against many aspects of the current American social-political system, Chicano power never amassed solid support in the Mexican American communities for revolutionary change. Another fatal flaw of the Chicano nationalist movement was that its male-dominated leadership was sexist.[67] It embraced patriarchal notions in the name of an authentic Mexican American experience while ignoring the important issues of women, many of whom were genuinely committed to all facets of the Mexican American struggle for equality. It was women who shouldered the double burden of racial and gender discrimination. Their role as participants and organizers in various Mexican American organizations served as a catalyst for turning them into self-conscious feminists who would critique sexism and analyze the role of Chicana women in American society. Through grassroots support and dynamic leadership, Mexican American women would help define the politics of protest in the 1980s.

Behind the surface glamour, nagging factionalism and dissension plagued the Chicano movement. Heated battles over the fine points of dogma divided many Chicanos. In the midst of this war of words and tumult of opinions, militants, student activists, and antiwar radicals soon discovered that the United States did not hesitate to violently crush outbreaks of dissent. COINTELPRO launched a dirty war against Mexican Americans. The fervor of the national Chicano movement of the 1960s had burned out by the 1970s. Political activism became more problematic; yet the Chicano movement continued to grow in different manifestations.

The Vietnam conflict encouraged social turmoil in the United States. As the war dragged on and the death toll of Mexican Americans mounted, the antiwar sentiment among Mexican Americans grew. Mexican Americans spoke out strongly against the Vietnam War and immediately began organizing opposition on college campuses and elsewhere. Mexican American women played a pivotal role in the movement to end the war in Vietnam, bringing not only their organizational skills, experience, and hard work but also their strength and courage to Mexican American opposition to the war. The war heightened Mexican American consciousness and helped further politicize them as a result of their being made clearly aware of the paradox of fighting for democracy abroad when they did not have it at home. The August 1970 National Chicano War Moratorium was a seminal event.

The Texas-based La Raza Unida Party emerged because many Mexican Americans drifted away from the Democratic Party, disillusioned by the horse-trading between the Party and Mexican American political leaders. RUP strove to empower Mexican Americans politically. Like all third parties, it was successful on the local and state levels rather than on a national level. Plagued by personality clashes and shortages of funds and a tendency toward using anti-Anglo, anticapitalist rhetoric that alienated many established Mexican American elected officials, RUP as an independent political party never attained the level of power its founders envisioned. Moreover, RUP established its power in declining Texas farm counties that were being abandoned by Mexican Americans fleeing the poverty resulting from Anglo landowners' converting their properties to ranching. Nevertheless, Mexican Americans had built their own political organization, spurned the two national political parties, and gained self-respect and the potential for future self-government.[68] A new breed of political activists emerged with knowledge and skills on many public policy issues to improve the political and economic life of Mexican Americans.

The Democratic Party's identification with welfare spending, school busing, racial preferences, and other unpopular issues, along with the disastrous race riots of the 1960s, created a powerful white backlash in America. Conservatives reacted to and used the escalating racial tensions to lure the formerly Democratic working class to the Republican banner. Under President Richard Nixon, the Cabinet Committee on Mexican American Affairs became the Cabinet Committee on Opportunities for Spanish-Speaking People. The Cabinet became less an advocate for the Spanish-speaking people and more an apologist for the federal government. Many of the Cabinet's efforts were not to produce programs for the Spanish-speaking people but rather to promote the Nixon administration and the reelection of the president.[69]

The progress of Mexican Americans as a whole was uneven in the late 1970s and became stagnant in the early 1980s. The Economic Opportunity Act of 1964 was weakened by administrative problems and short-changed by a growing conservative Congress that refused to remedy the hard realities of poverty in America. Furthermore, many Americans blamed the poor for their own plight and expressed anger over the use of their tax dollars for poverty programs. The barrier of racism remained a formidable factor.

Federal legislation set up affirmative action in employment and higher education. However, Title VII of the Civil Rights Act of 1964 upheld the postwar emphasis of prohibiting job discrimination rather than promoting minority employment. In

California, median incomes of Mexican Americans were only three-fourths of those of white families. Mexican American Vietnam veterans who had incomplete educations and no skills when they went into the military discovered when they got out that there were no jobs. Although the bracero program was terminated in 1964, Mexican Americans along the United States–Mexico border and in cities far from the border faced stiff competition for work from increasing numbers of workers coming in from Mexico, owing to the creation of the Border Industrialization Program (BIP), and from tens of thousands of aliens who crossed the border legally as commuters or as unauthorized migrants. In the 1970s impoverished Mexicans continued to flee their homeland of Mexico by the tens of thousands to come to the United States.

With the right-wing turn in America as a backdrop, many of the educational and income gains Mexican Americans achieved through federal and state affirmative action programs were attacked. Only a fourth of Spanish-surnamed males held white-collar jobs in 1970, compared with more than half of Anglo men. There was no improved school achievement by Mexican Americans owing to their high concentration in dreadful inner-city schools. Mexican Americans were still underrepresented in colleges and universities, which remained elitist and racist. Because debates continued over affirmative action, programs in Chicano studies and in bilingual/bicultural education constantly met opposition. Anglos increasingly challenged government programs in the courts as reverse discrimination, such as the Bakke decision in 1978, which put affirmative action on trial and was a slap in the face to Mexican Americans and other minorities.

Although the Mexican American struggle for equality made considerable gains for America's second largest minority group, Mexican Americans continued to suffer from discrimination in society as a whole. The large gap between Mexican Americans and Anglos persisted and led to racial antagonisms and tensions and many other problems that remained unresolved in the 1980s.

## NOTES

1. Grebler, Moore, and Guzmán, *Mexican American People*, 18–23. Speaking before the Senate Committee on Labor and Human Resources in 1967, Chavez explained the dilemma faced by farm workers who attempted to strike for higher wages and improved working conditions: "As long as . . . Mexican farm workers keep our place and do our work we are tolerated, but if the Mexican worker joins a union, if he stands up for justice and if he dares to strike, then all the local institutions feel duty-bound to defend what they consider to be their ideal of the American way of life. . . . For all these . . . years . . . when the farm workers strike and their strike is successful, the employers go to Mexico and . . . use illegal alien strikebreakers to break the strike. And . . . the Immigration and Naturalization Service has . . . assisted in the strikebreaking . . . The growers have armed their foremen. They have looked to professional agencies to provide them unlimited numbers of armed guards . . . who are given a gun and a club and a badge and a canister of tear gas and the authority . . . to break the strike by using this unchecked raw power against our people." U.S. Senate Committee on Labor and Human Resources, *Hearings Before the Committee on Labor and Human Resources,* 96th Cong., 1st Sess., 1967.

2. Grebler, Moore, and Guzmán, *Mexican American People,* 18–23. In 1960, journalist Edward R. Murrow's television documentary *Harvest of Shame* captured the deplorable plight of farmworkers and shocked the nation.

3. Ibid., 560–562, 591.

4. James L. Sundquist, "Has America Lost Its Social Conscience—And How Will It Get It Back?" *Political Science Quarterly* 101, no. 4 (1986): 513–514.

5. Jacques E. Levy, *César Chavez: Autobiography of La Causa* (New York: Norton, 1975), 179–182; Florence M. White, *César Chavez: Man of Courage* (Champaign, IL: Gerrard, 1973), 59. The bracero program had ended the previous year, but a new agreement between the United States and Mexico allowed growers to import Mexican workers if they were paid $1.25 an hour.

6. Nelson Lichtenstein, *The Most Dangerous Man in Detroit: Walter Reuther and the Fate of American Labor* (New York: Basic Books, 1995), 410; Levy, *César Chavez,* 202–203; Dick Meister and Anne Loftis, *A Long Time Coming* (New York: Macmillan, 1977), 138–139; J. Craig Jenkins, *The Politics of Insurgency: The Farmworkers Movement in the 1960s* (New York: Columbia University Press, 1985), 142–143.

7. Grebler, Moore, and Guzmán, *Mexican American People,* 464–465; "Grapes of Wrath," *Time,* December 10, 1965, 96. The California Rural Legal Assistance (CRLA) organization enlisted itself in the cause of the farm workers. In May 1966, the Office of Economic Opportunity (OEO) funded the creation of the CRLA, thus establishing a network of rural law offices to take on individual cases and class action suits. Lawyers teamed up with migrant farmworkers to fight for better working and living conditions. The CRLA forced the federal government to stop importing braceros; protected striking California farmworkers from eviction by their employer-landlords; and demanded that Spanish-speaking children, labeled "mentally retarded" based on English-language test scores, be retested in their native language.

8. Lawrence E. Davies, "Grape Growers Score Gov. Brown as March Ends," *New York Times,* April 11, 1966, 18; "Grape Strike Chief Accepts a Proposal for Secret Election," *New York Times,* April 9, 1966, 52; Peter Bart, "Schenley to Bargain with a Grape Union," *New York Times,* April 7, 1966, 1, 28.

9. Tony Castro, *Chicano Power: The Emergence of Mexican America* (New York: Saturday Review Press, 1974), 81.

10. Campbell, *Gone to Texas,* 429; Richard Bailey, "The Starr County Strike," *Red River Valley Historical Review* 40 (Winter 1979): 49.

11. Lichtenstein, *The Most Dangerous Man in Detroit,* 410; Pycior, *LBJ and Mexican Americans,* 218–219; Arthur M. Schlesinger, Jr., *Robert F. Kennedy and His Times* (New York: Mariner Books, 2002), 790–792; Peter Matthiessen, *Sal Sí Puedes: César Chavez and the New American Revolution* (New York: Random House, 1969), 179–181.

12. "Ten Thousand Farm Workers on Strike in California," *El Malcriado,* September 1, 1970; Lichtenstein, *Most Dangerous Man in Detroit,* 432–433; Jenkins, *Politics of Insurgency,* 176–181; Levy, *César Chavez,* 453. By 1974, the UFWA was attempting to sign new contracts with grape and lettuce growers, some of whom signed sweetheart contracts with the Teamsters. The UFWA survived the threat. Dolores Huerta again organized picket lines, continued to lobby, and directed the UFWA's East Coast boycott of lettuce, grapes, and Gallo wines. "Chavez Speaks on UFW Fight," *El Malcriado,* January–February 1975, Section 1, 11.

13. Ruiz, *From Out of the Shadows,* 133–134.

14 Marc Simmons, *New Mexico* (Albuquerque: University of New Mexico Press, 1988), 182; Swadesh, "Alianza Movement," 297.

15. Simmons, *New Mexico*, 183; Swadesh, "Alianza Movement," 302; "The Agony of Tierra Amarilla," *Time*, November 29, 1968; Clark S. Knowlton, "Violence in New Mexico: A Sociological Perspective," *California Law Review* 58, no. 5 (October 1970): 1075.

16. Knowlton, "Violence in New Mexico," 1077–1079; Michael Jenkinson, *Tijerina* (Albuquerque, NM: Paisano Press, 1968), 47–57.

17  Nancie L. González, *Spanish Americans of New Mexico: A Heritage of Pride* (Albuquerque: University of New Mexico Press, 1969), 95; Simmons, *New Mexico*, 185.

18. González, *Spanish Americans of New Mexico*, 95–96; Simmons, *New Mexico*, 185; Swadesh, "Alianza Movement," 308.

19. González, *Spanish Americans of New Mexico*, 97–98; Simmons, *New Mexico*, 186; Swadesh, "Alianza Movement," 307, 309; Knowlton, "Violence in New Mexico," 1073, 1079.

20. Edwin A. Tucker and George Fitzpatrick, *Men Who Match the Mountains: The Forest Service in the Southwest* (Washington, DC: U.S. Department of Agriculture Forest Service, 1972), 289.

21. Ibid., 276–278; González, *Spanish Americans of New Mexico*, 98; Simmons, *New Mexico*, 186; Knowlton, "Violence in New Mexico," 1080. Alianza member Isabel García stated at the trial: "The purpose was that we would go to the Echo Amphitheater and if we were arrested, we would get our case in court and maybe go to the Supreme Court." Swadesh, "Alianza Movement," 308–309.

22. "The Agony of Tierra Amarilla"; Swadesh, "Alianza Movement," 303–304, 313; Knowlton, "Violence in New Mexico," 1081.

23. Knowlton, "Violence in New Mexico," 1082.

24. Ibid., 1054–1055; Richard M. Gardner, *Grito! Reies Tijerina and the New Mexico Land Grant War of 1967* (New York: Bobbs-Merrill, 1970), 164.

25. González, *Spanish Americans of New Mexico*, 98; Knowlton, "Violence in New Mexico," 1081. Governor David Cargo warned: "It's the right of every citizen to petition government. However, I will not tolerate violence or destruction of property." Simmons, *New Mexico*, 186.

26. Pycior, *LBJ and Mexican Americans*, 224, 226–227; Simmons, *New Mexico*, 187; Swadesh, "Alianza Movement," 312. Typical of this reaction was a revealing poster on the University of New Mexico campus in May 1966: "We true Spanish are white, and we are Catholics. We fight communists. We don't care for foreigners, Negro or white, to come and lie about our race. The only race problem is the one brought in by dirty communists who try to pass as Spanish to get our land grants." González, *Spanish Americans of New Mexico*, 103–104.

27. González, *Spanish Americans of New Mexico*, 98–99; Knowlton, "Violence in New Mexico," 1081; Simmons, *New Mexico*, 187.

28. Alicia R. Schmidt Camacho, *Migrant Imaginaries: Latino Cultural Politics in the U.S.–Mexico Borderlands* (New York: New York University Press, 2008), 155.

29. Knowlton, "Violence in New Mexico," 1084.

30. Christine Marín, *A Spokesman of the Mexican American Movement: Rodolfo "Corky" Gonzales and the Fight for Chicano Liberation, 1966–1972* (San Francisco: R. and E. Research Associates, 1974), 2; Tom I. Romero, "Wearing the Red, White, and Blue Trunks of Aztlán: Rodolfo 'Corky' Gonzales and the Convergence of American and Chicano Nationalism," *Aztlán: A Journal of Chicano Studies* 29, no. 1 (Spring 2004): 101–102.

31. Romero, "Wearing the Red, White, and Blue Trunks," 103; Ernesto B. Vigil, *The Crusade for Justice: Chicano Militancy and the Government's War on Dissent* (Madison: University of Wisconsin Press, 1999), 20–21.

32. Romero, "Wearing the Red, White, and Blue Trunks," 107–108; Vigil, *Crusade for Justice*, 25–26.

33. Carlos Muñoz, *Youth, Identity, and Power: The Chicano Movement* (New York: Verso Books, 2007), 75–78; Alma M. García, ed., *Chicano Feminist Thought: The Basic Historical Writings* (New York: Routledge, 1997), 1:296.

34. Pycior, *LBJ and Mexican Americans*, 224, 226–227; Marín, *A Spokesman of the Mexican American Movement*, 7.

35. Ernesto Vigil, *El Gallo: La voz de la justicia*, April 1973. Denver police arrested a man for jaywalking in front of crusade headquarters, and this touched off a confrontation between the crusade and the city's irate police officers. The course of events accelerated in September 1975 when Denver police arrested two men in an alleged plot to blow up a police substation in the southwest part of the city. One of the men arrested was crusade founder John Haro. Aided by an odious Mexican American sneak who supplied the Denver police with incriminating information, undercover police tailed Haro and captured him transporting the bomb. Haro and a codefendant were acquitted in the bomb plot, but Haro was found guilty of possession of explosives and was given a six-year prison sentence.

36. Laura Pulido, *African American, Brown, Yellow, and Left: Radical Activism in Los Angeles* (Berkeley: University of California Press, 2006), 115.

37. Ibid., 115–116. Such was the case when someone started a fire in the Biltmore Hotel as Governor Ronald Reagan was giving a speech. Known as the L.A. Thirteen, Brown Beret members and other activists were arrested for conspiring to riot, disrupt the public schools, and disturb the peace.

38. Dolores D. Bernai, "Grassroots Leadership Reconceptualized: Chicana Oral Histories and the 1968 East Los Angeles School Blowouts," *Frontiers: A Journal of Women Studies* 19, no. 2 (1998): 114; Kaye Briegel, "Chicano Student Militancy: The Los Angeles High School Strike of 1968," in *An Awakened Minority: The Mexican-Americans,* ed. Manuel P. Servín (New York: Macmillan, 1974), 215.

39. Armando Navarro, *Mexican American Youth Organization: Avant-Garde of the Chicano Movement in Texas* (Austin: University of Texas Press, 1995), 80, 134. See also José Angel Gutiérrez, *We Won't Back Down: Severita Lara's Rise from Student Leader to Mayor* (Houston, TX: Arte Publico Press, 2005).

40. Navarro, *Mexican American Youth Organization*, 118–125; Campbell, *Gone to Texas,* 430.

41. Ignacio M. García, *Chicanismo: The Forging of a Militant Ethos Among Mexican Americans* (Tucson: University of Arizona Press, 1997), 56–57.

42. Muñoz, *Youth, Identity, and Power,* 76–84. MECHA brought together the United Mexican American Students (UMAS), the Mexican American Student Association (MASA), the Mexican American Student Confederation (MASC), the Mexican American Youth Organization (MAYO) of Texas, and the Committee for the Advancement of the Mexican American (CAMA). The Association of Mexican American Educators, founded in 1965, acted as an advisor to state and local boards of education on the educational needs of Mexican American youths.

43. Jorge Mariscal, "Left Turns in the Chicano Movement," *Monthly Review* 54, no. 3 (July-August 2002): 59–60. In 1970, the brigade's Mexican American caucus reported on the New Mexico land grant movement, the Denver Youth Conference, the student walkouts, and the Chicano Moratorium Committee antiwar demonstrations held in December 1969 and in February 1970. The seminar ended with the following declaration: "Our political activities have now transcended reformist demands. Now the U.S. government

knows that before it tries another Bay of Pigs, it will first have to contend with the South-west. Chicanos will help bring the struggle of liberation home to Latin Americans within the United States." Sandra Levinson and Carol Brightman, eds., *Venceremos Brigade: Young Americans Sharing the Life and Work of Revolutionary Cuba* (New York: Simon and Schuster, 1971), 235.

44. García, *Chicanismo*, 14–15; Ruiz, *From Out of the Shadows*, 108–109; Ramon Gutiérrez, "Community, Patriarchy and Individualism: The Politics of Chicano History," *American Quarterly* 45, no. 1 (March 1993): 49; Perlita R. Dicochea, "Chicana Critical Rhetoric: Recrafting La Causa in Chicana Movement Discourse, 1970–1979," *Frontiers: A Journal of Women Studies* 25, no. 1 (2004): 77–92.

45. Mirta Vidal, "The Unity of 'La Raza,'" *International Socialist Review* (October 1971).

46. Martha P. Cortera, *The Chicana Feminist* (Austin, TX: Information Systems Development, 1977), 33–47.

47. García, *Chicano Feminist Thought*, 21–24, 113–116; Ruiz, *From Out of the Shadows*, 108, 115–116; Marta Vidal, "New Voice of La Raza: Chicanas Speak Out," *International Socialist Review* 39, no. 9 (October 1971): 7; Mariscal, "Left Turns," 60–61. Reporting on the 1972 Third World Women's Conference, Enriqueta Longeaux y Vásquez wrote: "There is a need for . . . unity of all peoples suffering exploitation and colonial oppression here in the U.S . . . to identify ourselves as Third World peoples in order to end this economic and political expansion." García, *Chicana Feminist Thought*, 173. See also Maylei Blackwell, "Contested Histories: Las Hijas de Cuauhtémoc, Chicana Feminisms, and Print Culture in the Chicano Movement, 1968–1973" in *Chicana Feminisms: A Critical Reader*, ed. Gabriela Arredondo (Durham: Duke University Press, 2003), 59–89.

48. Lorena Oropeza, *¡Raza Sí! ¡Guerra No! Chicano Protest and Patriotism During the Viet Nam War Era* (Berkeley: University of California Press, 2005), 126–127; Pulido, *African American, Brown, Yellow, and Left*, 75.

49. Lisa Hsiao, "Project 100,000: The Great Society's Answer to Military Manpower Needs in Vietnam," *Vietnam Generation* 1, no. 2 (1989): 14–37; Robert McNamara, "Memorandum for the President: Subject: Project One Hundred Thousand," July 25, 1967. United States. Congress. House. Committee on Appropriations. Hearings, Part 1, 1968, p. 637.

50. Pulido, *African American, Brown, Yellow, and Left*, 74–75. In 1966, Corky Gonzales again spoke out eloquently against the war: "The American people are daily faced with news that attempts to brainwash them into approving of a war that can only bring shame and disgrace to the most powerful nation in the world along with misery and destruction to weak and helpless people. Would it not be more noble to portray our great country as a humanitarian nation with the honest intentions of aiding and advising the weak rather than to be recognized as a military power and hostile enforcer of our political aims?" Mariscal, "Left Turns," 63; Vigil, *Crusade for Justice*, 28.

51. At Kent State University on May 4, 1970, Ohio National Guardsmen advanced on a student antiwar rally, fired indiscriminately, and killed four students and wounded nine others. Eleven days later, two African American students were killed at an antiwar protest on the campus of Jackson State University in Mississippi.

52. Mariscal, "Left Turns," 67.

53. Edward J. Escobar, "The Dialectics of Repression: The Los Angeles Police Department and the Chicano Movement, 1968–1971," *Journal of American History* 79, no. 4 (March 1993): 1500–1504; Pulido, *African American, Brown, Yellow, and Left*, 75.

54. For the government's war on radicals, see, for example, Nelson Blackstock, *COINTEL-PRO: The FBI's Secret War on Political Freedom* (New York: Pathfinder Press, 1975) and

Ward Churchill and Jim Vander Wall, *The COINTELPRO Papers: Documents from the FBI's Secret Wars Against Dissent in the United States* (Boston: South End Press, 1990).

55. James T. Patterson, *America's Struggle Against Poverty in the Twentieth Century* (Cambridge, MA: Harvard University Press, 1986), 134–135; Pycior, *LBJ and Mexican Americans,* 151–158.

56. Joan W. Moore and Ralph Guzmán, "New Wind from the Southwest," *Nation,* May 30, 1966, 646; Armando Rendón, "La Raza Today Not Mañana," in *Mexican Americans in the United States: A Reader,* ed. John Burma (Cambridge, MA: Schenkman, 1970), 307–324.

57. Grebler, Moore, and Guzmán, *Mexican American People,* 590–593.

58. Ibid., 586.

59. Pycior, *LBJ and Mexican Americans,* 236–239; Muñoz, *Youth, Identity, and Power,* 99–113; José Angel Guiterrez, "Aztlán: Chicano Revolt in the Winter Garden," *La Raza Magazine* 1, no. 4 (Spring 1971): 35–40.

60. Pycior, *LBJ and Mexican Americans,* 239; José Angel Gutiérrez and Rebecca E. Deen, "Chicanas in Texas Politics," JSRI Occasional Paper # 66, The Julian Samora Research Institute, Michigan State University, October 2000, 11.

61. Pycior, *LBJ and Mexican Americans,* 239–240.

62. Between 1978 and 1982, the number of Mexican American voters in Texas rose from 591,950 to 832,398, an increase of 41 percent.

63. McGovern pointed out: "If the Democratic Party does not take positive steps to include America's minorities in—and not just with rhetoric but a full share of power—the day will surely come when those minorities will leave the Democratic Party out in the political cold. You can't play games with people any more. You either give them what they deserve or they will give you what you deserve." Olga Rodriguez, ed., *The Politics of Chicano Liberation* (New York: Pathfinder Press, 1977), 63.

64. Moore and Guzmán, "New Wind from the Southwest," 645; Grebler, Moore, and Guzmán, *Mexican American People,* 584, 586, 595.

65. Pycior, *LBJ and Mexican Americans,* 225; Levy, *César Chavez,* 289–290; Schlesinger, *Robert Kennedy and His Times,* 914; Patricia Cronin Marcello, *Gloria Steinem: A Biography* (Westport, CT: Greenwood Press, 2004), 107.

66. Grebler, Moore, and Guzmán, *Mexican American People,* 584.

67. See "The Angry Chicano," *Wall Street Journal,* June 11, 1970.

68. Pycior, *LBJ and Mexican Americans,* 239, 241.

69. Grebler, Moore, and Guzmán, *Mexican American People,* 583. In a speech on the floor of the U.S. Senate in 1972, presidential candidate George McGovern addressed the conundrum of the returning Mexican American Vietnam veteran: "The unemployment rate among returning Vietnam veterans between 20 and 24 years of age is 12.4%. These difficulties are even worse for veterans from minority groups, including Mexican-Americans who have contributed more than their fair share to this war. Fifteen percent of California's casualties, and ten percent of all casualties in the Southwest, have been Mexican-Americans. What Mexican-Americans want to know is why are they first in war, but last in peace? Why are they good enough to lead men in combat in Vietnam, to carry the heavy responsibility of life and death, but not good enough to handle a desk in Washington?" Jorge Mariscal, ed., *Aztlán and Viet Nam: Chicano and Chicana Experiences of the War* (Berkeley: University of California Press, 1999), 15.

# CHAPTER 11

✦

# Mexican Americans at the End
# of the Twentieth Century

In the decade of the 1970s the Mexican population in the United States nearly doubled from 4.5 to 8.7 million persons. This total figure included approximately 1.1 million unauthorized immigrants from Mexico. By 1980 nearly 73 percent of all Mexican Americans lived in California and Texas, and Illinois and Arizona together contributed sizeable Mexican American populations.

Many Mexican Americans attained success, as the well-educated among them broke down barriers of discrimination and entered better paying professional jobs. However, many more Mexican Americans were profoundly affected by the crisis ushered in by the restructuring of the United States economy and faced a shrinking job market. Those in the Midwest were hard hit by the savage unemployment precipitated by deindustrialization. The decline of American manufacturing and the continued integration of the Southwest border region with Mexico produced the second highest unemployment rate among the nation's Spanish-speaking population. Levels of poverty for them were three times higher than for Anglos. Inequality increased under the Reagan administration of the 1980s at the very time that civil rights implementation was reversed and social programs eliminated. Many of the gains Mexican Americans and African Americans had made during the previous two decades were wiped out.[1]

Mexican Americans would be significantly influenced by national public policy for the remainder of the late twentieth century as a conservative movement dubbed the "New Right" emerged as a potent force in American politics, bolstered by a reaction to the social upheavals that accompanied the civil rights movement of the late 1960s and early 1970s. It decried the rapid expansion of government power and, taking a conservative civil rights stand, labeled federal initiatives such as busing, affirmative action programs, and the proposed Equal Rights Amendment as intrusions on individual rights. Ronald Reagan laid out this position in his inaugural address on January 20, 1981. "Government is not the solution to our problem. Government is the problem." Concerned with the growth of bilingualism on a national scale, the New Right mobilized conservative Republican voters as a core constituency. The nationwide English-only movement and later the passage of Proposition 187 in California were examples of this retrenchment period that also saw Mexican Americans joining the New Right chorus. The most prominent Mexican Americans who defected to the right were essayist Richard Rodriguez and conservative pundit Linda Chavez. Chavez was especially hostile to affirmative action in all forms and demanded an end to bilingual education and welfare. Both instead advocated Mexican American integration into mainstream American society.

As electoral politics replaced social movements, Mexican Americans began participating in the political process at the local, state, and national levels. This electorate played an important role in Democratic and Republican Party politics and created a base of some influence in each, especially the Democratic Party. Mexican Americans made significant progress in being elected to public office as reapportionment and redistricting increased the number of districts containing majority Spanish-speaking populations and because of successful legal challenges to voter inequality.[2] What resulted was empowerment through the reallocation of political power at the local and state levels.

President Ronald Reagan's new cold war nationalism depicted the Soviet Union as an evil, totalitarian empire and fueled a massive military buildup. Reagan's concern about Third World radicalism in Central America resulted in America's support for right-wing torture and violence, sponsoring surrogate wars in Guatemala and El Salvador, and backing the Contra wars to overthrow the Sandinistas in Nicaragua. Mexican Americans protested against U.S. involvement in Central America and actively participated in human rights groups such as the sanctuary movement to end Central America's bloody wars and to aid people fleeing the horrendous violence in El Salvador and Guatemala, facing deportation, or threatened by the government with legal action. Because low-income minority communities were the principal victims of environmental pollution as a result of deliberate government or corporate decisions, Mexican Americans also came together on a wide array of environmental justice issues to protect their neighborhoods.

Reflecting the growth of racial intolerance in the 1980s, a time when guaranteeing civil rights was not a priority, racially motivated attacks and other harassment directed at minorities increased. White racism and limited opportunities stirred feelings of alienation, frustration, and anger among young Mexican Americans who fully recognized their marginality in America. Tracked into noncollege courses, Mexican Americans became the nation's most segregated students, suffering from dropout rates as high as 50 percent.[3] These school dropouts became prone to involvement in gang warfare. For minorities the 1980s not only brought continuing problems of joblessness and public schools that only served as stopping places until they went off to jail or prison but also violent and deadly gang warfare fueled by a drug epidemic of crack cocaine and heroin in many inner cities where poverty was widespread. Mexican Americans also became victims of an incarceration epidemic brought about by "tough on crime" legislation such as moderate to minimum sentencing, three-strikes-you're-out laws, and the "war on drugs."

After a twenty-year lull, the flow of unauthorized migration from Mexico as a whole increased significantly, so that by the early 1980s it accounted for an estimated two-thirds of all Mexican immigrants in the United States. Between 1970 and 1988 the number of Mexican immigrants increased five times, tripling the nation's Mexican-born population. In 1989 this population was estimated at 12,565,000, a 45 percent increase from 1980, largely due to high immigration and rising birth rates.[4] It would continue growing at an accelerated pace in the 1990s.

Accounting for this upsurge in immigration were the conditions in Mexico that placed pressure on Mexico's workers to migrate north: an economic slump, the worst since the Great Depression; population growth that averaged 3 percent per year since 1960; and a 50 percent underemployment rate. Many Mexican immigrants came to stay and induced their women family members to come north to take advantage of work opportunities. One in two immigrants from Mexico went to California, principally concentrating in the southern part of the state. Many became citizens and encouraged additional migration from Mexico to the United States.[5]

The anger and frustration about the growing number of unauthorized Mexicans and the cultural changes their presence imposed produced a backlash. This neo-nativism, fueled by the politics of fear, scapegoated immigrants. Because of the protracted recession in California, state governor Pete Wilson cut billions of dollars from schools and other public programs through Proposition 187. This initiative was a response to the rapid growth of the Latino population, the increase of new immigration, and the general anti-immigrant sentiment that blamed immigrants for the ills that befell California's economy.

The resurgence of racism fueled resentment by whites of the gains made by racial minorities that they believed came at their own expense. These feelings of "reverse discrimination" produced the Reagan assault on affirmative action, a campus backlash against minorities, and a wave of campus-based racial incidents by decade's end. In California, Proposition 209 abolished all public-sector affirmative action programs in employment, contracting, and education. This came at a time when Mexican American college attendance was declining while high school graduation rates continued to rise and as deep cuts were made in funding for public education.

Despite the gains made by Mexican American workers, they still had not achieved wage parity with Anglo workers and tended to be relatively concentrated in unskilled occupations. Furthermore, their modest gains were wiped out by the recession of the early 1970s and the deindustrialization that followed in the 1980s. The wave of extreme antilabor sentiment in the United States ushered in by the Reagan era and sustained by the first Bush administration witnessed Mexican and Mexican American men and women workers fight back through strike actions.[6] This infusion of Latino worker energy revitalized the American labor movement—ironically, one that aggressively resisted organizing immigrant workers.

The North American Free Trade Agreement (NAFTA) aptly demonstrated that American corporations were more loyal to their bottom line than to their workers, for it transformed the U.S.–Mexico border into the world's most dynamic free-market region. NAFTA promoted outsourcing of work, subcontracted work, and other labor forms detrimental to Mexican Americans and other American workers and contributed to a growing low-paid feminized workforce across the border in Mexico. NAFTA also helped transform Mexican immigration from a regional southwestern occurrence affecting California, Texas, and Arizona to a national one affecting all fifty states.[7]

Because of economic globalization, Los Angeles by 1990 had one of the world's largest Spanish-speaking populations, and it had become the nation's premier immigrant capital, followed by the city of New York. These two global cities contained more than five million immigrants, one-fourth of the more than twenty million immigrants in the United States. The immigrants became more segregated socially and economically from whites in those communities in which their numbers grew rapidly, resembling the balkanized ethnic enclaves satirized by T. Coraghessan Boyle in his novel *The Tortilla Curtain*. The nation's growing Spanish-speaking population—now referred to officially as Latino—raised serious questions regarding American national culture and identity. Because of the high immigration levels from the Americas and Asia, the Spanish-speaking population increased by 50 percent and the Asian population doubled, so that people of color composed a fourth of the total U.S. population.[8] All of these conditions set the stage for Mexican Americans in the new millennium.

## MEXICAN AMERICANS AND REAGAN'S "NEW MORNING IN AMERICA"

The inflationary trend in the United States that began in the late 1960s continued unabated through the 1970s, so that by 1980 the nation's economy was in shambles. Real wages peaked in 1973 but because of inflation declined 18 percent. A major oil shortage and the subsequent oil price increases added to double-digit inflation and higher deficits, as did growing foreign imports of automobiles and electronics. The American economy was restructuring itself; high-wage, high-skilled manufacturing jobs were disappearing and being replaced with low-wage, low-skilled service jobs.[9]

The 1980s marked the end of the New Deal social contract that was extended through legislative action into the 1960s. A new mood of social meanness now pervaded America, and many Americans resented having to provide for the underprivileged. Critics charged that taxes replenished the welfare state and its minority clientele at the expense of productive taxpayers. Specifically, Democratic leadership had developed programs to redistribute social and economic benefits to minorities, who were seen as unfairly receiving preferential treatment with regard to jobs and educational opportunities. Affirmative action policies, moreover, created reverse discrimination—echoing President Reagan's arguments, whites were now claiming to be the victims of discrimination in education and the job market.[10]

A "new morning in America" dawned with Ronald Reagan's election as president of the United States. Reagan harnessed the simmering discontent among large numbers of whites who felt threatened by the racial policies of the past two decades. To Reagan, the civil rights revolt had subverted the constitutional guarantees designed to ensure racial equality. Fervently opposed to affirmative action, he withdrew funding for and ended demands on unnecessary social programs and increased racist, conservative resistance responding to those demands. "Ronald Reagan," said African American editor Acel Moore of the *Philadelphia Inquirer*, "presided and helped create an age in which too many people felt free to express their bigotry. Ignorance had a holiday."[11]

Constitutionally protected rights were cut back when Reagan named William H. Rehnquist Chief Justice of the Supreme Court and Antonin Scalia and Anthony Kennedy to serve alongside Rehnquist. Reagan also selected a record number of conservative judges to the federal bench, all of these appointees openly hostile to affirmative action. The president cut the funding of the Office of Federal Contract Compliance and the Equal Employment Opportunity Commission (EEOC) and backed the repeal of key sections of the Voting Rights Act. In 1981, Reagan appointed conservative African American lawyer Clarence Thomas and California businessman Clarence M. Pendleton, Jr., to the EEOC. Both were averse to affirmative action. It was Pendleton who declared, "We are working on a color blind society that has opportunities for all and guarantees for none." In frequent attempts to discredit established black civil rights leaders, Pendleton called them "the new racists" for advocating affirmative action. These and other minorities who were insensitive on civil rights and poverty issues assisted the Reagan administration in tilting the nation to the political right in the matter of race relations.[12] Like Clarence Thomas and other African Americans, Mexican American "safe" minorities were incorporated into the nonracialism of the Republican Party and served as influential ideologues of the Reagan revolution.

The book *Hunger of Memory: The Education of Richard Rodriguez* earned its author, Richard Rodriguez, a prominent place in American literature for its reflections on the role of language in determining one's cultural identity. Rodriguez's New Right admirers believed *Hunger of Memory* was primarily concerned with explaining to white Americans why affirmative action programs failed. A Mexican American unabashedly seeking the abolition of affirmative action was staunch conservative Linda Chavez. Mentored by neoconservatives Albert Shanker and William Bennett, Chavez, as president of the grassroots organization U.S. English, also sought the elimination of bilingual education and instead advocated English as the nation's official language.[13]

A senior fellow of the conservative Manhattan Institute, Linda Chavez had come to Washington in the early 1970s as a committed civil rights activist. However, Chavez gradually moved to the right politically. In the early 1980s Chavez worked for the American Federation of Teachers (AFT). A series of articles written by Chavez and published in the AFT magazine urging "traditional values" in teaching to reverse America's cultural decline brought her to the attention of the White House. In 1983, Reagan appointed Linda Chavez staff director of the U.S. Civil Rights Commission. The Mexican American archconservative gained instant notoriety for advocating "go slow" policies in many civil rights areas such as busing and affirmative action and for opposing the Equal Rights Amendment. In her polemical book *Out of the Barrio: Toward a New Politics of Hispanic Assimilation*, Linda Chavez bashed Mexican American political leaders such as Arnold Torres, LULAC's executive director. In one of her many diatribes against them she declared, in *Out of the Barrio,* "[These] leaders seem more intent on vying with African Americans for permanent victim status than on seeking recognition for genuine progress by Hispanics over the last three decades." In 1986, Linda Chavez ran unsuccessfully for a Maryland Senate seat on the Republican ticket. Her nomination by President Reagan as his secretary of labor collapsed with the so-called "Nannygate." A question was raised about Chavez's character because it was reported that Chavez, ignoring labor laws and tax requirements, employed an unauthorized Guatemalan immigrant in her home as a domestic.[14]

The Republican Party broadened its support among Mexican Americans, as Mexican Americans were added to the ranks of conservative voters. Those under thirty-five who experienced economic and educational upward mobility embraced Republican ideals of free-market enterprise, the limited role of government, and strident individualism. Having won one-third of the Spanish-speaking vote in Ronald Reagan's 1980 sweep, Republican strategists made sure that in 1984 Reagan would hold onto his share of this vote. However, as the dimensions of the Reagan landslide emerged, the Republican Party concluded it would not need Latino votes to win in 1984.[15]

The development of greater class differentiation through upward mobility among Mexican Americans did not lead to a growth in their political conservatism and support of the Republican Party. As with African Americans, class did not eliminate for Mexican Americans the importance of race, civil rights, and group identification. Immigration policy, the English-only movement, and other issues united Mexican Americans as an electorate.

## "TÚ VOTO ES TÚ VOZ" (YOUR VOTE IS YOUR VOICE): MEXICAN AMERICANS AND THE POLITICAL PROCESS

Between the 1972 and 1992 presidential elections Mexican American voter registration and voter turnout more than doubled. The enactment of the Twenty-fourth Amendment eliminating the poll tax, the amended 1975 Voting Rights Act that extended to Mexican Americans in the Southwest, and the elimination of the English literacy requirement helped to increase the number of Mexican Americans elected to local and federal positions. Also of help was the fact that gerrymandering and minority-vote dilution processes no longer existed to reduce Mexican American electoral power. In 1986, on the heels of blanket amnesty for nearly three million Mexican immigrants, voter registration drives were launched to bring more than one million new voters to the polls. The Southwest Voter Registration Education Project, based in San Antonio and led by former La Raza Unida Party member Willy Velázquez, was credited with great success in building voter strength through registration in electorally critical Texas and California. Ten years later, the number of Mexican Americans registered to vote and hold political office doubled, despite the large number of youths and noncitizens. Mexican Americans continued to vote overwhelmingly Democratic, and Mexican American candidates received a broader base of support in their election efforts. However, Mexican Americans running for and holding office still dealt with discrimination. This included voter and campaign worker intimidation, racial appeals from opponents, and other barriers.[16]

It had been nearly 140 years since a Mexican American was mayor of San Antonio, Texas. In 1981, former White House Fellow Henry G. Cisneros ran for mayor of San Antonio and won, becoming the first Mexican American to head a major American city. The popular mayor was reelected to three additional two-year terms. Instead of requesting federal funds to improve San Antonio and expand social programs, Cisneros worked to attract high-tech companies to the city to bolster the economy and generate more jobs.[17] The improvements Cisneros brought to San Antonio enhanced his stature; it gave him credibility and standing and gained him national attention. In 1984, Democratic presidential candidate Walter F. Mondale considered Cisneros as his running mate. The following year, Cisneros was elected to a one-year term as president of the National League of Cities.[18]

In Denver in 1983, a coalition of Mexican Americans and Anglos helped Federico Peña, formerly minority leader of the Colorado House of Representatives, narrowly capture City Hall as the first Mexican American mayor. Fulfilling his campaign slogan "Imagine a Great City," Mayor Peña modernized Denver.[19] Preempting the Rainbow Coalition politics of Jesse Jackson, Mexican Americans with Puerto Ricans in Chicago in 1983 played an important role in the bitter election that saw Harold Washington defeat Richard Daley's political machine to become the first African American mayor of the Windy City. Mexican Americans and Puerto Ricans helped Washington get reelected for a second mayoral term in 1987. In 1983, voters in New Mexico elected Toney Anaya governor. The progressive Anaya opposed the death penalty, declared New Mexico a sanctuary for political refugees from Central America, and stood firm against discriminatory immigration legislation. In Texas, twenty-four Mexican Americans won seats in the state legislature, and in California a Mexican American was elected to the state assembly for the first time. The Mexican American vote was predicted to play a key role in the outcome of gubernatorial elections in both Texas and California.[20]

Mexican American women became more central to politics as their participation in the political process and their numbers as elected officials grew rapidly during this time. It was accomplished through the Democratic Party because women rallied against Reagan's domestic federal spending cuts, increases in defense spending, and the inequities of his administration's economic policies favoring the rich. By the 1990s, through party and electoral support, Mexican American women accounted for 20 percent of elected officials. They ran as major party candidates for state legislatures and congressional offices in primaries or in general elections. These female candidates were well educated, held professional or managerial positions, and had party or organizational experience. For example, in 1972 a former labor activist and White House staff member under President Johnson, Polly Baca-Barragán, became the first Mexican American woman to be elected to the Colorado Senate and the first in the nation to serve in a leadership position in any state senate. In 1980 and again in 1984, Baca-Barragán was elected cochair of the Democratic National Convention and chaired the Colorado delegation. In the 1970s, Gloria Molina served in the San Francisco Department of Health and Human Services and then in the Carter White House. She was elected

**City Councilwoman Gloria Molina with Mayor Tom Bradley, 1987.**
CREDIT: uclamss_1429_b3824_304820. UCLA Charles E. Young Research Library, Department of Special
Collections, *Los Angeles Times* Photographic Archives, ©Regents of the University of California, UCLA Library.

to the California State Assembly in 1982 and the Los Angeles City Council in 1987. In 1991, Gloria Molina became the first Mexican American woman elected to the Los Angeles County Board of Supervisors.[21] These women elected representatives proved themselves effective leaders.

Overall, between 1974 and 1984, the number of Spanish-speaking elected officials at all levels of government more than doubled, from 1,539 to 3,128, and between 1983 and 1993 increased about 41 percent, with most representatives elected at the local level. California, Texas, and New Mexico accounted for 80 percent of these Spanish-speaking elected officials. Historically excluded from the inner political policy-making process, Mexican Americans achieved greater representation through the increased presence of Mexican Americans in city and county bureaucracies. These leaders used their positions to defend community interests such as a higher degree of police accountability and expanded educational, employment, and political opportunities for their constituents.[22]

The Mexican American political organizations that emerged in the 1960s and 1970s were disbanded and replaced by newer ones crafted to coordinate projects and other initiatives. The National Association of Latino Elected and Appointed Officials (NALEO) and the Congressional Hispanic Caucus (CHC), both founded by Congressman Edward B. Roybal (D-California), were the most powerful and active organizations. NALEO started an educational fund to assist Spanish-speaking people to participate fully in the American political process. Also founded in 1976, the CHC was a legislative service organization of the U.S. House of Representatives. Composed mostly of Spanish-speaking Democratic congressional members, the CHC dedicated time and staff resources to collective activities in working with Democratic Party politics, addressing issues of the committee system, and serving the particular interests of CHC members and national constituency causes.[23] The CHC played a role in the policy-making process by shaping party and committee action and also monitored actions by the executive and judicial branches. Dedicated to voicing and advancing through the legislative process issues affecting Spanish-speaking Americans in the United States and Puerto Rico, the CHC addressed international issues and the impact these policies had on the Latino community. One important issue in the 1980s was bringing Reagan's proxy wars in Central America to an end.

## MEXICAN AMERICANS AND THE CIVIL WARS IN CENTRAL AMERICA

Mexican Americans once again questioned and then voiced strong disapproval of the foreign policies of the United States. Backing up his bold rhetoric that Communism had to be stopped at the U.S. border, President Reagan launched bloody covert operations against the Sandinistas in Nicaragua and the antigovernment forces in El Salvador. United States' opposition to the newly democratically elected government of Nicaragua and to the insurgency in El Salvador dismayed many Mexican Americans. Favoring nonintervention and economic aid, large numbers through grassroots movements protested American military intervention in Central America.[24] Liberation theology also raised political, social, and economic issues that the Catholic Church began to address at this time. Mexican American peace and justice activists learned that anti-Communist death squads were targeting Catholic nuns and priests who worked with the poor in El Salvador, along with conducting the mass execution of peasants. The subsequent slaughter of unarmed men, women, and children in the village of El Mozote by a U.S.-backed Salvadoran battalion fueled further Mexican American opposition to United States policy in Central America. Mexican American support for the Reagan administration's ventures in Central America quickly dwindled. Appointed to the bipartisan Kissinger Commission on Central America, San Antonio Mayor Henry Cisneros declared: "Latinos . . . are bailing out early on Reagan in Central America. Latinos favor a peace plan, not a war plan." Mexican Americans were among the one hundred thousand demonstrators from major labor, religious, and political groups who marched at the national April Mobilization for Justice and Peace in Central America and South Africa in 1987 in Washington, DC. The Southwest Voter Research Institute, joined by LULAC, initiated projects for educating and involving Mexican Americans in the national debate on American foreign policy in Central America. For its part, LULAC in 1984 initiated the Latin American Project to involve this organization's leaders in the national debate on U.S. policy in Latin America.[25] Many Mexican Americans were at the forefront of the dissident political activities of the Committee in Support of El Salvador (CISPES) and consequently were targeted for investigation by the FBI, which was attempting to stifle dissent, for their support of international terrorism. One of the most active Mexican American peace activists was Elizabeth "Betita" Martínez. Martínez participated in the 1983 hearings against human rights violations in Guatemala held in Madrid, Spain.[26]

United States' covert assistance to drug-running, right-wing Central American military regimes during the Reagan years displaced close to two million peasants and workers from their homelands. It also shaped policy toward Central American refugees seeking entry into the United States who took up unauthorized residence in Los Angeles, San Francisco, Washington, DC, and other cities. Mexican Americans became actively involved in the sanctuary movement to bring El Salvadoran and Guatemalan war refugees into the United States, many of the exiles bearing the marks of torture on their bodies. The city of Los Angeles declared itself a sanctuary, along with the state of New Mexico. More than five hundred thousand El Salvadorans, along with significant numbers of Nicaraguans and Guatemalans, escaped death squads and political persecution at home and eventually settled in the United States. Mexican Americans in the 1980s supported other progressive positions, from curbing hunger and poverty in sub-Saharan Africa to promoting a nuclear freeze to stopping environmental pollution.[27]

For many of America's minority communities, race and social and economic status were linked to chronic exposures to greater than acceptable levels of environmental pollution. Communities in which racial minorities were the majority population got less attention when it came to enforcing environmental laws, because in many instances representatives who would be concerned with these issues were missing from local governments that decided these matters. Three out of every five African Americans and Mexican Americans lived in communities with uncontrolled toxic waste sites. Policy makers viewed East Los Angeles as a poor, crime-ridden, and politically powerless community and selected it for a hazardous waste incinerator. Mexican American residents of East Los Angeles strongly objected and launched a grassroots effort. Leading this drive was the Mothers of East Los Angeles (MELA). Founded in 1984 and numbering three thousand supporters made up mostly of women, MELA proved these policy makers wrong in justifying "dumping everything no other community wanted in East Los Angeles." The residents also vigorously opposed the building of a state prison in their community.[28]

## UNEMPLOYMENT, DRUGS, GANG WARFARE, AND THE 1992 RODNEY KING RIOTS

A greater problem facing many Spanish-speaking communities was the rise of open gang warfare. The recession, high unemployment, increased foreign competition from Europe and Asia, and an immigrant influx fueled rising racial tensions in America. Racism ignited the major cities of the United States in the 1980s. The decade began with the 1980 Miami riots, triggered by the acquittal of four white police officers in the beating death of an African American man, and ended with the 1989 race murder of a sixteen-year-old African American by young whites in Bensonhurst, Brooklyn, New York. There were civil disturbances involving Mexicans and Central Americans in Los Angeles and along the U.S.–Mexico border, where U.S. immigration officials with impunity conducted sweeps and harassed Spanish-speaking residents. With fears that immigrants were overrunning the nation, the number of neo-Nazi hate groups grew, many tapping the rising numbers of alienated working-class whites for membership. Prominent among the organizations were Tom Metzger's White Aryan Resistance (WAR) and the Ku Klux Klan.[29]

The 1980s racial incidents were provoked by unnecessary and excessive police abuse that included beatings, unjustified shootings, and the use of police dogs against African Americans and Mexican Americans. In June 1981, the U.S. Commission on Civil Rights report to the White House and Congress confirmed with alarm the "widespread acts of animosity . . . and rising numbers of civil disorders triggered by violent treatment of minorities by law enforcement officials."[30]

Linked inextricably to rampant poverty, high rates of joblessness, and school dropout, a wave of gang violence and crack cocaine use swept through many inner-city neighborhoods from 1985 through 1990. Luis Rodríguez's moving autobiographical novel *Always Running* captured the pervasive and deep sense of despair that led young, urban Mexican Americans in Los Angeles into gang activity. Gangs developed economic functions; they became deeply involved in the lucrative drug trade as a replacement for the federal government's abandonment of youth employment and urban renewal projects and the dearth of jobs. This hellish nightmare of unceasing gunfire, police sirens, and helicopters flying overhead was wrought on the city's minority working-class communities by the large-scale destabilizing forces and marginalization resulting from changes in global capitalism. The social calamity of drugs and gang members murdering gang members would claim the lives of twenty-five thousand young people.[31] The nearly one thousand gangs with two hundred thousand gang members in Los Angeles made the city the youth gang capital of the United States. Racial troubles and police violence continued to burden America at the end of the twentieth century as demands for more law and order measures grew.

Federal and state officials in Reagan's war on drugs ("Just Say No") responded with draconian antidrug and antigang legislation that sent a disproportionate number of poor African Americans and Mexican Americans into federal and state prisons, with younger adults incarcerated in youth authority institutions. "Lock-'em-up and throw-away-the-key" police suppression and the general lack of equality before the law for Mexican Americans is dramatically evident in the nation's racist criminal system. Although the incarceration rates of African Americans and Mexican Americans have always exceeded their representation in the general population, their numbers grew increasingly top-heavy throughout the prison explosion of the 1980s. Prison populations in essence became minority populations. Here prison guards routinely pitted rival African American and Mexican American gang members in organized "gladiator combats" in the exercise yards, the fighting ended by guards shooting the antagonists apart with rubber bullets, followed by high-impact explosive rounds. This trend of high rates of minority incarceration, in which offenders are convicted of nonviolent, drug-related third strikes, continued into the 1990s as the law and order campaign of the Clinton administration rivaled that of the Reagan-Bush era.[32] "Law and order" meant not giving Mexican Americans probation or parole, as well as racially motivated police violence and misconduct in the form of terrorizing Mexican American males suspected of being gang members through "stop and search" activities. For example, in southern California, two Huntington Park policemen were prosecuted for torturing a gang member with an electric cattle prod, and, in a federal class action suit filed by eighty-one minority victims, they accused twenty-two sheriffs from the Lynwood station of "systematic acts of shooting, killing, brutality, terrorism, house-trashing, and other acts of lawlessness and wanton abuse of power." It was later found out that the Lynwood sheriffs belonged to a white-supremacist gang.[33]

America's cities were increasingly segregated by race, ethnicity, and class. The sharp economic decline in the inner cities by the concentration of poverty and joblessness led to interracial competition and tensions. In 1990, nearly two-thirds of Los Angeles residents were of minority groups (40 percent Mexican or Central American, 13 percent African American, and 9 percent Asian). Most were desperately poor people. In this overlap between economic disadvantage and race, the impoverished Mexican and Central American immigrants who flooded into South Central Los Angeles competed with poor African Americans for low-paying jobs and low-cost housing. Police abuse, gangs, drugs, poverty, and racial tensions transformed this section of Los Angeles into a tinderbox, and in April 1992 it exploded in minority fighting minority. In combination with these precipitating factors, the acquittal of four white Los Angeles police officers who beat African American motorist Rodney King (the police had been videotaped attacking him) touched off six days of rioting in South Central Los Angeles and other parts

**Rodney King Riots, 1992.**
CREDIT: "Guardsman Standing Near Burning Building," AAFG002598, ©David Butow/CORBIS SABA.

of the city. The rioting produced 2,383 injuries, 8,000 arrests, 51 deaths, and the burning or destruction of more than 10,000 businesses. Property damage was estimated at over $1 billion. The 1992 Los Angeles race riot was viewed as involving only African Americans. However, many of the participants, as well as victims, of the riots were either Latino or Asian. The largest outbreak of racial violence since the race riots of the 1960s, the Los Angeles uprising was actually a major response by poor minorities to the economic and policy shifts and other manifestations of racism sweeping through cities all across America.[34] Federal government reform of immigration policy created further cultural division in the United States.

## THE 1986 SIMPSON-MAZZOLI ACT OR IRCA, THE ENGLISH-ONLY MOVEMENT, AND PROPOSITION 187

In 1985, one year before the Congressional elections, President Reagan seized the issue of unauthorized immigration and transformed it into a question of national security by asserting that the United States had "lost control" of its border with Mexico to an "invasion" of unauthorized migrants. Subsequently, immigration was linked in the minds of Americans with invaders, criminals, and drug smugglers who menaced the nation's border with Mexico. Mexican Americans also made their case against expanded immigration; they argued that increased restrictions on immigration were necessary and that immigrants from Mexico who were already here had to integrate into American society.[35]

The following year, the United States responded to the problem of unlawful immigration from Mexico through the passage of the Simpson-Mazzoli Act or, as it became known, the Immigration and Control Act of 1986 (IRCA). IRCA prohibited American employers from hiring unauthorized aliens, penalized employers for noncompliance, and increased border patrol enforcement across the U.S.–Mexico border. Under its two amnesty programs, IRCA provided 2.3 million Mexican immigrants who had been in the country continuously since 1982 with the opportunity to become legal U.S. residents. Apprehensions and arrests of unauthorized Mexicans along the border dropped by more than half from 1986 to 1989. However, the new immigration bill proved controversial. It came at a time when unemployment remained high along the U.S.–Mexico border; there was widespread fear that amnesty for immigrants would put an extra burden on social services; and American employers who continued to hire unauthorized workers would go unpunished.[36]

Despite the new IRCA legislation, hundreds of thousands of Mexican immigrants every year continued to flee the severe poverty and misery ravaging Mexico and crossed into the United States, many of them clandestinely. The 8.7 million immigrants who arrived in America in the 1980s accounted for nearly 40 percent of U.S. population growth in this decade. By 1988, the Mexican-born population of the United States had grown to 12.1 million, largely from recent, sharp increases in immigration. In the 1990s, the deindustrialization of Mexico's manufacturing sector, the privatization of land in that country, and the implementation of the North American Free Trade Agreement (NAFTA) would eventually displace millions of Mexicans, who then crossed the border into the United States to seek work.[37]

The growing numbers of unauthorized Mexicans aroused anger and hostility among whites nationwide. Many especially feared the changes in culture and language that the presence of immigrants imposed on the homogeneity of the United States. Along with welfare reform, opposition to immigration became one of the main focuses of racism, as a national movement for U.S. English took hold. Challenging bilingual education as an instrument of acculturation, the English-only movement spearheaded a drive to add an amendment to the U.S. Constitution that would mandate English as the official language of the United States.

English-only referendum campaigns between 1984 and 1987 were launched in four states with high percentages of Spanish-speaking residents: Florida, California, Arizona, and Colorado, and it spread to a fifth, Texas, through voter initiative campaigns. (The Texas English-only campaign failed to achieve its aim.) In the 1986 election in California, Proposition 63 to make English the state's official language won by a three-to-one margin. Several California cities had already passed similar resolutions. Proposition 63, however, had little effect in containing the use of Spanish and of the bilingual curricula in California. Virginia, Indiana, Tennessee, Kentucky, Arkansas, Mississippi, North Carolina, South Carolina, North Dakota, and Georgia adopted official-language policies in their state legislatures or had petitioned Congress to adopt the English-only amendment. Efforts to dislodge Spanish from the U.S. school system intensified. The success of the English-only amendments at the state level attested to the deepening of anti-Spanish feelings, because Congress cut back sharply on the $140 million annual apportionment for bilingual education in the 1980s.

America's most impoverished urban communities became its most racially diverse as large numbers of immigrants from Mexico, Central and Latin America, and the Spanish-speaking Caribbean continued to join African Americans, Mexican Americans, and Puerto Ricans in America's cities. In the context of the economic crisis of the early 1990s, industrial restructuring, high jobless rates, and the further demise of the welfare state, the racism against America's black and brown domestic minorities demonized a new scapegoat—immigrants. Latino immigrants were soon blamed for poor urban conditions, soaring welfare rates, and the deterioration of the national economy.[38]

Growing legal and unauthorized immigration to the United States gave rise to immigrant bashing. This nativism—the racist blowback of economic globalization—was especially felt in the metropolitan areas of Los Angeles, Chicago, New York, Boston, and Miami. The increasing Latinization of these cities through immigration and high birth rates came under sustained attack by conservative anti-immigrant organizations. Extreme right-wing groups such as the Minutemen used the anti-immigrant sentiment to recruit new foot soldiers of hate.[39]

The anti-immigrant scapegoating of the late twentieth century echoed many of the sentiments directed a century earlier against immigrants from southern and eastern Europe. In California, the new politics of nativist hate corresponded to the alleged tax burden caused by immigrants because of their costly use of social services. California's Proposition 187, the "Save Our State" initiative, targeted the state's rapidly increasing immigrant population by barring them from receiving state-funded health, social, and educational resources and services. The nativist movement in California, in which 60 percent of all unauthorized Mexicans were located, spread. It was most intense in states bordering Mexico, especially Arizona and Texas. The Republican Party during this time used California to generate a mean-spirited national debate on immigration issues connected with health care, affirmative action, and bilingual education.[40]

In the early 1990s, California went into the worst economic decline since the Great Depression. Federal spending cuts further hurt the state. An economic downturn coupled with strong reactions against the "flood" of Asian immigrants and unauthorized aliens and their "drowning" of California generated widespread anger among nativists and immigrant bashers. Reactionary critics of immigration contended that unauthorized immigrants were heavy users of state services; that is, that foreign households received 32 percent of all public cash assistance without paying taxes. However, studies such as those conducted by the Claremont Graduate School and the Urban Institute showed that unauthorized immigrants paid more to California in taxes than they cost in government services and that they did not put any extra strain on social services. Nevertheless, public opinion polls showed widespread support for cutting off public education, nonemergency health care, and social services benefits to unauthorized immigrants. The media fanned the flames of nativism by damning immigrants for a host of social ills, from unemployment to street crime. This happened because California governor Pete Wilson and other politicians intentionally perpetuated the negative stereotype of the "brown peril" as state voters considered voting for Proposition 187.[41]

In an atmosphere of escalating nativism, the large unauthorized Mexican presence in California thus provided Governor Wilson, who was seeking reelection in 1994, with the opportunity to demonize a new scapegoat through rhetorical excesses. Using the poll results to blame California's problems on unauthorized immigrants who seemed poised to overrun California, Governor Wilson claimed the state spent more than $2 billion per year providing public services for them. The strategy proved successful. California voters passed Proposition 187 in its 1994 statewide elections. Fifty percent of California's African American voters cast votes for Proposition 187, as did 31 percent of the state's Spanish-speaking voters. Half of California's Latino respondents to the opinion polls had supported Proposition 187; however, by election day this support had declined.[42]

The day after Proposition 187 passed, eight lawsuits were filed in state and federal courts in California to prevent its implementation. The opponents of Proposition 187 questioned its constitutionality, arguing that it violated the Fourteenth Amendment of the U.S. Constitution that forbids any state from denying any person equal protection under the law. A San Francisco superior court judge ruled that the Proposition 187 measure could not be enacted. A similar order was granted to California's public colleges and universities allowing them to provide aid to students regardless of their resident status. If the courts found Proposition 187 illegal, the state of California would have to fund benefits for unauthorized immigrants. Punctuating his speeches with divisive attacks on immigrants, Governor Wilson used "illegals" to deflect his inability to manage the state's budget: "3.4 million illegals requiring state services placed California on the verge of bankruptcy." Wilson, who had also called for the denial of citizenship to the U.S.-born children of unauthorized immigrants, argued that if President Clinton wanted unauthorized immigrants to have government services, then the federal government should provide the funding. Resistance to Proposition 187 mobilized thousands of its opponents. Large numbers of high school students walked out of school to protest Proposition 187. A handful of California school districts joined in lawsuits to challenge the denial of public education as unconstitutional. However, these legal threats triggered recall campaigns against public officials who voted to spend tax dollars to fight Proposition 187. In October 1994, seventy thousand demonstrators marched in downtown Los Angeles to denounce Proposition 187. The rally was coordinated by Fabian Nuñez of the Los Angeles County Federation of Labor and Juan José Gutiérrez of One Stop Immigration. Opposition to Proposition 187 also came from Republican ranks, because William Bennett and Jack Kemp stated that it fostered an "anti-immigrant climate." Proposition 187 was finally declared unconstitutional by a federal district court.[43]

Proposition 187 became a lightning rod of the divisive politics in California as the future of immigrants remained a volatile issue. Wilson's backing of the malicious state initiative triggered the mobilization of Latino voters and pushed them into the Democratic Party. The Southwest Voter Registration Education Project, La Hermanídad, and the Los Angeles County Federation of Labor helped to bring in 1.3 million new Latino voters. Six Mexican Americans were elected to the California State Legislature in 1996. In the same year in Orange County, Mexican American Democrat Loretta Sánchez defeated eight-term Republican Representative Robert K. Dornan in a hotly contested congressional House race. The archconservative Dornan disputed the results. As an example of how much nativist racism had shaped modern conservative Republican politics, Dornan claimed that bad ballots cast by people who were not American citizens or who were unauthorized aliens stole the election from him. In response to the mounting anti-immigrant backlash, 255,000 Mexicans became citizens in 1997, the largest single-nation naturalization record in American history.[44]

Mexican Americans next became embroiled in the great furor and hostility to affirmative action programs. The process of dismantling affirmative action in the state of California had begun twenty years earlier with the *Regents of the University of California v. Bakke* court case. Like Proposition 187, the drama of the fight over affirmative action that played out in California was one that had repercussions all across the United States.

## "FIGHT THE POWER": FROM THE BAKKE DECISION TO PROPOSITION 209

The social discontent that burst forth in the 1960s and early 1970s among minority academics, students, and women opened the doors for Mexican Americans to previously all-Anglo academic departments. Many Mexican Americans preferred a history of their own to claiming a place in a larger national history that had virtually ignored their place in it. The Mexican American feminist movement was sufficiently well established. Emma Pérez, Deena González, and other feminist scholars through their work expanded the category "woman" to include the experiences of Mexican American women. Other Mexican American scholars, such as Mario Barrera, provided new insights into how such categories as race and class have intersected in the United States.[45] However, conservative intellectuals were complaining loudly about "political correctness." The shift to the right became evident in the halls of academia in the fight over the proliferation of area studies programs and the growing presence of minority faculty and students.

Many Anglo faculty members and university administrators did not consider Chicano studies, African American studies, or ethnic studies as legitimate academic disciplines but rather as political enclaves of propaganda foisted on unwilling universities by minority faculty and students. The hiring and promotion of minority faculty, recruitment and support services for minority students, and affirmative action programs soon came under siege. Minority faculty and students, the former stereotyped as "witless affirmative action hires" and the latter as "special admits," were perceived to have benefited from illegitimate group-based advantages.

By the year of the *Regents of the University of California v. Bakke* Supreme Court ruling in 1978, a growing number of opponents of affirmative action saw racial preferences as unjust. They argued that affirmative action discriminated against white males in college admissions and employment and stigmatized minorities as needing preferential treatment and that campus speech codes endangered freedom of expression. The defenders of affirmative action, on the other hand, countered that studies showed that affirmative action did not have a large negative impact on white males. They pointed out that white males still held disproportionate power in American society and that laws and programs mandating affirmative action were one way to combat this inequality. In fact, it was white women who were the greatest beneficiaries of affirmative action, and their successes kept whites overrepresented in faculty and administrative positions.[46] Racial confrontations between minority and white students broke out on a number of college campuses and in certain instances escalated into violence. This violence was one more barometer of a shifting racial climate in American society.

*Regents of the University of California v. Bakke* was a "reverse discrimination" case that imposed limitations on affirmative action to ensure that providing greater opportunities for minorities did not come at the expense of the rights of the majority. The case involved the University of California-Davis Medical School, which had two separate admission pools, one for standard applicants and another for minority and economically disadvantaged students. The medical school reserved sixteen of its one hundred places for this latter group.[47] In *Regents of the University of California v. Bakke,* the Supreme Court ruled that although race was a legitimate factor in school admissions, the use of such inflexible quotas as the UC-Davis Medical School had set was not. However, the Supreme Court was split 5–4 in its decision on the Bakke case and addressed only a minimal number of the many complex issues that had sprung up about affirmative action.[48]

The Bakke decision mobilized minorities on the issue. Because affirmative action benefits were extended to Mexican American claimants, the Mexican American Legal Defense and Education Fund monitored the effects of the Bakke decision, along with the NAACP and other civil rights organizations. Vilma Martínez, the head of MALDEF and a member of the University of California Board of Regents, was sharply critical of the feeble efforts by the University of California to recruit more minority students.

The hard facts were that immigration and a higher birth rate increased California's Spanish-speaking people to nearly 20 percent of the state's population. Students of Mexican origin were fast becoming the largest segment in California's public schools. Their presence in Los Angeles was large and growing rapidly; the city's schools were 30 percent Spanish speaking. In kindergarten Spanish-speaking students made up 50 percent of the student body.

Mexican Americans were California's biggest and fastest growing minority, but they were the most underrepresented group in the University of California system. Only 4.5 percent qualified for admission to UC campuses. This low percentage was due to several factors. Reflecting the widespread trend in America's public schools toward more segregation, most Mexican American and African American high school students in California attended schools in failing city school systems, in which minorities made up 50 percent of enrollment, dropout rates were high, and the percentage of graduates going on to college remained flat. Eighty-five percent of those Mexican Americans who attended college were enrolled in two-year colleges; however, the transfer rate of these junior college students to four-year colleges was low.

Demographics in California were consequently putting pressure on the University of California to take action. A 15-percent decline in the state's college-age population was projected to take place between the 1980s and the early 1990s. State funding was tied to enrollment—the University of California had to attract a large proportion of minority students into the system or else the state's educational and social needs would go unmet and enrollments would suffer.

Anglos in California seethed with resentment against affirmative action. Republican governor Wilson saw an attack on racial preferences as another hot-button issue, joined in the criticism, and in doing so reinforced his image as an extremist. As with banning state aid to unauthorized immigrants, Wilson believed outlawing affirmative action could catapult him into the presidency of the United States. Despite a history of support for civil rights legislation, President George W. Bush proved he was no friend of civil rights legislation or affirmative action programs. Bush vetoed the Civil Rights Act of 1990, calling it a "quota bill." Bush became the first president since Andrew Jackson to veto a civil rights bill. A year later, the passage of the Civil Rights Act of 1991 reversed many of the Supreme Court's cutbacks on affirmative action. The act made it easier for individuals to sue employers for discrimination (but not for individual or monetary relief). The 1991 law was a response by the Republican Party to deflect charges of racism, as the presidential election was a year away. Also, in 1990, avowed racist nationalist David Duke had run for the U.S. Senate from Louisiana on the Republican ticket.[49]

**Proposition 209 Demonstrator, 1996.**
CREDIT: "Student Demonstrating on Affirmative Action Proposition," AAEH001510, ©Kim Kulish/CORBIS.

Proposition 209 was a 1996 ballot initiative that sought to amend the state constitution of California to prohibit public institutions from discriminating on the basis of race, sex, or ethnicity. It would outlaw affirmative action in hiring, contracting, and college admissions in the state. Proposition 209 had support from the California Civil Rights Initiative Campaign led by conservative University of California Regent Ward Connerly, handpicked by Governor Wilson in 1993. Pro-affirmative action advocacy groups rallied to oppose Proposition 209, but it was voted into law on November 5, 1996, with 54 percent of the vote.

Three weeks later, on the November 27, U.S. District Court Judge Thelton Henderson blocked enforcement of Proposition 209. Despite numerous lawsuits in state courts, in April 1997 the Ninth U.S. Circuit Court of Appeals ruled that Proposition 209 was legal, citing the nearly five million California residents who approved the so-called California Civil Rights Initiative.[50] Civil rights groups petitioned U.S. Supreme Court Justice Sandra Day O'Connor, who handled emergency requests from California, to block enforcement of the new law, but failed. The controversial Proposition 209, which outlawed affirmative action in state and local agencies, went into effect in August 1997. California Governor Pete Wilson lauded Proposition 209 as an opportunity to create the nation's first color-blind society.

The effect of Proposition 209 was immediately evident in the first year, when its impact on college admissions in the University of California system was witnessed.

At UC-Berkeley's Boalt Hall Law School, admissions of African American applicants dropped by 80 percent and those of Spanish-speaking applicants by 50 percent. The University of California remained a bastion of white privilege. The battle to dismantle affirmative action in the universities elsewhere in the nation moved forward.

At the University of Texas Law School at Austin, Texas, Cheryl Hopwood and three other white law school applicants, with financial support from the right-wing Pioneer Fund, challenged the school's affirmative action program. In their lawsuit, the plaintiffs asserted that they were rejected because of unfair preferences toward less qualified minority applicants. The Fifth U.S. Court of Appeals ruled in favor of the plaintiffs and suspended university affirmative action admissions programs in Texas and at state universities in Mississippi and Louisiana. Mexican American enrollment at the University of Texas Law School declined as Hopwood ended a legacy established in 1947 with the Herman Sweatt desegregation case. The University of Texas Law School had enrolled and graduated the most Mexican lawyers of any law school in the nation.[51]

The battles over multiculturalism, curricular innovation in the schools and colleges, speech and harassment codes, and canon revision and critical theory were part of a white backlash against the growing presence of minorities on America's college and university campuses. The racial polarization further heightened a sense of alienation among Mexican American faculty and students.

## MEXICAN AMERICAN WORKERS ORGANIZE

Meanwhile, Mexican American and Mexican workers refused to accept corporate demands for wage concessions and benefit cuts. Instead, they chose to fight back militantly and, in doing so, gave new life to the American labor movement.

Business took an adversarial position against labor in the 1970s, not only forcing union wages downward but launching efforts to break unions altogether. In 1974, two thousand female Mexican American and Mexican workers at the Farah Pants Company in El Paso, Texas, went on strike to protest low wages, poor benefits, and the unfair treatment of women employees by management. The Farah Pants walkout gained nationwide support and triggered a consumer boycott of Farah products that had considerable effect. Facing a range of discriminatory practices, 1,472 workers walked out of the Coors Brewery in Golden, Colorado, on April 5, 1977. Mexican Americans made up much of the ranks of the strikers. The union representing the workers argued that Coors was not an equal opportunity employer and that the company was a union buster. The Coors Boycott and Strike Support Coalition of Colorado was formed to support the striking workers. In late 1978, Coors took back three-fourths of the strikers and hired new employees to replace the rest. The Coors boycott continued until 1987, when an agreement was reached between the brewery and its employees.[52]

Deindustrialization and globalization picked up speed in the 1980s. Basic manufacturing more and more headed overseas. The willingness of American workers to strike was hit hard by the bad economy. Unemployment reached a postwar high of 9.7 percent in 1982. During the 1980s employers began hiring permanent replacements more frequently than they had in the previous decade. This strategy became a staple for management in dealing with unions in subsequent years (e.g., Caterpillar, Eastern Airlines, International Paper) following President Reagan's permanently replacing more than thirteen thousand air traffic controllers during the 1983 Professional Air Traffic Controllers Organization (PATCO) strike over higher wages, a shorter work week, and better retirement benefits. This assault on labor did not stop Mexican American workers from striking.

In 1983, a strike by mostly Mexican American Arizona copper mine workers unfolded against the Phelps Dodge Corporation after it rejected contract terms. Phelps Dodge permanently replaced its striking workers to rid itself of the union. By 1985, the unions that had represented the copper mine workers were decertified, ending decades of union representation.[53] This resistance by Phelps Dodge provoked a confrontation with the miners' union, the United Steel Workers of America, and the families and communities of its employees. Women once more proved their mettle as militant strikers and strike supporters. When court injunctions prohibited striking miners from picketing, women set up their all-female picket line. Soon they were traveling on speaking tours and disseminating news worldwide about their strike.

Phelps Dodge reopened its mining facilities with the help of four hundred state troopers, armored personnel carriers, Huey helicopters, and seven units of Arizona National Guard. The mining communities reeled under martial law; hundreds of strikers were arrested. The small union local and its supporters hung on for eighteen months. Also at this time Mexican American autoworkers at the General Motors plant in Van Nuys, California, began their battle to keep their auto plant open in the wake of plant closings and wage concessionary bargaining sweeping the nation. In Austin, Minnesota, Mexican American packinghouse workers joined their coworkers in a protracted strike at the local Hormel plant as members of United Food and Commercial Workers, Local P-9.[54]

Women represented nearly half of the total number of Mexican immigrants in the United States. With a 69 percent labor force participation rate, these Spanish-speaking female workers played a prominent role in the growing resistance to the assault by employers. Beginning in the fall of 1985, Mexican and Mexican American women frozen-food workers in Watsonville, California, waged a courageous though unsuccessful eighteen-month-long strike. In northern California an organization drive strengthened by family and kinship networks was undertaken by Mexican women hotel workers against abusive conditions on the job and low wages.[55]

During the 1980s, unionization efforts of the United Farm Workers union declined in California. California Republican governors George Deukmejian and Pete Wilson were less sympathetic to labor; they gutted the Agricultural Labor Relations Board and relaxed enforcement of the state's tough labor laws. Hard-won worker benefits achieved through the UFW's years of organizing struggles were eliminated. The living and working conditions of farmworkers steadily declined. Union workers were fired, and growers replaced them with unauthorized workers from Mexico. By relying on these poor migrants, American growers established a wage structure that discouraged American citizens from seeking farmwork.

The cultivation of high-value specialty crops such as strawberries became the fastest growing and most profitable segment of California's farm economy and one of the most dependent on the availability of cheap, foreign-born Mexican labor willing to work long hours for low wages without complaint. Widely reviled and depicted as welfare cheats, these Spanish-speaking workers were subsidizing one of the most important sectors of the California economy.[56] Unauthorized workers were increasingly being used not just to pick fruits and vegetables but to pack them as well. Automated packinghouses employing union workers as a result rapidly went out of business.

At the beginning of the 1980s the UFW had perhaps sixty thousand members. This number shrank to less than ten thousand. César Chavez was still struggling to bring labor rights to the nation's farm workers. In 1987, Chavez and consumer advocate Ralph Nader urged a boycott of all grapes sprayed with pesticides deemed potentially hazardous by the U.S. Environmental Protection Agency. The following year Chavez fasted for thirty-six days to call attention to farmworkers' children who were dying of cancer because of pesticides in grapes. Five years later Chavez was dead. The nonviolent movement of farmworkers he led in essence came to an end.

César Chavez died on April 23, 1993, near Yuma, Arizona, a short distance from the small family farm in the Gila River Valley where he was born. With Dolores Huerta, the founder and president of the United Farm Workers of America had turned this union into a mass movement twenty-eight years earlier. Chavez was in Yuma helping UFW attorneys defend the union against a lawsuit brought by Bruce Church, Inc., a giant lettuce and vegetable producer based in Salinas, California. Bruce Church, Inc., demanded that the UFW pay millions of dollars in damages resulting from a boycott of its lettuce during the 1980s. Six days after Chavez's death, more than forty thousand mourners came to honor the charismatic labor leader at the UFW Field Office at "Forty Acres," the site of his first public fast in 1968 and his last in 1988. Nearly everyone in attendance was overcome with emotion. Dolores Huerta delivered the eulogy at Chavez's burial site. Chavez's birthday, March 31, is celebrated in California as a state holiday, though controversy would surround establishing a national holiday honoring Chavez. The late Mexican American labor leader received the Medal of Freedom from President Bill Clinton in 2003, and the U.S. Postal Service honored Chavez with a postage stamp.

In the Midwest, the Farm Labor Organizing Committee began organizing the estimated sixty thousand farmworkers who traveled from Texas and Florida each year to work on the small tomato and cucumber farms in Indiana, Michigan, and Ohio. Headed by Baldemar Velázquez, FLOC would engage in three-way negotiations with corporations, producers, and workers.

In 1978, Velásquez organized a strike by FLOC against the Campbell Soup Company and, with church and student support, launched a consumer boycott of the company's products. Five years later, Velázquez led FLOC farmworkers on a six-hundred-mile march from Toledo, Ohio, to the Campbell Soup headquarters in Camden, New Jersey. FLOC signed three-year labor contracts with Campbell Soup and its subsidiary Vlasic Pickles in February 1986. The following year, FLOC signed a three-year contract with H. J. Heinz Company, and in 1991 more than seven thousand farmworkers worked under FLOC contracts. In 1993, Baldemar

Velásquez formed the Farm Worker Network to increase collaboration between U.S. and international farmworker organizations.[57] In 1998, Velásquez organized a national boycott of the North Carolina-based Mt. Olive Pickle Company, the South's largest pickle producer. The Mt. Olive labor struggle in that year was the first step toward building a farmworker labor movement in the South. FLOC improved wages for farmworkers, got them field sanitation facilities and pesticide protection, and eliminated child-labor practices. In addition, FLOC worked with unions in Mexico to equalize pay and labor conditions on both sides of the U.S.–Mexico border. Baldemar Velásquez has received numerous honors for his life's work to improve the working and living conditions of migrant farm workers and their families.[58]

## "NAFTA'S GONNA SHAFT YA": MEXICAN AMERICANS AND THE NORTH AMERICAN FREE TRADE AGREEMENT

Meanwhile, hemispheric trade policies through NAFTA changed American labor politics to job competition and accelerated Mexican immigration to the United States.

Over the opposition of organized labor and the Democratic Party, President Clinton joined like-minded Republicans in supporting and passing the North American Free Trade Agreement of 1993. Through NAFTA, capital and goods streamed to the *maquilas* (or runaway shops) owned by American, Japanese, and Korean companies located along the two-thousand-mile U.S.–Mexico border that soon became one of the world's most rapidly developing regions. The multinational corporations did this mainly through the exploitation of low-wage Mexican labor, principally that of young Mexican women. Women made up 85 percent of the quarter million workers employed by these multinational firms. By the year 2000, as more and more multinational companies set up factories along the border, this labor force mushroomed to three million workers. So did the seemingly unstoppable flow of Mexicans heading north for the higher U.S. wages.[59]

While Mexican American trade unionists staunchly lined up against NAFTA, Mexican American organizational support for NAFTA came from the Hispanic Alliance for Free Trade, as well as from Mexican American civil rights organizations such as MALDEF, the National Council for La Raza, and the Southwest Voter Research initiative through the Latino Consensus on NAFTA. These Mexican American organizations were not motivated by free-market policies but by the desire to gain recognition and a measure of political empowerment for the Mexican American community in the United States. For almost two decades Mexican American leaders held the belief that a close association with Mexico could help them politically with regard to U.S. domestic policy related to Mexican Americans. Mexico's corrupt ruling class greedily lined up in support of NAFTA, and it courted the Mexican American lobby in the United States to do the same. At a speech delivered at the eleventh annual banquet of MALDEF in Chicago on April 10, 1991, Mexico's President Carlos Gotarí Salinas invited Mexican Americans "to be the most fervent promoters in the [United States] of this Trilateral

Trade Agreement."[60] In return for its help, the Mexican American pro-NAFTA lobby wanted concessions from Mexico: environmental upgrading and economic development in areas where NAFTA would cause job loss and retraining and job creation programs for workers displaced by NAFTA.[61] Even though most American labor unions opposed NAFTA, César Chavez of the UFW supported the fast-track negotiation of the trade agreement. Chavez did this in return for the Salinas government's agreeing in 1990 to cover the costs of medical services in Mexico for the dependents of its citizen workers in the United States.[62]

NAFTA proved disastrous for both American workers and their counterparts in Mexico; it failed to deliver on jobs and sustainable development in Mexico. During the first ten years of NAFTA, more than one million jobs were lost in the United States, resulting in demonstrations across the country. American workers who lost good paying jobs with benefits were only able to find service-sector jobs that paid from 25 to 75 percent less and offered few or no benefits. Latino workers were the hardest hit; in 1999, the Labor Council for Latin American Advancement (LACLAA) reported that nearly one of every two workers (47 percent) who lost jobs in this year as a direct result of NAFTA were Spanish speaking.

NAFTA's negative economic impacts have been long-lasting and complex. It did not solve Mexico's high unemployment, nor did NAFTA create the quarter million jobs projected to grow in the United States as a result of the implementation of this trade agreement. What NAFTA did instead was to speed up the collapse of the living standards of workers and peasants in Mexico and to reorder the U.S. labor force by further perpetuating the influx of Mexican workers into the low-wage manufacturing and service sector.[63]

**Anti-NAFTA Demonstrations, Austin, Texas, 1993.**
CREDIT: 0000291105-11, © Bob E. Daemmrich/Sygma/Corbis.

In the 1990s Mexican immigrants began playing a main role in the reemergence of rank-and-file unionism in America, particularly in California's top economic sectors of apparel and construction that depended exclusively on immigrant labor. These workers engaged in strikes to win higher wages and better working conditions. They formed the core of union mobilization in the 1992 southern California drywall strike and the Justice for Janitors campaign.[64]

In 1995, the AFL–CIO's national labor federation's "New Voice" reform slate included organizing more minority workers and increasing their presence within labor's leadership ranks. The election of Mexican American Linda Chavez-Thompson as executive vice president of the AFL–CIO was part of this reform slate. Chavez-Thompson was the first person to hold the post of AFL–CIO executive vice president, and she was the first minority to be elected to one of the federation's three highest offices, a two-year term on the AFL–CIO's executive council. A native of Lubbock, Texas, Linda Chavez-Thompson joined the labor movement in 1967. After serving in a variety of posts with the American Federation of State, County and Municipal Employees union in San Antonio, Texas, Chavez-Thompson became this union's international vice president in 1988. She held this position until 1996. During this time Chavez-Thompson served as a national vice president of the Labor Council for Latin American Advancement.[65]

The national labor federation also committed resources to organizing industries employing large numbers of immigrant workers. As Chavez-Thompson said: "When you look at any large organizing drive going on today, for the most part, you see Latinos." At its 1996 convention, the Labor Council for Latin American Advancement delegates for their part introduced resolutions on increased organization and participation of Latinos in the labor movement and defending immigrant rights, among other issues.[66]

In February 1999, the AFL–CIO's executive council reversed its longtime policy on immigration when it called for blanket amnesty for unauthorized workers in the United States and for repeal of the 1986 IRCA, which criminalized the hiring of unauthorized workers. The AFL–CIO concluded that only by steering tens of thousands of low-wage service workers onto membership rolls could it reverse the decline in union membership and fight for free trade with labor rights so as to preserve the basic rights of all workers regardless of their legal status.[67] The national federation joined the battle worldwide against worker discipline and social inequality ushered in by market-oriented economic policies put in place by international financial institutions and their governments.

At the end of November 1999, Seattle, Washington, saw major governments participate at a World Trade Organization (WTO) meeting to discuss various trade rules. Protesters from all over the world also came to Seattle. They included human rights groups, students, environmental groups, religious leaders, and labor rights activists, all wanting fairer trade with less exploitation. Even right-wing protectionist groups came to Seattle arguing against the current corporate-led free trade. Enormous public protests ensued. Seattle saw a free-speech crackdown in the name of free trade. Six months later, on June 10, 2000, the AFL–CIO held its immigration forum in Los Angeles. The speakers included AFL–CIO vice president Linda Chavez-Thompson, one of the speakers at the anti-WTO demonstration in Seattle the previous year; California Assemblyman Gil Cedillo; Antonio Villaraigosa, former assembly speaker, union organizer, and candidate for mayor of Los Angeles; and Bert Corona, who for years had urged labor to change its position on immigration. All of these Mexican American activists had fought against a range of inequities in championing the rights of Mexican American and Mexican workers, who now were officially referred to as Latinos.

## LATINO: A NEW NATIONAL IDENTITY AND CONTINUED LATINO IMMIGRATION

Coined by the Nixon administration in the early 1970s, the word *Hispanic* became the official term used by the Department of Health, Education, and Welfare. It was ingrained in the language by usage. The term *Latino* in turn was imposed over the term Hispanic. The word Latino helped create, as well as express, a sense of identity among the heterogeneous Spanish-speaking population in the United States.

Latinos became America's fastest growing minority at the end of the twentieth century. Continued immigration from Mexico, Central America, and Latin America, as well as Asia, turned many cities in the United States into Third World metropolises. New York City was a magnet for Latinos from the Caribbean and South America; Miami's Cuban, Latin and Central American, Caribbean, and Mexican populations likewise dramatically reshaped this city racially and ethnically; and Los Angeles had the second largest number of Mexicans in the world and more Salvadorans than San Salvador. Los Angeles had become the premier immigrant capital of the world. Los Angeles contained more than five million immigrants and, together with New York City, contained 25 percent of the national total of 19.8 million immigrants counted in the U.S. Census.[68]

The upsurge in anti-immigrant sentiment in the 1990s saw unjustly harsh immigration controls intended to halt unauthorized immigration and to lower annual quotas for new arrivals. The Illegal Immigration Reform and Individual Responsibility Act of 1996, signed into law by President Clinton, expanded the list of crimes for which legal resident aliens could be deported, regardless of when the crime was committed. The new immigration law also provided for a policy of "expedited removal"; aliens could be deported immediately and banned from reentry for five years without a hearing or judicial review. Through militarization as well the U.S. government was determined to control its 2,076-mile border with Mexico against unauthorized crossers, as well as the trafficking of illicit drugs. "Operation Hold the Line" began in the early 1990s in El Paso, Texas, and reduced the flow of unauthorized workers by nearly three-fourths. On the heels of Operation Hold the Line, "Operation Gatekeeper" was a two-year effort in the San Diego area, where half of all unauthorized workers crossed into the United States. Operation Gatekeeper reduced the flow of unauthorized workers by one-third as the INS apprehended over a million immigrants. In 1995, the U.S. Justice Department allocated a quarter of a billion dollars to the U.S.–Mexico border and deployed additional agents that brought the total to more than five thousand. Helicopters, night-vision scopes, ground sensors, and computers borrowed from the Pentagon were now used at unprecedented levels. The U.S.–Mexico border became a virtual war zone, pitting the U.S. Border Patrol and the INS against unauthorized immigrants who, hungry and desperate for work, risked their lives to feed their families by crossing clandestinely into the United States.[69]

## CONCLUSION

Most Mexican Americans never fully benefited from the social changes of the 1960s, and they were worse off by 1980. Spanish-speaking communities steadily lost their working-class industrial base and faced growing economic inequality, reflecting the overall decline in living standards of American workers that began in 1973. The concentration of unemployment, poverty, and cuts in social services in Mexican American, as in other minority communities, was produced by the changes of the American economy to a postindustrial one in which low-wage service jobs replaced the high-wage manufacturing jobs. This growing pauperization was further aggravated by severe reductions in federal funding for social services and the privatization of public services in the wake of deregulation. Mexican Americans, who were unemployed in far greater numbers than Anglos, also suffered from the erosion of affirmative action, as a stronger backlash against affirmative action programs took place during the Reagan years.

At this time, conservatives launched a powerful attack on preferences in hiring or promotion of groups that had historically suffered discrimination. In addition to undermining affirmative action, President Ronald Reagan fought against extension of the civil rights law, paralyzed the U.S. Civil Rights Commission, and stacked the Supreme Court with right-wing, anti-affirmative-action appointees. Outspoken Mexican American conservative Linda Chavez added her voice to the shrill denunciations of bilingual education, affirmative action, and multiculturalism by the New Right.

Yet it was largely through the mechanism of affirmative action that the number of college-educated Mexican Americans increased in the 1970s, 1980s, and 1990s and entered corporate, educational, governmental, and professional positions of authority and mobility that had been previously closed to them. Mexican Americans made incredible economic progress. However, colleges and universities became the primary site for the struggle over affirmative action. The attacks on multiculturalism reflected the fears of white Americans about losing their social dominance, their apprehension prompted by economic globalization and dramatic demographic shifts in the United States.

The Reagan and first Bush administrations' policies vastly widened the gap between the rich and the poor in America. In the 1980s and early 1990s public policy rested increasingly on market models that emphasized individual rather than social responsibility. Empowerment Zones–Enterprise Communities, or EZECs, were rooted in the idea that industrial self-interest rather than government assistance would end poverty. Reducing funding, tightening eligibility standards for public assistance, and emphasizing sanctions to force the poor into the workforce redesigned what remained of poverty programs.[70]

Mexican Americans were no longer without the benefit of political power. This was the primary lesson conveyed by pro-immigrant Mexican American individuals and organizations. Confidence that important changes could be achieved through politics within the system escalated. Political advancement did not translate to Mexican Americans' influencing the larger political process. Nor were Mexican Americans able to fully convert political power into improved economic and social conditions. A polarization of the Mexican American community in terms of economic and social status continued to unfold, with the ranks of the poor growing at a much faster rate than the middle class.

Mexican Americans became the target of the renewed menace of racism. Race played an important role in the "right turn" in American politics as critical changes took place in welfare, civil rights policies, education, and immigration. The goal of the English-only movement was to discourage the creation of a separate language enclave in America through the maintenance of bilingual education and the use of non-English ballots and election materials. The rise of racism, racially motivated incidents, and race-hatred groups fostered an atmosphere in America as potentially explosive as the riot-torn 1960s.

Mexican American youths became mired in the turmoil of urban violence because of the escalation of street-gang activity. Gangs were the product of poverty, unemployment, poor race relations, and sharp deindustrialization. Imprisonment became commonplace among young minority men throughout the 1980s and 1990s.

The dramatic changes within the Mexican American communities of the United States were paralleled by the large immigration flows from Mexico, which IRCA sought to correct. IRCA facilitated the rapid naturalization of 2.5 million Mexicans but did relatively little in the way of curbing immigration from Mexico.

Many Mexican workers were foreign born, and, because substantial numbers were undocumented, they continued to be seen by employers as a valuable source of low-wage, pliable labor. This employer preference on the one hand accounted for the low rates of Mexican unemployment; the immigrants had no adverse effect on the earnings and employment opportunities of U.S. citizens. Yet Mexican immigrants and their offspring, on the other hand, were scapegoated for driving population growth, causing poverty, increasing health and educational needs, and placing stress on local communities. Mexican Americans once again assessed the effects of Mexican immigrants on their identity and culture, their economic status, and their political future in the United States.

Union membership declined significantly in the 1980s, as did union political influence, because American workers fell into disorganization. American workers nonetheless put up the good fight against the employers' defensive maneuvers. In the twilight years of the UFW, through strikes, marches, and boycotts, FLOC secured better treatment for its workers, most of whom were U.S. citizens or documented workers. Mexican American workers in Arizona, California, Colorado, and Minnesota went on strike against antiunionism and concessionary bargaining. The labor insurgency of the 1990s linked union revitalization with wider political struggles for reform that culminated in 1999 with globalization and WTO issues in the mass demonstrations in Seattle.

The attraction of jobs and family reunification to unauthorized immigrants undercut attempts to stem their greatly increased flow into the United States. America's 32 million Latinos, two-thirds of Mexican origin, made the United States the world's fifth largest Spanish-origin country. Latinos outnumbered African Americans in six of America's ten biggest cities, and, in three of these cities, they outnumbered non-Latino whites. The Latino population grew in the last decades of the twentieth century at ten times the rate of non-Latino whites, making the latter "majority minorities" in several states. Overwhelmingly urban, Latinos represent 50 percent of the population growth in ten states. By the late 1990's California's Spanish-speaking residents numbered ten million, or nearly a third of the state's population. The migration flows have become self-sustaining through strong social networks that link places of origin and destination.[71] Migration from Mexico and Central and Latin America inaugurated a new era in the history of Mexican Americans, for it marked the beginning of the development of a Latino community in America.

# NOTES

1. Latino unemployment was one and one-half times the national average. David G. Gutiérrez, "Migration, Emergent Ethnicity, and the 'Third Space': The Shifting Politics of Nationalism in Greater Mexico," *Journal of American History* 86, no. 4 (September 1999): 508; Anne M. Santiago and Margaret G. Wilder, "Residential Segregation and Links to Minority Poverty: The Case of Latinos in the United States," *Social Problems* 38, no. 4 (November 1991): 492–515.
2. Harry Pachon and Louis DeSipio, "Latino Elected Officials in the 1990s," *PS: Political Science and Politics* 25, no. 2 (June 1992): 212.
3. Gutiérrez, "Migration, Emergent Ethnicity, and the 'Third Space,'" 508.
4. Ibid., 505; Frank D. Bean and Marta Tienda, *The Hispanic Population of the United States* (New York: Russell Sage, 1987); U.S. Census, The Hispanic Population, 1990.
5. Gutiérrez, "Migration, Emergent Ethnicity, and the 'Third Space,'" 505; Gregory DeFreitas, *Inequality at Work: Hispanics in the U.S. Labor Force* (New York: Oxford University Press, 1991), 44–45.
6. Zaragosa Vargas, "Rank and File: Historical Perspectives on Latino/a Workers in the United States," in *The Latino Studies Reader: Culture, Economy and Society,* ed. Antonia Darder and Rodolfo D. Torres (Oxford: Blackwell, 1998), 243–246.
7. Gutiérrez, "Migration, Emergent Ethnicity, and the 'Third Space,'" 505–506; Jorge Durand, Douglas S. Massey, and Emilio A. Parrado, "The New Era of Mexican Migration to the United States," *Journal of American History* 86, no. 2 (September 1999): 519, 523–525.
8. Fernando Torres-Gil, "The Latinization of a Multigenerational Population," *Daedalus* 115, no. 1 (Winter 1986): 336. Many critics of America's immigration policies declared that its uncontrolled state "would seriously harm the U.S. and its institutions." Richard Lamb and Gary Imhoff, *The Immigration Time Bomb: The Fragmenting of America* (New York: E. P. Dutton, 1985), ix.
9. MacLean, *Freedom Is Not Enough,* 238, 290. The auto industry alone lost 250,000 jobs between 1979 and 1982. From 1979 to 1985 low-paying jobs accounted for 40 percent of the job growth, with high-paying jobs constituting only 10 percent.
10. MacLean, *Freedom Is Not Enough,* 249.
11. Acel Moore, "Left Out of Morning in America," *Philadelphia Inquirer.*

12. MacLean, *Freedom Is Not Enough*, 312–313. On the response by LULAC and the Congressional Hispanic Caucus to the revision of Executive Order 11246 on affirmative action in federal contracting, see MacLean, 306.

13. Richard Rodriguez, *Hunger of Memory: The Education of Richard Rodriguez* (New York: Bantam Books, 1983), 149; MacLean, *Freedom Is Not Enough*, 241. See also Linda Chavez's biography, *An Unlikely Conservative: The Transformation of an Ex-Liberal (Or, How I Became the Most Hated Hispanic in America)* (New York: Basic Books, 2002).

14. Linda Chavez, *Out of the Barrio: Toward a New Politics of Hispanic Assimilation* (New York: Basic Books, 1992), 6.

15. Susan González Baker, "Su Voto Es Su Voz: Latino Political Empowerment and the Immigration Challenge," *PS: Political Science and Politics* 29, no. 3 (September 1996): 467–468. In the 1980s Reagan took more than a third of the Mexican American vote in each election, as would George W. Bush in 1992. Although three-fourths of Mexican Americans identified as Democrats, the Democratic Party in California did not know how to tap the Mexican American vote. This proved to be a factor in George Deukmejian's narrow victory over Los Angeles Mayor Tom Bradley for the office of governor of California. Two-thirds of the Latino vote went to Bill Clinton, who took 71 percent of the Latino vote in California. Ibid.

16. Thomas Byrne Edsall, *The New Politics of Inequality* (New York: Norton, 1984), 194; Harry Pachon and Louis DeSipio, "Latino Elected Officials in the 1990s," *PS: Political Science and Politics* 25, no. 2 (June 1992): 212–213, 216; González Baker, "Su Voto Es Su Voz," 466, 468; Pycior, *LBJ and Mexican Americans*, 239–240; Ignacio M. García, *United We Win: The Rise and Fall of La Raza Unida Party* (Tucson: University of Arizona Mexican American Studies and Research Center, 1989), 202–213; Greenstein, "Fire in the Belly," *Texas Observer*, July 29, 1988.

17. Carlos Muñoz, Jr., and Charles Henry, "Rainbow Coalitions in Four Big Cities: San Antonio, Denver, Chicago, and Philadelphia," *PS: Political Science and Politics* 19, no.3 (Summer, 1986): 602, 604.

18. President Bill Clinton asked Cisneros to join his administration as the Secretary of Housing and Urban Development. Henry Cisneros's dramatic rise was cut short by scandal. In March 1995 Attorney General Janet Reno asked for an independent counsel to investigate charges that Cisneros had lied to the FBI about secret payments to a former mistress. See Stephen Labaton, "Ex-Housing Secretary Cisneros Charged in 18-Count Indictment," *New York Times*, December 12, 1997, A1, A18.

19. Muñoz and Henry, "Rainbow Coalitions in Four Big Cities," 606–606. Peña later served as U.S. Treasury Secretary from 1993 to 1997 and as U.S. Energy Secretary from 1997 to 1999 during the presidency of Bill Clinton.

20. Edsall, *New Politics of Inequality*, 195.

21. Ibid.; Pachon and DeSipio, "Latino Elected Officials in the 1990s," 215; Pycior, *LBJ and Mexican Americans*, 221, 240.

22. Pachon and DeSipio, "Latino Elected Officials in the 1990s," 213–214.

23. Rodolfo O. de la Garza " 'And then there were some . . . ': Chicanos as National Political Actors, 1967–1980," *Aztlán* 15, no. 1 (Spring 1984): 1–24.

24. Antonio González, "Chicano Politics and U.S. Policy in Central America, 1979–1990," in *Chicano Politics and Society in the Late Twentieth Century*, ed. David Montejano (Austin: University of Texas Press, 1999), 157–158; Antonio González and Richard Nuccio, eds., "Views of Latino Leaders: A Roundtable Discussion on U.S. Policy in Nicaragua and the Central America Peace Plan," *Southwest Voter Research Institute: Latin America Project Report* 1 (1988), 31–32.

25. Hedrick Smith, "Split Is Reported in Kissinger Panel over Salvador Aid," *New York Times*, December 13, 1983, 1; González, "Chicano Politics," 160–163.

26. Rodolfo Acuña, *Anything But Mexican: Chicanos in Contemporary Los Angeles* (New York: Verso Books, 1996), 119–120; Gary M. Stern, *The FBI's Misguided Probe of CISPES*, CNSS Report No. 111 (Washington, DC: Center for National Security Studies, June 1988), 2. Elizabeth Martínez was active in the campaign against Proposition 187 and protested against attacks on affirmative action programs. In addition to writing extensively on Spanish-speaking women's issues, Martínez in 1996 helped found the Institute for MultiRacial Justice in San Francisco, California. Martínez, whose book *De Colores Means All of Us* was published in 1998, has received numerous honors for her work as a journalist, writer, and activist.

27. Estrada, *Los Angeles Plaza*, 256; González, "Chicano Politics," 162; Muñoz, *Youth, Identity and Power*, 182; Bill Richardson, "Hispanic American Concerns," *Foreign Policy* 60 (Fall 1985): 38. On the sanctuary movement, see Elizabeth G. Ferris, *The Central American Refugees* (Westport, CT: Praeger Publishers, 1987), especially Chapters 2 and 7.

28. Ruiz, *From Out of the Shadows*, 142–143; Mary S. Pardo, *Mexican American Women Activists: Identity and Resistance in Two Los Angeles Neighborhoods* (Philadelphia: Temple University Press, 1998), 63; Nina Schuyler, "L.A. Moms Fight Back," *Progressive* 58, no. 3 (August 1992). See also *Toxic Waste and Race in the United States* (New York: United Church of Christ's Commission for Racial Justice, 1987).

29. House Committee on the Judiciary, *Increasing Violence Against Minorities: Hearings Before the Subcommittee on Crime of the House Committee on the Judiciary*. 96th Cong., 2nd sess., 1980, 2.

30. Monte Piliawsky, "Racial Equality in the United States: From Institutionalized Racism to 'Respectable' Racism," *Phylon* 45, no. 2 (1984, 2nd Qtr.): 137.

31. Gutiérrez, "Migration, Emergent Ethnicity, and the 'Third Space,' " 516; Mike Davis, *Magical Urbanism: Latinos Reinvent the U.S. City* (New York: Verso Books, 2000), 128; Cara Buckley, "A Fearsome Gang and Its Wannabes," *New York Times*, August 19, 2007; W. Triplett, "Gang Crisis," *CQ Researcher* 14 (2004), 421–444; Irving A. Spergel, "Youth Gangs: Continuity and Change," *Crime and Justice* 12 (1990): 171–175. During the 1980s many children and their families from El Salvador fled to the United States to escape armed conflict. These Salvadoran immigrant youths came into contact with Mexican American youth culture alienated from the larger society. In East Los Angeles Salvadorans established a gang culture distinct from that of Mexican Americans. *La Mara Salvatrucha* (also known as MS-13) and *Los de la 18* (18th Street Gang) were the most violent and powerful Salvadoran gangs.

32. Marc Mauer, *Race to Incarcerate: The Sentencing Project* (New York: New Press, 1999), 1; National Council of La Raza, *Lost Opportunities: The Reality of Latinos in the U.S. Criminal System* (Washington, D.C.: National Council of La Raza, 2004). In 2007, almost 2.7 times as many Latinos inhabited prison cells as college dormitories. See Stephen Ohlemacher, "More Blacks and Latinos in Prison than Dormitories," *Oakland Tribune*, September 27, 2007.

33. See Amnesty International Index AMR 51/76/92.

34. Daniel B. Wood, "L.A.'s Darkest Days," *Christian Science Monitor*, April 29, 2002. Approximately 1,200 Latino rioters were turned over to the Immigration and Nationalization Service. Ibid.

35. Durand, Massey, and Parrado, "The New Era of Mexican Migration," 521; Rodolfo O. de la Garza, "Interests Not Passions: Mexican American Attitudes Toward Mexico,

Immigration from Mexico, and Other Issues Shaping U.S.–Mexico Relations," *International Migration Review* 32, no. 2 (Summer 1998): 409–410.

36. Durand, Massey, and Parrado, "The New Era of Mexican Migration," 523.

37. Antonia Darder and Rodolfo D. Torres, "Latinos in Society: Culture, Politics, and Class," in *The Latino Studies Reader: Culture, Economy and Society,* ed. Antonia Darder and Rodolfo D. Torres (Oxford: Blackwell, 1998), 15; Ruben G. Rumbaut, *Origins and Destinies: Immigration, Race, and Ethnicity in America* (Belmont, CA: Wadsworth, 1996), 16, 19; Ruben Martínez, "The Shock of the New," in *Latino Studies Reader,* 176–177; Kim Moody, *Workers in a Lean World: Unions in the International Economy* (New York: Verso Books, 1997), 162.

38. Different races and ethnicities and legal status cut across the Latino population: negros, mestizos, mulattoes, blancos, Indians, Chicanos, Mexicans, Puerto Ricans, Dominicans, Cubans, Salvadorans, Guatamalans, Hondurans, American citizen, documented and undocumented immigrant. Moody, *Workers in a Lean World,* 159–163.

39. Rumbaut, *Origins and Destinies,* 16; Moody, *Workers in a Lean World,* 155; Darder and Torres, "Latinos in Society," 14–15.

40. Durand, Massey, and Parrado, "The New Era of Mexican Migration," 520–521.

41. Philip Martin, "Proposition 187 in California," in *New American Destinies: A Reader in Contemporary Asian and Latino Immigration,* ed. Darrell Y. Hamamoto and Rodolfo D. Torres (New York: Routledge, 1997), 327. Most California voters rejected Proposition 187 because it was too blunt an instrument to deal with the issue of undocumented immigration.

42. Ibid., 329; González Baker, "Su Voto Es Su Voz," 468; *Time,* November 21, 1994, 53; Yossi Shain, "The Mexican American Diaspora's Impact on Mexico," *Political Science Quarterly* 114, no. 4 (Winter 1999): 688.

43. Martin, "Proposition 187 in California," 327–330; Gutiérrez, "Migration, Emergent Ethnicity, and the 'Third Space,' " 481; Patrick J. McDonnell and Robert J. López, "70,000 March through L.A. against Prop. 187," *Los Angeles Times,* October 17, 1994, A1, A19; *La Opinión,* October 17, 1994.

44. Martin, "Proposition 187 in California," 331; Victor M. Valle and Rodolfo D. Torres, *Latino Metropolis* (Minneapolis: University of Minnesota Press, 2000), 170–171; González Baker, "Su Voto Es Su Voz," 467.

45. Mario Barrera, *Race and Class in the Southwest: A Theory of Racial Inequality* (Notre Dame, IN: University of Notre Dame Press, 1977).

46. Ellen Messer-Davidow, "Manufacturing the Attack on Liberalized Higher Education," *Social Text* 36 (Fall 1993), 40–80; Fred L. Pincus, *Reverse Discrimination: Dismantling the Myth* (Boulder, CO: Lynne Rienner, 2003), 120.

47. Allan Bakke, a white applicant, was rejected twice even though there were minority applicants admitted with significantly lower scores than his. Bakke maintained that judging him on the basis of his race was a violation of the Equal Protection Clause of the Fourteenth Amendment.

48. MacLean, *Freedom Is Not Enough,* 223–224.

49. The Willie Horton campaign advertisements were enormously effective in helping George H. W. Bush defeat Michael Dukakis in the 1988 presidential campaign.

50. California State Attorney General Dan Lundgren, a major candidate for the Republican gubernatorial nomination, jumped on the anti-affirmative action bandwagon and praised the decision.

51. Gerald Torres, "Grutter v. Bollinger/Gratz v. Bollinger: View from a Limestone Edge," *Columbia Law Review* 103, no. 6 (October 2003): 159. The court ruled that the 1978 *Bakke* decision was invalid—although *Bakke* rejected racial quotas, the decision maintained that race could serve as a factor in admissions. In addition to remedying past discrimination, *Bakke* maintained that the inclusion of minority students would create a diverse student body and that that was beneficial to the educational environment as a whole. The Hopwood court decision rejected the legitimacy of diversity as a goal of the University of Texas, asserting "educational diversity is not recognized as a compelling state interest." The U.S. Supreme Court allowed the ruling of the Fifth U.S. Court of Appeals to stand. Admissions offices at private universities in Texas followed this ban on race-based admissions. *Gratz v. Bollinger,* 539 U.S. 244 (2003). The Pioneer Fund also gave financial backing to a lawsuit filed by white students at the University of Michigan who charged that the university denied admissions to whites in favor of less qualified African American students. A federal judge on December 13, 2000, ruled in *Gratz v. Bollinger* that the use of race as a factor in admissions at the University of Michigan was constitutional. The gist of the University of Michigan's argument in its defense of affirmative action was as follows: just as preference is granted to children of alumni, scholarship athletes, and others groups for reasons deemed beneficial to the University of Michigan, so too does the affirmative action program serve "a compelling interest" by providing educational benefits derived from a diverse student body. Scholars have challenged research that identifies either principled opposition or racist action as the reason that self-identified whites oppose affirmative action. Their findings suggest that white opposition to affirmative action is the product of the desire to protect fellow whites. See, for example, Brian S. Lowery, Miguel M. Unzueta, and Eric D. Knowles, "Why White Americans Oppose Affirmative Action: A Group Interest Approach," *Latino Policy and Issues Brief* 15, April 2007, http://www.chicano.ucla.edu/press/briefs/documents/LPIB_15.pdf.

52. Edsall, *New Politics of Inequality,* 157–159; MacLean, *Freedom Is Not Enough,* 177–179; Ramos, *American GI Forum,* 111–116; Molly Ivins, "Union's Survival Is at Stake in 14-Month Strike at Coors Brewery," *New York Times,* June 12, 1978, A16.

53. Government officials, an obliging NLRB office, and promanagement academics substantially abetted this strategy.

54. Vargas, "Rank and File," 246; Eric Mann, *Taking On General Motors: A Case Study of the UAW Campaign to Keep GM Van Nuys Open* (Los Angeles: University of California, Institute of Industrial Relations, Center for Research and Education, 1987), 97–98.

55. Vargas, "Rank and File," 250–251.

56. See Eric Schlosser, "In the Strawberry Fields," *Atlantic Monthly* 276 (November 1995), 80–108, and Miriam J. Wells, *Strawberry Fields: Politics, Class, and Work in California Agriculture* (Ithaca, NY: Cornell University Press, 1996).

57. Velázquez expanded FLOC membership and focused on education, food and fuel cooperatives, and legal services for farmworkers. Velásquez formed the Donlop Commission and another independent commission in Mexico to negotiate collective bargaining rights for farmworkers.

58. Baldemar Velásquez earned advanced degrees in practical theology from Florida International Seminary in 1991 and was ordained a minister by Rapha Ministries. Baldemar Velázquez was also awarded honorary doctor of humane letters degrees from Bowling Green State University in 1996 and from Bluffton College in 1998. These awards include the John D. and Catherine T. MacArthur Fellowship (1989) and the Aguila Azteca Medal (1994), the highest award Mexico bestows to noncitizens.

59. Vargas, "Rank and File," 248; Oscar J. Martínez, *Troublesome Border* (University of Arizona Press, 1988), 126–128; Rachael Kamel, "'This Is How It Starts': Women Maquila Workers in Mexico," *Labor Research Review* 11 (Fall 1987): 17–18.

60. Patricia H. Hamm, *Mexican-American Interests in U.S.-Mexico Relations: The Case of NAFTA* (Irvine: University of California Center for Research on Latinos in a Global Society, 1996), 29. This paper is posted at the Scholarship Repository, University of California. http://repositories.cdlib.org/crlgs/WP4.

61. Ibid., 18–21; Teresa Puente, "Hispanic Support Builds for NAFTA Fast Track," *Hispanic Link Weekly Report* 9, no. 19 (May 13, 1991): 1–2; Yossi Lapid, "Ethnic Political Mobilization and U.S. Foreign Policy: Current Trends and Conflicting Assessments," in *Studies of Contemporary Jewry: An Annual. III: Jews and Other Ethnic Groups in a Multiethnic World,* ed. Ezra Mendelsohn (New York: Oxford University Press, 1987), 10; de la Garza, "Interests Not Passions," 404, 407–408. See also Center for the Public Interest, *The Trading Game: Inside Lobbying for NAFTA* (Washington, DC: Center for the Public Interest, 1993).

62. Hamm, "Mexican-American Interests in U.S.-Mexico Relations," 29; Sergio Muñoz, *Los Angeles Times,* May 30, 1991.

63. For the human impact of NAFTA and globalization along the U.S.–Mexico border, see David Bacon, *The Children of NAFTA: Labor Wars on the U.S./Mexico Border* (Berkeley: University of California Press, 2004).

64. SEIU Local 1877, a statewide janitor's union with 8,500 members in Los Angeles County, is composed almost entirely of Latino immigrants.

65. Nelson Lichtenstein, *State of the Union: A Century of American Labor* (Princeton, NJ: Princeton University Press, 2002), 261.

66. Rumbaut, *Origins and Destinies,* 17–18. In 1995, 14.2 percent of whites in the nonagricultural civilian labor force were members of unions, whereas 19.9 percent of African Americans were members. Latinos and other minorities were slightly more unionized than whites. Moody, *Workers in a Lean World,* 161.

67. Mark Anner, "Labor and the Challenge of Cross-Border, Cross-Sector Alliance," in *Latin America After Neoliberalism: Turning the Tide in the 21st Century?* ed. Eric Hersberg and Fred Rosen (New York: New Press, 2006), 311.

68. Rumbaut, *Origins and Destinies,* 30, 38, 40.

69. Gutiérrez, "Migration, Emergent Ethnicity, and the 'Third Space,'" 512; Moody, *Workers in a Lean World,* 163; Rumbaut, *Origins and Destinies,* 24.

70. The literature on so-called federal Empowerment Zones is substantial. However, see Stuart M. Butler, *Enterprise Zones: Pioneering in the Inner City* (Washington: Heritage Foundation, 1981); Marilyn Gittell et al., "Expanding Civic Opportunity: Urban Empowerment Zones," *Urban Affairs Review* 33 (March 1998), 530–558; and Renee Berger, "People, Power, Politics: An Assessment of the Federal Empowerment Zones," *Planning* (Fall 1997), 4–9.

71. For the contemporary role of chain occupation and chain migration of Latino immigrants, see Alejandro Portes and Robert L. Bach, *Latin Journey: Cuban and Mexican Immigrants in the United States* (Berkeley: University of California Press, 1985).

# CHAPTER 12

⚘

# Epilogue

## Mexican Americans in the New Millennium

In the late twentieth century immigration from Mexico to the United States was at its highest level since the early part of that century. Finding work was the primary incentive for Mexican immigrants to leave their home country. New employers, labor brokers, and cross-border social networks of relatives and friends linked American industries, occupations, and areas to communities in Mexico that sent migrants north to the United States.[1] These immigrants have enriched and replenished Mexican American communities and at the same time have caused profound change to America's social and cultural life, its politics, and its demographics. The immigrants' race and ethnic character has also brought about increased hostility and xenophobia not seen since the nineteenth century.

NAFTA and other trade agreements accelerated restructuring in Mexico. The human side of these free-trade initiatives is that they are leaving widespread and increasing poverty in their wake. From 1994 to 2002, 1.3 million jobs were lost in Mexico's agricultural sector due to NAFTA—a 15-percent decline—and wages in that country decreased by 14 percent. This left dirt-poor farmers and low-wage workers little option other than to come north to the United States. Many free-trade proponents in the United States believed that NAFTA would substantially curb migration from Mexico, but instead it increased both legal and unauthorized immigration. Since NAFTA's implementation, half a million Mexicans have entered the United States annually. Nearly 85 percent of the immigrants are unauthorized. They form a caste of marginalized workers who do the menial work of American society and are vulnerable to numerous forms of exploitation. Pushed to American society's margins, they have no legal protection, no job protection, no personal injury protection, and no benefits. Women endure some of the worst mistreatment. American employers know that if the immigrants were to acquire the same rights as the native workforce, they would then lose their special attraction as cheap and expendable labor.[2]

Deteriorating economic conditions in Mexico and the dependence of great numbers of U.S. employers on cheap Mexican labor thus generated much of the 58 percent growth in the nation's Spanish-speaking population.[3] More than half of the population remains concentrated in California, Texas, and Florida, though significant numbers migrated to the Central Plains states, the Midwest, and the South. In line with the growth of the U.S. economy and employment between 2000 and 2004, the South experienced the nation's second highest level of Latino migration after the Southwest. Indeed, the expanding low-cost, nonunion Latino labor force fueled the South's booming economy in construction, agriculture, textile manufacturing, and maintenance and service. Whereas in 1995 approximately 3.7 million Latinos resided in the South, by 2003 their numbers had climbed to 6.1 million. Over time immigrant networks replaced recruitment activities in drawing Latino newcomers to the region, so that the settlement patterns are now self-perpetuating. The sharp population growth of immigrants dramatically transformed the racial and ethnic composition of the South that is now home for a third of all Latinos in the United States.[4]

As elsewhere in the United States, unauthorized immigrants in the South remain in a precarious position, because state and local governments fail to enforce labor standards, turn a blind eye to their exploitation, or pass stringent anti-immigrant ordinances. The immigrants in large part experience overcrowded and substandard housing, language barriers, difficulties with access to health care and education, and laws that prohibit their children from obtaining a college education without proper documentation. Another problem is southern racism in the form of activities by a resurgent Ku Klux Klan and other organized hate groups that harass and attack immigrants.[5]

Anti-immigrant racism was not confined to the South, for the United States as a whole witnessed a rising tide of xenophobia directed at Mexicans and other Latino immigrants. Insisting on gaining control of America's borders and reducing the flow of unauthorized immigration, immigration politics as an economic concern and social issue moved to the forefront of national and international debate. To assuage Republican anti-immigrant rhetoric, the George W. Bush administration in 2000 held binational talks with Mexican President Vicente Fox to legalize the status of more than three million unauthorized Mexicans based on the eligibility requirement of employment history and length of residence in the United States. Bush and Fox also discussed reinstituting a contract labor program modeled after the early postwar bracero program. However, an economic recession and the 9/11 attacks stopped support for these plans as the United States government hardened its immigration policy.[6]

Since 9/11, regulation of the status of unauthorized immigrants in the United States shifted to a formal policy of preventing foreigners from entering the country to possibly engage in and commit terrorist attacks. The Immigration and Naturalization Service was reorganized and halted the processing of immigration and visa applications. One branch, the U.S. Citizenship and Immigration Services, serves legal immigrants. The agency's other branch, Immigration and Customs Enforcement, or ICE, focuses on enforcement. The Department of Homeland Security administers both branches.[7]

The pent-up frustrations of many Latino immigrants at increasing exploitation, rampant racism, and their marginal place in American society ignited a large-scale mobilization of immigrants. The new era's immigrant social movement began in September 2003, when one thousand immigrant workers boarded buses in ten cities to help promote legal status and civil rights for the estimated 12 million unauthorized workers in the United States. Modeled after the Freedom Riders of the early 1960s who challenged segregation in the South, the historic Immigrant Workers Freedom Ride consisted of a coalition of workers, labor unions, church groups, and other activists converging from ten cities. It was launched by the AFL–CIO to revive the movement on immigration legislation halted in the wake of 9/11. At one time the main advocate of immigration restriction, the AFL–CIO has become the champion of immigrants. The national federation correctly recognized the need to organize the huge Latino labor sector and accommodate the increasing transnational patterns of America's ongoing economic integration. The AFL–CIO was against the possible reintroduction of a guest worker program because it would create as many problems as it would solve. It favored instead permanent residence visas for immigrants so that they will have human and labor rights.[8]

After stopping in 103 cities, where they held rallies, walked picket lines, and met with legislators to build support for immigrant civil and worker's rights, the new Freedom Riders caravan, consisting of more than one thousand participants made up of some fifty nationalities, arrived in Washington, DC, and twelve days later, on October 4, held a mass rally in New York City's Flushing Meadows attended by one hundred thousand people. Speeches were made on the issues of immigration reform—demand for a road to citizenship for immigrant workers instead of President Bush's guest worker program with no eventual legalization, a right to family unification, and protection of worker rights and civil rights for all people.[9] The momentum in support of gaining rights for unauthorized immigrants spread from the confines of progressive and humanitarian circles to a broad national movement.

Demonstrations planned by churches, labor unions, and immigrant rights groups in Los Angeles, Chicago, New York, Atlanta, Washington, DC, Phoenix, Dallas, Houston, Tucson, Denver, and other cities began on or near March 31, the day that many American cities celebrate César Chavez's birthday. This "national day of action" was followed ten days later, on April 10, by the National Day of Action for Immigration Justice protest, drawing more than two million protestors in over one hundred cities. The mass mobilizations were in response to the Republican-sponsored bill H.R. 4437, passed by the House of Representatives in December 2005, that sought increased enforcement against immigrant communities and strengthening militarization of the border. Major provisions of the bill called for arresting and deporting unauthorized immigrants by imposing criminal status on them as felons and criminalizing those who provide medical, legal, or pastoral assistance to aliens; building a seven-hundred-mile fence along the border and heightening its militarization with advanced technology—more cameras, sensors, radar, satellite, and unmanned aerial vehicles; increasing the size of the U.S. Border Patrol, with an addition of one thousand port-of-entry inspectors and the training of 1,500 K-9 units; and penalizing employers who hire unauthorized immigrants. The legislation was complemented by a plan to create a path to citizenship for unauthorized immigrants through a guest worker registration program. Then on May 1 more than three million immigrant workers and their supporters in scores of American cities staged a one-day economic boycott and

**Day Without an Immigrant Demonstration, Los Angeles, California, 2006.**
CREDIT: "Mega-Marcha: Los Angeles" ©2006 Harry Gamboa, Jr.

work stoppage named the "Great American Boycott 2006: A Day Without an Immigrant." In conjunction with the boycott, immigrant advocacy groups launched voter registration and citizenship drives to increase Latino voting for the November 2006 midyear elections. This was done to apply direct pressure on the U.S. Congress to legalize unauthorized immigrants with civil, labor, and human rights protections, including U.S. permanent residency and citizenship.[10]

Through the Internet and Spanish-language mass media, organizers tapped a network of unionists, pro-immigrant-rights organizations, and other groups to plan boycott events timed to coincide with International Workers' Day. Celebrated around the world, International Workers' Day commemorates the day—May 1, 1886—that America's immigrant industrial workers took dramatic actions in Chicago to demand an eight-hour work day, fair wages, and safe working conditions.[11] In a nationwide show of solidarity, truckers in California did not report for work; meatpacking companies in the West and Midwest shut down their plants; scores of growers in California and Arizona let workers take the day off; and protesters closed Tijuana, Juarez-El Paso, and several other crossings along the two-thousand-mile border, halting international commerce between the United States and Mexico. Meanwhile, tens of thousands of Latino students coordinated their walkouts by cell phone to join the local protests, despite march organizers' urging them to stay in school.[12]

The huge and peaceful demonstrations advocating for immigrants' rights were unprecedented in American history. The crowds chanted: "USA! USA!

USA!" and, borrowing a tactic that the United Farm Workers used in the 1970 Salinas lettuce strike when its opponents attacked the union's red flags, carried American flags to send a symbolic message—to show the immigrants' allegiance to their new homeland. The immigrant-rights movement initially spread, but by the summer it lost momentum and dissolved, owing to a break between those who worked directly with immigrant communities and those from traditional advocacy groups. A series of marches on and around Labor Day as a result attracted far fewer people than those just several months before.[13]

Nevertheless, "A Day Without an Immigrant" forced Republican House Majority Leader J. Dennis Hastert and Senate Republican Leader Bill Frist to repudiate the controversial component of House Bill H.R. 4437 that made being an unauthorized immigrant in the United States a criminal offense and that penalized churches, humanitarian groups, and social service agencies that assisted unauthorized immigrants. Congress had once again failed to enact comprehensive immigration reform legislation.[14]

Education is the last great equalizer in the United States. Yet a half century after the Supreme Court ended enforced segregation in *Brown v. Board of Education of Topeka,* Latinos experience resegregation throughout the educational system. Latinos in areas of concentrated poverty endure more severely segregated and overcrowded schools than do blacks and have less qualified teachers and inferior educational resources. This has come about through Supreme Court rulings that limit judicial enforcement of desegregation, through the spread of housing segregation, and through the increase in minority populations and the decrease of white school populations. In the first decade of the twenty-first century, almost three million Latino students were enrolled in California's public schools and accounted for almost half of all students. Plagued with high dropout rates, California's Latinos fail to go on to college because one in four students—one in three in Los Angeles—quit school. Latinos in Texas make up more than a third of this state's public school students, yet because of high dropout rates, less than one in ten obtains a bachelor's degree.[15]

By 2007, between fifty and sixty-five thousand Latino students who had been in the United States more than five years but who were without citizenship status had graduated from American high schools each year.[16] These youths face limited education and employment prospects because they were originally brought into the country by parents lacking immigration status or who did not have their children naturalized. For such students with blocked aspirations, there was potential for help from a Senate action, the Development, Relief and Education for Alien Minors, or DREAM, Act. Part of the Comprehensive Immigration Reform Act, or CIR bill, the DREAM Act would have removed the section of the 1996 Illegal Immigration Reform and Responsibility Act that discourages states from providing lower in-state tuition (based on state residence and a green card) for students who are unauthorized. It would have also created the opportunity to achieve permanent resident status once a student is accepted to a college or university, graduates from high school, obtains a general equivalency diploma (GED), or serves two years in the military.

Critics decried the DREAM Act as amnesty and mobilized against it because they opposed any kind of accommodation for unauthorized immigrants. Concerned about high education costs reflecting shrinking state and local budgets, rising school enrollments, and overcrowded schools, the DREAM Act's opponents argued that Latino youths are no longer children but young adults who know they are in the United States unauthorized. The naysayers were especially angered that unauthorized immigrants were being favored over low- and middle-income Americans who compete to get state education scholarships and admission to public colleges. In November 2007, following the defeat of the Comprehensive Immigration Reform bill, the DREAM Act failed to pass by eight votes. This happened even though the bill's Democratic supporters made the possession of a green card applicable only to high school graduates who had completed two years of military service.

There is a corollary between Latino low educational achievement and rising military enlistment rates among this minority group. Stints in the military are often the last resort for many of the young and poor adults who cannot afford college, do not see higher education as a viable option, or fear eventual deportation. Recognizing that Latinos have few avenues to achieve equality, the United States government has selected them as its new foot soldiers in its wars overseas.

The percentage of Latinos in the military remains lower than the percentage in the general population, but efforts were made to increase their numbers. In the first years of the twenty-first century, the number of Latino enlistments in the army rose 26 percent, despite the overall low educational levels of this minority group—a 30 percent dropout rate for Mexican American high school students and a 61 percent dropout rate for immigrant Latinos. The army accommodated them by raising the number of enlistees without high school diplomas. This occurred at a time when the Army was struggling to recruit additional soldiers and when the enlistment of African Americans had dropped off sharply because of their disillusionment with the war in Iraq. Poor, uneducated, and on the path toward downward mobility, Latino men and women enlist in the military for the money, job training, and education benefits.[17] Many enlistees are immigrants or the children of immigrants drawn to military service by the incentive of procuring U.S. citizenship. President Bush helped them on July 3, 2002, when he signed Executive Order No. 13269 eliminating the three-year military service requirement for active-duty personnel seeking citizenship. In addition, the Armed Forces Naturalization Act of 2003 reduced the qualifying time to apply for citizenship from three years to one year for nonresidents serving in the military. These actions put immigrants who hold green cards and enlist in the military on a fast track to becoming Americans.[18]

Patriotism and economic hardship alone do not account for the rise in Latino military enlistments, because one result of the increases was the army's multimillion dollar marketing campaign targeting Latinos. As the Strategic Partnership Plan for 2002–2007 stated, "priority areas [for recruitment] are designated primarily as the cross section of weak labor opportunities and college-age population as determined by both [the] general and [Latino] population." In addition to advertising on Spanish-language television networks, on the radio, and in Latino magazines, army recruiters increased their presence in predominantly low-income Latino schools and neighborhoods, using bilingual recruiters to reach out to potential recruits. To persuade Latinos to enlist, recruiters deliberately glossed over the risks of military service and misled potential recruits and their parents about free money for college and travel and other inducements. Parents are susceptible to a recruiter's persistence; oftentimes they do not speak English or know little about the military.[19]

Former Secretary of the Army Louis Caldera initiated the army's aggressive Latino recruitment campaign. On one occasion Caldera enthused "[Latinos] have a natural inclination for military service," adding that army service could "provide the best education in the world." The army's Latino recruitment campaign also has the support of LULAC and the National Council for La Raza, as these organizations likewise view military service as a path to Latino social and economic advancement. All of them ignore the fact that Latino service personnel overseas are at high risk for serious multiple body part injuries from improvised explosive devices (IEDs), that Latino war veterans will not receive quality care in military and Veterans Administration hospitals once they return to the United States, and that chronic war-related posttraumatic stress disorder (PTSD) has been linked consistently to poor employment outcomes. Clear-thinking Latinos, on the other hand, launched a counterrecruitment movement to blunt U.S. Army recruitment drives in Spanish-speaking neighborhoods and to help immigrant parents and their sons and daughters learn of their rights.[20] These and other critics of the stepped-up recruitment of Latinos for military service noted that it is one way the government speeds up the acculturation of immigrants. Harvard professor Samuel Huntington made this position clear in his controversial book *Who Are We?* Huntington states, "Without a major war requiring substantial mobilization and lasting years . . . contemporary immigrants will have neither the opportunity nor the need to affirm their identity with and their loyalty to America as earlier immigrants have done." Still, many young Latino immigrants believe that military service is their pathway to citizenship. As long as American citizenship remains a kind of salvation myth for the Latino community, military recruiters will be able to exploit their desire for it. The disparity is that, even while the United States actively seeks Latino youths for military service to defend the nation, it continues to portray Spanish-speaking communities as a foreign menace to America's national identity.[21]

Disenchantment with the military quickly became apparent among Latino parents whose sons and daughters were killed in the war in Iraq. They founded organizations such as Latinos for Peace to protest the war in Iraq and joined nationwide protest demonstrations such as the one held in Los Angeles in 2006 at which some of the participants carried photos of their dead children.

Following 9/11, the increased militarization of the Mexico–U.S. border took on a new intensity with the advent of the war on terrorism and its accompanying rhetoric of fear. The response to the 9/11 attacks by policy makers was the passage of the U.S. Patriot Act of 2001 and the Homeland Security Act of 2002, which, respectively, enhanced law officials' and immigration agents' powers in detaining and deporting the unauthorized. Neo-nativist and xenophobic groups that had long denounced unauthorized migrants crossing the southern border latched onto a new way to rally broader opposition. For this fringe group, the immigrants not only brought crime and disease with them but also terror.[22] Carrying high-powered rifles, two-way radios, and wearing camouflage fatigues, the Minutemen lump together the war on terror and immigration as constituting a threat to "American

**Anti-Iraq War Protest, Los Angeles, California, 2005.**
CREDIT: 42-15823326, ©Emilio Flores/Corbis.

culture and values." They take the law into their own hands and ignore due process, human rights, and civil liberties to forcefully detain migrants before turning them over to U.S. Border Patrol agents.[23] The Minutemen are the most extreme symptom of racism in the contentious immigration debate because of their willingness to shoot immigrants and their ties to white-supremacist groups. To counter the expansion of the Minutemen project and other vigilante groups, border commu-nity groups, along with the American Friends Services Committee, formed the Border Community Alliance for Human Rights. In addition to confronting vigi-lante group activists, the Border Community Alliance for Human Rights works to combat the increased militarization of the border and to prevent the deaths of immigrants attempting to cross the border.[24]

As unauthorized immigration rose, the U.S. Border Patrol also grew. With almost twelve thousand agents and a budget of over $1 billion in 2006, the U.S. Border Patrol is the nation's largest police force. In addition, the 2006 U.S. Secure Fence Act authorized the building of seven hundred miles of walls along the U.S.–Mexico border.[25] Although it drew public approval and is perceived as a successful policy in affirming an image of U.S. sovereignty, the federal border blockade has proven to be costly and ineffective—it has impeded the flow of unauthorized migrants but not stemmed it. These efforts have diverted the unauthorized migrant flows from traditional crossing routes near San Diego and El Paso to new and less defensible crossing points in Arizona, New Mexico, and South Texas. With no work for them in their own country, thousands of desperate migrants continue to venture inland across rugged and more dangerous terrain, risking death from dehydration, heat stroke, drowning, and hypothermia, all harrowing experiences captured by

John Annerino in his book *Dead in Their Tracks*. The border crossers also expose themselves to human rights abuses in the form of attacks by vigilantes, bandits, and the immigration mafias that traffic migrants from Mexico as a business. American policies to close the border have had the effect of containing unauthorized immigrants in the United States; untold numbers are not returning to their home country for fear of being caught. As the United States blockades its southern border and criminalizes unauthorized workers, it continues to promote regional economic agreements such as the Central American Free Trade Agreement (CAFTA) to develop more free markets in the Americas for investments and commerce. These new trade policies will only bring in more immigrants to the United States.[26]

Immigrants are scapegoats for the effects of globalization on a faltering U.S. economy, and they are also seen as threatening America's national values and institutions. Globalization's impact on the United States has stirred economic uncertainties and heightened racial and anti-immigrant hostilities. The fear is that America will throw open the doors to immigration of groups who do not want to assimilate into American culture and society but want to enjoy its benefits. Americans are opposed to granting legal status or citizenship to the unauthorized. Instead, they favor consistent, across-the-board enforcement of existing immigration law, deterrence, and increased deportation. Motivated by fear, racism, and xenophobia, local legislatures adopted a harsh law-and-order politics. Action to tighten restrictions on unauthorized immigrants has included sanctions on employers and landlords who hire and give leases to unauthorized immigrants; allowing police officers to cooperate with federal immigration agents in enforcing immigration law; tightening driver's license requirements; proposing state referenda to make English the official language; and denying local, county, and state benefits to unauthorized immigrants. In the first half of 2007, state legislatures considered 1,404 immigration measures and enacted 107 of them. Such legislation has been supported by anti-immigrant groups such as the Federation for American Immigration Reform (FAIR). After appeals from immigrant advocacy groups, judges have struck down many of these laws.[27]

U.S. Immigration and Customs Enforcement (ICE) agents continue to conduct widely publicized raids in which they employ strong-arm tactics and excessive use of force in targeting individuals whom they think are unauthorized and thus deportable. In a six-month period between June 2006 and January 2007, ICE's "Operation Return to Sender" arrested more than thirteen thousand unauthorized immigrants. Most of those unauthorized immigrants were held by ICE in detention, often running longer than forty-five days, and were later released. In many cases the immigrant detainees are those who have overstayed visas or were caught when they tried to cross the border, then failed to appear at hearings, leading judges to order them to be deported. Citing human rights violations, organized labor, legal, religious, civil, and immigrants' rights organizations have called for an immediate end to community and work site raids by ICE that target immigrants.[28]

In the late nineteenth century Theodore Roosevelt remarked, in reference to the vast territory the United States gained from Mexico following the Mexican War: "It was . . . desirable for the good of the humanity at large that the American people should ultimately crowd out the Mexicans . . . from their . . . Northern provinces."[29] Today, the American people protest that they are the ones being crowded out by Mexicans. Racial conflict in the United States in the new millennium remains a struggle over national identity and the basic definition of citizenship. By the 2008 presidential campaign, America's Latinos could no longer tolerate the assaults on the Latino communities in the form of huge immigration raids in their neighborhoods and at their workplaces and the questioning of their loyalties and legality. Moreover, like other Americans, they were worried about the economy and viewed the wars in the Middle East as a failure.

America's two national political parties see the nation's Latino population as an important voting bloc worth cultivating. The growth in the numbers of immigrants with voting rights willing to participate in electoral politics first came about as a result of amnesty in the landmark 1986 legislation that added more than three million U.S. citizens through naturalization. The factors that brought Latinos to the polls were the increased immigrant-bashing rhetoric and national restrictions on immigration. Latinos voted en masse against Republican national candidates who used immigration as a divisive wedge issue against them to mobilize voters and win elections. The new generation of Latino voters set itself on a course of influencing national policy decisions regarding fair and humane immigration reform.[30]

Barack Obama's campaign for the presidency of the United States was rife with questions about citizenship, and antagonism toward his race became a primary focus of voters. Obama understood the critical importance of these two issues to the Latino vote when he appeared with Los Angeles Mayor Antonio Villaraigosa at the LULAC annual convention in Washington, DC, in July 2008. For them Obama's life story was similar to the lives of millions of Latinos. Yet even after Obama's election, right-wing protestors, many of them openly toting handguns and assault rifles to town hall meetings, deeply distrusted the ability of a president who is black to address domestic issues effectively. While reasserting their false sense of entitlement as white males, this fringe group of dispossessed Americans had no solutions or other ways to respond to falling incomes and failing employment. They failed to realize that the reason for the erosion of their social power is that they too are globalization's losers.

The United States economy has been in a recession since December 2007, as an endless shift of jobs from the United States to countries with low wages continues. The longest recession since the 1930s is having a serious effect on both U.S.-born and foreign-born Latinos. Unemployment among the former is 10.9 percent, whereas it is 8 percent for the latter. The reason is that Latinos are disproportionately concentrated in construction, blue-collar, or service industry jobs. As a result, Latinos and blacks are losing jobs faster than the general population. Insecurity over American job loss affects even well-educated Latinos in professional occupations. They have lost their jobs to the offshoring of white-collar jobs to India and China, as well as to labor market discrimination. New Latino college graduates face fewer job prospects and lower wages than preceding classes.

The major Latino migrations are unquestionably changing the racial and ethnic composition of the United States and redefining the social meanings of race, ethnicity, and American identity. Culturally, Latinos have both adapted to

**Barack Obama and Antonio Villaraigosa at the LULAC National Convention, 2008.**
CREDIT: 81865092, ©Chip Somodevilla, Getty Images News/Getty Images.

American culture and enriched it. Economically, they have contributed greatly in various ways to the vitality of the United States. In the twenty-first century, immigration is hotly debated in the public arena, and it remains a divisive and emotional issue. Economic crises and social frustration are exacerbating xenophobic reactions among large segments of the American population. Many of the problems regarding discrimination against minorities will persist. The racial strife surrounding immigration has sparked a political awakening among a new generation of Mexican Americans who as Latinos are now demanding the equality America promises but fails to deliver. The United States continues to be a destination for immigration, no matter how restrictive immigration policies become, because increased human mobility is one enduring impact of globalization.

## NOTES

1. Judith Adler Hellman, "Give or Take Ten Million: The Paradoxes of Migration to the United States," in *Latin America After Neoliberalism: Turning the Tide in the 21ˢᵗ Century?* ed. Eric Hersberg and Fred Rosen (New York: New Press, 2006), 219; Wayne A. Cornelius, "The Embeddedness Demand for Mexican Immigrant Labor: New Evidence from California," in *Crossings: Mexican Immigration in Interdisciplinary Perspective,* ed. Marcelo M. Suarez-Orozco (Boston: David Rockefeller Center Series on Latin American Studies, Harvard University Press, 1998), 126; Christine Marie Sierra, Teresa Carillo, Louis DeSipo, and Michael Jones-Correa, "Latino Immigration and Citizenship," *PS: Political Science and Politics* 33, no. 3 (September 2000): 535.

2. Nancy Foner, "Immigration Policy: Bringing in the City, State, and Region," *Labor: Studies in Working Class History of the Americas* 5, no. 2 (Summer 2008): 65; David J.

Tichenor, "Strange Bedfellows: The Politics and Pathologies of Immigration Reform," *Labor: Studies in Working Class History of the Americas* 5, no. 2 (Summer 2008): 58; Sierra et al., "Latino Immigration and Citizenship," 537–538. Mexican men and women were first drawn to the U.S.–Mexico border region to work in the maquila plants. Latinos account for more than 13 percent of the nation's total labor force, and their numbers are growing at five times the national average. U.S. Census Bureau, "Facts for Features, Hispanic Heritage Month 2007: Sept. 15–Oct. 15." Available from: www.census.gov/Press-Release/www/.../010327.html. At great risk, unauthorized immigrants have engaged in unionization efforts to gain labor rights and to improve working conditions in immigrant-driven labor sectors such as construction, manufacturing, elder care, domestic services, and other low-paid industries.

3. Hellman, "Give or Take Ten Million," 215–216; Eric Schmitt, "Census Shows Big Gain For Mexican-Americans," *New York Times*, May 10, 2001, A. 28; Sierra, Carillo, DeSipo, Jones-Correa, "Latino Immigration and Citizenship," 535; Luis Fraga, John García, Rodney Hero, Michael Jones-Correa, Valerie Martínez-Ebers, and Gary M. Segura, *Redefining America: Key Findings from the 2006 Latino National Survey*. Available from: http://depts.washington.edu/uwiser/. Forty percent are first-generation immigrants. Thirty-four percent are 18 or younger (compared to 26 percent of the United States population), and 88 percent of those under age 18 were born in the United States. Ibid. In 2007, approximately 44.5 million Latinos resided in the United States comprising about 15 percent of the nation's total population.

4. Lynette Clemetson, "Latinos Now Largest Minority, Census Shows," *New York Times*, January 22, 2003, A.1; David Kirp, "The Old South's New Face," *Nation*, June 26, 2000, 27–30; Hellman, "Give or Take Ten Million," 215; Justin Akers Chacón and Mike Davis, *No One Is Illegal: Fighting Racism and State Violence on the U. S.–Mexico Border* (Chicago: Haymarket Books, 2006), 157. Half the immigrants have been pulled into the labor-intensive manufacturing industries or into the low tiers of these firms' subcontractors.

5. Chacón and Davis, *No One Is Illegal*, 257; Bill Poovey, "Hispanics New Target of Hate Groups," *The America's Intelligence Wire*, Associated Press, July 29, 2005.

6. Hellman, "Give or Take Ten Million," 229; Philip Martin, ed., *Migration News* 8, no. 11 (November 2001): 1; Tomas Rivera Policy Institute, *Latinos, Foreign Policy and Contemporary International Relations* (Claremont, CA: Tomas Rivera Policy Institute, 2002), 4.

7. Hellman, "Give or Take Ten Million," 222, 229–230; Chacón and Davis, *No One Is Illegal*, 220. In 2005, Congress introduced the "Clear Law Enforcement for Criminal Alien Removal Act" (H.R. 2671). The Clear Act would give 660,000 state and local police officers the authority to enforce all federal immigration laws, offer financial incentives to states and localities to comply, criminalize all immigration law violations, place the names of any individuals believed to be in violation of immigration laws in the National Crime Information Center (NCIC) database, and fund the building of twenty immigration detention centers.

8. Sierra et al., "Latino Immigration and Citizenship," 539.

9. Chacón and Davis, *No One Is Illegal*, 284–285; Alan Maas, "Freedom Ride for Immigrant Rights," *Socialist Worker*, October 3, 2003; Bernardo Ruiz, "Freedom Riders Push for Immigrant Rights," *Progressive*, September 25, 2003; Vanessa Tait, *Poor Workers' Unions: Rebuilding Labor from Below* (Boston: South End Press, 2005), 217–218.

10. Chacón and Davis, *No One Is Illegal*, 292; "Immigrants Take to U.S. Streets in Show of Strength," *New York Times*, May 2, 2006, A.1; William I. Robinson, "'Aquí estamos y no

nos vamos!': Global Capital and Immigrant Rights," *Race & Class* 48, no. 2 (2006): 78, 84; Tomas Rivera Policy Institute, *New Dimensions of Latino Participation* (Claremont, CA: Tomas Rivera Policy Institute, October 2006), 2; Randy Shaw, *Beyond the Fields: Cesar Chavez, the UFW, and the Struggle for Justice in the 21st Century* (Berkeley: University of California Press, 2008), 234.

11. Robinson, "'Aquí estamos y no nos vamos!,'" 78; Chacón and Davis, *No One Is Illegal,* 290–291.

12. Robinson, "'Aquí estamos y no nos vamos!,'" 78–79; Chacón and Davis, *No One Is Illegal,* 291.

13. Shaw, *Beyond the Fields,* 230–231.

14. Robinson, "'Aquí estamos y no nos vamos!,'" 79.

15. John Arono and Raquel Donoso, *Beyond the Classroom: An Analysis of California's Public School Governance,* Latino Issues Forum, Summer 2006, 1–2, http://www.lif.org/download/lif_education_report.pdf; Tatsha Robertson, "In School, Latinos Find Fewer Resources, Ethnic Isolation," *Boston Globe,* May 17, 2004; Mitchell Landsberg and Howard Blume, "1 in 4 California High School Students Drop Out, State Says," *Los Angeles Times,* July 17, 2008; William C. Velásquez Institute, *The State of Latinos in Texas* (San Antonio, TX: William C. Velásquez Institute, 2000), 3; Jorge Mariscal, "Homeland Security, Militarism, and the Future of Latinos and Latinas in the United States," *Radical History Review* 93 (Fall 2005), 45. Emphasizing the disparity in education, Latinos made up just 1.9 percent of those entering graduate and professional schools.

16. Mariscal, "Homeland Security, Militarism, and the Future of Latinos and Latinas," 45. This is a paltry number given that the dropout rate among first-generation Mexican students was 61 percent.

17. Roberto Lovato, "The War for Latinos," *Nation,* September 15, 2005; Richard Morín and Dan Balz, "Most Latinos Say Iraq War Was Wrong," *Washington Post,* October 28, 2004, A08; Lizette Alvarez, "Army Focuses on Recruitment of Latinos," *New York Times,* February 13th, 2006; Tim Weiner, "Latinos Gave Their Lives to New Land," *New York Times,* April 4, 2003, B.10. Of the approximately 69,300 foreign-born men and women in the U.S. military at this time, nearly half, or 43 percent, are non-U.S. citizens.

18. Alvarez, "Army Focuses on Recruitment of Latinos"; Weiner, "Latinos Gave Their Lives"; Mariscal, "Homeland Security, Militarism, and the Future of Latinos and Latinas," 46. Due to limited opportunities, Latino reenlistment rates are the highest among any group of soldiers. In 2002, the army initiated the Foreign Language Recruitment Initiative intended to provide recent immigrants with intensive courses in English. Ibid. The Armed Forces Naturalization Act of 2003 also grants posthumous citizenship to Armed Forces personnel killed in battle. Hector Amaya, "Dying American or the Violence of Citizenship: Latinos in Iraq," *Latino Studies* 5, no. 1 (2007): 3.

19. Alvarez, "Army Focuses on Recruitment of Latinos"; Mariscal, "Homeland Security, Militarism, and the Future of Latinos and Latinas," 45–46.

20. Mariscal, "Homeland Security, Militarism, and the Future of Latinos and Latinas," 46, 49; Lovato, "The War for Latinos."

21. Mariscal, "Homeland Security, Militarism, and the Future of Latinos and Latinas," 50. Robert Lovato, "Becoming Americano: The Ascent of the New Latino Right," *Public Eye Magazine,* Spring 2007.

22. Hellman, "Give or Take Ten Million," 228; Chacón and Davis, *No One Is Illegal,* 255; Robinson, "'Aquí estamos y no nos vamos!,'" 80. See also Shan Cretin, "Communities Stand Up to Anti-Immigrant Patrols," *Quaker Action* 86, no. 3 (Fall 2005).

23. The group Civil Homeland Defense insists that U.S. citizens have the right to guard the border, and Ranch Rescue describes the border crossers as "drug smugglers, criminal gang members, bandits, thugs and international terrorists." The American Border Patrol (ABP) has links to the racist Neo-Nazi National Alliance and the right-wing Council of Conservative Citizens (CCC), the latter one of the largest white-supremacist groups in the country. Chacón and Davis, *No One Is Illegal*, 252–254, 257.

24. Cretin, "Communities Stand Up to Anti-Immigrant Patrols."

25. Chacón and Davis, *No One Is Illegal*, 225–226; Tomas Rivera Policy Institute, *Latinos, Foreign Policy and Contemporary International Relations*, 4; Peter Andreas, *Border Games: Policing the U.S.–Mexico Divide* (Ithaca, NY: Cornell University Press, 2000), 89; Wayne Cornelius, "Death at the Border: Efficacy and Unintended Consequences of U.S. Immigration Control Policy," *Population and Development Review* 27, no. 4 (2001): 661–689; Tony Payan, *The Three U.S.-Mexico Border Wars* (England: Greenwood, 2006), 56.

26. Hellman, "Give or Take Ten Million," 225, 227; Sierra et al., "Latino Immigration and Citizenship," 536.

27. Foner, "Immigration Policy: Bringing in the City, State, and Region," 66–67; Chacón and Davis, *No One Is Illegal*, 220. Violators faced fines of up to $500, with each day considered a separate violation. A federal judge issued an order halting enforcement of this ordinance, ruling that only the federal government could determine whether a person is in the United States legally. Julia Preston, "Surge in Immigration Laws Around U.S.," *New York Times*, August 6, 2007.

28. The unauthorized immigrants apprehended are released on humanitarian grounds, but they cannot work while they await their deportation hearings.

29. Lars Schoultz, "Latin America and the United States," in *Latin America After Neoliberalism*, ed. Eric Hersberg and Fred Rosen, Latin America After Neoliberalism: Turning the Tide in the 21st Century? (New York: The New Press, 2006), 63.

30. Tichenor, "Strange Bedfellows," 58; Jeffrey S. Passel, "Growing Share of Immigrants Choosing Naturalization," Pew Hispanic Center, March 27, 2007; Sierra et al., "Latino Immigration and Citizenship," 538.

# INDEX

AAA. *See* Agriculture Adjustment Administration
Abernathy, Ralph, 312
A. B. Frank plant, 224
Abiquiú, 16, 64
Abolitionism, 82, 101, 113, 123
Abortion issue, 324
Abrego, Mónico de, 134
Acoma Indians, 9, 10
ACSSP. *See* American Council of Spanish-Speaking
    People
Act for the Government and Protection of Indians of
    1850, 104
Acuña, Rodolfo, xv
Adams-Onís Treaty, 30
Affirmative action, xvii, 337–38, 344, 345, 346, 347–48,
    359–63, 370, 376n51
AFL. *See* American Federation of Labor
AFL-CIO. *See* American Federation of Labor-Congress
    of Industrial Organizations
African Americans, xiii. *See also* Mulattos; Negroes;
    Slavery
    affirmative action and, 361, 363
    in early 20th century, 178, 192
    at end of 20th century, 344, 348, 349, 353, 354, 372
    Great Black Migration, 196, 204
    Indian Wars and, 135
    in late 19th to early 20th century, 151–52
    Mexican Americans self-distinguished from, 205,
        305n74
    in mid-19th century, 112, 113
    military enlistment rates in, 383
    Plan de San Diego and, 186
    police brutality and, 353, 355–56
    in postwar years, 274, 275, 281, 288–89, 291, 292,
        293, 294, 295, 299
    Proposition 187 vote, 358
    in protest era, 307, 332
    Roybal's campaign and, 282
    women, 260
    in World War II era, 248, 249, 259, 265, 266, 267
    Zoot Suit Riot and, 254
African American studies programs, 360
Afromestizos, 6
Agricultural Labor Relations Board, 364
Agricultural workers. *See* Farm workers
Agricultural Workers Organizing Committee (AWOC),
    279, 310–11

Agricultural Workers' Union (AWU), 229
Agriculture
    in colonial era, 3, 14, 21, 28
    in late 19th to early 20th century, 144, 145, 168–69
Agriculture Adjustment Administration (AAA), 214,
    221
Agua Prieta, 167
Aguilera, Diana, 322
Aguilera, Tony, 258
AIM. *See* American Indian Movement
Air traffic controllers' strike, 364
Alabama, 53
Alamo, 20
Alamo, Battle of, 58–59, 60, 99, 137
Alarcón, Martín de, 20
Alaska, 25
Albuquerque, 14, 40, 87, 132, 155
Alianza Federal de Mercedes, 295, 314, 315–18
Alianza Hispano-Americana, 162, 169–70, 203, 289
Alien Land Law of 1887, 174n37
Alinsky, Saul, 282
Alta California, 1, 3, 4–5, 25–29, 30, 65, 67, 105
Altar Valley, 153
Alvarado, Concepción, 262
Alvarado, José, 91
Alvarado, Juan Bautista, 69, 71, 81
Alvarado, Manuel, 28
Alvárez, Anita, 286
Alvarez, Everett, 326
Alvarez, Manuel, 86
*Always Running* (Rodríguez), 354
Amador, José María, 69
American Border Patrol (ABP), 391n23
American Civil Liberties Union, 286, 288, 289
American Civil War. *See* Civil War
American Committee for the Protection of the Foreign
    Born, 281, 286, 287
American Committee on Race Relations, 283
American Council of Spanish-Speaking People
    (ACSSP), 285, 288, 289, 290
American Expeditionary Force, 189, 206
American Federation of Labor (AFL), 179, 183, 202,
    218, 233
American Federation of Labor-Congress of Industrial
    Organizations (AFL-CIO), 313, 368, 380
American Federation of State, County, and Municipal
    Employees, 368

American Federation of Teachers (AFT), 348
American Friends Services Committee, 385
American GI Forum, 281, 284, 287, 289, 291, 312, 332
American Indian Movement (AIM), 320, 321
Americanization movement, 200–201
American Legion, 226, 280
American Nazi Party, 294
American Revolution, 19, 21, 31
*América Tropical, La* (mural), 219
Anáhuac, 57
Anarcho-syndicalism, 179, 183, 205
Anaya, Pedro María, 99, 101
Anaya, Toney, 350
Angney, Witham, 89
ANMA. *See* National Association of Mexican
    Americans
Annerino, John, 386
Antietam, Battle of, 132
Antivagrancy laws, 116
Antón Chico community land grant, 157
Antuna, Philip, 255
Antuna, Ralph, 255
Apache Canyon, 87, 130
Apache Indians, 2, 11, 14, 16, 18, 19, 20, 22–24, 31, 39,
    40, 42, 43–44, 48, 87, 104, 114, 134, 135–36, 144
Appomattox Court House campaign, 132
*Arab* (steamer), 94
Arapaho Indians, 135
Aravipa Apache Indians, 135–36
Arbol Verde, 194
Arcero, Rafael, 234
Archuleta, Diego, 86, 87, 88–89
Archuleta, Juan Andrés, 88–89
Arista, Mariano, 84
Arizona, 1, 4, 16, 20, 40–41, 43, 104, 105, 106, 113, 364
    Confederate Territory of, 128, 132
    in Depression era, 218
    designated a territory, 113–14
    English-only movement in, 357
    Indian Wars and, 135–36
    in late 19th to early 20th century, 144, 152–54
    Mexican immigration in, 177, 188, 218, 344, 358
    mining industry in, 153–54, 181–82
    in postwar years, 283
    statehood issue, 163, 164–65, 171
    in World War II era, 247, 248–49
Arizona National Guard, 181, 364
Arizona Rangers, 154
Arizona State Federation of Labor, 183
Arkansas, 53, 294
Arkansas River, 23
Arkansas River Valley, 195, 247
Armed Forces Naturalization Act of 2003, 383, 390n18
Armijo, Antonio, 64
Armijo, George Washington, 164
Armijo, Manuel, 49, 62, 81, 86, 87, 106
Armour, Hammond, and Omaha, 196
Army of the West, 86, 87
Arroyo Hondo River, 25
Asociación de Jornaleros, La, 228, 229
Asociación de Trabajadoras Domésticas, 223
Atchison, Topeka, and Santa Fe Railroad, 155, 161, 166,
    167, 195
Atkinson, Henry, 157
Austin, 123
Austin, Moses F., 30, 52
Austin, Stephen F., 52, 53, 55–56, 57, 58, 60
Automobile industry, 189, 192, 196, 198–99, 219,
    234–35, 364

AWOC. *See* Agricultural Workers Organizing
    Committee
AWU. *See* Agricultural Workers' Union
Aztlán, 308, 320

Babocómari Creek, 114
Baca-Barragán, Polly, 350
Baca Hall, 158
Back of the Yards neighborhood, 235
Back of the Yards Neighborhood Council, 282
Bailey, Joseph W., 203
Baja California, 26, 27, 28
Bakke, Allan, 375n47. *See also Regents of the University
    of California v. Bakke*
Baldwin, Roger, 290
Balerio, Cecilio, 134
Balerio, Juan, 134
Bandini, Juan, 66
Banditry, 112, 119–23
Barkley-Cantú, David, 190–91
Barrera, Mario, 360
Barrera y Garza, Tomás Sánchez de la, 133
Barrios, 16, 138, 307
Barter economy, 40, 46
Bary, Arthur, 285
Bataan, 247
Bataan Relief Organization, 256
Baylor, John R., 128, 129, 132
Bear-baiting, 116
Bear Flag Rebellion, 86, 92–93, 94
Beaubien, Carlos, 88, 89
Beaubien, Narciso, 89
Beaubien-Miranda grant, 88
Bee, Hamilton P., 132–33
Bee County, 276
Beef, 21, 117
Belén, 14, 16
Belgium, 189
Belvedere, 193
Benavides, Basilio, 133
Benavides, Cristóbal, 133
Benavides, Placido, 60
Benavides, Refugio, 133
Benavides, Santos, 133–34, 137, 151
Benito Juárez Mutual Aid Society, 195
Bennett, William, 348, 359
Bent, Charles, 87, 88, 89
Benton, Thomas Hart, 54, 92
Bering Strait, 25
Bernal family, 28
Bethlehem Steel, 196
Beveridge, Albert J., 163–64
Beveridge Report, 164
Béxar, 21–23, 30, 41, 50, 53, 57, 58, 292
Bidwell, John, 67
Bigler, John, 120, 139n19
Bilbo, Theodore G., 277
Bilingual Education Act, 332
Bill S101, 276–77
Billy the Kid, 155
Bisbee deportations, 181–82
Black, Joseph, 316
Black Muslims, 295
Black Panthers, 321
Black power movement, 273
Blue Devils, 258
Board of Land Commissioners, 116, 117
Bonney, William ("Billy the Kid"), 155
Border Community Alliance for Human Rights, 385

Border Industrialization Program (BIP), 338
Border Patrol, U.S., 221, 297, 370, 380, 385
Bosque Redondo reservation, 135
Boston, 357
Botellier, Joaquín, 120
Bourbon Reforms, 1, 3, 4
Boxcar communities, 192, 193
Boyle, T. Coraghessan, 347
Braceros, 220, 246, 263, 267, 272, 278, 281, 297, 298, 338, 379
Bradley, Tom, 351(figure), 373n15
Branciforte, 27
Brazito, 88, 89
Brazos River, 52, 59
Brenham, Richard F., 62
Brite Ranch, 187
Brooks, Homer, 230, 231
Brown, Edwin, 311, 312
Brown Berets, 308, 321, 329
Brownsville, 125, 126, 133, 134, 147, 150
*Brown v. Board of Education of Topeka*, 288, 290, 292, 298, 382
Bruce Church, Inc., 365
Bryant, Sturgis, and Company, 63
Buena Vista, Battle of, 95, 99
Buffalo, 18, 21, 45–46, 105
Buffalo Soldiers, 135
Bulge, Battle of the, 255
Bull-baiting, 116
Bullfights, 138
Bunker Hill, 275
Burger, Warren, 318
Burgwin, John, 90
Burlington Northern Railroad, 195
Bush, George H. W., 346, 355, 370
Bush, George W., 361, 373n15, 379, 380, 383
Bushmasters, 257
Bustillos, Francisco, 60
Butterfield Stagecoach route, 135

Caballeros de Labor, Los, 161–62
Cabello y Robles, Domingo, 23
Cabinet Committee on Mexican American Affairs, 332, 337
Cabinet Committee on Opportunities for Spanish-Speaking People, 332–33, 337
Cadena, Carlos C., 290
CAFTA. *See* Central American Free Trade Agreement
Cahuenga
    Battle of, 81
    Treaty of, 98, 102
Cahuenga Pass, 98
Cajón Pass, 64, 69
Caldera, Louis, 384
Calhoun, John C., 101
California, 1, 39, 41, 45, 46, 112, 114–23, 157, 168–69, 350, 351. *See also* Californios
    Alta, 1, 3, 4–5, 25–29, 30, 65, 67, 105
    annexation of, 94
    Baja, 26, 27, 28
    banditry in, 119–23
    Civil War and, 127–28
    deportations in, 287
    in Depression era, 216, 220
    in early 19th century, 63–65
    English-only movement in, 357
    farm workers of, 233–34, 277, 364–65
    golden age of ranching in, 67–70
    gold rush in, 102–3, 106, 113, 114, 115–16, 120, 128

in late 19th to early 20th century, 145–46
    Mexican American War and, 86, 88, 91–98
    Mexican immigration in, 177, 220, 344, 346, 357–59, 378
    Mexico compensated for loss of, 101
    mission system of, 65–67
    number of Spanish-speaking residents, 372
    in postwar years, 274, 280, 283
    Proposition 10, 275
    Proposition 63, 357
    Proposition 187, 344, 346, 357–59
    Proposition 209, 346, 362–63
    revolts against Mexican rule, 70–71, 72
    school system of, 289, 321–22, 361, 382
    statehood granted to, 103, 106
    struggle over ownership of, 79, 80, 81–82, 83
    in World War II era, 247, 249, 262
California Alien Labor Act, 217
California Civil Rights Initiative Campaign, 362
California Commission on Immigration and Housing, 180
California Mountaineers Battalion, 128
California National Guard, 179
California Rangers, 120–21
California Rural Legal Assistance (CRLA), 339n7
California Sanitation Canning Company (Cal San), 234
California Trail, 135
California Walnut Growers' Assocation, 234
Californios, 41, 63, 92, 94, 95, 96, 97–98, 102, 106, 116–18
    golden age of ranching, 67–71
    revolt, 80, 81
Calleros, Cleofas, 220
Cambodia, 328
Cameron County, 150
Camino Real Trail, 64
Campa, Arturo, 264
Campbell, Jack, 315
Campbell Soup Company, 365
Camp Cody, 189
Camp Gordon, 189
Camp Grant Massacre, 136
Canales, Alma, 333
Canales, José Tomas, 187, 208n30
Cananea, 154
Canby, Edward S., 130
Cantaloupe workers' strike, 202, 211n78
Caribbean, 369
Carillo, Joaquín, 120
Carillo, José Antonio, 103
Carleton, James H., 135
Carnegie Steel Corporation, 196
Carranza, Venustiano, 187, 208n27
Carrillo, José Antonio, 96
Carrillo family, 28, 67
Carrizo, Battle of, 134
Carson, Christopher ("Kit"), 88, 96, 97, 129, 130
Carter, Jimmy, 350
Cart men, 50, 51, 124
Cart war, 124
Cass, Lewis, 124
Castro, José María, 28, 71, 81, 92, 93, 95
Castro, Manuel, 98
Castro family, 67
Caterpillar, 364
Catholic Church, 53, 63, 65, 66, 67, 70, 83, 84, 162, 163, 195, 199, 282. *See also* Indians, religious conversion of; Missionaries; Missions
    in colonial era, 1–2, 3–4, 6, 11–12

confiscation of property, 87
  in Depression era, 217
  farm workers' strike and, 311, 335
  liberation theology and, 352
  Mexican American War and, 87, 88, 99, 101
Catití, Alonzo, 7
Catron, Thomas B., 157, 158
Cattle, 14, 21, 68, 117, 145, 150, 156
Cattle rustling, 146–47, 187
Caucasian Race-Equal Privileges resolution, 265
Causa, La, 311, 335
Cavelier, Rene-Robert (Sieur de la Salle), 13
CCC. See Civilian Conservation Corps
Cebolleños, 43
Cebolleta, 14
Cedillo, Gil, 369
Celery workers, 233
Célis, Eulogio de, 93
Central America, 345, 352–53, 369, 372
Central American Free Trade Agreement (CAFTA), 386
Cerro Gordo, Battle of, 99
Chacón, Rafael, 130, 131(figure)
Chacón, Virginia, 280
Chain migration, 188, 192, 206
Chapin, 150
Chapultepec Castle, 100
Charles III, King of Spain, 25
Chattanooga, 132
Chaves, J. Francisco, 129, 162
Chaves, Manuel, 130
Chavez, César, 279, 297, 307, 309–13, 317, 329, 335, 338n1, 365, 367, 380
Chavez, Dennis, 227, 247, 276, 283, 293
Chávez, Ignacio, 60
Chavez, Linda, 345, 348–49, 370
Chavez, Manuel, 89
Chavez Ravine, 275
Chavez Ravine Training Base, 254
Chavez-Thompson, Linda, 368
CHC. See Congressional Hispanic Caucus
Cherokee Indians, 44, 55
Cheyenne Indians, 135
Chicago, 191, 192, 196, 197–98, 235–36, 246, 261, 275, 350, 357
Chicana Caucus, 320
Chicana Service Action Center, 325
Chicana women's movement, 299, 308, 324–25, 336
Chicano movement, xvi, xvii, 273, 274, 295–96, 299, 307–8, 318–24, 335–36
  objectives of, 307
  sexism in, 320, 324, 337
  student activism in, 321–24
Chicano studies programs, 360
Chicano Youth Liberation Conference, 319–20, 321, 328
Chickamauga, 132
Chihuahua, 15–16, 24, 31, 43, 46, 47, 48, 51, 62, 72, 86, 87, 88, 89, 98–99, 100–101, 114
Chihuahua Trail, 40, 63
Child labor, 195, 215, 366
Children. See also Education and schools
  deportations and, 220, 287
  in Depression era, 213, 220
  of farm workers, 277
  as strikebreakers, 233
Chimáyo Rebellion, 49, 79. See also New Mexico, revolt of 1837
Chinese Americans, 102, 112, 115, 116, 145, 172n8
Chinese Exclusion Act of 1883, 137
Chiracahua Apache Indians, 153

Chiso Indians, 22
Chivington, John, 130
Choate, D. P., 148
Cholam Pass, 69
Cholos, 118
Chumash Indians, 29
Ciboleros, 45–46, 74n15, 85
Cigar workers' strike, 223, 230
Cimarron cutoff, 135
CIO. See Congress of Industrial Organizations
CIR bill. See Comprehensive Immigration Reform Act
Cisneros, Henry G., 350, 352, 373n18
Cities. See Urban development; Urbanization
Citizens for Farm Labor, 311
Citizenship and Immigration Services, U.S, 379
Citizenship/naturalization
  for Indians, 42
  for Mexicans, 98, 102, 112, 151–52, 201, 283, 359, 380, 383–84, 387
  military enlistment and, 383–84
Citizen's Protective League, 182
Citrus industry, 168–69, 194
Ciudad Juárez Railroad, 166
Civil Homeland Defense, 391n23
Civilian Conservation Corps (CCC), 227, 230
Civil Rights Act of 1964, 294, 337
Civil Rights Act of 1990, 361
Civil Rights Act of 1991, 361
Civil Rights Commission, U.S., 317, 332, 348, 354, 370
Civil Rights Congress, 281, 285, 286, 287
Civil rights movement, 273–74, 294–97, 298–99, 307, 344
  litigation in, 288–90
  shifts in, 291–92
Civil War, xvi, xvii, 46, 126–34, 137, 160, 163
  Confederate Mexican Americans in, 113, 132–34
  number of Mexican Americans in, 126
Clamor Publico, El, 118–19, 138
Claremont Graduate School, 358
Clay, Henry, 54
Claypool-Kinney Bill, 202
Clear Law Enforcement for Criminal Alien Removal Act, 389n7
Clifton-Morenci strike, 181–82
Clinton, Bill, 354–55, 359, 365, 366, 369, 373n15,18
Coahuila, 21, 22, 26, 43, 52–53, 54, 55, 56, 57
Coahuiltec Indians, 22
Coal miners' strikes, 178, 180–81, 214–15, 225–27, 237
Cockfighting, 116
COINTELPRO, 331, 336
Coke, Richard, 146
Cold war, xvii, 272, 277, 345. See also Communism, postwar crackdown on
Colfax War, 155
Colleges and universities. See Higher education
Colonia del Nuevo Santadar, 20
Colonialism, 1–38. See also Northern frontier
  objectives for, 1–2
  three periods of, 1
  United States during, 3, 19–22, 24–25, 29, 31, 32
Colorado, 16, 18, 19, 44, 83, 113, 128, 130, 155, 157, 160, 161, 194–95, 202, 350
  in Depression era, 216, 222–23
  English-only movement in, 357
  farm workers in, 222–23, 232, 277
  Indian Wars and, 135
  Mexican immigration in, 188, 195
  mining industry of, 178
  in World War II era, 247–48

Colorado Federation of Miners, 181
Colorado Fuel and Iron Company (CFI), 180–81
Colorado National Guard, 181, 216
Colorado River, 26, 64, 101
Colorado Volunteers, 130
Colquitt, Oscar B., 150
Comanche Indians, 2, 15, 16, 17, 18, 20, 22–24, 39, 40,
    42, 43, 44, 45, 51–52, 53, 61, 62, 77n70, 104, 135
Comanchería, 40, 77n70
Comancheros, 40, 45–46, 315
Comisión Feminil Mexicana, 325
Committee in Support of El Salvador (CISPES), 352
Committee of Public Safety, 135–36, 148
Committee of Religious Concern, 311
Committee on Territories, 163
Communism, xvii
    in Central America, 352
    in Depression era, 215, 221, 225, 226, 229, 230, 231,
        232, 237
    postwar crackdown on, 272, 273, 277, 279, 281–82,
        283, 284–86, 290, 298
    Red Scare, 180, 191, 273, 284–86, 298
Communities Organized for Public Service, 334
Community Service Organization (CSO), 273, 279,
    282–84, 287, 298, 309
Compadrazgo, 21
Company A (356th Infantry Regiment), 191
Company B (355th Infantry Regiment), 190
Company E (141st Infantry Regiment), 258
Compeán, Mario, 323, 329, 333
Composiciones de tierra, 14
Comprehensive Immigration Reform Act (CIR bill),
    382–83
Compromise of 1850, 103, 104, 162
Concepción de Acuña, 20
Confederación de Pueblos Libres, La, 317
Confederación de Trabajadores Mexicanos (CTM), 229
Confederación de Uniones Campesinos y Obreros
    Mexicanos (CUOM), 202
Confederate Territory of Arizona, 128, 132
Conferencia de Mujeres por la Raza, La, 325
Congregación, 3
Congreso del Pueblos de Habla Español. See Congress
    of Spanish-Speaking Peoples
Congressional Hispanic Caucus (CHC), 351–52
Congress of Industrial Organizations (CIO)
    in Depression era, 215, 228, 229, 233–36, 237
    Political Action Committee, 262
    in postwar years, 279
    War Relief Committee, 262
    in World War II era, 248, 250, 260, 262
Congress of Spanish-Speaking Peoples, 244, 249–50,
    251
Connelly, Henry, 129, 130
Connerly, Ward, 362
Conscription. See Draft/conscription
Conscription Act of 1862 (Confederacy), 131
Constitution, Arizona, 164–65
Constitution, California, 103
Constitution, Mexican, 41, 55, 66
Constitution, Texas, 57, 123
Constitution, U.S., 118, 357
    Fourteenth Amendment, 152, 290, 358
    Twenty-fourth Amendment, 349
Contras, 345
Cook, Phillip St. George, 86
Cooke, William G., 62
Coors Boycott and Strike Support Coalition, 363
Coors Brewery, 363

Copper mining
    in Depression era, 218
    in early 20th century, 181–82, 203
    at end of 20th century, 364
    strikes by workers, 181–82, 364
    in World War II era, 248
Cordero, Antonio, 25
Corona, Bert, 369
Corpus Christi, 83, 84, 148, 246
Corpus Christi, Battle of, 132
Correa-Bary, Anna, 285, 298
Corregidor, 247
Corridos, 150
Cortera, Martha P., 325
Cortez, Gregorio, 148–50
Cortez, Manuel, 90
Cortez, Romaldo, 148
Cortina, Juan Nepomuceno, 113, 124–26, 131,
    133, 134, 137, 147, 148, 187, 333
Cortina War, 124–26, 131
Cortinistas, 113, 147
Cos, Martín Perfecto de, 58
Cosmopilita, El, 196
Cosmopolitan Company, 66
Cotton Acreage Control Law, 216
Cotton industry, 57, 168, 169, 189, 215–16, 218, 220,
    222, 229, 233
Council of Conservative Citizens, 391n23
Court of Private Land Claims, 155
Coyotes (alien smugglers), 192
Coyotes (mixed-race persons), 16
Crack cocaine, 345, 354
Creoles, 6, 30
Crime
    at end of 20th century, 345
    in mid-19th century, 112, 119–23
    in World War II era, 249
Cristero Revolution, 199
Crockett, Davy, 59
Croix, Teodoro de, 4
Crónica, La, 183, 184, 185, 208n17
Crusade for Justice, 307, 317, 318–21, 329, 331, 335–36
Crystal City, 294–95, 322–23, 333
CSO. See Community Service Organization
CTM. See Confederación de Trabajadores Mexicanos
Cuba, 94, 164
Cuban Americans, 369
Cuban Revolution, 281
Cuerno Verde, 19
Cuervo y Valdéz, Francisco, 14
CUOM. See Confederación de Uniones Campesinos y
    Obreros Mexicanos

Daley, Richard, 350
Dan Ryan Freeway, 275
Davila, Armando, 214, 285
Davis, Edmund J., 133, 134
D-day, 255, 256, 258
Dead in Their Tracks (Annerino), 386
De Anza, Juan Bautista, 16, 19, 26
Death squads, Central American, 352, 353
Debt peonage, 48, 50
Deindustrialization, 344, 346, 363
De la Fuente, Elvira, 295
De la Garza, Eligio, 306
De la Garza, José Antonio, 52
De la Garza, Joseph, 132
De la Garza, Rafael, 60
De la Guerra, Antonio María, 120, 128

De la Guerra, Pablo, 93(figure)
De la Guerra family, 28
De la Luz Sáenz, José, 191
Delaware Indians, 43
Delgado, María, 190(figure)
*Delgado v. Bastrop ISD,* 289
Deming, 155
Democratic Party, 318
    in Depression era, 215, 232, 234, 237
    in early 20th century, 203
    at end of 20th century, 345, 347, 349, 350, 359
    in late 19th to early 20th century, 146, 151
    in mid-19th century, 82, 112, 115, 119, 125
    in postwar years, 283, 292–94, 299
    in protest era, 325, 331–32, 333–34, 337, 343n63
De Neve, Philipe, 26–27
*Dennis v. United States,* 303n45
Denver, 195, 247–48, 276, 318–19, 320, 350
Department of Agriculture, U.S., 232, 267
Department of Homeland Security, U.S., 379
Department of Justice, U.S., 323, 335, 369
Department of Labor, U.S., 199, 287
Department of War, U.S., 246, 265
Deportations, 369
    Bisbee, 181–82
    in postwar years, 281, 282, 284–88, 298
    repatriation campaign, 213, 217–20
    in World War I era, 191
Depression of 1920-1921, 177, 191, 196
Depression of 1930s. *See* Great Depression
Detroit, 192, 198–99, 219, 275
Detroit Federation of Labor, 219
Detroit Institute of Arts, 219
Deukmejian, George, 364, 373n15
Development, Relief and Education for Alien
    Minors (DREAM) Act, 382–83
Dewey Canyon III, 331
DeWitt, Green, 56
Diaz, José, 250–51
Díaz, Porfirio, 126, 166, 167, 184
DiGiorgio Fruit Corporation, 278, 311, 312
Diphtheria, 229
Disenfranchisement, 150, 151–52, 153, 204
Dr. Jordan's Museum of Anatomy and
    Natural Science, 121
Dodger Stadium, 275
Dolores, 21
Domínguez, Manuel, 103, 118
Dominguez Ranch, Battle of, 96
Doniphan, Alexander William, 87–88, 89, 98
Don Lucas Ranch, 233
Dornan, Robert K., 359
Dorothy Frocks Company, 224, 230
Draft/conscription
    Civil War, 131
    in colonial era, 4
    in post-independence era, 48–49
    Vietnam War, 328
    World War I, 189
    World War II, 244, 246–47, 248, 249, 266
DREAM Act. *See* Development, Relief and
    Education for Alien Minors Act
Driscoll Independent School District, 289
Droughts, 117, 216
Drug abuse and trafficking, 345, 354, 369
Drywall strike, 368
Duff, James, 132
Duke, David, 361
Durán, María, 282, 283, 297

Durango, 85, 86
Durst Ranch, 179, 180
Dust bowl, 216

Eagle Pass, 123, 125, 166
Eastern Airlines, 364
East Los Angeles, 193, 308, 321, 322, 337, 353
Echeandia, José María, 71
Echo Amphitheater campground occupation, 315–16,
    318
Economic Opportunity Act of 1964, 299, 337
Economy. *See also* Depression of 1920-1921; Great
    Depression
    barter, 40, 46
    at end of 20th century, 346, 347
    in late 19th to early 20th century, 165–70
    in the new millennium, 387
Ecueracapa, 19
Education and schools. *See also* Higher education
    bilingual programs, 332, 333, 345, 348, 357
    dropout rate, 248, 306, 345, 361, 382, 383
    in early 20th century, 178, 201, 205
    at end of 20th century, 345, 346, 348, 357, 361
    in late 19th to early 20th century, 162, 163
    "Mexican," 288, 289
    in the new millennium, 382–83
    in postwar years, 273, 274, 275–76, 283, 288–89,
        291–92, 298
    in protest era, 306, 308, 320, 321–23, 332, 333, 337
    walkouts and boycotts, 308, 320, 321, 322–23
    for women, 184
    in World War II era, 245, 247–48
Edwards, Haden, 54–55
Eighth Texas Infantry, 132
Eighty-eighth Infantry Division, 258
80 percent law, 181
Eisenhower Freeway, 275
El Camino Real, 135
El Centro School District, 289
Elias, Cornelio, 136
Elias, Jesús María, 135–36, 137
Elias, Luis, 136
Elias, Ramón, 136
El Monte Boys, 119
El Paso, 4, 41, 51, 87, 101, 147, 166, 167, 181, 216, 223
    Mexican immigration in, 188, 189, 219, 220, 369
    sinarquistas in, 252–53
El Paso and Southwestern Railroad, 167
El Paso del Norte, 14, 88
El Pueblo de Nuestra Señora la Reina de Los Angles de
    Porciuncula, 26
El Salvador, 345, 352, 353
Embudo, 90
Eminent domain, 275
Empire Zinc Company, 280
Empowerment Zones-Enterprise Communities
    (EZECs), 370
Empresario system, 52, 53, 56
Enabling Act, 162, 163, 164
Encinias, Miguel, 247, 268n10
England. *See also* American Revolution
    advice on Texas annexation, 83
    California sale to considered, 81, 91
    California trade monopoly, 63
    colonialism and, 1, 15, 20, 25, 29
    Mexico's debt to, 79
    Oregon boundary dispute and, 82
English-only movement, 344, 348, 357, 371, 386
Entrada, 1

Environmental issues, 345, 353, 365
Environmental Protection Agency, U.S., 365
Equal Employment Opportunity Commission (EEOC), 348
Equal Opportunities Act of 1964, 294
Equal Rights Amendment, 344, 348
Escandón, José de, 20, 21
Espejo, Antonio de, 9
Espíritu Santo land grant, 124, 125
Espíritu Santo Mission, 20
Estrella, La, 118
Evangelical churches, 199–200
Examiner, The, 254
Executive Order 8002, 248
Executive Order 8803, 259
Executive Order 9346, 248
Executive Order 13269, 383
Expansionism of U.S., 19–22, 24–25, 30, 31, 32, 39, 41–42, 43, 44–45, 50, 63–64, 72–73, 82–83

Factories in the Field (McWilliams), 233
Fages, Pedro, 26
FAIR. See Federation for American Immigration Reform
Fair Employment Practices Committee (FEPC), 248, 259, 262, 264, 266, 276–77, 280, 283
Fair Labor Standards Act of 1938, 231, 332
Falcón, Cesario, 134
Farah Pants Company, 363
Farm Labor Organizing Committee (FLOC), 312, 365–66, 371
Farm Security Administration, 232
Farm Worker Network, 366
Farm workers
    in Depression era, 214, 215–16, 221–23, 232, 233–34
    in early 20th century, 179–80, 192, 194
    at end of 20th century, 364–66
    in late 19th to early 20th century, 168
    in postwar years, 277–79, 297
    in protest era, 307, 309–13, 335
    strikes by, 179–80, 194, 221–23, 233, 278, 307, 310–13, 335, 365–66
    in World War II era, 245, 246, 263, 267
Fascism. See Sinarquistas
FBI. See Federal Bureau of Investigation
F Division, 327
Federal Alliance of Land Grants. See Alianza Federal de Mercedes
Federal Bureau of Investigation (FBI), 279, 281, 285, 319, 335, 336, 352
Federal Housing Authority, 274
Federalist-Centralist wars, 133
Federal Land Grant Act of 1851, 116–17
Federal Writers Project, 227
Federation for American Immigration Reform (FAIR), 386
Federation of Mexican Societies, 202
Female workforce
    in Depression era, 213–14, 215, 222, 223–25, 233–34, 237
    in early 20th century, 178, 188–89, 192, 194, 196, 197, 206, 210n64
    at end of 20th century, 364, 366
    in late 19th to early 20th century, 145
    in World War II era, 243, 248, 259–63, 266
Feminism, 184, 308, 324–25, 336, 360
Feminist Pacifist Group, 184
FEPC. See Fair Employment Practices Committee

Ferdinand Maximilian Joseph, Emperor of Mexico, 126
Fernández, J. A., 150
Fifty-fifth Alabama Infantry, 132
Figueroa, José, 66, 69
Figueroa family, 67
Filibusters, 52, 54, 125, 292
Filipinos, 233
Fillmore, Millard, 103
Finck Cigar Company, 223
First Battalion of the Native Cavalry of California, 127, 128
First Cavalry Division, 326–27
First Marine Division, 327
First New Mexico Cavalry, 134–35
First New Mexico Infantry, 129
First New Mexico Volunteers Regiment, 130, 135
First Texas Cavalry (Confederate), 132
First Texas Union Cavalry, 133
Fisher Freeway, 275
515th Coast Artillery Regiment, 255–56
Fleteros, 51
FLOC. See Farm Labor Organizing Committee
Floods, 117
Flores, Ceferino, 149
Flores, José María, 93, 96, 98
Flores, Manuel, 60
Flores, Salvador, 58, 60
Flores Magón, Enrique, 154
Flores Magón, Ricardo, 154
Florida, 3, 13, 30, 357, 378
Food for Victory campaign, 262
Ford, Edsel, 219
Ford, Henry, 198(figure), 219
Ford, John ("Rip"), 125
Ford Foundation, 290, 297
Ford Motor Company, 198
Foreign Language Recruitment Initiative, 390n18
Foreign Miners Tax, 115–16
Forest Service, U.S., 314, 315, 316
Forgotten People: A Study of New Mexicans (Sanchez), 247
Fort Craig, 128, 130
Fort Fillmore, 129
Fort Lyon, 156
Fort Marcy, 130
Fort Ross, 25
Fort Sumner, 135
Fort Sumter, 131
Fort Texas, 84
Fort Union, 130
Four Freedoms, 243
Four-Minute Men, 189
Fourteenth Amendment, 152, 290, 358
Fourth New Mexico Infantry, 129
Fox, J. M., 187
Fox, Vicente, 379
France, 92
    colonialism and, 1, 13, 15, 20, 21, 22
    French and Indian War, 25
    Louisiana transferred to, 24
    Mexico occupied by, 126
    World War I and, 189, 191
    World War II and, 255
Franciscans, 1, 8, 9, 10, 12, 13, 20, 26, 28, 29, 65, 66
Fraternal organizations, 188, 199, 201–5, 206
Fredericksburg, Battle of, 132
Fredonia Rebellion, 55, 56
Freedom Riders, 380
Freeways, 275

Frémont, John C., 88, 92, 94, 95, 98
French and Indian War, 25
Frist, Bill, 382
Fuentes, Albert, 295

Gadsden, James, 104, 105
Gadsden Purchase, 105, 114
Gaines' Mill, Battle of, 132
Galarza, Ernesto, 263, 264, 272, 278–79, 297
Galindo family, 28
Gallup, 155, 214–15, 225–27, 237
Galván, Robert, 285, 298
Gálvez, José de, 1, 25–26
Gamboa, Harry, Jr., 322
Gangs, 345, 353, 354, 355, 371
García, Alonso, 7, 12
García, Bernardino ("Three-Fingered Jack"), 120, 121
García, Gus, 290
García, Hector P., 284, 332
García, Juan, 120
García, Macario, 258–59, 265
Garment workers, 150, 223–25, 230
General Motors, 234, 364
Genízaros, 6, 15, 16, 48
Germany
    World War I and, 187, 189, 191
    World War II and, 255
Gerrymandering, 151, 306, 349
Gettysburg, Battle of, 132
GI Bill, 274
Gigedo, Revilla, 23
Gila Apache Indians, 105
Gila River, 101, 105
Gilbert Islands campaign, 256
Gillespie, Archibald H., 95–96, 97
Globalization, xvii, 347, 363, 371, 386, 388
Glorieta Pass, Battle of, 129, 130, 132
Glover, Robert M., 149
Gold, 9
Gold rush, 102–3, 106, 113, 114, 115–16, 120, 128
Gold Star Mothers, 262
Goliad, 41, 53, 58, 59, 60, 61, 99, 124, 148
Gomez, Anna Nieto, 324
Gómez Farías, Valentín, 66, 83, 99
Gonsalves, Harold, 257
Gonzales (county), 148, 149
Gonzales (village), 57, 58, 123
Gonzales, José, 49
Gonzales, Manuel C., 203, 264
Gonzales, Rodolfo ("Corky"), 307–8, 318–21, 328, 329, 330, 335–36, 342n50
González, Deena, 360
González, Henry B., 291–92, 293, 294, 306
González, José Elias, 118
González, M. C., 288, 290
González-Monroy, Jesús, 179
Good Neighbor Policy, 244, 248, 264, 265, 281, 288
Gorras Blancas, Las, 144, 158–62, 161, 171
Gotarí Salinas, Carlos, 366–67, 382
Granado, Francisco, 60
Gran Concilio de la Orden Caballeros de Honor, 183
Gran Liga Mexicanista de Benefinencia y Protección, La, 184
Grant County Herald, 158
Grape pickers' strike/boycott, 310–13, 335, 365
Grapes of Wrath, The (Steinbeck), 233
Gratz v. Bollinger, 376n51
"Greaser" (pejorative term), 112, 118, 124
"Greaser Law," 116

Great American Boycott 2006: A Day Without an Immigrant, 381–82
Great Black Migration, 196, 204
Great Coalfield War, 181
Great Comanche War Trail, 43
Great Depression, xvi, xvii, 191, 207, 213–42, 346
    Mexican immigration during, 213, 214, 217–20
    plight of Mexicans in early years of, 215–17
Great Society, xvii, 306–7, 327, 335
Great Western Sugar, 195
"Gringo against greaser" war, 112
Grito del Norte, El, 317, 328, 329
Guadalajara, 85
Guadalupe Gallegos, José, 129
Guadalupe Hidalgo, Treaty of. See Treaty of Guadalupe Hidalgo
Guadalupe River, 21
Guanajuato, 85
Guatemala, 345, 353
Guevara, Che, 329
Gulf of California, 23
Gulf of Mexico, 20, 21, 23, 101
Guonique, 51
Gustave Line, 258
Gutiérrez, José Angel, 322, 333
Gutiérrez, Juan José, 359
Gutiérrez, Nicolas, 71
Guzmán, Ralph, 292

Halff Company, 224
Hammond, Thomas C., 96, 97
Haro, John, 341n35
Harrington, Michael, 278
Hastert, J. Dennis, 382
Hate strikes, 259
Haynes, John L., 134
Headright system, 134
Head Start, 332
Head tax, 189
Heintzelman, S. P., 125, 126
Henderson, Thelton, 362
Hendley, Israel R., 89–90
Henry Ford Service School, 198
Herald Express, 254
Hermanídad, La, 359
Herminadad, 324
Hernández v. the State of Texas, 290
Heroin, 345
Herrera, José Joaquín de, 83–84
Herrera, Juan José, 160, 161
Herrera, Nicanor, 160
Herrera, Pablo, 160
Herrera, Rafael, 60
Hidalgo, Miguel, 30
Hidalgo County, 150, 277
Hidalgos, 28, 118
Higher education, 321–22, 346, 360–63, 370
Híjar, José María, 66–67
His-oo-sán chees, 43, 44(figure)
Hispanic (coining of term), 369
Hispanic Alliance for Free Trade, 366
Hispanic-American Alliance. See Alianza Hispano-American
Hitler, Adolf, 237
H. J. Heinz Company, 365
Hobby, William P., 187
Ho Chi Minh, 329
Holy Order of the Knights of Labor, 144, 158, 160, 161, 162, 170, 171

Homeland Security Act of 2002, 384
Homesteading, 116
Hondo River, 25, 114
Hood, John Bell, 132
Hoover, Herbert, 217–18
Hoover, J. Edgar, 319
Hop-Fields Riot, 179–80
Hopi Indians, 9
Hopwood, Cheryl, 363
Hormel, 364
Horses, 14, 15, 21, 23, 66, 69, 145
Hos-Ta, 17(figure)
House Un-American Activities Committee (HUAC),
   281
Housing, 169, 193, 197–98
   in the new millennium, 382
   in postwar years, 273, 274–75, 283, 291
   residential segregation, 138, 146, 249, 274–75, 283,
      382
   in World War II era, 244, 246, 249, 262, 267
Housing Act of 1964, 294
Housing Authority, U.S., 249
Houston, Sam, 57, 59–60, 125
H.R. 4437, 380, 382
HUAC. See House Un-American Activities Committee
Huerfano County, 180
Huerta, Dolores, 279, 296, 297, 307, 309–13, 335, 365
Hunger of Memory (Rodriguez), 348
Hunt, G. W. P., 181
Hunting, 18, 45–46, 105
Huntington, Samuel, 384

Ia Drang Valley, Battle of the, 327
ICE. See Immigration and Customs Enforcement, U.S.
Idar, Clemente, 183
Idar, Eduardo, 183
Idar, Jovita (daughter of Nicasio), 183, 184–85, 206
Idar, Jovita (wife of Nicasio), 183
Idar, Nicasio, 183–85, 208n17
ILGWU. See International Ladies' Garment Workers
   Union
Illegal Immigration Reform and Individual
   Responsibility Act of 1996, 369, 382
Illinois, 15, 344
Illinois Steel, 197
ILWU. See International Longshoremen and
   Warhouseman's Union
Immigration
   from Latin America, 369
   from Mexico (see Mexican immigration)
   to Texas, 24, 25–29, 41, 51–56
Immigration Act of 1929, 217
Immigration and Control Act of 1986 (IRCA), 356,
   368, 371
Immigration and Customs Enforcement, U.S. (ICE),
   379, 386
Immigration and Naturalization Service (INS), 280,
   285, 287, 297, 369, 370, 379
Immigration Bureau, U.S., 191, 217, 218, 221, 229,
   232, 250
Imparcial de Texas, El, 203
Imperial Valley, 169, 202, 203, 277
Imperial Valley Workers Union, 202
Imuris, 114
Incarceration rates, 354–55, 371
Indentured servants, 68
Independent Partisan Rangers, 133
Independent Progressive Party (IPP), 280–81, 282
Indiana, 196–97

Indians. See also individual tribes
   captives and, 2, 6, 16, 42, 43, 44, 51, 105, 153
   in Civil War, 127, 128
   in colonial era, 1–31
   enslavement of, 2, 4, 9, 10, 11, 15, 16, 42, 43, 64
   extermination of, 105, 114–15
   in late 19th to early 20th century, 145
   Mexican American War and, 79, 85, 86, 87
   in mid-19th century, 112, 113, 114–15
   Plan de San Diego and, 186
   in post-independence era, 39–41, 42–45, 48–49,
      67–70
   in protest era, 320
   raids by, 2, 5–6, 14, 16–19, 22–24, 42–44, 51–52,
      62–63, 65–66, 69–70, 104–5
   religious conversion of, 1–2, 3, 8, 9, 11, 23, 28–29,
      31, 65–66
   Texas independence and, 55
   treaties with, 19, 23, 24, 42, 51
   tribute from, 3, 10, 11, 31
   women, 2, 11, 27, 29, 65, 66
   in World War II, 257
Indian Wars, 134–36
Industrial capitalism, 144, 155, 159
"Industrial Detroit" murals, 219
Industrial Workers of the World (IWW), 154, 178,
   179–80, 181–82, 195, 202, 205
Infant mortality rates, 193, 274, 291
Inland Empire, 194
Inland Steel, 196–97
INS. See Immigration and Naturalization Service
Inter-Agency Committee on Mexican American
   Affairs, 332
Internal Provinces, 24, 26
Internal Security Act of 1950, 284
International Brotherhood of Teamsters. See
   Teamsters Union
International Ladies' Garment Workers Union
   (ILGWU), 214, 224–25
International Longshoremen and Warehouseman's
   Union (ILWU), 234
International Mexican Railroad, 167
International Paper, 364
International Union of Mine, Mill, and Smelters
   Workers (Mine Mill), 272, 279–80, 281
International Workers' Day, 381
Interracial relations, 2, 7, 10–11, 27. See also
   Miscegenation
Iraq war, 383, 384
IRCA. See Immigration and Control Act of 1986
Irigoyen, José María, 43
Italy, 258
Itliong, Larry, 310, 311
Iwo Jima, 256
IWW. See Industrial Workers of the World

Jabón de lejía, 45
Jackson, Andrew, 54, 361
Jackson, Jesse, 350
Jackson State University shootings, 342n51
Jano Indians, 22
Japan, 255, 256–58, 265
Japanese Americans, 170, 233, 265
Jefferson, Thomas, 24
Jesuits, 28
Jews, 253, 311
Jicarilla Apache Indians, 17, 19, 105
Jim Crow system, 151, 288, 291
Jimenez, María, 333

*Joaquin Murieta: The Celebrated California Bandit*
    (Ridge), 140n33
Jobs for Progress, 319
John Birch Society, 294
John King's Saloon, 121
Johnson, Albert, 122
Johnson, Edwin C., 216
Johnson, Lyndon B., xvii, 299, 306–7, 311, 319, 327,
    328, 332–33, 350
Jones, Thomas C., 91
Jones and Laughlin, 196
Joseph, Antonio, 163
Juárez, Benito, 118, 126
Juáristas, 133
Junta Femeníl Pacifista, 184
Jury service, 274, 283, 289–90, 291, 306
Justice for Janitors, 368

Kahlo, Frida, 219
Kansas, 195–96
Kansas City Consolidated Smelting and Refining
    Company (ASARCO), 167
Karnes County, 124
Kazen, Abraham, 292
Kearny, Stephen Watts, 80, 86, 87, 88, 96, 97–98
Kearny Code, 87
Kemp, Jack, 359
Kenedy, Mifflin, 132, 133
Kennedy, Anthony, 348
Kennedy, Ethel, 313
Kennedy, John F., 292–93, 299, 318–19
Kennedy, Robert F., 312, 313, 322, 335
Kent State University shootings, 342n51
Khe Sanh base siege, 327
Khrushchev, Nikita, 286
Kickapoo Indians, 42, 144
King, Coretta Scott, 313
King, Martin Luther, Jr., 297, 312, 313, 317
King, Rodney, 355–56
King Ranch, 186
Kiowa Indians, 16, 39, 42, 43, 45, 51, 62, 104, 135
Kirker, James, 43
Kissinger Commission on Central America, 352
Kit Carson National Forest, 315–16, 317
Kivas, 11
Knights of Honor, 183
Knights of Labor. *See* Holy Order of the Knights of
    Labor
Knights of the Golden Circle, 126
Know-Nothing Party, 123
Korean War, 279, 281, 285, 308
Ku Klux Klan, 203, 285, 354, 379

La Bahía, 20, 21, 22, 23, 24, 41
La Bahía de Espíritu Santo, 21
Labor Council for Latin American Advancement
    (LACLAA), 367, 368
Labor force. *See also* Female workforce; Strikes;
    Unemployment; Unions; Wages
    in Depression era, 213–42
    in early 20th century, 177–83, 188–89, 196–99,
        201–3, 206–7
    at end of 20th century, 346, 363–66
    in late 19th to early 20th century, 144–45, 146,
        153–54, 165–70
    in postwar years, 276–80
    in protest era, 337–38
    in World War I era, 189
    in World War II era, 243–50, 259–63, 266

La Cañada, 90
LACLAA. *See* Labor Council for Latin American
    Advancement
La Follette, Robert, 233
La Follette Civil Liberties Committee Hearings, 233
Laguna Park rally, 329–30
Lamar, Mirabeau B., 62, 133
La Mesa, Battle of, 98
Land
    in early 20th century, 183, 184
    enclosure of, 150, 159–62
    headright system, 134
    in late 19th to early 20th century, 144, 145,
        146, 150, 155–56, 157–58, 159
    in mid-19th century, 113, 114, 116–18, 123,
        124, 137, 139–40n19
    open-range system, 156
    partitioning of, 157, 159
    in post-independence era, 52, 53, 54–55, 57, 61
    speculation, 54, 57, 61, 117, 157
Land Act of 1820, 52
Land grants
    adjudications of, 156–58
    attempted reclamation of, 295, 313–18, 321
    in colonial era, 2, 14, 21, 28, 29
    in mid-19th century, 116–18
    in post-independence era, 46, 51, 67
    post-Mexican American War, 102
    struggle to protect, 158–62
Landrum-Griffin Act, 301n18
La Purísima Mission, 66
Lara, Severita, 322
Laredo, 21, 43, 84, 104, 123, 134, 166
Larkin, Thomas Oliver, 91–92
Las Animas County, 180
Las Cruces, 155
Las Vegas, 155, 158, 159–62
Las Vegas Grant, 159–62
Las Vegas Land and Cattle Company, 159
Las Vegas Land Grant Defense Association, 161
Latin America, 372
    dictatorships supported by U.S., 281
    Good Neighbor Policy, 244, 248, 264, 265, 281, 288
    immigration from, 369
Latin American Project, 352
Latino Consensus on NAFTA, 366
Latinos, xiii, 372
Latinos for Peace, 384
Latin Protective League, 202
Law No. 23, 202
Law of April 16, 1830, 56
Laws of Discovery, 8
League of United Latin American Citizens
    (LULAC), 178, 348, 387
    in Depression era, 214, 223, 231
    at end of 20th century, 352
    founding philosophy of, 203–5
    in the new millennium, 384
    in postwar years, 281, 284, 287, 289, 298
    in protest era, 312, 332, 334
    in World War II era, 264
League of Workers and Peasants, 219
Leal, James W., 89
Lee, Robert E., 126
Lee, Stephen Luis, 89
Lenin, V. I., 323
Lesbians, 325
Lettuce pickers' strike/boycott, 313, 335, 365, 382
Leyva, Abdon, 122

Leyva Armendaríz, Jesús, 258
Liberation theology, 352
*Life and Adventures of Joaquín Murieta, The* (Ridge), 121
Liga de Obreros y Campesinos, La, 219
Liga Femenil Mexicanista, La, 184
Liga Instructiva Mexicana, La, 203
Liga Obrera de Habla Español, La, 195, 226, 232
Liga Protectora Latina, 202
Liga Protectora Mexicana, La, 203
Lincoln, Abraham, 118, 127
Lincoln County Stock Growers Association, 156
Lincoln County War, 144, 155, 156
Lincoln Heights, 276
Lipan Apache Indians, 22, 24, 42, 51, 133
Little Salt Lake, 64
Livestock, 14–15, 21, 41
López, Ignacio, 283
López de la Cruz, Jessica, 313
López Tijerina, Cristobal, 316
López Tijerina, Reies, 162, 295–96, 307, 313–18, 335
López Tijerina, Rosa, 316
Lorenzana, Apolinaria, 29
Loreto, 26
Los Adaes, 22, 23
Los Angeles, 5, 26, 70, 116, 217, 224–25, 233–34, 287
   East, 193, 308, 321, 322, 337, 353
   founding of, 27
   gangs in, 354
   Mexican American War and, 88, 94, 95–96, 98
   Mexican immigration in, 188, 192, 218–19, 220, 347, 357
   Mexican settlement patterns in, 193–94
   population growth in, 145–46
   in postwar years, 274–75, 276
   race riots in, 244, 355–56
   total immigrant population of, 369
   in World War II era, 249–50, 252–53, 259–60
   Zoot Suit Riot, 253–55, 266
Los Angeles American Unity Committee, 254, 255
Los Angeles County Federation of Labor, 359
Los Angeles Gas Works, 179
Los Angeles Labor Federation, 217
Los Angeles Pacific Electric Railway, 193
Los Angeles Plaza, 118, 193
Los Angeles Police Department, 224, 255, 276, 355
Los Angeles River, 193
*Los Angeles Star,* 118, 122
*Los Angeles Times,* 254–55, 330
Los Baños strike, 278
Los Patricios, 134
Louisiana, 15, 21, 22, 24, 44, 53, 55, 363
Louisiana Purchase, 24, 30, 37n78, 54, 101
Love, Harry, 120, 121, 140n29
Loyalty Leagues, 189
Lucas, María Elena, 313
Ludlow Massacre, 178, 181
Luján, José Ignacio, 160
Luján, Manuel, 318
LULAC. *See* League of United Latin American Citizens
Luna, Maximiliano, 164, 165(figure)
Lunch counter integration, 294
Lynchings, 113, 116, 118, 119, 145, 146–47, 183–84, 187, 285

MacArthur, Douglas, 256, 257
Machado, Rafael, 96
MacKenzie, Alexander, 94
Magoffin, James W., 86

Magónistas, 154, 179
*Major Problems in Mexican American History* (Vargas), xv
Malcolm X, 329
MALDEF. *See* Mexican American Legal Defense and Educational Fund
Manauila Creek, 124
Manifest Destiny, xvii, 45, 82, 83, 86, 102, 105, 112
Mansfield, Battle of, 132
Manso Indians, 22
Mao Ze-dong, 323
MAPA. *See* Mexican American Political Association
Maquilas, 366
March on Washington for Jobs and Freedom, 297
Marcy, William L., 86
Marsh, John, 67
Marshall, Lupe, 235(figure), 236
Marshall Plan, 281
Martínez, Alonzo, 10
Martínez, Antonio José, 89
Martínez, Antonio María, 30, 52
Martínez, Elizabeth, 317, 318, 325, 329, 352–53, 374n26
Martínez, Kiko, 331
Martínez, Manuel, 60
Martínez, Refugio, 214, 235, 285
Martínez, Vilma, 361
Martínez de Lejanza, Mariano, 81
Marxism, 323. *See also* Communism
Matagorda Bay, 20, 21
Matamoros, 43, 84, 85
"Maximum feasible participation" doctrine, 332
Maxwell, Lucien B., 156
Maxwell Land Grant, 156, 158
MAYO. *See* Mexican American Youth Organization
Mayordomos, 68
Mazatlán, 85
McCarran-Walter Act, 281, 283, 284, 285, 286
McCarthy, Joseph, 286
McCarthyism, xvii, 272, 273, 284, 286. *See also* Communism, postwar crackdown on
McCorkle, Joseph Walker, 139n19
McGovern, George, 334, 343n63,69
McMillan, Samuel H., 90
McWilliams, Carey, xiv–xv, 233, 250
Meany, George, 335
Meatpacking industry, 189, 192, 195, 196, 197, 246, 364
MECHA. *See* Movimiento Estudiantil Chicano de Aztlán
Medicare, 307
Medina River, 58
Mediola, Rafael Antonio, 56–57
Medrano, Francisco, 294
Memorial Day Massacre, 235–36
Menchaca, Antonio, 60
*Mendez v. Westminster,* 289
Mendoza, Hope Schecter, 282, 283, 297
Mercedes, 150
Mervine, William, 96
Mescalero Apache Indians, 24, 135
Mesilla, 128, 129
Mesilla Valley, 132
Mestizaje, 6
Mestizos, 6, 7, 9, 11, 12, 16, 20, 22, 26, 32, 40, 118
Metamoros, 134
Metzger, Tom, 354
Mexican American Democrats, 334
Mexican American Legal Defense and Educational Fund (MALDEF), 290, 334, 361, 366
Mexican American Legislative Caucus, 334

Mexican American National Issues Conference, 325
Mexican American Political Association (MAPA), 292–93, 297, 325, 332
Mexican American studies programs, 308
Mexican American Unity Council, 334
Mexican American War, xiv, xvi, xvii, 61, 62, 63, 67, 71, 73, 79–111, 112, 114, 116, 119, 124, 133, 137, 231, 386. *See also* Treaty of Guadalupe Hidalgo
    casualties in, 100
    issues leading to, 79–84
    occupation of California, 91–94
    occupation of New Mexico, 85–88
    outbreak of, 84–85
    Taos Revolt, 80, 88–91, 162
Mexican American women
    in American GI Forum, 284
    Chicana movement, 299, 308, 324–25, 336
    in civil rights movement, 296
    in CSO, 282–83
    in early 20th century, 184, 200
    education for, 184
    at end of 20th century, 350–51
    Mexican American War and, 96
    in the political process, 350–51
    in postwar years, 297
    in protest era, 320, 333, 337
    strikes supported by, 272, 279, 280, 364
    in the workforce (*see* Female workforce)
Mexican American Youth Organization (MAYO), 322–23, 329, 333
Mexican Bar Association, 334
Mexican Central Railway, 166
Mexican Colony Law of 1824, 67, 156
Mexican Feminine Commission, 325
Mexican Feminist League, 184
Mexican immigration, xvii. *See also* Deportations
    Americanization movement, 200–201
    amnesty programs, 349, 356, 387
    chain, 188, 192, 206
    in Depression era, 213, 214, 217–20
    in early 20th century, 177–78, 188–89, 191–93, 195, 199–201, 204–6
    at end of 20th century, 344, 345–46, 347, 349, 356–59, 368–70, 371–72
    intensified border control, 369–70, 384–86
    in late 19th to early 20th century, 145, 146, 165–70, 171
    NAFTA impact on, 347, 356, 378
    in the new millennium, 378–91
    restrictions on, 202, 214, 356
    social and cultural change, 199–201
    in World War I era, 191, 206
    in World War II era, 250
Mexican Instructive League, 203
Mexican League of Beneficence and Protection, 184
Mexican Mutual Aid Society of the Imperial Valley (MMAS), 202
Mexican National Railroad, 166, 167
Mexican Protective League, 203
"Mexican Question in the Southwest, The" (Brooks), 231
Mexican Railway, 150
*Mexican Reglamento,* 67
Mexican Revolution, xvii, 177, 184, 188
Mexican scale wages, 153, 179, 181, 225
Mexico
    colonial, 1–38
    debt to England, 79
    expansionism of U.S., 19–22, 24–25, 30, 31, 32, 39, 41–42, 43, 44–45, 50, 63–64, 72–73, 82–83

French occupation of, 126
    independence from Spain, 1, 24, 30, 50
    manumission of slaves, 56
    post-independence, 39–78
    railroad system of, 166–67
    reconquest, 1, 13–20
Mexico City, 3, 6, 31, 62, 83, 84, 87, 94, 99, 100, 166
Miami, 353, 357, 369
Micheltorena, Manuel, 71, 81
Michigan, 198–99, 246
Mier y Terán, Manuel de, 56
Migrant workers, 215–17. *See also* Farm workers
Military enlistment rates, 383–84, 390n18
Mine Mill. *See* International Union of Mine, Mill, and Smelters Workers
Minimum wage, 189, 312
Mining, 105. *See also* Coal miners' strikes; Copper mining
    in colonial era, 3, 4, 10, 13, 16, 20, 25
    in early 20th century, 180–82, 202
    in late 19th to early 20th century, 144, 153–54, 155, 167, 169, 170, 171
    in mid-19th century, 135, 136
    in postwar years, 272
    strikes by workers, 154, 180–82, 272, 279–80
Minnesota, 199
Minutemen, 357, 384–85
Miscegenation, 6, 7. *See also* Interracial relations
Mission (town), 150
Missionaries. *See also* Franciscans; Jesuits
    Catholic, 1–2, 3–4, 8–9, 28–29, 31, 65
    Protestant, 199–200
Mission Church of San Gerónomo, 90
Missions, 1, 3–4, 5, 8, 20, 21, 22, 26, 27, 28–29, 31, 65–67
    life on, 65–66
    Pueblo Revolt and, 11–12
    secularization of, 21, 23, 29, 41, 65, 66–67, 69, 71
Mississippi, 53, 294, 363
Mississippi Freedom Summer, 317
Mississippi River, 3, 13, 21, 24, 44, 64
Missouri, 16, 40, 46, 47, 53, 62
Miwok Indians, 69
Mobilization for Justice and Peace in Central America and South Africa, 352
Mohammed, Elijah, 295
Mojados, 272, 278, 287, 297
Molina, Gloria, 350–51
Mondale, Walter, 312, 350
Monongahela Valley, 199
Monroe Doctrine, 91
Montana, 195, 277
Monterey, 4, 5, 25, 26, 70, 71, 81, 91, 103
Monterey Bay, 94
Monterey Harbor, 91
Monterrey, Battle of, 94–95
Montoya, Joseph, 306, 318
Montoya, Nestor, 162
Montoya, Pablo, 88, 90
Moore, Acel, 348
Moore, Benjamin D., 97
Moore, Carlos, 295
Mora, 90
Moraga family, 28
Morales, Manuel, 187
Morales, Pedro, 60
Moreno, Dorinda, 280
Moreno, Guadalupe, 194
Moreno, Luisa, 234, 249

Moreno, Rudy, 194
Morin, Jesse I., 90
Morris, W. T. ("Brack"), 148–49
Mothers of East Los Angeles (MELA), 353
Mt. Olive Pickle Company, 366
Movimiento Estudiantil Chicano de Aztlán (MECHA), 323
Mujeres por la Raza, 325
Mulattos, 6, 7, 9, 20, 22, 26
Muñiz, Ramsey, 333
Muñoz, Carlos, 295
Muñoz, Rosalio, 329
Muriati, Joaquín, 120
Murieta, Joaquín, 120–21, 140n33
Mutual aid societies, 138, 169–70, 178, 188, 199, 201–5, 206
Mutual Protection Society of Mexican Workers, 202
Muzquiz, Virginia, 295, 297

NAACP. See National Association for the Advancement of Colored People
Nacogdoches, 20, 21, 22, 23, 24, 25, 41, 52, 55, 60, 61
Nacozari Railroad Company, 167
Nader, Ralph, 365
NAFTA. See North American Free Trade Agreement
NALEO. See National Association of Latino Elected and Appointed Officials
Nannygate, 349
Nashville, 53
Nashville, Battle of, 132
Natchitoches, 24, 25
Nation, The, xiv
National Association for the Advancement of Colored People (NAACP), 289, 298, 361
National Association of Latino Elected and Appointed Officials (NALEO), 351
National Association of Mexican Americans (ANMA), 273, 280–82, 285, 298, 302n31
National Beet Growers Association, 232
National Catholic Welfare Conference, 220
National Chicano Moratorium Against the War, 308, 321, 328–31, 337
National Council for La Raza, 366, 384
National Day of Action for Immigrant Justice, 380
National Farm Labor Union (NFLU), 278
National Farm Workers Association (NFWA), 279, 309, 310–11
National Industrial Recovery Act (NIRA), 214, 221
National Labor Relations Act (NLRA), 233, 250, 311, 332
National Labor Relations Board (NLRB), 234, 236
National League of Cities, 350
National Miners Union (NMU), 214–15, 225–27, 237
National Negro Congress, 244
National Peace Action Coalition, 331
National Recovery Act (NRA), 214, 221–23, 225, 236
National Tube, 196
National Youth Administration (NYA), 227
Native Americans. See Indians
Nativism
    in Depression era, 207, 213
    in early 20th century, 200
    at end of 20th century, 246, 357–58
    in late 19th to early 20th century, 163, 171
    in mid-19th century, 112
    during World War I, 191
Naturalization. See Citizenship/naturalization
Nava, Julian, 321
Nava, Pedro de, 24

Navajo Indians, 11, 14, 18, 19, 39, 40, 42–43, 48, 87, 104, 105, 134, 135, 257
Navarrete, Gabriel L., 258
Navarro, José Ángel, 132
Navarro, José Antonio, 52, 57, 58, 60, 62
Nazism, 244, 294. See also Neo-Nazi groups
Nebraska, 195
Negroes, 2, 6, 22
Neighborhood Youth Corps, 319, 332
Neo-Nazi groups, 294, 354
Neo-Nazi National Alliance, 391n23
Netherlands, 15
Neutral ground agreement, 25
Nevada, 113, 181
New Deal, 214, 226, 227–28, 232, 234, 236, 237, 243, 247, 265, 293, 347
New Mexico, 4, 24, 30, 42–43, 45–49, 54, 55, 82, 113, 114, 181–82, 202, 350, 351
    Civil War and, 127, 128–30
    common property rights in, 102
    in Depression era, 216–17, 236
    designated a territory, 113
    founding of, 8–11
    Indian Wars and, 134–35
    land grant adjudications in, 156–58
    land grant restoration movement in, 295, 313–18, 321
    land grant struggle in, 158–62
    in late 19th to early 20th century, 144, 154–65
    Mexican American War and, 85–91
    Mexican immigration in, 177, 188, 195
    Mexico compensated for loss of, 101
    in mid-19th century, 104–5, 106
    in postwar years, 283
    reconquest of, 1, 13–20
    revolt of 1837, 39–40, 48–49, 62, 72, 79
    statehood issue, 162–65, 171
    struggle over ownership of, 79–80, 81
    in World War II era, 247
New Mexico Land and Livestock Company, 157
New Mexico National Guard, 247, 317
New Orleans, 24, 53, 54, 61
New Right, 344–45, 348, 370
New Spain, 1–38. See also Northern frontier
New Town, 159
"New Voice" reform slate, 368
New York, 191, 347, 357, 369
NFLU. See National Farm Labor Union
NFWA. See National Farm Workers Association
Nicaragua, 345, 352, 353
Niles' National Register, 90
NIRA. See National Industrial Recovery Act
Nixon, Richard, 325, 328, 334, 337, 369
NLRA. See National Labor Relations Act
NLRB. See National Labor Relations Board
NMU. See National Miners Union
Noachian Deluge of California Floods, 117
Nogales (Arizona), 5, 167
Nogales (Sonora), 167
Nolan, Phillip, 36n77
Nonviolent protest, 312, 313
Nootka Treaty, 29
Normandy invasion, 255, 258
North American Free Trade Agreement (NAFTA), xvi, xvii, 346–47, 356, 366–67, 378
Northern borderlands, 39–78
    men of, 45–46
    opening of commercial markets, 46–48
Northern frontier, 1–38

guarding the periphery, 25–29
institutions and society of, 3–8
Texas as a buffer zone, 20–22
*North from Mexico* (McWilliams), xiv–xv
*Not with the Fist* (Tuck), 193
NRA. *See* National Recovery Act
Nuclear proliferation, 281
Nueces River, 41, 50, 51, 54, 58, 60, 61, 63, 79, 82–83, 95, 133
Nueces strip, 82–83, 84, 123, 125, 134, 147
Nuecestown, 147
Nuestra Señora Dolores, 21
Nuestra Señora Purisima, 20
Nueva Vizcaya, 26
Nuevo Leon, 21
Nuñez, Fabian, 359
NYA. *See* National Youth Administration

Obama, Barack, 387, 388(figure)
Obrajes, 11
Obregón Park rally, 329
Ocampo Quesada, Dora, 245(figure)
*Occupied America: A History of Chicanos* (Acuña), xv
Ochoa, Antonio, 131, 137
Ocomorenia, Joaquín, 120
O'Connor, Sandra Day, 362
Office of Economic Opportunity (OEO), 307, 332
Office of Federal Contract Compliance, 348
Office of the Coordinator of Inter-American Affairs, 265
Office of the Surveyor General, 157
Oil prices, 347
Okinawa, 256–57
Oklahoma, 16, 104, 135, 163
Old Spanish Trail, 46, 63–64, 114
Omaha, 195
Omnibus Bill of 1902, 163
Oñate, Juan de, 1, 9–10
158th Regimental Combat Team (RCT), 257
101st Airborne Division (Vietnam), 326(figure)
101st Airborne Division (WWII), 255
141st Infantry Regiment, 258
One Hundred Percent Americanism, 189
165th Infantry Regiment, 257
120th Engineer Regiment, 247
One Stop Immigration, 359
Onion pickers' strike, 228–29
Open-range system, 156
Operation Gatekeeper, 369
Operation Hold the Line, 369
Operation Return to Sender, 386
Operation Terror, 286–88, 298
Operation Wetback, 273, 286–88, 290, 298
Orange County, 194, 233
Oregon, 82
Organic Bill, 152–53
Ornelas, William R., 255
Ortega family, 28
Ortiz, Juan Felipe, 89
Ortiz, Tomás, 88–89
O'Sullivan, John L., 82
Otermín, Antonio de, 12, 13
Otero, Antonio José, 87
Otero, Miguel A., Jr., 164
*Other America, The* (Harrington), 278
Oury, William S., 135, 136
*Out of the Barrio* (Chavez), 348–49
Oxnard, 170

Pacheco Pass, 69
Pachucos, 251
Padilla, José Leon, 159
Padrés, José María, 66–67
Paiute Indians, 64
Palacios, Enriqueta, 295
Palmer raids, 182
Palo Alto, Battle of, 84–85, 124
Pan American Federation of Labor, 183
Pan American Union, 263
Panic of 1819, 52
Panoche Pass, 69
Papago Indians, 136
Paredes y Arrillaga, Mariano, 84, 85, 94
Partido del Pueblo Unido, El, 162
Partido Liberal Mexicano (PLM), 154
PASSO. *See* Political Association of Spanish-Speaking Organizations
Patrónes, 50, 150
Pawnee Indians, 15, 16
"Peace by purchase" policy, 19
Pearl Harbor, Japanese attack on, 256, 265
Pease, Elisha M., 124
Pecan shellers' strike, 229–31
Pecan shelling industry, 222
Pecos River, 135
Pedraza, Gómez, 99
Pellagra, 216
Peña, Albert R., 292, 328
Peña, Elena, 264
Peña, Federico, 350
Peña, Miguel, 125
Peñaloza, Joseph M., 132
Pendleton, Clarence M., Jr., 348
Peninsulares, 6, 22
Pennsylvania, 199
Peonage, 48, 50–51, 150
Peónes, 50–51
People's Coalition for Peace and Justice, 331
Perales, Alonso, 203, 212n85, 264
Peralta, Pedro, 10
Peralta family, 28, 67
Pérez, Albino, 39–40, 48–49, 72, 88
Pérez, Emma, 360
Pérez, Eulalia, 29
Pérez de Almazán, Fernando, 23
Pesqueíra, 114
Phelps Dodge Corporation, 167, 180, 364
*Philadelphia Inqiurer*, 348
Philip II, King of Spain, 9
Philippine Islands, 247, 255–56, 258
*Phillip Millhiser et al. v. José Leon Padilla*, 159
Pico, Andrés, 93, 96–97, 98, 120, 128
Pico, Jesús, 98
Pico, José Ramón, 127–28
Pico, Pío de Jesús, 28, 71, 81, 93, 94
Píco, Simón, 121
Pico family, 67
Pierce, Franklin, 104
Pike, Zebulon, 19–20
Pile, William, 174n49
Pinckney Treaty, 24
Pino, Miguel, 129, 130
Pino brothers, 89
Pioneer Fund, 363
Pizaña, Aniceto, 185
Plains Indians, 15, 39, 40, 42, 45–46, 134
Plains region, 45–46, 194–96
Plan de San Diego, El, 150, 178, 185–87, 206

Plan de Santa Barbara, El, 323
Plan de Tomé, 49
Plan Espiritual de Aztlán, El, 320, 321
*Plessy v. Ferguson,* 151
Poblaciones, 2
Pobres, 40, 49
Poinsett, Joel R., 54
Police brutality
    at end of 20th century, 353, 354, 355–56
    in postwar years, 273, 276, 283
    in protest era, 319
    in World War II era, 250, 255, 262
Political Association of Spanish-Speaking
        Organizations (PASSO), 292–93, 294–95, 312, 332
Polk, James K., 83, 84, 85, 86, 92, 94, 95, 101
Polka Rebellion, 99
Poll tax, 151, 283, 294, 295, 334, 349
Poor People's March, 317, 320, 321
Popé, 11–13
Populist Party, 144, 151, 162, 171
Porfiriato, 167
Portolá, Gaspar de, 26
Portugal, 29
Porvenir Massacre, 187
Powderly, Terrence, 161
President's Commission on Migratory Labor, 277
Presidial Lancers, 96, 97
Presidios, 1, 2, 3, 4–5, 16, 20, 23, 26, 27, 39, 41
Price, Sterling, 87, 88, 89, 90, 100–101
Primer Congreso Mexicanista, El, 184
Prince, LeBaron Bradford, 160, 161–62
Professional Air Traffic Controllers Organization
        (PATCO), 364
Progressive Citizens of America, 281
*Progresso, El,* 184
Project 100,000, 328
Proposition 10, 275
Proposition 63, 357
Proposition 187, 344, 346, 357–59
Proposition 209, 346, 362–63
Protestant missionaries, 199–200
Provincias Internas. *See* Internal Provinces
Public Law 45, 263
Public Law 78, 279
Public Works Administration (PWA), 227
Puebla, 85
Pueblo Indians, 9–14, 16, 19, 43, 49, 86, 88
Pueblo Revolt, 1, 2, 7, 11–13, 31
Pueblos, 1, 27. *See also* Towns
Puerto Ricans, 350
Puerto Rican Young Lords, 321
Puerto Rico, 281
PWA. *See* Public Works Administration

Querétaro, 101

Race riots, 244, 337, 353
Racism
    during Civil War, 129
    in colonial era, 6–8
    in early 20th century, 180, 201
    at end of 20th century, 345, 353–54, 371
    in late 19th to early 20th century, 144, 145, 162, 163,
        170
    Mexican American War and, 86, 94–95, 101
    in mid-19th century, 112, 113, 114, 118–19, 123, 124
    in the new millennium, 379
    in postwar years, 273
    in World War II era, 247, 258–59

Railroads, xvii, 104, 136, 138, 144–45, 146, 150, 153,
        155, 165–68, 171, 188, 189, 192, 195, 196. *See also*
        individual railroads
    female workforce, 248, 261
    Las Gorras Blancas' attacks on, 161
    in Mexico, 166–67
    strikes by workers, 160, 179
Rainbow Coalition, 321, 350
Ramírez, Francisco, 118–19
Ramón, Domingo, 35n60
Ranching
    in colonial era, 21, 28
    golden age of, 67–70
    in late 19th to early 20th century, 150, 155
    in mid-19th century, 80, 117–18
    in post-independence era, 40, 41, 50–51, 63, 67–70
Rancho de San Francisco, 94
Rancho San Ramón, 69
Ranch Rescue, 391n23
Randolph, A. Phillip, 265
Rape, 2, 11, 29, 65, 71, 156
Rapido River Crossing, 258
Raton, 155
Raymondville, 150
Raza, La, 308, 335
Raza Unida Party, La (RUP), 308, 320, 323, 325,
        331–34, 337, 349
Reagan, Ronald, 344, 345, 346, 347–49, 350,
        352, 353, 354, 355, 356, 370, 373n15
Reclamation Act of 1902, 150
Reconquest, 1, 13–20
Reconstruction, 146, 151
*Recopilación,* 14
Red baiting, 272, 281
Red Cross, 189, 206, 262, 265, 266
Red River, 22, 23, 30, 148
Red River campaign, 132
Red Scare, 180, 191, 273, 284–86, 298
Red Squad, 224, 233
Refugio, 148
*Regents of the University of California v. Bakke,* 338,
        359, 360–61, 375n47, 376n51
*Reglamento para el governo de las provincias de
        Californias,* 27
Regulation of 1729, 23
*Regulations and Instruction for the Presidios...of New
        Spain,* 23
Rehnquist, William H., 348
Relief (public assistance), 213, 214, 216–17, 219–20,
        222, 223, 236, 314
Reno, Janet, 373n18
Repatriation campaign, 213, 217–20
Republican Party
    Civil War and, 127
    in early 20th century, 203
    at end of 20th century, 345, 348, 349,
        358, 359, 361, 366
    in late 19th to early 20th century, 154, 163
    in mid-19th century, 113, 119
    in the new millennium, 379, 380, 387
    in protest era, 333, 337
Republic of Fredonia, 55
Republic of San Joaquín del Cañón de Río de Chama,
        315–16
Republic of the Sierra Madre, 125
Republic Steel, 235
*Re Rodriguez,* 152
Resaca de la Palma, Battle of, 84–85, 124
Reuther, Walter, 294, 311, 335

"Reverse discrimination," 346, 347, 360
Revivalism, 199–200
Ricos, 15, 40, 47–48, 49, 65, 72, 79, 81, 85, 86, 114, 154, 157
Ridge, John Rollins, 121, 140n33
Right-to-work laws, 277
Riley, Bennet, 103
Río Abajo, 12, 14, 85
Río Arriba, 12, 14, 85, 88
Río Arriba County, 314
Río Arriba County Courthouse, 316
Río Arriba rebellion, 49
Río Grande, 9, 10, 12, 14, 19, 21, 24, 30, 40, 41, 43, 50, 55, 56, 63, 84, 85, 123, 130, 132, 144, 147, 148, 150
    as Mexico-U.S. boundary, 101
    as Texas-U.S. boundary, 54, 60, 79, 82–83, 106
Río Grande City, 126
Río Grande Valley, 21, 43, 124, 125–26, 133, 134, 150, 151, 178, 206, 229, 253, 277
    Mexican immigration in, 189
    racial violence in, 183–87
Río Hondo. See Hondo River
Ríos, Antonio, 282, 283
Río San Francisco valley, 114
Ritch, William G., 158
Rivera, Diego, 219
Rivera, Pedro de, 20, 23
Rivera y Moncada, Fernando de, 26
Robert Marshall Civil Liberties Trust, 289, 290
Robledo, Martín, 149
Robledo, Refugia, 149
Rockefeller family, 180
Rocky Mountain region, 18, 180, 194–96, 202, 280, 281
Rodríguez, Ambrosio, 60
Rodríguez, Antonio, 183–84
Rodríguez, Augustín, 8–9
Rodríguez, Joe, 235
Rodríguez, Julia, 262
Rodríguez, Luis, 354
Rodríguez, Ricardo, 151
Rodriguez, Richard, 345, 348
Rodríguez, Thomas A., 151
Romero, Tomás, 88, 89, 90
Romero, Trinidad, 158
Romero v. Weakley, 289
Roosevelt, Eleanor, 254
Roosevelt, Franklin D., 214, 215, 234, 237, 243, 244, 259, 262, 264
Roosevelt, Theodore, 164, 386–87
Rosario, 20
Ross, Edmond, 156
Ross, Fred, 282, 283, 309
Rough Riders, 164
Rowland, William Richard, 122
Roybal, Edward B., 282–84, 292, 293, 306, 332–33, 351
Rubí, Marqués de, 23
Ruiz, Alejandro R., 257
Ruiz, José Francisco, 51, 52, 57, 58, 60
RUP. See Raza Unida Party, La
Russia, 1, 25

Sabine River, 25, 30, 55, 83
Sacco, Nicola, 202
Sacred Expedition, 26
St. Francis of Assisi Mission, 26
St. Louis Railroad, 150, 167
St. Vrain, Ceran, 89, 90
Saiz, Herman, 258
Salazar, Luz, 214

Salazar, Ruben, 330
Salcedo, Manuel María de, 25, 30
Salcedo, Nemesio, 24–25
Saldívar, Juan de, 10
Saldívar, Vicente de, 10
Salman's Scouts, 156
Saltillo, 95
Salt of the Earth (film), 280
Salt of the Earth strike, 279–80
Salt River Valley, 153
Salt War, 147
Salvatierra v. Del Rio Independent School District, 205
San Antonio, 4, 18, 21, 23, 31, 60, 61, 150, 194, 223, 224, 229–31, 236
    Mexican immigration in, 188–89, 192, 246
    political gains in, 350
San Antonio de Béxar, 20, 23, 24, 52, 53, 57, 58
San Antonio de Valero, 20
San Antonio Express, 147
San Antonio River, 20, 21, 22, 50, 230
San Antonio River Walk, 230
San Augustine, 22
San Benito, 122, 150
San Bernardino, 193
Sánches Chumascado, Francisco, 8–9
Sánchez, Alfonso, 316
Sánchez, Corinne, 324
Sánchez, David, 329, 331
Sanchez, George, 247, 264
Sánchez, José Antonio, 128
Sánchez, Loretta, 359
Sánchez family, 28
Sanctuary movement, 345, 353
San Diego (California), 4, 5, 25, 26, 27, 28, 29, 41, 82, 369
    Mexican American War and, 88, 94, 95, 97–98
    trade in, 91
San Diego (Texas). See Plan de San Diego, El
San Diego Bay, 65
Sandinistas, 345, 352
San Felipe de Albuquerque, 14
San Fernando Mission, 98
San Fernando Valley, 98
San Francisco, 4, 5, 26, 27, 29, 41, 191
San Francisco Alta California, 121
San Francisco Bay, 26, 65
San Francisco Canal, 153
San Francisco de la Espada Mission, 20
San Gabriel Mission, 26, 64, 69, 119
San Gabriel River, 98
Sangre de Cristo Grant, 156
San Ignacio Babocómari land grant, 114
San Ildefonso, Treaty of, 24, 37n78
San Jacinto, Battle of, 59–60
San Jacinto River, 59–60
San Joaquín communal land grant, 316
San Joaquin Valley, 233
San José, 5, 81
San José de Guadalupe, 27
San José y Miguel de Aguayo Mission, 20
San Juan Basin, 114
San Juan Bautista Mission, 69
San Juan Capistrano, 20, 69
San Juan Mission, 81
San Luis Obispo, 69, 88
San Luis Potosí, 95
San Luis River Valley, 247
San Miguel County, 158–62
San Miguel de Aguayo, Marqués de, 21

San Miguel del Vado, 14
San Pasqual, Battle of, 96–97
San Patricio, 148
San Pedro, Battle of, 96
San Pedro River, 114, 136
San Salvador, 369
Santa Anna, Antonio López de, 47, 48, 49, 67, 81, 105
    Mexican American War and, 85, 94, 95, 99–100
    Texas independence movement and, 57, 58–60, 61
Santa Barbara, 5, 26, 27, 66, 70, 88, 93, 94, 96
Santa Clara de Asís, 27
Santa Clara Mission, 5
Santa Cruz, 27
Santa Cruz de la Cañada, 49
Santa Cruz de Rosales, 100–101
Santa Cruz Valley, 114
Santa Fe, 4, 11, 12, 13, 14, 16, 31, 40, 46, 49, 62, 82,
    130, 132
    Mexican American War and, 87, 88, 89
    as New Spain capital, 10
    trade in, 79, 85, 86
Santa Fe Railroad, 145, 155, 167, 195, 238n14. See also
    Atchison, Topeka, and Santa Fe Railroad
Santa Fe Ring, 144, 154, 157–58
Santa Fe Trail, xvi, 44, 46–48, 49, 64, 72,
    73, 88, 128, 135, 155
Santa Inés, 88
Santa María, 40
Santa Rita, 105
Santa Rosa de Lima, 14
Santa Ynez, 66
Scalia, Antonin, 348
Scalp hunting, 43, 114
Scarlet fever, 66
Schenley Industries, 311–12
Schnabel, Mr., 149
School Improvement League, 205
Schools. See Education and schools
Scott, Winfield, 95, 99, 100
Second Bull Run, Battle of, 132
Second New Mexico Infantry, 129
Second Pueblo Revolt, 13
Second Texas Cavalry, 134
Second Texas Mounted Rifles, 132
Second Texas Union Cavalry, 133
Seguín (town), 123
Seguín, Erasmo, 52, 55–56, 60
Seguín, José Erasmo, 30
Seguín, Juan Ángel, 52
Seguín, Juan Nepomuceno, 57, 58, 60, 61
Selective Service Act of 1917, 189
Selma march, 294
September 11 terrorist attacks, 379, 380, 384
Sepulveda family, 67
Serna, Marcelino, 190
Settlement houses, 198, 200
Seven Years' War, 4, 25
Sexually transmitted diseases, 29, 66
Shanker, Albert, 348
Shawnee Indians, 43
Sheep, 14–15, 21, 40, 117, 118, 145, 155
Sheepherders, 145, 156
Sheepshearers, 118
Sheldon, Lionel, 158
Sibley, Henry H., 128, 130, 132
Silver, 9, 13, 16, 25, 46
Silver City, 155
Simpson-Mazzoli Act. See Immigration and
    Control Act of 1986

Sinaloa, 26, 65
Sinarquistas, 244, 252–53
Siqueiros, David Alfaro, 218–19
Sixth California Infantry, 128
Sixth Missouri Infantry, 132
Sixth Texas Infantry, 132
Slaughter Hill, Battle of, 257
Slavery, 79, 102, 119, 162
    abolitionism vs., 82, 101, 113, 123
    Civil War and, 127, 134, 137
    Indians in, 2, 4, 9, 10, 11, 15, 16, 42, 43, 64
    Mexico's manumission, 56
    in Texas, 53, 54, 55–56, 57, 58, 59, 61, 72,
        73, 82, 106, 123, 125, 126
    underground railroad and, 123
    Wilmot Proviso on, 101, 103
Sleepy Lagoon Defense Committee (SLDC), 250, 251
Sleepy Lagoon incident, 250–52, 266
Slidell, John, 83, 84, 85
Sloat, John D., 94
Smallpox, 19, 23, 66, 130
Smeltertown, 167
Smith Act, 285, 303n45
Smuggling, 147
SNCC. See Student Nonviolent Coordinating
    Committee
Snyder's Store, 122
Socialist Party, 179
Socialist Workers Party, 325
Social Security, 232
Sociedad Proteción Mutual de Trabajadores
    Unidos, 202
Socorro, 40
Sonoma, 65, 92, 94
Sonora, 26, 31, 39, 65, 114, 116, 120, 128, 135, 153,
    167, 170
Sonora Exploring and Mining Company, 135
Sonora Railroad Company Limited, 167
Sonora Town, 146
Sons of America, 203
Soto, Miguel, 119
South America, 369
South Boyle Heights, 193
Southern Dixiecrats, 277, 292
Southern Manifesto, 290, 292
Southern Pacific Railroad, 145, 155, 167, 218, 248
Southern Pecan Company, 230–31
Southern states, 379
South Platte River Valley, 195
South Texas, 185–87, 274, 283, 289, 291
Southwest
    on the eve of Mexican American War, 81–84
    in late 19th to early 20th century, 144–76
    postconquest, 113–19
    in postwar years, 274
Southwestern Railroad, 160
Southwest Voter Registration Education Project,
    334, 349, 359
Southwest Voter Research initiative, 366
Southwest Voter Research Institute, 352
Soviet Union, 345
Spain. See also Colonialism
    Bourbon Reforms, 1, 3, 4
    Mexico independence from, 1, 24, 30, 50
    reconquest, 1, 13–20
    Spanish American War, 164
    war with France, 21
Spanish-American Alliance, 289
Spanish American War, 164

Spanish-Speaking Workers' League. *See* Liga Obrera de Habla Español, La
Spears, Bob, 125
Speedups, 234
Spencer, T. Rush, 157
Spiritual Plan of Aztlán. *See* Plan Espiritual de Aztlán, El
Springer, 155
Squatters, 53, 56, 103, 112, 116
Stalin, Joseph, 286, 323
States' rights, 277, 290
Steel industry, 189, 192, 196–97, 235–36, 246, 260–61
Steel Workers Organizing Committee (SWOC), 234, 235–36
Steinbeck, John, 233
Stockholm Peace Appeal, 281
Stockton, Robert F., 88, 94, 95, 97–98
Strategic Partnership Plan, 383
Strikes
   autoworkers', 234–35
   coal miners', 178, 180–81, 214–15, 225–27, 237
   copper miners', 181–82, 364
   in Depression era, 221–31, 233, 234–35, 237
   in early 20th century, 178, 179–82, 202
   at end of 20th century, 346, 363–66, 368
   farm workers', 179–80, 194, 221–23, 233, 278, 307, 310–13, 335, 365–66
   hate, 259
   miners', 154, 180–82, 272, 279–80
   pecan shellers', 229–31
   in postwar years, 277
   railroad workers', 160, 179
   vaqueros', 170
Student Nonviolent Coordinating Committee (SNCC), 317
Sugar Act of 1937, 232
Sugar beet industry, 168, 170, 194–95, 196, 216, 222–23, 232
Supreme Court, U.S., 117, 285
   on affirmative action, 360–61, 362
   on common property rights, 102
   on jury service, 290
   land grant cases in, 156
   racial segregation upheld by, 151
   Reagan appointees, 348, 370
   on school desegregation, 292, 298, 382
Sutter, John, 67, 78n87, 102
Sutter's Fort, 92, 94
Sutter's mill, gold discovered in, 102
Sweatt, Herman, 363
Swift and Company, 196
SWOC. *See* Steel Workers Organizing Committee
Syphilis, 29

Taft, William Howard, 164
Taft-Hartley Act, 277
Tamaulipas, 54, 126, 147
Tampico, 20, 21
Taos, 15–16, 40, 46–48
Taos Revolt, 80, 88–91, 162
Tapia, Primo, 178
Tapia, Tiburcio, 69
Tarawa, Battle of, 256, 257(figure)
Taylor, Zachary, 84, 85, 94, 95, 98, 103, 124, 162
Teamsters Union, 294–95, 312, 313
Teatro Campesino, El, 311
Tehuacán, 100

Tejanos
   in Civil War, 131–34
   defined, 30
   in Depression era, 216, 228–29
   disenfranchisement of, 150, 151–52
   as freedom fighters, 183–85
   independence from Spain and, 30
   in late 19th to early 20th century, 144, 146–50, 170–71
   in mid-19th century, 79, 112–13, 123–26
   Plan de San Diego and, 150, 178, 185–87, 206
   in post-independence era, 41, 50–51, 52–53, 62–63, 72
   slavery opposed by, 123
   Texas independence and, 54, 56, 57, 59, 60–61
   Treaty of Guadalupe Hidalgo and, 102
   unionism struggle, 228–29
   World War II and, 246–47, 258
Tejón Pass, 69
Telles, Raymond, 292
Tenayuca, Emma, 214, 229–32, 237
Tennessee, 53, 132
Tenth Cavalry, 113
Tenth Texas Cavalry, 132
Tet Offensive, 326, 327
Texan Mounted Volunteers, 130
Texas, 1, 3, 4, 14, 16, 18, 26, 31, 32, 41, 43, 50–51, 52–63, 80, 112–13, 137, 144, 168, 170–71, 350, 351, 363. *See also* Tejanos
   American immigration to, 24, 25–29, 41, 51–56
   annexation of, 58, 61, 62, 73, 79, 82–83, 101, 106, 152
   Apache and Comanche threat in, 22–24
   attempt by U.S. to purchase, 54
   border region, 123–26
   as a buffer against expansion, 20–22
   Civil War and, 127, 128, 129, 130, 131–34
   Comanche raids in, 51–52
   in Depression era, 215–16, 220, 222
   in early 19th century, 24–25
   in early 20th century, 183–87
   English-only movement in, 357
   farm workers in, 222, 277
   "gringo against greaser" war in, 112
   growing conflict with Mexico, 52–54
   independence from Mexico, 54–63
   independence from Spain, 30
   Indian Wars and, 135
   in late 19th to early 20th century, 146–50
   Mexican American War and, 85
   Mexican immigration in, 177, 188–89, 220, 344, 358, 378
   Mexico denies independence of, 79, 82–84
   in mid-19th century, 123
   New Mexico territory gained by, 104
   in postwar years, 274, 276, 283
   revolt of, xvi, 39, 40, 51, 72, 79, 92, 123
   school system of, 205, 289, 291–92, 322–23, 382
   South, 185–87, 274, 283, 289, 291
   statehood granted to, 83
   in World War II era, 246–47, 255, 264–65
   zona libre in, 147
Texas Agricultural Worker's Organizing Committee (TWOC), 229
Texas and Pacific Railroad, 167
Texas Army of the Republic, 58
Texas Brigade, 131–32
Texas Convention of 1845, 61
Texas Declaration of Independence, 58
Texas Industrial Commission, 231

Texas Rangers, 113, 120, 125, 126, 144, 146, 147, 148, 149, 170, 178, 184, 186, 228, 229, 294, 314
    Mexican American War and, 94–95, 99, 100
    Porvenir Massacre and, 187
Texas-Santa Fe expedition, 62
Texas State Federation of Labor, 183
Texians, 51, 56, 59, 72
Third Marine Division, 327
Third New Mexico Infantry, 129
Third Texas Infantry, 132
Thirtieth Infantry Regiment, 258
Thirty-third Texas Cavalry Regiment, 133, 134
Thomas, Clarence, 348
Thornton, Seth, 84
Thornton Skirmish, 84
Three-Fingered Jack. See García, Bernardino
355th Infantry Regiment, 190
356th Infantry Regiment, 191
360th Infantry Regiment, 191
313th Infantry Regiment, 258
Tierra Amarilla community land grant, 157
Tierra Amarilla Courthouse raid, 316, 317, 318
Title VII of the Civil Rights Act of 1964, 337
Tlaxcalan Indians, 13
Todd, William, 257
Torres, Arnold, 348
Tortilla Curtain, The (Boyle), 347
Towns, 3, 20, 21, 27. See also Pueblos
Trade. See also Central American Free Trade Agreement; Globalization; North American Free Trade Agreement
    in colonial era, 2, 15–16, 22
    in mid-19th century, 79, 81–82, 85, 86, 91, 106
    in post-independence era, 40, 41, 45, 46–48, 63–64, 72
Trade fairs, 15–16, 19, 40, 46–48
Transcontinental Treaty, 30
Travis, William, 57, 60
Treaties of Velasco, 60
Treaties with Indians, 19, 23, 24, 42, 51
Treaty of Cahuenga, 98, 102
Treaty of Guadalupe Hidalgo, xv, 80, 100–103, 106, 116, 124, 125, 152, 158, 164, 206, 273
    land grant restoration movement and, 295, 314, 315, 318
    negotiations and ratification, 101–2
Treaty of San Ildefonso, 24, 37n78
Tres Pinos, 122
Treviño, George, 134
Treviño, Juan Francisco, 11
Treviño, Ramón, 60
Trinidad War, 156
Trist, Nicholas P., 100
Trujillo, Antonio María, 90–91
Truman, Harry S., 259, 282
Tubac, 4, 40, 43, 114, 135, 153
Tuberculosis, 193, 229, 274, 282
Tuck, Ruth D., 193
Tucson, 4, 5, 31, 40, 43, 114, 135, 152, 153, 218
Tumacácori, 40
Turley, Simon, 89
Twenty-fourth Amendment, 349
Twenty-fourth Infantry Division, 258
TWOC. See Texas Agricultural Worker's Organizing Committee
200th Coast Artillery Regiment, 247, 255–56
Tydings Amendment, 246
Typhoid, 216

UAW. See United Auto Workers
UCAPAWA. See United Cannery, Agricultural, Packing and Allied Workers of America
UFC. See United Front Committee of Agricultural Workers Unions
UFW. See United Farm Workers of America
UFWA. See United Furniture Workers of America
UFWOC. See United Farm Workers Organizing Committee
UMWA. See United Mine Workers of America
Underground railroad, 123
Unemployment
    in Depression era, 215
    at end of 20th century, 344, 353, 356, 363
    in the new millennium, 387
    in postwar years, 291
    in protest era, 306
    in World War II era, 247
Unión de Trabajadores del Valle Imperial, La, 202
Union Pacific Railroad, 195
Unions. See also individual unions
    in Depression era, 214–15, 219, 228–29
    in early 20th century, 179–83, 189, 202, 205
    at end of 20th century, 366, 367, 368–69, 371
    in late 19th to early 20th century, 153–54, 169
    NAFTA opposed by, 366, 367
    in postwar years, 277
    in World War II era, 249, 265–66
United Auto Workers (UAW), 234–35, 294, 311
United Cannery, Agricultural, Packing and Allied Workers of America (UCAPAWA), 215, 229, 230–31, 232, 233–34
United Electrical, 234
United Farm Workers of America (UFW), 307, 309, 313, 321, 324, 329, 335, 364, 365, 367, 371, 382
United Farm Workers Organizing Committee (UFWOC), 311–13
United Food and Commercial Workers, 364
United Front Committee of Agricultural Workers Unions (UFC), 223
United Furniture Workers of America (UFWA), 234, 285
United Mine Workers of America (UMWA), 180–81, 226
United Nations, 332
United Nations Commission on Human Rights, 281
United Packinghouse Workers of America (UPWA), 285
United Service Organizations (USO), 265, 266
United States Magazine and Democratic Review, 82
United States Steel Corporation, 196
United Steel Workers of America, 364
United War Chest Campaign, 262
Unity Leagues, 283
University of California, 321, 360–63
University of California-Berkeley Boalt Hall Law School, 363
University of California-Davis Medical School, 360–61
University of California-Los Angeles, 297
University of California-Santa Barbara, 323
University of Texas Law School, 363
Urban development, 273, 274–75, 283
Urban Institute, 358
Urbanization, 196–99, 246
Urrea, José, 58
U.S. English movement, 348, 357
U.S. Patriot Act of 2001, 384
U.S. Secure Fence Act of 2006, 385
USO. See United Service Organizations

U.S.S. Portsmouth, 94
Utah, 104, 113, 181, 202
Ute Indians, 18, 19, 40, 42, 63–64, 87, 88, 105
Uvalde County, 123

Valdez, Daniel, 311
Valdez, Luis, 311
Valdez, Mike, 256–57
Valdez, Valentina, 317
Valencia family, 28
Valenzuela, Joaquín, 120, 121
Vallejo, Manuel, 28
Vallejo, Mariano, 92, 93, 103
Vallejo, Salvador, 93(figure), 128
Vallejo family, 67
Valley of Peace, 315
Valverde, Battle of, 129, 130, 132
Val Vita, 234
Van Camp Seafood Company, 234
Vancouver Island, 29
Van Ness, George, 62
Vanzetti, Bartolomeo, 202
Vaqueros, 21, 50, 51, 118, 145, 170
Varela, María, 317
Varela, Sérbulo, 96
Vargas, Aurora, 275(figure)
Vargas, Diego de, 13, 34n40
Vargas, Juan de, 1
Vásquez, Tiburcio, 120, 121–23, 137
Vásquez Borrego, José, 21
Vasquez de Coronado, Francisco, 9, 33n24
Vásquez y Longeaux, Enriquita, 317, 319,
    320, 325
Vecinos, 14, 16, 40, 43, 45, 48, 49, 85, 86
Vejar, Pablo, 97
Velasco, Treaties of, 60
Velasco Fort, 56
Velásquez, Baldemar, 312, 365–66
Velázquez, Willy, 349
Venceremos Brigade, 323
Veracruz, 94, 99
Veterans of Foreign Wars, 226
Victoria (town), 60, 61
Victoria, Manuel, 71
Victorio, Chief, 135
Vidal, Adrián J., 132–33
Vidal, Mirta, 324
Vidal, Petra Vela de, 132
Vietnam Veterans Against the War, 331
Vietnam War, xvii, 307, 322, 332, 338, 343n69
    antiwar movement, 308, 320, 321, 325–31, 336–37
    casualties in, 327–28
    cost of, 327
    Mexican American soldiers in, 308, 326–28
    prisoners of war, 326
Vigil, Cornelio, 89
Vigil, Donaciano, 87, 88, 91
Vigilantism, 112, 116, 119, 145, 146–47
Villa de Béxar, 20
Villaraigosa, Antonio, 369, 387, 388(figure)
Villarreal, Andrea, 206
Villarreal, Teresa, 206
Viva Kennedy Clubs, 292–93, 318
Vlasic Pickles, 365
Voluntarios, Los, 319
Voting. See also Disenfranchisement
    at end of 20th century, 349–52
    in mid-19th century, 135
    in the new millennium, 381, 387

in postwar years, 273, 274, 279, 291
in protest era, 306, 333, 334
women's suffrage movement, 185, 203
Voting Rights Act of 1965, 306
Voting Rights Act of 1975, 334, 348, 349
Voz del Pueblo, La, 159, 162

Wages
    of coal miners, 225
    in early 20th century, 178
    of farm workers, 246, 277
    Mexican scale, 153, 179, 181, 225
    in Mexico, 378
    of miners, 153–54, 180, 181
    minimum, 189, 312
    of railroad workers, 166, 168
Wakdi-Sarmi campaign, 257
Wallace, George, 325
Wallace, Henry A., 280–81, 282
War Manpower Commission, 261
War of 1812, 84
War of the Reform, 126
War on drugs, 345, 354
War on Poverty, 307, 319, 327, 332
War on terrorism, 384–85
Warren, Earl, 254, 290
Washington, Harold, 350
Washington-on-the-Brazos, 58
Water rights, 124, 146, 150, 153
W. A. Thulmeyer Ranch, 148
Webb County, 133
Weller, John B., 104
Wells, James B., 151
Western Federation of Miners (WFM), 154, 181
Wetback (pejorative term), 273
WFM. See Western Federation of Miners
Wheatland Strike, 179
White Aryan Resistance (WAR), 354
White Caps. See Gorras Blancas, Las
White Citizens' Councils, 290
Whiteness, 7, 118, 205, 264–65, 288–90, 298
White supremacists, 112, 123, 385
Who Are We? (Huntington), 384
Wilderness campaign, 132
Wilkerson, James, 25
Wilmot Proviso, 101, 103
Wilson, Pete, 346, 358–59, 361, 362, 364
Wilson, Woodrow, 182, 183, 184
Wilson and Company, 196
Wobblies. See Industrial Workers of the World
Women
    affirmative action and, 360
    African American, 260
    in colonial era, 10, 27
    feminism and, 184, 308, 324–25, 336, 360
    Indian, 2, 11, 27, 29, 65, 66
    Mexican American (see Mexican American women)
    suffrage movement, 185, 203
Women's Army Corps, 262
Wool, John E., 87, 88
Workers' Alliance of America, 230, 232
Workers Freedom Ride, 380
Workmen's Loyalty League, 182
Works Progress Administration (WPA), 227,
    230, 232
World Trade Organization (WTO), 368–69, 371
World War I, 177, 180, 187, 188, 189–91, 198, 205
    labor force during, 189
    Mexican immigration during, 191, 206

World War II, xvi, xvii, 220, 237, 243–71, 285, 308
    casualties in, 255, 256, 257, 258
    Mexican Americans on the eve of, 245–50
    Mexican Americans on the front, 255–59
    prisoners of war, 256, 258
    war industries, 243–44, 246, 247, 248–49, 259–60, 266
Wormser, Michael, 153
Wounded Knee demonstration, 320
WPA. *See* Works Progress Administration
Wyoming, 195, 277

Ximenes, Vicente, 332

Yaqui Indians, 127
*Yates v. United,* 303n45
YMCA, 200

Yokut Indians, 69, 70(figure)
Yorba family, 67
Yorty, Sam, 330
"Yo Soy Joaquín" (poem), 320, 335
Young Citizens for Community Action (YCA), 321
Youngstown and Inland Steel, 235
Yturri, Manuel, 132
Yturria, Francisco, 150
Yucatán, 105

Zacatecas, 9, 58, 85
Zambos, 6
Zapata, Clemente, 134
Zapata County, 131
Zavala, Lorenzo de, Jr., 60
Zona libre in Texas, 147
Zoot Suit Riots, 253–55, 266